Modernity and the
Hegemony of Vision

Modernity and the Hegemony of Vision

EDITED BY

David Michael Levin

UNIVERSITY OF CALIFORNIA PRESS

Berkeley   Los Angeles   London

University of California Press
Berkeley and Los Angeles, California

University of California Press
London, England

Copyright © 1993 by

The Regents of the University of California

Library of Congress Cataloging-in-Publication Data
Modernity and the hegemony of vision / edited by David Michael Levin
    p.   cm.
    Includes bibliographical references and index.
    ISBN 0–520–07972–8 (cloth: alk. paper).–ISBN 0–520–07973–6
(paper: alk. paper)
    1. Philosophy, Modern. 2. Vision. I. Levin, David Michael,
 1939– .
B846.M63 1993
128′.3–dc20   93–1523
                                              CIP

Printed in the United States of America

1 2 3 4 5 6 7 8 9

There are times in life when the question of knowing
if one can think differently than one thinks, and perceive
differently than one sees, is absolutely necessary
if one is to go on looking and reflecting at all.

MICHEL FOUCAULT, *The Use of Pleasure*

CONTENTS

CONTRIBUTORS

Mieke Bal

Professor in the Instituut voor Algemene Literatuurwetenschap at the University of Amsterdam, Dr. Bal is the author of *Narratology: Introduction to the Theory of Narrative* (1988) and *Femmes Imaginaires* (1986). Her most recent book is *Reading "Rembrandt": Beyond the Word-Image Opposition*.

Hans Blumenberg

Professor of Philosophy at the University of Münster, Dr. Blumenberg is the author of *The Legitimacy of the Modern Age* (1966), *The Genesis of the Copernican World* (1975), *Work on Myth* (1979), and many other groundbreaking works on culture and intellectual history.

Susan Buck-Morss

Professor of Political Philosophy and Social Theory in the Department of Government at Cornell University, Dr. Buck-Morss is the author of *The Origin of Negative Dialectics: Theodor Adorno, Walter Benjamin and the Frankfurt School* (1977) and, more recently, *The Dialectics of Seeing: Walter Benjamin and the Arcades Project* (1989).

Paul Davies

Currently teaching in the Department of Philosophy at the University of Sussex, Professor Davies has taught at the University of London (1983–1986), the University of Essex (1985–1987), Loyola University Chicago (1987–1990), and DePaul University (1990–1992). He is the author of *Experience and Distance: Heidegger, Blanchot, Levinas* (1990) and another book forthcoming, *Blanchot and Philosophy*.

Thomas R. Flynn
Dr. Flynn is Samuel Chandler Dobbs Professor of Philosophy at Emory University. He is the author of *Sartre and Marxist Existentialism: The Test Case of Collective Responsibility* (1986), and some recent studies on Foucault, ethics, and politics.

Stephen Houlgate
Formerly Research Fellow in Philosophy at Girton College, Cambridge University, and also at the University of Edinburgh, Dr. Houlgate is currently Associate Professor in the Department of Philosophy at DePaul University. He is the author of *Hegel, Nietzsche, and the Criticism of Metaphysics* (1986), *Freedom, Truth and History: An Introduction to Hegel's Philosophy* (1991), and numerous shorter studies.

Martin Jay
Professor of History at the University of California, Berkeley, Dr. Jay teaches European intellectual history and is the author of *The Dialectical Imagination* (1973), *Marxism and Totality* (1984), *Adorno* (1984), *Permanent Exiles* (1985), *Fin-de-Siècle Socialism* (1988), and most recently, *Force Fields* (1993). He is currently completing a book on ocularcentrism in Western thought.

Dalia Judovitz
Formerly on the faculty of the University of California, Berkeley, Dr. Judovitz is now Professor in the Department of French at Emory University. She is the author of numerous essays on philosophy and literature and on the aesthetics of the French baroque and classical ages. Her major work is *Subjectivity and Representation in Descartes: The Origins of Modernity* (1988). She is currently completing a book on Marcel Duchamp.

David Michael Levin
Dr. Levin is Professor of Philosophy at Northwestern University. He is the author of *Reason and Evidence in Husserl's Phenomenology* (1970) and a trilogy, *The Body's Recollection of Being* (1985), *The Opening of Vision* (1987), and *The Listening Self* (1989). He also edited and contributed to *Pathologies of the Modern Self: Postmodern Studies on Narcissism, Schizophrenia and Depression* (1988).

John McCumber

Formerly on the faculty of the New School for Social Research, Dr. McCumber is Professor of Philosophy at Northwestern University. He is the author of *Poetic Interaction: Language, Freedom, Reason* (1989), *The Company of Words: Hegel, Language and Systematic Philosophy* (1992), and of numerous studies on ancient Greek philosophy, aesthetics, and the philosophies of Hegel, Heidegger, and Habermas.

Andrea Nye

Associate Professor of Philosophy at the University of Wisconsin–Whitewater, Dr. Nye is the author of *Feminist Theory and the Philosophies of Man* (1988) and *Words of Power: A Feminist Reading of the History of Logic* (1990), as well as numerous essays in feminism. She is currently completing a new book on three women thinkers: Rosa Luxemburg, Simone Weil, and Hannah Arendt.

Herman Rapaport

Chairperson and Professor in the Department of Comparative Literature at the University of Iowa, Dr. Rapaport is the author of *Milton and the Postmodern* (1983) and *Heidegger and Derrida: Reflections on Time and Language* (1989), as well as numerous shorter works. His latest book is *Between the Sign and the Gaze.*

Robert D. Romanyshyn

Formerly Chairperson and Professor in the Department of Psychology at the University of Dallas, and currently Research Coordinator for the Doctoral Program at Pacifica Graduate Institute in California, Dr. Romanyshyn is the author of *Psychological Life: From Science to Metaphor* (1982) and *Technology as Symptom and Dream* (1989), as well as numerous shorter studies on science, culture, and psychology. A new book, *Method and Research in Psychology: Doing Research with Soul* is forthcoming. Dr. Romanyshyn maintains a private practice in clinical psychology.

Gary Shapiro

Formerly in the Department of Philosophy at the University of Kansas, Dr. Shapiro is Professor of Philosophy and Tucker-Boatwright Professor in the Humanities at the University of Richmond. He is the author of *Nietzschean Narratives* (1989) and *Alcyone: Nietzsche on Gifts, Noise and Women* (1991). He is also the editor of *After the Future: Postmodern Times and Places* (1990) and co-editor of *Hermeneutics: Questions and Prospects* (1984).

Georgia Warnke

Formerly in the Department of Philosophy at Yale University, Dr. Warnke is currently Professor of Philosophy at the University of California, Riverside. She is the author of *Gadamer: Hermeneutics, Tradition and Reason* (1987) and *Justice and Interpretation* (1993).

INTRODUCTION

David Michael Levin

Proclaiming his empiricism, his pride of distance from a past informed by myth, Heraclitus (500 B.C.) wrote: "Those things of which there is sight, hearing, knowledge: these are what I honour most" (Fragment 55).[1] For him, though, "the eyes are more exact witnesses than the ears" (Fragment 101a). He also insisted on the fact that "the eyes and ears are bad witnesses for me if they have barbarian souls" (Fragment 107). Furthermore, he wanted us to realize that "men are deceived over the recognition of visible things" (Fragment 56).

Reading the pre-Socratics and studying the archaic history of their cultural world, we are easily tempted to construct new narratives, letting something be seen that was unseen before. And why shouldn't we? It is through such narratives that we articulate our changing forms of self-understanding and continually remake ourselves. We can now see that, even before Plato—in fact long before Plato, not only in the extant fragments attributed to Heraclitus, but in fragments attributed to Parmenides (475 B.C.)—philosophical thinking in the Western world was drawn to the tuition, the authority, of sight. But also, we can see that these philosophical teachings repeatedly insisted on calling to mind all the dangers in placing too much trust in vision and its objects.

The dangers of which the philosophers warn us are not only the tricks and deceptions, the hermeneutics, of everyday perception—the stick, for example, that appears to be bent when placed in water—but also the illusions and superstitions of visionary religion. For, when we turn away from the discourse of philosophers to look into the origins of this discourse in archaic history, in the cultural lifeworld of the earliest ancients, we find an abundance of myths recounting visionary journeys of the

1

spirit, and we see, through the fragments of the past, the telling ciphers of occult visionary religions, visionary rituals and practices, visionary "technologies of the self." In the course of formulating his theory of recollection in *Meno*, Plato refers back, with appropriately encrypted words, to the archaic visionary Mysteries of Eleusis, where every spring for perhaps hundreds of years, hundreds of people gathered in the dark of a cave-like temple, awaiting initiation into the esoteric teachings of death, rebirth, and immortality bestowed by the goddess Demeter in luminous visions. Likewise, Plato's myth of the cave in *The Republic* refers back to the experiences of a visionary religion practiced, and perhaps abandoned, at the very beginning of our civilization.

This volume is a collection of essays on vision: not only vision itself but the culture of vision, and the many different discourses of vision. All the essays were written especially for this collection, except for the study by Hans Blumenberg, which was published in 1954 in his native language, and which is presented here in its first English translation.

In the same year another important study on vision appeared: an essay titled "The Nobility of Sight: A Study in the Phenomenology of the Senses," in which Hans Jonas examined the historical privilege of sight, which from the very dawn of our culture has been thought to be the noblest of the senses.[2] Reflecting on this essay some years later in *The Life of the Mind*, Hannah Arendt observed that "from the very outset, in formal philosophy, thinking has been thought of in terms of *seeing*. . . . The predominance of sight is so deeply embedded in Greek speech, and therefore in our conceptual language, that we seldom find any consideration bestowed on it, as though it belonged among things too obvious to be noticed."[3] But, some pages later, she noted: "Since Bergson, the use of the sight metaphor in philosophy has kept dwindling, not unsurprisingly, as emphasis and interest have shifted entirely from contemplation to speech, from *nous* to *logos*."[4]

For those of us who can see, vision is, of all the modes of perception, the one which is primary and predominant, at least in the conduct of our everyday lives. This does not seem open to much debate. More problematic, however, is the narrative that argues for the domination, the hegemony, of a visual paradigm in our cultural history. Can it be demonstrated that, beginning with the ancient Greeks, our Western culture has been dominated by an ocularcentric paradigm, a vision-generated, vision-centered interpretation of knowledge, truth, and reality? If so, many more questions follow. Can it be argued that, in the period we call "modernity" (the period beginning, say, with the "discovery" of perspectivism and the rationalization of sight in the Italian Renascimento of the fifteenth century), this ocularcentrism has assumed a distinctively modern historical form? How is the ocularcentrism of modernity different from that which prevailed in earlier ages? Has the *character* of the dominant vision changed in correlation with the evolution of modernity, its hegemony manifesting itself differently in each of the centuries since the Renascimento? What is left, today, of the rational vision of the Enlightenment? Has its institutionalization in the course of modernity given it historically distinctive forms of incorporation, power, and normativity? How has the paradigm of vision ruled, and with what effects?

There are difficult questions implicit here: questions regarding the historical connections between vision and knowledge, vision and ontology, vision and power, vision and ethics. How does vision figure in the methodology of the social sciences—in its hermeneutics of positions, perspectives, and horizons? Is visualism implicated in the problematics of relativism? Is it implicated in the narcissism of the will to power? Is it responsible in any sense for a dangerous politics?

In "The Turning," Martin Heidegger asserted that both our capacity for seeing and our capacity for hearing "are perishing through radio and film under the rule of technology."[5] Similarly, in *Dawn and Decline,* Max Horkheimer commented: "As their telescopes and microscopes, their tapes and radios become more sensitive, individuals become blinder, more hard of hearing, less responsive."[6] If they are right, and we are indeed becoming blinder all the time, how can vision still be hegemonic today? We may thus wonder, returning to Arendt's reflections on the discourse of the present, whether our contemporary culture is really still ocularcentric, whether it is in transition to a different, historically new paradigm, and whether she could be right about the future importance of the logos, of a paradigm based on speaking and listening. If we are becoming deafer, it may be doubted that our capacity for listening can be counted on to redeem the logic of our cultural history and its future. Is there a postmodern future beyond the governance of ocularcentrism? What would a postmodern vision be like?

There certainly is some evidence for a shift in our cultural paradigms: a shift, that is, from (the normativity of) seeing to (the normativity of) listening.[7] Thus Hans-Georg Gadamer appropriated the ocular concept of "horizon" and reinscribed it within a conversation-based hermeneutics of interpretation. And Jürgen Habermas, like John Dewey, has tried to replace the detached-spectator paradigm with a paradigm that recognizes the importance of democratic participation. Breaking away from a subject-centered rationality, Habermas has conceptualized a rationality that is grounded, instead, in the ethics of communicative processes. Moreover, he has attempted to displace the epistemological privileging of "the kind of objectification inevitable from the reflexively applied perspective of the observer," whereby "everything gets frozen into an object under the gaze of the third person," the gaze, that is, of the subject as observer-spectator.[8] His philosophical work is intended to contribute to the release of the modern subject from a terrible double bind. For, in the objectivist paradigm generated by traditional ocularcentrism, the subject is invariably positioned either in the role of a dominating observer or in the role of an observable object, submissive before the gaze of power.

The critiques of Gadamer and Habermas are indebted to earlier critiques. Already, in the nineteenth century, Friedrich Nietzsche was formulating a powerful critique of the privileging of vision and of the foundational position of vision-generated, vision-centered concepts and methods in the history of modern philosophy. Although he never discussed ocularcentrism as such, Nietzsche was certainly critical, like Heraclitus, of the vision constitutive of the "herd mentality," and he attacked our readiness to shut our eyes to the truth. But he was equally critical, if not more so, of the vision of the philosophers, which he thought too myopic, too abstract, too theoretical, too detached from practices, and even from their own senses and sensibility. Thus, in *The Genealogy of Morals,* he attacked the philosophers' presupposition of an eye outside time and history, "an eye that no living being can imagine, an eye required to have no direction, to abrogate its active and interpretive powers."[9] He immediately followed this attack by asserting that "all seeing is essentially perspective, and so is all knowing. The more emotions we allow to speak on a given matter, the more different eyes we can put on in order to view a given spectacle, the more complete will be our conceptualization of it, and the greater our 'objectivity.'" And in *The Will to Power,* he reminds us that "there are many kinds of eyes. Even the sphinx has eyes."[10]

In keeping with this project of multiplying perspectives, multiplying eyes, Nietzsche praises "fearless Oedipus eyes,"[11] but also expresses his admiration for "an eye like Goethe's, full of love and good will,"[12] for the eyes of the child ("On the Uses and Disadvantages of History for Life," section 5),[13] and for the "secure and calm" gaze of Epicurus, capable of moderation in its voluptuousness.[14] If such a commitment to perspectivism is sufficient to make one's thinking ocularcentric, then perhaps, in this sense, Nietzsche's philosophy is itself ocularcentric. But this sense of the term could not be more at odds with the sense in which the thinking of (say) Plato, Descartes, and Husserl may be described as ocularcentric. For, by *multiplying* perspectives, Nietzsche is effectively using an ocular metaphorics derived from the tradition to subvert the authority of ocular thinking: he turns the very logic of ocularcentrism against itself, altering forever the visionary ambitions of philosophy.

However, it would seem that, in spite of Nietzsche's efforts, our social life and culture are still being formed by the hegemony of vision. For, in the twentieth century, three major philosophers—Martin Heidegger, Michel Foucault, and Jacques Derrida—have argued that the thought and culture of modernity have not only continued the historical privileging of sight but allowed its worst tendencies to dominate—and in fact allowed sight to dominate in a distinctively modern way, very different from the ocularcentrism of earlier times.

For Heidegger, visionary experience has always dominated both the origin (*arché*) and the end (*telos*) of the discourse of metaphysics. But he saw in modernity an historically distinctive phase in the evolution of this ocularcentrism. Whereas, at the beginning, this hegemony brought forth glorious visions as well as visions of violence, it has, in modernity, turned increasingly nihilistic. For a tendency of dangerous character, which in his "Letter on Humanism" he calls the "malice of rage," has become increasingly dominant in ocularcentrism.[15] This cultural tendency he defines as *das Gestell*: often translated as "enframing," it is the universal imposition of an interpretative paradigm or *episteme*.

In terms of our sight, this means that the formation of the figure-ground structure (*Gestaltung*) of our perception (*Wahr-nehmung*), in which the alethic truth (unconcealment) of the ontological difference between being and beings must be sheltered and preserved (*bewahrt* and *gewährt*: words which, in German, let us hear their relation to truth), becomes increasingly reified, closed, restricted, narrowed, tightened, distorted, and destructively fixated in representations—of self, of others, of knowledge, truth, and reality—that interpret the visible world by imposing confrontations of opposition between subject and object. In the discourse of metaphysics, this tendency reflects, and is in turn reflected by, the technological transformation of life in the modern age.

In "The Age of the World Picture," Heidegger not only considers the hegemony of vision to have had its beginning in the culture and philosophies of ancient Greece but thinks it has continued into our own time. In fact, he thinks, the historical form that this hegemony has assumed in the latest phase of the modern period is particularly ominous, reducing everything to the ocularcentric ontology of subject-relative images or representations. Moreover, this historical development of our ontology as he sees it is so distinctive, so decisively different from the ontology of earlier historical periods that he argues for the recognition of a "new epoch," defined precisely in terms of this reduction of being to being-represented: "That what-is should become what-is in representation is what makes the epoch [*Zeitalter*] which gets to this point in a new epoch in relation to the preceding one."

In this "new epoch" the ocular subject finally becomes the ultimate source of all being—and the reference point for all measurements, all calculations of the *value* of being. The very being of the world is equated with our images and representations. As Derrida says in "Sending: On Representation": "The fact that there should be representation or *Vorstellung* is not, according to Heidegger, a recent phenomenon, characteristic of the modern epoch of science, of technique and of subjectness (*subjectité*) of a Cartesian-Hegelian type. But what would be characteristic of this epoch is rather the authority, the dominant generality of representation. It is the interpretation of the very essence of what is as an object of representation [that makes this epoch distinctive]. Everything which becomes present, everything which happens or presents itself, is apprehended [solely] within the [subjective] form of representation."[16]

According to Heidegger, the Platonism of the Greeks set in motion an ocularcentric metaphysics, a way of thinking of which the logic would eventually turn all being into being-represented, or being-imaged. Platonism effected this without being in an historical position to understand itself, from the standpoint of the future, as already setting the stage for this later development. Thus Derrida notes that, although representation is not merely, for Heidegger, an image in and for the subject, "to the extent that it is, this presupposes that the world is previously constituted as visible. Now if for the Greeks, according to Heidegger, the world is not essentially a *Bild*, an available image, a spectacular form offered to the gaze or to the perception of the subject; if the world was first of all a presence (*Anwesen*) which seizes man or attaches itself to him rather than being seen [as such], intuited (*angeschaut*) by him; if it is rather man who is taken over and regarded by what-is, it was nevertheless necessary for the world as *Bild*, and then as representation, to declare itself among the Greeks, and this was nothing less than Platonism."[17]

Although influenced by this analysis, Foucault was more disturbed by the social and political manifestations of this ontological reductionism. And, like Heidegger, he thought he could see striking correlations between this ontology and the modern hegemony of vision, modern technology, and modern forms of "governmentality." For Foucault, the enlightenment project constitutive of our modernity has been increasingly double-crossed by the panopticism of its technologies. Whether these be the technologies of production, the technologies of sign systems, the technologies of power, or the technologies of the self, in each of these economies Foucault sees an increasingly dangerous tendency—dangerous, but nevertheless resistible—pointing us toward conditions of totalization, normalization, and domination. If modernity is, as it seems, dominated by vision, earlier times may indeed have been ocularcentric; but the hegemony of vision at work in modernity is nevertheless historically distinctive, and functions in a very different way, for it is allied with all the forces of our advanced technologies. The power to see, the power to make visible, is the power to control. Panopticism is the political display of the "enframing," the *Gestell* that Heidegger sees ruling our time: it is the universal imposition of technologies of control. Only in modernity does the ocularcentrism of our culture make its appearance in, and as, panopticism: the system of administrative institutions and disciplinary practices organized by the conjunction of a universalized rationality and advanced technologies for the securing of conditions of visibility.

Derrida, likewise influenced by Heidegger's critique, sees a certain ocularcentrism concealing itself behind the history of the metaphysics of presence. Although, for him, this hegemony of vision is therefore very old and certainly traceable to Platonism, it appears to have adopted a different configuration in modernity. What is distinctive about ocularcentrism in the modern period? Derrida's answer seems to be that it has extended its hegemony beyond the margins of philosophical textuality into the politics of culture. In the eighteenth century, its politics was that of the Enlightenment. It supported a reflective, critical rationality and the visions of a utopian imagination. But in our own time, we can see the tain of the mirror: the other side, a phallocentric, logocentric "heliopolitics" driven by "the violence of light" and threatening to impose the ontological order of presence wherever its mastery can reach.

Heidegger, Foucault, and Derrida have all seen, traced, and attempted to understand the advent of a distinctively modern form of ocularcentrism. Each one, of course, in his own way and from his own perspective. But, for all their differences, each one has gone beyond critique, using the textuality, the *work* of critique to articulate and practice what might be called "countervisions": not only critical and strategically subversive observations, but also historically new ways of seeing, ways that model visions very different in character from the one that has become hegemonic.

In *The Economic and Philosophical Manuscripts of 1844,* Karl Marx pointed out that "the forming of the five senses is a labor of the entire history of the world down to the present."[18] Our vision continues to change. But do we know—can we tell from this history—the full extent of our sensibilities? Do we know of what further development our senses may be capable? Inspired by the enlightened humanism in the young Marx's vision, Herbert Marcuse asserted that "alternative cultural forms and practices, new ways of seeing and a new sensibility" are necessary today.[19]

The essays collected here represent many different points of view.

However different, they are all, I think, responsive to some of the needs and concerns of our time. They are, then, timely reflections on the present, opening up our moment in time to a past that was never fully present and a future always under way. The topic of ocularcentrism provides a unique opportunity for us to think about modernity from different points of view, yet also in a focused and coherent way.

Reading Heraclitus, Heidegger was led to the reflection that we are indebted to the light, and are "entrusted" with "preserving it and handing it down."[20] Perhaps this collection of essays, questioning the predominant character of our vision, examining the hegemony of vision in the life of our culture, and problematizing in different ways the ocular discourses, practices, and institutions that we have for so long simply taken for granted, will in its own way preserve and hand down this entrustment, this gift of light, making it possible for us—and for the generations following us—to cultivate a different sensibility and bring new visions into being.

The first chapter, by Hans Blumenberg, is on "Light As a Metaphor for Truth: At the Preliminary Stage of Philosophical Concept Formation." Opposed to the "notion that the philosophical logos has 'overcome' pre-philosophical mythos," and convinced that this reading of the history of philosophy "has narrowed our view," Blumenberg sets out to formulate a "philosophical metaphorology," documenting the "metaphorics of light in the history of metaphysics." His intention, he says, is "to show the way in which transformations of the basic metaphor indicate changes in world-understanding and self-understanding." Thus, in his carefully documented narrative, we see how the "history of man," a history conceived in terms of stories of redemption and stories of freedom, becomes an intricate "history of light" reflecting those many changes.

Beginning his story with Parmenides, Blumenberg takes us through the history of metaphysics. He tells us about Plato's myth of the cave, in which "the metaphorics of light already has a metaphysics of light implicit within it"; light in Hellenic skepticism and Stoicism; the vision of Neoplatonism; the precarious privilege that Jewish culture accorded to listening; Cicero's identification of light with the virtue of a moral consciousness; the Gnostic dualism of light and darkness; Augustine and the early Christian reception of the metaphorics and metaphysics of light; the scholasticism of the Middle Ages, where the light appears not in a cave but in a monastic cell and in a small study; and of course the Enlightenment, with its own critical transformation of the natural light doctrines that figured in seventeenth-century thought.

In a footnote bringing his narrative into the present, Blumenberg opines that, "with regard to the modern age, it evidently still needs to be proven that the history of metaphors of light *continues* at all." There is, then, for him, no hegemony of vision shaping our present world. However, in an analysis of today's "technologies of light" that may remind one of Heidegger and that certainly anticipates Foucault, he calls attention to the existence of a "coerced vision": "The connection between vision and freedom is being dissociated. Due to the dominance of the prefabricated and of technologically precast situations and aspects, the modern extension of sensory spheres has not become a source of freedom." Thus, while Blumenberg questions the view that the philosophical discourse of modernity, and, more generally, our modern culture, can be called "ocularcentric," what he sees today, when he looks around him, is a world in which vision is no longer a path to wisdom or redemption, no longer even a method for acquiring knowledge and achieving freedom, but rather a technology complicitous with domination—and forces that threaten a new "darkness."

For Descartes, darkness is a nightmare. There is nothing to be learned from entering its domain. He is a philosopher obsessed with clarity and light. If a discourse in which light, vision, and its metaphorics are constitutive of its very logic may be called ocularcentric, then it would be difficult to deny that Descartes's philosophy exemplifies ocularcentrism. In chapter 2, on "Vision, Representation, and Technology in Descartes," Dalia Judovitz recognizes this logic, but argues that Descartes not only limits but ultimately displaces both the priority of the eye and the centrality of its vision, in order to proclaim and affirm the sovereign power of a reason the intuitive nature of which is modeled—paradoxically—on our experience with vision. Concurring with Merleau-Ponty, who noted in "Eye and Mind" that the course of Descartes's thought is organized around two fundamental and related projects, namely (1) his "struggle against, and critique of, illusion," a struggle for certitude in knowledge that led him in the end to reject the visible world as a whole, and (2) his rational reconstruction of the visible domain "according to a figurative model based on mental schematism," Judovitz undertakes to demonstrate that, although Descartes acknowledged vision as the dominant sense and was sufficiently fascinated by the new science of optics, and by the new technologies that were suddenly augmenting the power and prestige of vision, to conduct optical experiments and write at length on his research, his much deeper commitment to rationalism disposed him to challenge, and ultimately repudiate, the power and nobility of vision. Ironically, at the same time that he criticized vision for its deceptiveness and attempted to separate mind from body, and reason from perception and imagination, he transferred the properties of the visible to the mental domain, "whence they will illuminate metaphorically the powers of reason to attain certitude as clear and distinct ideas." Henceforth an intuitive, inborn light free of sensory experience, reason is finally empowered to rationalize the visible world for the sake of science and technology. Thus, vision itself becomes merely a "construct" of the rational mind, and its referent becomes the optical projection of a geometric system.

Judovitz concludes her study by adumbrating her conviction that there are dimensions to vision not reducible to thought and that there are conditions limiting thought which Descartes, and the schools of thought he inaugurated, have failed to see.

The next chapter proposes a very different reading of Descartes. In "Vision, Reflection, and Openness: The 'Hegemony of Vision' from a Hegelian Point of View," Stephen Houlgate argues for the position that there is nothing inherently problematic—and, in particular, nothing inherently despotic—about making vision our model for knowing and thinking. Challenging the critique of ocularcentrism that sees in philosophical thought and its culture a tragic commitment to the metaphysics of presence and that connects the historical domination of this metaphysics with the hegemony of vision as our cultural paradigm of knowledge, truth, and reality, Houlgate says: "my intention in this essay is to examine, and indeed call into question, the conception of vision which constitutes the presupposition of that critique."

Houlgate opens his essay with some appreciative as well as critical reflections on Dewey, Rorty, and Heidegger. Dewey is of interest because he problematized the spectator theory of knowledge and argued for a participatory conception of knowledge based on the unity of theory and practice. Rorty is of interest because he has rejected the picture of the mind as a mirror of theoretical reflection, rejected ocular theories of truth that make it a matter of correspondence, and proposed a conception of truth and mind based, instead, on discourse. And Heidegger is of interest because he denied that our primary involvement with the world is theoretical, repudiated the reduction of knowledge to techniques of objectification aimed at mastery and control, and attempted to think a different way of experiencing our world. Noting that each of these philosophers was convinced of the hegemony of vision, that each argued against the continuation of this hegemony, and that each proposed an alternative paradigm, Houlgate examines the thought of Descartes, Berkeley, and Hegel in order to question these more contemporary critiques of vision and "visionary" thinking. Concluding his analysis of Descartes and Berkeley, he asserts that neither of these philosophers made vision by itself responsible for the reductive objectification and instrumentalization of our world.

Taking a position that differs from the one defined by Judovitz, he writes: "It may well be, as a study of Descartes suggests, that modern technological subjectivity rests not so much on the hegemony of vision, but rather on a certain narrow conception of thought. Furthermore, it may also be the case that vision is precisely what points the way to a richer, more open, less reductive conception of thought. One philosopher who to my mind is convinced of the intrinsic generosity of vision is G. W. F. Hegel." Pointing out that Hegelian vision is "a complex fusion of different levels of awareness," Houlgate maintains that, for Hegel, "objectifying, mastering subjectivity is not the product of the hegemony of vision . . . in human life, but rather the product of [a] conscious reflection" moved by "self-oriented desire." After drawing our attention to Hegel's articulation of "visual intuition"—a very different mode of vision, less reductive, more generous, and more in harmony with its objects, but no less oriented toward objective clarity—Houlgate concludes his study, inviting the cultivation of a philosophical vision that is genuinely open to its other and free of the need to dominate.

Following this reading of Hegel—the architect of a great philosophical system, one of the "grand narratives" that postmodern criticism would like to see us abjure—is a chapter on Nietzsche, the most passionate enemy of philosophical systems, who wrote of his "profound aversion to reposing once and for all in any one total view of the world," and of his "fascination for the opposing point of view: refusal to be deprived of the stimulus of the enigmatic."[21] Gary Shapiro's "In the Shadows of Philosophy: Nietzsche and the Question of Vision" skillfully moves through the labyrinths traced by Nietzsche's writings and enables us to put in historical perspective Nietzsche's many ways of seeing things, his discursive deployment of visual examples, his visual metaphors, his attitude toward dream and illusion, his critique of the visualism blinding philosophical discourse, and his relationship to modernity and its project of Enlightenment.

Shapiro holds that, contrary to what Heidegger contended, Nietzsche's philosophy does not continue the tradition's hegemonic conception of vision. Pointing out that Nietzsche's thinking delighted in the interplay of light and shadow, clarity and obscurity, the manifest and the hidden, presence and absence, he calls into question the interpretation according to which Nietzsche thought of vision as an instrument of the will inherently driven by a desire to make everything totally visible and totally clear. But if Nietzsche refused the nobility of a privileged vision captured by the metaphysics of presence, then neither, according to Shapiro, did he adopt an uncompromisingly antiocular position, substituting the auditory and the tactile for the visual. Shapiro shows that Nietzsche's break with the tradition of ocularcentrism in philosophy does not consist in avoiding all recourse to visual vocabulary, but rather in the strategic deployment of a visual vocabulary excluded by the tradition, thereby deconstructing the ocular support claimed for its epistemology and metaphysics. Rethinking vision, thinking toward the possibility of a vision no longer enslaved by metaphysics, Nietzsche calls for an abyssal vision, a fearless gaze willing to look into the abysses and face a world without any absolute grounding. Shapiro elaborates this vision.

In the "Economy" chapter of *Walden*, Thoreau asks an important question: "Could a greater miracle take place than for us to look through each other's eyes for an instant?" In "Sartre, Merleau-Ponty, and the Search for a New Ontology of Sight," Martin Jay defends vision and its philosophical discourse against the hostility of French philosophy in the twentieth century. Finally in revolt against the legacy of Cartesianism, many French philosophers of this century have sharply denounced what Jay calls a "spectatorial and intellectualist epistemology based on a subjective self reflecting on an objective world exterior to it," radically questioning the ocularcentrism of the dominant philosophical tradition, and finding support for their critique in the work of Husserl and Heidegger. According to Jay, these philosophers ultimately contributed, despite their own strongly ocularcentric vocabularies, to a decisive weakening of the ocular paradigm. Thus, for example, Husserl's concept of intentionality abolished the spectatorial distance separating subject and object and made it necessary to revise traditional theories of representation. Moreover, his late work on the prereflective lifeworld demonstrated that "phenomenology could mean something besides the search for pure essences."

As for Heidegger, Jay points out that, although Heidegger was always attempting to give thought to the advent of a new vision, he was extremely critical of Greek notions of *theoria*, theoretical vision and contemplation; that he lamented the reduction of *theoria* to observation in modern empiricism; that, like Dewey and Husserl, he contested the privileging of a spectatorial vision which endistances and estranges subject and object; that he repudiated ontologies which, "based on the synchronicity of a fixating gaze," made spatial existence prior to temporality; and that he regretted the degeneration of vision, its fall from the nobility and openness of wonderment in ancient Greece to the gaze driven by the will to power, the predatory possessiveness and calculating, self-interested curiosity that are distinctive, for him, of our contemporary world.

Analyzing all Sartre's major philosophical works, Jay carefully documents the evolution of Sartre's obsession with vision—his indictment of "the absolute look" and his critique of the hegemony of vision both in our social relations and in our philosophical discourse. Noting that, for Sartre, life is a constant struggle for power, and that he thought our sight to be partly responsible for the reifications, alienations, and humiliations of social existence, Jay can find no recognition in Sartre's work of any redeeming virtues, any more benevolent tendency and potential, in our capacity for sight—nothing worth cultivating.

With Merleau-Ponty, the story is very different—and also, as Jay shows, much more complex, much more ambiguous. For if it can be argued that he was a critic of ocularcentrism in the history of philosophy, it can also be argued that his own work is deeply ocularcentric, and that he made, as Jay puts it, "a heroic attempt to reaffirm the nobility of vision on new and firmer grounds" than those provided by the "scopic regime" of Cartesianism. To be sure, on the one hand, he dethroned the sovereign spectator, "the observing subject, whether Cartesian, Sartrean, Husserlian, or Marxist," brought the philosopher's "bird's-eye view" back down to earth, challenged philosophies of reflection, undermined the vision-generated dualism of subject and object, denied the possibility of Cartesian clarity and the rationalist assumption of transparency in meaning, and "raised invisibility to the same ontological status as visibility." On the other hand, he argued with eloquence for the primacy of perception, fought for perspectivism, and rejected both empiricism, which he accused of reducing vision to observation, and intellectualism, which he accused of transcendental narcissism, and of turning vision into an act of intellectual judgment.

Moreover, he attempted, as Jay points out, to articulate a "new ontology of vision," drawing on the resources of a hermeneutical phenomenology to bring to light a dialectical intersubjectivity of gazes, gazes constitutive of social relations oriented by mutual acknowledgment. And it may even be argued, as I have, that Merleau-Ponty's last writings, assembled in a volume titled *The Visible and the Invisible,* show how, in the process of "mirroring," the reflexive reversibilities of vision "double-cross" the moment of narcissism and constitute a "corporeal schema" that schematizes and grounds—or, say, provides fertile soil for the cultivation of—the normative principles of mutual acknowledgment, reciprocity, and justice.[22]

Nevertheless, Jay wants to conclude that, "even in his case, it can be demonstrated that the suspicions and doubts plaguing other twentieth-century French critics of ocularcentrism ultimately surfaced." For, while some philosophers have accused Merleau-Ponty of being too closely tied to the "exorbitant privilege of vision in our culture," Jay finds himself compelled to confess that the new ontology of sight which Merleau-Ponty adumbrates in his last writings—the project of an ontology which radically decenters the percipient subject—delivers a "vision" that is not easily recognizable as still human—or even, for that matter, as still what can be called "vision." Perhaps one of the most thought-provoking questions with which Jay leaves us, then, is, what sense can we make out of phenomenological "narratives" that radically deconstruct the subject-object structure which we moderns have come to identify with, or as, the essentially human: assertions, for example, that there is "an anonymous visibility," a reversible "vision in general" inhabiting us, that "I am all that I see," and that "through vision we [literally] touch the sun and the stars."

My own contribution is "Decline and Fall: Ocularcentrism in Heidegger's Reading of the History of Metaphysics." As earlier chapters have pointed out, Heidegger formulated a powerful double critique: first of all, a critique of our everyday way of seeing, the inauthentic way of seeing typical of everyone-and-anyone (*das Man*), which he regarded as calculative, narrowly instrumental, reifying, aggressive, and ontologically degenerate (i.e., forgetful of being); and second, a critique of the hegemony of vision, not only in the discourse of philosophy from Plato through Husserl but also in Western culture as a whole, and in modernity most of all. In this chapter, I place Heidegger's critique in the context of his reading of the history of metaphysics, and relate this critical reading to his interpretation of Western history. And I show that, although he was inclined to see our history through the optics of a conservative-Romantic narrative of decline and fall, he was also drawn to the consideration of a radically different way of seeing: as early as *Being and Time,* with its hope for a redeeming "moment of vision," and as late as *Gelassenheit,* with its attempt to envision an ontologically appropriate, ontologically thoughtful seeing which is open to "the lighting," the "unconcealment" of being, and capable of letting visible beings be what and as they are.

Proposing an interpretation that differs to some extent from Martin Jay's, I suggest that Heidegger was neither (in contrast to Derrida) against the *hegemony* of vision as such, nor even (in contrast to Descartes and Sartre) critical of *vision* as such. On the contrary, his thinking, ever inspired by the ocularcentric Greeks, was deeply beholden to vision-generated, vision-centered language. However, he was strongly critical of the *character* of the vision that has prevailed in our ocularcentric culture and its philosophical discourse. What disturbed him was increasing domination by a vision the character of which he held partly responsible for the increasing "darkness" of the world, our increasing "closure" to the lighting of being. This "pathological" vision was, he thought, particularly powerful in our present epoch. Indeed, the modern age was, for him, the age of the world picture, the age when being itself is finally reduced to the enframing of representation. And he turned to the Greeks, especially the pre-Socratics, not in order to repeat the past, not in order to retrieve intact their original vision, but rather to learn whatever he could from struggling to understand their thought, and to find, in the light of their accomplishments, a new beginning for vision, a way of seeing no longer bound to the will to power and the metaphysics of modernity.

Chapter 7, contributed by Herman Rapaport, is on "Time's Cinders." The focus of this chapter is Heidegger's lecture course "On the Essence of Human Freedom." In this course, which took place during the summer of 1930, Heidegger attempted to define the "essence" of freedom in relation to the truth (unconcealment) of being and to articulate this relation in terms of a hermeneutic phenomenology of lighting and vision. Thus, the question of freedom ultimately becomes, for Heidegger, a question of understanding how human beings can exist in the openness granted by the light of being. However, since he held that being must be interpreted "in the light of time," the logic of his analysis of human freedom led him into a continuation of his thinking, begun in earlier work, about the relation of time and being.

Paradoxically, this thinking continues to make use, as Rapaport shows, of a "visionary" discourse, in spite of the fact that, to some extent, Heidegger's critique of the Platonic and Aristotelian conceptions of being as a standing and persisting presence attributes the occlusion of temporality, and the consequent "substantializing" of being, to the ocular vocabulary of their metaphysics.

After exploring Heidegger's perplexing dependency on the metaphorics of light and vision in his interpretation of time and being—an interpretation intended, of course, to cast light on the "essence" of human freedom, Rapaport turns to consider Derrida's *Cinders,* a work that reminds us of the cinders that remained in the crematoria of the German death camps, and of the lights of the spirit suddenly extinguished by the fires of hate that raged in the Holocaust: events exemplifying the monstrousness of human freedom that is always a possibility in the openness of being; events that, in 1930, Heidegger's invocations of a lighting, fire, and flames of the spirit may be said, if only belatedly and after the fact, to have anticipated—or even, perhaps, in a most uncanny way, to have ignited.

Supplementing Derrida's critical reading of Heidegger—a deconstructive hermeneutics that brings to light some surprising textual traces of Heidegger's National Socialism—Rapaport indicates how Heidegger's thinking remains haunted by the flames and glowing cinders of the Shoah, in which the light of both truth and freedom was betrayed, and virtually extinguished—something about which Heidegger was loath to think and loath to see, in spite of his avowed commitment to freedom and truth.

Writing with Derrida's *Cinders* in mind, Rapaport gives us a reading of Heidegger's text "On the Essence of Human Freedom" that discovers in this discourse the evidence of a monstrous "truth of being" which Heidegger did not see. This tracework leaves no doubt: something was shadowing his vision of human freedom, something was being concealed: a truth already present and yet *not* already present, or *not yet* present. Thus, Rapaport also shows how Heidegger's understanding of the "essence" of freedom is related, in ways Heidegger himself did not expect to see, to the "indifference" of being: the "indifference" of an openness which allows for the possibility that the lighting of being may be turned into the fires of hell, the monstrous evil of the Holocaust.

What is absent from Heidegger's illumination of being? In the aftermath of the Second World War, the traces of evil were still present: cinders that spoke of all the absent ones—all those who were murdered in the name of the Spirit (*Geist*). In Germany, this Spirit fanned the flames of nationalism and racism. Reading Heidegger's lectures in the afterglow of this eerie light, Rapaport calls our attention to Heidegger's discussion of monstrousness as a human possibility, and also to his reflections on the temporal interpretation of being as presence and as absence. For the truth of the cinders in the crematoria, about which Heidegger never spoke, lies precisely in their uncanny position in our traditional ocular-centric ontology. There is no place for these cinders in the discourse of metaphysics. How do the cinders that remain to tell of the dead bring being into time and time into being? For Rapaport, this is a relation that can profoundly unsettle our understanding of ourselves and challenge our capacity for vision.

Chapter 8, by John McCumber, is on "Derrida and the Closure of Vision." McCumber begins his essay with a question: what is the connection Derrida makes, within the field of textuality, between metaphysics and vision? And he notes that, according to Derrida, metaphors of light and vision are central to the texts of metaphysics, and that these texts have always desired clarity, objected to shadows, refused to recognize shading (shades of meaning, the shade in which writing is cast), and betrayed their anxiety over perspectivism.

McCumber shows that Derrida's fascination with vision is twofold: (1) "If vision itself is external to [the texts and textuality of] philosophy, then a metaphorized version of vision is constitutive of it." (2) But what if, conversely, "vision itself, 'properly' understood . . . , is in truth merely an artifact of the metaphorical vision instituted by (and instituting) philosophy"? What then? In McCumber's reading, Derrida documents "four main characteristics" in the vision that philosophers have used as a model of knowledge in the texts of metaphysics. Working with these four traits, McCumber arrives at the paradoxical conclusion that, as Derrida's reading of Hegel shows, sound is really more visionary than sight itself, and the word does not deny vision its ideal of full presence, but rather fulfills it.

This story of the construction and use of vision in the texts of metaphysics leads McCumber to see in Derrida's critique of ocularcentrism the at least provisional assumption of a distinction between vision as it has been represented in the history of metaphysics and a vision "uncontaminated" by that history, "liberated" from "its metaphysical subjection to form and the voice." And he argues that Derrida wants not merely to trace the origin of this constructed vision in the history of philosophy but also to question it. But then, when we take into account Derrida's deconstructive strategies, which problematize all distinctions—e.g., that between vision and hearing, interiority and exteriority, intellect and perception, the pure and the contaminated—it is not easy to see how such liberation could be accomplished. Nor is it even easy to say what "liberation" could possibly mean here.

Derrida seems to be caught in a double bind; but McCumber shows that his way out is a double gesture. If the concept of vision has been used by metaphysics to support presence, then he must continue to use this concept, but use it in a way that is disruptive and deconstructive: to designate a certain blindness—"or better: a blind spot." This disruptive, non-metaphysical vision is accordingly "organized around its own blind spots," and its objects are not forms that are totally present, but rather what Derrida calls "traces": an unseen that nevertheless "affects what we do see, the shape and scope of our visual field," a "supplementarity" that, in spite of its being unseen, or precisely because it *is* unseen, "opens and limits visibility." Thus, "Derrida's criticism of metaphysical vision is made, not from a standpoint supposed to be wholly beyond vision, or from that of a 'purer' (intellectual) vision, but from the limits of vision," from an immanent articulation of the conditions under which the metaphysics ruling in our vision becomes impossible. However, as already noted, Derrida also uses the auditory realm to unsettle the visual paradigm of knowledge. A second front of attack.

McCumber then points out that Derrida's disruptive vision does not, and indeed, if Derrida's deconstruction of absolute boundaries is to be taken seriously, could not entirely break with the tradition. There is continuity first of all, because, long before Derrida, Hegel was already challenging vision's predominant tendencies, attacking the modeling of knowledge on vision, and forfeiting the privilege given to vision over voice and speech. However, Hegel's critique is directed only against intellectual vision—the "reflexive vision" analyzed in Houlgate's essay—and is conceived in the name of a still purer vision. Thus, McCumber finds that, contrary to one's first impressions, Derrida's critique of vision is really more radical than Hegel's. There is also, for McCumber, a second point of continuity between Derrida and the tradition: although Derrida's critique of logocentrism substitutes something seen ("writing") for something heard (logos), "writing" seems to bear some of the very traits to which he so insistently objects in vision. The traits of metaphysics paradoxically reappear, albeit transfigured, in the articulation of *écriture,* despite—or rather because of—its traces, its supplementarity, its margins. Thus McCumber concludes his essay with the asseveration that Derrida's critique of ocularcentrism, though effectively incisive, fails to perform an absolutely decisive break with the tradition: when all is said and done, it both escapes and does not escape the artificial vision encoded within the textuality of metaphysics.

In chapter 9, Paul Davies reflects on "The Face and the Caress: Levinas's Ethical Alterations of Sensibility." As early as 1930, with the publication of the first major work on Husserl in France,[23] Levinas was engaged in the formulation of critical arguments against the primacy of theoretical consciousness and its gaze: the "imperialism" of ocularcentric philosophy, which in the modern age has imposed on the world of its representation an ethics which either reduces the human other to transcendental sameness or exposes the other to the most dehumanizing exile and estrangement, an otherness in which the humanity of the other cannot be recognized. Thus, according to Derrida, Levinas was the first philosopher to give thought to the "ancient clandestine friendship between light and power, the ancient complicity between theoretical objectivity and technico-political possession."[24]

Davies contends that, despite Levinas's early critique of the cultural hegemony of vision, especially as it has operated within the discourse of philosophy, he has not completely disconnected his ethics from visionary thinking. On the contrary, he has attempted to articulate, within the domain of sensibility, and thus within our experience of seeing others, the phenomenology of an ethical predisposition, an ethical relationship to the other: an "immediate" ethical acknowledgment of the other which *precedes and makes possible* all our mediated knowledge of the other—all the cognitive identifications, typifications, and classifications that figure in the representations of our ontology.

In *Minima Moralia,* Theodor Adorno observed that "the possibility of pogroms is decided in the moment when the gaze of a fatally wounded animal falls on a human being. The defiance with which he repels this gaze—'after all, it's only an animal!'—reappears irresistibly in cruelties done to human beings, the perpetrators having again and again to reassure themselves that it is 'only an animal.'"[25] And he reflected that, in "repressive society the concept of man is itself a parody of divine likeness. The mechanism of 'pathic projection' determines that those in power perceive as human only their own reflected image, instead of reflecting back the human as precisely what is different."[26]

According to Levinas, when we encounter others face to face, we are immediately affected by the ethical demands, the ethical claims, that their presence makes on us. We are touched and moved: "The visible," he says, "caresses the eye. One sees and hears like one touches."[27] The argument he makes for the priority of the ethical is accordingly fleshed out in a hermeneutical phenomenology that articulates our experience of being sensibly affected by what we see when we see the face of another. Derrida finds this narrative compelling, but he is not convinced that, with an articulation of the face, Levinas can escape the epistemology and ontology that seem to come with ocularcentrism. Thus, in "Violence and Metaphysics," Derrida is provoked to ask: "How . . . will the metaphysics of the face as the *epiphany* of the other free itself from light?" Indeed: "What language will ever escape it?"[28]

The answer that Paul Davies wants to suggest here is that we must look to Levinas's "alterations of sensibility." Derrida is right in asserting that Levinas does not achieve a total break with the ocularcentric tradition. However, he does, in three crucial ways—ways that also figure in the last writings of Merleau-Ponty—decisively disengage from it; and he accordingly challenges us to rethink our understanding of how ethics and vision are related. First, by showing that "even in its subordination to cognition sight maintains contact and proximity," he breaks away from the ocular representation of subject and object, which assumes that the subject is a detached spectator-observer.[29] Second, by showing that the ethical claim of the other is first of all a matter of being sensibly affected, rather than being presented with an object for cognition, he breaks away from the cognitivism of the tradition—the ocular privileging of theoretical knowledge. And third, by articulating the visual interaction in terms of the caress, he radically contests the hegemonic representation of the "nature" of vision.

And yet, when we turn our eyes away from the culture of books and take a look at the world around us, what we could see might make us sadly doubtful about the prospects for ending this hegemony. In "Children As Moral Observers," Robert Coles reported what a black child of eleven, a child living in Soweto, South Africa, told him in the summer of 1979: "One day, I'm ready to go die for my people. It's that bad. We are treated like dogs. . . . When I go to Joburg [Johannesburg], I look at the white people, and there is fear in their faces. They can't see us, but we see them. They don't want to see us, but we have to see them! I hope, some day, God helps us settle this; He will have to come down here again, and open a lot of eyes!"[30] For this child, the connections between vision and domination, vision and violence, could not be more visible.

With chapter 10, by Thomas Flynn, we turn to "Foucault and the Eclipse of Vision." According to Flynn, Foucault's work must be read as a postmodern critique of the hegemony of vision in Western life and culture: Foucault rejected not only the detached, contemplative, spectatorial vision of Platonism but also the domination-oriented gaze of modernity. And yet, he notes, Foucault's style of critique, and the epistemology behind it, are unmistakably ocular. Is this a paradox? Flynn contends that Foucault used vision to undermine vision—or, more specifically, he used his own way of seeing, which Flynn describes as "diacritical," and the "force" of the images it produced, to challenge the way of seeing that today is hegemonic, and to promote by his example the learning of a very different way of seeing.

Flynn traces the trajectory of Foucault's historical work, from his early practice of "archaeology," mainly focused on making visible the correlations between vision and truth, to his later practice of "genealogy," concerned with making visible the correlations between vision and power. He notes, however, that even in *The Birth of the Clinic,* a work from the early "archaeological" period, Foucault was already distancing himself from certain doctrines central to the Enlightenment, disputing, for example, "the great myth of the free gaze," a gaze that, "freed from darkness, dissipates darkness," and declaring that "the gaze that sees is the gaze that dominates." Thus, even in his early work, the involvement of vision in the operations and institutions of power was already in question. But it was only later, in his genealogies—and most especially in his account of the birth of the prison—that he elaborated his quarrel with the legacy of the Enlightenment.

Through Foucault's eyes, we see how, in the historical evolution of modernity, "vision has become supervision," as Flynn puts it so accurately. "The hegemony of vision in Foucault's modernity is the hegemony of power," increasingly internalized in the disciplinary practices of individuals: not only self-observation and self-examination, but also continuous, ever-watchful self-monitoring. Thus, the shift from the sovereign power of the classical period to the disciplinary power of the modern is to be correlated, for Foucault, with a shift in the mode of vision dominant in our political institutions: the shift, namely, from governmentality organized around the gaze of the sovereign to governmentality organized by surveillance, panopticism, the normalizing gaze dispersed throughout the social system, maintaining civil order.

In his concluding pages, Flynn questions whether or not Foucault's gaze completely breaks away from the hegemony of that mode of vision distinctive of modernity. And he questions whether or not the critical postmodern gaze that Foucault's life exemplifies can be sufficient for the needs of our time. Don't we need, he asks, a "narrative vision" and a "temporalized reason"? Don't we need, in fact, many *different* ways of seeing, and many different methods and practices of reason? In particular, don't we need a gaze of mutuality and reciprocity, a gaze moved by generosity and friendship?

In chapter 11, on "Ocularcentrism and Social Criticism," Georgia Warnke examines the arguments that Martin Jay has formulated against the many contemporary critics of ocularcentrism in Western culture. Focussing on ideology and social criticism, Warnke acknowledges Jay's point that "for [many] contemporary critics . . . ideology is no longer to be connected to distortions in vision but rather to distortions in language," but she problematizes his claim that this historical shift "follows from a renewed respect for the truths of interpretation over the methods of scientific observation."

According to Warnke, Jay takes these critics to believe that connecting ideology to obscured vision assumes that the social critic is somehow privileged, able to see social reality for what it is, and that, by contrast, connecting ideology with language opens up possibilities for critical interpretation. But she questions Jay's assumption that the repudiation of seeing and the privileging of listening and interpretative processes are necessarily more congenial to an extremely past-oriented, tradition-bound, and conservative social theory, and that, by contrast, the privileging of vision will necessarily keep us more firmly situated in a present we can see—critically—for ourselves. Jay finds support for this position in the social theory of Jürgen Habermas, in spite of the fact that Habermas has been as critical as Heidegger and Merleau-Ponty of the subject-centered observer-spectator paradigm in epistemology, and has connected social emancipation to an ideal of unconstrained communication and to a communicative rationality. Warnke calls into question Jay's reading of Habermas, asking: "Just how tied to a privileging of vision over the truths of an interpretation is Habermas's model of a critical social theory?"

Warnke contends that Jay exaggerates the extent to which Habermas's conception of social critique supports objectivist epistemology, and that he correspondingly plays down the critical function of communicative processes in Habermas's theory. But she also suggests that, instead of taking ocularcentrism to support an objectivist epistemology, we might think of it as supporting the cultivation of social and ethical perception. This proposed revision of the idea of ocularcentrism then leads her to question whether Habermas's account of the critique of ideology sufficiently appreciates the importance of this sense of ocularcentrism, and to suggest that, in the hermeneutics of Hans-Georg Gadamer, this sense is given the recognition it deserves. Here she notes that Gadamer formulated his own critique of the objectivist epistemology as paradigm for the social sciences and the humanities, but argues that, unlike Habermas, he gave insufficient theoretical acknowledgment to the hidden connections between interpretative processes and power.

In the concluding pages of her essay, pages that continue the thinking of Marx, Dewey, and Marcuse, Warnke moves beyond the opposition between the ocular and the discursive—the opposition Arendt articulated in terms of nous and logos, and develops the idea that the cultivation of perception and sensibility exemplified by an "aesthetic education" could multiply our perspectives, expand our horizons, and deepen our moral vision, contributing significantly to the discursive formation of those fusions in the horizons of our understanding that could bring us closer to the achievement of moral consensus.[31] Appreciating that human freedom "is rooted in the human sensibility," and that we need to open up sensibility to "a new dimension of history," Marcuse was led to pose a difficult question: "how can the human sensibility, which is *principiuum individuationis*, also generate a *universalizing* principle?"[32] Warnke's contribution to this collection, putting together Gadamer's hermeneutics of culture and Habermas's theory of communicative action, may be read as the beginning of an answer to this question.

Walter Benjamin would certainly have approved this attention to perception and sensibility. He once wrote: "I have nothing to say, only to show." Words that could also have been uttered, perhaps, by Foucault. In chapter 12, "Dream World of Mass Culture: Walter Benjamin's Theory of Modernity and the Dialectics of Seeing," Susan Buck-Morss writes about the *Arcades* Project. This is perhaps Benjamin's most important work, for in it he formulated a critical theory of modernity and a materialist dialectics of seeing, using material from his experiences in the Arcades of Paris, vast shopping theatres in which he loved to stroll, simultaneously marveling—like a child—at the variety of riches displayed there, before his eyes, but also reflecting very deeply and critically on the intangible, more invisible dimensions of significance in his experiences. He had a way of highlighting and reframing familiar things, penetrating the logic of their re-enchantment under capitalism to see into their ideologically concealed social and cultural reality: he saw the suffering behind their presence, saw the exploitation, alienation, surplus labor, and relations of power behind their construction, saw their secretly calculated fetishism.

If writing to produce dialectical images and transform the way we see things could be sufficient to make one an "ocular" thinker and writer, then Benjamin would certainly count as an "ocular" thinker and writer. Like Nietzsche, like Foucault, Benjamin was a teacher of vision, of vision as social criticism. He wrote, as did they, to make visible what others could not, would not, dared not see. He struggled to overcome the habits of social normalization, socially induced blind spots—ours and his own. He understood the distinctiveness of modernity to be captured in, and by, its visual productivity and visual obsessions. For him, modernity under late capitalism is dominated, and haunted, by dream-images and commodified visual fetishes: visual processes re-enchanting the world which the Enlightenment, and then Marxism, had struggled to free from illusion; processes masking once again the violence of social reality. However, there is insufficient textual evidence for us to say that, for Benjamin, modernity is (distinctively) ocularcentric. To be sure, the modernity about which and for which he wrote is a world of images made visible to us through his clear-sighted, deeply penetrating eyes: a world reflected in store windows and mirrors, a world enchanted and dazzled by the shining objects, the fetishized commodities of late capitalism. Using words to create images, he showed us what Foucault would have called the "micro-physics" of power: no detail of the workings of power in everyday life was too small to escape his notice. In "Types of Lighting," for example, he anticipated Foucault's analysis of panopticism with observations about the early years of electricity that already saw potential danger in nineteenth-century projects for city lighting based on the "idea of universal illumination," an idea which of course captured the imagination of the Enlightenment.

Although the *Passagenwerk* puts into practice a theory of modernity and a theory about seeing, the two theories never converge in a conceptualization of modernity as distinctively ocularcentric. And yet, Benjamin clearly understood the significance of his work with vision for modernity, because his *appeal* to his time, his claim on his contemporaries, was to a large extent framed in terms of images and solicited our capacity to see the world of our own making in a new way, without the illusions and deceptions that have been controlling our lives. Believing that how we see our world is responsible for its production and reproduction, he understood the extent to which changing how we see can be instrumental in changing the world.

Does changing the world require ending the hegemony of vision?

Echoing the critical judgments of Heidegger and Horkheimer (quoted near the beginning of this introduction), Michel de Certeau has argued: "From television to newspapers, from advertising to all sorts of mercantile epiphanies, our society is characterized by a cancerous growth of vision, measuring everything by its ability to show or be shown, and transmuting communication into a visual journey."[33] The argument in the next chapter agrees that media images are increasingly dominant in our psychological, social, and cultural life; but it contests such sweeping condemnations, and looks instead for the signs and symptoms that might foreshadow a redeeming potential in this bewildering culture of vision.

Chapter 13, by Robert D. Romanyshyn, is on "The Despotic Eye and Its Shadow: Media Image in the Age of Literacy." Like Benjamin, Romanyshyn believes that critical attention to the cultural production, reproduction, and circulation of images, representations, and the entire commodity "phantasmagoria" of late modern capitalism is crucial to our understanding of what modernity is all about. According to Romanyshyn, "we stand today at a crossroads." Until recently, modernity was determined by the hegemony of a "literate" vision, the vision that created and reproduced a culture of the book. This vision, abstract, emotionally detached, disembodied, monadic, and linear, is, however, increasingly disappearing, yielding its hegemony to the very different vision of media image consciousness and its culture of image technologies. This historically new mode of vision, immediate, emotionally engaged, participatory, rooted in the body of experience, no longer confined to the metaphysical dualisms of modernity (subject-object, center-periphery, foreground-background), is a way of looking and seeing that corresponds to the omnipresence of television, and it challenges the older mode of vision that corresponds to the modern culture of the book.

For Romanyshyn, television is "the shadow side" of a book consciousness that he identifies with the history of modernity. Examining the character of the vision that figures in Descartes's *Meditations* and the vision brought into being with the invention of linear perspective in the fifteenth century, he explores two crucial "generative sites of modernity," and recovers the historical connection between the ocularcentrism that has been distinctive of this period and the familiar character of our book-centered, ego-centered culture. Thus, he argues that, instead of subjecting television and the image industries to a sweeping condemnation, we should consider them to be "symptomatic" of the present condition of modernity: "as the shadow of the book, [television] makes visible the pathology of verbo-ocular-ego-consciousness by challenging its values of linear rationality, contextual coherence, focused concentration . . . and neutral objectivity."

We may regret the fact that television perpetuates an ocularcentric culture, but we must nevertheless understand the ways in which it also "revisions the eye." Our increasing seduction and narcotization by the images that support a market economy—the same process of reenchantment which Benjamin wanted his dialectic of images to disrupt—is, for Romanyshyn too, a very real danger. But the response he proposes, instead of a defense of visions past, is that we begin to take responsibility for the world our vision has created, and transform this danger into an opportunity. Can we learn from our symptoms? Can we remember what our culture of vision has occluded? These are the questions with which he wants to leave us.

In chapter 14, "Assisting at the Birth and Death of Philosophical Vision," Andrea Nye carries forward the critique of speculative metaphysics and its vision proposed by Luce Irigaray. According to Irigaray, this metaphysical vision originated in Plato's allegory of the cave. Although the mythic dimensions of this cave are chthonic, matriarchal, and in the keeping of the feminine spirit, the allegory itself is unmistakably patriarchal, and celebrates a vision made possible by the triumph and domination of men. For Plato, this vision is glorious and noble, the achievement of a calm and dispassionate contemplation of immutable Forms, a gaze turned away from the sensible, material world of becoming, to abide with eternal truths in a light visible only to the purified reason of the philosopher. And he thought of the allegory as a narrative of rebirth, a passage in which men, having rejected the world of their bodies and senses, of women and sexuality, but still lost in a "shadow theater of deceptive images," could be reborn to a vision of the Forms.

Nye, however, like Irigaray, sees this vision differently—as a vision turned away from life. And as a vision complicitous with war and domination: "The metaphysician's eye," she says, "is a refinement of the general's eye: abstract, all-encompassing, unemotional, pitiless." If this assertion seems extreme, it is worth noting that it echoes an observation made once by Emerson: "The will, the male power, imposes its own thought and wish on others, and makes that military eye which controls boys as it controls men."[34]

But if "Plato's universe of Reason, as Irigaray records it, is the vision of a young man," Nye finds herself "thinking of another man, a later version of this vision of a man, Ludwig Wittgenstein." For, in his *Tractatus Logico-Philosophicus,* "the rectification Plato described has rectified itself in the perfection and purification of a fully mathematized photologicism. Gone is Plato's flickering Aryan fire, the Sun-God, the glittering, blinding reflections of Form. Wittgenstein's metaphysical vision is finally removed from any reference to physical things, detached from any spoken language. . . . Only the purest of representational symmetry remains between logical form and the necessary form of the world."

Whatever radiance remained in Plato's noble vision is, with Wittgenstein, totally suppressed. His eye, a monocular eye, is the dead eye of the strictly "logical subject." "The metaphysician's philosophical vision is finally blind."

For Nye, the character of the vision that has been dominant in the history of ocularcentrism, dominant in the hegemony of vision as paradigm for knowledge, truth, and reality, is, then, the death of vision, a dead vision, a vision of death; and it is related to the death of language, a dead language, a language of the dead, a language of death, and a silence that belongs only to death. But—she conjectures—perhaps understanding this from the depths of our suffering can prepare us for the birth of another vision. If from the maternal womb of Mediterranean culture there could emerge a vision that supported all the great empires of the Western world, then perhaps, in the wake of the nihilism to which this vision has led us, another vision—or say other ways of seeing—could be brought into being.

What is now possible? Nye contends that Irigaray is herself caught in the living death of the very metaphysics from which she struggled to escape. Avoiding Irigaray's blind passageway, Nye's reflections lead her to some provocative questions. What would have happened, she wonders, if those Greek men had turned back, after learning from their vision of the Forms, to look at one another, their gazes engaged by the interactions of friendly conversation? And what would have happened if they had turned and looked at women, looked with eyes moved by feelings of friendship, admiration, and respect?

Finally, in chapter 15, "His Master's Eye," Mieke Bal challenges the very framework of premises in terms of which the question of the hegemony of vision in modernity, and the question of the patriarchal character of this vision, have been formulated, contesting the assumption "that it is possible to define vision in some unified, if not essentialist way." Her challenge to this framework clears a space for the suggestion that "differentiating modes, if not kinds of vision—multiplying perspectives, proliferating points of view," may be "a more useful strategy for examining the ideological, epistemological, and representational implications of the dominating modes of vision, including their illusory monopoly." And she supports her argument for a differentiating, pluralizing conception of vision with an analysis of two historically important "cases": first, the painting *Danae* by Rembrandt and its critical reception in the seventeenth and twentieth centuries; then the painting *Olympia* by Manet, its contemporary reception, and the interpretation of that reception in the critical discourse of present-day art history.

Strongly opposed to "grand narratives" with a totalizing view of modernity, Bal attempts to deconstruct a critical discourse that has supported the domination of a *single* mode of vision. At the same time, she attempts to display and subvert the *character* of this mode of vision, showing us gazes that differ from, and oppose, the patriarchal gaze which has dominated our lives and our culture. If, as Thoreau once said, "the perception of beauty is a moral test,"[35] then Bal's analysis of the critical discourse in art history is more than an argument for different ways of seeing or reading these works of art; it is an indictment of our moral culture.

Working through a detailed analysis of these two paintings, and of their reception in a critical discourse controlled by men, Bal frees the gazes of the women in the paintings from the long history of critical interpretations that obscured their truths: she shows us their defiant looks, resisting the objectifications and typifications of male fantasy, refusing to satisfy the gazes of men; but she also shows us looks exchanged by friends, and looks reciprocating forms of respect. She thereby demonstrates, at the same time, that there are other ways of looking at these paintings—and indeed, more generally, other critical, art-historical points of view, other visions, no less legitimate, the exclusion of which we must no longer tolerate. Practicing art history in a way that makes it a form of social criticism, Bal enables us to see the distinctive spirit of modernity in Rembrandt, and of course later, Manet, a spirit figured in the "enlightened" character and artifice of their gestures, both of them painting works of art that confront and question the domination of our cultural life by the forceful gaze of the sovereign male subject: works of art that also project gazes freed from that domination, gazes moved by quite other visions. Bal's essay will thus leave us, at the end of this book, with an unsettling question: Whose eye is ultimately master?

I would like to let this question close my introduction, if not the book, because it is, I think, an opening for our vision.

NOTES

1. All references to the pre-Socratics are drawn from Kathleen Freeman's *Ancilla to the Pre-Socratic Philosophers* (Cambridge: Harvard University Press, 1978).

2. Hans Jonas, "The Nobility of Sight: A Study in the Phenomenology of the Senses," *Philosophy and Phenomenological Research* 14, no. 4 (June 1954): 507–519. This study was later expanded, and appeared in his book *The Phenomenon of Life: Towards a Philosophical Biology* (New York: Harper & Row, 1966), pp. 135–156.

3. Hannah Arendt, *The Life of the Mind* (New York: Harcourt Brace Jovanovich, 1978), pp. 110–111.

4. Ibid., p. 122.

5. Martin Heidegger, "The Turning," *The Question Concerning Technology and Other Essays* (New York: Harper & Row, 1977), p. 48.

6. Max Horkheimer, *Dawn and Decline: Notes 1926–1931 and 1950–1969* (New York: Seabury Press, 1978), p. 162.

7. See David M. Levin, *The Listening Self: Personal Growth, Social Change, and the Closure of Metaphysics* (London: Routledge, 1989).

8. Jürgen Habermas, "An Alternative Way Out of the Philosophy of the Subject: Communicative vs. Subject-Centered Reason," *The Philosophical Discourse of Modernity* (Cambridge: MIT Press, 1987), p. 297. Also see the chapter "The Entwinement of Myth and Enlightenment: Horkheimer and Adorno," esp. p. 129, where he speaks of the "cramped optics that render one insensible to the traces and the existing forms of communicative rationality," and p. 128, where he argues against "the gaze of contemporary diagnosis," which is incapable of breaking through a dangerously aestheticized "horizon of experience."

9. Friedrich Nietzsche, *The Genealogy of Morals* (New York: Doubleday Anchor Books, 1956), Third Essay, note 12, p. 255.

10. Nietzsche, *The Will to Power* (New York: Random House Vintage Books, 1968), note 540, p. 291.

11. Nietzsche, *Beyond Good and Evil* (New York: Random House Vintage Books, 1966), note 230, p. 161.

12. Nietzsche, *The Will to Power*, note 1031, p. 532.

13. Nietzsche, "On the Uses and Disadvantages of History for Life," *Untimely Meditations* (New York: Cambridge University Press, 1983), section 5, p. 83.

14. Nietzsche, *Joyful Wisdom* (New York: Frederick Ungar, 1960), note 45, p. 82.

15. Heidegger, "Letter on Humanism," *Martin Heidegger: Basic Writings* (New York: Harper & Row, 1977), p. 237.

16. Jacques Derrida, "Sending: On Representation," *Social Research* 49 (1982), p. 310.

17. Ibid., p. 312.

18. Karl Marx, *The Economic and Philosophical Manuscripts of 1844* (New York: International Publishers, 1964), p. 141.

19. Herbert Marcuse, *One-Dimensional Man: Studies in the Ideology of Advanced Industrial Society* (Boston: Beacon Press, 1964), p. 165.

20. Heidegger, "Aletheia (Heraclitus Fragment B16)," *Early Greek Thinking* (New York: Harper & Row, 1975), p. 121.

21. Nietzsche, *The Will to Power*, note 470, p. 262.

22. See David M. Levin, "Justice in the Flesh," in Galen Johnson and Michael Smith, eds., *Ontology and Alterity in Merleau-Ponty* (Evanston, Ill.: Northwestern University Press, 1991), pp. 35–44, and "Visions of Narcissism: Intersubjectivity and the Reversals of Reflection," in Martin Dillon, ed., *Merleau-Ponty Vivant* (Albany: State University of New York Press, 1991), pp. 47–90.

23. See Emmanuel Levinas, *The Theory of Intuition in Husserl's Phenomenology* (Evanston: Northwestern University Press, 1973).

24. Derrida, "Violence and Metaphysics: An Essay on the Thought of

Emmanuel Levinas," *Writing and Difference* (Chicago: University of Chicago Press, 1978), p. 91.

25. Theodor Adorno, *Minima Moralia: Reflections from Damaged Life* (London: New Left Books, 1988), p. 105.

26. Ibid., p. 105.

27. Emmanuel Levinas, *Collected Philosophical Papers* (Dordrecht: Martinus Nijhoff, 1987), p. 118. For a charming example of this vision-in-touch, see Sir Philip Sidney's *Arcadia,* which describes the blush in such a moment: "and once his eye cast upon her and finding hers upon him, he blushed: and she blushed, because he blushed: and yet streight grew paler, because she knew not why he had blushed." Quoted in Mario Praz, *Mnemosyne: The Parallel Between Literature and the Visual Arts* (Princeton: Princeton University Press, 1970), p. 104.

28. Derrida, "Violence and Metaphysics," p. 92.

29. Levinas, p. 118.

30. Robert Coles, "Children As Moral Observers," *The Tanner Lectures on Human Values,* vol. 2 (Salt Lake City: University of Utah Press, 1981), p. 138.

31. Warnke's project here is supported by Yaron Ezrahi's new book, *The Descent of Icarus: Science and the Transformation of Contemporary Democracy* (Cambridge: Harvard University Press, 1991). Ezrahi sees a historical evolution in the political culture of popular vision: a paradigm shift from the "celebrative" mode of seeing dominant during the age of monarchies and spectacular displays of power, to the "attestive" mode of seeing, the empirical, objective, observer-spectator model prominent in the modern age of experimental democracies; and now, another shift, from the "attestive" to the "reflexive," a relativized, more participatory, more discursive mode of seeing, more in keeping with contemporary critiques of objectivism, the subject-object dualism, and the correspondence theory of truth.

32. Marcuse, *Counterrevolution and Revolt* (Boston: Beacon Press, 1972), pp. 71–72.

33. Michel de Certeau, *The Practice of Everyday Life* (Los Angeles: University of California Press, 1984), p. xxi.

34. See Ralph Waldo Emerson, "Education," in M. van Doren, ed., *The Portable Emerson* (New York: Viking Press, 1946), p. 269.

35. H. D. Thoreau, *The Journal of Henry David Thoreau,* vol. 2 (New York: Dover Publishing, 1906), p. 43. The entry is dated June 21, 1852.

ONE

Light as a Metaphor for Truth

At the Preliminary Stage of Philosophical Concept Formation

Hans Blumenberg

If indications are not misleading, a revival of philosophical research into the history of concepts is imminent. Several factors are behind this trend, including a recognition of the futility of the conceptual neoproduction that has erupted during the last decades, increasing embarrassment about the difficulties of mutual understanding in philosophy, and paradigmatic accomplishments in theology with regard to research on concepts.

If this long-neglected work is profitably to be taken up again, one will, above all, have to revise the scope of the term *philosophical concept*, as compared with earlier approaches. Because of the peculiarity and history of philosophical statements, *terminology* has a much broader meaning here than in other disciplines, which have either drawn their concepts from philosophy itself or been able to construct their own conceptual apparatus by establishing unambiguous definitions. In constantly having to confront the unconceptualized and the preconceptualized, philosophy encounters the means of articulation found in this nonconceptualizing and preconceptualizing, adopts them, and develops them further in separation from their origin. The notion that the philosophical logos has "overcome" prephilosophical mythos has narrowed our view of the scope of philosophical terminology; besides concepts in the strict sense, which are offset by definition and fulfilled intuition [*Anschauung*],[1] there is a broad range of mythical transformations, bordering on metaphysical conjectures, which find expression in a metaphorics with diverse forms.

This preliminary stage of a concept is, in its "aggregate state," more

Originally published under the title "Licht als Metapher der Wahrheit: Im Vorfeld der philosophischen Begriffsbildung," in *Studium General* 10, no. 7 (1957). Translated by Joel Anderson.

vivid, more sensitive to the ineffable, and less dominated by fixed traditional forms. Often, what could not find a medium within the rigid architectonics of systems found expression here. Careful research in this area should be able to unearth a wealth of resources. The hope is that the present study of metaphors of light and their accompanying milieu will contribute, in both content and method, to a philosophical "metaphorology."[2]

In their expressive power and subtle capacity to change, metaphors of light are incomparable. From its beginnings, the history of metaphysics has made use of these characteristics in order to give an appropriate reference to its ultimate subject matter, which can no longer be grasped in material terms. Again and again, this cipher has been used in attempting to show that there is more to the concept of Being [*des Seins*] than an empty abstraction which one could extract from beings [*dem Seienden*] as their most general real predicate.[3] The relation of unity to plurality, of the absolute to the conditional, of origin to descent—all found a "model" of sorts here.

Light can be a directed beam, a guiding beacon in the dark, an advancing dethronement of darkness [*Finsternis*],[4] but also a dazzling superabundance, as well as an indefinite, omnipresent brightness containing all: the 'letting-appear' that does not itself appear, the inaccessible accessibility of things. Light and darkness can represent the absolute metaphysical counterforces that exclude each other and yet bring the world-constellation into existence. Or, light is the absolute power of Being, which reveals the paltriness [*Nichtigkeit*] of the dark, which can no longer exist once light has come into existence. Light is intrusive; in its abundance, it creates the overwhelming, conspicuous clarity with which the true "comes forth"; it forcibly acquires the irrevocability of Spirit's consent. Light remains what it is while letting the infinite participate in it; it is consumption without loss. Light produces space, distance, orientation, calm contemplation; it is the gift that makes no demands, the illumination capable of conquering without force.

The intent here is not to fill in the details of this short and doubtless fully incomplete outline of the expressive potential of metaphors of light, but rather to show the way in which transformations of the basic metaphor indicate changes in world-understanding and self-understanding. What we call "history" in a fundamental sense is of course always in conflict with the essential inertia of the materials providing the evidence in which a basic change in the conception of reality not only can become manifest but can actually, for the first time, achieve articulation. Here, however, it is precisely traditional philosophical terminology, as it populates indices and specialist dictionaries, that is capable of only the slowest shifts of meaning. In the history of ideas, settled definitions that emerge from the reshuffling of concepts tend to be genuinely "slow on the up-take," just as, in philosophy, by the time a "system" comes together, the underlying substructure is usually already in motion again. These conditions explain the significance of immature, groping, tentative modes of expression, among which metaphors of light have a privileged position. Outstanding achievements have already been made in research on individual periods,[5] but only a more comprehensive periodicization can make apparent the real "achievement" of these metaphors.

In all likelihood, the concept of light originally belonged to a dualistic conception of the world, as the second part of Parmenides poem [*The Way of Opinion*][6] documents for us (and for the Pythagorians, according to Aristotle's report).[7] Light and darkness are, like fire and earth, fundamental primordial principles. Their enmity leads to the awareness that Being is nothing assured, that truth is nothing self-evident. But the fact that Parmenides situates this dualism in the *second* part of the poem already points toward its being overcome; it belongs to the sphere of *doxa*. At the beginning of the poem, the path to the truth leads *eis phaos*.[8] In the center of his work, Parmenides uproots the dualism of Being and not-Being, truth and appearance, light and darkness: Being does not exist *because* it is not not-Being (since not-Being would then be *necessary* for its Being),[9] and light is not *essentially* the opposite of darkness; rather, in the essence of light, darkness is destroyed and overcome. Thus, Plato was not the first to release the concepts of Being, truth, and light from a dualistic reliance on their opposite. Plato was, however, the first to demonstrate, by means of metaphors of light, that this splitting-in-two implies what can be termed the *naturalness* of the connection between Being and truth.

What this means is that Being *is*, as "nature," *of its own accord* (not in virtue of its opposite), and that, in exactly the same way, it is true, i.e., it is true of its own accord and not in virtue of a subsequent process of thought discovered in a situation of un-truth. Truth is light upon Being itself, Being as light, i.e., Being as the *self-presentation* of beings. That is why cognition in its highest form bursts out of the inactive, calm contemplation of *theōria*. That is why, in Platonic *anamnēsis*, the truth that has already been seen penetrates, again and again, into that which is forgetful of its origin. That is why, in the *Republic*'s allegory of the cave, an original situation is constructed with a perfectly artificial and forcible screening-off of "natural" light, a situation that no longer has anything dualistic about it and which only later must be bent back into a dualistic schema. The drama of truth is not a cosmic *agon* between light and darkness but rather only a process of man's withdrawing himself or handing himself over—a matter, thus, of paideia.[10] Truth is not only present, it is insistent.

In the Platonic allegory of the cave, it is said of the Idea of the Good—
which figures there as the sun that puts everything in the light of Being—
that (as the origin of knowability, Being, and essence) it is not itself a
being, but rather something that stands out, in virtue of its dignity and
strength, above beings.[11] This statement is not at all metaphysically lad-
en: that which gives everything else visibility and 'objecthood' cannot, in
the same way, itself have the character of an object. Light is only seen
in what it lets become visible. The "naturalness" of light consists precisely
in this, that it only "dawns," in its own sense, with the visibility of things,
and thus is itself not of the same nature as that which it evokes. But already in Plato, this *difference* is tinged with *transcendence*; the *metaphorics*
of light already has a *metaphysics* of light implicit in it. A way of expressing the naturalness of truth turns into its opposite: truth becomes "localized" in transcendency.

Despite an abundance of gods of nature, Greek religion did not have
a deity of light,[12] precisely because light was too comprehensive to be
grasped: it is the *wherein* of nature, not its component part, "daylight as
the brightness in which one moves, in which the world articulates itself,
in which it becomes surveyable and understandable, in which the distinction between here and there, between this and that, is possible ... and
which, at the same time, thereby makes existence [*Dasein*] understandable to itself."[13] Spirit and material things are equally in this brightness.
"Illumination" is not an inner as opposed to an outer occurrence; rather,
ontic and ontological elucidation [*Erhellung*] are identical. There is no
mysticism of light in Plato; light is not a peculiar, special dimension of experience.[14] Aristotle formulated the same point in more sober terms
when he said that that which sees becomes colored itself, so to speak,
and that the reality of the perceived and the reality of the perceiving are
identical.[15]

Therein lies the radical difference between light and darkness: darkness is unable to bring about this identity; it is ontically and ontologically
impotent. From this perspective, it is easy to grasp the full difference
that exists with regard to the meaning of "light" and "darkness" in the
Neoplatonism of late antiquity. There, they become antagonistic forces
that dispute with each other over the soul; they exercise, seize, and "incorporate" force.

Thus, in order to see what precisely "light" meant at the time, one
must pay attention to how "the dark" is to be understood as well. There
is an autonomous, "romantic" darkness [*Dunkelheit*] of the dark, and
there is a darkness [*Dunkel*] that lies under the light and in the light.
Corresponding to the perspective of classical Greek philosophy developed here, the following can be said of Greek tragedy: "Classical tragedy indeed shows the dark underground of human existence, but not as

something that is to be sensed dimly. On the contrary, it elucidates this dark underground with a ruthlessly bright light."[16]

The transcendency of light implied in the Platonic allegory of the sun becomes dominant in Hellenistic thought. The brightness that fills the cosmos like a medium is withdrawn, concentrated, objectified as a metaphysical pole. Radiance comes to mean a decline, a loss of darkness [*Dunkels*]; and consumption comes to signify loss. The "unnatural" protection of the cave is extended to the cavernous nature of the entire cosmos, which seizes light, swallows it, and exhausts it. The previously translucent surfaces of the spheres thicken into cave walls. Light, now otherworldly and pure, does not allow for theoretical lingering in joyful contemplation; it demands extraordinary, ecstatic attention, in which fulfilling contact and repellent dazzling[17] become one. Few are equal to this task. The deadly light must be made available to mortals in the more cautious dosages of the *phōtismos* of mysteries. Thus, light becomes a metaphor for "salvation," for immortality.

The cosmic *flight of light* is the precondition for the concept of "revelation," which announces a return of light as an eschatological event and bids man prepare himself for it. By holding the transcendent in reserve, light demands a purer condition of humanity than now happens to be the case.[18] It is no longer being *in* the light and seeing that offers man fulfillment; instead, what drives him on is the idea of looking *into* the light itself and letting everything else that is visible be extinguished. Light's flight from the world results in man's urge to enter the light. This leads directly to the Neoplatonism of late antiquity and to gnosis. Here, the classical conception of *theōria* has lost its footing: Being is no longer the self-presentation of beings; it has become something "formless that cannot be glimpsed";[19] it does not open eyes but shuts them. Absolute light and absolute darkness collapse into each other. Consistent with this, the areopagite of all mysticism will give the phrase *theion skotos* its initial coining.

Until now, this particular dimension (the 'de-lumination' of the world) has been given more attention than the unanimity of other dimensions of Hellenistic and late Classical thought. What has been overlooked above all is that skepticism, too, represents a reply to the cosmic flight of light. Indeed, it is not at all an elementary "accident" (of the school) that skepticism breaks out in the middle of the Platonic Academy. Here too, a position is being taken with regard to the fundamental ontological event of light's transcendency, and it is an attitude of flight, of shutting out the world, of rejecting *theōria* for *epochē*. One needs only to remind oneself that Socrates, in the *Phaedo,* has to experience the way in which turning toward reality itself dazzles the eye, and that the conclusion he draws from this is to escape to logoi and to observe in them the truth of beings.[20] Vision wants to defend itself from this dazzling immediacy; it does not want to look into the sun and is content with the stand-in mediacy of logos.

Skepticism can situate itself in this tradition; it simply takes the next step, following the proven failure of logos in the dispute among the schools. It does not concern itself with the experience of light and dark at all. But before this step can be taken, the classical connection between *eudaimonia* and *theōria* had to be broken. A completely happy existence is presupposed for man as an *inner* possibility. But in skepticism, this interior is peculiarly *empty*; it is the sheer difference that remains after the subtraction of any connection to the world. *That* something remains in *epochē,* and *what* it could be never came into question for skepticism; like Epicureanism, it took for granted the assumption that happiness was guaranteed simply by protection against unhappiness, confusion, and pain. The skeptic is the negative version of the mystic: he too closes his eyes, not against the dazzling abundance of absolute light, but against the questioning and confusing urgency of *obscuritas rerum.* In shutting off the *outer* dark, however, the *inner* light has still not yet been won. This is the point on which the Stoics brought their moral absolutism to bear. Consistent with this, they sought a *positive* definition of the concept of happiness and connected it with the inner self-evidence of ethical life.

This engagement of the various Hellenistic schools of thought with one another on the basis of their mutual ontological implication becomes clear in Cicero. He coined the concept of "natural light" for the tradition.[21] And he linked the metaphor of light with inner moral self-evidence. For Cicero, light is no longer the universal brilliance in which all beings are found equally; rather, a sort of anthropocentric *economy* is attached to light. Human life finds itself in a clearing [*Lichtung*] appropriate to its necessities. In the theoretical sphere, the gleam of probability, to which the "naturalness" of truth is reduced, "suffices." In the practice of methodically playing theses off each other, as the Academic skeptics engaged in it, *probabile* "shines" forth.[22] Wanting to go further is *arrogantia,* upon which the teleological economy of truth does not look highly. Outside the clearing that is economically appropriate to man, the dark is given its due. Among the *vitia* that violate the norm of *sapientia,* he mentions not only carelessness in giving approval, but also an orientation toward *res obscurae* and *non necessariae.*[23]

This sort of exclusion would have been unthinkable earlier, given the ontological assumptions of classical ancient philosophy. The natural striving for knowledge, as Aristotle formulates it at the beginning of the *Metaphysics,* moves in a sphere of *universal* theoretical brightness and visibility, and *theōria* represents the comprehension (via imaginative reenactment) of an absolutely divine act. Cicero sees knowledge in the context of human specificity and neediness; theoretical activity comes to have moral premises. Under the title of *curiositas,* the Middle Ages will continue this trial in terms of theoretical hubris.[24]

For Cicero, it is in accordance with practical principles that light and dark are divided in the theoretical domain. The claim upon beings that is open to man is not primarily *scire* but *uti*.[25] Thus, light's center of intensity must lie in the principles of human action; only in these *res necessariae* are full light and compelling self-evidence assured. Plato's self-luminous *agathon,* which gives light to everything else, is not extended into transcendency but rather internalized in the most intimate immanence of moral consciousness—which *also* means, however, that it is theoretically hidden. Cicero accepts the Stoic principle that if one has any doubt whatsoever as to the rightness or wrongness of an act, one should refrain from performing it at all.[26] But the acceptance of this presupposition lands him in an unnoticed contradiction with his own Platonic "residuum of light." For can there be any doubt about right or wrong at all if what is stated in the next sentence is true? *Aequitas lucet ipsa per se, dubitatio cogitationem significat iniuriae.* If the good presents itself as self-luminous, then doubt alone is enough to indicate that a wrong is being considered. The good is so authentically in-the-light that it rules out doubt.[27] Corresponding to the internalization of pure light are the inward forms of its obscuration by the passions.[28] But, at the same time, internalized light also pushes its way out again: Cicero treats *gloria* as the "emanation" of *virtus* that has been taken up and confirmed by the *communitas*; virtue shines forth and commands the respect of the human community.[29] Moral quality is still related to aesthetic quality and, at its highest level, can turn into it—a Platonic inheritance!

EXCURSUS: THE CAVE

Darkness, as the power dualistically opposed to light, as a vanquished emptiness, as the natural background zone of the economic clearing of the humanly knowable, as a dazzling envelope of pure and absolute light—these are the correlates of the metaphorics of light considered thus far. In this field of signification, metaphors of the cave gain a special position. The cave is not simply the world opposed to light in the way that darkness is the "natural" opposite of brightness. The world of the cave is an "artificial," indeed perfectly violent underworld, relative to the sphere of natural light and natural dark: a region of screening-off and forgetting, a surrogate and derivative of Being. It is appropriate to address metaphors of the cave at this point, since it is Cicero who, in his discussion of a cave allegory found in an early Aristotelian dialogue, exemplifies most pronouncedly the just-mentioned features of cave metaphors.[30]

In this connection, the Stoic Balbus attempts to show that the *admirabilitas* of the world have paled for us as a result of our becoming accustomed to them, and that people who had always lived under the earth would, upon surfacing and beholding the cosmos, instantly believe in the existence and effectiveness of gods. The most important difference from the allegory of the cave in Book 7 of Plato's *Republic* is that, in Cicero, the situation in the cave is merely a thought experiment for hypothetically reducing the factor of being accustomed. The normal situation (*haec loca, quae nos incolimus*) is outside the cave, within sight of the cosmos in a constant and thus experientially flattened way. In Plato, the space outside the cave is the extraordinary residing place of the wise, whereas the situation in the cave represents our "normal" condition; the people in the cave are precisely not *atopoi*, as Glaucon asserts, but rather *homoioi hēmin*, as Socrates declares in rebuke. Already, in Plato, the artificiality of the cave world of objects is implied: the shadows that appear on the cave wall are generated by artificial equipment, artistic forms, and all sorts of productions by human hands.

Nonetheless, the Platonic cave is impoverished compared to that of Cicero. There, the emphasis is on brilliance and splendor, in order to prevent the slightest feeling of dissatisfaction or malcontent. Everything is there, *quibus abundant ii, qui beati putantur*. Cicero's cave world is one of "urban" luxury, a dazzlingly appointed sphere of culture, which captivates in virtue of its sheer attractiveness. In the Platonic cave, by contrast, man is chained and is in a situation of constraint which, although it is presupposed, virtually forces the question—which is not stressed until Neoplatonism—of what caused this. For Cicero, it is crucial that the cave world seem able to "compete" with the upper world, since the ascent out of this sphere is conceived as a matter of pure coincidence and is only considered in terms of the surprise that it effects.

In Plato, by contrast, the release from the chains, the painful reorientation, and the climb up the steps of disillusionment make up the crucial notion of paideia, which is meant to create an awareness, in retrospect, of the cave world as a sphere in which Being and truth were lacking. In Cicero, in spite of all the brilliance with which the actual cosmos is portrayed, the realm of artificial light has nothing horrifying about it. Cicero has become familiar with the economy of the dark. One might almost say that he might have had a certain affinity for his conception of the cave, in which nature has been turned completely into *res obscura* and all certainty continues to be allocated to the *inner* light.

The expressive power of Cicero's cave metaphor lies precisely in the fact that the cave has lost its (*sit venia verbo*) "existential seriousness"; it has become a hypothesis, a mental exercise. The contrasting background of *obscuritas rerum*, along with the internalization of *lumen naturae* corresponding to it, have undermined the assumptions behind the image of the cave.[31] From here on, radical reinterpretations of "cave" become possible. The entire cosmos had been equated with a cave once before by the pre-Socratics;[32] but it is Neoplatonism that, for the first time, really makes something of this identity.

Partly as a result of vivid allegorical readings of Homer, the grotto of the nymphs in the *Odyssey* gets cosmologically extended in meaning, as in the *De antro nympharum* of Plotinus's student Porphyry, where cosmos and cave exist for each other. The one is the *symbolon* of the other, and man is the *tertium*, who is prevented by temptation and gentle force from reaching his cave-transcending destiny. Here, the cave, identified with the cosmos, issues in a scenario of the incarnation characteristic of Eastern Christian symbolism: Christ is born in a cave instead of a stable, and Justinian insists that the cave cult of Mithras is a diabolical usurpation of this symbolic locus.[33] The topos of "the light in the cave" has become possible only as a result of this constellation.[34] The paideutic path no longer leads out of the cave; the gaze is directed into the dark, because in it the unbelievable—that light could appear *here*—has become believable. The Platonic opposition of the cave fire to the sun of the Good has been eliminated: the light in the cave is of one essence with its origin; it is its steward and guarantor, and not a deceitful source of shadows. The inside of the cave has been reassessed positively.

As individualized caves, the small room and the monastic cell become, in the Middle Ages, places where the truth is openly present, an indication that now everything can be expected *from within*. *Intra in cubiculum mentis tuae, exclude omnia praeter Deum*[35] is a new motto that generates caves and chambers in which one can *wait* for the light, as the belief in *grace* implies. But this conception immediately turns into a metaphor for the "inner space of self-possession," as Montaigne understands "cave" (*tanière*).[36] The cave remains in use as a contrasting metaphor vis-à-vis the new and emergent. Francis Bacon formulates the awkwardness of the individual within its subjective world under the title *idola specus*;[37] disposition, education, and experience represent each person's own particular cave, which breaks and weakens the "natural light" for each. The "cave" denotes the facticity of the subject, the world of its own in which the subject always already finds itself. Significantly, Bacon renders *idia phronēsis*, the phrase used by Heraclitus, to whom he refers by name, as "own little world." And leaving the cave is now no longer the paideutic path of the wise individual into full light, but rather a *method,* a "technique" for the production of a "greater common world" for all.

Leaving the cave becomes a metaphor within the philosophy of history; it denotes a *new epoch* of humanity. This is how Descartes used the metaphor. He compares the Scholastics' fight against the new science to the ways of "a blind man, who, to fight without a handicap against someone who is sighted, makes his opponent go into the depths of a very dark cave"; in publishing his method, by contrast, he "would be doing almost the same as if [he] were to open some windows and make some light of day enter into that cave where they have descended to fight."[38] This is a significant new image in place of the paideutic path out of the cave, for here the space itself is transformed. It does something not only to man but *to the world,* something that no longer depends on the individual's education and will. This is not, however, a momentary act, but rather a historically continuous path of dis-covering the truth, *qui ne se découvre que peu à peu.* The window metaphor takes this into account with its implication of light gradually gaining access. Recall the significance of the closed, medieval chamber in Descartes's portrayal of the turning point in his thinking: "I remained for a whole day by myself in a small stove-heated room."[39] Here the relation of the room to the world is still completely medieval: the "direction" is from the outside to the inside.

Nicholas of Cusa illustrated this with the image of a cosmographer (*Compendium* 8). In order to produce a map of the world, the cosmographer first collected all the empirical data, *clauditque portas et ad conditorem mundi internum transfert intuitum . . .* This internal 'ground' of the world is the immediate relationship between man's mind and God's, the *signum conditoris, in quo vis creativa . . . relucet.* In the medieval chamber's screening-off of the world, the creative potency of man lights up for the first time. Only through asceticism does man take hold of the world.

From this point on, the cave becomes the accepted metaphor in the philosophy of history for the point from which "progress" must begin. The problems of human socialization are exemplified by the hypothetical situation of leaving the primordial cave (where, quite fittingly, the relics of primordial man are also sought and found). The topos of the history-initiating departure from the cave was already given an initial form in antiquity. In Vitruvius, for example, it is the flames of a forest fire that lure people out of the cave and socialize them for the first time;[40] in Cicero, it is rhetoric that manages to "convince" them to come out of an isolated cave existence and enter into community.[41]

This ambiguity between an automatic instinctual process and a primordial intellectual accomplishment runs through the entire history of the motif of leaving the cave. The return to the cave, by contrast, is a matter of deviant curiosity, as in Don Quixote's descent into a cave (*Don Quixote de la Mancha*, vol. 2, chaps. 22 and 23) or in the remarkable imitation of Cicero's allegory of the cave in Jean Paul,[42] where the hero, Gustav, in accordance with a condition of his parents' marriage contract, spends the first eight years of his life underground "for heaven" (in the Stoic sense!), with the paideutic idea of keeping the child from "being hardened to both the beauty of nature and the distortions of humans"; and it is expressly confirmed later that the plan worked, for "the beauty of nature was the only thing he could talk about enthusiastically with other (viz. female) beauties;—and he could condense, in the most lively way, all the world's charms into *one* morning, when he described his entrance up out of earth into the great hall of the world."[43] But the return to the cave, whence humanity stepped forth into its "progress," can also signify a distancing from this progress: the cave thus becomes a locus of aristocratic seclusion, of withdrawal from the lowly spheres of the commonly human, of the desire for a reorientation of movement in history. Zarathustra's cave is of this type. [End of excursus.]

Returning to the point where this digression began, we can say that the transcendency of light, on the one hand, and its internalization on the other, characterize the transition from the metaphorical to the metaphysical usage of the notion. Both correlates of this development are linked by a crucially new idea: light acquires a *history*.

The inner light of the mind [*Geist*] is descended from transcendent light: not, however, by means of "illumination" but by means of "dispersal"; not because of a message but due to an "accident" of theft, of illegitimate cosmic implication. The drama of the diaspora and reunification of absolute light is the fundamental conception of gnosis. Light no longer shines into the world in order to wake it into Being; instead, it gets lost in an alien and enemy sphere; it must be liberated and led back to its origin. The paideutic history of *man*, who comes out of the dark into the light, has been transformed into a history of *light*, which loses itself to the dark and returns to itself. Man is only a "vehicle" for this history, which is not a human but a cosmic drama. With this, the concept of "world" lands in an irresolvable ambiguity: without the descent [*Herabkunft*] of divine light, there would be no visibly formed cosmos, no origin of the material world; at the same time, however, this creation of the world represents the metaphysical ruin of pure light, the contamination and distortion of the absolute.

Plotinus, too, in his discussion of the origin of *kakon*, describes the emergence of the cosmos and the origin of evil *at the same time*.[44] For Plotinus, the pure light of the Good and the pure dark of matter are each *mē on.* The drama of intermingling, from which *to on* emerges, is played out between these two poles; from the perspective of this origin, what is [*das Seiende*] has a negative value. This negativity of what is corresponds to that of *logos.* Whereas Socrates, in the *Phaedo,* sought refuge in *logoi,* now the mind must be awakened from its state of laboring under *logoi* and redirected to the ineffable and nonconceptual contemplation of pure light.[45] Likenesses no longer refer back to the original, as in Plato, but rather deceitfully seduce one away from it; only those who look, know.[46] There is only one "object" of true knowledge: light itself and itself *an sich. Descent is, by itself, decline.* Therein lies an irrevocable immanent conclusion of the metaphysics of light: light, as the Good, represents self-squandering and self-emanation; precisely thereby, however, light also represents distancing from itself, loss of self, and self-humiliation. This will be the main difficulty in the Christian reception of the metaphorics of light: *kakon* cannot emerge as a result of God's self-emanating, luminous essence. This is the central problem in Augustine's metaphysics, which he sets out to solve in his argument with Manichean gnosis. The cosmos, as the God's "creation," can no longer represent light's mésalliance.

The starting point for the *Christian reception* of the metaphorics and metaphysics of light is the peculiar separation that the biblical report of Creation makes between the origin of "light" (on the first day) and that of "lights" (on the fourth day). This provided an easy entrance, which could hardly be missed, for the idea of a light that cannot be localized in the cosmos and that precedes all beings. The Christian tradition's extremely rich "language of light" took its point of departure from this approach.

We are not concerned here with an inventory; instead, our attention is directed, once more, to transformations of meaning occurring in the transition to and reception of this language of light. Central themes of this transformation can already be found in Genesis: the light of the first day represents *created* light. It has its source in a divine command; its opposition to darkness is not a primordial dualism but is based on God's positing and dividing. God Himself is beyond this opposition and has it at His disposal. This requires a reversal of the initial, dualistic cast that late antiquity gave to metaphors of light.

Far more important, however, is the unavoidable collision that occurs between the implications of that conception of light, on the one hand, and the fundamental assertion of the *willful* positing of beings on the other. If the connection between phenomenal beings and the 'ground' of Being is understood in terms of the "model" of light, then the implication of a "natural" overflowing of light onto the lit, of the emanative transformation of "ground" into "grounded" cannot be ruled out. This is indeed what metaphors of light have a tendency, immanently, to assert: that the entirety of a "ground" squanders and expresses itself, yet without diminishing. Implicit in metaphors of light is, further, the idea that they presuppose, if not a dualistic counterprinciple, then certainly a reflecting and passive underlying "ground": the substratum entailed by the classical concept of *hulē*, which appears in the light. This is where differences emerge between the language that has been handed down and what it now has to say.

With his attempt to transform biblical statements into Greek metaphysics, the Alexandrian Jew Philo had already decided how the image of light would be received. In his allegorical reading of Genesis, *De opificio mundi*, Philo succumbs almost completely to his "guiding image" of light. Just as he puts the light of the first day and the lights of the fourth day in the *genetic* context of aesthetic light emerging out of noetic light, he understands *noēton phōs* as "emission" rather than "creation."[47] The introduction of the concept of will was not able to stave off the "naturalism" of this image, because the concept of will is synonymous, for Philo, with that of the Platonic Ideas, which the Academic Antiochus had already dynamized.[48] Attempts have repeatedly been made since then to apply metaphors of light to an effective form of divine will, viewed as "emanation."[49] There is, however, an insurmountable heterogeneity here between metaphysical fact and metaphorical category. In Philo, the accent is suddenly shifted, in the Platonic sense: light is not the worldly first-created, but is rather the otherworldly creator; as Creator, God is *phōs*,[50] is Himself *noētos hēlios*,[51] the original source of the light of Being.[52] This "naturalization" of the biblical idea of creation remains the essential indication of how metaphors of light are used until the High Scholastic Middle Ages.

The association of metaphors of light with Gnostic dualism slowed their Christian reception but did not prevent it. By developing a concept of freedom, and by strictly formulating the *ex nihilo* of creation thinking, Augustine undermined dualism and prepared the way for the final Christian legitimation of *illuminatio*. Never before and never since has the language of light been handled in such a subtle and richly nuanced way. The predominantly epistemological interest in *illuminatio* has not yet been able to generate a suitably encompassing study; for that reason, we will neglect this (epistemological) dimension here, in order to draw attention to what has usually been neglected. Most important is the way in which Augustine distances himself from the Gnostic usage of metaphors of light. He accuses the Manicheans of not distinguishing *inter lucem quod est ipse Deus* from *lucem quam fecit Deus*. God is not simply light; He is *lucifa lux*.[53]

Augustine renounces the idea of the emanative homogeneity of the light of Being (from absolute light to noetic light to aesthetic light), and thereby renounces the idea of a magnificently unified conception as well. He calls for metaphysical divisions: as between uncreated and created, so too between light *qua cernimus* and light *qua intelligimus*.[54] In our terminology, he *traces the metaphysics of light back to the metaphorics of light*! He argues with rhetorical vehemence against the Manichean *fabella* of light's primordial struggle with darkness, against the entire dramatic mythology of defeat, consumption, and degradation by darkness and light's reliberation, purification, and elevation—all with the help of man.[55] Not only is Augustine's God beyond the reach of such an attempt to grasp Him, but light, which God gives to humans, is not *tale lumen, quod ab aliquo possit obtenebrari*.[56] This is not only a matter of the incontestability of His saving Will but also of the illuminative underpinnings of the truth that is accessible to man. Man himself cannot be light: *Lumen tibi esse non potes; non potes, non potes*.[57] Man is not light [*Licht*] but only a light [*Leuchte*] that has been lit by light: *Lucerna et accendi potest, et exstingui potest; lumen verum accendere potest, exstingui non potest*. This talk of *lumen illuminatum* and of *participando illuminari* is meant not only to set out a strict distinction of *Being* but also to signify the absolute character of the *truth* available to man.[58]

Augustine made this discovery against the background of Academic skepticism. In contrast to the Neoplatonists' ecstatic concept of truth, in which the highest level of the disclosure of truth is seeing-into-the-light, Augustine returns to the classical form of the metaphor of seeing-in-the-light: we can recognize the light only by the certainty that it grants us in elucidated beings.[59] Light is always, so to speak, "behind us," and that is true precisely for *lux interior*, which is responsible for things being laid plain to us—*qua res quaeque manifesta est*.[60] In itself, this hiddenness of revealing light is indicated, in the same place, by the paradoxical and (in spite of being analogous to Neoplatonic formulations) completely autochthonous talk of *insensibilieas tenebrae huius lucis*. Notwithstanding the oft-desired terminological harmonization with Plotinus—e.g., in the case of *attingere* and *amplecti*—the sheer inwardness of *illuminatio* rules out an interpretation in terms of ecstasy.[61] In Augustine, the "locus" of *illuminatio* is the "depths" of the soul, especially *memoria*'s "ground" of inwardness.[62] What the ec-static act would have to have missed is precisely the "direction" from which *illuminatio* comes.

Instead, the paideutic moment associated with the metaphorics of light becomes prominent again: the crucial drama is not the history of light but human *conversio*. To put it in the language of Plato's allegory of the cave, the accent is on turning away from the shadows, or more narrowly and precisely, on breaking the chains that forced the gaze toward the shadows. Everything depends on something that, in Plato, the prisoners in the cave were not able to accomplish by themselves, although this is treated as incidental there and is given no importance in comparison with the path of paideia. At the start of the path of paideia, there is now an all-important condition, namely, the act of *gratia,* which can be grasped in the experience of *conversio.* Augustine's doctrine is a "metaphysics of conversion."[63]

Finally, it should be noted that Augustine's aversion to the implication of "flow" in the language of light represents an essential difference from the Neoplatonist metaphysics of light. He sets the emanantistic *fluere* in strict opposition to one of his favorite terms, the substantialist *manere: nihil est omne quod fluit . . . est autem aliquid, si manet, si constat, si semper tale est.*[64] The development of the idea of *creatio ex nihilo* implies a sharper outline of what is [*des Seienden*] than the Neoplatonic overflow of light onto the dark 'ground' of primordial matter; against the background of nothingness, the moment of keeping oneself in Being, of *custodire se velle* (as an intensification of the Stoics' *suum esse conservere*), establishes itself as a basic characterization of all that is [*alles Seienden*] (after *existentia* and *essentia*), for which Augustine reinvents the term *manentia.*[65]

The light of the Neoplatonists, which flows out in stages and which hypostatically multiplies and forms itself, is also the target of the Augustinian creation terminology, with its emphasis on the momentary totality of the creative act. This is evinced most succinctly in the *ictus condendi,* in the "push" that "grounds" Being, which expressly exceeds the "flow" of *gradibus attingere* and *gressibus pervenire.*[66] Augustine cannot accept the "naturalness" (in the sense of *natura non facit saltus*) implied by the metaphorics of light, as long as he holds onto the idea of the radical originating "leap" [*Ur-"sprung"*] of Being via the *mandavit* (viz. *Deus*) *et creata sunt.* In the medieval tradition, these boundaries of the metaphorics of light have all too often become blurred. The figurative as well as phonetic affinity between *lumen* and *flumen* comes to assert itself once again, in spite of Augustinian reservations.

EXCURSUS: THE EYE AND THE EAR

In the language of the metaphorics of light, the eye (as the *organ* associated with light) does not become explicitly significant until the correspondence between elucidation and vision has partly or even completely ceased to be obvious. Such a process (of ceasing to be a matter of course) can mean a return either to a dazzling, extreme brightness which hurts the eye, blinds it, and forces it to shut itself, or to a dulling of the eye itself, due to everything from the impurity of those who see, to the willful and culpable shutting of the eye against what is, by nature, its to see.

In Plato's allegory of the cave, the relativity of the disruption of sight is seen in terms of the starting situations relative to different paths: both the one who comes out of the light into the darkness and the one who steps out of the dark into the light cannot see at first, because the organ cannot immediately make the transition.[67] Becoming accustomed to the light diminishes its dazzling effects. At the same time, however, it is also an essential source of deception about one's own standpoint vis-à-vis Being, since it functions ambivalently: after a while, one sees as well in the half-light of the cave as in daylight.

The absolutely dazzling, to which no one can ever become accustomed, first emerges in Neoplatonism. But here it comes to mean something positive: the coincidence of seeing and not-seeing found in the dazzling effect of pure light is the fundamental confirming experience of all mysticism, in which the presence of the absolute attests itself, in which all thinking and speaking is surpassed, and which represents the uniquely adequate way of encountering transcendency.[68]

At the same time, by way of painful presence, of the eye-penetrating violence of that which is seen, the sense of sight passes into a perception by the sense of touch, a "contact." The distance involved in vision is lost; in its place, the highest grade of evidence for the reality of the "object" comes to be that of the tactile faculty. With the loss of the distance and standpoint involved in sight, the one who previously had been "only" someone who saw has simultaneously become another; he is no longer this self and no longer himself; he *belongs* to the Other, which cannot be regarded purely theoretically. To want (and to be able) to do that, would be an illusion.[69] With this moment of nonvisual "belonging" [*Gehören*],[70] however, the language moves into another sensory realm: from seeing to hearing, from metaphors of light to those of the word, from the eye to the ear as the relevant organ. This is a transition that always bears on the possibility of *freedom* as well.

In addition to the meaning it has in the context of imperative dazzling, the shutting of the eyes can also represent the introduction of introversion, of inner contemplation, the free act of turning one's gaze inward. This is the characteristic attitude in Augustinian soliloquies, sustained by the emphasis on the inner *illuminatio* in contrast to the ecstatic encounter with the absolute. But Plotinus, too, was familiar with this screening-off of the gaze directed outward at the tempting and self-alienated world, which must be traversed, either into transcendency or into inwardness, if one is not to succumb to it.[71] From this point on, the entire mystical tradition is situated in this ambiguity of shutting one's eyes.

Augustine gives the metaphor of shutting one's eyes yet another meaning: it is useless to open one's eyes in the darkness, but it is also useless to "be in the light" and to keep one's eyes shut.[72] The first image illustrates the situation of the "good heathen," the impotence of a subjective desire to see, in the absence of grace, the objective condition for vision. The second image illustrates the situation of the "bad Christian," who subjectively spoils the objectively given possibility of vision. This opposition could not have been articulated within the classical approach to metaphors of light, for it presupposes the involvement of the eye.

There is yet another, extreme form that this metaphor can take, one that can be asserted only after "darkness" [*Dunkelheit*] has gained a positive value, as in the Romantic concept of night and darkness [*Dunkelheit*]. Novalis will speak, in his first "Hymn," of the "infinite eye, which opens the night to us." Here, the light of the diurnal world signifies limitation and unfreedom through its association with the finitude of a gaze that is bound to and determined by material things, whereas the dark of the night signifies the diminishment of material determination, which makes it possible for the horizonless entirety of Being to be affectively present as a unity.

For Greek thought, all certainty was based on visibility. What *logoi* referred back to was a sight with form [*gestalthafter Anblick*], i.e., *eidos*. Even etymologically, "knowledge" [*Wissen*] and "essence" [*Wesen*] (as *eidos*) are extremely closely related to "seeing" [*Sehen*]. *Logos* is a collection of what has been seen. For Heraclitus, eyes are "more exact witnesses than ears."[73] This is a formulation that deeply shaped the Occidental tradition precisely when it found itself faced with a conception of a completely different type, namely, the conception found in the biblical intellectual world's concept of certainty. For the Greeks, "hearing" is of no significance for truth and is initially nonbinding. As an imparting of *doxa*, it represents an assertion that must always be confirmed visually.

For the Old Testament literature, however, and for the consciousness of truth it documents, seeing is always predetermined, put into question, or surpassed by hearing. The created is based on the Word, and in terms of its binding claim, the Word always precedes the created. The real reveals itself within a horizon of its signification, a horizon allocated by hearing. Just how inaccessible the biblical meaning of "hearing" must have been for those thinking within the Greek tradition is brought out in the first fundamental confrontation of these two intellectual worlds, which we find documented in Philo Judaeus, who tried to make the meaning of the Old Testament intelligible within the Greek cultural horizon. What is remarkable there is that he must *translate* at precisely the point where the moment of "hearing" is involved. In this way, as has already been shown, the Creation image of the Word calling out of the void is transposed into an image of light emanating into the darkness [*Dunkel*] of matter, and his explicit view is that the only seeing which does not deceive is that through which beings are presented in their Being.[74] Consistent with this, Philo's personified "logos" must first of all prepare the organs that will receive its revelation, which it does by *transforming* human ears into eyes. It is then to these that logos manifests, as light, its nonverbal essence.[75] And Philo reinterprets the fundamental event of the Old Testament—the giving of the law on Sinai—as an experience of "illumination."[76]

In the New Testament, hearing the Word is the source of faithfulness. Not wanting to hear, means rejecting an offer of salvation.[77] But this already anticipates the form of the harmonization with Greek *theōria*, which then takes place in the work of the Church Fathers and the Scholastics, where vision comes to represent a mode of eschatological finality. The history-ending Second Coming (which has been held in reserve) consists in God, who until this point has been hidden, becoming visible. From this, the allocation of the classically ideal *theōria* to *status gloriae* develops. Thereafter, questions of human knowledge are interpreted in terms of a deficiency vis-à-vis *status viae*, which needs hearing as a guiding anticipation of conclusive *visio*.

This is a complete transformation of the Old Testament account, where the impossibility of beholding God is absolute and not merely temporary. The provisionality of hearing in the New Testament is further confirmed by the primacy of seeing in John, who represents most powerfully the arrived presence of the *eschaton*. In exactly the same way, the eschatologically pregnant Easter event shows the moment of the has-been-seen to its best advantage in comparison with mere hearing. There are plenty of approaches here for *theōria* (which has been eschatologically held in reserve) to stream back into worldly existence. "Hearing" restricts itself again: hearing [*Vernehmen*] the Word gets reduced to "heeding" [*Gehorchen*].

In Augustine, this meaning component forges links with the Roman idea of obligation found in *auctoritas*: following the Skeptics' undermining of "seeing," an equivalence of the instances of *ratio* and *auctoritas* becomes possible.[78] "Truth" becomes the integration of "hearing" and "seeing." But even within Augustine's thought, this equilibrium between the two "witnesses" to truth is fleeting: in the late writings, "hearing" the Word about divine predestination displaces vision's aspiration to seek *insight* into the reasons of the divine will. Once again, we see that the metaphorics of the *eye* is crucially connected to the concept of *freedom*, whereas the metaphorics of the *ear* indicates the limits or even suspension of freedom.

The "qualities" of the "eye" and the "ear" that let them say something metaphorically imply an entire phenomenology of the senses.[79] For example, the attitude of not wanting to hear is marked, even if only metaphorically, as more serious than the attitude of not wanting to see, since the ear is, by nature, always open and cannot be shut. Thus, not hearing presupposes a greater degree of contrariness and of intervention in nature than does not seeing. Compared to the language of "illumination," the Gnostic metaphor of the "call" found in the Mandean and Manichean doctrines points toward a more compelling, more powerfully "gripping" phenomenon, that of the absolute claim to *metansia*. Luther's language in *De servo arbitrio* plays metaphors of the ear against those of the eye: the merciful Lord's offer allows none of the distance for free consideration that two parties have when they catch sight of each other.[80] That which is not expected and has not been prepared for, the character of "grace" as a pure event, comes through in the language of "hearing."

The eye wanders, selects, approaches things, presses after them, while the ear, for its part, is affected and accosted. The eye can seek, the ear can only *wait*. Seeing "places" things; hearing is placed. The term "listener" [*Zuhörer*] lacks the sense of disengagement implied by "onlooker" [*Zuschauer*]. Correspondingly, the "Word" does not have the cosmic universality of "light." The Word is essentially "directed at" something; one can obey it and submit oneself to it, but one cannot stand "in" the Word, in the sense of *in luce esse*. That which demands unconditionally is encountered in "hearing." Conscience has a "voice," not light. For Kant, the moral ought is *given* as an unavoidable "fact of reason" before it can be deduced—that is, before insight into it can be achieved—from its premise of freedom. Accordingly, Kant speaks of the "voice of reason," which is "with respect to the will . . . so distinct, so irrepressible, and so clearly audible to even the commonest man."[81] Here, the structures of "hearing" can still be found beyond all transcendental metaphysics.

Finally, metaphors of "hearing" are also significant for grasping the phenomenon of *tradition*. "Seeing" is oriented toward the *repetition* of eyewitness experience, most clearly in the restoration of the phenomenon itself in all experimental methodology. The demand for the *presence* of the object under study is the point of departure for the modern idea of science, and in Bacon and Descartes, this demand is formulated in opposition to the validity of *auctoritas*. Here, needing to rely on tradition appears as a lack of knowledge which can, in principle, be remedied. Implicit in this reproach is the assumption that reason does not need to "hear," because it can, at any time, make the objects under study accessible to sight (experimentation) and insight (deduction). Ontologically, this means that every condition is *iterable*; there is no unique and actual experience. Or rather, such experience has no significance for the human fund of knowledge. Only if the actual-and-unique is essential for man, does "hearing" a tradition have binding force. Only then must man allow something to be "handed down" to him without being able to expect to see it himself.

In judging the value of tradition, a teleological moment is always implied, namely, that "truth" is *intended for man* and that it is for that reason that it *reaches* him via the precarious stream of cultural transference. The denial of vision that is entailed in listening to tradition always includes an element of teleological trust that "theoretically" cannot be justified. For this reason, in the attitude of "hearing" (i.e., in being dependent on tradition), there is often a hidden insufficiency, which presses for a shift from *veritas asserentis* to *evidentia obiecti*, to put it Scholastically. The metaphorical language indicates this insufficiency primarily where the facts of tradition—of *auctoritas*, and thus of "hearing"—appear in metaphors of light.

Cicero seems, once again, to have been at the start of this. Thus, in connection with his "translation" of Greek philosophy into the Latin medium, he speaks of *lumen litterarum Latinarum* (*Tusc.* 1. 5), of *lux auctoris* (1. 5. 11). Rhetoric becomes the primordial form of this light. In *Scienza Nuova*, Vico portrays the history of jurisprudence as light spreading over the obscurity [*Dunkelheit*] of facts (4. 14. 2). And at the end of *Démocratie en Amérique*, Tocqueville says, negatively, that ever since the past stopped shedding its light on the future, the human spirit has been lying in darkness. [*End of excursus.*]

The path of metaphors of light in the Middle Ages needs to be sketched only briefly here, not only because comprehensive studies of it are already available but also because its course has already been decided in the transition from antiquity to the Middle Ages. Arabic and Jewish Prescholaticism amalgamated Neoplatonism and Aristotelianism, in that "light" was equated with "form": *forma est lumen purum.*[82] Albertus Magnus passed this amalgam on to Latin Scholasticism in *De causis et processu universitatis*, in which there is a striking ease in the way he adopts the metaphor of "flux" (*influentia constitutionis ad esse*) or adopts *diffusio intellectus* as *lumen luminis rei.*[83]

Thomas Aquinas is completely hostile to the "language of light," because, in his view, it blurs the distinction between metaphysics and metaphorics. For him, light is a *qualitas per se sensibilis et species quaedam determinata in sensibilibus,* and, in this respect, "light" may be spoken of, in intellectual contexts, only *aequivoce vel metaphorice,* where the *ratio manifestationis* of what is [*des Seiende*] (i.e., its ontological truth) is concerned.[84]

His contemporary Bonaventure, by contrast, handles the metaphorics of light with a mastery comparable only to that of Augustine. Light is the *natura communis* of what is [*des Seienden*],[85] a fundamental state and underlying determination of all things, even before their differentiation. In Bonaventure, however, dawn breaks primarily in the inwardness of man, whose light is a *possession*—not a gradually elucidating *acquisition*—which precedes and makes possible all cognition, just as all truths are based on "truth." Light changes and becomes one with the 'ground' of identity of the subject itself. Thus, God is *secundum veritatem in anima*—not, however, as its object or idea, but rather as its capacity for truth and, in this respect, *intimior animae quam ipsa sibi.*[86] What this very bold wording of the internalization of *illuminatio* means is this: the subject can always become objective to itself in reflection, and to the extent to which it can do so, a light is required that must thus be "more internal" to the subject than the subject is to itself. This provides a formulation for the discovery of the idea, already suggested in Augustine, that inner light has to be "behind" the self, so that looking into the light becomes impossible here. The *lux veritatis, in qua cuncta relucent,*[87] is "given" only in the self-certainty of the subject's capacity for truth: not in *cognitio* (for that, Bonaventure allows for the possibility of an Aristotelian tabula rasa) but in *notitia,* as Being's radical prefamiliarity with the subject.[88]

Thus we find, formulated in the metaphorics of light, something that in terms of cognition is *more* than mere receptivity. The mystical emotion of *amor* (which is the vehicle of all relations of Being) and the sustaining pretheoretical *notitia* are but two aspects of *one* fundamental relation: *Amor et notitia animae connaturales sunt.*[89] Here, it becomes possible to grasp the philosophical "achievement" of illuminative representations: they point to a radical *unity* of the mind, beyond the psychological plurality of its "faculties." And they point, in the same way, to the ultimate unity of the horizon, in which all that is becomes phenomenal [*in dem alles Seiende zur Gegebenheit kommt*].

Consistent with this, Duns Scotus, in whose works the Augustinian tradition has to assert itself within the constraints of Aristotelian axioms, carries out an extreme (though stabilizing) *reduction* of *illuminatio.* He lets *illuminatio* be rooted in the *one* original phenomenon, the *primum obiectum* associated with the univocal concept of Being.[90] Here, *esse* is not *esse commune,* at the last derivative of abstraction, but rather the first and total anticipation of the meaning of all merely possible phenomena. In this way, with the help of the illuminative representation, the "naturalness" of truth, its antecedence relative to all that is predicatively true, receives a subtle articulation yet again.

This "yet again" is explained by the fact that it is precisely in Duns Scotus that the Augustinian tradition takes a direction in which "natural light" increasingly obscures itself, in order to focus the situation of man (vis-à-vis the absolute) entirely on "hearing the Word." Nominalistic fideism needs the backdrop of a darkening of the world in order, once again, to drive out the *credo quia absurdum*; the doctrine of *Deus absconditus* no longer allows for the "naturalness" of truth. Nor is this tendency halted, in the fifteenth century, by Nicholas of Cusa's development of the "language of light," which he treats in all its richness, yet also in a way that unmistakably and excessively grants metaphor independent status as metaphysics (for example, in the dualism of *De coniecturis*). His *Magnaie potentiae veritas est* [91] remains a historically isolated experience at the close of the Middle Ages.

What is more essential is that the medieval "internalization" of light prevents the worldly dark from fully penetrating and disempowering the subject. To keep with the metaphor, so much transcendent light has "passed over" to the subject that the subject has become "self-luminous." Augustine's principle within the illumination doctrine—*Lumen tibi esse non potes*—emerges weakened by the change in the language of light that begins at this point. In the late-medieval experiment, where it is left to itself vis-à-vis *Deus absconditus*, the human mind proves itself to be authentic light. This is shown, purely grammatically, by the fact that in the expressions *lumen rationis, lumen intellectus*, and so on, the *genitivus objectus* becomes the *genitivus subjectus*.

There are transitional forms that remain indeterminate, such as Francis Bacon's *lumen experientiae*, in which the object of experience as well as the act of experience can be "light." [92] The luminarity of the human mind can be seen precisely in the fact that the analysis and subsequent elimination of the obscurations and misdirections of this light come to be understood as the new task of philosophical "method." [93]

What characterizes the dawn of a new epoch here, indicated in the metaphors of light, is that it can be said of man—at least in his highest realization, *studiosus homo*—that he is *naturalis lux*. [94] Man does not find already in place an objectively fixed world structure that obligingly presents itself and to which he has to adapt himself; rather, he becomes, himself, the principle of a structural formation that emanates from him. And by realizing himself as *sapiens*, he gains that emanative force: self-realization becomes a condition for world-realization. *Sapientes* "realize" the world in that they *quodlibet ad proprium finem ducunt*. [95] Cognizing the world and the *rite uti* of its things is not a relation of *receiving* but of *giving*. In cognizing and in using, man remedies the one great deficiency of Being, namely, that Being *is* everything, but is everything *unknowingly*.[96] The physical only becomes "fulfilled" in the mental. Theory and practice are no longer derivatives of an all-binding nature, but are rather its integration and its fulfillment of Being. *Homo denique fulgor est, scientia, lux et anima mundi.* . . .

Once this turn has been taken, we are not far from the comprehensive historical significance of the concept of "enlightenment," whose descent from the language of light is so tangible in French[97] and English: *siècle des lumières, progrès des lumières,* the *Aufklärer* (enlightenment figure) as an agent of light, *qui propage les lumières,* as well as the English word "enlightenment."

With the emergence of the Enlightenment, "light" moves into the realm of that which is to be accomplished; truth loses the natural *facilitas* with which it asserted itself. Even (or rather, only) in caricature does the now-broken connection between metaphors of light, on the one hand, and trust in the "naturalness" of self-presenting truth, on the other, demonstrate itself. Thus, in the *Dialogo* (*Dialogue on the Two Chief World Systems*), Galileo endowed Simplicio—the figure of the Scholastic, often ironically characterized as "Middle-Aged"[98]—with this trust, now exposed as careless confidence. There is, for example, a discussion of the problem of the cause of the tides, in which Simplicio says that although there can be only *one* cause, there are many opinions about this and that one has to take into account that the true explanation will not be among them; otherwise, it would certainly be most astonishing for the true not to emit so much light as to shine out through the darkness of such mistakes.[99]

As a result of the inversion of metaphors of light during the Enlightenment, it is precisely this conception of truth (as that which is self-luminous and penetrating) which becomes a way of reproaching the Middle Ages for its credulity, for not noticing its own darkness. According to d'Alembert, the principles of science and the arts were lost during the twelve centuries of the Middle Ages because the beautiful and the true, which *seem* to reveal themselves to people from all sides, do not actually get through to people until they have them pointed out.[100] The ignorance of the Middle Ages must thus be attributed precisely to the illusion that the truth "reveals itself." The truth does not reveal itself; it must *be revealed.* "Natural" luminosity cannot be relied on; on the contrary, truth is of a constitutionally weak nature and man must help it back on its feet by means of light-supplying therapy, as it were, *parce que rien n'est si dangereux pour le vrai et ne l'expose tant à être méconnu que l'al-*

liage ou le voisinage de l'erreur. That is the exact, literal opposite of the state that Galileo had Simplicio attribute to the true!

In this characterization of truth as weak and in need of assistance, the background of the late-medieval concept of God is still perceptible: d'Alembert compares the universe to a literary work *d'une obscurité sublime,* whose author tries, again and again, by means of "flashes of hope," to give the reader the illusion of having understood almost everything. As it is found, "natural" light thus acquires virtually the function of misleading: in the labyrinth of the world, once we have left the path, the few *éclairs* can just as well lead us further away from the path as back to it.[101] In such a world, which has become the playing field for a divine game (*où l'Intelligence suprême semble avoir voulu se jouer de la curiosité humaine*), the value of an individual truth is ambiguous—it can be either a beacon or a will-o'-the-wisp—as long as its sporadic character has not been put into a *systematic* context. "Truth," as such, is dubious [*zwielichtig*], as long as it lacks a well-ordered origin in *method* and a well-ordered position in a *system.* The dictionary and the encyclopedia become exemplary instruments of the Enlightenment: d'Alembert wrote not only the introduction but (along with it) the metaphysics of the great *Encyclopédie.*

In the idea of "method," which originates with Bacon and Descartes,[102] "light" is thought of as being at man's disposal. Phenomena no longer stand in the light; rather, they are *subjected to the lights of an examination*[103] from a particular perspective. The result then depends on the angle from which light falls on the object and the angle from which it is seen. It is the conditionality of *perspective* and the awareness of it, even the free selection of it, that now defines the concept of "seeing." The significance, for the modern age, of perspective and a consciousness of location would require a study of its own. All that can be done here is to indicate the way in which *technological* figures come to invade the metaphorics of light, the way in which light turns into an encompassing medium of the focused and measured ray of "direct lighting."

The status of this development as a historical signature is best illustrated in painting. During the sixteenth and seventeenth centuries, the idea of light as the homogeneous, unquestioningly presupposed medium of visibility that ensures the unaccented presence of that which is to be represented, turns into a localized factor which can be "adjusted." Caravaggio and Rembrandt already engage in something like "a staging of lighting," although the "quantity" of light—subject to the law of inverted quadratic proportion—is still limited. Not until the nineteenth century do Drummond's "lime" lights put the *theater* in a position to generate, in combination with concave mirrors, lighting "effects," a development which begins to open up new possibilities for an accentuating approach to vision, an approach that always takes as its point of departure, the dark as *the "natural" state*.

But it is only because these possibilities for *directed* light were discovered at all, that the technology for this discovery could ultimately make possible the most violent of methods and devices; and it is significant that the term *lighting*[104] is used to refer to thoughtless accentuation by artificial light, as well as to the technological selection and overemphasis of the work of man, which—as the only things thought to be worth seeing—is to be made impossible to overlook. This manipulation of light is the result of a long process.

In nocturnal spaces, an "optics of prefabrication"[105] is being developed, which eliminates the freedom to look around within a general medium of visibility, and confronts modern man with ever more situations of coerced vision [*Zwangsoptik*].[106] The connection between vision and freedom is being dissociated. Due to the dominance of the prefabricated and of technologically pre-cast situations and aspects, the modern extension of sensory spheres has not become a source of freedom.[107] The structure of this world of optical prefabrications and fixations of the gaze is once again approaching that of the "cave." (W. H. Auden portrays the cave situation of modern man in *Age of Anxiety*.) As a paideutic metaphor, "leaving the cave" is regaining real relevance.

Man—on whom the technological light of "lighting" has imposed, in many forms, an 'optics' that goes against his will—is the historical antipode of the classical *contemplator caeli* and his freedom to gaze. Today, there are even people who have never seen a star. "Stars? Where?" This is the unbelieving (but now believable) cry of the modern metropolitan lyricist.[108]

NOTES

1. In philosophical texts, "intuition" is the standard rendering of *Anschauung*, but it should be understood not in its contemporary sense of nonrational perception but rather in its older sense, stemming from the Latin *intueri* ("to gaze upon"), where the visual dimension found in the German (*Schauen*, to look) is implicit. See Robert M. Wallace, "Translator's Notes," in *The Genesis of the Copernican World* (Cambridge, Mass.: MIT Press, 1987), p. 692—*Trans*.

2. For more recent contributions to a philosophical "metaphorology," see Hans Blumenberg, *Work on Myth* (Cambridge, Mass.: MIT Press, 1985); see also

The translator would like to thank Paulien Kleingeld, Patrizia Nanz, and David Michael Levin for their assistance.

The Genesis of the Copernican World—especially part 4, "Vision in the Copernican World"—and *Höhlenausgänge* (Frankfurt a.M.: Suhrkamp, 1989).—*Trans.*

3. This distinction is notoriously difficult to translate. Here, *das Sein* has been translated as "Being," while *das Seiende* has been rendered either (in the plural) as "beings" or (less commonly) as "what is"; in the latter case, the German is always given in brackets.—*Trans.*

4. In German, there are several words for darkness: *Finsternis,* which has connotations of utter and foreboding darkness; *Dunkelheit,* which connotes an obscuration of vision; and *das Dunkel,* which generally corresponds to the English "the dark." In this essay, *Finsternis* is the most common term. Whenever "darkness" has been used to translate either of the other terms, the original German will be given in brackets.—*Trans.*

5. The work that must be mentioned first of all remains Cl. Baeumker's "Witelo, ein Philosoph und Naturforscher des XIII. Jahrhundert," *Beiträge zur Geschichte der Philosophie des Mittelalters* III:2 (Münster, 1908), incomparable in its collection of material. Concerning antiquity, see R. Bultmann, "Zur Geschichte der Lichtsymbolik im Altertum," *Philogus* 97 (1948): 1; J. Stenzel, "Der Begriff der Erleuchtung bei Platon," *Die Antike* 2 (1926): 235–257. On the Middle Ages: "Die Abstraktionslehre in der Scholastik bis Thomas von Aquin mit besonderer Berücksichtigung des Lichtbegriffs," *Philosophisches Jahrbuch* 44 (1931) and 45 (1932); M. Honecker, "Der Lichtbegriff in der Abstraktionslehre des Thomas von Aquin," *Philosophisches Jahrbuch* 48 (1935): 268; L. Baur, "Die Philosophie des Robert Grosseteste," *Beiträge zur Geschichte der Philosophie des Mittelalters* 18 (Münster, 1917): 4–6; P. Garin, *Le théorie de l'idée suivant l'école thomiste* (Paris, 1930); and R. Carton, *L'expérience mystique de l'illumination intérieure chez Roger Bacon* (Paris, 1926). With regard to St. Augustine, Bonaventure, mysticism, and Nicholas of Cusa, the relevant literature contains a wealth of material, of which insufficient use has been made. With regard to the modern age, it evidently still needs to be proven that the history of metaphors of light *continues* at all.

6. H. Diels, *Die Fragmente der Vorsokratiker,* 3 vols. (Berlin, 1939), 28 B 9; in this connection, see also Simplicius's commentary on fragment 8, 53–59.

7. Aristotle, *Metaphysics* 1. 5. 986a 25.

8. Diels, 28 B 1, 10.

9. Diels, 28 B 2, 5.

10. Martin Heidegger, "Plato's Doctrine of Truth," trans. John Barlow, in *Philosophy in the Twentieth Century: An Anthology,* vol. 3, ed. William Barrett and Henry D. Aiken (New York: Random House, 1962), pp. 257–258. [Original German edition of 1947, pp. 25–26.]

11. Plato, *The Statesman* 509 B.

12. U. v. Wilamowitz-Moellendorff, *Der Glaube der Hellenen,* 2d ed. (Darmstadt, 1955), vol. 1, p. 135.

13. R. Bultmann, p. 13.

14. J. Stenzel, p. 256.

15. Aristotle, *De Anima* 3. 2. 425b 20–27. Cf. W. Bröcker, *Aristoteles* (Frankfurt, 1935), p. 148: "Aristotle takes seeing to be not primarily some occurrence in the subject, but rather the visible's showing itself."

16. K. v. Fritz, "Tragische Schuld und poetische Gerechtigkeit in der griechischen Tragödie," *Studium Generale* 8 (1955), p. 228.

17. The German here (*Blendung*) has a range of meaning, extending from "confusion" and "deception" to "the act of blinding a person." It has been rendered throughout as "dazzling" in order to capture the broad sense of a (painful) bewilderment caused by light.—*Trans.*

18. Seneca, *Epist. Mor.* 102:

> Cum venerit dies ille, qui mixtum hoc divini humanique secernat, corpus hic, ubi inveni, relinquam, ipse me diis reddam (22). Alia origo nos expectat, alius rerum status. Nondum caelum nisi ex intervallo pati possumus. (23 sq.) . . . aliquando naturae tibi arcana retegentur, discutietur ista caligo te lux undique clara percutiet. Imaginare tecum, quantus ille sit fulgor tot sideribus inter se lumen miscentibus. Nulla serenum umbra turbabit: aequaliter splendebit omne caeli latus: dies et nox aeris infimi vices sunt. Tunc in tenebris vixisse te dices, cum totam lucem et totus aspexeris, quam nunc per angustissimas oculorum vias obscure intueris, et tamen admiraris illam iam procul: quid tibi videbitur divina lux, cum illam suo loco videris? (28).

19. Plotinus, *Enneads* 6. 7. 17: *amorphos kai aneideos.*

20. *Phaedo* 99E–100A.

21. W. Dilthey, *Gesammelte Schriften* 2 (Leipzig, 1923), p. 177.

22. *De officiis* 2. 2. 8: "Contra autem omnia disputantur a nostris (sc. academicis), quod hoc ipsum probabile elucere non possit, nisi ex utraque parte causarum esset facta contentio." Typical of the unclarity of the meaning of metaphors of light is the transitive rendering that K. Atzert gives *elucere* in his translation (Limburg, 1951): "Das geschieht deshalb, weil sich das Wahrscheinliche erst *ins rechte Licht rücken* läßt, wenn man . . . " ["This happens because the apparently true lets itself *be put in the proper light* only when one . . . "] K. Büchner (*Vom rechten Handeln* [Zürich, 1953]), by contrast, renders it adequately: "weil eben *dieses Einleuchtende* nicht *aufstrahlen* könnte, wenn nicht . . . " ["because just *this plausibility* cannot *shine forth,* when not . . . "]. Atzert basically brings the modern transformation of metaphors of light into Cicero, while Büchner does well to leave the skeptic with the remainder of Platonic presuppositions at which he hints. The Academic skepticism is generally "more Platonic" than it wants to know. Not only does it "break out," institutionally, in Plato's school, but it is moreover a result of Platonism itself, of Platonism's transcendency of Ideas. The rumor about Arcesilas passing on Platonic orthodoxy to an esoteric circle of pupils (Sextus Empiricus, *Pyrrh. Hyp.* 1. 33. 234) while pretending to be a skeptic, fits perfectly in this regard. Above all, however, the Platonic remainder is in the meaning of the apparently true. In this concept, the difference between Idea and appearance is transferred to "truth" itself. Cicero translates the Skeptics' *pithanon* as *verisimile* and initially retains the metaphorical character of this with a *quasi* (*Luc. 32*), only then to terminologize it. The apparently true not only "appears" (in the sense of deception) to be the true, but is the "showing-through" [*Durchscheinen*] of the true, the appearance of the true that is sufficient for man. In his dispute with Academic skepticism (*Contra Academ.* 2. 27), Augustine draws a connection to the presupposition of *verum* in *verisimile.*

23. *De officiis* 1. 6. 18.

24. In his paraphrase of *De officiis*, St. Ambrose already goes beyond Cicero in polemicizing against his making an exception for geometry and astronomy. For Ambrose, that which is set aside is a "matter of salvation" and not, as with Cicero, of *societas* (*De officiis ministorum* 1. 26. 122). The idea of leaving *res obscurae* alone is already suggested to the Christian in the belief in a judge, "whose notice the hidden does not escape" (1. 26. 124). It is easy to see how the stage is already set here for the medieval identification of *curiositas* with natural science.

25. *De divinatione* 1. 35: "Latet fortasse (sc. causa) obscuritate involuta naturae. Non enim me deus ista scire, sed his tantummodo uti voluit." The importance for Cicero of this view has been pointed out by G. Gawlick in studying the phrase *Perdifficilis et perobscura quaestio* in his dissertation *Untersuchungen zu Ciceros philosophischer Methode* (Kiel, 1956). See, there, the extensive further evidence documenting the "natural" darkness [*Dunkelheit*] of things outside the "economic" clearing of Being [*Seinslichtung*] centered around human beings.

26. *De officiis* 1. 9. 30: "Quocirca bene praecipiumt, qui vetant quicquam agere, quod dubites acquum sit an iniquum."

27. Several editions have wanted to polish away the inconsistency here by placing an *enim* after *acquitas*. Atzert, for example, corrects (without any justification in the apparatus criticus) his own edition of 1939 in the revised edition of 1949, but does not properly consider the unmotivated *enim* in his 1951 translation. This can also be said of Büchner and Gignon.

28. *Tusc.* 3. 2: "Nunc parvulos nobis dedit (sc. natura) igniculos, quos celeriter malis moribus opionibus depravati sic restinguimus, ut nusquam naturae lumen appareat."

29. *De officiis* 2. 9. 32: "Etenim illud ipsum, quod honestum decorumque dicimus, quia per se nobis placet animosque omnium natura et specie sua commovet maximeque quasi perlucet ex iis, quas commemoravi, virtutibus, idcirco illos, in quibus illas virutes esse remur, a natura ipsa diligere cogimur." In Kant's concept of "respect," the accent is shifted almost entirely to *cogimur*: "Respect is a tribute we cannot refuse to pay to merit whether we will or not." *Critique of Practical Reason*, trans. Lewis White Beck (New York: Macmillan, 1956), p. 80. Here, metaphors of light are no longer of use.

30. *De natura deorum* 2. 37. 95. V. Rose (1886), R. Walzer (1934), and W. D. Ross (1955) have no doubts with regard to this quote. Without further consideration, W. Jaeger (*Aristoteles* [Berlin, 1923], p. 167) sees it as providing evidence for the proximity to Plato, as well as the young Aristotle's reconstruction of Plato. A comment of Erich Burck's led me to wonder about the authenticity of the text under discussion: there is, indeed, too much Stoicism in it. But that can still be laid at the doorstep of Cicero's understanding of "translation." G. Gawlick (op. cit.) has produced important new evidence in support of this. The whole question probably cannot yet be answered definitively. We are on firm ground, however, when we utilize the text only for the context in which, for us, the question occurs.

31. Cf. Heidegger, "Plato's Doctrine of Truth," p. 261 [German, p. 53]: "Where the truth is of another essence and is not unhiddenness or at least where

unhiddenness is not a component of this definition, an 'allegory of the cave' has no basis from which it can be clarified." The depth and "exactness" with which Plato's metaphor of the cave is supported can, in fact, be seen in its rehearsal at *Phaedo* 109E, where the mistaking of Being [*Seinsverwechselung*] and the ascent out of the deceiving depths are already implicit.

32. Pherecydes of Syros, Diels, 7 B 6.

33. *Dialogus cum Tryphone Judaeo* 78. 5–6 (possibly in response to *Protev. Jacobi* 18. 1). On this, cf. C. Schneider, *Geistesgeschichte des antiken Christentums I* (München, 1954), p. 250, where (Ps.) Basilius, *Hom. in nativ. Christi* is again referred to. See also E. Benz, "Die heilige Höhle in der Alten Christenheit und in der östlichen orthodoxen Kirche," in *Eranos-Jahrbuch* 22 (1953).

34. A most recent reflection of this is in Ezra Pound's "Canto XLVII": "The light has entered the cave. Io! Io! / The light has gone down into the cave, / Splendour on splendour!"

35. Anselm of Canterbury, *Proslogion*, c. 1.

36. Cf. H. Friedrich, *Montaigne* (Bern: Franke, 1949), p. 307.

37. *Novum Organum* 1. 42:

> Idola specus sunt idola hominis individui: Habet enim unusquisque (paeter aberrationes naturae humanae in genere) specum sive cavernam quandam individuam, quae lumen naturae frangit et corrumpit . . . ut plane spiritus humanus (prout disponitur in hominibus singulis) sit res varia, et omnino perturbata, et quasi fortuita: unde bene Heraclitus, homines scientias, quaerere in minoribus mundis, et non in maiore sive communi.

38. *Discourse on Method* 6, trans. Donald A. Cress (Indianapolis: Hackett, 1980), p. 38; first French edition, p. 71.

39. Ibid., p. 6; French edition, p. 11.

40. *De architectura* 2, prooemium.

41. *De inventione* 1, prooemium.

42. *Die unsichtbare Loge: eine Biographie* (1793), section 3.

43. Ibid., section 30.

44. *Enneads* 1. 8.

45. Ibid., 6. 9. 4.

46. Ibid., 6. 9. 9.

47. *De opificio mundi* c. 8 (ed. Cohn, 1889, p. 9).

48. W. Theiler, *Die Vorbereitung des Neuplatonismus* (Berlin, 1930), p. 50.

49. An illustrative example is found in Salomon ibn Gabirol (Avicebron), *Fons vitae* 4, 31 (ed. Baeumker, p. 254): "Dubitas quod lumen infusum in materia [!] sit defluxum ab alio lumine, quod est super materiam, scilicet lumine, quod est in essentia virtutis agentis? Et hoc est voluntas, quae eduxit formam de potentia ad effectum." In Moses Maimonides (*Dux neutrorum* 1. 72), a metaphor of light is applied to the motor force emanating from the first sphere of heaven.

50. *De somniis* 1. 13. 75 (ed. Cohn-Wendland).

51. *De virtutibus* 22. 164.

52. *De Cherubim* 28. 97.

53. *Contra Faustum Manichaeum* 22. 8.

54. Ibid., 20. 7.

55. Ibid., 13. 18.

56. *Enarratio in Psalmum* 26. 2. 3.

57. *Sermo* 182. 5.

58. *Epist.* 140. 7.

59. *Epist.* 120. 10: "sed invisibiliter et ineffabiliter, et tamen intelligibiliter lucet, tamque nobis certum est, quam nobis efficit certa quae secundum ipsum (sc. lumen) cuncta conspicimus." Deviating from his stance on Manichaeism, Augustine attempted to harmonize his relation to the Neoplatonists and thus did not stress the distinctions in the metaphysics of light sharply enough. (*De civitate dei* 10. 2). Even in the phrases that sound Neoplatonic and esoteric—such as, *sed paucissimis (sc. conceditur) videre quod verum est* (*De div. quaest.* q. 46)—what is meant, in fact, is only reflection upon the origins [*Herkunft*] of certainty, not ecstatic, mystical contemplation of its source [*Quelle*].

60. *De genesi ad litteram imperfectus liber* 5. 24: "Convenienter autem lucem hanc dici concedit, quisquis condedit recte dici lucem, qua res quaeque manifesta est . . . haec lux qua ista manifesta sunt, utique intus in anima est, quamvis per corpus inferantur quae ita sentiuntur."

61. Pace J. Barion, *Plotin und Augustinus* (Berlin, 1935), p. 152.

62. *De Trinitate* 14. 6. 8–7. 10; see also *Confessiones* 10. 20.29–21. 30.

63. E. Gilson, *Introduction à l'étude de St. Augustine* (Paris, 1929). German edition (Hellerau, 1930), p. 399.

64. *De beata vita* 2. 8.

65. *Epist.* 11. 3.

66. *De genesi ad litteram* 4. 33. 51.

67. *The Statesman* 518 A.

68. It is perhaps Nicholas of Cusa who has best expressed this mystical, methodological function of darkness [*Dunkelheit*] as the criterion of the correct path, in order, significantly, to justify the obscurity [*Dunkelheit*] of his own metaphysics: "It is just as in the case of someone who seeks the sun and approaches it in the correct manner: as a result of the overpowering light of the sun, darkness emerges in his weak eye; and for him, who seeks the sun, this fog is a sign that he is on the right path, and were the dark not to appear, then he would not be on the path to that brilliant light." (Letter to the Abbot of the Tegersee Cloister, September 14, 1453 [Vansteenberghe, ed., *Autour de la docte ignorance* (Münster, 1915), p. 113, n. 5].) This fits perfectly with Nicholas's metaphysics of *coincidentia oppositorum*. In a single sentence, he effortlessly carries out the objectification of subjective mystical experience: *Deus est maxime lux, quod est minime lux* (*De docta ignorantia* 1. 4). The pseudo-hermetic *Liber XXIV philosophorum* (prop. 21) of medieval mysticism had already given this a proto-formulation: *Deus est tenebra in anima post omnem lucem relicta.* And Bonaventure says: *Exceaecatio est summa illuminatio* (*In Hexaem.* 22. 11). In Nicholas of Cusa's *docta ignoratio*, this entire tradition is given its densest wording.

69. Plotinus, *Enneads* 6. 9. 10: *hoion allos genomenos kai ouk autos oud'antou.*

70. Blumenberg is making use here of an untranslatable German homophony between *Gehör* ("the sense of hearing") and *gehören* ("to belong to").—*Trans.*

71. *Enneads* 1. 6. 9; 5.5. 7.

72. *Enarratio in Psalmum* 25. 2. 14.

73. Diels, *Die Fragmente der Vorsokratiker,* 22 B 101a. Cf. the parallels quoted by Diels.

74. *De fuga et inventione* 208: *apseudes d'horasis, hēi ta onta ontōs katanoeitai.*

75. Cf. H. Leisegang, *Der heilige Geist* (Leipzig, 1919), p. 215.

76. Ibid., p. 219.

77. Gerhard Kittel, *akouō,* in *Theologisches Wörterbuch zum Neuen Testament* (Stuttgart: Kohlhammer, 1933), vol. 1, pp. 216–225. See, there, all the evidence for the following.

78. *De ordine* 9. 29: *Ad discendum necessario dupliciter ducimur auctoritate atque ratione.*

79. Cf. H. Jonas, "The Nobility of Sight: A Study in the Phenomenology of the Senses," *Philosophy and Phenomenological Research* 14 (1954): 507–519. See further the analyses by H. Lipps, *Die menschliche Natur* (Frankfurt, 1941), p. 25, 76.

80. The way in which the humanist Melanchthon returns from the language of hearing back to that of seeing is characteristic: "Lux quid sit cerni rectius potest, quam dici, estque illa ipsa claritas quae cernitur, quae omnie ostendit, sic et in corde nostro, clara ostensio, lux est." (*Commentarius in Genesin* c. 1 [*Corp. Reform.* 13, p. 767].)

81. *Critique of Practical Reason,* trans. Lewis White Beck (New York: Macmillan, 1956), p. 36. Cf. *Studium Generale* 6 (1953): 179.

82. Ibn Gabirol *Fons vitae* 4. 14.

83. *De causis et processu universitatis* 1. 1, c. 1.

84. *Sententiarum* 2, dist. 13, q. 1, a. 2.

85. Ibid. 2, dist. 12, a. 2, q. 1, arg. 4.

86. Ibid. 1, dist. 1, a. 3, q. 2, concl. Characteristically, just this wording returns, extracted from the metaphorics of light, in Luther, in reference to the *verbum dei* (*Werke* 9 [Weimar]: 103), that is, as the absolute intimacy of "hearing."

87. *Interarium mentis* 2. 9.

88. *Sent.* 2, dist. 39, a. 1, q. 2, concl.

89. Bonaventure *Sent.* 1, dist. 3, p. 2, a. 2, q. 2, concl. What is of primary importance here is that emotion—which the classical tradition had judged to be *obscuring of Being* [*seinsverdunkelnd*]—experiences a positive reevaluation and gains an *elucidating* function. The connection of a positive doctrine of emotions with the usage of metaphors of light also becomes quite clear in (Ps.) Witelo's *Liber de intelligentiis* (ed. Baeumker): *amor* and *delectatio* are the soul's primary "answers" to the luminosity of Being; in them, the *appetitus substantiae cognoscentis ad ipsum cognoscibile* emerges, without which the gaze would not be open for phenomena; it would be an *ordinatio huius ad hoc* preceding all spiritual "acts" (prop. 18).

90. Cf. E. Gilson, "Avicenne et le point de départ de Duns Scot," *Archives d'histoire doctrinale et littéraire du moyen-age* 2 (1927): 116.

91. *De apice theoriae.*

92. *Novum Organum* 1. 49. Cf. 1. 56, where the difference in kind among intellects is determined according to *admiratio antiquitatis* or *amor novitatis,* and

where it is then said, "veritas autem non a felicitate temporis alicuius, quae res varia est, sed a lumine naturae et experientiae, quod aeternum est, petenda est."

93. *Novum Organum* 1. 49: "intellectus humanus luminis sicci non est: sed recipit infusionem a voluntate et affectibus."

94. Carolus Bovillus (Charles de Bovelles), *Liber de sapiente* (*Studien der Bibliothek Warburg* 10 [1927], ed. Klibansky), c. 51. This statement cannot be put in the same context with the fact that Aristotle represented *nous* in its active-passive double function as *phōs* (*De anima* 3. 5. 430a 14–17). This *nous* is genuinely cosmic, and associated with the human soul only "from the outside" in cognitive accomplishment. The "direction" of this light is thus from the inside to the outside; what is crucially new is the inversion of this direction.

95. Bovillus *Liber de sapiente*, c. 19.

96. Ibid. "Omnia siquidem est mundus: scit tamen novitque nihil. Porro exiguum et fere nihil est home: scit attamen novitque universa."

97. The transition is, in the simultaneity of its nuances, particularly tangible in Pascal's language, for example, in Fragment 337 (ed. Brunschvicg): "par une nouvelle lumière, par une autre lumière supérieure, selon qu'on a de lumière." In the first fragment of Pascal's study *De l'esprit géométrique*, *lumière naturelle* is both the limit of the human mind with regard to its aspiration to prove all its premises *and* the foundation of those exacting proofs which are in fact possible for the mind, in spite of its limitations.

98. The German here (*mittelalterlich*) can mean both "middle-aged" and "medieval."—*Trans.*

99. "Dialogo IV," *Opere*, ed. Albèri, 1. 456: "anzi cosi credo esser veramente perchè gran cosa sarebbe che il vero potesse aver si poco di luce, che nulla apparisse tra le tenebre di tanti falsi." The connection of *simplicitas*—though in a positive sense!—with this basic view is found, with exceptional expressiveness, in a thirteenth-century tract, *De usuris*, written by Aegidius of Lessines as an exegesis of the first sentence of Aristotle's *Metaphysics*: "Quam (sc. veritatem) si quis concupiscit vero corde, et eam quaesierit in simplicitate cordis sui, ipsa seipsam manifestabit . . ." Cited in M. Grabmann, *Mittelalterliches Geistesleben II* (Munich, 1936), p. 522.

100. *Discours Préliminaire de l'Encyclopédie*, ed. Picavet: "Les principes des sciences et des arts étaient perdus, parce que le beau et le vrai semblent se montrer de toutes parts aux hommes, ne les frappent guère à moins qu'ils n'en soient avertis."

101. It would require a separate study (which would be part of the history of the concept of "probability") to demonstrate this ambivalence in the change of meaning of *verisimile*. Originally, the "appearance" of the apparently true is entirely appearance as pale reflection of the *proximity* of truth (cf. footnote 22 above). [The author's use of metaphors of light here cannot be rendered fully in English: "Der 'Schein' des Wahrscheinlichen ist ursprünglich durchaus Schein als Abglanz der Nähe der Wahrheit."—*Trans.*] This understanding of the term has, however, metaphysical premises that no longer hold for Descartes. For him, "appearance" means possible deception; the apparently true (or probable) is only something that looks like the true and must therefore be methodologically 'bracketed'. Until an object can be confirmed by *clare et distincte percipere*, it is

without significance for truth [*wahrheitsindifferent*]. "Certum etiam est, cum assentimur alicui rationi quam non percipimus, vel nos falli, vel casu tantum incidere in veritatem . . . " (*Principia philosophiae* 1. 44). The idea that one could "hit upon" the truth "by chance" is a previously unthought and unthinkable thought, one in which the entire tradition of the metaphorics of light is negated and raised to a higher level [*aufgehoben*]. "Method" then takes this annoying element of chance by the hand and puts it at man's disposal.

102. Cf. *Studium Generale* 5 (1952): 133–142.

103. *Beleuchtet*: the translation here attempts to capture the double meaning that Blumenberg is playing on here: *beleuchten* can mean both "to shine light on something" and "to examine."—*Trans.*

104. The German here, *Illumination*, refers primarily to artificial outdoor lighting.—*Trans.*

105. *Optik des Präparats*. Consistent with his general emphasis on the intimate interrelations between science and *mentalité*, Blumenberg here uses *Optik* ("optics") to refer not to a specific science but to a view of light and vision that is embedded in a general consciousness. *Präparat* generally refers to a laboratory or pharmaceutical "preparation," but it is rendered as "prefabrication" to convey the central idea that, in the world of artificial lighting, visual possibilities are shaped in advance.—*Trans.*

106. Today, one speaks of the "technology of light" in a sense not at all limited to the generation of light or to the "lighting" [*Beleuchtung*], but rather one which understands light as a construction unit like steel, concrete, etc. See the book by W. Köhler and W. Luckhardt, *Lichtarchitektur* (Berlin, 1956).

107. Whether it has become a source of truth is a question that W. Wagner has raised: "Versuch zur Kritik der Sinne," *Studium Generale* 4 (1951): 256.

108. Gottfried Benn, *Gesammelte Gedichte* (Zürich, 1956), p. 98.

TWO

Vision, Representation, and Technology in Descartes

Dalia Judovitz

The mystery of the world is the visible, not the invisible.
OSCAR WILDE

Commenting on René Descartes's *Optics,* Maurice Merleau-Ponty observes in *Eye and Mind* that the visible is exorcising the specters of illusion, as well as being redefined according to a model based on the clarity of thought:

> How crystal clear everything would be in our philosophy if only we could exorcise these specters, make illusions or object-less perceptions out of them, keep them on the edge of a world that does not equivocate!
> Descartes's *Dioptrics* is an attempt to do just that. It is the breviary of a thought that wants no longer to abide in the visible and so decides to construct the visible according to a model-in-thought. It is worthwhile to remember this attempt and its failure.[1]

Merleau-Ponty's pointed remarks isolate in Descartes's thought two fundamental and related tendencies. The first involves Descartes's struggle against, and critique of, illusion. Illusion in all its forms, be it reflection, *trompe-l'oeil* or artifice, threatens by its deceptive character to impede the search for truth. By relegating illusion to the status of an objectless perception, Descartes seeks to eradicate the question of doubt from the elaboration of certitude understood as objective truth. Merleau-Ponty's subsequent observation underlines Descartes's rejection of illusion by extending it to the visible world as a whole. No longer abiding in the visible, Descartes constructs it according to a figurative model based on mental schematism. This study will demonstrate that, while interested in optics as a physical science, and in vision as the dominant sense, Descartes is in fact systematically undermining in both his scientific and philosophical writings the role of vision and its perceptual domain. Instead, the properties of the visible will be transferred to the mental do-

63

main, whence they will illuminate metaphorically the powers of reason to attain certitude as clear and distinct ideas.

This essay examines Descartes's theory of vision in the larger context of his scientific and philosophical writings. Rather than restricting the analysis to the scientific articulation of the concept of vision in the *Optics* (*Dioptrique*; 1637), this study examines its foundation in Descartes's critique of illusion in his earlier writings, the *Observations* (*Experimenta*; 1619) and *Rules for the Direction of the Mind* (*Regulae ad directionem ingenii*; written in 1628 and published posthumously in 1701).[2] Rather than merely noting the suppression of illusion by the emergence of the discourse of certitude, this study contextualizes the status of illusion in terms of the Renaissance and baroque traditions that define it scenographically and pictorially. Particular attention will be paid to anamorphosis as a technical and pictorial device and its impact on Cartesian epistemology. How does Descartes's ostensible rejection of these traditions, where illusion functions as a reflection on the allegorical nature of truth, enable him to posit a concept of truth based on its homology to a mathematical model (*mathesis universalis*)?

Descartes's theory of vision espoused in the *Optics* will be in question insofar as it involves a rejection of ocular vision, in favor of a concept of vision which affirms the arbitrary relation between the object of vision and the impression that object generates. Based on technical experiments, involving the use of lenses and the telescope, as well as perspective in art, Descartes establishes the arbitrary character of vision by analogy to language. In so doing, he opens up the possibility of an inquiry into the relationship between vision, understood as a theory of representation, and its instrumentalization as a technical device. Descartes's interpretation heralds the demise of illusion associated with perceptual vision and the birth of a concept of reason whose intuitive character relies upon figurative notions based on mathematical schematism. The question is how the reabsorption of visual categories into a mathematical and discursive schematism enables Descartes to exclude visual sensation as the site of error. Extending his critique of vision from sensation to the imagination, Descartes reframes the visible world through the paradoxical affirmation of the autonomy of reason.

THE SCENOGRAPHY OF ILLUSION

Painting is nothing but the intersection of the visual pyramid following a given distance, a fixed center, and a certain lighting.
ALBERTI

From Descartes's earliest writings, *Preliminaries* (*Praeambula*; 1619), to his more elaborate philosophical disquisitions, such as *Discourse on the*

Method (*Discours de la méthode*; 1637) and the *Meditations on First Philosophy* (*Meditationes de Prima Philosophia*; 1641), the same concern continues to be reiterated in different ways: that of the danger of illusion. This invocation of illusion is invariably tied to deception and the problem of the unreliability of the senses.[3] One only needs to think of the *Meditations* where deception is so pervasive as to threaten the very definition of the thinking subject. The power of illusion is so persuasive as to cast doubt on one's ability to distinguish being awake from being asleep, and sanity from madness, culminating in the fiction of total deception engineered by the evil genius. It is this fiction of a total deception, rather than partial or occasional error, that leads Descartes to discover his own indubitable existence and its inalienable definition through thought.[4] Given this scenario in the *Meditations*, which is but the repetition of many such scenarios in his other writings, we must ask why is illusion, and particularly visual illusion, so central to Descartes's articulation of his philosophical project? Is the fear of illusion merely a conceit invoked by the discoverer of truth as certitude, or does it embody a baroque world view, to which Descartes resorts in order to dismiss it once and for all?

Descartes's early interest in the generation and manipulation of optical illusions is recorded as the *Observations* in the *Cogitationes privatae* (1619). In these notes, Descartes captures the power of illusion through an evocation of its spectral properties: (1) one can make shadows in a garden, so as to represent trees; (2) cut hedges so that from a set perspective they represent various figures; (3) control the passage of sunlight into a room, through certain openings, so as to generate numbers and shapes; (4) conjure up, in a room, limbs of fire, chariots of fire, and other spectral figures based on mirrors that reassemble our visual rays; (5) manipulate the reflection of the sun with parabolic mirrors so as to make it appear to be shining always from the same direction, or to be rising in the west instead of the east (*CMS* 1, 3). Alluding to the illusionism that characterizes the baroque gardens of his time, Descartes's observations on the projection of shadows, or the manipulation of perspectival effects, reveals his fascination with artifice and *trompe-l'oeil*. Not content with the manipulation of scenographic effects, Descartes also itemizes types of optical illusion, which confound through reflections and mirrors the perceptual experience of the observer. In these notes, Descartes's exploration of illusion reduces nature to an elaborate theater, one in which its very "nature" is in question as an effect of human artifice. Illusion is presented as a mechanical effect, whose optical-mathematical character underlies even its most fantastic and magical apparitions.

These allusions to optical and scenographic illusions in Descartes's early writings reflect the scientific and artistic concerns of the late sixteenth and early seventeenth century. They correspond to a renewal of interest in perspective, both as a technical and artistic fact. In his correspondence, Galileo Galilei mentions an anamorphic image and notes the divergent perceptions it engenders from two different points of view.[5] When the image is seen obliquely from the side, a human figure comes into view. When viewed frontally, the same image dissolves into a chaos of figures and colors that barely resembles landscapes, clouds, and spectral forms. According to Jurgis Baltrusaitis, Galileo's description presents a kind of allegorical poetry in which the "images and the meanings flow out of each other and change according to the direct or oblique perspective of the concept."[6] But Galileo's account of anamorphosis also suggests that visual experience corresponds to the oblique rather than the direct inscription of a subjective viewpoint into the image. Anamorphosis reflects the fascination with illusion at the dawn of the age of experimental optics. A theoretical analogue of technical devices, such as telescopes and lenses, anamorphosis represents an effort to rethink the visible by instrumentalizing the notion of pictorial perspective.

A quick review of Descartes's predecessors and contemporaries who devoted themselves to the study of perspective reveals the extraordinary scientific, artistic, philosophical, and magical significance of perspective. In Salomon de Caus (1576–1626), whose book *Perspective* (London, 1612; Paris, 1624) ranges from the mechanics of vision to hydraulic machines and automatons, and in *Curious Perspective* (1638) and *Thaumaturgus opticus* (1646) by Jean François Niceron (1613–46), we have discussions of perspective which mix purely technical and mechanical details with occult and hermetic considerations. In these works, "science unfolds in a fairy-tale atmosphere," since perspective is treated both as a legitimate tool for artistic and scientific knowledge, and as a device whose potential to manipulate and distort reality is equated with "artificial magic."[7] Niceron summarizes its impact when he explains: "the true magic or the perfection of sciences consists in Perspective, which enables us to know and discern more perfectly the beautiful works of Nature and Art."[8] The magical potential of perspective lies in its efficacy as a technical and artistic instrument to organize knowledge and define its criteria.

The development of experimental optics leads to a renewed inquiry into the philosophical and metaphysical potential of artistic perspective. As the scenographic depiction of rationalized space, pictorial perspective becomes the impetus for a combined approach to mathematics and philosophy, as a figurative science of measure, order, and proportion.[9] Whereas perspective represents an effort to rationalize and thereby normalize the visible, anamorphosis, on the contrary, represents a rejection of visual semblance, in favor of a schematism that deliberately distorts the visible. Unlike perspective, anamorphosis does not reduce forms to their visible outline. Rather, it distorts them through a process that projects them outside themselves. While perspective identifies the point of view with the centrality of vision and the subjective eye, anamorphosis relies on the decenterment of vision.[10] It implies a displacement of the subject and its reinscription according to a trajectory of obliqueness. Anamorphosis supplants the frontality of the visible, since the position of the viewing subject is now constituted outside the parameters that define visual semblance.

The legacies of perspective and the aperspectivism that defines anamorphosis are visible in the tensions that define Descartes's earliest philosophical writings. Starting with the *Rules for the Direction of the Mind* (written in 1628 and published posthumously in 1701), Descartes explicitly warns the reader against the danger of undirected reflection and the fascination with illusion for its own sake:

> For it is very certain that unregulated inquiries and confused reflections of this kind only confound the natural light and blind our mental powers. Those who so become accustomed to walk in darkness weaken their eyesight so much that afterwards they cannot bear the light of day. [Rule 4; *HR*, 1, 9]

For Geneviève Rodis-Lewis, this passage embodies Descartes's overt rejection of the occult and hermetic traditions that use mathematics and optics as magic, merely to astonish the learned through the illusion of knowledge.[11] However, a closer inspection of this passage reveals that Descartes's purpose, to demystify knowledge which is not based on method, involves the effort to equate all illusion with blindness. Alluding to Plato's allegory of the cave in the *Republic*, Descartes suggests that the allegorical nature of truth may be corrected by the discovery and methodical use of the light of reason. Not content to critique previous Platonic and Aristotelian traditions, Descartes suggests that the mediated relationship of the sensible and the intelligible may be overcome once the light of reason no longer refers to vision but to purely "mental powers." Descartes's attempts to supersede Platonic allegory through the rejection of the interplay of illusion and truth result in the paradoxical position of positing truth as an allegory which abolishes the notion of allegory.

In spite of his rejection of the illusionism associated with ocular vision in the *Rules*, Descartes resorts to visual metaphors to describe the nature of intuition as mental "vision." When describing the passage of deduction to intuition, he appeals to pictorial principles in order to displace visual with figurative considerations. In Rule 7, Descartes explains how the mind attains intellectual vision:

> It is in precisely the same fashion that though we cannot with one single gaze distinguish all the links of a lengthy chain, yet if we have seen the connection of each with its neighbor, we shall be entitled to say that we have seen how the first is connected to the last. [*HR* 1, 20–21]

Intellectual vision is not ocular, and consequently it is no longer subject to illusion. Rather, it is a new kind of vision that the understanding rescues from the limitations of the gaze. It is based on understanding how the chains in an argument are connected, thereby enabling one to arrive at intuitive understanding through the schematic and figurative reduction of arguments. Combining rhetorical and mnemonic strategies, intuition is presented as the figural realization of the process of deduction.[12] Based on the Renaissance traditions of the *ars memoriae* that seek to reduce memory to compendious abbreviations or schematic figures, Descartes's elaboration of intuition seeks to escape the constraints of the visible by abstracting and reifying its character through its implicit reliance upon scenographic and pictorial traditions.[13]

In Rule 12, Descartes explores how the understanding is able to arrive at a "distinct intuition" when it deals with matters that touch upon the body. It is in this context that Descartes's rejection of visual semblance becomes explicit, as he attempts to disenfranchise objects of their visible nature. He explains that the understanding does not proceed from a "multitude of objects," since the focus is on how to "deduce one thing from a number of objects" (*HR* 1, 40). This process of abbreviation of the field of objects, according to a principle of logical inclusion, is accompanied by their instrumentalization and reduction, since "we must banish from the ideas of the objects presented whatsoever does not require present attention" (*HR* 1, 40). Descartes concludes by claiming that "it is not on those occasions that the objects themselves ought to be presented to the external senses, but rather certain compendious abbreviations" (*HR* 1, 40). At this stage of the argument, neither objects nor our ideas of them have any direct pertinence. They are replaced by schematic or notational devices which are presented to the external senses, ostensibly to guard against lapses of memory. Thus the power of the understanding to arrive at a "distinct intuition" involves displacing the validity of perception with conceptual devices.

In order to preclude deceptions of the visible, Descartes valorizes the capacity of the understanding to represent things according to a set of procedures that elides visual considerations. For it seems that Descartes's interest lies less in the ocular evidence of external objects than in the effort to avoid conceptual distortions. Descartes's arguments in the *Rules* attest to his effort to discover a philosophical analogue to the technical and artistic devices which are redefining the concept of vision. While Baltrusaitis, on the basis of historical evidence, argues for Descartes's interest in anamorphosis, his definition of anamorphosis leaves open the question of its precise impact on Cartesian philosophy:

> Anamorphosis—a word that makes its appearance in the seventeenth century but for a device already known—plays havoc with elements and principles; instead of reducing forms to their visible limits, it projects them outside themselves and distorts them so that when viewed from a certain point they return to normal. The system was established as a technical curiosity, but it embraces a poetry of abstraction, an effective mechanism for producing optical illusion and a philosophy of false reality.[14]

Defined as a technique for the manipulation of optical illusion, anamorphosis emerges as a device whose speculative impact lies in the conceptual redefinition of the visible. Anamorphosis means a return to form, from the Greek *ana* (back) and *morphē* (form). But this return to visual form relies on the technical redefinition of vision, as mediated either by the reconstruction of the visual field or by the use of devices such as mirrors. Anamorphosis announces a new relation to the visible, one which conceives visual form not as a given but as a conceptual and technical construct.

Descartes's critique of illusion in general, and of visual semblance in particular, marks the convergence of his philosophical strategy to orchestrate the emergence of the discourse of truth with the technical and artistic experiments of his contemporaries with anamorphosis. In both contexts, visual illusion is manipulated technically in order to reduce the world to a false reality. Visual distortion stages the discovery of that particular point where optical illusion dissolves into truth, like the vantage point in anamorphic art. Thus Descartes's critique of illusion cannot be construed as a critique of anamorphosis, as Rodis-Lewis contends.[15] Rather, it represents Descartes's assimilation of anamorphosis to his elaboration of a rationalism founded on mathematical schematism. As a technique that reduces the visible world to a false reality, and ordinary vision to a kind of blindness, anamorphosis announces the emergence of a new concept of vision and a new philosophical outlook. The rejection of visual semblance and its relocation within a mathematical schematism constitutes a new point of view, based on the instrumentalization of both optics and pictorial perspective. As the pages that follow demonstrate, Descartes's inquiry into the nature of vision leads to an exploration of optics that displaces both the priority of the eye and the centrality of vision.

THE ECLIPSE OF THE EYE

Blame not on eyes the error of the mind.
LUCRETIUS

Descartes begins the *Optics* with a praise of the senses, among which vision is singled out as the most universal and noble. However, Descartes immediately qualifies his privilege of vision, by affirming the necessity for technical innovations that would augment its power. The question of what constitutes vision is addressed only to the extent of the need to develop technical devices or "artificial organs" to correct it. Descartes's fascination with lenses that expand human vision brings the imperceptible, the previously invisible, within the domain of human perception, extending "our vision much further than our forebears could normally extend their imagination" (*CSM* 1, 152). Descartes's effort to address the perceptual domain coincides with the attempt to redress its limits: he corrects errors and expands its scope so that it no longer has anything to do with visual perception, in a human rather than a purely technical sense. The development of instruments that expand the scope of vision coincides with the instrumentalization of visual perception as a whole, since technology enables a greater and more perfect knowledge of nature. Descartes connects the perfectibility of human knowledge with the extension of human perception through artificial organs. They expand the horizon of perception while erasing its experiential, all-too-human character.

In order to discuss the nature of light, how visual rays enter the eye and are reflected by physical objects, Descartes proposes the analogy of walking in the dark along an uneven path with the help of a stick. He suggests that its function is that of a hypothesis which in spite of its falseness may enable us to arrive at some true conclusions:

> No doubt you have had the experience of walking at night over rough ground without a light, and finding it necessary to use a stick in order to guide yourself. You may then have been able to notice that by means of the stick you could feel the various objects situated around you, and that you could even tell whether they were trees or stones or sand or water or grass or mud or any other such thing. It is true that this kind of sensation is somewhat confused and obscure in those who do not have long practice with it. But consider it in those born blind, who have made use of it all their lives: with them, you will find, it is so perfect and so exact that one might almost say that they see with their hands, or that their stick is the organ of some sixth sense given to them in place of sight. [*CSM* 1, 153]

Descartes's analogy of the walking stick to light recasts the act of vision: it replaces visual identification with a blind vision whose clarity is mediated by one's familiarity with the stick as a conduit for sensation. The attempt to discuss the nature of light by analogy not merely to night but to a different sense altogether, is surprising. Surprising, if only because the effort to think of light by reducing it to blindness eliminates its most distinctive feature: its ubiquity, either as luminous source or as illuminating force (as generator of reflections), that is, the very horizon of its phenomenal domain. Comparing the blind with those who "see with their hands," Descartes equates vision with touch, a sense which he considers to be more certain and less vulnerable to error than vision.

Before we examine Descartes's attempt to privilege touch, it suffices to note that the value of touch lies in the fact that it does not presuppose any resemblance between experience and its physical causes. It is the sensation of physical resistance or of movement that informs our perception of the object, rather than the medium, be it the sense of touch or, by analogy, that of vision. By taking recourse to blindness and to the "seeing stick," Descartes transforms seeing into a purely mechanical operation, one determined by the position and activity of the seeing subject in regard to the passive object of sight. It is no longer the object or its position in the visual field which is significant, but rather the manner in which sight is instrumentalized, transformed by analogy from a "walking" into a seeing "stick," that is, an extension of the subject. The transparency of vision is now equated with the opacity and blindness of touch, so that the act of vision becomes indirect, to the extent that it stumbles on, points at, and projects the existence of objects through a mechanics of movement. It brings them within the purview of a clarity illuminated by blindness.

In *The World* (whose subtitle is "Treatise on Light"), Descartes discusses the nature of light by stating that there is a difference between the sensation of light and its cause, the latter being identified with "the idea of light which is formed in our imagination by the mediation of our eyes" (*CSM* 1, 81). In order to argue that there is no similarity between ideas and their physical causes, Descartes resorts to an analogy to language.[16] The aim is to demonstrate that in spite of its dissimilarity to the things it represents, language can provide us with information about the world:

> Now if words, which signify nothing except by human convention, suffice to make us think of things to which they bear no resemblance, then why could nature not also have established some sign which makes us have the sensation of light, even if the sign contained nothing in itself which is similar to this sensation? [*CSM* 1, 81]

The analogy of the sensation of light to that of language reduces nature to a world of signs, whose meaning must be deciphered independent of any similarity between the sign and the sensation it signifies. While nature provides us with visible signs, the attempt to decipher them no longer demands that this process take place within the register of the visible. Like speech, the visible becomes legible at the moment that it becomes something different from itself. Once the visible is reduced to a sign, what matters is not its relation to what it ostensibly signifies, but its function in the order of signification. Reduced to mathematical conventions, to the language of universal mathematics (*mathesis universalis*), nature signifies not as an image, but as a rational schema. Its visible character is no longer at issue: it is a question of logic rather than mimesis.[17] In other words the visible can only be addressed because its figurative character conforms to pregiven conventions. The logic of these conventions lies in the design of geometry rather than experience.

Now we begin to understand why, for Descartes, touch is more reliable than vision: it "makes us conceive many ideas which bear no resemblance to the objects which produce them" (*CSM* 1, 82). Descartes proceeds to cite a number of instances in which the sensation of pleasure or pain is generated (an infant tickled with a feather, or the soldier's experience of an illusory wound), in order to argue that sensation need not reflect the object that causes it. He asks the reader: "Do you think the idea of tickling, which he [the child] conceives, resembles anything present in this feather?" (*CSM* 1, 82). While revealing the existence of external objects, through the fugitive contact with their sensation as pleasure and pain, Descartes disenfranchises in the same gesture the qualitative differences of sensation. The idea that sensation need not resemble its particular physical cause, suggests that ultimately we may be unable to distinguish between the touch of a feather and the caress of a hand.

It is this dissimilarity between things and the ideas that they produce in us, that interests Descartes and that leads him to conceive vision according to a nonmimetic and, ultimately, nonreferential model. At issue for him is the effort to deliver us from the notion of *intentional species,* attributed to Aristotle and the Scholastics, which contends that there is something in the object itself that resembles the ideas we have of them (*CMS* 1, 153). But in attempting to deliver us from what appears to be the dominion of things and their reflections, Descartes is in fact submitting us to the mastery of the subject, whose perceptual reality like that of nature has been reduced to mechanical reality. In part 2 of the *Optics,* entitled "Refraction," Descartes compares light rays with bouncing balls which move in straight lines, whose angles vary depending on the surfaces they encounter (*CMS* 1, 158–175). In so doing, he suggests that visual reflection is merely a mechanical projection. This equation of felt experience and physical motion, which now homogenizes our sensations of vision and touch, elides something fundamental: that the visual image is not merely a mechanical reflection but a conceptual construct that embodies and represents the physical world.

What then is the status of visual images? In the *Optics,* Descartes warns the reader not to envisage visual perception according to a pictorial model, that is, as images that are sent to the brain. Such a model is based on the mimetic traditions of painting, where an image of the object leads us to conceive the object itself, and hence projects it, as it were, through the senses to the brain. However, for Descartes, "our mind can be stimulated by many things other than images—by signs and words, for example, which in no way resemble the things they signify" (*CSM* 1, 165). Rejecting resemblance once again as a perceptual model, Descartes goes on to suggest that the very lack of resemblance assures the accuracy of the perception of certain images. To illustrate his point, Descartes mentions etchings where forests, cities, men, and battles become merely traces of ink on the paper (*CSM* 1, 165). If on a flat surface figures are distorted, since circles are represented by ovals and squares by rhombuses, then distortion is made necessary by the very laws of perspective. Descartes's allusion to perspective in this context clarifies the fact that his theory of vision is a theory of representation, an interpretation of the visible as a symbolic form. Vision is merely a construct whose pictorial referent is the projection of a geometric-optical system.

Merleau-Ponty suggests that the impact of the Cartesian rejection of resemblance has implications that go beyond questions of visual illusion and pictoriality. The implications touch upon the question of how the mind conceives, how it reflects both upon itself and the external world:

> If the reflection resembles the thing itself, it is because this reflection acts upon the eyes more or less as a thing would. In the world there is the thing itself, and outside this thing itself there is that other thing which is only reflected light rays and which happens to have an ordered correspondence with the real thing; there are two individuals, then, bound together by external causality. As far as the thing and its mirror image is concerned, their resemblance is only an external denomination; the resemblance belongs to thought. [What for us is] the "cross-eyed" relationship of resemblance is—in things—a clear relationship of projection. ["EM,"170]

Merleau-Ponty's comments clarify Descartes's particular contribution to a theory of knowledge that seeks to move beyond resemblance in order to banish illusion and anchor itself within difference. This difference is not only constitutive of sensation, but of the physical world as a whole. The effort to establish a theory of perception—which on the one hand designates the object (the thing itself), and designates on the other hand its mirror reflection as another kind of a thing (which has an "ordered correspondence with the real thing"), while binding them together by the same mechanical causality—is to create an empirical world, in the modern sense of the word. What we are witnessing here, in effect, is the creation of things, whose identity is defined by the particular manner in which they become objects of rational cognition. Their presence as objects is no longer defined by the phenomenal domain, but by their adequation to a schema that privileges the immediacy of touch (the presence-at-hand) over the mediating reflection of the visible. It is a world where reflections cease to exist, where objective reality undermines by its mechanical veracity the capacity of the imagination to define thought.

THE VISIONARY "I": THE SEAL AND THE WAX

Anamorphosis is as soft and flexible as the wax on which the philosopher meditated.
BALTRUSAITIS

The questions that Descartes raises in regard to visual perception are questions that apply to sensation, in general. Starting with the *Rules*, and continuing through the *Meditations* and the *Search After Truth*, Descartes consistently pursues the question of the relationship of the mind to the senses. However, whereas in the *Rules* he still appears to recognize the capacity of the external world literally to impress itself upon the body and thus define it through sensation, later on sensation is denied its scriptorial character. Its signatory imprints will be associated with error rather than with information. In the later writings, we witness the evacuation of the body and its sensorial domain, in order to ascertain the indubitable master of the mind over all aspects of physical reality. This transformation can be seen in Descartes's deliberate choice of metaphors, in the *Rules*, that of describing the body as a piece of wax which receives impressions from a seal. However, in the *Meditations*, this analogy no longer refers to the body, but solely to the objects of perception. There we see the transformation of a piece of wax into a material substance, whose mutable nature challenges the capacity of the external world to signify, and thus to generate meaning.

If according to the *Rules* understanding alone is "capable of perceiving the truth" (Rule 12; *HR* 1, 35), the question remains what is the status of the body and "how it is 'informed' by mind" (*HR* 1, 36).[18] Descartes formulates this problem in the *Rules* as follows:

> all our external senses, insofar as they are part of the body, and despite the
> fact that we direct them towards objects, so manifesting activity, viz. a

movement in space, nevertheless properly speaking perceive in virtue of passivity alone, just in the way that wax receives an impression (*figuram*) from a seal. And it should not be thought that all we mean to assert is an analogy between the two. We ought to believe that the way *is entirely the same* in which the exterior figure of the sentient body is really modified by the object, as that in which the shape of the wax is altered by the seal. [*HR* 1, 36]

While Descartes underlines the passivity of the senses, he elaborates their receptive character by analogy to the impression that wax receives from a seal. Using the Platonic analogy, that of the "mind's likeness to wax" (*Theatetus* 194d), Descartes now defines the body as a material substance, a piece of wax which bears upon itself the impressions of the physical world.[19] This analogy of the body with wax expresses the recognition that the "external sense is stimulated [*movetur*] by the object" (*HR* 1, 37). In the case of vision, the "first opaque structure in the eye receives the figure impressed upon it by the light" (*HR* 1, 37). However, Descartes subsequently clarifies his position by noting that "the figure which is conveyed to it is carried off to "the common sense, in the very same instance and without the passage of any real entity from one to the other" (*HR* 1, 37). Descartes thus establishes the formal character of sensation, where stimulation is figurative and belongs to the order of movement. In other words, the modalities of impression of the external world are schematic rather than anchored in an image which reflects the actual visual semblance of objects.

Descartes goes on to describe the function of common sense by pursuing the analogy of the wax seal. Common sense "impresses on the fantasy or imagination, as though on wax, those very figures and ideas which come *uncontaminated and without bodily admixture from the external senses*" (*HR* 1, 38; emphasis added). As Descartes's analysis unfolds we are witnessing the gradual disenfranchisement of the senses of any material and bodily qualities. The activity of common sense upon the imagination is exercised through the reification of the senses. Only those impressions which are in abstraction of the senses are to be conveyed. Descartes goes on to privilege the understanding as a faculty which is not only moved by the imagination but can "act on it" (*HR* 1, 39) in turn.[20] This valorization of the understanding ultimately leads him to dismiss the input of the imagination:

> if the understanding deals with matters in which there is nothing corporeal or similar to the corporeal, it cannot be helped by those faculties, but that, on the contrary, to prevent their hampering it, the senses must be banished and the imagination as far as possible divested of every distinct impression. [*HR* 1, 39]

This dismissal of the imagination and the senses, as regards their power to inform the understanding, elucidates Descartes's contention that the power by which we know things is "purely spiritual." It is no less distinct from the body as a whole, as the hand is from the eye, and thus it represents a single and unique agency which is properly the mind (*HR* 1, 38). But, as Descartes explains, the attempts of the understanding to address the phenomenal or physical world lead to the reduction of objects to "compendious abbreviations," schematic figures which are presented to the external senses (*HR* 1, 40). Thus the "objects themselves," as the insignia of the external world, only have meaning to the extent that they have undergone a process of reduction that denies their material nature in favor of a schematism that affirms figuratively their indirect mode of existence.

While recognizing that the mind is a cognitive power, that it may be both passive and active, resembling "now the seal and now the wax" (*HR* 1, 39), Descartes seeks however to dissociate this analogy from corporeal things (*HR* 1, 39). Consequently we are witnessing a model for both perception and conception that is created by analogy to a scriptorial/figurative model. This model is constituted as an apparatus, a machine which is intended to both capture and communicate the translation of the sensible into the intelligible. However, following the logic of Descartes's argument, the reader discovers that this concept of translation no longer refers to the experiential world. What is being expressed has little to do with experience in a phenomenal sense. Rather, the invocation of this system of mediation only exists as a way of erasing the world of sensation in favor of a schematism that both predicts and predates it. Cognition thus becomes the site of confirmation, that of acknowledging the priority of mind and its power to produce, rather than reproduce, experiential reality. In spite of the invocation of a scriptorial/figurative model the experiential world recedes, since its mimetic dimensions only testify to its inadequacy to inform the power of understanding.

This failure of experiential reality to inform, that is, to mediate how the mind conceives, is made explicit in the failure of perception. In the *Meditations,* the metaphor of the piece of wax reappears not as analogy for perception but as the index of the failure of experience to provide meaningful information about itself. Having determined that he is a thinking thing, Descartes proceeds in the Second Meditation to broach the question of the status of the things that surround him. Whether by accident or design, his reflection on the bodies that we touch and see takes the form of "this piece of wax" (*HR* 1, 154). The piece of wax in the *Meditations* is very different from the metaphor of the wax and seal that we encountered in the *Rules.* The piece of wax is no longer an analogy or device to think about the mechanisms of perception: it is now merely the vehicle for delimiting the conceptual implications of perception.

When Descartes examines the piece of wax he is struck by its perceptual qualities, its color, odor, figure and size. But as soon as he approaches the fire, the piece of wax is altered in his hands, the "smell evaporates, the color alters, the figure is destroyed, the size increases, it becomes liquid, it heats, scarcely can one handle it, and when one strikes no sound is emitted" (*HR* 1, 154). These perceptual shifts, involving the wax, lead him to question its material nature: "Does the same wax remain after this change?" (*HR* 1, 154). The material liquefaction of the wax casts into doubt the solidity of the senses to provide information about the external world:

> What then did I know so distinctly in this piece of wax? It could certainly be nothing of all that the senses brought to my notice, since all these things which fall under taste, smell, sight, touch and hearing, are found to be changed, and yet this same wax remains. [*HR* 1, 154]

The senses lose their solidity before the material substance of the object in question. What was previously perceptible in one form is "now perceptible under others." It is only by "abstracting" these forms of perception from the wax that Descartes is able to examine what remains. This remainder, however, no longer refers to the perceptual domain, but to a conceptual one.

This process of abstraction and reduction leads Descartes to conclude that "nothing remains excepting a certain extended thing which is flexible and movable" (*HR* 1, 154). However, this Cartesian definition of the wax as an "extended thing" no longer refers to "this same wax," since its self-identity is not defined in relation to the phenomenal world. Rather, the definition of the wax in terms of extension and movement inscribes its material identity within the immaterial reality of a geometric and mechanical schematism. The failure of the imagination to function as a vehicle for "understanding" this piece of wax is recuperated by the mind "alone which perceives it" (*HR* 1, 155). Perception is thus transferred from the senses and the imagination to the "understanding" or the "mind." But as Descartes explains, perception in this context has a different meaning:

> But what must particularly be observed is that its perception [that of the wax] is neither an act of vision, nor of touch, nor of imagination, and has never been such although it may have appeared formerly to be so, but only an intuition of the mind (*mens*), which may be imperfect and confused as it was formerly, or clear and distinct as it is at present. [*HR* 1, 155]

Having declared the signatory or defining properties of the wax to be purely illusory, Descartes reserves for the mind those perceptual qualities that until now defined the mind's objects. When the mind perceives, it does so in exclusion of sensation. It forms a clear and distinct idea of objects, by having reduced and abstracted their material character into an entity whose transparency is the result of the homology of the mind and the mathematical schematism that the mind imposes upon the world. Hence the experiential world recedes in its material opacity, because and in spite of the illusory transparency of vision.

Unable to dismiss the power of vision, because it now describes the capacity of the mind to attain certitude, Descartes obsessively returns to meditate on vision's powers. He considers the possibility that he knew the wax "by means of vision and not simply by the intuition of the mind" (*HR* 1, 155). This option is rapidly dismissed by invoking the absurd notion that the men who pass in the streets are "automatic machines," that is, spectral illusions designed to confound us. This paranoid plot, intended to deceive him (by whom? and by what agency?), is settled by the paradoxical reaffirmation of the *cogito,* not as a thinking thing (the *Discourse*) but as a seeing thing:

> For it may be that what I see is not really wax, it may be also that I do not possess eyes with which to see anything; but it cannot be that when *I see, or (for I no longer take account of the distinction) when I think I see,* that I myself who think am nought. . . . And there are so many other things in the mind itself which may contribute to the elucidation of its nature, that those which depend on body such as these just mentioned, hardly merit being taken into account. [*HR* 1, 156–157; emphasis added]

In this passage the conclusion of the First Meditation, "I am, I exist," is fleshed out in order to include sight as a defining characteristic of the topology of being. The distinction between thinking and seeing is eliminated at the point where the subject posits the indubitability of its existence. When perception is reintroduced, its only function is to reconfirm the identity of being as self-reflection. Removed from its contact with the external world, vision in this context only validates the autoaffective character of thought: it now becomes a passion of the soul. The *cogito* of the *Discourse* is now redefined as the visionary "I" of the *Meditations.* The term *visionary* in this context refers to Descartes's paradoxical reappropriation of vision by reason, which corresponds to an act of denunciation of its phenomenal and experiential character.

In the Third Meditation, Descartes proceeds to elaborate the visionary character of the "I" by analogy to his idea of God's existence. Returning implicitly to the metaphor of the wax and seal, he now designates himself as the bearer of the imprint of God's workmanship:

And one certainly ought not to find it strange that God, in creating me, placed this idea within me to be like the mark of the workman imprinted on his work; and it is likewise not essential that the mark shall be something different from the work itself. [*HR* 1, 170]

As Férdinand Alquié observes in his annotations to the *Meditations*, the idea of God is innate and it infuses consciousness so pervasively as to be confused with consciousness itself. Thus Descartes becomes the very *sign* of God, and the *cogito* is but the idea of God.[21] However, the purpose of this study is less to elucidate the character and status of innate ideas in the *Meditations* than to raise a different question altogether. Why does Descartes return to a scriptorial/figurative model, involving the notion of signatory imprints, when he has refused to concede to the external world the capacity to perceptually inform and mark his own consciousness?

It is important to recall that, earlier in the Third Meditation, Descartes underlines the "difference between the object and its idea" (*HR* 1, 161). He discovers two completely diverse ideas of the sun in his mind. The first is derived through the senses and thus belongs to the category of "adventitious ideas," according to which the sun is "extremely small." The second is derived through "astronomical reasonings, i.e., is elicited from certain notions that are innate in me, or else it is formed by me in some other manner; in accordance with it the sun appears to be several times greater than the earth" (*HR* 1, 161). While both of these ideas resemble the sun, reason leads him to conclude that the idea based on ordinary experience is the one most "dissimilar" to the sun. Descartes's valorization of astronomical observation and its equation with reason and innate ideas, reveals the technological character of his thought. The world of experience is reduced to illusion, whereas the mathematical-optical world view more intimately corresponds to and reflects the nature of human reason.

Now we begin to understand why the wax-and-seal metaphor that appears in the *Rules*, as an analogy for the passage of the sensible to the intelligible, disappears altogether in the *Meditations*. The capacity of the external world to imprint itself upon Cartesian consciousness is denied totally, since the materiality of the wax dissolves under the scrutiny of reason. The wax is nothing more than an object, a thing defined by extension and movement, that is, by its conformity, not to its perceptual but to its conceptual nature. It is no longer the natural world that forms and informs reason, like a seal, but rather reason that seals the fate of nature by the imposition of its own signatory character. Thus it comes as no particular surprise that in the Third Meditation Descartes concludes that God alone has the power to impress upon consciousness the idea of his existence. By assigning this power to God alone, Descartes can suc-

cessfully prevent the external world from acting on his own consciousness. Whether we choose to interpret the Cartesian gesture as a gesture
of faith or as a gesture of pure cynicism, one thing becomes clear. The
analogy of the mind with God's seal results in the identification of the
mind with its divine author. And thus by extension, it affirms the indubitable power of the mind to apply its own authoritative and decisive seal
upon the shape and character of the external world.

THIS WANING WORLD:
THE ANAMORPHOSIS OF THE VISIBLE

Any theory of painting is a metaphysics.
MERLEAU-PONTY

Descartes's visionary interpretation of the mind in the Third Meditation
as the bearer of God's seal and thus as the sole authoritative source of
true knowledge, becomes the turning point in his efforts to separate the
intellect from the imagination. The conceptual threat posed by the imagination's power to visualize things is countered by Descartes's strategy to
separate conception from the imagination. In the Sixth Meditation,
Descartes attempts to settle the "difference between the imagination and
pure intellection" (*HR* 1, 185). Taking the example of a chiliagon, he affirms the power to conceive it and the impossibility to imagine it:

> But if I desire to think of a chiliagon, I certainly conceive truly that it is a
> figure composed of a thousand sides, just as easily as I conceive of a trian-
> gle that it is a figure of three sides only; but I cannot in any way imagine
> the thousand sides of a chiliagon [as I do the three sides of a triangle], nor
> do I, so to speak, regard them as present [with the eyes of my mind]. [*HR*
> 1, 185–186]

Descartes concludes that this particular "effort of mind in order to effect
the act of imagination" clearly manifests the difference between imagination and pure intellection (*HR* 1, 186). Taking as an example the chiliagon, a mathematical figure whose thousand sides resist visualization,
Descartes frames the imagination by staging its limits. He introduces visual considerations in the context of mathematical schematism, thereby
deliberately confusing the figurative character of mathematical schematism with that of vision.

The power of mathematical schematism to hypothesize is opposed
to the failure of the imagination to see, that is, to regard something as
"present [with the eyes of my mind]." This failure to visualize a hypothetical mathematical object as an ordinary object serves to distinguish the
power of imagination from that of pure intellection or conception. This

thousand-sided geometric figure posits a challenge to the imagination, by bracketing its figurative character through the hyperbolic power of conception. The power of the mind to conceive figures such as a chiliagon or a myriagon is constituted through the invocation of a mathematical sublime, that is, figures that stand in for a concept of mathematical infinity.[22] The capacity of the mind to hypothesize in the context of mathematical schematism is pitted against the imagination's figurative character which resists such schematization. Defined by its ability to exceed figurative determinations, the mind is constituted as a trope, whose sublime character rhetorically sublates and reinscribes the imagination.

Consequently, the imagination is relegated to a subsidiary status, no longer intrinsic to the "essence" of the mind. For Descartes the imagination is "in no wise a necessary element in my nature," since it involves a turn "towards the body" (*HR* 1, 186). The imaginative function of the mind is dismissed because its figurative character does not conform to the epistemological constraints of the Cartesian method. Descartes's definition of the intellectual activity of the mind, which "in some manner turns on itself and considers some of the ideas which it possesses in itself" (*HR* 1, 186), corresponds to a process of self-inspection and self-validation that defines the mind's rational character. The manner in which the mind reflects upon itself, by considering in itself particular ideas, and by scrutinizing itself as a totality, implies the paradoxical affirmation of perspective and also its denunciation. This is why only visually unrepresentable geometric figures can embody the conceptual aptitude of the mind. As hypothetical projections of mathematical species, they challenge the figurative nature of the imagination by their appeal to indeterminacy and thus to the unimaginable. However, this paradoxical appeal to indeterminacy in the context of mathematical determinism, must be understood as the effort to validate, through the projection of a fictitious exteriority, the axiomatic character of *mathesis*. In the effort to validate itself, the Cartesian mind becomes an instrument of its own projection: an unimaginable point that determines the domain of the imagination.

The dominance of the conceptual power of the mind over the imagination represents Descartes's effort to shift attention away from the image to the order of representation to which the image belongs. In *The Search After Truth*, Descartes discusses the failure of the imagination in pictorial terms. As Epistemon explains, only the mind can produce "good pictures," since the senses are like "bad painters":

> The senses, the inclinations, our masters and our intelligence, are the various painters who have the power to execute this work; and amongst them, those who are least adapted to succeed in it, i.e. the imperfect senses, blind instinct and foolish nurses, are the first to mingle themselves with it. . . .

> But it [intelligence] is like a clever painter who might have been called upon to put the last touches on a bad picture sketched out by prentice hands, and who would find it vain to employ all the rules of his art in correcting little by little first a trait here, then a trait there, and finally be required to add to it from his own hand all that was lacking, and who yet could not prevent great faults from remaining in it, because from the beginning the picture would have been badly conceived, the figures badly placed, and the proportions badly observed. [*HR* 1, 312]

This analogy of intelligence with a master painter should not deceive the reader into believing that the visible is brought back within the purview of consciousness. Rather, the opposite is the case. Descartes's appeal to a pictorial model serves here as a vehicle for affirming the mastery of the mind to conceive things correctly. Since the senses are like "bad" painters, the problem is not that of retouching and correcting particular faults. Such a gesture is deemed insufficient. By correcting what is lacking, the painter fails to address the issue that the picture is badly conceived. This emphasis on intelligence as a "clever painter" underlines its conceptual function, as organizer of the placement of the figures and their proportions.

Eudoxus responds to Epistemon's comparison by suggesting that the artist would be better off effacing with a sponge all the features of the drawing in order to "begin entirely over again rather than lose his time in correcting it" (*HR* 1, 312). This suggestion, to remove from the imagination "all the inexact ideas which have hitherto succeeded in engraving themselves upon it" (*HR* 1, 312), reveals Descartes's radical effort to efface its figurative impact. The master painter, like the philosopher architect in the *Discourse,* must start with a clean slate. Just as the painter sketches a formal outline, so does intelligence impose its own conceptual order as a plan that predetermines and thus defines the nature of the elements deployed. This pictorial scheme sets the scene for the criteria that define the visual rendering of the elements involved. Descartes's appeal to intelligence as a "master" painter redefines the pictorial not in mimetic terms, but as a symbolic form that constructs figures in conformity to the rationality of its design. This analogy suggests that the purpose of the pictorial is not to reproduce a reality already given, but to create an image of how it ought to be conceived.

This emphasis on the technical rather than mimetic aspects of pictorial composition, rather than its consideration as a medium for artistic reproduction is addressed by Descartes in the First Meditation. In his discussion of visual images in dreams, he affirms their connection to external reality, only to reaffirm the fact that this connection is not referential, but refers instead to shared compositional elements:

For, as a matter of fact, painters, even when they study with the greatest skill to represent sirens and satyrs by forms the most strange and extraordinary, cannot give them natures which are entirely new, but merely make a certain medley of the members of different animals; or if their imagination is extravagant enough to invent something so novel that nothing similar has ever before been seen, and that their work represents a thing purely fictitious and absolutely false, it is certain all the same that *the colors of which this is composed are necessarily real.* [*HR* 1, 146; emphasis added]

While this analogy to painting pertains to dream images as "counterparts" of external reality, Descartes subsequently expands this pictorial analogy to apply to "all these images of things that dwell in our thoughts, whether true and real and fantastic or false" (*HR* 1, 146). Thus whether it is a question of dream images or paintings, be they realistic or fantastic, what matters is less the particular content of the image than its compositional elements, such as color.[23] Their truth value depends less upon their referential quality than upon the universality of color, as a constitutive property shared by all images.

Descartes's reliance upon color as a compositional element, reflects less his interest in pictorial issues (those of visual semblance or resemblance) than his conceptual concern with how images are constructed. For color in this context does not signify a shared material substrate, but rather a universal element of design. Hence it is not surprising that Descartes follows his discussion of color and the composition of images with an inquiry into scientific reason when applied to "composite things" (*HR* 1, 147). His conclusion is that certitude can only be attained in the context of arithmetic and geometry, that is, sciences "which only treat of things that are very simple and general" (*HR* 1, 147). What is important for him is not whether such things are "existent or not," but that they "contain some measure of certainty and an element of the indubitable" (*HR* 1, 147). Descartes conceives certitude as an element of design, defined by its appurtenance to a rationally defined order. By interpreting certitude as subject to the overall design of mathematical constraints and conventions, Descartes identifies its congruence to the function of color in painting. Thus a theory of pictorial design is conflated with a mathematical schematism leading to the technical redefinition of both vision and the visible.

The defining elements of Cartesian thought have nothing to do with visual semblance, which is the reflective shimmer of objects. Rather, the elements are defined by mathematical principles that contain the space of figuration and that predict the types of figures that are available to define thought. The Renaissance and baroque paradigms that problematized the question of representation (the world as theater) are displaced by the emergence of a concept of truth that elides its own representational character. Henceforth, it is the sensible world which takes on a spectral quality, while reason aspires to a reality free of both artifice and illusion. Human invention reduces illusion to technical artifice, transforming nature into a mechanical phantom. Like an automaton that supplants its human model through a haunting resemblance, so does the Cartesian fiction of rationality threaten to render obsolete the perceptual world.

In his essay "The Age of the World Picture" (1938), Martin Heidegger remarks that the "fact that the world becomes picture at all is what distinguishes the essence of the modern age."[24] Heidegger's comment on the Cartesian legacy to modernity underlines the fact that the "world picture" in this context does not have pictorial referent, but rather refers to the manner in which the world is conceived, that is, represented (both composed and apprehended). As this essay has shown, Descartes's deliberate use of pictorial analogies is not intended for the exploration of the visible, but rather its foreclosure. For the significance of painting in Descartes's work is purely conceptual. It provides a model for intellectual thought, a theory of representation whose schematic character denies ocular vision. This model of conception relies upon the deliberate distortion and technical reconstruction of the visible in order to resituate its logic in the order of anamorphosis. Descartes thus redefines both our access to the visible and the meaning of vision. If modern metaphysics takes painting as its conceptual prototype, we are left to wonder about the possible meaning of vision beyond its identification with thought. Along with Merleau-Ponty, we conclude by asking whether there are dimensions to vision which are not exhausted by its equation to thought: "But *it is not enough* to think in order to see. Vision is conditioned thought; it is born as occasioned by what happens in the body; it is incited to think by the body."[25] Merleau-Ponty's reminder reinstitutes the body as the enigmatic site that conditions the question of vision. The failure to think through the conditional character of thought reflects Descartes's legacy to modern metaphysics. It is this metaphysical destiny which relegates the body to an enigma, a tendentious and mysterious passivity which challenges the limits of representation.

NOTES

1. Maurice Merleau-Ponty, "Eye and Mind," *The Primacy of Perception*, ed. James M. Edie and trans. Carelton Dallery (Evanston, Ill.: Northwestern University Press, 1964), p. 169, henceforth abbreviated as "EM" and page number.
2. This study will refer to the most widely available translations of Descartes:

Elisabeth S. Haldane and G. R. T. Ross, *The Philosophical Works of Descartes* (New York: Cambridge University Press, 1969), henceforth abbreviated as *HR*, volume, and page number; and John Cottingham, Robert Stoothoff, and Dugald Murdoch, *The Philosophical Writings of Descartes* (Cambridge: Cambridge University Press, 1985), henceforth abbreviated as *CMS*, volume, and page number.

3. For an analysis of illusion, its relations to the senses in the context of the emergent discourse of science, see Sylvie Romanowski, *L'illusion chez Descartes: La structure du discours cartésien* (Paris: Klincksieck, 1974), pp. 15–30.

4. For an analysis of the totalizing character of doubt in Descartes's philosophy, see my *Subjectivity and Representation in Descartes: The Origins of Modernity* (Cambridge: Cambridge University Press, 1988), pp. 140–159.

5. See E. Panofsky, *Galileo As a Critic of Art* (The Hague, 1954), p. 13, and "Galileo" *Opera* 9:129.

6. Jurgis Baltrusaitis, *Anamorphic Art*, trans. W. J. Strachan (New York: Harry Abrams, 1977), p. 56.

7. See Baltrusaitis's discussion, pp. 38–39.

8. *Thaumaturgus opticus, seu Admiranda optices per radium directum, catoptrices per radium reflectum* (Paris, 1646); quoted by Baltrusaitis, p. 39.

9. For an analysis of perspective as a rational space and its impact on the emergence of modern philosophy, see Erwin Panowsky's conclusions in *La perspective comme forme symbolique* (Paris: Minuit, 1975), pp. 156–159.

10. Jean Pélerin Viator, *De artificiali perspectiva* (Toul, 1505).

11. "Machineries et Perspectives curieuses dans leurs rapports avec le Cartésianisme," *XVIIe Siécle* 140 (1956): 466–467.

12. It should be noted, however, that Descartes's use of intuition is explicitly presented as an overt challenge and critique of memory.

13. For a detailed account of the traditions of the *arts of memory*, see Francis Yates, *The Art of Memory* (Chicago: University of Chicago Press, 1966).

14. Baltrusaitis, p. 1.

15. See Rodis-Lewis's comments, p. 474.

16. See John W. Yolton's analysis of signs and ideas in *Perceptual Acquaintance from Descartes to Reid* (Minneapolis: University of Minnesota Press, 1984), pp. 22–27.

17. Cf. Louis Marin, *La Critique du discours sur la "Logique de Port-Royal" et les "Pensées" de Pascal* (Paris: Minuit, 1975), p. 91.

18. Alquié points out that Descartes's use of the word *inform* captures the Aristotelian conception of the relation of body and soul. He also observes that this notion stressing the codependence of mind and body, appears to be contradicted in Descartes's later writings by the effort to establish a fundamental distinction between mind and body. This distinction still claims the union of body and soul, but in terms of their conjoint rather than their reciprocal character.

19. It is important to note that Plato's analogy is based on a Homeric analogy, that the impressions that come through the senses are stamped on the tables of the "heart" (*Iliad* 2. 851; 16. 554). Thus Plato himself adopts the notion of sensorial impression in order to describe the workings of the mind rather than the passions of the body. Although Descartes gives the impression of returning

to Homer's analogy, his explicit effort to privilege the mind undermines this possibility.

20. Jean H. Roy notes the active role of the understanding both in terms of images and the imagination; see *L'imagination selon Descartes* (Paris: Gallimard, 1944), pp. 41–42.

21. *Oeuvres Philosophiques de Descartes,* ed. Ferdinand Alquié (Paris: Garnier, 1967), vol. 2, p. 453.

22. Descartes's invocation of a mathematical sublime anticipates Immanuel Kant's elaboration in *The Critique of Judgement,* trans. James Creed Meredith (Oxford: Clarendon Press, 1973), pp. 98–103.

23. John D. Lyons interprets this passage in terms of a movement from optical properties to narrative ones, in David L. Rubin and Mary B. McKinley, eds., "Image and Imagination in Descartes's *Méditations," Convergences: Rhetoric and Poetic in Seventeenth-Century France* (Columbus: Ohio University Press, 1989), pp. 191–194.

24. This essay is a lecture given by Heidegger on June 9, 1938, under the title "The Establishing by Metaphysics of the Modern World Picture." See *The Question of Technology and Other Essays,* trans. and introd. by William Lovitt (New York: Harper Colophon Books, 1977), p. 130.

25. Merleau-Ponty, "Eye and Mind," p. 175.

THREE

Vision, Reflection, and Openness

The "Hegemony of Vision" from a Hegelian Point of View

Stephen Houlgate

I

In the twentieth century a number of philosophers have begun to be concerned about what they take to be the fateful consequences of holding human knowledge of the world to be analogous to visual perception. John Dewey argued in 1929, for example, that Western philosophy since Plato and Aristotle has been dominated by a "spectator theory of knowledge" in which "the theory of knowing is modeled after what was supposed to take place in the act of vision," and he criticized philosophy's corresponding insistence on the importance of unclouded observation and accurate representation of reality—on *seeing* the world clearly—for reinforcing "the traditional depreciation of practical activity on the part of the intellectual class."[1] In Dewey's judgment, the spectator theory of knowledge reflects the profound conviction (or prejudice) prevalent among Western philosophers that the aim of philosophical or scientific inquiry is to come to know reality—as we seem to do in vision—without in any way interfering with it or modifying it through practical activity. He claims, further, that the main consequence of this search for the accurate, undistorted representation of what is independently real has been the familiar, but in his view needless and fruitless, dispute between philosophers over which objects are in fact the most certain and most real—physical, mathematical, or logical objects—and over which kind of object genuine knowledge should seek to conform to.

As an alternative to the spectator theory of knowledge Dewey himself proposes a practical, participatory conception of knowledge based on the idea of experimentation. According to this model, the inquirer does not

87

seek a purely theoretical understanding of the world through endeavor-
ing to bring his thoughts into conformity with a reality which is assumed
to be independent of human activity, but rather operates on the objects
of study (for example, through adding chemicals to one another or
through changing the soil in which plants grow) and so participates in
generating the things that are known. If all genuine knowledge is understood according to this model of experimentation, Dewey maintains, the
object of knowledge will not be thought of as something fixed with "an-
tecedent existence or essential being," but will be seen to reside "in the
consequences of directed action" in whatever field we are working, be it
physics, chemistry, sociology, or psychology.[2] As a result, no single object
of knowledge can be held up as the most "real," because all the things we
know will be understood to be the products of specific practical operations on objects in the world which are designed to deal with specific,
equally pressing problems.

Dewey's concern about the spectator theory of knowledge is that it
pursues the certain, accurate perception of what is considered to be already given, and so diminishes our sense that we can and do make a
practical difference to the world we inhabit through the very process
whereby we come to understand and know that world. A similar critique
of the tendency of philosophy to understand knowledge as analogous to
visual perception has been propounded by a recent champion of
Dewey's pragmatism, Richard Rorty. In his book *Philosophy and the Mirror
of Nature* (1980), Rorty argues that "the picture which holds traditional
philosophy captive is that of the mind as a great mirror" and that, accordingly, knowledge has been viewed within the Western tradition as
analogous to "*looking* at something (rather than, say, rubbing up against
it, or crushing it underfoot, or having sexual intercourse with it)."[3] As
this somewhat flippant juxtaposition of looking with rubbing, crushing,
and sexual intercourse clearly indicates, Rorty considers the comparison
of knowledge with vision to be profoundly inappropriate, indeed arbitrary. Consequently, like Dewey, he considers skeptical worries about the
accuracy of what we know or "see," and the related search for foundations for knowledge which could provide us with the same kind of "compulsion to believe" as we feel "when staring at an object," to be inappropriate and arbitrary as well, or at least to be the products of an ancient
choice of perceptual metaphors for knowledge to which we now no
longer need to adhere.[4]

Rorty's alternative conception of knowledge is, however, somewhat
different from Dewey's. Whereas Dewey rejects the spectator theory of
knowledge in favor of an understanding of cognition as a form of practical interaction with things, Rorty's concern is to replace the idea that

knowledge is a direct, immediate relation to the objects we see with a conception of cognition as primarily discursive, that is, as comprising propositions *about* the world (together with reasons and arguments to support them), rather than clear, distinct, and accurate intuitions or representations of the world itself. Knowledge, for Rorty, is thus not a matter of "having our beliefs determined by being brought face-to-face with the objects of belief," of being "transfixed by a sight which leaves us speechless," and so of being "gripped, grasped and compelled" by what is unveiled to us, but is rather a matter of trying to justify propositions by reference to other propositions, practices, or experiences in an ordinary, "common-sense" manner which does not seek final, absolute certainty, clarity, or accuracy of vision, but which is content to discuss and "keep conversation on the subject going" until agreement is reached and "everyone, or the majority, or the wise, are satisfied."[5] Rorty does not deny that we engage and "cope" with *reality* in our discussions and debates about the world, but he does deny that we can—or indeed should even particularly wish to try to—intuit or "mirror" that reality with perfect accuracy. For him, what we should aspire to in knowledge is not "some unimaginable sort of immediacy which would make discourse and description superfluous," but an agreed and workable understanding of how to deal with things which is attained through conversation and the "continual adjustments of ideas or words,"[6] that is to say, something more modest, more ordinary and humdrum, and perhaps—in Rorty's eyes at least—something more recognizably human than the pure, objective, "divine" insight at which (according to him) philosophy has traditionally aimed.

In addition to Dewey (and Wittgenstein), Rorty acknowledges Heidegger to be one of those—in his view, all too few—thinkers who have been concerned "to explore the way in which the West became obsessed with the notion of our primary relation to objects as analogous to visual perception."[7] Heidegger's concern with this issue is clearly evident in *Being and Time* (1927) where he claims that "the tradition of philosophy has been oriented from the beginning primarily towards 'seeing' (*Sehen*) as the mode of access to beings *and to being*," and that such theoretical "looking" (*Hinsehen*) has tended to narrow down the multiple ways in which things can be to "the uniformity of what is simply present before us" (*die Einförmigkeit des puren Vorhandenen*), that is, to what is simply there, given as what it is in and by itself, without (apparently) any intrinsic relation to any space of awareness or disclosure.[8] This primacy given to seeing or intuition (*Anschauung*) by philosophy has gone hand in hand, according to Heidegger, with a primacy given to statements (*Aussagen*) and judgments as the main locus of truth. Philosophical "vision" has thus traditionally consisted in recognizing that some object there, present before my eyes (or before the "eye of my mind"), has certain "properties," and in determining that object through citing the predicates which name those properties.[9]

From Heidegger's own existential perspective, however, things are not initially, or most commonly, encountered through being stared at or gaped at (*begafft*);[10] nor does the disclosure of what they are initially, or most commonly, take the form of noting their "objective" presence and properties. Things are initially encountered through being feared, welcomed, or prized, or through being used and, in use, being tacitly understood to be "to hand" or "handy" (*zuhanden*).[11] The deficiency of pure intuition or "seeing" as a mode of access to beings, for Heidegger, lies precisely in the fact that its basic conception of things as given, independent objects with determinate properties renders it incapable of understanding the genuinely intimate handiness of the hammer, or of encountering a threat *as* a threat, but only allows it to view things as having qualities that make them "objectively" valuable or dangerous for other objects or for human beings. Moreover, pure intuition is also considered by Heidegger to be deficient as a mode of access to the *being* of beings—to *how* rather than *what* they are—because intuition can only see being as objective, that is, as the substance, nature, or "what" of things, and thus as itself some "thing" which is present, given, and determinable in terms of its predicates.

Heidegger continues his critique of the objectification of being in the essay "The Age of the World Picture" (1938), where he once again suggests that such objectification is bound up with the fact that philosophy has tended to conceive of understanding and knowing as modeled on seeing. Admittedly, Heidegger's primary focus in this essay is on the connection between objectification and such concepts as the "world picture" (*Weltbild*) and "placing before oneself" (*Vorstellen*), rather than vision as such. Nevertheless, he does point out that Aristotle understood our relation to being to be one of *theōria* or "pure seeing" (*das reine Schauen*) and that Plato conceived of the being (*Sein*) of beings as "what is beheld" (*das Angeschaute*), and he notes that these conceptions, together with Plato's further determination of the "beingness" (*Seiendheit*) of beings as the *eidos* or "look" (*Aussehen, Anblick*) of things, constitute the long-concealed presuppositions of the modern (i.e. Cartesian and post-Cartesian) transformation of the world into a "picture" (*Bild*).[12]

The term "world picture," Heidegger explains, is not to be taken to refer to an image or copy of the world, but rather to what we have in mind when we say that we get the picture (*wir sind über etwas im Bilde*), that is, to what we actually understand and "see" when we understand something. To get the picture, Heidegger writes, is to realize that "the matter itself stands before us just as it stands with it for us" (*so, wie es mit ihr für uns steht*). Similarly, to put someone in the picture means "to place whatever is, itself, before us in the way that it stands with it, and to have it constantly standing (*ständig*) before oneself as placed in this way."[13] The "picture," in other words, is not just an image of the world, but is the world itself, understood as something there before us, about which we are informed and for which we are prepared. The age of the "world picture"—the modern age—is thus, for Heidegger, the age which conceives of whatever is as something "placed before us" (*vorgestellt*), as objective, that is, as something whose being lies in standing over against us—*there*—as an object (*Gegenstand*) which is present to us in all its clarity.[14]

Since, on this view, the being of things is held to reside in their actually being placed there before us—their actual *Vorgestelltheit*[15]—and so in their actually being present to us, their being must be conceived as that which *we* ourselves know to be present before us. Therefore, the modern age, for Heidegger, is not just the age which equates being with objectivity; it is at the same time the age which equates true objectivity with what we are certain of, the age in which the subject comes to enjoy pride of place among beings because it knows itself to be the arbiter of what is to count as present for it and thus as real and objective. Accordingly, objectivity in the modern age is always an objectivity which affords us a sense of *certainty* about the world and our own place in it, an objectivity which we can understand, explain, count on, reckon with, and so predict. Such objectivity is one which holds few surprises for us, one which we can thus learn to manage and manipulate according to our interests and, through such manipulation—that is, through technology—learn to control and master.[16]

This is the central connection that Heidegger wants to establish in this essay: that the modern conception of being as objective (*gegenständlich*)—as "placed before us" and so brought into view—gives rise to, or at least goes hand in hand with, a conception of subjectivity as able to survey and master that objectivity, as being the "scene" before which beings can come to be present and as being the power which disposes over and uses such beings as it wills.[17] For the Greeks (which in Heidegger's eyes means above all for the Pre-Socratics), what is (*das Seiende*) was thought to be "that which arises and opens itself" to those who hold themselves open to what is. The essence of humanity was thus not to control and master being, but "to be carried by it, to be driven about by its oppositions and marked by its discord . . . to remain exposed to all its sundering confusions."[18] For the modern age, however, such openness has given way to "mastering objectification": "representing (*Vorstellen*) is no longer the apprehending of that which presences (*das Vernehmen des Anwesenden*) . . . no longer a self-unconcealing for (*das Sich-entbergen für*) . . . but is a laying hold and grasping of. . . . What presences does not hold sway, but rather assault (*Angriff*) rules"—an assault whose most developed form is the "planetary imperialism of technically organized mankind" which seeks "technical mastery over the earth."[19]

Such "mastering objectification" concerns Heidegger not just because of the debilitating effect it may have on humanity, but because "where what is has become the object of representation which places things before us (*Vor-stellen*), it suffers a certain loss of being,"[20] and, as *Being and Time* makes clear, we are above all beings who are concerned about *being*. Heidegger's hope—if that is the right word—is that in the future humanity will become more open to being than is presently the case and that "the essence of the truth of being will lay claim more primally to the essence of humanity."[21] However, we cannot free ourselves from the sway of our objectifying will to power and open ourselves to being through our own efforts or through our own fiat (*Machtspruch*), any more than Luther could earn himself unconditional grace, or than Kundry, in Wagner's *Parsifal*, can by herself fulfill her desire to be freed from desire. We can at most turn our thinking toward the presupposition of our modern objectifying subjectivity, that is, toward the mode of disclosure of being—the "truth" of being—which underlies that subjectivity, and ponder the fact that "being subject as humanity has not always been the sole possibility belonging to the originary essence of historical humanity, nor will it always be."[22] Through this move, we will not be granted any immediate insight into being—into how things are—but we will at least loosen the hold that the conceptions of man as subject and of being as objectivity have on us by recognizing that those conceptions have arisen in history and could change in the future. This is the first step toward openness to being, because humanity will only be given over to the truth of being, according to Heidegger, "when it no longer represents what is as an object (*Objekt*)."[23]

For the Heidegger of "The Age of the World Picture," then, the alternative to a "spectatorial" mode of thinking founded on the idea of *Vorstellen* is not, as it is for Dewey, a conception of knowledge as something which unites theory and practice, nor, as it is for Rorty, a conception of knowledge as a conversation which helps us to "cope" or "deal" with reality better. Such talk of "practice" and "coping" and "dealing" with things, though abjuring the idea that knowledge entails staring at objects, would surely have struck Heidegger as still tied too much to the idea of beings as objects which are at our disposal, as still too much under the sway of practical, technological, mastering subjectivity, and thus as still too removed from genuine openness to the being of beings. For Heidegger, it seems, all relation to things as objects which are there _for us_—whether theoretical or practical—is inevitably associated with, or at least risks future association with, mastering subjectivity, and is thus incompatible with genuine enduring openness and attentiveness of mind. Heidegger's alternative to mastering _Vor-stellen_ cannot therefore take the form of a new openness to objects as available _objects_—as something _vorgestellt_—but must be an attentiveness and openness to what is not an object, what is not available or at our disposal, what is not a "what" but perhaps rather a "how"—that is, to _being_. Such an openness to being may well be inseparable from a relation to ordinary things—to beings—since being is after all the being of beings, not some otherworldly "beyond." Nevertheless, being "itself," for Heidegger, is not some determinate substance, object, or thing there in the world before us, not something _vorgestellt_. The openness to the being of beings which Heidegger calls for cannot therefore continue to regard things solely as _objects_ which simply stand before us, always present and available for study or use, and so cannot just look to discern _what_ things are, the manifold qualities and properties which are apparently given to and present to our mind. Rather, such openness must entail attending to _how_ things are, to their way of being, their self-disclosing and self-concealing, their coming into and withdrawing from presence, which is never itself simply _present_ for us to observe.

This connection between openness, nonpresence, and nonobjecthood is also evident in Heidegger's lecture and dialogue on _Gelassenheit_. In the lecture, given in 1955 in his hometown of Meßkirch, Heidegger states that it is not possible for humanity simply to deny or escape from the technological character of the modern world, but that it is possible to prevent ourselves from becoming slaves to the technological machines and devices which we utilize. We can do this, he says, by learning to say both yes and no to the objects and instruments of technology at one and the same time, that is, by using them as they are intended to be used but also learning to "let go of them" (_sie . . . loslassen_) and to "leave them to themselves" ([_sie_] _auf sich beruhen lassen_) as things "which do not concern us in our innermost and authentic being."[24] This nontechnical, nonmastering attitude toward things Heidegger terms _Gelassenheit_: being released to things, or letting things be. It immediately becomes clear, however, that this new way of relating to the things which we usually view as objects under our technical control—this letting things be—is inseparably bound up with an openness to what is not an object at all, to what Heidegger calls the "mystery" or _Geheimnis_.[25]

We do not know in what direction the modern technological era is headed, Heidegger says, but we do know that it is headed somewhere, that it harbors within itself a hidden orientation, direction, or "*Sinn*."[26] We can catch a glimpse of this orientation in the developments which our technological world undergoes, but it remains essentially withdrawn and hidden from us. It is our destiny and yet we can never fully understand what it is, can never "place it before ourselves" as a clearly defined present object which we can count on, predict, and master. As such, this hidden, nonobjectifiable orientation of the modern world is a mystery to us. If we can reflect upon this mystery, hold ourselves open to, and abide with it in thoughtful consideration without seeking to master it, Heidegger suggests, we may be able to gain—or be granted—a new way of dwelling in the world which is no longer oriented solely toward objects that are present to us and no longer dominated by the desire to take hold of and control the things among which we live. A nontechnical, *gelassen* relation to things is thus not to be achieved by understanding what is present before our eyes more clearly. On the contrary, only a thoughtful openness to the mystery in things, to what is not a present object for us, will release us from mastering subjectivity and so enable us to leave things to themselves and let them be.

In his dialogue on *Gelassenheit* (1944–45), Heidegger's conception of nonobjectifying thinking is given further eloquent expression. The discussants in the dialogue sound the familiar note that through ordinary representative thinking or *Vorstellen* everything is encountered as present to us or as standing over against us within a given field of vision or "horizon." They also remark, however—in a manner reminiscent of, but also subtly different from Kant—that things do not always have to be thought of as standing over against *us* or as presenting *us* with a specific view, but can be thought of as "gathered together" (*versammelt*) in their nearness and distance from one another and, as it were, as resting within themselves.[27] The space or "region" (*Gegend* or *Gegnet*) in which things are gathered—indeed, which is the gathering, the being together of things—is understood by Heidegger to constitute the openness of things to view, an openness which lets things be encountered in countless specific ways and from countless specific perspectives, but which is not itself a specific way of appearing or of being seen. Since, however, things always come before us within a particular perspective or field of vision and with a particular "look" (*Aussehen*),[28] that region of the utter openness of things is paradoxically not itself something with which we ever come directly face to face, but remains hidden from us as the concealed space of openness which always surrounds us and whatever we see. This region of openness, and the things which are gathered and lie open in that region, can thus never be *vorgestellt*, never be present to us as objects of scrutiny. Moreover, the open gathering of things cannot be "placed before us" for another reason: because we ourselves belong to that gathering, in that we are the space of disclosure (*Entschlossenheit*) in which things are to be gathered together in *thought* in their concealed openness. Since we are, as it were, "used" to gather things, indeed are ourselves the space of the thoughtful gathering of things, we cannot encounter that space as an object over against ourselves.[29]

How, then, can we think that region of openness and dwell with it as it is "within itself" (*in sich*)?[30] Only by holding ourselves open to something that is not an object, not a determinate thing that can become present to us. And we do this, we are told, by letting our thinking transform itself (or be transformed) from a *Vorstellen* into a waiting (*warten*) which is without an object, that is, into a waiting which does not wait for something anticipated and known in advance, but rather waits to be opened up to, to be released and let into, openness itself. Such a waiting waits to become, and so already is, *Gelassenheit*.[31]

It would be rash of me to claim that Heidegger's intentions in this dialogue are completely clear to me. They are not, and I must leave further clarification (if that is the appropriate word) to others who are more qualified than I. My concern here is simply to point to the fact that, for Heidegger, nonmastering openness of mind and being goes hand in hand with a thinking which seeks—or waits—to be free of the tendency to objectify and place before itself whatever it attends to. Such thinking does not, however, turn away from things completely; rather it is an attempt to think of the things around us as not just present to us, but as resting or abiding with themselves and one another. Furthermore, such nonobjectifying thinking of things does not altogether obviate the need for a calculative, technical, objectifying relation to things.

Heidegger insists, in his lecture on *Gelassenheit*, that both calculative and noncalculative thinking are justified and necessary in the modern world, that we must thus both count on and use things to achieve our practical, utilitarian ends *and* let things go free.[32] However, it is clear that, although these two modes of thinking belong together (at least for the inhabitants of the modern technological world), they constitute two distinct ways of thinking about and relating to things. Heidegger does not seem to entertain the possibility that those two modes of thinking might be fused into one, such that we could be open to things, and let things be, as present *objects* (*Gegen-stände*), and such that we might be able to know things as objects over against us and yet as not *just* over against us, in one and the same thought. Heidegger cannot entertain such a possibility because for him *Vorstellen* is always considered to have prejudged the question of the being of things, and to get in the way of genuine openness to the way things may be in and from themselves, by reducing the being of things to what is simply there before us or over against us, and by turning all things into objects which are encountered within recognizable fields of vision. Genuinely open thinking, for Heidegger, may begin from, and coexist with, *Vorstellen*, but it becomes "purer"[33] and more genuine the more it eschews *Vorstellen*. Openness cannot therefore ever be construed as a mode of thinking which actually incorporates *Vorstellen* within itself, that is, as a mode of thinking which actually *is* a form of *Vorstellen* itself, at least to a certain degree.

With the exception of *Being and Time*, Heidegger's main concern in the texts I have been considering has not been so much with the objectifying tendencies inherent in the idea of knowledge as a form of vision or intuition, but rather with *Vorstellen*. As I pointed out in my comments on "The Age of the World Picture," however, Heidegger does see the visual metaphors which dominated Platonic and Aristotelian philosophy as paving the way for the later distortions of *Vorstellen*, and for this reason I have considered his analysis to be important for understanding what limitations (if any) visual metaphors place upon our thinking. The connection between vision itself and objectifying, mastering subjectivity is made much more directly in recent work by David Levin.

For Levin, vision is "the most reifying of all our perceptual modalities," the mode of perception which, more than any other, perceives things in the world as objects that are clearly there, present, and available for us to study and use.[34] Vision, accordingly, gives the observer a sense of security or certainty which derives from the conviction that what is seen is laid bare and so harbors no secrets which might surprise or disorient us—the conviction, that is, that what is seen can be surveyed at a distance, anticipated, and so mastered by being taken hold of and grasped. For Levin, therefore, there is an undeniable "power drive inherent in vision"—a tendency to expose and dominate the world around us, at the heart of the desire to see—and the drive toward total visibility is consequently equated with the desire for total control over things. The "hegemony of vision" in the modern world—the apparent dominance in the modern age of the conviction that vision provides us with the most appropriate paradigm for knowledge—is thus associated by Levin with what he sees as the will to power at work in modern social, economic, and political life, that is, in the modern scientific and technological exploitation of the earth, as well as in modern political surveillance.[35]

Yet, this is not the only tendency or potential which Levin finds in vision. Vision, for him, normally takes the form of focusing or "seizing" on what is there in front of my eyes and seeking to bring it directly into view. However, he believes that visual disclosure can also be more "relaxed, playful, gentle, caring," more *gelassen*, as Heidegger would put it.

It can become a gaze that is not "fixated" on the objects present before my eyes, but rather "diffused, spacious, open, alive with awareness and receptive to the presencing of the field as a whole," that is, a gaze that does not seek to control things, but lets things show themselves as they are, and so lets them *be*.[36]

But how can vision be rendered more subtle and supple in this way? How can the inherent orientation of vision toward a direct focus on objects that are present, available, and masterable be changed? Levin's answer, based on his reading of (among others) Heidegger, Nietzsche, and Merleau-Ponty, is that vision must be more attuned to what is *not* directly before my eyes but rather withdraws from presence and availability and thus from surveillance and control. Such are the "shadows" and "reflections" within our field of vision which are not themselves present as *objects*, but point to something else not directly seen (for example, a hidden source of light), and which "deepen, heighten, extend and enrich the field of visibility." Such also is the "horizon" or "background" which unifies the field of vision, but which is not itself an object within that field. A mode of vision attuned to such shadows and horizons would thus not be a "stare, an act of direct, frontal looking fixated on its object," but rather "a playful gaze . . . which delights in ambiguities, uncertainties, shifting perspectives and shades of meaning." And if we were to model or base our knowledge on this Nietzschean-Heideggerian vision, rather than on objectifying "Cartesian" vision, Levin claims, the grip of the will to power governing modern humanity could perhaps be loosened.[37]

We can therefore make a difference to the way in which we *see* things, in Levin's view. Vision is not always and irredeemably power-hungry. Yet, it is important to note that for Levin we do not transform our vision and our thinking into a more open, responsive form of disclosure by *seeing the objects before us more clearly or completely*, but rather by attending to what is not directly there before our eyes, indeed not directly present before us at all. Such attention to elusive horizons, shadows, and reflections affords us the more subtle, responsive vision which Levin hopes for. However, it does not render what is there before us completely or totally visible; rather, it gives us a vision which is more ambiguous and "shadowy" and which is for *that* reason more subtle. (Shadows cannot make for total visibility, in Levin's view, because total visibility is understood by him to be "shadowless.")[38] Thus, even though vision for Levin can be rendered more responsive and receptive, the capacity to be open to things and let them be does not appear to reside within totally clear and unambiguous visibility as such, which remains in itself a problem. If vision is to be opened up, it needs to be taken out of itself by being attuned to concealments and horizons which are *not* clearly and directly visible, because vision itself has an inherent tendency toward the objectifying, dominating gaze or stare. Indeed the stare, as far as Levin is concerned, is simply "the most extreme case of vision."[39]

But is this really true? Is vision (and the mode of thinking which is modeled on vision) inherently oriented toward surveying and dominating objects? Even if we grant that vision seeks the totally clear perception of objects present before us, need such objectifying vision always seek power and domination? Cannot the concern for total objective clarity of vision also be the concern to let things stand out for themselves? Moreover, if we are able to answer yes to this last question, would that not mean that the pursuit of total objective clarity of vision and thought is not so much the cause of the destructive modern drive for the technological domination of the earth, as rather precisely that which holds out the prospect for loosening the grip of that drive? And might not the vision which construes openness as attentiveness to what is not objectively present before us (as opposed to closer attentiveness to what is present and objective) run the risk of neglecting, or at least undervaluing, the qualities of determinacy, objectivity, and articulation which are inherent in vision and which are perhaps required if we are truly to let things be?

These questions are difficult to answer. Nevertheless, they strike me as essential for anyone who is persuaded by Heidegger's and Levin's analyses of the modern condition and by their responses to that condition, because they address the fundamental presupposition of those analyses and bear directly on the question of what kind of thinking, language, and style is appropriate for philosophy today. To my mind, if it could be shown that objective vision and objective thinking are not necessarily governed by a reductive will to power, but can be characterized by a genuine openness and attentiveness to the things of this world, this would have important consequences for the whole phenomenological and post-phenomenological project of deconstructing the "metaphysics of presence" and of undermining the "hegemony of vision" that is believed to give rise to this metaphysics; for to show that vision is inherently open and attentive, rather than reductive and constricting, would call into question the fundamental conception of vision which contemporary critics of the metaphysics of presence all too readily presuppose.

II

In what follows I propose to take the charge against vision seriously and literally. That is to say, I shall assume the charge to be that the choice of visual metaphors for knowledge in the Western philosophical tradition has been fateful because vision itself—actual *seeing*, not just "visionary" thinking—harbors within itself a tendency toward reification (though, of the philosophers I have discussed, perhaps only David Levin puts the matter quite this boldly). In order to try to evaluate this charge, I propose to examine how certain philosophers in the tradition have understood vision, and to investigate whether vision as they conceive it—and so any mode of thinking modeled on vision—is necessarily associated with reductive, reifying, technological subjectivity. In the course of this investigation I shall first look at texts by Berkeley and Descartes and then turn my attention to Hegel. This might perhaps seem to be a rather strange choice to make, since all three are considered by Heidegger and Levin to be under the sway of the metaphysics of presence and its accompanying ocular metaphors and so would seem to be immediately vulnerable to the critique of that metaphysics and those metaphors which we have been setting out. However, my intention in this essay is to examine, and indeed call into question, the conception of vision which constitutes the presupposition of that critique. I do not therefore intend to accept in advance that the positions of Berkeley, Descartes, and Hegel have already been fundamentally "deconstructed" by twentieth-century philosophy. Berkeley, Descartes, and Hegel are three very different thinkers whose views on vision are not necessarily compatible with one another. Nevertheless, I wish to consider them in this essay as partners in the contemporary discussion about vision whose conceptions of vision may hold some important lessons for their critics.

The charge which David Levin levels at vision, we recall, is that it is "the most reifying of all our perceptual modalities."[40] In support of this charge Levin cites, among others, Merleau-Ponty, who claimed that "visual experience . . . pushes objectification further than tactile experience."[41] However, if, by speaking of "reification" and "objectification," Levin and Merleau-Ponty mean to say that vision itself tends to see things primarily as objects (*Gegen-stände*) which stand over against us, this is not an interpretation which Bishop Berkeley would have endorsed. The notion of "standing over against"—of *Gegenständlichkeit*—implies that there is some observable distance between the observer and the object observed. In his *Essay Towards a New Theory of Vision* (1709, 1732), however, Berkeley insists that distance is not something which is ever immediately visible. "It is, I think, agreed by all," he writes, "that distance, of itself and immediately, cannot be seen. For distance being a line directed end-wise to the eye, it projects only one point in the fund of the eye, which point remains invariably the same, whether the distance be longer or shorter." Furthermore, though I may well believe that I see things at a certain distance from myself, I cannot mean by that that what I actually *see* is a yard or a mile off, "since that every step I take towards it the appearance alters, and from being obscure, small, and faint, grows clear, large and vigorous. And when I come to the mile's end, that which I saw first is quite lost, neither do I find anything in the likeness of it."[42]

All I actually *see*, Berkeley contends, are "lights and colors in sundry situations and shades and degrees of faintness and clearness, confusion and distinctness." These lights and colors may become more confused, more clear, or more faint, and, being "various in their bounds or limits," may grow greater or smaller; however, they are not actually seen to be at any distance from us and so cannot be seen to "approach or recede from us."[43] Berkeley does not deny that we *judge* that the things we see stand over against us in space, nor indeed that that judgment is so habitual and immediate that we do, to all intents and purposes, "perceive by sight the distance, magnitude, and situation of objects."[44] His point is simply that vision needs the help of another sense—touch—which provides us with the sensations of "solidity," "resistance," and "protrusion," in order to be able to "perceive" something as distant or spatially distinct from the viewer. Strictly speaking, then, "space, outness, and things placed at a distance are not . . . the object of sight." We only judge that what we see is located at a specific position over against us in space, according to Berkeley, because we immediately associate the colors and shades which we see with things which have a *tangible* spatial location and magnitude in relation to us.[45]

The contrast between Berkeley on the one hand, and Levin, Heidegger, and Merleau-Ponty on the other, is clearly illustrated toward the end of Berkeley's essay, when he speculates on what might be seen by "an intelligence, or unbodied spirit, which is supposed to see perfectly well . . . but to have no sense of touch." Such an intelligence would not, Berkeley explains, "have any idea of distance, outness, or profundity, nor consequently of space or body," and so would not, to use Heidegger's terminology, regard what it sees as *gegenständlich* or "objective." Furthermore, it would not be able to measure, calculate, or fix the location or magnitude of things either, because "the perpetual mutability and fleetingness of those immediate objects of sight [the colored areas we see] render them incapable of being *managed* after the manner of geometrical figures" (my italics).[46] In contrast to Levin and Heidegger, therefore, Berkeley does not associate the alleged philosophical ideal of pure, unadulterated vision with a sense of being able to survey, measure, and control what is seen, but rather with the opposite, with a sense of being exposed to something which is constantly changing and so which cannot be surveyed, measured, and controlled—that is to say, with a sense not unlike the one which Heidegger and Levin associate with being attuned to what is *not* directly visible.

Yet surely I have been missing the point somewhat in comparing Berkeley with Levin and Heidegger in this way. Berkeley may well distinguish between what is visible and what is tangible and point out that, strictly speaking, we do not *see* spatial depth and distance, but he still talks of what we do see as being the *objects* of sight. Moreover, he considers the field of vision to be occupied by given points or *minima visibilia*— all of which are visible, however dimly—and so still shows himself to be a philosopher who is concerned with what is present to the mind and eye, and who consequently evinces no attentiveness to the hidden openness of things.[47]

This is no doubt true enough. Nevertheless, the "lights and colors" which constitute the objects of sight for Berkeley are subtly different from the measurable, quantifiable, *vorhanden* or *vorgestellt* objects which Heidegger and Levin associate with the vision or thinking that is not yet attuned to the "open." Such objects of sight may be said to be present to us, but they cannot be said to stand "over against" us, to be "before" our eyes, or even to be "there" (as opposed to "here"), since sight by itself, according to Berkeley, does not yield any sense of determinate, measurable spatial relation to the viewer at all. The colors and lights which we see are thus not present to us in a *gegenständlich* or *objective* way, and so do not constitute determinate, spatially distinct objects that can be managed or mastered by us. A philosopher of presence Berkeley may well be; that I do not wish to dispute. All I wish to suggest is that the mode of presence which he associates with vision does not seem to be allied with any reifying, mastering subjectivity, and so does not seem to be vulnerable to the kind of charge that Heidegger and Levin level at the "traditional" metaphysics of presence—unless, of course, one has already decided that all orientation toward presence is suspect and that the only real alternative to mastering subjectivity involves an openness to what is not present and not unambiguously visible. But that surely would beg the question of the nature of vision and of presence.

Yet it could still be argued that my analysis misses the point. After all, what Levin, at least, is arguing is not just that pure visual sensation by itself reifies and objectifies being, but that our ordinary, everyday visual perception of actual concrete things tends to reduce those things to objects, that is, that "normal perception, the ontical perception of anyone-and-everyone, is inveterately grasping."[48] However, even if—and I stress *if*—Berkeley were to agree with this judgment, he would still point out that ordinary "visual" perception of objects in measurable space involves both vision and touch, and indeed that an awareness of spatial depth, distance, and resistance—and thus *objectivity*—is specifically provided by touch rather than vision itself. For Berkeley, therefore, it is touch which

objectifies things—which perceives things to be over there in front of us—
and if normal vision seems to relate to objects which are at a clear, measurable distance from us (and which are therefore able to be surveyed
and managed), this is only because the lights and colors we see are immediately associated with known *tangible* depth and distance. Thus even if
Berkeley were to agree with Levin's misgivings about normal, everyday
vision, he would still ask: why is the sense of *vision* in particular singled
out for criticism, since touch is just as much implicated in the generation
of "visual" distance and objectivity as vision itself? Furthermore, he
might also point out that the description of normal perception as inveterately "grasping" suggests that it is in fact touch—at least a certain kind
of touch—rather than vision per se which really worries Levin.

A slightly different light is cast by Descartes on this problem. Whereas
Berkeley endeavors to explain, on the basis of the sensations that are
given to us, the actual experience we have of outness and profundity—
that is, "the *phenomena* of distance"[49]—and is not concerned, at least in
the essay on vision, with investigating how we come to have the sensations we have, Descartes is very much interested in studying the relation
between our sensations and the external world which gives rise to them,
and so seeks to provide a largely mechanistic, physiological, and geometrical account of vision.

For Descartes, light is "nothing other than a certain movement, or
very rapid and lively action, which passes to our eyes through the
medium of the air and other transparent bodies," and vision arises because the objects of sight produce, "through the medium of the interven-
ing transparent bodies, local motions in the optic nerve-fibers at the back
of our eyes, and then in the regions of the brain where these nerves originate."[50] In spite of the fact that he is often considered to be one of the
most visually minded of philosophers, it is thus immediately apparent
that Descartes actually has a remarkably nonvisual understanding of vision itself. What reaches the eye and brain from the objects we see are
not "little images flitting through the air," nor indeed are we even to suppose that there is something in the objects we see which resembles the
ideas, sensations, or images that we have of them.[51] All that reaches the
brain from external objects, according to Descartes, are the "corporeal
motions" of our nerves which have been triggered by the light from objects hitting the eye and which in turn stimulate the soul to produce certain sensations or images which are "innate" to the mind and bear no
similarity to the corporeal motions themselves or to the objects that trig-
ger them. Vision does not actually see or "represent" the qualities of objects, therefore; rather, the mind is indirectly stimulated by certain "dis-
positions" in the objects to have various visual sensations.[52] Nor are we to

assume—"as our philosophers commonly do—that in order to have sensory perceptions the soul must contemplate certain images transmitted by objects to the brain . . . as if there were yet other eyes within our brain with which we could perceive [such images]."[53]

Contrary to what Rorty asserts, therefore, Descartes does not believe in an "eye of the mind" or an "inner eye" which "*inspects* entities modeled on retinal images."[54] Indeed, in an almost proto-Rortian fashion, Descartes points out that philosophers only posited the idea of internal images before an inner eye because "they saw how easily a picture can stimulate our mind to conceive the objects depicted in it, and so it seemed to them that, in the same way, the mind must be stimulated, by little pictures formed in our head, to conceive the objects that affect our senses." Such philosophers overlooked the fact, however, that "our mind can be stimulated by many things other than images—by signs and words, for example, which in no way resemble the things they signify."[55]

For Descartes, then, vision—at least at the physiological level, prior to conscious visual sensation as such—entails a mechanical relationship between the human body and external objects which is comparable to the relation which a blind person has to things. Indeed, in the *Optics* (1637), Descartes explicitly likens the way our eyes and optic nerves are moved by incoming light to the way a blind man's stick is moved by the changing contours of a body.[56]

As far as the level of *conscious* visual sensation itself is concerned, Descartes anticipates Berkeley in maintaining that light and color are "the only qualities belonging properly to the sense of sight," and that we thus do not, strictly speaking, *see* the position of objects in space.[57] Distance can, to a degree, be discerned from the distinctness or indistinctness of the shapes seen, Descartes says, but our knowledge of the position of objects and of their distance from the viewer is not just derived from what we see. Rather, we perceive position and distance "by means of our eyes exactly as we do by means of our hands," that is, by noting changes in the position of the tiny parts of the brain where the nerves originate, which result from changes in the position of our sense organs.[58] We thus determine the position of objects in space, not so much from visual images or sensations themselves, but rather by noting the direction in which we have to turn the eyes in order to see objects, and the extent to which we have to alter the shape of the eye and the angle between the eyes in order to obtain a clear image of objects. This awareness of the location of objects in relation to our body is not to be confused with the sensations we derive from touching things, since touch, for Descartes, only provides us with sensations such as hardness, heaviness, heat, and humidity. Our awareness of place and location is to be understood as the result of a "rational calculation" by which the soul can somehow "immediately" detect the movements in its accompanying body, and, "as if by a natural geometry," determine its spatial relation to the other objects with which it comes into contact.[59] The notion of a "natural geometry"—an awareness of our location in space which is not based solely on the content of our visible or tangible sensations—is, of course, one of the main targets of Berkeley's later critique of Descartes. Nevertheless, in spite of the evident differences between Descartes and Berkeley, what is important for our analysis is that both agree that vision *by itself* is not responsible for locating objects over against us in space.

Both Descartes and Berkeley insist, then, that spatial location and distance are not something we simply *see*. They differ, however, in that Berkeley considers the combination or cooperation of visual and tactile sensation to be sufficient to yield perceptual experience of "outness," whereas Descartes claims that, by themselves, "sensations . . . do not represent anything located outside our thought,"[60] and that, consequently, we need an *intellectual* consciousness of that which is distinct from us (together with our capacity for "natural geometry") in order to be able to experience a realm of objects or bodies outside or over against us. Descartes's point is not just that the intellect grants us access to external objects which we presume to exist; he is arguing, as Kant will do 150 years later, that the intellect is what enables us to conceive of such a thing as an external object in the first place. We believe that we *see* objects and bodies in space, Descartes explains, but careful analysis reveals that "bodies are not strictly speaking perceived by the senses at all, but only by the intellect."[61]

How, then, does the intellect make possible the experience of distinct, external objects? Descartes's answer is simple: the intellect makes such experience possible by being nothing other than the *thought* of that which is distinct. The intellect is the consciousness of clear and distinct ideas and truths, but, more importantly, it is the consciousness of that which is itself distinct, namely substance. In the *Principles of Philosophy* (1644), Descartes defines substance as "a thing which exists in such a way as to depend on no other thing for its existence"; but then, having recognized that God is the only thing which truly satisfies this definition of substance, he promptly admits that there is actually "no distinctly intelligible meaning of the term which is common to God and his creatures."[62] However, if one attends carefully to what Descartes has to say about substance, it becomes clear that there is in fact a distinctly intelligible, univocal meaning of the term in his texts: quite simply, being a substance means being a *distinct* thing. Substances, Descartes tells us, are *conceptually* distinct from their attributes, *modally* distinct from their modes, and *really* distinct from one another, that is to say, they are "things which are separate from other things."[63]

The two basic substances in the world (apart from God who created the world) seem to be derived by Descartes from this notion of distinctness itself, though he himself does not present the matter in this way. On the one hand, there is the distinct activity of drawing distinctions—of distinguishing—which is above all the activity of distinguishing *itself* (through abstracting from whatever is given to it) as that activity, that is, as itself, as *a* self, as an inner sphere of distinct ideas. This is the sphere of thought. On the other hand, there is that which is clearly distinct from thought, that *from* which thought distinguishes itself, but which cannot distinguish itself as a self, and which is thus not a self, not inner, but rather external. This is the sphere of extension, of geometrical space. It is this distinction which thought draws between itself and what is distinct from itself that, in the Cartesian scheme of things, constitutes for thought a space of extended, natural objects or *Gegen-stände*. For Descartes, then, our relation to external, natural objects is an intellectual one: objects are things which we *understand* to be there. Consequently, when we "see" a colored object such as a lighted torch in front of us, we do not actually *see* the object itself; rather, we refer our visual sensations to the thing—the torch—which we suppose to be the cause or ground of our sensations and (mistakenly) regard the colors and shape that we see as the actual, objective qualities of that thing, "in such a way that we think that we see the torch itself."[64]

Since we know natural objects to exist in a geometrical space which we can understand, measure, and survey, we are able, according to Descartes (or at least we believe we are able), to make ourselves "the lords and masters of nature." Whether this makes Descartes into the father of modern mastering, objectifying, and dehumanizing subjectivity, I could not say; indeed, it seems to me rather unlikely considering his reverence for "the law which obliges us to do all in our power to secure the general welfare of mankind."[65] Be that as it may, those who do choose to see his philosophy as motivated by a certain will to power must at least recognize that this is *not* the consequence of any "hegemony of vision" in his thinking. If anything dominates Descartes's thinking, it is not so much vision as the intellectual interpretation of being in general as clearly and distinctly itself, that is, as substance or "thinghood," and the intellectual interpretation of nature in particular as measurable, surveyable geometrical space.

In *Being and Time,* of course, Heidegger also points to the dominance in Descartes's philosophy of the concept of substance; but he connects this to the idea that Descartes's thinking is governed by what he regards as the traditional philosophical conception of being as "permanent presence at hand" (*ständige Vorhandenheit*) and the traditional philosophical conviction that intuition (*Anschauung*), or theoretical "seeing," is the appropriate mode of access to beings.[66] This reading of Descartes assumes, therefore, precisely what I have been trying to call into question, namely that Descartes's philosophy is indeed under the sway of a visual conception of knowledge and *for this reason* objectifies being. Heidegger's reading thus presupposes that the concept of distinct substance, objectivity or *Gegenständlichkeit* is intimately bound up with a mode of thinking—intuition—which is modeled on seeing, and so implies that the only way to loosen the hold of objectifying thinking is to loosen the hold of such intuition. What this fails to allow for, however, is that visually conceived thought, though oriented toward presence, might not be intrinsically connected with the notion of distinct substance after all, and so might not be as reductive or narrowly objectifying as has frequently been claimed.

What I should like to suggest here—pace Heidegger, Levin, and Rorty—is that it is not so much the hegemony of *vision* or of *Anschauung* which restricts or distorts our thinking in the modern world, but rather the Cartesian *concept* of substance and the association of clarity with distinctness—with "either/or" thinking—which narrows down and distorts our vision. But, if this is so, then perhaps what is required to open our vision and our thought is not that we attune ourselves to what is *not* directly visible—to the hidden openness of things or to the horizons or shadows on which we can never directly focus—but rather that we attend a little more closely to the character of what *is* directly visible, without assuming in advance that what we shall see will be distinct substances or things which can be surveyed and mastered.

III

My aim in examining the theories of vision offered by Berkeley and Descartes is not to argue that they are correct in every detail, but simply to show that alternatives to the conception of vision offered by writers such as David Levin are possible, and that, consequently, the claim that modern objectifying, technological subjectivity is the result of our construing our knowledge and access to beings in terms of vision and visual metaphors is contestable. It may well be, as a study of Descartes suggests, that modern technological subjectivity rests not so much on the "hegemony of vision," but rather on a certain narrow conception of thought. Furthermore, it may also be the case that vision is precisely what points the way to a richer, more open, less reductive conception of thought.

One philosopher who to my mind is convinced of the intrinsic generosity of vision is G. W. F. Hegel.

In his *Encyclopaedia* (1830) Hegel explains that vision (*Sehen*) must be regarded as a "concrete habit, which *immediately* unites the many determinations of sensation, consciousness, intuition (*Anschauung*), understanding and so on in one simple act."[67] Vision is thus a complex fusion of different levels of awareness, each of which has to be understood in its difference from and relation to all the others, if we are fully to comprehend what it means to see.

The first level to consider is that of sensation (*Empfindung*). All sensation, Hegel contends, unites two "moments" or "sides." On the one hand, sensation is a form of self-relation, the *felt* awareness which an animal or human being has of itself. On the other hand, sensation is also a relation between the living organism and something which is different from it, a felt awareness of something given, something which stems from the world outside. These two sides do not simply coexist, however; they form *one* united relation. The sensing organism or "soul" (*Seele*) thus feels itself and its own being in and through feeling itself to be determined or "affected" in a particular way, that is, in and through experiencing particular sensations such as sounds, smells, tastes, and so on. The soul feels a difference between itself and its particular sensations in that it does not feel itself restricted to one given sensation or mode of sensation: it is not just aware of itself as the hearing of this sound, or indeed just as hearing. Yet, equally, the soul feels no difference between itself and its particular sensations, since each sensation is experienced as its *own* (*Eigenstes*), as a particular modification of the soul itself. There is, therefore, no distinct awareness of the self as such, as separate from its particular experiences of color, sound, taste, and so on; the soul simply feels itself *in* experiencing the particular sensations it has. I see red or hear a certain note and I find myself as—feel myself as—this seeing of red or this hearing of the note. That is to say, in seeing and hearing, I am simply "with myself" (*bei mir selbst*).[68]

Sensation is thus not marked by any clear difference between subjectivity and a distinct, external object: "the subjectivity of the sensing soul . . . insofar as it *only* senses, does not yet understand itself as something subjective standing over against something objective" (*als ein einem Objektiven gegenüberstehendes Subjektives*). That is to say, there is not yet any distance between subjectivity and what it is aware of. Accordingly, Hegel argues, visual sensation (*das Gesicht*) by itself gives us no sense of things being "over there," no sense of depth or three-dimensional space, but only makes us aware of light, color, and flat, two-dimensional planes.[69]

The only sense which does give us a sensation of spatial depth, Hegel claims, is touch, since it senses the weight, resistance, and three-dimensional shape (*Gestalt*) of material bodies, and thus makes us aware that things extend away from us in all directions.[70] Yet touch has to be in direct contact with things to sense their shape, depth, and distance and so cannot be directly aware of things which are at a tangible distance from us but with which we are not actually in physical contact. That is to say, it cannot be directly aware of any distance which might lie *between* my body and things, separating things from the organs of touch. We do, however, become directly aware of a distance separating us from things, according to Hegel, when we learn that visible size and areas of visible darkness— shadows—correspond to, and so are the visible indications of, tangible depth and distance, and when we thus learn to *see* depth and distance—to *see* things "over there"—even in the absence of any corresponding tangible contact with the things which we see:

> Initially, the child only has a sensation of light, through which things are made manifest to it. This mere sensation misleads the child into grasping at distant objects as if they were near at hand. However, the child learns about distances through the sense of touch. Thus it acquires a sense of visual proportion [*Augenmaß*] and casts what is external outside itself.[71]

Hegel's account of visual sensation is clearly very close to Berkeley's; indeed it may even be partly derived from Berkeley's writings, since Hegel comments briefly on the Irish empiricist's theory of vision in his lectures on the history of philosophy.[72] However, Hegel goes beyond Berkeley by arguing that the visual sensation of depth and distance, which is made possible by the association of visible and tangible sensation, does not yet amount to a clear consciousness of genuine objectivity. The ability to see distance is certainly needed if a living being is to become conscious of things as distinct from it, but it is not by itself sufficient for such consciousness to arise, as is evident in the case of animals. Many kinds of animals can see things at a distance, but they do not regard these things as distinct objects standing over against them, because they are not yet aware of themselves as distinct subjects confronting things, that is to say, they are not yet *conscious* of themselves as being an "I."

For Hegel, there is an important difference between mere sensation and consciousness. Sensation involves seeing colors and hearing sounds which are felt as modifications or "states of mind" of the soul itself. Thus, even though the sensing soul can progress as far as seeing colors and shapes (and, presumably, hearing sounds) as distant, it is only aware of what it itself actually sees and hears, and can never abstract what is sensed from the sensing of it, so as to regard it as having an existence of its own. Consciousness, on the other hand, is precisely the awareness that what I see and hear is something that is there, even if I am not actually seeing or hearing it. Consciousness is the awareness that colors, shapes, sounds, and so on, *are* in their own right, that they exist in themselves and constitute a world that is independent of me (*selbständig*). It is for consciousness, therefore—not for sensation—that things appear as distinct objects standing over against the self, as *gegenständlich* or *gegenübertretend*, that is, as things which stand at a real distance from the self.[73]

This distinction between self and object arises because—in an act which Hegel calls an act of reflection (*Reflexion*)[74]—the self distinguishes itself from what it sees and hears by, as it were, turning or bending back into itself out of its immersion in the flux of sensations and so becoming conscious of itself as having an identity and being of its own, an identity that is separate from the particular colors, shapes, and sounds it sees and hears. Consciousness thus actually has a double object: it is conscious of its *Gegenstand* and of itself at one and the same time, because "it is only by my coming to grasp (*erfassen*) myself as an I, that the other becomes objective (*gegenständlich*) for me."[75] Consequently, Hegel sees consciousness as marked by an inevitable tension. On the one hand, the conscious self knows the object to be over against itself as a wholly independent, objective other. On the other hand, however, it understands its own certainty of itself to be inseparable from its certainty of the object, and so regards the object as something which is not simply independent of it, but which mediates its self-consciousness and self-certainty and is thus there *for* the self.

Let us consider the "objectifying" side to consciousness first. Hegel reminds us that consciousness does not have a different content from sensation, but rather regards the content of sensation in a new, objective way. The most basic level of consciousness, which Hegel calls sense-certainty, simply regards what it senses as colors, shapes, and sounds that are actually there before it and really exist. However, just as the conscious self is "reflected" back into itself out of the object, so the object itself is known by consciousness to be reflected back into itself and to have an independent identity of its own which is not immediately revealed through present sensation. The modes of consciousness which think of objects in this way are called by Hegel perception (*Wahrnehmen*) and understanding (*Verstand*). For both these modes of consciousness, the colors, shapes, and sounds we see and hear do not exhaust all there is to know of things; they are simply the observable properties or qualities of things whose own identities and manifold relations to other things cannot themselves be directly observed, but are known through thought to exist. Perception begins from the observation of sensuous material, Hegel says; yet "it does not limit itself to smelling, tasting, seeing, hearing, and feeling, but proceeds necessarily to relate what is sensed (*das Sinnliche*) to a *universal* which is not immediately to be observed."[76] Perception and understanding do not just see red, therefore, but see some *thing* which is red; or rather—to be more precise—*know*, in seeing a red shape, that there is a red thing there whose visible properties we are able to observe. The visible properties themselves are thus understood to refer beyond themselves (*hinausweisen*) to a network of interconnected existing things which form the intelligible, nonobservable ground or presupposition of all that we observe, and which, as intelligible, can be comprehended in terms of mathematical and scientific concepts and laws.[77]

It is clear, then, that with perception and understanding—the forms of consciousness which Hegel considers to be characteristic of Kantian philosophy and the natural sciences—we have reached a mode of awareness or disclosure similar to the one which we found earlier in Descartes, and to the one which Heidegger and Levin believe reduces being to "the uniformity of what is simply present":[78] that is, *Vorstellen*. Like *Vorstellen*, perceiving consciousness views things as objects standing over against the subject, and it thinks of these objects as distinct things whose properties and relations with other things can be adequately presented in judgments or statements (what Heidegger calls *Aussagen*). Like *Vorstellen*, perceiving consciousness also combines certain knowledge of objects and *self*-certainty into one mode of knowing. Furthermore, if we turn to the other "side" of consciousness which we mentioned above, we shall see another parallel between consciousness and *Vorstellen*.

As I indicated, consciousness, for Hegel, does not just regard the object as independent, but also at one and the same time as that which mediates the subject's own certainty of itself. The object is thus viewed as not just there for its own sake, but as there *for me*, as that through which I become aware of myself and of my own power over things. Just as Heidegger associates *Vorstellen* with technological, mastering subjectivity, so Hegel associates consciousness with *desire*—the desire to afford oneself a sense of self-satisfaction through appropriating and consuming available objects and thereby negating their independence.[79] It is clear, then, that even though Hegel says consciousness "releases" (*entläßt*) the object and lets it go free as an independent thing,[80] the conscious self does not actually have the "freedom" of the object uppermost in its mind. Indeed, how could it do so, since the objectivity the self confronts is only "released" or placed before it so that the self can become certain of its own distinctness as a self?

In spite of these similarities between Hegel, Heidegger, and Levin, however, there are very significant differences between them. For Hegel, in contrast to Heidegger and Levin, objectifying, mastering subjectivity is not the product of the hegemony of vision or *Anschauung* in human life, but rather the product of conscious *reflection*. As we have noted, visual sensation, in Hegel's view, does not reify or objectify what we see. Visible shapes and colors are only turned into the shapes and colors of *objects* by an act of conscious reflection in which the self bends back into itself by distinguishing itself from what it sees and hears, and at the same time understands what we see and hear as referring back to—as being reflected back into—an objective identity which constitutes the invisible, intelligible ground of the properties we observe. Such reflection is an important moment of vision because it lends objectivity to what we see, but it is different from visual sensation and, as we shall see, does not suffice to yield full visual intuition. Nor should the term *reflection* be understood in a visual way. Reflection, for Hegel, does not mean "mirroring," but rather a mode of thought which doubles back on itself and withdraws into itself while at the same time stepping down into the intelligible ground of what it sees, that is, into the presupposition of what it sees, into the realm of what is *not* directly visible.

Hegel's analysis of consciousness thus suggests the same conclusion as Descartes's analysis of vision, namely that a particular kind of *thinking*, not visual sensation itself, is responsible for reducing the world to a realm of manipulable objects. Hegel does not share Descartes's view that our belief that the colors we see are real is a mistake, the simple result of our habitual confusion of what we see with the things we judge, through the intellect, to exist outside ourselves. Hegel holds that things in the world about us really are colored, and he tries to prove this in his philosophy of nature. However, he does agree that (at the level of consciousness) we do not actually see the substantial identity or thinghood of things, and that we regard the colors we see to be objective because we conceive them through *thought* to be distinct from us. For Hegel, then, we do not see objectively existing colors by visual sensation alone; rather, it is conscious reflection which throws the content of our sensations outside us and so constitutes or discloses a realm of objective sensory qualities for us. Insofar as we do seem actually to *see* colors and shapes as over against us, as *gegenständlich*, it is our reflexive consciousness, which combines with our visual sensations to produce visual consciousness of distinct objects, that we must consider responsible.

But such visual consciousness—rather than mere visual sensation—is surely what we ordinarily mean by vision. To say that reflection objectifies things would thus in fact seem to be the same as saying that *vision* (in the ordinary meaning of the term) objectifies things, even though visual

sensation by itself does not objectify things. Why, then, do I insist that reflection rather than vision gives rise to the narrow objectification of
things? Is this simply the consequence of stubbornly understanding vision to mean visual sensation only? Or could it be that reflexive visual
consciousness does not actually amount to vision as we usually experience it? This indeed is what Hegel maintains.

Vision as we usually experience it is not simply equivalent to the visual
sensation of colors and shapes, nor does it just amount to knowing colors and shapes to be there, to be the visible properties of things. Vision
in its proper sense entails the awareness of the presence of concrete, unified objects (of various forms and colors) in continuous, surrounding
space. The name Hegel gives to vision so conceived is the same name
Heidegger gives to theoretical "seeing," namely "intuition" (*Anschauung*).
Like reflexive consciousness, intuition is a fusion of visual sensation and
thought: it is a mode of awareness which has a sensory content, but
which conceives of that content in a particular way. Moreover, visual intuition actually incorporates the moment of visual consciousness within
itself, insofar as it, too, conceives of what it sees as objective. Yet intuition is not simply a further mode of reflexive consciousness, but is distinguished from reflection by the more generous, less reductive way in
which it conceives of its objects.

Reflection is a mode of thought which is reflected back into itself, into
its own awareness of itself as a distinct "I," and which at the same time
regards objects as reflected back into their own independent identity and
ground. The objects it is aware of are understood to be what underlie
the properties we see, and so are not directly observable as things, nor
even directly *present* to thought. Reflection thus does not so much know
things in themselves as know *that* they are there. Insofar as it is reflected
back into itself, however, reflection stands in a contradictory relation to
its objects. On the one hand, it assures itself of its own identity by distinguishing itself from things and, as it were, pushing them away as something outside and independent of itself. On the other hand, since it can
only become certain of itself by distinguishing itself from these objects, it
regards them as mediating its own self-identity, and so tacitly views them
as having no independent value, but as simply being there for me and
my own self-satisfaction. In both cases, reflection views objects as something negative: either as something which is distinct from, and therefore
not, me, or as something which, in comparison with myself, is of no value
in itself.[81]

Intuition views objects very differently. It does not think of itself as reflected *back* into itself and thus as standing over against its objects, but
rather knows itself to be united with and in "harmony" with its objects.[82]

In intuition, therefore, our own identity is not defined in opposition to—through the negation of—what is outside of us, but rather is gained through attending to and affirming the presence of what is outside of us. That is to say, we are aware of ourselves and present to ourselves in and as the *opening* of ourselves to, and the beholding of, other things. These things themselves thus cannot be viewed simply as residing over against or outside a self that is distinct from them, but must be seen as revealed within the space of our own open awareness, that is, as fully present to us. And they must be viewed, not just as present to us "over here," but as present within the space of our awareness, as it were, *over there*. In intuition, then—that is, in concrete, fully rounded vision—I do not regard myself as simply distinct from objects, because I understand the space of my awareness itself to extend outside me and to disclose the objects which I see. In this sense, Hegel says, we are in visual intuition "outside ourselves" (*außer uns*).[83]

Visual intuition, for Hegel, does not mark itself off from objects, stand over against and survey them, or reduce them down to mere objects "for us." Rather, it gives itself to objects and lets them stand free, because it is itself nothing other than being attentive and open to, and so being filled with, what is independent of and outside of us. Visual intuition thus does not just view the object as a "relative other," as something whose objectivity lies essentially in its external relation to *me*; but it discloses the way in which the object is itself "the other of itself," that is, the full objectivity of things themselves.[84]

The intrinsic self-externality of things which visual intuition discloses is space. Visual sensation and visual consciousness are spatial, for Hegel, to the extent that I can see depth and distance (as well as two-dimensional planes), and be conscious of what I see as over against me. However, such space is at most relative, perspectival space, the spatial distance at which things stand in relation to me. Furthermore, the colors and shapes which we see—whether viewed as subjective sensations or as objective qualities—are always sensed or perceived individually, or as aggregates of properties which refer back to intelligible grounds, and are not understood as themselves forming any interconnected spatial order or whole that is present to view. Only visual intuition is aware of what it sees as objects standing in their own determinate, objective relations to one another and so as constituting a continuous spatial *presence* or whole—because only visual intuition opens itself to the full objective presence of things, to what things themselves objectively *are*.

It should perhaps be noted at this point that intuition is a form of *thinking* which is not restricted to the visual awareness of things in space, but is also aware of space (and time) in conjunction with other senses.

Nevertheless, Hegel seems to regard spatial awareness as the mode of intuition in which we are most properly "outside ourselves" (time, after all, can be experienced internally in a way that space cannot); and, since he considers vision to be the sense through which we are able to have the clearest awareness of spatial depth and distance, he regards vision as the sense by means of which we are most properly able to intuit, as *der eigentliche Sinn der Anschauung*.[85]

Intuition is thus primarily visual intuition, for Hegel. Moreover, visual intuition, as I have suggested, is vision in its full and proper sense, the concrete awareness of actual things in space, rather than the mere sensing or consciousness of visible shapes and colors. If we accept that vision is properly to be identified with the blending together of visual sensation and spatial awareness in visual intuition, then we can see that, at least as Hegel presents it, vision does not effect the kind of narrow reduction of things to mere disposable objects, and does not have an "inveterate tendency to grasp, secure, master and dominate," as David Levin, for example, suggests.[86] Visual intuition certainly relates to objects: it places objects before itself and thus incorporates within itself the moment of consciousness or *Vorstellen*. But it does not just think of these objects as things which are reflected back into themselves and which stand over *against* us, presenting their visible properties to view and being available for use. Visual intuition does not push objects away from it, or appropriate them, in order to gain greater certainty of itself; it attends to objects— opens and gives itself to them—and discloses the concrete, unified presence of the objects themselves by letting them stand out in space, that is, *by making space for them*—a space which is known to be real and present all around us and to be the space which we ourselves share. Visual intuition is, indeed, precisely what Heidegger appears to leave out of consideration, namely a mode of openness which lets things stand out before us as present *objects* (*Gegenstände*) and yet which does not just regard them as objects over against us to be surveyed and mastered, but rather sees them as things with which we dwell and share a common space.

If Hegel is right in viewing visual intuition as generous in this sense, then there is nothing particularly sinister about modeling knowing or thinking on vision. Hegel himself considers it to be extremely important that people speak from a lively "intuition" of the matter at hand in all branches of knowledge, especially philosophy, and he spells out some of the qualities which he thinks a philosopher or historian needs to take over from intuition: the ability to recognize the interconnected structure, substance, or whole—*das Ganze*—of a particular matter (rather than disconnected details), as well as the willingness to give oneself over, to yield, to the matter itself, and let it hold sway and guide our thinking ([*die Sache*] *gewähren lassen*).[87]

Hegel does not think that we should remain content to encounter the world through (metaphorical or literal) intuition alone, whether it be visual, aural, or tactile. He well understands the need for practical interaction with the world; and he argues that, in order to know things—and especially human beings—fully, we need to proceed to pure conceptual reason which has been freed from sensuous externality and which can think the inner nature or immanent, rational structure of things. Yet he argues that even pure thought has some of the qualities which belong to intuition. Like intuition, pure thought is the direct awareness of being itself (rather than an internal representation of being), and like intuition, it must be able to comprehend the whole and let itself be guided by the matter itself. Indeed, in the opening chapter of the *Science of Logic,* Hegel seems actually to equate the pure thought of being with pure intuition itself.[88]

Berkeley, Descartes, and Hegel all agree that visual sensation does not reify what is seen or turn what is seen into manipulable objects placed before me. Hegel's analysis suggests that visual intuition—vision proper—does not reify what is seen in any technologically exploitative way either. If we as individuals, or indeed whole ages and cultures, nevertheless do regard things or people as objects to be pinned down, surveyed, and mastered, this must be due, according to the Hegelian view, to our *reflexive* consciousness which narrows down our vision and deprives it of its intrinsic generosity, by changing it from genuine openness and attentiveness to things into a vision which gazes with lustful, self-oriented desire on what it sees.

Yet Dewey, Rorty, Heidegger, and Levin all insist that the problems they analyze—technological subjectivity, modern skepticism, or quietism—have arisen because of the Western philosophical tradition's tendency to model knowledge on vision and to regard it as a theoretical "seeing." Given that Hegel agrees with a good deal of what Heidegger and Levin say about the deficiencies of modern society, however, does it really matter that he singles out reflexive consciousness as the source of the problem, rather than vision and visual metaphors for knowing? I think it does, for the focus of so many twentieth-century writers on the problematic nature of vision and theoretical "seeing," and their corresponding lack of focus on the problematic nature of reflection as Hegel understands the term, leads them to overlook the reflexive features which continue to haunt their own thinking, and to undervalue many of the qualities of visual intuition which Hegel values strongly.

This continuing reflexivity is most evident in Dewey and Rorty. Both seek to replace the "spectator theory of knowledge" with a conception of knowledge based on the pragmatic idea of "coping" or "dealing" with the world. From Hegel's perspective, however (indeed, from Heidegger's, too), this pragmatic conception of knowledge still seems to perpetuate the reflexive or technological idea that our primary relation to the world is that of making something of the world for ourselves, rather than disclosing the world or letting it be whatever it is in itself (though it should be said that both Dewey and Rorty have an open-ended conception of making something of the world, which is not as intent on completely subordinating the world to the interests of subjectivity, as the reflexive desire or technological *Vorstellen* described by Hegel and Heidegger). Dewey and Rorty would probably not view the absence of any concept of "letting be" in their thinking as a deficiency. But that does not alter the fact that their alternatives to knowledge-as-vision are still reflexive in character. In particular, Rorty's step back from direct, face-to-face contact with things or from the accurate mirroring of the world (both of which he considers to be fictions) into the sphere of propositions, arguments, and conversation *about* the world, that is, into the sphere of mediation—of knowledge *that* such and such is the case, rather than immediate knowledge *of* objects—seems to be a quintessentially reflexive move. Indeed, Hegel specifically identifies "knowledge that" (*wissen, daß*)—albeit a very minimal and abstract form thereof—with the standpoint of reflexive consciousness.[89]

The reflexive features of Heidegger's and Levin's thinking are perhaps a little less obvious, but they are nonetheless real. Unlike Dewey and Rorty, both Heidegger and Levin are concerned to prepare the way for a mode of comportment which is open to things and which lets them be. However, since they associate the form of vision or intuition which is oriented toward visible objectivity and presence (i.e. *Vorstellen*) with technological control, both seek to open us up to being by attuning our thinking or seeing to what is not directly visible, not objective, not there before us. *Gelassenheit,* for Heidegger, is the waiting for the opening of the "region" (*Gegnet*), the waiting to be let into the region by the region itself. This region is not an object before us, nor indeed any determinate field of objects before us, but rather the openness of things which surrounds us and with which, *as* that which surrounds us, we can never come face-to-face. As nonobjective, non-"thing-like," the region would appear to elude the grasp of reflexive thinking. Yet is not such a region thought as *reflected* back into itself precisely by being thought as that which is turned away from us and concealed from us, as the sphere of what is "turned in on itself" (*in-sich-gekehrt*)?[90] Furthermore, in spite of Heidegger's insistence (or rather the insistence of the participants in his dialogue) that neither the relation between the region and *gelassen* thinking, nor the relation between the region and things, is a "horizontal-transcendental" one, must not the thought of the region be viewed as the product of "transcendental" reflection, precisely because it is the thought of that which "lets the thing while (*weilen*) in itself as the thing" and of "that which lets the horizon be what it is," and thus is a thought which we can only open ourselves to and wait for by turning our attention from what is present *back* to that which allows what is present to become present, but which is never present before us itself?[91] That is to say, does not thinking remain reflexive, even if it seeks to avoid the reductive reification of being, as long as its fundamental move remains that of *stepping back* from what is present into what lets what is present come to be present, rather than that of attending to and disclosing that which is itself present, and letting it stand out in all its objective clarity?

A similar point could be made about Levin's suggestion that vision can only be genuinely opened up by being attuned to "circumambient regions of darkness" and "necessary concealments."[92] Like Hegel, Levin does not regard vision as irretrievably reductive and reifying, but conceives of a mode of "circumspective" vision which is aware, not just of isolated objects and qualities, but of "a whole." However, Levin considers this "whole" to be a field of vision gathered together within a "horizon" or "background," and the vision he favors entails the "capacity to experience the presence of the horizon without seeing it as another object," that is, to "perceive the background *as* background."[93] It is true that Levin does speak here of experiencing the *presence* of this horizon; but the presence of the horizon is not objective presence, not clearly visible presence, but an ambiguous, background presence which is largely concealed and thus shades into nonpresence and invisibility. Indeed, Levin explicitly states that the style of vision he seeks to encourage is "the playful gaze" which delights in being "drawn into the invisible."[94] From a Hegelian perspective, then, such a mode of vision, which must turn its attention from the front to the side in this way, and so turn *back* from the things present before us to the ground or field within which they are present, still remains a *reflexive* mode of vision.

Hegel does not deny that our world can be viewed as having a horizon or "infinite periphery."[95] However, the notion of a periphery or horizon only makes sense in relation to a center on which one's attention is focused. It is thus only when one focuses one's eyes on what lies straight ahead, and at the same time bends one's attention back to the side, that the things we see appear to recede into a background or toward a periphery. The distinction between a center and a peripheral horizon is consequently a reflexive one, which is made by a mode of consciousness which is able to center its vision on what is over there in front of it. Mere visual sensation does not distinguish between a center and periphery, because it is not yet aware of what it sees as being over there in front of it, but just sees colors and shapes, clearly or not clearly as the case may be. Furthermore, even when it is the visual sensation of depth and distance, it cannot detect a *periphery* as such because it is not able to abstract or bend its attention back to the side away from what is immediately present to it.

But neither is visual intuition bound to the idea of a periphery or horizon. Visual intuition obviously cannot see in all directions at once, and so cannot see what is in front of and behind the head at the same time. Furthermore, visual intuition does not see everything clearly because not all our visual sensations are clear. However, it knows the objects it sees to be connected with other objects which surround us and which, though not directly visible at the moment, are nevertheless all there as present objects. Visual intuition thus does not regard what it sees as receding toward a "periphery" or as existing within a disappearing "horizon," but rather as constituting an interconnected spatial continuity, or whole, in which each object is equally *present*. And it knows that if it turns its eyes and attention to what appears to be at the periphery of vision, new *objects* will immediately be disclosed to view.

This is not to deny that some of our visual sensations are clear and others unclear and that, *if* we focus on what is ahead of us and see it clearly, our unclear sensations will take on the status of a periphery or horizon. Nor is it to deny that, *if* we identify objective presence with what is immediately and clearly there before us, then what is not clear before us will be regarded as a region of concealment and ambiguity, a region that is not fully and objectively present. But note that we only interpret our unclear sensations as "peripheral" or "in the background" if we regard what is clearly there in front of us as constituting the "center" of our attention. If we wish to experience or "open" ourselves to the background *as* background (as Levin does), therefore, we must in fact continue to focus our attention resolutely toward the front while bending our attention back to what is not in front of us; otherwise we will have no center of focus or point of reference in contrast with which we can see the background *as* a background. But this means that it is only frontally oriented, reflexive vision which can "open" itself to the background as such. By contrast, visual intuition (that is to say, normal vision) is aware that things belong to an omnipresent, all-encompassing space, and thus does not fix its attention on what is in front of us or over against us, but directs its attention toward what is present *both* before us *and* all around us—to the things among which and with which we dwell. Consequently, such intuition or vision does not regard the region of unclear vision at the edge of what we see clearly as a permanently receding periphery or horizon, but rather as indicating the direction in which we can turn in order to see new objects clearly.

Both Levin and Hegel want to conceive a mode of vision that is open to what is not just in front of us. But, whereas for Levin such openness consists in turning from directly visible, frontal presence to its concealed, receding "ground," such openness for Hegel involves being able to turn from the presence of one set of objects to the presence of others, and so being able to open out onto a whole surrounding, omnipresent space.

This difference between what we might call "reflexive" and "intuitive" openness of vision and thinking has important ramifications for philosophical style. Hegel, who regards reflection as the source of reductive, mastering subjectivity, sees nothing particularly "despotic" about vision, indeed he regards visual intuition as a mode of genuine openness toward things. Vision, for him, is thus not oriented primarily toward something merely *vorgestellt* or over against us which we seek to survey and dominate through our gaze, but rather *opens up* a space of objective presence which we know both to stand before us as *vorgestellt* and to extend all around us beyond what we actually see at any particular moment. Consequently, philosophical thinking which seeks to open itself to and let itself be guided by the matter at hand, rather than control the path of thinking itself, does not need to eschew the typically visual qualities of objectivity and presence, even though it must be strictly conceptual and not merely sensuous or intuitive. Like visual intuition, philosophical thinking, as Hegel construes it, conceives of being as that which is *present* to mind; and like visual intuition, Hegelian philosophical thinking recognizes definite, determinate differences in the world and so lets things stand out objectively as what they are, at the same time as it understands how things are interconnected with other things in one whole. Furthermore, Hegel does not only believe that ordinary understanding can be brought to understand philosophical dialectic if it is prepared to let go of its habitual fixed distinctions; he also believes that the "abstract" ideas which philosophy develops are rendered *anschaulich* or incarnate for visual intuition in nature, art, and religion. The world which philosophy discloses, for Hegel, is thus the same world we disclose in vision.

For Levin and Heidegger, on the other hand, vision (or intuition or *Vorstellen*) is the source of reductive, reifying, mastering subjectivity, so a mode of thinking or "seeing" which seeks to avoid such mastering reification and hold itself open to being, must, to some degree at least, eschew the visual qualities of objectivity and presence. This does *not* mean that such thinking eschews intelligibility and rigor; but it does mean that, in spite of its commitment to openness, such thinking feels drawn toward concealments, receding horizons, and invisible regions, and so is not as open as thought is able to be, since it cannot let what it opens itself to stand out objectively before it as something that can be—though need not merely be—*vorgestellt*. Such nonreductive, "open" thinking cannot conceive of what it opens itself to as objective because it courts an openness which is still essentially reflexive rather than intuitive, that is, which requires that thinking *turn back from* objective presence to concealed peripheries and horizons. Thus, though this reflexive openness seeks to be genuine openness to what is other, it constantly runs the risk of mirroring reflexive consciousness by withdrawing into—reflecting itself back into—its own space of inwardness. Such inwardness perhaps finds expression in Levin's work in a certain subjectivism suggested by his emphasis on the importance of "felt experience" as opposed to "cold" objectivity;[96] and it perhaps finds expression in Heidegger in a vocabulary which contains words whose meanings, if not exactly private, cannot be rendered explicit for or shared with *Vorstellen,* but have to be approached, waited on, and perhaps understood in silence, and which thus, for *Vorstellen,* must remain obscure. (The researcher in Heidegger's dialogue on *Gelassenheit* admits at various times that he cannot *vorstellen* what terms such as *Gelassenheit* and *Gegnet* really mean.)[97] What dangers, or—in spite of my reservations—what potential for renewal there may be in such inwardness is not something I have space to discuss here. The point I wish to make is simply that Levin and Heidegger are required to turn inward by their concern to free thinking from what they perceive to be the fateful limitations of narrowly objectifying vision or intuition, and that they might not be required to make this turn if they interpreted vision and intuition in a different way.

There are clearly many similarities between Hegel's project and the projects pursued by Heidegger and Levin. I hope, however, that what I have suggested here sheds some light on the ways in which their respective conceptions of the nature and potential of vision differ from one another, and on the ways in which these differences determine their respective conceptions of thoughtful openness.

NOTES

1. John Dewey, *The Quest for Certainty* (Gifford Lectures, 1929) (New York: Putnam, 1960), pp. 23, 214.

2. Ibid., pp. 22, 196.

3. Richard Rorty, *Philosophy and the Mirror of Nature* (Oxford: Blackwell, 1980), pp. 12, 39.

4. Ibid., pp. 159, 162.

5. Ibid., pp. 159–160, 163, 375–376.

6. Ibid., p. 375.

7. Ibid., pp. 162–163.

8. Martin Heidegger, *Sein und Zeit* (Tübingen: Max Niemeyer Verlag, 1927, 14th ed. 1977), pp. 138, 147, 171, 358.

9. Ibid., pp. 154, 158.
10. Ibid., p. 69.
11. Ibid., p. 69.
12. Heidegger, "Die Zeit des Weltbildes," *Holzwege,* (Frankfurt: Vittorio Klostermann, 1950, 6th ed. 1980), pp. 89, 100.
13. Ibid., p. 87.
14. Ibid., p. 106.
15. Ibid., p. 88
16. Ibid., pp. 87, 106–107.
17. Ibid., pp. 84, 89, 106.
18. Ibid., pp. 88–89.
19. Ibid., pp. 106, 109.
20. Ibid., p. 99.
21. Ibid., p. 110.
22. Ibid., p. 109.
23. Ibid., p. 110.
24. Heidegger, *Gelassenheit* (Pfullingen: Günther Neske Verlag, 1959, 9th ed. 1988), p. 22.
25. Ibid., p. 24.
26. Ibid., pp. 23–24.
27. Ibid., pp. 39–40.
28. Ibid., p. 36.
29. Ibid., pp. 59, 62–64.
30. Ibid., p. 39.
31. Ibid., pp. 42–43, 50.
32. Ibid., pp. 13, 22–23.
33. Ibid., p. 59.
34. David Levin, *The Opening of Vision* (New York and London: Routledge, 1988), p. 65.
35. Levin, "Existentialism at the End of Modernity: Questioning the I's Eyes," *Philosophy Today,* vol. 34, no. 1/4 (Spring 1990), pp. 88-90.
36. Levin, *The Opening of Vision,* pp. 238, 240.
37. Ibid., pp. 79, 428, 432.
38. Ibid., p. 427.
39. Ibid., p. 438.
40. Ibid., p. 65.
41. Ibid., p. 65.
42. George Berkeley, *Philosophical Works* (London: J. M. Dent, 1975, 1983), pp. 9, 20.
43. Ibid., pp. 22, 31, 243.
44. Ibid., pp. 9, 51.
45. Ibid., pp. 21, 48.
46. Ibid., pp. 53–54.
47. Ibid., pp. 22, 33, 41.
48. Levin, *The Opening of Vision,* p. 234.
49. Berkeley, *Philosophical Works,* p. 11.

50. *The Philosophical Writings of Descartes,* trans. J. Cottingham, R. Stoothoff, and D. Murdoch, 2 vols. (Cambridge: Cambridge University Press, 1985), 1:153, 333.

51. Ibid., 1:153–154.

52. Ibid., 1:284–285, 304.

53. Ibid., 1:165, 167.

54. Rorty, *Philosophy and the Mirror of Nature,* pp. 45, 105.

55. *The Philosophical Writings of Descartes,* 1:165.

56. Ibid., 1:153.

57. Ibid., 1:167.

58. Ibid., 1:169–170.

59. Ibid., 1:170, 281–282; 2:295.

60. Ibid., 1:219.

61. Ibid., 2:95.

62. Ibid., 1:210.

63. Ibid., 1:215.

64. Ibid., 1:337.

65. Ibid., 1:142–143.

66. Heidegger, *Sein und Zeit,* p. 96.

67. G. W. F. Hegel, *Werke,* ed. E. Moldenhauer and K. Michel, 20 vols. (Frankfurt: Suhrkamp Verlag, 1969–), 10:186 [Enc §410 Remark].

68. Ibid., 9:432; 10:98 [Enc §351 Addition; §400 Remark].

69. Ibid., 10:100, 104 [Enc §400 Addition, §401 Addition].

70. Ibid., 9:466; 10:106 [Enc §358 Addition; §401 Addition].

71. Ibid., 10:80, 104 [Enc §396 Addition, §401 Addition].

72. Ibid., 20:274.

73. Ibid., 10:98, 118–119, 199 [Enc §400 Remark, §402 Addition, §413].

74. Ibid., 10:199 [Enc §413].

75. Ibid., 10:201 [Enc §413 Addition].

76. Ibid., 10:209 [Enc §420 Addition].

77. Ibid., 10:118 [Enc §402 Addition]; 19:211.

78. Heidegger, *Sein und Zeit,* p. 138.

79. Hegel, *Werke,* 10:215–219 [Enc §§426–429].

80. Ibid., 10:199 [Enc §413].

81. Ibid., 10:237 [Enc §443 Addition].

82. Ibid., 10:232 [Enc §441 Addition].

83. Ibid., 10:256 [Enc §450 Addition].

84. Ibid., 10:249–250 [Enc §448 and Addition]: see "Sichhingeben an die Sache," "Sicherfüllen mit einem Inhalte," "das Andere seiner selbst."

85. Ibid., 10:251 [Enc §448 Addition].

86. Levin, *The Opening of Vision,* p. 236.

87. Hegel, *Werke,* 10:254 [Enc §449 Addition].

88. Ibid., 5:82–83.

89. Ibid., 10:244 [Enc §445 Addition]; Rorty, *Philosophy and the Mirror of Nature,* pp. 146–147.

90. Heidegger, *Gelassenheit,* p. 40.

91. Ibid., pp. 37, 53–54.
92. Levin, *The Opening of Vision,* pp. 426–427.
93. Ibid., p. 79, 234–235.
94. Ibid., p. 438.
95. Hegel, *Werke,* 10:120 [Enc §402 Addition].
96. Levin, *The Opening of Vision,* p. 117.
97. Heidegger, *Gelassenheit,* pp. 34, 41.

FOUR

In the Shadows of Philosophy

Nietzsche and the Question of Vision

Gary Shapiro

I. LEARNING TO SEE:
NIETZSCHE'S LANGUAGE OF VISION

In the preface to *Human, All Too Human* Nietzsche indicates that he is a philosopher of suspicion, and he describes that suspicion in highly visual terms. He looks more closely where others are naive and he stays with the surface more rigorously than do those thinkers who posit a reality behind the appearances:

> in fact I do not myself believe that anyone has looked into the world with an equally profound degree of suspicion . . . and anyone who could divine something of the consequences that lie in that profound suspiciousness, something of the fears and frosts of the isolation to which that unconditional *disparity of view* (*Verschiedenheit des Blicks*) condemns him who is infected with it, will also understand. . . . What I again and again needed most for my cure and self-restoration, however, was the belief that I was *not* thus isolated, not alone in *seeing* as I did—an enchanted surmising of relatedness in eye and desires, a blindness in concert with another without suspicion or question-marks, a pleasure in foregrounds, surfaces, things close and closest, in everything possessing color, skin and apparitionality (*Scheinbarkeit*). [*HAH*, preface][1]

The poles of Nietzsche's "method" then are a deeply suspicious look and an intense desire that others share his point of view. On the one hand an evil eye (*böse Blick*) for that which is questionable, on the other a willingness to suffer illusion for the sake of a presumed common perspective. That Nietzsche should describe his approach so frequently in the language of vision gains a poignancy when we recall the failing eyesight of which he complained in almost illegible letters; beyond that (although we can never really leave the oedipal theme here) the problematic intensifies when Nietzsche turns his suspicion to the question of vision itself and when his desire is that we share his vision of vision.

Nothing is more of a commonplace in speaking of Nietzsche than to point out that he is not a systematic thinker and to observe that he is capable of writing apparently contradictory statements on what appears to be the same topic. In the case of everything connected with vision, the reader faces some difficulties. On the one hand, Nietzsche never produced an extended treatment of the question or the issues that might be comparable to what he has to say about philosophy or tragedy or morality; on the other hand, his writing is suffused with what seem to be visual metaphors, some of which are developed with great elaboration, but which seem to point in many different directions. One might suspect that the second of these tendencies is simply a symptom of the prevailing ocularcentrism that many take to characterize almost all of the Western intellectual tradition (later I will consider such characterizations by Martin Heidegger and Luce Irigaray). Perhaps Nietzsche does no more than adopt the language of vision, the eye, perspective, noon and midnight, shadow and sun, illumination which is part of the heritage of the West at least from the time of Plato's story of the cave and the sun.[2]

Human, All Too Human is often described as belonging to Nietzsche's "enlightenment" or "positivistic" phase. Here, if anywhere, we might expect to find him accepting some version of the hegemony of vision, where vision is understood in terms of the metaphysics of presence. Certainly the book, in all of its parts, constitutes one of Nietzsche's attempts to come to terms with modernity. But even in this most "enlightened" of his writings there is no uncritical acceptance of either of these positions. This is true in spite of certain appearances to the contrary. Early in the book, for example, Nietzsche gives an account of the "logic of the dream" in which he adopts the rhetoric of nineteenth-century psychology (*HAH* 13). There he suggests that when we are asleep (or even when our eyes are closed while we're awake) "the brain produces a host of light-impressions and colors, probably as a kind of afterplay and echo of those effects of light which crowd in upon it during the day." But we cannot tolerate a mere chaos of impressions and are unconsciously compelled to organize these random data into

> definite figures, shapes, landscapes, moving groups. What is actually occurring is again a kind of inferring of the cause from the effect; the mind asks where these light-impressions and colors come from and supposes these shapes and figures are their causes: it regards them as occasioning these lights and colors because, by day and with eyes open, it is accustomed to

finding that every color, every light-impression does in fact have a cause
that occasions it . . . as with a conjurer, a confusion of judgment can here
arise. [*HAH* 13]

Characteristically Nietzsche adds that this process of confused inference
is all too easy for us and that we live about half our lives still in this condition of interpreting as in fantasy and dream. Nietzsche, then, would
seem to be adopting a Cartesian, Humean, or Russellian account of vision according to which what we see is a construct, more or less justified,
that arises from a series of discrete visual impressions. Ambiguity, confusion, or uncertainty are to be ascribed not to the data but to our own
processes of construction and inference.

However, just a few aphorisms later, Nietzsche discusses "Appearance
and Thing Itself" in a way that modifies the apparent reductionism
of "Logic of the Dream." There he compares philosophers to spectators standing before a painting and attempting to interpret it correctly.
They disagree as to whether this painting is an informative indication of
the thing in itself (for example, Descartes) or if the connection is completely indeterminate (for example, Schopenhauer). Both make the same
mistake:

> Both parties, however, overlook the possibility that this painting—which we
> call human life and experience—has gradually *become,* is indeed still fully in
> course of *becoming,* and should thus not be regarded as a fixed object on
> the basis of which a conclusion as to the nature of its originator (the suffi-
> cient reason) may either be drawn or pronounced undrawable. [*HAH* 16]

If the painting has acquired color over many years, Nietzsche adds, we
may forget that "we have been the colorists." So the suggestion here is
that vision itself is in flux, that the very idea of there being constant data
for it is an illusion. There never was a firm bedrock of visual impressions
that could have served as the basis of inferences, conscious, unconscious,
or philosophical.

One might expect that in a work entitled *Twilight of the Idols,* Nietzsche
would be concerned with just those subtle shadings or chiaroscuro of the
Zwielicht or *Dämmerung* that might provide an alternative to the all too
bright and illusory light of the Enlightenment. He is, but it's difficult to
discover whether he holds a consistent view or even if there is some law
that would make comprehensible his apparent shift of positions. Here in
a chapter on "What the Germans Lack" Nietzsche suggests that they require an education in seeing (*Sehen*):

> One has to learn to *see,* one has to learn to *think,* one has to learn to *speak*
> and *write*: the end in all three is a noble culture.—Learning to *see*—habituat-
> ing the eye to repose, to patience, to letting things come to it; learning to

defer judgment, to investigate and comprehend the individual case in all its aspects . . . the essence of it is precisely *not* to "will," the ability to defer decision. [*T*, "What the Germans Lack," 6]

It's not immediately clear to what extent *seeing* functions here as a name for a dimension of all education and culture and to what extent it is modeled on the specific activity or experience of ocular vision. We might say that we shall have to *see*, in the sense of reading and thinking with care and not leaping to premature judgments. The need for such a phil-ological approach (philology is defined as the art of "slow reading" in the preface to *Daybreak*) could also be signaled by encountering what Nietzsche says just a few pages later in *Twilight* where he condemns ob-servation for its own sake and couches the entire aphorism in the lan-guage of the eye, vision, and painting, suggesting that such observation will produce a "false optics" and a "squint":

> To experience from a *desire* to experience—that's no good. In experiencing one *must* not look back towards oneself, or every glance becomes an "evil eye" (*jeder Blick wird da zum "bösen Blick"*). A born psychologist instinctively guards against seeing for the sake of seeing; the same applies to the born painter. He never works "from nature"—he leaves it to his instinct, his *cam-era obscura*, to sift and strain "nature," the "case," the "experience." . . . What will be the result if one does otherwise? Carries on colportage psy-chology in, for example, the manner of Parisian *romanciers* great and small? . . . just see what finally emerges—a pile of daubs (*Klecksen*), a mosaic at best, in any event something put together, restless, flashy. . . . Seeing *what is*—that pertains to a different species of spirit, the *anti-artistic*, the prosaic. One has to know *who* one is. [*T*, "Skirmishes," 7]

We might attempt to harmonize these two statements by pointing out that in the first case Nietzsche is discussing the minimal conditions of culture, not its highest attainments, while in the second he is prescribing for the psychologist in particular who must not remain at the level of naive observation; we might also say that in the first aphorism he ad-dresses the deficiency of the Germans, while in the second he speaks of what the French (or their psychologists) possess too much of. Such a reading would tend to reduce the specifically visual nature of Nietzsche's language to a general way of speaking about observation and knowledge. Now while Nietzsche can hardly avoid the strong relation between seeing and knowing that is embedded in the Western languages and their philosophies, there are other elements at work here. In the first apho-rism Nietzsche focuses on the importance of learning to see *before* one does anything else, and he emphasizes the powerful self-restraint that is necessary to prevent oneself from yielding to the first stimulus that comes along. In the second, he compares the psychologist to a painter, that is, to one who is actively involved in shaping objects for vision. The painter and his kin are explorers and researchers in the realm of the visual, Nietzsche assumes, and so they must create and constrain. The visionary artist, the Apollonian, is not merely receptive; he or she may put out of play Dionysiac exuberance and multiplicity, but such an artist *invents* and does not merely observe.

II. THE EVIL AND THE RADIANT EYE

One of the key terms that appears in the second aphorism and throughout Nietzsche's writing is "the evil eye" (*böse Blick*). Nietzsche uses the expression to the same effect later in *Twilight* when he criticizes the idea of art for art's sake and specifically Schopenhauer's conception of art as a release from the will: this, he says, is "a pessimist's optics and an 'evil eye'" (*T,* "Skirmishes," 24). To have an evil eye for something or somebody is to see that object in its worst possible light; it is to wish that the thing or person not shine forth, not be glorious, not be a center of radiance. Nietzsche alludes to a common usage of "evil eye" in which the expression designates an envious attitude in which the one with the evil eye wishes the injury or destruction of another just because the envier resents the success, beauty, or glory of what is envied.[3] The evil eye is a pervasive phenomenon in certain cultures, especially peasant and "primitive" cultures in which one person's gain is typically another person's loss and where consequently people worry that their good fortune will be the subject of a malicious, devouring envy. The evil eye is reductionistic or nihilistic; it reduces whatever it sees to the lowest common denominator of sameness. As Jacques Lacan observes, "It is striking, when one thinks of the universality of the function of the evil eye, that there is no trace anywhere of a good eye, of an eye that blesses."[4] (But is this true? Later I will suggest that such a "trace" is to be found in Nietzsche.) Lacan may be drawing on Freud's suggestion that sight was the last of the human senses to be developed; consequently it could be supposed that there is some lingering trauma connected with the shift from living on all fours and finding one's way about by touch and smell to standing erect and perceiving the world visually.

Yet Nietzsche frequently writes of the good, the clear, or the purified eye, in apparent opposition to the evil eye. When Zarathustra, emerging from ten years of solitude, is recognized by the hermit on his mountain, the latter says "His eye is pure (*rein*), and around his mouth there hides no disgust" (*Z* 10–11). Nietzsche also speaks of "*the purifying (reinmachende) eye*" in *Daybreak,* where he contrasts two sorts of genius—those like Schopenhauer whose genius is an extension of their nature or character, and those like Plato who possess the *pure, purifying eye* which seems not to have grown out of their temperament and character but free from these and usually in mild opposition to them, looks down on the world as on a god and loves this god. But even they have not acquired this eye at a single stroke: seeing needs practice and preschooling, and he who is fortunate enough will also find at the proper time a teacher of pure seeing. [*D* 497]

"Radiant eyes" have the capacity to bless and seduce:

> *Applause itself as a continuation of the play.* Radiant eyes and a benevolent smile is the kind of applause rendered to the whole great universal comedy of existence—but at the same time a comedy within the comedy aimed at seducing the other spectators to a *"plaudite amici."* [*AOM* 24]

The pure, radiant, clear eye is enthralled and entranced by the spectacle and has no need to dominate it. Eyes not only have the capacity of objectifying and reducing but of receiving and honoring. Vision, whether understood literally as one of the senses or metaphorically as a general way of apprehending and contemplating, is not a single thing. It should not be surprising that for the thinker of perspectivism there is no such thing as vision in itself; there is, as he frequently insists, only a perspectival seeing and knowing. (We could multiply the modalities by recalling Zarathustra's "last men" who blink in their facile state of contentment—distracted, not wanting to look at anything too long or too hard, having neither the pure nor the evil eye, they distractedly flip the channels.)

III. TOWARD A HISTORY OF VISION: BEYOND THE METAPHYSICS OF PRESENCE

Vision has a history and this history is one both of seeing and of making things to be seen. What is perhaps Nietzsche's fullest consideration of the structure of a possible history of vision occurs in a long aphorism in *Assorted Opinions and Maxims* (222). There he interrogates the presuppositions of an evolutionary account of the development of religious images or representations of the divine. It is tempting to believe, Nietzsche suggests, that there has been a "gradual evolution of *representations of gods* (*Götterdarstellung*) from clumsy stones and blocks of wood up to complete humanization." We might loosely call such an evolutionary narrative Hegelian, insofar as it would depict human beings as moving by intelligible steps from a position in which they confront the religious as something mysteriously other and transcendent to one in which they acknowledge their own nature in the highest reality, finally representing it to themselves in the beautiful images of the Greek gods.

This story, according to which we have come to understand ourselves ever more completely and in which the dimension of sheer otherness is overcome, would suggest that vision and the production of images are destined to approach and capture reality, to make it all present with no unrepresentable residue. This would be to subordinate the history of the visual to the metaphysics of presence. It is to suppose that the deepest intention of visual images has always been to make everything present. This was of course a familiar narrative in nineteenth-century histories of painting and the visual arts; inspired by Italian Renaissance painting and its tradition, critics and historians found it easy to see art history as a progressive conquest of the world of appearances. The pattern is already present in Vasari's *Lives of the Painters,* in which the line from Giotto to Michelangelo is represented as a successive series of discoveries of the world of sight with respect to perspective, color, modeling, and texture.

Contained in this narrative is a certain imperial, hegemonic conception of the visual that takes painting to be a kind of science, a paradigm of human knowledge which must have as its goal the ability to lay everything before us open to inspection. It is the "empire of the gaze" (as Martin Jay calls it) in which the monocular, absolute perspective of Alberti and his disciples join hands with Cartesian method and optics. Merleau-Ponty analyzed this reductive approach to vision in his "Eye and Mind," where he demonstrates how Descartes provides "the breviary of a thought that wants no longer to abide in the visible and so decides to construct the visible according to a certain model-in-thought."[5]

In Descartes's optics and in his remarks on painting we find an account of vision as a deciphering of signs in which visual clues allow us to reconstruct the genuine, geometrical order of the world; color, depth, the intermingling of objects, and above all the complicity of the viewer in the scene beheld are excluded from this attempt to construe vision on the model of line drawings, diagrams, and engravings. By the nineteenth century, philosophical modernity had made common cause with an evolutionary history of religion and symbols, so that the movement that Vasari saw beginning with Giotto could now be read back into the earliest forms of the production of images and deployed to explain the history of religion.

It is in this context that we should understand Nietzsche's intervention and interrogation of what might be called the aesthetics of presence and its history of images. The context of Nietzsche's discussion of the history of visual images, then, is the typical belief of the nineteenth century that everything has become visible, that the development of visual representation and seeing have been a steady progress toward the light.

Nietzsche describes the original images of the gods not in terms of an aesthetics of presence but in terms of a play of the present and the absent, the clear and the obscure, the manifest and the hidden; and he insists that this has nothing to do with an incapacity of the artists or an incipient process of image-making that is just finding itself:

> The oldest image of the god (*Götterbild*) is supposed to *harbor and at the same time conceal* the god—to intimate his presence but not expose it to view. No Greek ever truly *beheld* his Apollo as a wooden obelisk, his Eros as a lump of stone; they were symbols whose purpose was precisely to excite fear *of* beholding him. . . . In the incompleteness, elusiveness or overladenness of these figures there lies a dreadful holiness which is supposed to *fend off* any association of them with anything human. It is not at an embryonic stage of art at which such things are fashioned: as though in the ages when such figures were revered men were *incapable* of speaking more clearly, representing more accurately. What was the case, rather, was that one thing was specifically avoided: direct statement. As the cella contains the holy of holies, the actual *numen* of the divinity, and conceals it in mysterious semi-darkness, *but does not wholly conceal it*; as the peripteral temple in turn contains the cella and as though with a canopy and veil shelters it from prying eyes, *but does not wholly shelter it*: so the image is the divinity and at the same time the divinity's place of concealment. [*AOM* 222]

Nietzsche goes on to give an account of how "plastic art in the grand style" (*die grosse Plastik*) emerged after the Greeks became accustomed to viewing statues of the victors in the Olympic games, statues that were set up outside the temples. This was not an inevitable historical progression, but the consequence of a concatenation of events and circumstances that might have been otherwise. The flickering quality of the early image is a constant possibility of our vision. This flickering is elaborated at many levels in Nietzsche's works, for example in his fondness for titles such as Daybreak (*Die Morgenröte*) and Twilight of the Idols (*Götzen-Dämmerung*), which suggest the value of those circumstances in which outlines waver, objects are in shadow, and the full presence sought by philosophers since Plato is not to be found. This system of "metaphors" could be expanded to include perspectivism with its insistence that the notion of a single, absolute perspective is impossible and the necessity of a dialogue with the personified "Shadow" of the Wanderer or Zarathustra.

To the extent that full clarity and presence are obtainable in vision, Nietzsche suggests, they take the form of illusion rather than truth. Consider the description of the Apollonian dream world as one where "we delight in the immediate understanding of figures (*Gestalt*); all forms speak to us; there is nothing unimportant or superfluous" (*BT* 1). The dream is *Schein*, illusion or appearance. We could say that Nietzsche seems to reverse the traditional cognitive values of dream or illusion on the one hand and sight in general on the other. The dream is not the locus of confusion and obscurity, but of luminous illusion subject to the principle of individuation. The dream is exceptional in relation to vision as a whole, in which the dominant theme is the duality of concealing and revealing, light and shadow, dawn and dusk. When clarity emerges it always does so out of a context of darkness. This is the analysis that Nietzsche gives a little later in *The Birth of Tragedy* of the appearance of the tragic hero, whose apparently clear outlines and definition he ascribes to something like an optical illusion. We should not take vision and illusion to be mere metaphors here, for the appearance of the hero on stage is, for Nietzsche, very much a visual phenomenon:

> suppose we disregard the character of the hero as it comes to the surface, visibly—after all, it is in the last analysis nothing but a bright image projected on a dark wall, which means appearance (*Erscheinung*) through and through; suppose we penetrate into the myth that projects itself in these lucid reflections (*hellen Spiegelungen*): then we suddenly experience a phenomenon that is just the opposite of a familiar optical phenomenon. When after a forceful attempt to gaze on the sun we turn away blinded, we see dark-colored spots before our eyes, as a cure, as it were. Conversely, the bright image projections (*Lichtbilderscheinungen*) of the Sophoclean hero— in short, the Apollonian aspect of the mask—are necessary effects of a glance into the inside and terrors of nature; as it were, luminous spots to cure eyes damaged by gruesome night. [*BT* 9]

Clarity is illusion; beautiful illusion, but illusion nonetheless. Presence is obtainable only in and through illusion. In his accounts of the genesis and nature of dreams and other Apollonian illusions we could take Nietzsche to be providing an analysis of a conception of vision that could be called the aesthetics of presence. In recent years, following Martin Heidegger and Jacques Derrida, we have come to say that the central tendency of the Western metaphysical tradition has been to valorize the absolutely present, whether under the form of the Platonic ideas, the Cartesian *cogito,* or the Hegelian absolute spirit.

The aesthetics of presence would hold that paradigmatic sensory experiences, especially that of visual images and works of art, must also be understood in terms of their success or failure at realizing a full presence or manifestation, in which nothing remains obscure or concealed. There would then be a high degree of complicity between a metaphysics and an aesthetics of presence, a complicity that is evident in the tradition that runs from Plato's appeal to the vision of the ideas to Husserl's *Wesenschau* of ideal essences.

One response to both the metaphysics and aesthetics of presence has been to challenge the supremacy they accord to sight. It's suggested by pragmatists, for example, that we are tactile, kinesthetic beings, involved in a surrounding world that must always be in large part implicit; or some feminists have argued that the focus on sight is gendered, males having a tendency for the imperial, objectivizing gaze, while women have a more diffuse, plural, and decentered sensory repertoire. Often the attempt at revaluation reverts to founding texts of the tradition, especially Plato's, in order to point out how a certain conception of vision has established itself and to indicate how it might be interrogated.

Both Martin Heidegger and Luce Irigaray have produced extended readings of Plato's account of the myth of the cave in the *Republic* that attempt to exhibit the strategies by which the hegemony of vision is instituted and, by means of this articulation, to suggest how alternatives that were neglected could be developed. In "Plato's Doctrine of Truth," Heidegger systematically discloses the visual import of notions such as *eidos* and *theōria*, which help to found the metaphysics of presence. For Heidegger the scene of instruction in and out of Plato's cave is the point at which philosophy founded itself in an ocular metaphysics of presence and in which the more primordial conception of truth as unhiddenness (*a-letheia*) is repressed.

Since Heidegger's history of metaphysics as vision both parallels and diverges from Nietzsche's, it is worth considering his account of Plato's image of the sun and its heritage. Heidegger begins by telling us what Plato did *not* do:

> In the "allegory of the cave" the force of the clarification does not spring from the image of being enclosed in a subterranean vault and imprisoned in this enclosing; it does not even spring from the aspect of the openness outside of the cave. The image-making interpretative force of the "allegory" is gathered together for Plato rather in the role of the fire, the firelight and the shadows, the brightness of the day, the sunlight and the sun. Everything depends upon the shining of the phenomenal and the possibility of its visibleness. To be sure, unhiddenness is named in its various stages, but one can only consider it in the way it makes the phenomenal accessible in its outward appearance (*eidos*) and the way it makes this emerging (*idea*) visible.[6]

The nerve of Heidegger's story of philosophy, the plot of his metanarrative, consists in claiming that we have never ceased to be in thrall to the Platonic principle that "everything depends on the *orthotes,* the correctness of the glance."[7] The culmination of this story, for Heidegger, lies in Nietzsche's declaration that truth is the kind of error that is necessary for life:

> Nietzsche's concept of truth is an example of the last reflection of the extreme consequence of that changing of truth from the unhiddenness of beings to the correctness of the glance. The change itself takes place in the

definition of the Being of beings (i.e., according to the Greeks, the presence of what is present) as *idea*.[8]

Luce Irigaray undertakes a similar project in "Plato's *Hystera*" which provides a detailed reading of the complicity of ocularcentrism and phallogocentrism in Plato's myth of the cave. She argues that Western logic, as instituted by the Greeks, submerges the nature of woman's desire. As Irigaray says in "This Sex Which is Not One":

> Within this logic, the predominance of the visual, and of the discrimination and individualization of form, is particularly foreign to female eroticism. Woman takes pleasure more from touching than from looking, and her entry into a dominant scopic economy signifies, again, her consignment to passivity: she is to be the beautiful object of contemplation. While her body finds itself thus eroticized, and called to a double movement of exhibition and chaste retreat in order to stimulate the drives of the "subject," her sexual organ represents the *horror of nothing to see*. A defect in this systematics of representation and desire.[9]

While Heidegger and Irigaray both seem to challenge the tradition, they may be confirming it in another sense. It may be that these two critics of the visual are simply reverting to an age-old suspicion, one that may in fact antedate the origin of metaphysics, the suspicion named "the evil eye."

IV. THE ABYSS OF VISION

Where does Nietzsche stand with respect to these interrogations of the visual? On a certain reading of the Apollonian/Dionysian binary he could be construed as favoring the tactile, the kinesthetic, the auditory, and the musical over the visual. A closer examination, however, shows that there are several distinct and related strategies at work in Nietzsche's treatment of sight and its modes. If vision is thought of in terms of the metaphysics of presence, then it is to be opposed to what *The Birth of Tragedy* calls the "truly existent primal unity, eternally suffering and contradictory," although even there we are cautioned to remember that such unity "also needs the rapturous vision, the pleasurable illusion for its continuous redemption" (*BT* 4).

Yet, as I've already suggested, there is another, complementary line of thought at work in which Nietzsche seeks to articulate a sense of vision not as presence but as presence/absence or concealing/disclosing. Perhaps the most significant site of this tendency is the chapter "On the Vision and the Riddle" (*Vom Gesicht und Räthsel*) in *Thus Spoke Zarathustra*. This chapter, where the thought of eternal recurrence is broached for the first time in Nietzsche's story, is concerned not only with the riddle of recurrence but with the riddle of vision itself. Recurrence is first brought to speech as the result of a vision and the vision contains a discussion of vision itself. Zarathustra says to the adventurous sailors who constitute his audience, "To you alone I tell the riddle that I *saw*, the vision of the loneliest." A riddle is usually thought of as strictly linguistic, perhaps (as Freud might suggest) as the inverse of a joke. But here the riddle, Nietzsche emphasizes, is *seen*. Throughout the chapter the visual context is explicit. The narrative proper begins by setting the scene: "Not long ago I walked gloomily through the deadly pallor of twilight (*leichenfarbne Dämmerung*). . . . Not only one sun had set for me." In the duality or ambiguity of twilight things lose the simple outlines that they might appear to have at high noon.

What Zarathustra will ask here is: "Is seeing itself not—seeing abysses?" (*Ist Sehen nicht selber–Abgründe sehen?*) To see abysses is to become aware of the absence or failure of the ground, of that which would be present. Twilight is the time for discovering the abyssal nature of vision. Its duality is not to be despised, but to be welcomed as a condition of discovery. But sight requires courage, especially in such conditions, since we are constantly threatened by dizziness or vertigo when looking into an abyss: "Courage also destroys vertigo (*Schwindel*) at abysses: and where does man not stand at an abyss?" From the courageous point of view, vision is never all-encompassing and imperial; courageous vision is always at risk, always looking into the abyss.

But the point is made more sharply when Zarathustra's spirit of gravity, the dwarf that he has been painfully carrying on his back, jumps off his shoulders. The two of them now engage in a dialogue on vision, a dialogue that is doubly or even triply inscribed as such: by the chapter's title (*Vom Gesicht und Räthsel*), by the fact that what is in dispute is how to read or see the visible scene before them (the paths that join at the gateway), and by the title inscribed on the gateway itself, *Augenblick*. The *Augenblick* is conventionally translated as the moment, the *what* of eternal recurrence. But it is also a momentary glance, a twinkling of the eye; this sense is often emphasized in *Zarathustra*, as in "The Tomb Song," where Zarathustra addresses and laments what is lost:

> O you visions and apparitions of my youth (*Gesichte und Erscheinungen*)!
> O all you glances of love (*Blicke der Liebe*), you divine moments (*göttlichen Augenblicke*)!

Recall that Heidegger says that for Nietzsche everything depends upon the correct orientation of the glance (*Blick*). Verbally this is clearly the case, since in addition to the constant "metaphorics" of vision that I have already noted, Nietzsche's heaviest thought concerns the nature of the *Augenblick* itself.

Very little attention has been paid to the visual language within which Nietzsche formulates or alludes to this thought, perhaps because it has all too easily been assumed that Nietzsche speaks within the tradition's hegemonic conception of vision. From that assumption it follows, as Heidegger was the first to demonstrate, that Nietzsche is dominated by that very tradition in ways that he could not imagine. Now whatever Nietzsche's unthematized indebtedness to the metaphysical tradition may be, I want to suggest that he questions the visual metaphysics of presence in his thought of the abyssal dimension of the *Augenblick*.

While much has been said about the difficult thought of eternal recurrence, the thought that is called the most abyssal or the most heavyweight of all thoughts, it has not been much noticed how specifically what recurs is, in the first instance, something visual. Perhaps the obstacle to reading Nietzsche here lies in the unacknowledged influence of the metaphysics and aesthetics of presence. That is, it may be assumed too easily that *if* Nietzsche were emphasizing the visual dimension of the *Augenblick* then he would be endorsing the recurrence of what is most fully present. But if seeing, or courageous seeing, is always of abysses, then the *Augenblick*, the glance of the eye, is precisely an abyss.

Let us now read Zarathustra's colloquy with the dwarf, which is a confrontation between courageous vision and dwarf-vision. The dwarf has been taunting Zarathustra, enviously hissing at him that "You threw yourself up high, but every stone that is thrown must fall." The evil eye is at work here; from the perspective of dwarf-vision everything must be reduced to the lowest common denominator. For the dwarf, as for the evil eye in general, all seeming greatness must be shown to be nothing but a repetition of the same. From Zarathustra's point of view the same verbal formula will have the sense of a celebration of the depth, complexity, and abyss of the same.[10] Zarathustra replies to the reductionism of the evil eye by sharpening the alternative: "Dwarf! It is you or I!" The place where the decision is to be made is the gateway marked *Augenblick*, and the *agon* will take the form of a dispute about how to read a visual image or text. The scene is a vision within a vision, for the two have come to a halt and are looking at the scene before them. Zarathustra begins:

"Behold this gateway, dwarf!" I continued. "It has two faces. Two paths meet here; no one has ever followed either to its end. This long lane stretches back for an eternity. And the long lane out there, that is another eternity. They contradict each other, these paths; they offend each other face to face; and it is here at this gateway that they come together. The name of the gateway is inscribed above: '*Augenblick.*' But whoever would follow one of them, on and on, farther and farther—do you believe, dwarf, that these paths contradict each other eternally?"

The demand is that the dwarf *see* the gateway in all its depth and complexity, with all its contradictions. But what does he see?

"All that is straight lies," the dwarf murmured contemptuously. "All truth is crooked; time itself is a circle."

The dwarf sees both more and less than is there. More, because he claims that apparently straight and diverging lines really do circle around to meet. But this more is also less, less because the seeing of the paths as circular eliminates the clash and mutual offense that Zarathustra sees. And what of the gateway itself, the site of the clash? The dwarf doesn't describe it at all, perhaps he doesn't notice it. For the evil eye, everything is to be leveled down: Zarathustra will fall, and each moment will simply be submerged in the uniform figure of the circle, a figure of perfect uniformity. The gateway is inscribed, but dwarf-vision overlooks the inscription as it overlooks everything specific about the scene. Isn't the inscription a doubling and a deepening of *this* moment, *this* gateway that Zarathustra wants to see?

The inscription of the *Augenblick* as *Augenblick* sets up a *mise en abime*; it marks the vision as the vision of abysses. We are always at the abyss, at every moment, and it is a question of whether we have the courage to see that and to endure and overcome the vertigo induced by the abyss. Who might do this? The courageous ones, like the sailors who must have a sharp eye for the sea and the sky in all sorts of weather, who must be alert to the subtlest variations in what they see. Artists too (visual artists in particular) are also "bold searchers and researchers" (*Suchern, Versuchern*) who are "drunk with riddles, glad of the twilight." It is the task of the artist as explorer to look into the abyss and to prevent the facile acceptance of simplified visions.

In *Truth in Painting*, Jacques Derrida suggests (with no explicit reference to Nietzsche) that the figures of the circle and the abyss may define the discourse of aesthetics and the place of the visual within that discourse. The circle is invoked throughout the history of aesthetics as the form of the beautiful, and it is often transferred, as in Hegel and Heidegger, to the form of aesthetic discourse itself; it is already there in the prehistory of aesthetics in the Pythagorean cult of geometry and in the Platonic and Aristotelian passion for the supreme beauty of the circular orbits of the heavenly bodies. Commenting especially on the figure of the circle in the aesthetic discourse of Hegel and Heidegger, Derrida observes that the figure imposes a certain enclosed totality on both the subject matter (art and beauty) that it purports to encompass and on the capacity of thought itself to think of its other:

> This autodetermination poses singular problems of priority. The mind must put itself into its own product, produce a discourse on what it produces, introduce itself of itself into itself. This circular duction, this introduction to oneself, calls for what Hegel names a "presupposition" (*Voraussetzung*). In the science of the beautiful, the mind presupposes itself, anticipates itself, precipitates itself.[11]

Now one of the odd things about the aesthetic tradition, Derrida also claims, is that in spite of its reputation for valorizing the visual, in its most complete statements (in Hegel and Heidegger) it subordinates all the arts to speech.[12] This subordination, he implies, may itself be a turning away from the abyss of vision to the full presence that seems to be promised by live speech, by language in which everything can be said. One may very well ask, then, whether there really has been a hegemony of vision, or of vision construed as the metaphysics of presence understands it.

There are at least two interpretations of the thought of eternal recurrence that are bound up with the two perspectives on the vision of the *Augenblick*. In the figure of the circle everything is made schematic; it is as if one could stand outside the whole of time and comprehend it with one's gaze. To see the abyssal character of the *Augenblick* is to know the vertigo of vision; it is to see so deeply into the moment that one realizes its infinite depth. These perspectives emerge with variations in later sections of *Zarathustra*. When his eagle and snake tell Zarathustra that they *know* what he teaches, they recur to the figure of the circle, although in an ecstatic tone that contrasts with the dwarf's cynicism: "Everything goes, everything comes back; eternally rolls the wheel of being . . . eternally the ring of being remains faithful to itself." But this account is met with the rebuke, "O you buffoons and barrel organs! . . . have you already made a hurdy-gurdy song of this?" (Z 217–218). The Midnight Song that Zarathustra sings to celebrate eternal recurrence repeats that the world and eternity are *deep* and this abyssal depth is contrasted with the illusions of the dream and the superficial thought of the day:

O man, take care!
What does the deep midnight declare?
"I was asleep—
From a deep dream I woke and swear:
The world is deep,
Deeper than day had been aware.

Deep is its woe;
Joy–deeper yet than agony:
Woe implores: Go!
But all joy wants eternity–
Wants deep, wants deep eternity."
[Z 324]

V. THE WANDERER AND HIS SHADOW

My eyes get worse every day, and, unless someone comes along and helps me, I shall probably be blind by the year's end. So I shall decide not to read and write at all–but one cannot stick it out when one is completely alone.
[NIETZSCHE TO HIS MOTHER, MAY 1885][13]

To his mother (and to others) Nietzsche repeatedly writes of his failing eyes and his fear of blindness. He had too many reasons, among them human, all too human reasons, for associating his own destiny with that of vision itself. Following Heidegger's reading of Nietzsche as the culmination of Western thought's pursuit of presence, we could read his struggle to see as an emblem of philosophy's impossible desire. Heidegger hints that philosophy should be read as the tragic unfolding of a certain *hubris* that enters the stage with Plato's sun. If Nietzsche's work constitutes the last act of this tragedy, then the analogy with Oedipus is even stronger when we hear these laments for failing eyes. We discover Nietzsche moving among a range of views and positions by means of which he attempts to work out his relation to vision. These may now be schematically sorted out into three major modes. The first, or hegemonic position, is the one that Heidegger attributes to Nietzsche, in which vision is thought to yield presence and to be the primary sense, the sense that is exemplary of knowledge in general. In the second position, Nietzsche puts the dominance of sight into question by stressing, for example, the auditory and the musical or the tactile. The opposition between these two positions is in fact the most familiar of Nietzsche's thoughts, the contrast of the Apollonian and the Dionysian. The third position is one that may be a bit less familiar, and the one which I have stressed in this essay: it is the position that vision ought not to be construed according to the metaphysics of presence but courageously understood as "seeing abysses." It is no longer a question of valorizing or devalorizing vision but of rethinking vision—whether we are speaking of eyesight in the everyday sense or of the mind's eye.

The Wanderer and His Shadow perhaps names this third position; the text is framed by two dialogues between the title characters. The suggestion is that thinking, the work of the mind's eye, occurs in this dialogical space, a place of shadows and rapid changes of light and perspective. We will be tempted to identify the Wanderer with Nietzsche, the author, but any such identification will be rendered problematic by the splitting of the figure into a primary self and a shadow. The same duality is at work in *Zarathustra* when the Shadow enters into the drama of Zarathustra's encounter with the Higher Men. Jung seems to have been much affected by this theme, to the extent of incorporating some of Nietsche's terms as well as his thoughts. Surprised by the appearance of his speaking Shadow, the Wanderer is forced to thematize the play of light and shadow, and so to acknowledge a certain distance from the optics and metaphysics of presence that might otherwise have not been made explicit. The Wanderer confesses:

> You will know that I love shadow as much as I love light. For there to be beauty of face, clarity of speech, benevolence and firmness of character, shadow is as needful as light. They are not opponents: they stand, rather, lovingly, hand in hand, and when light disappears, shadow slips away after it.

The two, we suppose, now settle down to a conversation which is echoed in some way by the text that bears their names. But the communication of this conversation is hedged about with certain restrictions. The Shadow, in keeping with his retiring nature, begs the Wanderer to "promise you will tell no one how we talked together!" The Wanderer knows that a flat record of the colloquy would lack the appropriate shadings:

> *How* we talked together? Heaven defend me from long-spun-out literary conversations. . . . A conversation that gives delight in reality is, if transformed into writing and read, a painting with nothing but false perspectives: everything is too long or too short. But shall I perhaps be permitted to tell *what* it was we were in accord over?

This is then the visual protocol for reading Nietzsche's writing and specifically his aphorisms. Each must be understood as the fruit of a dialogue between light and shadow. The dialogue is taken up again explicitly after the series of aphorisms. It is getting darker and the Shadow must reckon with his own imminent disappearance. At this point all that the Wanderer can do for the Shadow is to move in such a way as to prevent the latter's being lost in the encroaching darkness. The Shadow begs for a small favor, and in doing so recalls a philosophical anecdote. All that the Wanderer can do for him now is this:

> Nothing, except perhaps that which the philosophical "dog" [Diogenes the Cynic] desired of the great Alexander: that you should move a little out of the sunlight, I am feeling too cold.

Of course, since it is the Shadow who speaks, the situation has been reversed from the original. Diogenes wanted light in order to be able to see clearly and without obstruction. The Shadow requires light simply in order to be. When darkness falls, the Shadow vanishes and the conversation ceases. Is this Nietzsche's way of suggesting that thought occurs neither in the glaring Platonic sunlight, nor in its all too facile negation, but in the flickering, twilight play of light and shadow?

NOTES

1. References to Nietzsche's writings are generally to numbered sections; references to *Thus Spoke Zarathustra* are to the page numbers of the English translation cited below. I employ the following abbreviations and translations (with some modifications of the latter): *AOM: Assorted Opinions and Maxims* (published with *HAH*); *BT: The Birth of Tragedy*, trans. Walter Kaufmann (New York, 1967); *HAH: Human, All Too Human*, trans. R. J. Hollingdale (New York: Cambridge University Press, 1986); *T: Twilight of the Idols*, trans. R. J. Hollingdale (Baltimore: Penguin Books, 1968); *WS: The Wanderer and His Shadow* (published with *HAH*); *Z: Thus Spoke Zarathustra*, trans. Walter Kaufmann (New York: Penguin Books, 1978).

2. References to some of the vast literature on the philosophical understanding and critique of vision may be found in the following: Martin Jay, "In the Empire of the Gaze: Foucault and the Denigration of Vision in Twentieth-Century French Thought," in David Hoy, ed., *Foucault: A Critical Reader* (New York: Blackwell, 1986); David Michael Levin, *The Opening of Vision* (New York: Routledge, 1988) and *The Listening Self* (New York: Routledge, 1989).

3. Cf. my article "Nietzsche on Envy," *International Studies in Philosophy* 1983, pp. 3–12 and the works cited there; to these there should be added: Alan Dundes, "Wet and Dry, the Evil Eye: An Essay in Indo-European and Semitic World-View," in *Interpreting Folklore* (Bloomington, Ind.: Indiana University Press, 1980); Clarence Maloney, ed., *The Evil Eye* (New York, 1976); Lawrence Di Stasi, *Mal Occhio: The Underside of Vision* (San Francisco: North Point Press, 1981).

4. Jacques Lacan, *The Four Fundamental Concepts of Psychoanalysis*, trans. Alan Sheridan (New York: Norton, 1978), p. 115.

5. Maurice Merleau-Ponty, "Eye and Mind," trans. Carleton Dallery, in *The Essential Writings of Merleau-Ponty*, ed. Alden L. Fisher (New York: Harcourt, Brace and World, 1969), pp. 252–286.

6. Martin Heidegger, "Plato's Doctrine of Truth," trans. John Barlow, in Henry Aiken and William Barrett, eds., *Philosophy in the Twentieth Century* (New York: Random House, 1962) 3:261.

7. Heidegger, "Plato's Doctrine of Truth," p. 265.

8. Ibid., p. 267.

9. Luce Irigaray, *This Sex Which Is Not One*, trans. Catherine Porter (Ithaca: Cornell University Press, 1985), pp. 25–26.

10. Cf. Heidegger's formulation of this point in *Nietzsche*, vol. 2: *The Eternal Recurrence of the Same*, trans. David Farrell Krell (New York: Harper & Row, 1984), p. 182.

11. Jacques Derrida, *The Truth in Painting*, trans. Geoff Bennington and Ian McLeod (Chicago: University of Chicago Press, 1987), p. 26.

12. Ibid., p. 23.

13. *Selected Letters of Friedrich Nietzsche*, ed. and trans. Christopher Middleton (Chicago: University of Chicago Press, 1969), p. 242.

FIVE

Sartre, Merleau-Ponty, and the Search for a New Ontology of Sight

Martin Jay

But all of a sudden I hear footsteps in the hall. Someone is looking at me! What does this mean?
JEAN-PAUL SARTRE[1]

I would like to see more clearly, but it seems to me that no one sees more clearly.
MAURICE MERLEAU-PONTY[2]

Despite the challenge of Bergson before the First World War and the Surrealists' embrace of Hegel after it, mainstream French philosophy remained in the thrall of neo-Kantian and positivist tendencies until well into the 1930s. In fact, in the broadest sense, it had never been able to throw off many of the fundamental assumptions bequeathed to it by Cartesianism. Among the most stubbornly persistent was its spectatorial and intellectualist epistemology based on a subjective self reflecting on an objective world exterior to it. Here the most zealous guardian of the flame was Léon Brunschvicg, whose dominance at the Sorbonne stretched from 1909 until the German occupation of Paris in 1940.[3]

The story of how a group of young, restless, and extraordinarily gifted thinkers in the interwar years—including Gabriel Marcel, Paul Nizan, Jean Wahl, Jean Hyppolite, Claude Lévi-Strauss, Simone de Beauvoir, and most notably Jean-Paul Sartre and Maurice Merleau-Ponty—rebelled against the hegemony of Brunschvicg and the orthodoxies of Third Republic philosophy has been told too often to repeat here.[4] Their tutelage in Hegelian dialectics in the lectures of Alexander Kojève, rediscovery of history and politics, impatience with Eurocentric models of culture, and search for a philosophy of the concrete to replace the stale abstractions of neo-Kantianism are all now widely appreciated. Less well-known, however, is their radical questioning of the ocularcentric bias of the dominant tradition, which complemented in important ways other French critiques beginning with Bergson. Although in many ways different from Georges Bataille and the Surrealists, whose work in fact they often maligned,[5] Sartre and Merleau-Ponty nonetheless shared with them

a deep-seated suspicion of the Cartesian perspectivalist gaze, which often
extended to the primacy of vision itself.

They also shared no less profound a debt to German critics of ocularcentrism, whose ideas they helped disseminate, if often in creatively garbled form, in France. For the generation of Sartre and Merleau-Ponty,
the main inspiration from across the Rhine came from phenomenology,
in particular the philosophy of Edmund Husserl and Martin Heidegger.
The Husserl discovered by Sartre and Merleau-Ponty in the early 1930s
might not, at first glance, seem very much like a critic of ocularcentrism.
In such works as the *Cartesian Meditations* of 1931,[6] he defined phenomenology as a kind of neo-Cartesianism, concerned with the rigorous scientific investigation of ideas in all their conceptual clarity and distinctness. Husserl, moreover, defended the need to purify philosophy of the
psychological residues he saw lurking even in Descartes in order to become genuinely transcendental. Phenomenology should.be what he
called an "eidetic science," able to gain intuitive insights into essences.
Intuition, contrary to Bergson's use of the concept, could reveal more
than the interior experience of lived temporality. The phenomenological
"reduction" (or *epoché* as he often called it) led back (the Latin word *re-
ducere*) to the source of existence and meaning. By bracketing the "natural standpoint," which takes for granted normal perceptual experience
and identifies reality with the ensemble of empirical "facts," and then
painstakingly describing the data of the consciousness that remained, the
phenomenologist could gain access to a more fundamental level of
reality.

That Husserl chose to call the eidetic intuition a *Wesenschau* (literally a
look into essences) suggests the persistence of ocularcentric premises in
his thought. In fact, as early as 1930, in one of the first French appreci-
ations of his work, Emmanuel Levinas's *Theory of Intuition in Husserl's
Phenomenology,*[7] Husserl's reliance on ocular metaphors in describing intuition and theory was singled out for critique. More recently, in *Speech
and Phenomena*, published in 1967, Derrida criticized Husserl's privileging of the *Augenblick*—the timeless blink of an instant in which the "scene
of ideal objects" appears to consciousness—as complicitous with the
Western metaphysics of presence.[8] And in 1976, Marc Richir, a follower
of Merleau-Ponty, claimed that Husserl's great mistake was the "installation of pure seeing in the position of an absolute overview [*survol*] vis-à-
vis the world."[9]

How then, we must ask, did Husserl help furnish Sartre and Merleau-
Ponty with arguments against ocularcentrism? First, however much
Husserl may have retained a visual bias in the idea of *Wesenschau*, how-
ever steeped his rhetoric in visual metaphors of clarity, he subtly under-

mined the spectatorial distance between viewing subject and viewed object in the Cartesian epistemological tradition. Although he wanted to make phenomenology a science, he was careful to avoid equating science with its Galilean version. For consciousness was not independent of its object, nor was an object a thing standing apart to be viewed from afar; consciousness was always *of* something. This complicated notion of intentionality, which Husserl had adopted from Franz Brentano, may have been cast in terms of a ray or beam emanating from the subject, but it nonetheless suggested that traditional philosophical notions of representation had to be revised.

The mind was not completely distanced from a world which was represented to it as images in its metaphorical eye. Nor was it sufficient to trust the physiological experience of seeing one aspect of an object, for the intended object transcended any of its specific profiles or representations. Even Bergson's distinction between intuited experiences of internal *durée* and intellectual knowledge of objects in external space failed to register the primordial unity of all consciousness prior to its dissociation. Husserl's famous call to return to "the things themselves" meant regaining the experience of the intertwining of subject and object, which was lost in all dualistic philosophies.

Second, although Husserl's early work sought to defend the concept of the transcendental ego, which might be construed as a residual version of the Cartesian *cogito,* his later work, most notably *The Crisis of European Sciences and Transcendental Phenomenology* of 1936,[10] put the stress on the prereflective *Lebenswelt* (lifeworld) instead. Here both the cultural/historical variations of everyday life (the *doxa* of opinion prior to the *episteme* of science) and the lived body played a central role. Although most commentators deny that the *Lebenswelt* simply replaced the transcendental ego in Husserl's thinking, Merleau-Ponty in particular was able to seize on it as the means to strip phenomenology of its Cartesian residues.[11] Now phenomenology could mean something besides searching for pure essences through eidetic intuition; it could mean as well exploring impure existence, which resisted reduction to the object of a gaze, phenomenological or otherwise.

That Merleau-Ponty was able to interpret Husserl in this way was in part made possible by the more explicit critique of visual primacy already present in Heidegger's phenomenology, which also entered the French debates in the 1930s. For all his fascination with certain Hellenic models, Heidegger can be construed as recovering the Hebraic emphasis on hearing God's word rather than seeing His manifestations.[12] Whether or not Heidegger's restoration of hearing can solely be derived from Old Testament taboos on graven images—his general attitude toward the Jews was, to put it mildly, less than admiring—he was certainly critical of many of the aspects of Greek thought that permit it to be called the fount of Western ocularcentrism. The Apollonian impulse in Greek art, with its privileging of beautiful form, and the visually oriented concept of *theōria,* were among his favorite targets.[13] His hostility to the heliocentric rationalism of Platonism was no less explicit, as was his rejection of the dualism of subject and object entailed by privileging distantiating vision. Like Bergson, although with important differences, Heidegger bemoaned the neglect of temporality in Western metaphysics since Heraclitus in favor of a spatializing ontology based on the synchronicity of the fixating gaze.

Heidegger's critique of the ocularcentrism of post-Socratic Greek thought extended as well to the dominant Western philosophical and scientific tradition:

> In *theōria* transformed into *contemplatio,* there comes to the fore the impulse, already prepared in Greek thinking, of a looking-at that sunders and compartmentalizes. A type of encroaching advance by successive interrelated steps toward that which is to be grasped by the eye makes itself normative in knowing.[14]

A further step occurred when *theōria* was conflated with observation, which in German (*Betrachten*) contains residues of the Latin *tractare,* to manipulate and work over. The science based on visual manipulation was thus anything but disinterested.

Contrasting the early Greek attitude of wonder, which lets things be, with that of curiosity, which is based on the desire to know how they function, Heidegger linked the latter with the hypertrophy of the visual. In *Being and Time,* he wrote: "the basic state of sight shows itself in a peculiar tendency of Being which belongs to everydayness—the tendency towards 'seeing'. We designate this tendency by the term 'curiosity'."[15] The ultimate triumph of curiosity over wonder was an essential component in the hegemony of the technological world-view in the modern era.[16] Technology was deeply problematic for Heidegger because it carried to an extreme the distancing of subject and object, which had come into its own in modern philosophy with Descartes. It drew on the mode of relating to Being he called *Vorhandenheit* (presence-at-hand), which posited something in front to be seen, rather than *Zuhandenheit* (readiness-to-hand), which meant using something practically without visualizing it first. For Heidegger, the tendency latent in Plato's doctrine of Being as *eidos* became fully manifest in what he called the modern "age of the world picture." So fateful was this development that he could claim that "the fundamental event of the modern age is the conquest of the world as picture."[17] It was so profoundly significant because it facilitated the birth of the modern humanist subject, who stood apart from a world he surveyed and manipulated. Even when the sophist Protagoras had declared that "man was the measure of all things," he was still operating with a concept of truth that was not yet representational, not yet based on the correspondence of object and mental image. Only the modern age had allowed what Heidegger called enframing (*Ge-stell*) to gain full sway, turning the world into a "standing reserve" for arrogant human domination. What such an attitude forgot was that "world is never an object that stands before us and can be seen. World is the ever-nonobjective to which we are subject as long as the paths of birth and death, blessing and curse transport us into Being."[18]

Heidegger's critique of the primacy of vision is so sweeping that many commentators have been led, as we noted above, to stress his privileging of the ear instead.[19] There can be no doubt that in many ways this claim is valid, especially if we recall his growing fascination with poetry, namely Hölderlin's, in the 1930s, but it is not the entire story. For at times, Heidegger also employed visual metaphors of his own to evoke his alternative to the dominant metaphysical/scientific tradition, metaphors which have even encouraged some commentators to place him in the Romantic lineage of visionary innocence.[20]

Heidegger's debt to Husserl's "phenomenological seeing" meant that the road to ontology, the revelation of Being, was through an uncovering of what was hidden.[21] "Because *logos* lets something be seen," he wrote in *Being and Time*, "it can *therefore* be true or false. But everything depends on staying clear of any concept of truth construed in the sense of 'correspondence' or 'accordance.'"[22] If such a concept of truth as revelation or unhiddenness (*aletheia*) rather than correspondence could be defended, so too could a more attractive notion of *techne* than that associated with the modern technological world view. "There was once a time when it was not technology alone that bore the name *techne*," Heidegger claimed. "Once that revealing which brings forth truth into the splendor of radiant appearance was also called *techne*. . . . The poetical brings the true into the splendor of what Plato in the *Phaedrus* calls *to ekphanestaton*, that which shines forth most purely."[23]

Such a shining forth took place in what Heidegger came to call a *Lichtung* or forest clearing, in which Being discloses itself. "What is light in the sense of being free and open," Heidegger cautioned, "has nothing in common with the adjective 'light' which means 'bright,' neither linguistically nor factually. . . . Still, it is possible that a factual relation between the two exists. Light can stream into the clearing, into its openness, and let brightness play with darkness in it. But light never first creates openness. Rather, light presupposes openness."[24] Here the thinking

subject does not cast his light, the searchlight of curiosity, onto mute and
opaque objects, but rather Being is allowed to manifest itself to *Dasein*.
Traditional philosophy, he complained, "does speak about the light of
reason, but does not heed the opening of Being. The *lumen naturale*, the
light of reason, throws light only on openness. . . . No outward appearance without light—Plato already knew this. But there is no light and no
brightness without the opening."[25]

A key difference between these two modes of vision, one which we
might call epistemological, the other ontological, concerns the spectatorial distance of the former in comparison with the embeddedness of the
latter. David Levin captures Heidegger's argument about the shortcom-
ings of epistemological vision:

> The visible deeply *objects* to our habitual objectification; it will not fully give
> itself, will not wholly yield itself, to our desire. The most extreme evidence
> in which this is visible appears when we engage in an exercise in intensive
> staring: "a fixed staring at something that is purely present-at-hand (*vorhan-
> den*)." In German, the word which we translate as "re-presentation" is
> *Vorstellung*. Now, this word signifies a gesture of setting down (*stellen*) in
> front (*vor*), a gesture which corresponds to the "frontal" ontology of our
> modern, nihilistic world. I submit that the concealed essence of "re-presen-
> tation" begins to appear through this interpretation, and that it is, in a
> word, *staring*.[26]

The more benign version of sight, which refuses to stare aggressively
at its objects, is dependent on a primordial opening to Being which is
prior to the very differentiation of the senses. After the differentiation,
it is maintained by what in *Being and Time* Heidegger calls *Umsicht*, prereflective, circumspect vision. Here the viewer is situated within a visual
field, not outside it; his horizon is limited by what he can see around
him. Moreover, his relation to the context in which he is embedded is
nurturant, not controlling: "Letting something be encountered is primarily circumspective; it is not just sensing something, or staring at it. It implies circumspective concern."[27]

One way to define the opposition between the two visual modes in
Heidegger is suggested by Levin's distinction between the "assertoric"
and "aletheic gaze."[28] The former is abstracted, monocular, inflexible,
unmoving, rigid, ego-logical and exclusionary; the latter is multiple,
aware of its context, inclusionary, horizontal, and caring. Although
Heidegger deeply regretted the power of the former in Western thought
and practice, he nonetheless held out some hope for the reinstatement
of the latter. He was thus never simply hostile to sight per se, but only to
the variant that had dominated Western metaphysics for millenia. In the
French reception of his ideas, complicated by the spotty availability of his

texts, both dimensions of Heidegger's thought were not always equally appreciated. While Merleau-Ponty favored what might be called an "aletheic gaze," Sartre was far more hostile to any redemptive notion of vision.

Sartre's critique of ocularcentrism was especially powerful because he conflated many of the complaints expressed by other critics into one relentless, overwhelming indictment. Not only, he claimed, does the hypertrophy of the visual lead to a problematic epistemology, abet the domination of nature, and support the hegemony of space over time, but it also produces profoundly disturbing intersubjective relations and the construction of a dangerously inauthentic version of the self. Sartre's interrogation of the eye thus included social, psychological, and indeed existential dimensions, which he invariably described in the most frighteningly negative terms.

Sartre was profoundly curious in the sense of that term defined by Heidegger in *Being and Time*: he passionately wanted to penetrate the world's secrets and reveal them to his pitiless gaze. But Sartre was no less sensitive to the dangers of visually incited curiosity, both for the gazer and the object of the gaze. The result was a personal and intellectual dialectic of attraction and repulsion, avowal and denial, rivaling that of the Rousseau famously portrayed by Jean Starobinski.[29]

Sartre's obsessive hostility to vision—by one estimate, there were over 7,000 references to "the look" in his work[30]—was so unremitting that it has been tempting to account for it as a personal problem. As in the case of Bataille, whose scatological and violent preoccupations also invite speculations of this kind, Sartre's ocularphobia has been interpreted in biographical terms, including even the impact of his physical make-up. And far more than Bataille, whose career was pursued in relative obscurity, Sartre solicited such interpretations by deliberately exposing himself to public view.

As early as 1952, Sartre's phenomenology of sight was subjected to a psychoanalytic reading by René Held, who claimed that his celebrated treatment of "the look" in *Being and Nothingness* disclosed less about its ostensible subject matter than about its author.[31] Sartre's frightening description of visual interaction, he charged, demonstrated extreme castration anxiety, a narcissistic fear of splitting the body from the self, and masochistic fantasies about enslavement to dominating figures. In 1976, François George, less beholden than Held to the Freudianism Sartre himself so distrusted, probed what he called *le regard absolu* in Sartre's work.[32] Having the benefit of reading Sartre's childhood reminiscences, *The Words,* which had appeared in 1964, George was able to discern the

paternal behind the divine eye. Or more precisely, he was able to see the
residue of the dead father's gaze—Jean-Baptiste Sartre having died when
his son was only fifteen months old—in the imagination of the orphan.
An orphan, he noted, feels especially guilty in the sight of his absent parents. "It is a question of an imaginary look, of a look supposed to be cast
on the child by the father, condemning him at the same time to aban-
donment."[33] Although Sartre loudly denied that his father's death was
traumatic,[34] its residues were obvious to George: "the look is always absolute, it emanates from a pitiful, dead transcendence, which makes reciprocity unthinkable."[35]

The Words in fact provides considerable material for such interpretations of Sartre's visual obsessions. Often, he recalled, he had felt defined
by being caught in a field of gazes: "My truth, my character, and my
name were in the hands of adults. I had learned to see myself through
their eyes. . . . When they were not present, they left their gaze behind,
and it mingled with the light. I would run and jump across that gaze,
which preserves my nature as a model grandson."[36] So bewitched was he
by the experience, Sartre even believed that he was the handsome boy
his family insisted he was. "Dozens of photos are taken of me, and my
mother retouches them with colored pencils . . . my mouth is puffed
with hypocritical arrogance: I know my worth."[37] The inevitable disillusionment that followed created in him, so it seems, a lifelong distrust for
the illusions of sight and the treachery of definition by the gaze of others. His actual ugliness, he ruefully concluded, was "my negative principle, the quicklime in which the wonderful child was dissolved."[38]

Its implications are probed with great finesse in the most extensive biographical account of his visual obsessions, Alain Buisine's *Laideurs de
Sartre (Sartre's Uglinesses)*.[39] Divided into three sections, "The Public
Philosopher," "The Squinting (*louche*) Philosopher,"[40] and "The Blind
Philosopher," the book examines a series of variations on the ocular
theme in Sartre. The first concerns his drive to be fully transparent to his
audience, which recalls the exhibitionist openness to the multitude
sought by Rousseau two centuries earlier. Sartre's desire for perfect
transparency, like that of Rousseau's, was thwarted by obstacles he could
not fully overcome. "There reigned in my spirit," Sartre masochistically
confessed, "a pitiless clarity; it was an operating theater, hygienic, without shadows, without dark corners, without microbes under a cold light.
And yet, as intimacy doesn't allow itself to be completely banished, there
was nonetheless beyond, or rather in the sincerity of public confession, a
type of bad faith in me . . ."[41] Even while he was struggling to reveal himself to the world, the reputation of Sartre as master intellectual, celebrity,
even institution, got in the way. Buisine concludes that Sartre came to

understand that the very project of total transparency was inherently unrealizable, for if all subjects were totally transparent to each other, then there would be nothing strictly speaking left to see. Indeed, Sartre's early decision to dedicate himself to writing, to words, was a dim anticipation of this realization. As he put it in his autobiography, "I was born of writing. Before that, there was only a play of mirrors."[42] Although Sartre came to bemoan the sterility of mere writing in comparison with the action he advocated during his most militant period, he never wanted to return to the hall of mirrors in which he had been trapped as a child.

Mirrors, in fact, were fraught with danger for Sartre because they provided reminders of the bad faith involved in accepting the look of the other as true. "The mirror had taught me," he confessed, "what I had always known: I was horribly natural. I have never gotten over that."[43] In the second section of his book, Buisine explores the implications of Sartre's wall-eyed squint, which developed after he left the paradise of his family's idealizing gaze. Not only would looking in the mirror disabuse one of the mistake of identifying with the other's gaze, but it would also provide evidence of the meaninglessness of one's own corporeal existence. Commenting on the scene in Sartre's novel *Nausea,* in which the hero Roquentin examines his face, Buisine notes that for Sartre, "regarding oneself for a long time in the glass, the petrified subject assists in the obscene return of a flesh which is beyond sense, a literally insignificant return of the organic and even the inorganic, of the geologic, of the primitive, of an upsurge of the aquatic in the reflection of the face."[44]

In his final section, Buisine speculates about the implications of Sartre's near blindness at the end of his life. Discussing his works on painters like Tintoretto and Titian, he contends that Sartre's disgust for color is due to its being an experience only available to the eyes. He further argues that Sartre's disdain for abstract painting, for example that of Picasso, was due to its lack of tactility, of weight. And he concludes that "probably never has a critic of art denied and denigrated the power of the eye as much as Jean-Paul Sartre."[45] His final image is that of the elderly Sartre, now almost totally sightless, sitting in a hotel in Venice, the most visually stimulating of cities, comforting himself by listening to music on the radio.

The persuasiveness of these psychological and biographical treatments of Sartre's highly charged attitude toward vision depends not only on the plausibility of psychoanalytic explanations, but also on the trustworthiness of Sartre's own recollections. The author of *The Words* may well have projected his later theories back onto his childhood experiences. But however we understand their origins, there can be no doubt that the results found a ready audience, including figures like Lacan, Foucault, and Irigaray, already primed to be suspicious of the hegemony of the eye.

What precisely was the nature of Sartre's critique? It took, in fact, many forms. Although Sartre was deeply indebted to Husserl's phenomenology, he immediately detected problems with the idea of a transcendental ego, which he interpreted in visual terms. In Sartre's first major work, *The Transcendence of the Ego*, written in 1936, he complained that Husserl's strong notion of an "I" introduced opacity into consciousness. By positing a self-reflecting ego, "one congeals consciousness, one darkens it. Consciousness is then no longer a spontaneity; it bears within itself the germ of opaqueness."[46] Instead, true consciousness was pure translucence, unburdened by positivity. Although later Sartre would nuance his categorical opposition between transparent consciousness and the alien opacity introduced into it from without, in the first phase of his work it reigned supreme.

If, however, pure consciousness was understood as transparency rather than opacity, how can we say Sartre was simply antivisual? Wasn't he merely contrasting a good vision, which sees through things, with a bad one which reaches no further than their opaque surfaces? The answer appeared in his next two works of philosophy, which dealt with the issue of images and the imagination, *Imagination: A Psychological Critique* (1936) and *The Psychology of Imagination* (1940).[47] Here Sartre posited a radical difference between sense perception and the imagination. Like Bergson, he criticized the belief that images were only likenesses of external objects reflected in consciousness. "We pictured consciousness," he wrote, "as a place peopled with small likenesses and these likenesses were the images. No doubt but that this misconception arises from our habit of thinking in space and in terms of space. This we shall call: *the illusion of immanence*."[48] Philosophers like Hume, who confused images with sense data, were wrong; for the former were best understood as acts which intend an object that is either absent or doesn't exist. Here Husserl was a better guide than Bergson, who lacked a positive understanding of intentionality.[49]

For Sartre, although images may draw on analogies with objects of perception, they themselves are unreal. In fact, imagination is precisely that active function of consciousness which transcends or nihilates the reality of the perceived world. As such, it serves as a model for the negation and lack that Sartre would soon identify with the "for-itself" in *Being and Nothingness*. What is vital for our purposes is that Sartre distinguished images from perception, visual or otherwise, and identified them with the intentionality of action instead. As a result, he was able to describe consciousness less in terms of visual transparency than in those of pure nihilating action. Although nonperceptual images teach us nothing about the external world, their very "no-thing-ness" or invisibility suggests a critical link to human freedom, as Sartre interpreted it. In short, the Sartre who could escape from the play of mirrors and the defining power of adult gazes by immersing himself in words, now posited a radical break between sight and consciousness, which directly challenged the ocularcentric tradition's equation of the "I" and the "eye."

Before Sartre spelled out the full ontological implications of the new view of consciousness in *Being and Nothingness,* he anticipated certain of its arguments in *Nausea,* the literary work published in 1938 that elevated him from an esoteric philosopher to a full-fledged culture hero.[50] Here too, visual themes play a prominent role. Implicitly drawing on Heidegger's distinction between *Zuhandenheit* and *Vorhandenheit,* Sartre contrasted tactile with visual experience. As Alain Robbe-Grillet notes in his essay on the novel, "the first three perceptions recorded at the beginning of the book are all gained by the sense of touch, not that of sight. The objects which provoke revelation are, in effect, respectively, the pebble on the beach, the bolt of a door, the hand of the Self-Taught Man."[51] Sartre thus anticipated his later political defense of "dirty hands" against the clean hands of the nonengaged, contemplative observer above the fray.[52] But now what made such hands superior was their ability to reveal existential truths, unavailable to the eye, rather than political ones.

Sartre's critique of visual distance is perhaps most notably expressed in the celebrated scene in which Roquentin confronts the source of his existential nausea by understanding the meaningless thingness of the root of a chestnut tree. "Even when I looked at things," Roquentin muses, "I was miles from dreaming that they existed: they looked like scenery to me. I picked them up in my hands, they served me as tools, I foresaw their resistance. But all that happened on the surface."[53] In touching and smelling the black root, he realizes that vision by itself is insufficient: "I did not simply *see* this black; sight is an abstract invention, an idea that has been cleaned up, simplified, one of man's ideas. That black there, amorphous, weakly presence, overflowed sight, smell and taste."[54]

His epiphanous experience leaves Roquentin with the feeling "there was nothing more, my eyes were empty and I was spellbound by my deliverance."[55] But then sight once again intrudes, as he notices the movement of the tree's branches: "No more than three seconds and all my hopes were swept away. Viewing these hesitant branches groping around like blind men, I could not succeed in grasping the process of coming into existence."[56] Even shutting his eyes doesn't help, since "the images,

forewarned, leaped up and filled my closed eyes with existences: existence is a fullness from which man can never get away. Strange images.
They represent a multitude of things. Not real things; other things which
looked like real things."[57] Here not even the derealizing power of the
imagination serves to release Roquentin from his torment. For the imagination, he realizes, is parasitic on the prior existence of meaningless matter, which comes to us primarily through sight. "To imagine nothingness," Roquentin laments, "you had to be there already, in the midst of
the World, eyes wide open and alive; nothingness was only an idea in my
head, an existing idea floating in this immensity; this nothingness had
not come *before* existence."[58]

One reading of Roquentin's struggle to make sense of his nausea
might conclude that the most basic prereflective level of human interaction is essentially tactile or visceral, as we blindly muck about in the
slimy, viscous reality in which we are immersed. Visual reflection, consciousness in the mode of *Vorhandenheit*, then tries to master this experience by turning it into conceptual ideas, finding essences where there
is nothing but brute existence. But these efforts fail to overcome the
meaningless, absurd thingness of the world. Shifting metaphors, Sartre is
thus able to claim that ideas cannot "digest" reality. Hence the nausea of
existence.

But another reading, which recalls Roquentin's experience in the mirror mentioned above, would claim that sight too can be an organ capable
of disabusing us of the fallacies of essentializing conceptualization. For if
we can see our ugliness or the sheer thingness of our bodies, we are prevented from accepting the idealizing images foisted on us by the flatter-
ing gaze of others. Rather than being only the means of essentializing an
absurd existence, vision can also reveal the excess of "thatness" over the
"whatness" that is the source of human anguish. However construed, vision thus provides us with no way out of the dilemmas of our alienated
existence.

Thus far, we have identified three main manifestations of Sartre's critique of sight. The first is his rejection of an opaque transcendental ego
intruding into the translucency of pure, active consciousness. The second is his radical separation of perception, visual or otherwise, from the
de-realizing, nihilating imagination, which proves in *Nausea* not to be so
radically pure after all. And the third is the failed attempt of vision to impose concepts and ideas on the recalcitrant meaninglessness of the material world, which is more directly available to our other senses, or perhaps better put, is a primordial reality prior to the very differentiation of
the senses. Vision is thus insufficient as a means to conceive the subject,
or what he will call the "for-itself," and no less problematic in its attempts
to conceptualize the object, or the "in-itself."

The opposition between "for-itself" and "in-itself" was most clearly developed in *Being and Nothingness: An Essay on Phenomenological Ontology* (1943), where Sartre reprised all of these themes and fleshed them out by offering the detailed ontology absent from his earlier work. In addition, he provided a profoundly troubling discussion of intersubjective and intrasubjective interactions based on the exchange of gazes. Here Hegel's celebrated master-slave dialectic, interpreted by Kojève to maximize its reciprocal violence rather than the mutual recognition stressed by others, was recast in the register of sight, with the horrifying results that invited the psychological explanations detailed above.

For Sartre, the domination of the object world by a distant subject, facilitated by the hegemony of sight, became a model as well for intersubjective relations. Departing from Husserl, whose treatment of personal interaction depended on reciprocal empathy, Sartre emphasized the hostile contest of wills between competing subjects.[59] Explicitly rejecting Heidegger's irenic notion of *Mit-sein* (co-being), in favor of conflict as the original meaning of being-for-others,[60] Sartre elevated his own experience as the victim of the look—or what he recalled as such—into something very much like a universal human condition.

Addressing the hoary philosophical question of how we know the existence of other selves, other interiorities, Sartre contended that "my apprehension of the Other in the world as *probably being* a man refers to my permanent possibility of *being-seen-by-him*; that is, to the permanent possibility that a subject who sees me may be substituted for the object seen by me. 'Being-seen-by-the-Other' is the *truth* of 'seeing-the-Other.'"[61] There is always an oscillation between these two modes of relating to the Other. Although it can be produced by other perceptual experiences, such as the sound of footsteps or the movement of a curtain, "what *most often* manifests a look is the convergence of two ocular globes in my direction."[62]

When this happens, the uncanny experience of being looked at completely blots out the possibility of returning the gaze.

Significantly, Sartre distinguishes between the eye as the object of a look and the look itself. "It is never when eyes are looking at you that you can find them beautiful or ugly, that you can remark on their color," he writes. "The Other's look hides his eyes; he seems to go *in front of them*."[63] This inability is tied, Sartre claims, to the incommensurability between perception and imagination, which he had examined in *The Psychology of Imagination*. "This is because to perceive is to *look at,* and to apprehend a look is not to apprehend a look-as-object in the world (unless the look is not directed upon us); it is to be conscious of *being looked at.*"[64] But now, perception is understood as an act in the sense that it transforms the object of the gaze, whereas imagination is identified less with derealizing freedom than with the paralyzing internalization of the Other's gaze.

The nonreciprocity between look and eye, between being the subject and object of the gaze, is in fact related to a fundamental struggle for power. For the one who casts the look is always a subject and the one who is its target is always turned into an object. Or at least, objectification is the *telos* of the look, even if it comes up against the ultimate barrier of the "for-itself's" constitutive nothingness. That fundamental property of the subject is, however, threatened when the self identifies with the Other's look. Here the Cartesian self-reflecting *cogito* is replaced by a self that is constituted by the gaze of the Other: *l'Autre me voit, donc je suis,* as François George nicely puts it.[65]

Taking into itself the opacity of an object which contradicts its pure transparency, the self becomes like the mistaken notion of the transcendental ego posited by Husserl. Sartre describes the process in his celebrated vignette of the voyeur caught looking through the keyhole. Whereas, before being caught, the viewer is a pure, acting consciousness unself-consciously experiencing the emotions, such as jealousy, that accompany it, once seen, he is turned into something else: "first of all, I now exist as *myself* for my unreflective consciousness . . . I see *myself* because *somebody* sees me."[66] Second, the result is colored by a new emotion, that of shame, which is "the *recognition* of the fact that I *am* indeed that object which the Other is looking at and judging."[67] Shame can perhaps be called the transcendental emotional *a priori* of Sartre's universe of threatening gazes, so pervasive is it in his description of the result of being seen.

But the stakes are higher than mere embarrassment or humiliation, for it is human freedom itself which is undermined by the look of the Other. "I grasp the Other's look at the very center of my *act* as the solidification and alienation of my own possibilities. . . . The Other as a look is only that—my transcendence transcended. Of course I still *am* my possibilities in the mode of non-thetic consciousness (of) these possibilities. But at the same time the look alienates them from me."[68] Like Bergson, Sartre sees the loss of human freedom partly in terms of visual spatialization: "The Other's look confers spatiality upon me. To apprehend oneself as looked-at is to apprehend oneself as a spatializing-spatialized."[69] Even when he adds that it is temporalizing as well, he claims that the time it imposes on the "for-itself" is that of simultaneity, which denies the forward thrust of individual potentiality.

The sinister dialectic of gazes also plays itself out with reference to our corporeal self-consciousness. When the body is on display to the gaze of the Other, it becomes a fallen object, which is the original meaning of our sense of shame at being caught naked. "To put on clothes," Sartre contends, "is to hide one's object-state: it is to claim the right of seeing without being seen; that is, to be pure subject. That is why the Biblical symbol of the fall after the original sin is the fact that Adam and Eve 'know that they are naked.'"[70] Here too, the internalization of the Other's shame-engendering look produces a disastrous outcome, as the body loses its *ur*-function as the agency of human action and becomes an object of the other's vision for oneself as well.

The social interactions promoted by vision as Sartre understood it were no less problematic. A salient example was the inability to create a meaningful community, which in the Hegelian terminology he adopted at the same time as he was learning phenomenology was called the project of totalization. Indeed, from *Being and Nothingness* to the *Critique of Dialectical Reason* (1960), if not to the very end of his life, Sartre was haunted by the question of achieving a totalistic knowledge of reality (or at least of the social world), and the concomitant possibility of a normative totalization overcoming the various alienations of human existence.[71] Totalizing cognition and totalizing action were closely related, as dialectical sides of the same coin, although how closely Sartre did not realize until his embrace of Marxism after the war.

The primary impediment to knowing the whole, as Heidegger had also pointed out in his discussion of *Umsicht*, was the situated nature of our individual vantage point, which could not see beyond a limited horizon of knowledge. It is impossible to transcend this specificity, Sartre insisted, "because I exist as myself on the foundation of this totality and to the extent that I am engaged in it."[72] Indeed, not even a God's-eye view would provide a perspective on the whole.[73] In his most Marxist moments in the 1950s and 1960s, Sartre never found a way to overcome this pessimistic conclusion; no metasubject able to totalize the whole and see its totalization, such as the proletariat posited by Hegelian Marxists like Lukács, was ever possible. Without even Heidegger's faith in alethetic vision, the revelation of the truth of Being in a primal *Lichtung*, Sartre resolutely refused to posit a redemptive notion of the visual.

If such an outcome was denied on the macro-scopic level of knowing the totality, it was no less rejected on the micro-scopic level of human relations at their putatively most reciprocal: the interaction of lovers. Not even their mutual glances of tenderness, captured in the ambiguous meaning of the word "regard," can overcome the frightening dialectic of subject and object posited by Sartre.[74] Desire, he claims, is always the yearning to possess the subjectivity of the other, appropriating him or her as flesh. Although the expression of desire is often tactile, coming through the caress, it has an inevitably visual component as well. "I am possessed by the Other," Sartre writes, "the Other's look fashions my body in its nakedness, causes it to be born, sculptures it, produces it as it *is*, sees it as I shall never see it. The Other holds a secret—the secret of what I am."[75] Lovers, for Sartre, are engaged in a mutual dialectic of possession, which goes beyond the Hegelian master-slave interaction because "the lover wants the beloved's freedom *first and foremost*,"[76] wants, that is, to have it entirely for himself.

The result is a series of moves and countermoves, which can only be described in terms of sado-masochism acted out through a contest of gazes. But the sado-masochistic dialectic of the look is doomed to failure for both lovers, as there is no way to reconcile human freedom with the desire to possess. To make his point, Sartre invokes the passage from Faulkner's *Light in August* in which the castrated and dying black man, Christmas, looks at his executioners "with his eyes open and empty of everything save consciousness . . . for a long moment, he looked up at them with peaceful and unfathomable and unbearable eyes."[77] And he concludes: "here once more we are referred from the being-in-the-act-of-looking to the being-looked-at; we have not got out of the circle."[78]

That Sartre never felt we can get out of the circle is amply demonstrated by the many other invocations of the visual in his subsequent work, literary, critical, and political. Perhaps its most sustained application came in his remarkable 1952 study of the writer Jean Genet.[79] The original, defining moment in Genet's personal formation is described in the terms of the voyeur at the keyhole in *Being and Nothingness*. As the ten-year-old boy unself-consciously reaches into a drawer, he is suddenly *"caught in the act.* Someone has entered and is watching him. Beneath this gaze the child comes to himself. He who was not yet anyone suddenly becomes Jean Genet. . . . A voice declares publicly: 'You're a thief.'"[80] Although the labeling is verbal, Sartre leaves no doubt what came first: "Pinned by a look, a butterfly fixed to a cork, he is naked, everyone can see him and spit on him. The gaze of the adults is a *constituent power* which has transformed him into a *constituted nature.*"[81]

Not only is Genet condemned to his identity as a thief by the look of the other, so too his sexual self-image is fixed by visual objectification, indeed penetration: "Sexually, Genet is first of all a raped child. This first rape was the gaze of the other, who took him by surprise, penetrated him, transformed him forever into an object."[82] Ultimately, Genet came to take on these objectifications willingly, even heroically, as his own identity. "What he desires is to be manipulated passively by the Other so as to become an object in his own eyes."[83] Although on one level a surrender, on another level this decision allowed Genet to come to the same bleak conclusion reached by Sartre himself in *Being and Nothing-*

ness: "Exhausted but not appeased, Genet gazes at the beautiful, tranquil appearance which has taken shape again beyond his reach, and he concludes: 'Love is despair.' But we now know that this despair is willed and that he first rejected the only chance of salvation through love: reciprocity."[84] His homosexual relationships may have once been an attempt to communicate with other men, but Genet, according to Sartre, realizes the failure of such efforts: "He has gone out of himself, he has gone toward his fellow man and encountered only appearances. He now returns to himself. He is alone beneath the fixed light which has not ceased to traverse him."[85]

Genet is thus far superior to those like the Surrealists who seek visionary redemption. Although not himself attracted by Genet's personal alternative, Sartre clearly identifies with his attempt to deal with the dilemmas of his existence through words, through exercising the same literary imagination to which the young Sartre himself had turned for relief. "The glamorous word repeats, while effacing it, the original crisis: it too hits him in the face and reveals the existence of Another, of a Gaze directed at Genet; but this Other is kindly, for it is the I-who-is-Another, it is Genet himself."[86] Significantly, the "non-Apollonian" poetry Genet writes has nothing to do with the traditional apotheosis of formal beauty: "Genet's art does not aim, will never aim, at making us see. . . . The avowed aim of his magnifying attempts is to annihilate the real, to disintegrate vision."[87] Thus, he is the opposite of Breton, who tries to use words to give us a revelatory vision of the Word; Genet instead uses language to nihilate the real, to deny the very possibility of any higher reality to be revealed. "Genet's poems flee from him into the consciousness of the Other, he writes them blindly, in the darkness. They deserve, much more than do those of Henri Thomas, to be called 'Blind Man's Work.'"[88]

"Blind Man's Work" might also be the motto for Sartre's own relentless critique of the gaze. Not all French phenomenologists, however, were as ruthlessly hostile as he, even if they shared his rejection of the discredited Cartesian perspectivalist scopic regime. Paradoxically, Sartre's radical distinction between the "for-itself" and the "in-self," as well as his categorical opposition between perception and imagination, came themselves to be faulted as expressions of a residual debt to Descartes's dualism. Instead, Heidegger's notion of a Being prior to the split between subject and object and his belief in a social *Mitsein* more fundamental than the interminable conflicts posited by Sartre found a ready hearing. Could they be reconciled with a more benign notion of vision than that found in Sartre's playhouse of disillusioning mirrors and crossfire of wounding gazes? Could a new ontology of vision replace the pernicious spectatorial epistemology, that all phenomenologists found so wanting? Answers to these questions were sought and sought again in the work of Maurice Merleau-Ponty. In fact, if any serious philosophical attempt to check the momentum of the antiocularcentric discourse in France can be located, it would thus be his remarkable exploration of the "madness of vision,"[89] to which we now must turn.

Lacking Sartre's compulsive need for confessional self-transparency, Merleau-Ponty left no autobiographical reflections comparable to *The Words*.[90] Despite the loss of his father during the First World War, when Merleau-Ponty was six, he seems to have had a relatively secure and happy childhood, free from the visually induced mortifications apparently suffered by the young Sartre.[91] If his personal sense of being victimized and objectified by the gaze of others was less intense than Sartre's, it is not surprising that his work presented a far less bleak analysis of vision's ontological as well as social implications. In fact, Merleau-Ponty's meditations on the visual, every bit as obsessive and incessant as Sartre's, came to conclusions that seem diametrically opposed to those of his friend. His version of phenomenology may thus plausibly be called a heroic attempt to reaffirm the nobility of vision on new and firmer grounds than those provided by the discredited Cartesian perspectivalist tradition.

And yet, even in his case, it can be demonstrated that the suspicions and doubts plaguing other twentieth-century French critics of ocularcentrism ultimately surfaced. Although many later commentators, such as Lyotard and Irigaray, would condemn him for being too hopeful about redeeming the visual, certain anticipations of their qualms can be discerned in his work as well. Merleau-Ponty thus occupies a pivotal place in any narrative of the French critique of visual hegemony. Registering the collapse of the dominant Cartesian perspectivalist scopic regime, he attempted to defend an alternative philosophy of the visual, which would have beneficial social implications as well. But his project, cut short by his untimely death at the age of fifty-three, was never satisfactorily completed. That it was almost universally read as a failure by the generation that followed suggests how powerful the accumulated force of the antiocularcentric discourse had become by the time of his departure from the scene in 1961.

Merleau-Ponty's fascination with perception in general and vision in particular was evident at the very outset of his career, even before the impact of Husserl on his thought. In 1933, he drew up a thesis proposal called "On the Nature of Perception," which disputed Brunschvicg's contention that the world of sensible perception was ultimately reducible to intellectual relations and scientific knowledge.[92] Here his main theoretical inspiration came from Gestalt psychology, recently introduced to France by Aron Gurwitsch, and Anglo-American philosophical "realism," rather than from the phenomenology to which he was so decisively drawn shortly thereafter. That event took place when he encountered Husserl's *Crisis of the Empirical Sciences and Transcendental Phenomenology* in 1936, which led him to devour the rest of Husserl's published work and seek out unpublished manuscripts in the newly created archive in Louvain, Belgium. At about the same time, he became familiar with Heidegger's version of phenomenology, which would have an increasingly powerful impact on his ruminations about the visual, and much else as well, in the decades to come.

Although Merleau-Ponty's preoccupations remained obstinately consistent throughout his career, justifying Sartre's remark that he was "always digging at the same place,"[93] his development is generally divided into two major phases.[94] The first, whose most notable achievements were *The Structure of Behavior*, published in 1942, and *The Phenomenology of Perception*, which appeared three years later, expressed his most optimistic hopes in the possibility of a post-Cartesian philosophy grounded in perception.[95] After an interregnum, filled principally by his meditations on history, Marxism, and contemporary politics,[96] Merleau-Ponty returned to his earlier philosophical concerns. In several of the essays appearing in *Signs* in 1960, in "The Eye and the Mind" of 1961, and the posthumously published, uncompleted manuscript known as *The Visible and the Invisible*, he deepened and problematized the analysis of the issues he had treated in the 1930s and early 1940s.[97]

In a report he wrote for his candidacy to the Collège de France in 1952, Merleau-Ponty himself distinguished between the phases of his development in the following terms: "My first two works sought to restore the world of perception. My works in preparation aim to show how communication with others, and thought, take up and go beyond the realm of perception which initiated us to the truth."[98] To what extent, we have to ask, was his recognition that the mere restoration of perception alone would not provide us with access to "the truth" a subtle departure from the assumption that the nobility of sight could be renewed after the collapse of Cartesianism? What effect did his interest in intersubjective communication and what he called the "prose of the world"[99] have on his earlier celebration of perception? How significant was his assimilation of psychoanalytic and linguistic motifs, which were to become even more influential in France after his death, in the decline of his faith in a phenomenology of perception as a sufficient foundation for a new ontology? In short, did the ambiguities that were never resolved in his thought work against his apparent intentions and inadvertently contribute to the continuing crisis of ocularcentrism?

Merleau-Ponty's first sustained effort to grapple with the enigmas of perception, *The Structure of Behavior,* was published during the war, but completed in 1938, when he had only haltingly entered the world of Husserl and Heidegger. It was written largely within the universe of discourse of experimental psychology, whose scientific approach to the mind was precisely what phenomenologists had spurned as "psychologism." Rather than adopting this hostility, Merleau-Ponty sought to draw on the insights of contemporary psychological research, while criticizing its unreflective and reductionist ontological assumptions.

Carefully examining such competing schools as Pavlovian reflexology and atomistic behaviorism, Merleau-Ponty concluded that the most promising approach was that of the Gestaltists. Their emphasis on the structural component of perception and the formal determination of reflex behavior meant that they were sensitive to the ways in which the mind was active, without being beholden to the intellectualist categories posited by transcendental philosophies like neo-Kantianism. Unidirectional causal explanations of perception informing sensationalist epistemologies were equally surpassed, because the Gestaltists registered the circular, interactional nature of sense experience. As the Gestaltists had demonstrated, figures needed grounds and vice versa. The human retina was thus more than a passive screen registering impressions from without. In fact, whatever the object to be investigated, whether it be the nonvital physical world, the biological order, or the realm of human symbolic exchange, relational structuralism was the most appropriate approach.

Moreover, Merleau-Ponty insisted, the structural dimension of perception was fully compatible with the meaningfulness that we perceive in the world. Unlike the later Structuralists of the 1960s, he believed that at least in the human order formal structure and subjective meaning were intertwined, not opposed. For—and here the effect of Husserl was evident—structuration was an intentional phenomenon. Prior to all of the ways in which we conceptualize phenomena was a primordial order of signification, which tied together what transcendental and sensationalist philosophies had torn asunder. Gestalt psychology was useful in reaching this understanding, but it had not gone far enough in rejecting what Merleau-Ponty called the realist epistemology of "the outside spectator,"[100] who believed the structures he saw were wholly independent of his constitutive powers. In fact, as Bergson had recognized, perception was active, rather than contemplative, although he wrongly confined such action to the sphere of vitality alone.[101] "Life" was an insufficient category to capture the richness of the "orders of signification" in which humanity was embedded, and which played a central role in constituting perceptual experience.

In his account of that experience, Merleau-Ponty reached several arresting conclusions about its visual component. *The Structure of Behavior* began with an account of the distinction between the scientific understanding of light, which he called "real light," and the qualitative experience of light in naive consciousness, which he termed "phenomenal light." Rather than accepting the radical cleavage between the two, Merleau-Ponty contended that the Gestaltist nature of nonscientific perception meant that a continuum existed between them. Science thus grew out of natural perception, rather than being its antithesis or corrective. Thus the seeming inconsistency between two notions of light did not mean that vision was self-contradictory and even in some sense "irrational," but rather that subjective visual experience and its scientific redescription were ultimately part of the same order of signification.

Second, Merleau-Ponty discussed the implications of the inevitably perspectivalist dimensions of all-seeing. Against both the transcendentalists, who feared that this acknowledgment would mean cognitive relativism, and the Nietzscheans, who reached the same conclusion but welcomed it, he followed Husserl in arguing that multiple profiles indicated the existence of an actual "thing" in the world transcending all of its aspects. "Perspective does not appear to me a subjective deformation of things," he argued, "but, on the contrary, to be one of their properties, perhaps their essential property. It is precisely because of it that the perceived possesses in itself a hidden and inexhaustible richness, that it is a 'thing.'"[102] Rather than shutting man off in a little camera obscura of his own, nontranscendental perspectivalism reunited him with the objective world. "Far from introducing a coefficient of subjectivity into perception, it provides it on the contrary with the assurance of communicating with a world which is richer than what we know of it, that is, of communicating with a real world."[103]

Third, Merleau-Ponty directly challenged the Cartesian account of vision, critically examining, as he would on several subsequent occasions, *La Dioptrique*. Descartes was right, he concluded, in abandoning the medieval notion of "intentional species" flying through the air from object to eye, and with it, the resemblance theory of vision. For if such entities existed, the different perspectival profiles of perception would be impossible. But Descartes still remained too beholden to the realist paradigm, which turned vision into a view *on* the world, rather than *in* it. He also erred in giving too constructive a role to the intellect, the *cogito*, with its projection of natural geometry onto the observed world. Playfully taking liberties with Descartes's celebrated claim that it is not the eyes but the soul which really sees, Merleau-Ponty reinterpreted the spiritual category in his own terms and opposed it to something else: "it is the soul which sees and not the brain; it is by means of the perceived world and its proper structures that one can explain the spatial values assigned to a point of the visual field in each particular case."[104] The "soul" did not see intelligible essences, but rather things with existential or real presence. "The universe of consciousness revealed by the *cogito* and in the unity of which even perception itself seemed to be necessarily enclosed," he charged, "was only a universe of thought in the restricted sense: it accounts for the thought of seeing, but the fact of vision and the ensemble of existential knowledges remain outside of it."[105]

If the Cartesian account of vision was thus deficient because of its inattention to the existential presence of the objects on view, what of the explicitly existentialist alternative being developed simultaneously by Sartre? Even though the fully worked out account we have described above was still in the making, Merleau-Ponty had encountered enough of his friend's early work to become suspicious of certain of its implications. Although he shared Sartre's distaste for Husserl's transcendental ego, approved of his stress on the "lived body," and even anticipated his critique of Surrealism, Merleau-Ponty distanced himself from his friend on two fundamental issues.

First, whereas Sartre had invidiously compared the de-realizing imagination with the mundane world of perceptual observation, Merleau-Ponty refused to separate the two realms so categorically. As he noted in a later treatment of the same theme, Sartre himself had acknowledged certain confusions between the two in his discussion of illusions, and thus "necessarily suggests the possibility of a situation anterior to the clear distinction between perception and imagination which was made at the start."[106] Perception, Merleau-Ponty implied, was intertwined not only with the scientific and rational intellect, but with the artistic imagination as well.

If Merleau-Ponty resisted Sartre's distinction between perception and imagination, he also subtly distanced himself from the unreciprocal social relations to which Sartre's still dualist ontology inevitably led. More faithful than his friend to the dialectic of recognition in Hegel and the analysis of *Mitsein* in Heidegger, Merleau-Ponty emphasized the potential for communication through shared signification, which was evident on the prereflective level of perception. Intersubjective relations are not thus constituted by a duel of objectifying gazes; indeed, they cannot be reduced to their visual component alone. Nor of course could perception as a whole. In a telling footnote near the end of his text, Merleau-Ponty pondered Heidegger's claim that we have a primordial perception of the "world" prior to sight. Reserving judgment about its full implications, he nonetheless concluded that "what is certain is that the perceived is not limited to that which strikes my eyes. When I am sitting at my desk, the space is closed behind me not only in idea but also in reality."[107] Sight, in other words, had to be integrated with the other senses in order for us to "make sense" of our experience of the world.[108]

If *The Structure of Behavior* concentrated on the attempts of experimental psychology and certain philosophies to conceptualize perceptual experience, Merleau-Ponty's next work turned directly to that experience itself. A much more thickly textured, arduously labored, convoluted book than its predecessor—perhaps because it strove to emulate the ambiguities of perception rather than master them with categorical distinctions—*The Phenomenology of Perception* has spawned a small cottage industry of interpretation, culminating in a full-length book devoted entirely to its paraphrase.[109] This is not the place for yet another rehearsal of its complex arguments; instead, only certain points warrant emphasis.

Setting out to provide no less than an "inventory of the perceived world,"[110] Merleau-Ponty proceeded by systematically criticizing classical prejudices about perception, which he grouped in two camps called "empiricist" and "intellectualist." The former assumed that sensations were produced by the impingement of stimuli entirely from without on the passive receptive apparatus of the sensorium. It thus reduced vision to the tradition of observation. The latter posited an absolute subjectivity, which constituted the world it perceived entirely out of the subject's own interiority. Here the alternative tradition of speculation, in which the subject only sees a mirror image of itself, was dominant.

For Merleau-Ponty, both traditions were equally at fault for factoring out the actual phenomenon of perception itself, empiricism because it turned the subject into an object in the world like all others, intellectualism because it made the cognitive subject all-powerful, turning perception into a mere function of thought, an effect of judgment. In both cases the world was construed as a spectacle to be observed from afar by a disembodied mind. It was necessary instead to delve into the experience of perception prior to the constitution of the body as object and the *cogito* as rational subject. Although his own philosophical tools were inevitably reflective, Merleau-Ponty sought to explore the prereflexive phenomenal field he called "being in the world."[111] He did so by drawing on the results of psychological examinations of perceptive disorders, which revealed the suppressed assumptions of "normal" perception. These abnormalities he then interpreted through phenomenological descriptions, which, however, explicitly spurned Husserl's goal of escaping the imperfect world of existence for the purer world of eidetic essences.

If Merleau-Ponty rejected the visual traditions of observation and speculation, can we say that he adopted a third alternative, that of revelatory illumination, which the Surrealists in certain moods were seeking to revive at around the same time? If the goal of the seer is understood to be the attainment of perfect transparency, fusion with the divine light, or clairvoyant purity, then obviously Merleau-Ponty with his celebration of the interminable ambiguities of visual experience was not of their number. Contrary to certain interpretations,[112] he never sought a mystical unity in which all shadows were dissolved in a flash of unearthly brilliance. Although he may have wanted to redeem the primacy of perception and spoke of a primordial sensorium prior to the differentiation of the senses, he never believed perception was the realm of redemption in the mystical sense of perfect reconciliation.

Still, in two ways, certain residues of the visionary tradition may perhaps be discerned in Merleau-Ponty, which became even more evident in his later work. First, his insistence on mingling the viewer with the world on view meant an ecstatic decentering of the subject, an acknowledgment that however active perception may be, it also meant a kind of surrender of the strong ego, a willingness to let things be, which has invited comparison with the ideas of Meister Eckhart.[113] Second, contact with the visible world did not produce nausea in Merleau-Ponty as it did in Sartre, but a sense of wonder instead. Never perhaps fully throwing off the Catholicism of his early training,[114] he reveled in the richness of created, incarnated Being available to the eyes.

By and large, there is little in *Phenomenology of Perception* to sustain an explicitly visionary interpretation of Merleau-Ponty's restoration of perception. After a lengthy introductory section devoted to demolishing the classical prejudices, the book begins with a detailed examination of the lived body in its physiological, psychological, sexual, and expressive modes. The second part of the book examines the perceived world, focusing on sensing, space, the natural world, and the human world. The final part treats being-for-itself and being-in-the-world, with special attention paid to the issues of the *cogito,* temporality, and human freedom.

In many ways, his arguments deepened the conclusions he had already reached in *The Structure of Behavior.* Thus, for example, he frequently emphasized the imbrication of the senses, each of which creates its own perceived world and at the same time contributes to an integrated world of experience. In particular, the role of touch needed emphasis, Merleau-Ponty going so far as to claim that it even played a role in our perception of color, which was dependent on light cast on the textured surface of objects in the world.[115]

Recognizing the existence of a primordial, prereflexive perceptual relation to the world helped resolve such time-honored puzzles as that posed by Molyneux in his famous letter to Locke concerning the implications of a newly sighted blind man. The empiricist solution—that each sense was utterly distinct—and the intellectualist alternative—that a transcendental knowledge of space exists prior to sense experience—were both inadequate, because they failed to register the primary layer of intersensory experience in the body anterior to the differentiation of the senses and their resynthesis on the level of reflected thought. Instead, Merleau-Ponty claimed, the unification was like the merging of binocular into monocular vision, produced by a kind of bodily intentionality before mind distinguished itself from matter. "The senses," he contended, "translate each other without any need of an interpreter, and are mutually comprehensible without the intervention of any idea."[116]

Because of the importance of the intentional component in perception, Merleau-Ponty echoed Bergson in stressing temporality as one of its constituent elements. The lived body was not reducible to a static image observed from without. Thus, Zeno's paradoxes, at least those that applied to human movement, were based on a false reduction of motion to an intellectual judgment about a succession of static states, like the stop-action frames of chronophotography.[117] Although Merleau-Ponty did not share Bergson's distrust of the cinema, he agreed that "the lived perspective, that which we actually perceive, is not a geometric or photographic one."[118] Thus, in "The Eye and the Mind," he would take the side of painters like Géricault against photographers like Marey in their depiction of movement, and cite approvingly Rodin's verdict that "it is the artist who is truthful, while the photograph is mendacious; for in reality, time never stops cold."[119]

If the phenomenal field linking, but not fully uniting, lived body and natural environment was based on the communication of the senses, so too the human *Lebenswelt* entailed reciprocity rather than conflict. Indeed, the very bodily experience of being at once viewer and viewed, toucher and object of the touch, was an ontological prerequisite for that internalization of otherness underlying human intersubjectivity. The hoary philosophical problem of other minds was thus poorly posed, because the primary experience of sympathetic understanding was preflexive and corporeal. Contrary to Sartre, and here the hints of a disagreement in *The Structure of Behavior* became a full-fledged critique, the "inhuman gaze"[120] of mutual objectification exists only on the level of thought, not on the level of interactive presence. For all his talk of situating consciousness in bodily experience, Sartre had thus missed the existence of the intersubjective (or intercorporeal) dimension that always subtends the seemingly self-contained subject. A Cartesian in spite of himself, Sartre failed to acknowledge the dialectical interplay of bodily intentionalities prior to the duel of wounding gazes.

As a result, the only way Sartre could conceptualize a community was through the gaze of a third person external to the fragile collective subject it creates from without. In contrast, Merleau-Ponty more optimistically posited a cooperative, complementary world of intersubjectivity in which mutual regard is a visual as well as an emotional phenomenon. What he would call "tele-vision"[121] meant a kind of transcendence of the isolated subject and a sympathetic entry into the subjectivity of others. Although the ambiguities of communal existence meant that the realization of its full potential was still a historical task, which Merleau-Ponty in his more Marxist moments assigned to the proletariat, he was careful to distance himself from Sartre's *a priori* dismissal of the possibility of *Mitsein*. The objectifying look of the other was unbearable, he insisted, only "because it takes the place of possible communication," but "the refusal to communicate . . . is still a form of communication."[122] *Phenomenology of Perception* thus concluded with a far more hopeful account than Sartre's of vision's role in the nurturing of human freedom. In spite of the divisions between them, the two managed to work together on *Les Temps Modernes* after the Liberation. But in the years that followed, their friendship foundered as political disputes compounded theoretical ones. Only near the end of Merleau-Ponty's life did a hesitant rapprochement begin. Significantly, their differing attitudes toward vision permeated their political disagreements. Merleau-Ponty's lengthy attack on Sartre's "ultra-Bolshevism" in *The Adventures of the Dialectic* of 1955 is a case in point. Sartre's fellow-traveling support of the Communist Party, Merleau-Ponty charged, revealed his identification of it with a pure, transcendental subject gazing from afar at a recalcitrant, opaque object entirely external to it. That object was the proletariat, which was robbed of its own subjectivity as a result. "For Sartre," Merleau-Ponty complained, "the relationships between classes, the relationships within the proletariat, and finally those of the whole of history are not articulated relationships, including tension and the easing of tension, but are the immediate or magical relationships of our gazes."[123] The institutional interworld that makes up the recalcitrant stuff of history was thus lost, as Sartre once again failed to find a mediation between the nihilating, objectifying gaze and its opaque, meaningless object.

Ultimately, Sartre came to see the power of much of Merleau-Ponty's criticism and sought in *The Critique of Dialectical Reason* to wean himself from the Cartesian residues in his thought. How successful his efforts actually were has been a point of dispute ever since.[124] Although he abandoned his indifference to the interworld of mediations between subject and object and distanced himself from the existentialist despair of his early work, nowhere did Sartre explicitly repudiate his harsh description of the objectifying power of the gaze.

Merleau-Ponty, in contrast, returned with fresh eyes, as it were, to his initial formulations about the primacy of perception, and was in the process of a major revision of his thought when his work was abruptly cut short in May 1961. The earliest effort to realize his project, the unfinished manuscript written before 1952 called *The Prose of the World*, produced one lengthy article entitled "Indirect Language and the Voices of Silence," published in his lifetime.[125] In 1960, "Eye and the Mind" presented what appeared to be a preliminary statement of his general conclusions. After his death, Claude Lefort collected the first part of his manuscript and the notes for the second as *The Visible and the Invisible*.

Fragmentary, uncompleted, often obscure, this body of work is not easy to interpret in an unequivocal way. From one perspective, it may well appear to lend weight to the contention that Merleau-Ponty continued his search for a redemption of sight, even for a new ocularcentric ontology. Rather than talking of perception in general, with its implicit leveling of the hierarchy of the senses, he now concentrated on the sense of sight more than any other. Leaving behind his reliance on Gestalt psychology, whose spectatorial epistemological foundations he could no longer abide, Merleau-Ponty plunged more deeply than ever before into the enigmas of visibility and invisibility as the privileged avenue of entry into the question of Being. And he did so while still defending the special role of painting as opposed to other arts like music, which he never analyzed with any seriousness.

The text that best supports this interpretation is "Eye and the Mind," which begins with an invidious comparison between science and painting. Whereas the former looks on things from above, the latter immerses the viewer in the world on view. The painter does not depict representations in his mind, but rather paints with his body, which is mingled with the perceived world. The self revealed by painting is thus "not a self through transparence, like thought, which only thinks its object by assimilating it, by constituting it, by transforming it into thought. It is a self through confusion, narcissism, through inherence of the one who sees in that which he sees."[126]

The "narcissism of sight" is thus an appropriate phrase because "the world is made of the same stuff as the body."[127] And yet, although at one with the world, the painter is also apart from it, which is the paradoxical, enigmatic "madness" of vision: "painting awakens and carries to its highest pitch a delirium which is vision itself, for to see is *to have at a distance*; painting spreads this strange possession to all aspects of Being, which must in some fashion become visible in order to enter into the work of art."[128] It is precisely the revelation of the oneness and multiplicity of Being that makes painting so remarkable. Thus, with a sunny optimism that might have made Sartre shudder, Merleau-Ponty concluded: "the eye accomplishes the prodigious work of opening the soul to what is not soul—the joyous realm of things and their god, the sun."[129]

Interestingly, in presenting his defense of painting, Merleau-Ponty not only drew on modernists like Cézanne, Matisse, and Klee, but also on Dutch art, the "art of describing" that Svetlana Alpers has called an alternative to the Albertian perspectivalism of the Renaissance mainstream.[130] Citing Claudel's description of the "digestion" of empty interiors by the "round eye of the mirror" in many Dutch paintings, Merleau-Ponty remarked that "this prehuman way of seeing things is the painter's way. More completely than lights, shadows, and reflections, the mirror anticipates, within things, the labor of vision. . . . The mirror appears because I am seeing-visible [voyant-visible], because there is a reflexivity of the sensible; the mirror translates and reproduces that reflexivity."[131] The curved mirror was especially powerful in this regard because its tactile dimension helps to collapse the seemingly unbridgeable distance between the Albertian painter's disembodied eye and the scene before him on the other side of the window-like canvas.

This "defenestration" of the painter's eye, as Marc Richir has noted, was also extended by Merleau-Ponty to the philosopher's as well.[132] "Eye and Mind," in fact, turns directly from a consideration of Dutch painting to an analysis of Descartes's Dioptrique, "the breviary of a thought that wants no longer to abide in the visible and so decides to construct the visible according to a model-in-thought."[133] Among Descartes's failings was his inability to appreciate the ontological importance of painting, which "for him is not a central operation contributing to the definition of our access to Being; it is a mode or variant of thinking, where thinking is canonically defined according to intellectual possession and evidence."[134] Symptomatically, Descartes deemphasized color in favor of spatial design and denigrated texture in favor of form. Although he was correct to try to liberate space from the empiricists' fetish of surface appearance, "his mistake was to erect it into a positive being, outside all points of view, beyond all latency and all depth, having no true thickness."[135] In our post-Euclidean world, Merleau-Ponty insisted, we are now aware that space is no longer what it seemed to Descartes, with his geometer's eye outside and above the scene it surveyed. "It is, rather, a space reckoned starting from me as the zero point or degree zero of spatiality. I do not see it according to its exterior envelope; I live it from the inside; I am immersed in it. After all, the world is all around me, not in front of me."[136]

"Eye and Mind" would thus seem like an apotheosis of vision, understood, to be sure, in terms closer to Heidegger's horizontal Umsicht than Descartes's pensée au survol. And yet, read alongside the other fragments of his uncompleted project, it may betoken a less enthusiastic endorse-ment of the visual—understood in any of its conventional senses—than appears at first glance. First, his new emphasis on the "flesh of the world" rather than the lived, perceiving body meant that the notion of vi-sion itself began to assume a posthumanist inflection, which made it less obviously a term referring to what is normally thought of as human be-ings looking at the world. Second, Merleau-Ponty's increasingly sympa-thetic interest in psychoanalysis, including the work of Lacan, meant that he came to acknowledge certain of the problematic implications of the visual constitution of the self. And finally, his growing fascination with language, fueled in part by an enthusiastic, if garbled, reading of Saus-sure, would introduce a potential tension between perception and ex-pression, figurality and discursivity, which later thinkers would explicitly develop in antiocularcentric directions.

The posthumanist implications of Merleau-Ponty's concept of the flesh of the world were anticipated in several ways before *The Visible and the Invisible*. In a 1951 essay entitled "Man and Adversity," Merleau-Ponty had written:

> if there is a humanism today, it rids itself of the illusion Valéry designated so well in speaking of "that little man within man whom we always presup-pose." Philosophers have at times thought to account for our vision by the image or reflection things form upon our retina. This was because they presupposed a second man behind the retinal image who had different eyes and a different retinal image responsible for seeing the first.[137]

Such an assumption was, of course, false, so if humanism can be said to exist, it cannot be based on a notion of a disembodied observer, seeing with his mind's eye.

If the Cartesian I/eye was ruled out by Merleau-Ponty as a basis for humanism, so too was the existentialist alternative famously defended in 1946 by Sartre.[138] Merleau-Ponty, as we've already noted, distrusted his friend's identification of the subject with a nihilating "for-itself" opposed to being as the imagination was opposed to perception. In the introduc-tion to *Signs*, he contended that "it would be better to speak of 'the visi-ble and the invisible,' pointing out that they are not contradictory, than to speak of 'being and nothingness.'"[139] And he added in *The Visible and the Invisible* that

> the analytic of Being and Nothingness is the seer who forgets that he has a body and that what he sees is always beneath what he sees, who tries to force the passage toward pure being and pure nothingness by installing himself in pure vision, who makes himself a visionary, but who is thrown back to his own opacity as a seer and to the depth of being.[140]

Even Husserl's phenomenological version of the subject, Merleau-Ponty came to realize, was too beholden to a visually constituted humanism, still too much an idealist philosophy of consciousness and reflection. The very concept of intentionality presupposed a too-centered intending subject. Any philosophy of reflection, including Husserl's, was thus inadequate: "we reproach the philosophy of reflection not only for transforming the world into a noema, but also for distorting the being of the reflecting 'subject' by conceiving it as 'thought'—and finally for rendering unthinkable its relations with other 'subjects' in the world that is common to them."[141]

Finally, the collective meta-subject of history, which he had tentatively supported in his militant Marxist period, seemed no less problematic as a source of a viable humanism. No retrospective total knowledge of history would ever be possible, no sovereign, God's-eye survey of the whole would ever be granted to the proletariat or any other pretender to the role of subject/object of history. The flesh of history is as unsurveyable as the flesh of the natural world; we are always in the middle of a multi-layered process best understood in terms of the figure of speech known as chiasmus. The visible and the invisible was like a fold in Being, a crossing over, a hinge, not a flat landscape to be observed from afar.

Merleau-Ponty's dethroning of the observing subject, whether Cartesian, Sartrean, Husserlian, or Marxist, went so far that at times he seemed to deny not only the link between vision and the mind but also between vision and the lived body. In *The Visible and the Invisible,* he would write: "there is here no problem of the *alter ego* because it is not *I* who sees, not *he* who sees, because an anonymous visibility inhabits both of us, a vision in general, in virtue of that primordial property that belongs to the flesh, being here and now, of radiating everywhere and forever, being an individual, of being also a dimension and a universal."[142] It is precisely because of this remarkable anonymity that Merleau-Ponty began to talk of "the visible and the invisible," those utterly impersonal phenomena, rather than the viewer and the viewed. He thus contested the assumption that representation by itself could adequately capture the world, and contended that "what I want to do is to restore the world as a meaning of Being absolutely different from the 'represented,' that is, as the vertical Being which none of the 'representations' exhaust and which all 'reach,' the wild Being."[143]

Wild Being, the flesh of the world, thus became the fundamental category for Merleau-Ponty, grounding both subject and object, viewer and viewed, mind and body. But although ultimately one, thus allowing the narcissism of vision, the flesh is not a specular unity or Idealist identity. Instead, it contains internal articulations and differentiations, which

Merleau-Ponty struggled to capture with terms like dehiscence, separation (*écart*), latency, reversibility, and circularity. Neither purely transparent nor completely opaque, the flesh is an interplay of dimensionalities of light and shadow. Consciousness can never have a completely positive vision of reality as full presence, because it inevitably has a blind spot (*punctum caecum*): "*What* it does not see is what makes it see, is its tie to Being, its corporeity, are the existentials by which the world becomes visible, is the flesh wherein the *object* is born. It is inevitable that the consciousness be mystified, inverted, indirect, in principle it sees the things *through the other end*, in principle it disregards Being and prefers the object to it."[144] In spite of the apparent polarity one might infer from this passage, Being was not the simple obverse of objectness, as black to white, but rather the larger context in which the object was situated. What consciousness misses in Being is the invisible inextricably intertwined with the visible in a chiasmic exchange that never achieves dialectical sublation. Being is in the interplay of the visible and invisible, which no humanist subject can ever truly see.

If Merleau-Ponty's meditations on the flesh of the world thus undermined traditional notions of a coherent viewing subject and raised invisibility to the same ontological status as visibility, so too did his cautious embrace of psychoanalysis. The changes in his attitudes toward Freud are too complex to detail here, but it is clear that near the end of his career, he began to be more sympathetic to certain psychoanalytic ideas. Rather than construing Freudianism merely as a version of the causal psychology he damned in *The Structure of Behavior*, he began to appreciate its substantive contribution to the philosophical problems he so obsessively explored. One aspect of the unconscious which Merleau-Ponty found especially congenial complemented his earlier interests in the cognitive development of children, the role of the so-called "mirror stage" in creating the knowing self. In his 1960 essay "The Child's Relations with Others," Merleau-Ponty drew on psychologists like Henri Wallon and Paul Guillaume, who had discussed the cognitive implications of specular images.[145] What he called "autoscopy," or the external perception of a self, was responsible, among other things, for an ideal, uniform notion of space, which is assumed to be the same wherever the image of the child appears. It also has profound affective implications, which purely cognitive psychology fails to explain.

Here psychoanalysis, in particular the work of Jacques Lacan, provided a useful corrective. Having recently read Lacan's seminal papers, "The Psychic Effects of the Imaginary Mode" and "The Mirror Stage as Formative of the Function of the I," Merleau-Ponty noted that they accounted for an aspect of specularity that Wallon had noted but neglected to address: the child's jubilation on seeing itself for the first time. "Lacan's answer," he approvingly writes, "is that, when the child looks at himself in the mirror and recognizes his own image there, it is a matter of *identification* . . . until the moment when the specular image arises, the child's body is a strongly felt but confused reality. To recognize his image in the mirror is for him to learn that *there can be a viewpoint taken on him.*"[146] It thus makes possible narcissistic pleasure.

But in addition to registering the positive emotional implications of the mirror stage, Merleau-Ponty followed Lacan, as he read him, in discerning negative ones as well.

> Thereupon I leave the reality of my lived *me* in order to refer myself constantly to the ideal, fictitious, or imaginary *me,* of which the specular image is the first outline. In this sense I am torn from myself, and the image in the mirror prepares me for another still more serious alienation, which will be the alienation by others. For others have only an exterior image of me, which is analogous to the one seen in the mirror.[147]

One result is the conflict between the internal and external senses of the self, which leads to aggressive feelings as well as narcissistic jubilation. Another is the creation of the "specular I," which is different from the "introceptive *me.*"

In adopting Lacan's account so enthusiastically, Merleau-Ponty almost readmitted Sartre's bleak version of the dialectic of vision (which had directly influenced Lacan) through the back door. But in one telling way, he held onto a residue of his earlier phenomenological belief in the existence of a prereflective ego prior to its constitution by sight. "The personality before the advent of the specular image," he wrote, "is what psychoanalysts call, in the adult, the ego (*soi*), i.e., the collection of confusedly felt impulses. . . . With the specular images appears the possibility of an ideal image of oneself—in psychoanalytic terms, the possibility of a super-ego."[148] This equation of the mirror stage with the creation of the ego ideal or the superego was not, however, what Lacan had meant; he identified it squarely with the ego itself and thus explicitly jettisoned Merleau-Ponty's phenomenological notion of an ego prior to the *cogito*. For all his appreciation of Merleau-Ponty's positive appropriation of his work, Lacan thus carefully distanced himself from his interpretation of it in the tribute he wrote after the philosopher's death and in later statements.[149]

However imperfectly he may have understood Lacan's convoluted arguments, Merleau-Ponty took from him the recognition that the mirror stage could well be the source of an alienated self and conflict between visually constituted selves. He also seems to have been deeply impressed by Lacan's emphasis on the linguistic dimension of the unconscious, as demonstrated by his approving citation of the famous claim that it was "structured like a language."[150] Here too his grasp of the intricacies of Lacan's linguistics may have been unsure, but by stressing the role of language, he was subtly distancing himself from his earlier celebration of perception. As he put it in his posthumously published prospectus: "the study of perception could only teach us a 'bad ambiguity,' a mixture of finitude and universality, of interiority and exteriority. But there is a 'good ambiguity' in the phenomenon of expression."[151]

Merleau-Ponty, to be sure, had emphasized from the beginning the importance of signification, claiming that the world was replete with meaning and that perception was the ground of communication. But now at the end of his career, he started to explore the ways in which language worked at cross purposes with perception. The extent of his shift away from his original position is not absolutely certain, for as in many other respects, his final work is tantalizingly incomplete and fragmentary. Moreover, his appropriation of linguistic theory, especially that of Saussure, seems to have been partial and often based on misunderstandings.[152] Still, several generalizations can be hazarded with some assurance.

For all his fascination with the power of painters to evoke the primordial perceptual experience prior to the differentiation of the senses, Merleau-Ponty came to acknowledge that the meanings paintings conveyed remained mute.[153] Thus language is necessary to bring the meanings of perception into explicit speech. "In a sense the whole of philosophy, as Husserl says, consists in restoring a power to signify, a birth of meaning, or a wild meaning, an expression of experience by experience, which in particular clarifies the special domain of language."[154] For Merleau-Ponty, literary language in particular provides the demonstrative stories that inscribe the invisible in the visible.[155] Here the celebrated Heideggerian contention that language is the "house of Being" found its echo, as Merleau-Ponty came to see that sense and the senses were not mutually entailing.

At other times Merleau-Ponty turned to communicative language as an antidote to the inadequacies of visual interaction. Thus, in the introduction to *Signs,* where he talked of the enigma of "tele-vision," he asked the Sartrean question, "what is it like when one of the others turns upon me, meets my gaze, and fastens his own upon my body and my face?"[156] His answer was that "unless we have recourse to the ruse of speech, putting a common domain of thoughts between us and a third party, the experience is intolerable. There is nothing left to look at but a look. Seer and seen are exactly interchangeable. The two glances are immobilized upon one another. . . . Vision produces what reflection will never understand—a combat which at times has no victor. . . . Speech . . . would interrupt this fascination."[157]

But elsewhere, he recognized that language, spoken or not, could be less a supplement to perception than at odds with it, at least potentially. For all the interaction between the two, "there is all the same this difference between perception and language, that I *see* the perceived things and that the significations on the contrary are invisible. The natural being is at rest in itself, my look can stop on it. The Being whose home is language cannot be fixed, looked at . . ."[158] Still, the two were not to be conceptualized in terms of an opposition or a negation. If perception is a mute version of language, needing it to come into full speech, so too language bears within it the residue of its silent predecessor, which inaugurated the drama of meaningfulness that is our destiny.

In short, the precise relationship between vision and language remained very much to be worked out by Merleau-Ponty, whose journey away from his original phenomenological restoration of perception never reached a final destination. Its abrupt truncation is poignantly illustrated by a detail disclosed by Lefort. When Merleau-Ponty died suddenly on May 3, 1961, an open book was found on his desk: Descartes's *Dioptrique,* still the stimulus to fresh thoughts on the theme that had obsessed him for so many years.

Perhaps, of course, the "good ambiguity" that he claimed defined the relationship between perception and language could never be conclusively resolved. But perhaps also, the ambiguity may not have been so good after all, at least for the reception of Merleau-Ponty's thought. After his death, his star rapidly waned, and not merely because a later generation would grow impatient with his political vacillations.[159] Faithful disciples like Richir and Lefort aside, French intellectuals lost interest in phenomenology, with its stress on meaning and expression, and read the lessons of Saussure in a manner very different from Merleau-Ponty. So, too, the very project of grounding philosophy in perception or in Being seemed problematic to thinkers disdaining any version of foundationalist thought.

But perhaps the main source of criticism for many of those disenchanted with Merleau-Ponty's legacy was their belief that his work remained far too ocularcentric, despite all the counter-tendencies we have discerned in his later writings. Rather than celebrating the mutual imbrication of the discursive and the figural in the flesh of the world, they would question any positive resolution of the conflict between them, even one lacking the full dialectical sublation explicitly denied by Merleau-Ponty. Thus, J. F. Lyotard, himself an early defender of phenomenology, condemned Merleau-Ponty's defense of Cézanne for "remaining hostage to a philosophy of perception that grants to vision the rediscovery in the Cézannian disorder of a true order of the sensible and the lifting of the veil which Cartesian and Galilean rationalism has thrown over the world of experience."[160] René Magritte, the Belgian Surrealist, likewise complained that "Eye and Mind" turned the visible world into an overly meaningful, homcgeneous, expressive realm robbed of its ineradicable enigmas: "The only kind of painting Merleau-Ponty deals with is a variety of serious but futile divertissement, of interest only to well-intentioned humbugs. The only painting worth looking at has the same *raison d'être* as the *raison d'être* of the world—mystery."[161] Similarly, Luce Irigaray would attack the "labyrinthine solipsism" produced by the ungendered nature of Merleau-Ponty's musings on the narcissism of vision and conclude that he had "accorded an exorbitant privilege to vision—or rather, he expressed the exorbitant privilege of vision in our culture."[162] Foucault would include Merleau-Ponty's search for lost origins in perception in the category of "transcendental narcissism," which he condemned in *The Archaeology of Knowledge*.[163] And Christian Metz, damning as bedfellows the phenomenological account of perception and the experience of being seduced by the movies, would claim that it was "no accident that the main form of idealism in cinematic theory has been phenomenology."[164]

Such critics, however, underplayed the doubts that were developing in Merleau-Ponty himself about the primacy of perception in general and vision in particular. His effort to provide a more nuanced and less hostile account of vision than that found in Sartre was widely regarded as unsuccessful. By the 1960s, at a time when earlier critics of vision like Bataille were coming into their own, the antiocularcentric discourse became a pervasive, if not always coherently or self-consciously articulated feature of French intellectual life.[165] But however much they were "surpassed" by Structuralist and Poststructuralist critics of the eye, Sartre and Merleau-Ponty, I hope it has been amply demonstrated, must be credited with breaking much of the ground that others were so vigorously to till.

NOTES

1. Jean-Paul Sartre, *Being and Nothingness: An Essay on Phenomenological Ontology*, trans. Hazel E. Barnes (New York: Washington Square Press, 1966), p. 319.

2. Maurice Merleau-Ponty, *The Primacy of Perception*, ed. James M. Edie (Evanston, Ill.: Northwestern University Press, 1964), p. 36.

3. On Brunschvicg's role, see Colin Smith, *Contemporary French Philosophy* (London: Methuen, 1954) and Jacques Havet, "French Philosophical Tradition

Between the Two Wars," in Marvin Farber, ed., *Philosophic Thought in France and the United States* (Albany, N.Y.: State University of New York Press, 1950).

4. See Mark Poster, *Existentialist Marxism in Postwar France* (Princeton: Princeton University Press, 1975), and Vincent Descombes, *Modern French Philosophy*, trans. L. Scott-Fox and J. M. Harding (Cambridge: Cambridge University Press, 1980).

5. Sartre in particular was critical of Surrealism. See his hostile review of Bataille's *L'Expérience intérieure*, "Un nouveau Mystique" in *Situations I* (Paris: Gallimard, 1947), and his critique of Surrealism in *What Is Literature?*, trans. Bernard Frechtman (New York: Harper, 1949). For a general account of his attitude, see Michel Beaujour, "Sartre and Surrealism," *Yale French Studies*, 30 (1964). Merleau-Ponty seems to have been less engaged with their ideas.

6. Edmund Husserl, *Cartesian Meditations*, trans. D. Cairns (The Hague: Martinus Nijhoff, 1970).

7. Emmanuel Levinas, *The Theory of Intuition in Husserl's Phenomenology*, trans. André Orianne (Evanston: Northern University Press, 1973).

8. Jacques Derrida, *Speech and Phenomena and Other Essays on Husserl's Theory of Signs*, trans. David B. Allison (Evanston: Northwestern University Press, 1973).

9. Marc Richir, *Au-delà du renversement copernicien: La question de la phénoménologie et de son fondement* (The Hague: Martinus Nijhoff, 1976), p. 8.

10. Husserl, *The Crisis of European Sciences and Transcendental Phenomenology*, trans. D. Carr (Evanston: Northwestern University Press, 1970).

11. For an account of Merleau-Ponty's use of the later Husserl, see James Schmidt, *Maurice Merleau-Ponty: Between Phenomenology and Structuralism* (London: Macmillan, 1985), pp. 35–48.

12. Hans Jonas, *The Phenomenon of Life: Toward a Philosophical Biology* (Chicago: University of Chicago Press, 1982), p. 240.

13. See, for example, "The Origin of the Work of Art" (1935) in Martin Heidegger, *Basic Writings*, ed. David Farrell Krell (New York: Harper & Row, 1977), p. 158.

14. Heidegger, "Science and Reflection," p. 166. The Latin *contemplari*, he claims, comes from *templum*, the place which can be seen from any point and from which any point is visible.

15. Heidegger, *Being and Time*, trans. John Macquarrie and Edward Robinson (New York: Harper & Row, 1962), p. 214. For a very different analysis of the emancipation of curiosity, see Hans Blumenberg, *The Legitimacy of the Modern Age*, trans. Robert M. Wallace (Cambridge, Mass.: M.I.T. Press, 1983).

16. For a useful account of his views on the subject, see Harold Alderman, "Heidegger's Critique of Science and Technology," in Michael Murray, ed., *Heidegger and Modern Philosophy* (New Haven: Yale University Press, 1978).

17. Heidegger, "The Age of the World Picture" (1938), in *The Question Concerning Technology and Other Essays* (New York: Harper & Row, 1977), p. 134.

18. Heidegger, "The Origin of the Work of Art," (1935), in *Basic Writings*, p. 170.

19. See, for example, David M. Levin, *The Listening Self: Personal Growth, Social Change and the Closure of Metaphysics* (London: Routledge, 1989); and John

D. Caputo, "The Thought of Being and the Conversation of Mankind: The Case of Heidegger and Rorty," in Robert Hollinger, ed., *Hermeneutics and Praxis* (Notre Dame, Ind.: Notre Dame University Press, 1985), p. 255.

20. See, for example, Allan Megill, *Prophets of Extremity: Nietzsche, Heidegger, Foucault, Derrida* (Berkeley: University of California Press, 1985), p. 156. For a more sustained consideration of Heidegger's differentiated attitude toward vision, which stresses its positive dimension, see Levin, "Decline and Fall: Ocularcentrism in Heidegger's Reading of the History of Metaphysics," in this collection.

21. In his 1947 "Letter on Humanism," Heidegger even claimed that the language of *Being and Time* was "still faulty insofar as it does not yet succeed in retaining the essential help of phenomenological seeing and in dispensing with the inappropriate concern with 'science' and 'research.'" *Basic Writings*, p. 235.

22. Heidegger, Introduction to *Being and Time*, in *Basic Writings*, p. 80.

23. Heidegger, "The Question Concerning Technology," in *Basic Writings*, pp. 315–316.

24. Heidegger, "The End of Philosophy and the Task of Thinking" (1966), in *Basic Writings*, p. 384. He added that the clearing is also the place where echoes and resonances can be made present.

25. Ibid., p. 386.

26. Levin, *The Opening of Vision: Nihilism and the Postmodern Situation* (New York: Routledge, 1988), p. 68.

27. Heidegger, *Being and Time*, p. 176.

28. Levin, *The Opening of Vision*, p. 440.

29. Jean Starobinski, *Jean-Jacques Rousseau: la transparence et l'obstacle* (Paris: Gallimard, 1971).

30. See Alain Buisine, *Laideurs de Sartre* (Lille: Presses Universitaires de Lille, 1986), p. 103. He attributes the figure to an unnamed American psychoanalyst.

31. René Held, "Psychopathologie du regard," *L'Evolution psychiatrique* (April–June 1952), p. 228.

32. François George, *Deux études sur Sartre* (Paris: Christian Bourgois Éditeur, 1976), pp. 303–339.

33. Ibid., p. 307.

34. Sartre, *The Words*, trans. Bernard Frechtman (New York: Fawcett, 1964), p. 11. He claims it gave him freedom and no super-ego. He also asserted that his father was "not even a shadow, not even a gaze" (p. 12).

35. George, *Deux études sur Sartre*, p. 307.

36. Sartre, *The Words*, p. 52.

37. Ibid., p. 17.

38. Ibid., p. 158.

39. See note 30.

40. *Louche*, which also means suspicious-looking, equivocal, even weird, was one of Sartre's own favorite words.

41. Cited in Buisine, *Laideurs de Sartre*, p. 37.

42. Sartre, *The Words*, p. 95.

43. Ibid., p. 69.

44. Buisine, *Laideurs de Sartre,* p. 96.

45. Ibid., p. 133.

46. Sartre, *The Transcendence of Ego: An Existentialist Theory* of Consciousness, trans. Forrest Williams and Robert Kirkpatrick (New York: Noonday Press, 1957), pp. 41–42.

47. Sartre, *Imagination: A Psychological Critique,* trans. Forrest Williams (Ann Arbor: University of Michigan Press, 1962), and *The Psychology of Imagination,* trans. Bernard Frechtman (New York: Citidal, 1948). For helpful analyses of these works, see Hide Ishiguro, "Imagination," in Mary Warnock, ed., *Sartre: A Collection of Critical Essays* (Garden City, N.Y.: Anchor, 1971); Thomas R. Flynn, "The Role of the Image in Sartre's Aesthetic," in *The Journal of Aesthetics and Art Criticism* 33 (1975): 431–442; and Eugene F. Kaelin, "On *Meaning* in Sartre's Aesthetic Theory," in Hugh J. Silverman and Frederick A. Elliston, eds., *Jean-Paul Sartre: Contemporary Approaches to His Philosophy* (Pittsburgh: Dusquesne University Press, 1980).

48. Sartre, *The Psychology of Imagination,* p. 5.

49. Ibid., p. 85. Interestingly, Merleau-Ponty defended Bergson against Sartre in his review of the book in the *Journal de Psychologie Normale et Pathologique* 33 (1936): 761.

50. Sartre, *Nausea,* trans. Lloyd Alexander (New York: New Directions, 1949).

51. Alain Robbe-Grillet, "Nature, Humanism, Tragedy" in *For a New Novel: Essays on Fiction,* trans. Richard Howard (New York: Grove, 1965), p. 65.

52. Sartre, "Dirty Hands," in *No Exit and Three Other Plays,* trans. Lionel Abel (New York: Vintage, 1949).

53. Sartre, *Nausea,* p. 171. Here picking things up with the hands doesn't suffice, because objects are still understood in the mode of *Vorhandenheit,* as tools for visualized purposes.

54. Ibid., p. 176.

55. Ibid., p. 177.

56. Ibid., p. 178.

57. Ibid., p. 180.

58. Ibid., p. 181.

59. For a comparison of the two thinkers on this issue, see Frederick A. Elliston, "Sartre and Husserl on Interpersonal Relations," in Silverman and Elliston, eds., *Jean-Paul Sartre: Contemporary Approaches to his Philosophy.*

60. Sartre, *Being and Nothingness,* p. 525.

61. Ibid., p. 315.

62. Ibid., p. 316.

63. Ibid., pp. 316–317.

64. Ibid., p. 317.

65. George, *Deux études sur Sartre,* p. 321.

66. Sartre, *Being and Nothingness,* p. 319.

67. Ibid., p. 320.

68. Ibid., p. 322.

69. Ibid., p. 327.

70. Ibid., p. 354.

71. For an account of Sartre's attempt to resolve this issue in the context of the general Western Marxist search for a viable concept of totality, see Martin Jay, *Marxism and Totality: The Adventures of a Concept from Lukács to Habermas* (Berkeley: University of California Press, 1984), chap. 11.

72. Sartre, *Being and Nothingness*, p. 370.

73. Ibid.

74. For a useful comparison of Georg Simmel's notion of reciprocal visual interaction with Sartre's, which focuses on the issue of regard, see Deena Weinstein and Michael Weinstein, "On the Visual Constitution of Society: The Contributions of Georg Simmel and Jean-Paul Sartre to a Sociology of the Senses," in *History of European Ideas* 5, no. 4 (1984): 349–362. They conclude that both positions tell us something about the way in which vision contributes to social interaction.

75. Sartre, *Being and Nothingness*, p. 445.

76. Ibid., p. 452.

77. Ibid., p. 496.

78. Ibid., p. 497.

79. Sartre, *Saint Genet: Actor and Martyr*, trans. Bernard Frechtman (New York: Pantheon, 1963).

80. Ibid., p. 17.

81. Ibid., p. 49.

82. Ibid., p. 79.

83. Ibid., p. 81.

84. Ibid., p. 114. Presumably, the chance to achieve such salvation through reciprocity was not taken very seriously by Sartre.

85. Ibid., p. 137.

86. Ibid., p. 298.

87. Ibid., p. 440.

88. Ibid., p. 514. Thomas, born in 1912, is a French novelist and poet, who wrote *Travaux d'aveugle* in 1941.

89. Maurice Merleau-Ponty, *The Visible and the Invisible*, ed. Claude Lefort, trans. Alphonso Lingis (Evanston: Northwestern University Press, 1968), p. 75.

90. The most extensive biography of the young Merleau-Ponty can be found in Theodore F. Geraets, *Vers une nouvelle philosophie transcendentale. La genése de la philosophie de Maurice Merleau-Ponty jusqu'à la Phénoménologie de la perception* (The Hague: Martinus Nijhoff, 1971). See also Barry Cooper, *Merleau-Ponty and Marxism: From Terror to Reform* (Toronto: University of Toronto Press, 1979), and Schmidt, *Maurice Merleau-Ponty: Between Phenomenology and Structuralism*.

91. Sartre himself claimed that Merleau-Ponty's childhood was happy. See "Merleau-Ponty," *Situations*, trans. Benita Eisler (New York: George Braziller, 1965), p. 296.

92. For a discussion, see Geraets, *Vers une nouvelle philosophie*, pp. 9–10.

93. Sartre, "Merleau-Ponty," p. 322.

94. Other periodizations would emerge if Merleau-Ponty's political odyssey were examined, but here the criterion is only his attitude toward perception.

95. Merleau-Ponty, *The Structure of Behavior*, trans. Alden L. Fisher (Boston:

Beacon, 1963); *Phenomenology of Perception*, trans. Colin Smith (London: Routledge and Kegan Paul, 1962).

96. The most important results of these efforts were *Humanism and Terror*, trans. J. O'Neill (Boston: Beacon, 1969); *Sense and Non-Sense*, trans. H. L. and P. A. Dreyfus (Evanston: Northwestern University Press, 1964), and *The Adventures of the Dialectic*, trans. J. Bien (Evanston: Northwestern University Press, 1973).

97. Merleau-Ponty, *Signs*, trans. Richard C. McCleary (Evanston: Northwestern University Press, 1964); "The Eye and the Mind," in *The Primacy of Perception*, trans. James M. Edie (Evanston: Northwestern University Press, 1964); *The Visible and the Invisible*, ed. Claude Lefort, trans. Alphonso Lingis (Evanston: Northwestern University Press, 1968).

98. Merleau-Ponty, "An Unpublished Text by Merleau-Ponty: *A Prospectus of His Work*," in *The Primacy of Perception*, p. 3.

99. This was the projected title for a work never completed, whose fragments were published in 1969.

100. Merleau-Ponty, *The Structure of Behavior*, p. 162.

101. Ibid., pp. 164–165. For a comparison of the two thinkers' attitudes toward perception, see Augustin Fressin, *La perception chez Bergson et chez Merleau-Ponty* (Paris: Sedes, 1967).

102. Ibid., p. 186.

103. Ibid.

104. Ibid., pp. 192–193.

105. Ibid., p. 197.

106. Merleau-Ponty, "Phenomenology and the Sciences of Man," in *The Primacy of Perception*, p. 74. He made a similar point in *The Visible and the Invisible*, pp. 39, 266.

107. Merleau-Ponty, *The Structure of Behavior*, p. 249.

108. The multiple meanings of "sense" (*sens*) in French include the idea of direction, which fits well with the emphasis on intentionality in Merleau-Ponty. For a later discussion of the word's various meanings, see Jacques Rollande de Renéville, *Itinéraire du sens* (Paris: Presses Universitaires de France, 1982).

109. Monika M. Langer, *Merleau-Ponty's Phenomenology of Perception: A Guide and Commentary* (London: Macmillan, 1989). Other useful treatments can be found in Gary Brent Madison, *The Phenomenology of Merleau-Ponty: A Search for the Limits of Consciousness* (Athens: Ohio University Press, 1981); Remy C. Kwant, *The Phenomenological Philosophy of Merleau-Ponty* (Pittsburgh: Dusquesne University Press, 1963); Garth Gillan, ed., *The Horizon of the Flesh: Critical Perspectives on the Thought of Merleau-Ponty* (Carbondale, Ill.: Southern Illinois University Press, 1973); Samuel B. Mallin, *Merleau-Ponty's Philosophy* (New Haven: Yale University Press, 1979); Albert Rabil, Jr., *Merleau-Ponty: Existentialist of the Social World* (New York: Columbia University Press, 1967); and Schmidt, *Maurice Merleau-Ponty: Between Phenomenology and Structuralism*.

110. Merleau-Ponty, *Phenomenology of Perception*, p. 25.

111. Ibid., p. xiii.

112. See, for example, Eugenio Donato, "Language, Vision and Phenomenology: Merleau-Ponty as a Test Case," *Modern Language Notes* 85, no. 6 (December, 1970), p. 804.

113. Michel de Certeau, "The Madness of Vision," *Enclitic* 7, no. 1 (Spring 1983), p. 28.

114. For a discussion of his complicated and ambivalent relationship to religion, see Rabil, *Merleau-Ponty: Existentialist of the Social World*, chap. 9.

115. Merleau-Ponty, *Phenomenology of Perception*, p. 209.

116. Ibid., p. 235.

117. Ibid., p. 268.

118. Merleau-Ponty, "Cézanne's Doubt," in *Sense and Non-sense*, p. 14.

119. Merleau-Ponty, "The Eye and the Mind," pp. 185–186.

120. Merleau-Ponty, *The Phenomenology of Perception*, p. 361.

121. The term appears in various places throughout his work, for example in *Signs*, p. 16, and *The Visible and the Invisible*, p. 273.

122. Merleau-Ponty, *The Phenomenology of Perception*, p. 361.

123. Merleau-Ponty, *Adventures of the Dialectic*, p. 153.

124. For my own analysis of his success, see *Marxism and Totality*, chap. 11.

125. It appeared in *Signs*.

126. Merleau-Ponty, "Eye and Mind," pp. 162–163.

127. Ibid., p. 163. See also Levin, "Visions of Narcissism: Intersubjectivity and the Reversals of Reflection," in Martin Dillon, ed., *Merleau-Ponty Vivant* (Albany: State University Press of New York, 1990), pp. 47–90. [Levin argues that Merleau-Ponty's phenomenology shows how the reflective reversibilities of vision constitute a corporeal schema that grounds the principles of mutual recognition, reciprocity, and justice.—Editor]

128. Merleau-Ponty, "Eye and Mind," p. 166.

129. Ibid., p. 186.

130. Svetlana Alpers, *The Art of Describing: Dutch Art in the Seventeenth Century* (Chicago: University of Chicago Press, 1983).

131. Merleau-Ponty, "Eye and Mind," p. 168.

132. Marc Richir, "La défenestration," *L'Arc* 46 (1971).

133. Merleau-Ponty, "Eye and Mind," p. 169.

134. Ibid., p. 171.

135. Ibid., p. 174.

136. Ibid., p. 178.

137. Merleau-Ponty, "Man and Adversity," *Signs*, p. 240.

138. Sartre, "Existentialism Is a Humanism," in *Existentialism from Dostoevsky to Sartre*, ed. Walter Kaufmann (Cleveland: Meridian, 1963).

139. Merleau-Ponty, *Signs*, p. 21.

140. Merleau-Ponty, *The Visible and the Invisible*, p. 88.

141. Ibid., p. 43.

142. Ibid., p. 142.

143. Ibid., p. 253.

144. Ibid., p. 248.

145. Merleau-Ponty, "The Child's Relations with Others," in *The Primacy of Perception*, pp. 125–141. He distinguished the "specular image," which is a psychological phenomenon, from the "image in the mirror," which is merely physical.

146. Ibid., p. 136.

147. Ibid.

148. Ibid.

149. Jacques Lacan, "Maurice Merleau-Ponty," *Les Temps Modernes*, vols. 184–185 (1961), pp. 245–254; see also the confirmation of this judgment in Jacques-Alain Miller, ed., *Four Fundamental Concepts of Psychoanalysis*, trans. Alan Sheridan (New York: Norton, 1981), p. 119.

150. Merleau-Ponty, *The Visible and the Invisible*, p. 126. Sartre claimed that Merleau-Ponty agreed with Lacan on this issue. See "Merleau-Ponty," p. 306.

151. Merleau-Ponty, "An Unpublished Text by Maurice Merleau-Ponty," p. 11.

152. For an account of the confusions in his reading of Saussure, see Schmidt, *Maurice Merleau-Ponty*, pp. 105–116.

153. Merleau-Ponty, "Eye and Mind," p. 169, and "Indirect Language and the Voices of Silence," p. 81.

154. Merleau-Ponty, *The Visible and the Invisible*, p. 155.

155. This argument is developed by de Certeau, "The Madness of Vision," p. 30.

156. Merleau-Ponty, *Signs*, p. 16.

157. Ibid., pp. 16–17.

158. Merleau-Ponty, *The Visible and the Invisible*, p. 214.

159. For a good account of the radical shift in climate, political and theoretical, around 1960 in France, see Descombes, *Modern French Philosophy*.

160. Jean-François Lyotard, *Des Dispositifs pulsionnels* (Paris: Christian Bourgois Editeur, 1980), pp. 77–78. For a comparison of the two, see Jean-Loup Thébaud, "Le chair et l'infini: J. F. Lyotard and Merleau-Ponty," *Esprit* 66 (June 1982): 158–162.

161. René Magritte, Letter to Alphonse de Waehlens, April 28, 1962; reprinted in Harry Torczyner, *Magritte: Ideas and Images*, trans. Richard Miller (New York: Henry N. Abrams, 1977), p. 55.

162. Luce Irigaray, *Éthique de la différance sexuelle* (Paris: Minnit, 1984), pp. 148, 163. For another feminist analysis of Merleau-Ponty, see Judith Butler, "Sexual Ideology and Phenomenological Description: A Feminist Critique of Merleau-Ponty's *Phenomenology of Perception*," in Jeffner Allen and Iris Marion Young, eds., *The Thinking Muse: Feminism in Modern French Philosophy* (Bloomington: Indiana University Press, 1989).

163. Foucault, *The Archaeology of Knowledge and the Discourse on Language*, trans. A. M. Sheridan Smith (New York, 1972), p. 203. For an excellent comparison of the two on the question of painting, see Stephen Watson, "Merleau-Ponty and Foucault: De-aestheticization of the Work of Art," *Philosophy Today*, vol. 28, no. 2/4 (Summer 1984), pp. 148–166.

164. Christian Metz, "The Imaginary Signifier," *Screen,* vol. 16, no. 2 (Summer 1985), p. 54.

165. For an account of its importance with special reference to Foucault, see Martin Jay, "In the Empire of the Gaze: Foucault and the Denigration of Vision in Twentieth-Century French Thought," in David Couzens Hoy, ed., *Foucault: A Critical Reader* (New York: Blackwell, 1986).

SIX

Decline and Fall

Ocularcentrism in Heidegger's Reading of the History of Metaphysics

David Michael Levin

I

Heidegger's reading of the history of metaphysics is framed by an interpretation of modernity: a viewpoint strongly influenced by Nietzsche, but also by Jünger and Spengler, from which Heidegger sees modernity, and the metaphysics in its culture, in terms of a decline and fall with the promise of decisive interruption and a different beginning. Heidegger's viewpoint is hermeneutical, unconcealing. His words can sound kerygmatic, seeming to announce the apocalypse, the moment of crisis; but they address us as deeply encrypted, trembling with ironic overtones and undertones, undecidable reverberations, blinding insight with shades of meaning and self-deconstructive reflections. And while foreseeing a crisis, he was also looking, casting about, for hints, *Winke*, traces of the promise, signs of redemption: another beginning. This interpretation also figures in what Heidegger has to say about vision and the possibility of a different vision. I will argue that his metaphysics is often ocular, but not ocularcentric—especially not later, after the so-called turning in his thinking; that, although he never denounced ocularcentrism as such, he took a very critical position with regard to the everyday experience of seeing and the ocularcentric metaphysics which reflection on this experience has brought forth; and third, that he began to let his thinking shift from a vision-generated discourse to a discourse formed by listening.

In his 1935 *Introduction to Metaphysics*, Heidegger notes that the

> inflection of the noun is called *ptosis* (*casus*); that of the verb *enklisis* (*declinatio*). . . . The words *ptosis* and *enklisis* mean falling, tipping, inclining. This implies a deviation from standing upright and straight. But this erect stand-

ing-there, coming up (*zum Stande kommen,* coming to stand) and enduring (*im Stand bleiben,* remaining in standing) is what the Greeks understood by being.[1]

Later in the text, he glosses *enklisis* in terms of "deficiency" as well as "deviation."[2]

Continuing in this *Introduction* the work he began in *Being and Time,* Heidegger undertook a reading of the history of Western metaphysics, a history of the discourse, in which he tells a story of decline and fall. In effect, therefore, his story sets the history of this discourse within the frame of a larger, and indeed all too familiar story: the story of the decline and fall of Western civilization. This is, of course, an exceedingly questionable story. But beyond the specific questions that may be raised with regard to the validity of this particular story, questions difficult to settle may be posed with regard to the very possibility of such "grand narratives." I want to acknowledge here the importance of these questions; but I shall not consider them further in the context of this study. Rather, our concern here will be centered on the question of ocularcentrism as it figures in Heidegger's reading of the history of metaphysics.

Let us return now to this reading. I have suggested that Heidegger might seem to be telling the very *same* story that so many reactionary thinkers in Europe had been telling and repeating since the closing years of the nineteenth century: a story which, let us say, begins in nostalgia and concludes with a condemnation of modernity. There are, to be sure, some deep and profoundly disturbing affinities between Heidegger's account and the narratives in circulation among the forces of the German right. And yet, throughout Heidegger's text, there are also hints and traces of a "new beginning," a revolutionary "repetition" very different from the simple turn backward for which the conservatives among his contemporaries were preparing to battle—and also very different from the "new beginning" proclaimed by the official program of National Socialism.

In any case, Heidegger's reading of the history of metaphysics is framed by an interpretation of modernity that sees Western history in terms of a decline and fall. This interpretation also figures in what he has to say about vision. But this framing is treacherous, and perhaps even double-crossing. Looking back into the past, Heidegger's reading attempts to document the closure of metaphysics. But the differences separating his reading from other stories begin to show themselves once it is seen that this "closure" must be understood in two senses, call them (a) and (b), corresponding to the two grammatical readings (the subjective and objective genitives) that one may give to the little word *of.*

In the subjective sense, (a), of the preposition, the closure in question is something the discourse itself effects, a process at work *within* the discourse. The closure is a matter of how the discourse works or functions—say, by neglecting that open dimensionality of things, things such as physical nature (*physis*), law (*nomos*), and speech (*logos*), which Heidegger calls "being." The closure of metaphysics thus consists in its reductionism, its self-restriction, its narrowness of focus. Paradoxically, in the very act of asking the question by which the discourse of metaphysics is inaugurated, or say opened—namely, the question "Why is there something (anything at all), rather than nothing?"—philosophical thinking unknowingly closed itself off, protecting itself against the disturbing "solicitations" of the question, by interpreting the opening-up of our experience, experience called for precisely by the question of being, in such a way that an experience with the openness, the open dimensionality of being, would already be foreclosed. The story Heidegger tells, then, is a story that documents a process of decline and fall within the unfolding concept-formations important to metaphysics, a process ultimately of increasing restriction and reduction in our experience of being: a process for which, in the story Heidegger tells, the discourse of metaphysics itself is responsible. Thus, it may be said that, by telling this story of closure and bringing it to our attention, Heidegger was attempting simultaneously to accomplish the *closure* of a discourse that he read as increasingly closed to being, and to begin a process of *opening it up* (again), assuring its continued survival, but only by virtue of a new and truly appropriate beginning. (An "appropriate" beginning would be a beginning in which the discourse let itself be "appropriated" by the claim, the *Anspruch,* of being. What this means is that the discourse would attempt to keep its words open and receptive to that claim. I will say more about this claim later, specifying it as a claim on our vision, our capacity to see—a claim, in fact, on the *character* of our vision, and on our willingness and commitment to develop this capacity.)

This point leads us to an interpretation of "closure" based on the objective sense, (b), of the preposition. In terms of *this* sense, the closure in question is an ending: old-style metaphysics may perhaps continue; but in any event, it will not continue in its old form. Let me be more precise with regard to what continues and what so changes that the discourse may be described in terms of its closure. According to Heidegger, metaphysics is supposed to be concerned with the question of being, being as such. It is supposed to be, and on Heidegger's reading claims to be, the guardian of the "ontological difference," that is, the difference between being and beings. Metaphysics is the discourse of being. But, according to Heidegger, this "ontological vocation" is precisely what metaphysics has systematically neglected and forgotten, occupying itself instead with the ontic realm of beings, and even so deeply forgetting its calling that it has increasingly reduced being itself, being as such, to the ontic condition of a being—one being among many, albeit the highest or most universal being among all the (other) beings. So, in terms of this (objective) sense of the preposition, the closure *of* metaphysics would mean either (1) its total cessation, its ending, the end of all discourse (claiming to be) devoted to the question of being as such, or else (2) the continuation of this discourse, but in a radically different form: the form, namely, of a discourse still concerned with the question of being, but no longer relating to it in the old way, that is, no longer forgetting, neglecting, or denying the open dimensionality, the "clearing," of being, no longer reducing or restricting this dimensionality, no longer relating to the being of beings as if it were a being among beings. Just what this means in terms of vision will be considered shortly. Suffice it to say, for the moment, that we may think of this "open dimensionality" as a characterization of the field of illumination that figures in human vision.

I think the second alternative here is the one that for Heidegger better describes the situation projected by his work. By *opening up* the concepts (*logoi*) of the discourse to the question of being, and to its dimensionality, its reach and range, Heidegger *brings to a close* a discourse which has been, with and from its very inception, a curiously paradoxical discourse, both open and closed to ontological questioning and the experience that would involve—but closing, increasingly, in the course of its history. The original closure of metaphysics in sense (a)—that is, the closure of metaphysical thinking to the question of being that already took place at the very beginning—was never resisted or overcome. On the contrary, this closure, this forgetfulness, has persisted and continued, down through the ages, finally reaching such a state of reductionism that it now faces an abyss: the frightening groundlessness of nihilism. No longer claimed by the question of being, the discourse is in danger of becoming closed in the sense of "ended."

Is this danger—closure in the objective sense of the genitive—somehow *connected* with the fact that metaphysics has broached the question of being only to inscribe it within a process of closure in the subjective sense: the closure—say, the deafness and blindness—of the discourse to the open dimensionality of being, and thus, too, the closure, the reduction, of this dimensionality itself? If so, then Heidegger's attempt to open up the discourse and make it aware of, receptive, and open to the openness of being itself will be at once the closure of metaphysics, appropriately putting an end to its traditional relation to being, and also its opening, appropriately introducing a new ontological relationship—or rather, since it is a question of returning the discourse to its original (sense of) vocation, introducing a relationship radically *different* from the one which has prevailed.

More concretely understood, just what is at stake in Heidegger's insistence on the openness of being, and in his argument that we must retrieve and accomplish, in the discourse of metaphysics, our openness to the claim of being? In keeping with the conception of phenomenology and hermeneutics formulated very clearly in the introduction to *Being and Time,* the term "openness *of* being" stands for and encourages resistance to all forms of reification, totalization, and reductionism, while correspondingly the term "openness *to* being" stands for and encourages epistemological humility, a rigorously experimental attitude, always provisional, always questioning, always alert to the fact that the being of beings is such that beings continually offer themselves to a multiplicity of interpretations. Together, then, these two terms, functioning—in effect—normatively and critically, stand for a consistent perspectivism, truth without certainty, the end of essentialism, an uncompromising break with foundationalism, and a renunciation of the metaphysics of presence.

Moreover, since some of the beings in question are sentient, are animals, or are beings such as we are, these terms, charged with ethical significance, serve to remind us that our ontology and epistemology must never fail to recognize, respect, and protect the being of these beings. In a word, it is a question of openmindedness, for the question of being calls into question all totalizations, all reifications, all reductionisms: it opens all domains to the draft of being and holds them open—ethics and politics no less than ontology and epistemology. In principle, and regardless of what Heidegger himself may have thought, the discourse of being contests and breaches all forms of closure—including those tacitly at work in the liberal tradition of humanism; and it articulates the dimensions of a new humanism. Thus, for example, on the terrain of ethics, it shelters a deep respect for the differentness of others.

The argument I will be formulating here concerns seeing and the discourse of vision. There are, in this regard, many questions that need to be asked and that call for thought. Is it the case that vision, and the discourse of vision (visual images, visual metaphors, and vision-based or vision-centered concepts), have been hegemonic in and for modernity? And are they still? Is modernity, as Derrida claims, ocularcentric? Has it been dominated by a visual paradigm? If so, what is the *character* of this paradigmatic vision? And what are its effects? What can we learn from that history? Does it figure in the ancient world as well—say, in ancient Greece? Can it be recognized in the thinking of Plato, and in other thinkers of antiquity? And what is to be said about the philosophical discourse we identify with modernity? Is this a discourse dominated by vision? Has it, perhaps, been saturated by vision-based and vision-centered language, figured and disfigured by the character of our everyday vision? Can we discern, in this discourse, in its observations, reflections, and theoretical speculations, the hegemony of an ocularcentric paradigm of rationality—a reason conceived in and by our historical experience with sight?

If we affirm ocularcentrism and hold that vision has dominated modernity through the hegemony of a vision-generated paradigm of knowledge, truth, and reality, further questions then confront us: If the character of seeing is embedded in history, how have historical changes in our visionary experience, changes including our understanding of seeing and of ourselves as beings gifted with sight, affected the hegemonic history of the ocularcentric paradigm of rationality? Does vision display a distinctive character in modernity? Does vision—I mean, of course, vision of a distinctive character—assume a singular role in the philosophical discourse of modernity?

These questions prepare the ground for some critical normative questions that would challenge not only the hegemony of vision, but also the paradigm of rationality ruled by this hegemony and based on vision and its discourse. Do these questions effect a breach in the history of this hegemony and its paradigm of rationality? Do they ultimately point beyond the life-world we identify as the period of modernity, in the direction of a postmodern constellation of cultural experiences and understandings?

It is possible, I think, to argue that, in the course of a struggle to understand the texts of the Pre-Socratics and think philosophically about poetry and language, Heidegger found himself moving away from the unexamined ocularcentrism of the philosophical tradition. Indeed, it may be argued that, little by little, his thinking was beginning to drift away from the old rationality of vision, carried away perhaps by the very logic of this occupation with language, in the direction of the very different paradigm of rationality, and the very different way of seeing, that can be instituted on the normative ground of listening and hearing. The *Beiträge zur Philosophie (Vom Ereignis)*, written in the years 1936–1938, already strongly suggest this shift, working not toward a "moment of vision" but rather with a thinking attuned to, and attuned by, the echo, *der Anklang,* of being.[3]

Does Heidegger's thinking, struggling to listen and hear something still unthought in the shadowy traces of the Pre-Socratics and something still unspoken in the writings of poets, poets such as Hölderlin, Rilke, and Trakl, foreshadow a paradigm shift of major significance? Is Heidegger's late thinking, his thinking after the "turn," turned so decisively in the direction of auditory experience, resonating to the need for a different ontology? Perhaps it is responding to new possibilities in the history of (our experience of) being. Perhaps its distinctly different tone— this strange, *unheimlich* tone that depends so much on an effort to listen and hear, and becomes audible in the texts which follow the turn—is a tone attuned, somehow, to the tone set by being at the end of modernity, at that moment when the ocularcentric rationality which has ruled over the modern life-world can no longer contain the differential justice of the logos.

I will not attempt to answer all these large and difficult questions here. For the time being, I am satisfied with having broached them. Before leaving them, however, I would like briefly to suggest that, in the work of Habermas, in his discourse ethics and his theory of communicative rationality, precisely this shift of paradigms is at stake. Accordingly, if I may venture an hypothesis calling for further thought, I would like to propose that the problematization of ocularcentrism is also the problematization of modernity, and that, correspondingly, the increasingly widespread cultural drift toward a discursive conception of ethics and a truly communicative rationality, a drift greatly strengthened by the work of Habermas, sets the stage for a postmodern world in which the normativity implicit in speaking and listening can set the tone—not only for justice but for our claims to knowledge, truth, and the social construction of reality.

Reflecting on these questions, I find that there is a story waiting to be told. The frame for the story we shall be considering is a theory of modernity: an interpretation of modernity on the verge of a shift in paradigms. According to this interpretation, we have come to a moment in history when the negative factors at work in ocularcentrism, and the negative consequences of these factors, are becoming increasingly apparent, increasingly problematic. As this problematization takes place, the hegemony of a vision-based, visioned-centered *episteme* is weakened, and an experimental space is opened up, where it may be possible for people to practice and institute a new, postmodern paradigm for knowledge, truth, and reality, based and centered instead on the norms of a communicatively formed rationality that are implicit in our speaking and listening.

In this study, I shall for the most part limit myself to a hermeneutical reading of Heidegger's *Introduction to Metaphysics*. As for his earlier texts, suffice it to say that, despite his attempt to break away from the ego-logical idealism, the Cartesianism, of Husserl's phenomenology, they are saturated with vision-based and vision-centered language. Thus, for example, one finds in these works not only an unfolding examination of the nature of visual perception and its illusions, pathologies, and potentials but also penetrating inquiries into the history of reason as a source of "natural light"; reflections on phenomenology as a hermeneutics of bringing-to-light and making visible; provocative thoughts on the visibility of truth and the mind as mirror of truth; explorations of the practical importance of foresight (*Vorsicht*) and circumspection (*Umsicht*); bold suggestions regarding the existential "projections" of ontology; and challenging questions about the nature of observation in science and the rootedness of theory in theoretical vision.

In *Being and Time,* a work that first appeared in 1927, that is, before his *Introduction to Metaphysics,* Heidegger undertook a devastating critique of everyday seeing—a diagnosis, we might say, of the psychosocial pathology of everyday seeing—which he repeated, essentially unchanged, in his *Introduction*.[4] In the latter text, as we shall see, this critique would seem to be reinforced, and even extended, since the visual language Heidegger used in formulating his critique of modernity—he wrote of a "darkening of the world," a *Weltverdüsterung*—suggests that there may be some *connection* between this "darkening," the decline and fall of Western civilization, and the hegemony of vision as our paradigm for knowledge, truth, and reality.

Be this as it may, it must be noted that nevertheless, in the framework of *Being and Time,* this critique did not cause him to *abandon* the language of vision. Far from it. Seemingly acknowledging the domination of a visual paradigm, he observed that, "from the beginning onwards, the tradition of philosophy has been oriented primarily towards 'seeing' as a way of access to entities *and to Being*."[5] What immediately follows this is an unequivocal commitment to *continue* the discourse ruled over by this paradigm: "To keep the connection with this tradition, we may formalize 'sight' and 'seeing' enough to obtain therewith a universal term for characterizing any access to entities or to Being, as access in general."[6] In light of the fact that the text is structured to unfold into what Heidegger called a "moment of vision," I am inclined to explain this commitment by reference to the contention that appears in a chapter on "temporality and everydayness," where he declared his conviction that "a Dasein can, in existing, develop the different possibilities of sight, of looking around (*Sichumsehens*), and of just looking."[7]

Is this reference to a "moment of vision" only metaphor? Do these words refer to an actually lived experience of the eyes? I would say that, for Heidegger, they refer certainly to a moment of achieved understanding: a moment when one understands how all things "hang together," and enjoys a deepened sense of the meaning of human existence in relation to the question(ing) of being. But to say that this moment is one of understanding is not to deny that this understanding is, and must be, embodied—that it will only have been achieved in, and through, thought-ful work with our experience as visionary beings, our experience as be-ings endowed with the capacity to see, and that it will be manifest pri-marily in the way we actually look and see things—and manifest, too, in our views and viewpoints, our perspectives, our *Weltanschauung,* and the predominant historical understanding many of us living in the West share today regarding an apparently unavoidable perspectivism, or rela-tivism, in our cultural paradigm of knowledge, truth, and reality.

Among Heidegger's later writings, texts written later than both *Being and Time* and *An Introduction to Metaphysics,* there are some extremely im-portant works concerned with the historical character of vision, examin-ing this character in relation both to the historical conditions of moder-nity and to the philosophical discourse which, however obliquely, reflects those conditions, continually reinscribing their terms within its vision-saturated language. The texts I have in mind here are "The Age of the World Picture" (1938), "The Word of Nietzsche: 'God is Dead'" (1936–1943), "The Question Concerning Technology" (1949–1955), "The Turning" (1949), and "Science and Reflection" (1954). In all these texts there is a deeply critical examination of vision-based thinking and vision-centered discourse, situating this critique in relation to the vision distinc-tive of modernity and exposing the historical formation of this vision, be-ginning with the legacy of antiquity. These are very important texts, but they are not the only ones in which Heidegger examines and problema-tizes vision and its discourses. This problematization also figures, as we have already noted, in his reflections on the Pre-Socratics—Anaximander, Parmenides, and Heraclitus—and in all his thinking, early and late, about Plato.

There certainly is no sweeping disparagement of vision as such, nor of the discourse of light as such, when Heidegger reflects on Kalchas the seer in "The Anaximander Fragment." Nor is there any denigration of light and vision in his "Logos" study on Heraclitus, Fragment B50, and his "Alētheia" study on Heraclitus, Fragment B16. But Heidegger always attempts to articulate a difference (call it "an ontological difference") be-tween (1) the character of our habitual, "normal" vision, a way of seeing that he regards as forgetful of the lighting by grace of which we are en-abled to see, and which he therefore, in this sense, accuses of being de-generate and pathological, and (2) the character of a radically different way of seeing, a vision in which the potential for "recollecting" this light-ing, and seeing it "aletheically"—or say, in its unconcealment—as a gift of being, would be realized. Heidegger is therefore not at all antiocular; but he certainly is strongly critical of the *character* of vision that has prevailed in our civilization, and that still prevails in our time. Thus, for example, in his commentary on Heraclitus, he points to the fact that we "turn from the lighting, and turn only towards what is present," toward that which "immediately concerns" us in our "everyday commerce with one another."[8] In *Being and Time,* he is critical of a gaze turned only by self-interested "curiosity"[9] and speaks disparagingly of "the still covetous vision of things" in "What Are Poets For?"[10]

It must be noted, however, that his critique of our vision, and of the philosophical discourses informed by this vision, is often the beginning of an effort to think a new way of seeing. This effort is, I believe, at the very heart of a short text from his late period, *Zur Erörterung der Gelassenheit,* in which he attempts to think beyond the horizon determined by our present vision and to articulate a radically different figure-ground structure for perception in terms of an "attitude" or *Stimmung* that he calls *Gelassenheit,* letting-be. However, as I indicated earlier, we shall for the most part restrict our thinking here to Heidegger's *Introduction to Metaphysics.*

II

Our word *paradigm,* which we are using here to describe the role of vision in the philosophical discourse of modernity, is itself a vision-generated word. It derives from the word *paradeigma,* which means "model." This word can be traced back to the ancient Greek words *para,* meaning "next to" or "alongside of" and *deiknunai,* meaning "to show" or "to indicate." Thus, the composite carries the meaning of "to compare," "to exhibit," and "to point out for special attention." The verb *deiknunai* is related to *dikè,* the Greek word for "justice" and "right," as well as to the Latin *dicere,* meaning "say" and "tell."

In his *Introduction to Metaphysics,* Heidegger traces the genealogy of the concept of paradigm, showing its formation in a specific experience with vision. He notes that, at a certain moment in the history of philosophical thought,

> Being as *idea* is exalted, it becomes true being, while being itself, previously dominant, is degraded to what Plato calls *mē on,* what really should not be and really *is* not, because in the realization it always deforms the idea, the pure appearance, by incorporating it in matter. The *idea* now becomes a *paradeigma,* a model.[11]

Continuing this account, Heidegger points out how *idea* in the sense of "paradigm" derived from, and shaped in its turn, the nature and character of our experience with vision, and how that shaping of vision determined, beyond itself, the crucial philosophical distinction between appearance and reality and the no less fateful philosophical understanding of truth, which reduced truth as unconcealment to truth as correspondence, correctness of representation. Thus we see that, in the formation of some crucial philosophical concepts, the ocularcentrism of philosophical discourse has played a decisive, and by no means innocent role:

> From the standpoint of the idea, appearing now takes on a new meaning. What appears—the phenomenon—is no longer *physis*, the emerging power, nor is it the self-manifestation of the appearance; no, appearing is now the emergence of the copy. And since the copy never equals the prototype, what appears is *mere* appearance, actually an illusion, a deficiency. . . . The truth of *physis*, *alētheia* as the unconcealment that is the essence of the emerging power, now becomes *homoiosis* and *mimēsis*, assimilation and accommodation, orientation . . . , it becomes a correctness of vision, of apprehension as representation.[12]

Now, how does this fit into a story of decline and fall? Heidegger elaborates the significance of the foregoing account:

> Once we fully understand all this, it becomes undeniable that the interpretation of being as *idea* is a far cry from the original beginning. Yet, when we speak of a decline it should be noted that this decline remains lofty; it does not sink into baseness. We can judge this loftiness from the following. The great period of Greek being-there [*Dasein*] was essentially the only classical age; it was so great that it provided the metaphysical conditions underlying the possibility of all classicism. The basic concepts *idea*, *paradeigma*, *homoiosis*, and *mimēsis* foreshadow the metaphysics of classicism.[13]

So it would seem that we cannot expect to understand the history of metaphysics and epistemology in the West—nor even, perhaps, the historical course of ethics in the West—without first understanding, quite literally, the Greeks' *view* of being.

Let us now consider the visual generation of the *idea* in greater detail. According to Heidegger's reading of the ancient Greek texts:

> The word *idea* means that which is seen in the visible, the aspect it offers. What is offered is the appearance, *eidos*, of what confronts us. The appearance of a thing is that wherein, as we say, it presents, introduces itself to us, places itself before (*vor-stellt*) us and as such stands before us . . . and . . . is present, i.e., in the Greek sense, it *is*. This standing is the stability of that which has emerged from out of itself, of *physis*. But from the standpoint of man, this standing-there of the stable and permanent is at the same time the surface of what is present *through itself*, the apprehensible. In the appearance, the present, the essent [*Seiende*], presents its what and how. It is apprehended and taken, it is in the possession of an acceptance, its property (*Habe*), it is the accessible presence of the present: *ousia*. This *ousia* can signify both: the presence of something present *and* this present thing in the what of its appearance (*Aussehen*).[14]

This interpretation of the ocularcentric generation of the *idea* suggests that, although empiricism and rationalism belong to two distinct histories, two distinct conceptual formations, they are both rooted in visual experience and share an ocularcentric genealogy. According to empiricism, all our ideas either came directly from perceptual experience or are at least connected to ideas which do have a direct perceptual origin. Thus, the idea is, in the most literal sense, an abstraction prized away from the perceptual object that is its source and referent. An essent (*Seiende*) appears, presenting a face, an aspect. What is seen, perspectivally, is a surface the sensible qualities of which constellate, in their abstraction from the object, an *eidos*, an idea of what the appearing object is. According to rationalism, however, the idea is always a prototype, paradigmatic for perceptual experience; it is the source of the possibility of perceptual experience and the referent for the illumination of the meaning that the perceptual object is given. In the texts of Platonism, one of the earliest known forms of rationalism within the Western philosophical tradition, there is, of course, a familiar story regarding our perception of things in the world. This story, introducing definitions that differentiate shadows, images, opinions (*doxai*), appearances, knowledge, and wisdom (*sophia*), confirms the ocularcentric generation of the Platonic concepts of knowledge and truth. At the center of this story we find the doctrine of recollection (*anamnēsis*) and the myths Plato repeats concerning the transmigration of souls. According to this account, ideas serving as paradigms and prototypes are eternal; that means that they have existed *a priori*, prior to all our worldly experience, prior to our encountering them and participating in their work. Souls, our souls, disembodied, first encounter them during our spiritual wanderings prior to the time of incarnation. At this time, our souls forget their great encounter with these ideas; and they lose the illumination those ideas cast. However, when our souls, endowed by grace of their embodiment with organs of perceptivity, encounter things in the world, it is possible for them to be reminded of the forgotten ideas. This is the process that Plato calls *anamnēsis*, recollection, and it involves two moments, or phases: first, a moment of abstraction, the moment of the *eidos*, in which a striking aspect is discriminated and made visible as such: "what appears (in its shining forth, its seeming) shows an aspect."[15] Second there is a moment of recognition, when, because of a visible resemblance, this aspect awakens a recollection of the forgotten idea. Thereafter, this idea becomes—or rather, depending on the character, the virtue of the soul's worldly life, the idea may become—a paradigm or prototype, a shining exemplar and source of illumination, for the remaining years of the soul's journey through the visible world of the senses.

Here, I think, one can begin to discern the outline and direction of an interpretation that would show how deeply and extensively the nature and character of the ancient Greek experience with seeing must have determined the conceptualization of ontology and epistemology in the philosophical thinking of antiquity.

But it is Heidegger's contention that philosophical thinking, in the moment of its historical instauration, enjoyed what might be described as a "privileged" experience with vision, from which it unknowingly moved away, and that its loss of contact with this experience correspondingly affected its understanding of being and knowing. Here is what Heidegger says about the beginning of philosophical thinking:

> from the viewpoint of the beholder [von der Betrachtung her gesehen], that which stands-there-in-itself becomes that which re-presents itself, which presents itself in what it looks like. The Greeks call the appearance of a thing eidos or idea. Initially, eidos included a resonance of what we too have in mind when we say: the thing has a face, it can let itself be seen, it stands. The thing "sits." It rests in the manifestation, i.e., emergence, of its essence. . . . For the [early] Greeks, "being" basically meant this standing presence [Anwesenheit].[16]

But what happened in the course of time? "Greek philosophy never returned to this ground of being and to what it implies. It remained on the surface of that which is present."[17] "The transformation of physis and logos into idea and statement has its inner ground," says Heidegger, "in a transformation of the essence of truth from unconcealment to correctness."[18] This transformation "is a decline from the first beginning."[19] This

> essence of truth could not be maintained in its initial, original force. Unconcealment, the space created [gestiftete Raum—better translated, perhaps, as the space "founded" or "prepared"] for the appearing of the essent, broke down. "Idea" and "statement," ousia and kategoria, were saved from the ruins. . . . A ready-made [vorhandener] logos had to assimilate and accommodate itself to a ready-made essent as its object.[20]

"Yet," Heidegger adds, calling our attention to the way in which the character of this historical evolution becomes visible—how it shows up in, and also as, the character of our experience with vision, "a last glimmer and semblance [Schein und Schimmer] of the original essence of alētheia has been preserved. . . . But the remaining semblance of alētheia no longer has sufficient sustaining power or tension to be the determining ground for [our experience of] the essence of truth" in, and as it lays claim to, our visual experience.[21]

With painstaking hermeneutical attention to phenomenological details, Heidegger carefully documents the history of a decline in the wake of this great beginning. Remaining on the surface, for example, is an attitude or comportment that is peculiar to our capacity for vision—and it carries, as we shall see, quite distinctive ontological implications.

Heidegger avers that "Metaphysics belongs [*gehört*] to the nature of man."[22] The word *gehört*, however, also means "listens to" and "is obedient to." So metaphysics not only *belongs* to our nature; it is also *obedient* to its conditions. What does this purport? It means, among other things, that if there are any inveterate tendencies in human nature—limitations, say, in our visionary capacity—these tendencies or limitations would show up, would be reflected, in the discourse of metaphysics. This suggests some questions. Since metaphysics is the work of philosophers, and this work is a work of reflection based and centered on vision, it would seem reasonable to ask whether we can document a decline in the character of the philosophers' visionary experience, and, if so, whether that could be responsible for the decline that Heidegger documents in the history of this discourse.

After all, says Heidegger, "We know that the unconcealment of being is not simply given. Unconcealment occurs only when it is achieved by work: the work of the word in poetry, the work of stone in temple and statue, the work of the word in thought, the work of the *polis* as the historical place in which all this is grounded and preserved."[23] Could the decline which figures in metaphysics—a decline that disfigures by closing it to the openness which is being—perhaps be a symptom of the historical marginalization of the seers' great visions and, correlatively, the increasing domination, within philosophical discourse, of the more degenerate type of vision which has prevailed in everyday life?

Heidegger's argument is worth noting in this regard:

> Appearance, *doxa*, is not something beside being and unconcealment; it belongs to unconcealment. But *doxa* is itself ambiguous. It means the view [*Ansicht*] which something presents of itself and at the same time the view [*Ansicht*] that men have. Being-there [*Dasein*] defines itself in these views. They are stated and passed on. Thus *doxa* is a kind of *logos*. The prevailing views [*herrschenden Ansichten*] now block [*versperren*] men's view [*Aussicht*] of the essent. The essent is deprived of the possibility of appearing spontaneously and turning *toward* apprehension [*Vernehmen*]. The view [*Aussicht*] that usually turns toward us is distorted into an opinion [*Ansicht*]. The rule of opinions [*Die Herrschaft der Ansichten*] perverts and distorts the essent.[24]

There may be metaphor and allegory in these words, but, in any case, I think it is crucial that we take Heidegger's words as *directly referring* to our lived experience with seeing. Now, on my reading, this passage certainly seems to suggest that the prevailing "rule of opinions" and, in conformity with that, domination by a very "degenerate" type of vision—the type, namely, that tends to prevail in the ontological forgetfulness

(*Seinsvergessenheit*) of everyday life—eventually would have extended their corrupt hegemony into the domain of metaphysics, displacing the authority there of a very different philosophical experience with vision: above all, the visionary experience, eluding a metaphysics of presence, exemplified by the Pre-Socratics.

This is an interpretation that I find quite convincing. But it needs to be fleshed out in its phenomenological details, so that we can see how the domination of a degenerate type of seeing, ruling as our cultural paradigm for knowledge, truth, and reality, invaded the discourse of metaphysics and brought about its increasing closure: a process that Heidegger makes visible in his interpretation of "the transformation of *physis* to idea, and of *logos* as gathering to *logos* as statement"—and also, of course, in his tracework marking the historical "transformation" of truth as "unconcealment" to "truth as correctness."[25]

Heidegger takes us back to the ancient Greeks, back, in fact, to the Pre-Socratics. "Essent," according to his story of the glorious dawn of philosophical thinking, "is that which is permanent and represents itself as such, that which appears and manifests itself primarily and for the most part to vision."[26] Thus, says Heidegger, "We know that being disclosed itself to the Greeks as *physis*. [But *physis*, as the] realm of emerging and abiding, is intrinsically at the same time a shining appearing (*das scheinende Erscheinen*)."[27] And he adds that the "radicals *phy* and *pha* name the same thing. *Phyein*, self-sufficient emergence, is *phainesthai*, to flare up, to show itself, to appear [in the light]."[28]

Moreover, since appearing is "the power that emerges," and appearing makes manifest, makes visible, "we know that being, appearing, causes to emerge from concealment."[29] The essent thus emerges into unconcealment (*alētheia*, its truth), places itself within this space, this clearing, and there stands and stays in self-disclosure. Now, in appearing thus, every essent "gives itself as aspect, *dokei*. *Doxa* [in fact] means aspect, regard (*Ansehen*), namely the regard in which something stands."[30] It also means "glory."[31] When essents can stand in their truth—when they are allowed, by virtue of the way in which we look at and see them, to appear in their most radiant aspect (*Ansicht*), then they are present (*anwesend*) in their aletheic truth, as what they "most essentially" are. "For the Greeks, *on* [being] and *kalon* [the beautiful] meant the same thing: presence was pure radiance."[32] (In his *Journal*, Thoreau wrote: "The perception of beauty is a moral test."[33] I suggest that it is precisely as a test of the character, the virtue, of our vision, that Heidegger's "question of being" is related to our capacity for seeing. We shall return to this point shortly.)

"Now," says Heidegger, "we have come to the point at which we were aiming. Because being, *physis*, consists in appearing, in an offering of appearances and views, it stands, essentially and hence necessarily and enduringly, in the possibility of an appearance which precisely covers over and conceals what the essent in truth, i.e., in unconcealment, is."[34] In this way, appearing, in one of the senses of *Schein,* namely, as coming-to-light and becoming visible, becomes semblance, *Anschein.* Semblances, however, are without the beauty of *Schein* in the sense of radiance and glow: their coming-to-light is duller, dimmer, more superficial, and, most important, not as enduring.

Under the domination, then, of a way of seeing in the everyday character of which the will to power prevails, and in which, therefore, a strong affinity binds together an instrumental vision and a culture of technology, the "essent becomes an object either to be beheld (view, image) [*für das Betrachten (Anblick, Bild)*] or to be acted upon (product and calculation)."[35] The being of the essent, *das Seiende,* under the control of a willful vision, is ontologically reduced, either to the practical objectivity of a being always ready-to-hand (*Zuhandensein*) or else to the theoretical objectivity of a being always present-at-hand (*Vorhandensein*). What is *zuhanden* is seen, is visible, only instrumentally, as the means to an end in the context of some practical activity. We might say that the essent which is *zuhanden* is seen only peripherally, or rather that its being is being-seen but not being-looked-at. The *Zuhandene* is noticed, really seen, really made visible only, as Heidegger says, when there is an instrumental breakdown and the essent with which we are involved compels our attention. By contrast, what is *vorhanden* is given a central position in a field of inquiry: as the object of thought and the focus of questions, the *Vorhandene* is an end in itself, made visible for a theoretical gaze.

In both cases, however, "The original world-making power, *physis,* degenerates [thereby] into a prototype to be copied and imitated."[36] The original Greek ontology increasingly falls under the sway of a calculative and instrumental rationality: under the torsion of its vision, and under its mode of production. Ontology is thus increasingly bent to the service of a will to power. "The original emergence and standing of energies, the *phainesthai,* or appearance in the great [phenomenological] sense of a world epiphany [*Epiphanie,* a hermeneutical event, bringing the aletheic truth of beings into unconcealment], becomes a visibility of things that are already there, present-at-hand [*vorhandener Dinge*], and can be pointed out."[37] A vision of the eyes which originally acknowledged and accepted the luminous sway (*Walten*) of being, that which presences and gives itself to be seen (*den Entwurf*), "becomes," in Heidegger's words, "a mere looking-at or looking-over or gaping-at. Vision degenerates into mere optics."[38] "To be sure," he avers, "there are still essents. . . . But being has gone out of them. The essent has been made into an 'object' of endless and ever-changing activity, and only thereby has it retained an appearance of its permanence."[39]

To the extent that the will to power captures our capacity for vision, there is a strong inveterate tendency in our vision to fixate whatever our eyes behold, to "bring being to a stand," a standstill, in our grasp and hold.[40] Indeed, we say *Wahr-nehmung, per-ception,* stressing the taking (*nehmen*) rather than the protecting (*wahren*). Thus, "if the human being is to take over his being [*Dasein*] in the radiance [*Helle*] of being, he must bring this being to a stand, must endure it in appearance and against appearance, and he must wrest both appearance and being from the abyss of nonbeing."[41] Since the character of our everyday vision is such that we tend to reify, to substantialize, and to totalize, philosophical thinking, increasingly under the sway of a vision-based and vision-centered paradigm, represents itself as standing positioned in a relation of *opposition* to being: "In defining the opposition between being and thinking, we move in a familiar schema. Being is the objective, the object. Thinking is the subjective, the subject. The relation of thinking to being is that of subject to object."[42]

This structuring (*Gestaltung*) of our visionary encounter with (the being of) various essents needs to be considered further:

> From the vantage point to which our questioning has now brought us, we can survey another aspect. We have shown that, contrary to current opinion, the word "being" has a strictly circumscribed meaning. This implies that being itself is understood in a definite way. Thus understood, it is manifest to us. But all understanding, as a fundamental mode of disclosure, must move in a definite line of sight [*bestimmte Blickbahn*]. . . . The line of sight [*Blickbahn des Anblicks*] must be laid down in advance. We call it the "perspective" [*Perspektive*], the track of fore-sight [*Vorblickbahn*]. Thus we shall see not only that being is not understood in an indeterminate way, but that the determinate understanding of being moves in a predetermined perspective [*Vorblickbahn*].[43]

This prompts him to comment:

> To move back and forth, to slip and slide along this track have become second nature with us, so much so that we neither have knowledge of it, nor even consider or understand the inquiry into it. We have become immersed (not to say lost) in this perspective, this line of sight which sustains and guides all our understanding of being.[44]

This linear character of vision, determining, as it does, the modern experience of being (the being of beings, of essents), continues a history that Heidegger traces all the way back to the ancient Greeks. In modern times, to be sure, it assumes a distinctive—paradigmatic—force and weight. But the history of this "line of sight" already begins with the Greeks:

> what makes our immersion the more complete as well as the more hidden is that even the Greeks did not and could not bring this perspective [*Vorblickbahn*] to light, and this for essential reasons (not [only] for reasons of human deficiency). Still, the growth of the differentiation between being and thinking [in, e.g., the structure of subject and object] played an important part in forming and stabilizing this perspective in which the Greek understanding of being [already] moved.[45]

In modernity, the background illumination of the visual field, and also the presence of the horizon, simultaneously opening and delimiting this field, have become occluded. Vision narrows down to a line of sight, intensely focused on its object. In the ideal situation, this line of sight, its beholding moved, or rather driven, by the will to power, will position its objects directly in front, fixating and holding them in a structure ruled by opposition and confrontation. Corresponding to this visual attitude, a "frontal ontology" prevails. And, since the will to power drives our seeing, the presencing (*Anwesen*) of beings, of essents, is subject to reification and totalization. The "metaphysics of presence" is rooted in such vision, an observation or contemplation that is immobile and impassive, untouched and unmoved by what it sees—what it is *given* to see.

In *Zur Seinsfrage*, Heidegger observes that the *Gestalt* undergoes a fateful historical transformation at the beginning of modernity. The *Gestalt* is totalized and reified; it closes and becomes *Gestell*. In its general meaning, *Gestell* refers to the systematic, totalizing ordering of things according to the universal imposition of a principle and grid of ordering.[46] (Foucault's analytics of disciplinary power suggests a political interpretation of the *Gestell*.) Curiously, Heidegger does not explicitly deploy these interpretative concepts to account for historical processes in the realm of perception, in spite of the fact that, according to his own story, metaphysics is ocularcentric, and has been since its inception.[47] The story I am telling here draws attention to the perceptual matrix that has figured not only in the generation of our metaphysics, but also in the building of our society and culture.

In the modern epoch, and especially I think in the world of late capitalism, appropriately characterized by the predominance of the *Gestell*, the formation of the visual *Gestalt*, reduced to the subject-object relationship, tends to be, and often is, driven by the will to power, generated by possessive, predatory, and calculative desires. If we carry forward this hermeneutic reading of the Heidegger texts, giving them an interpretation in terms of perception, and more specifically an interpretation in terms of vision, then the "ontological difference" between beings (i.e., essents) and being (i.e., the being of beings) may be seen (becomes visible) as the forming of the differential figure-ground structure—the primal, inaugural moment in the field of vision, opening up a *space of difference* within which the perceptual act (activity) can take place. (It may seem that this interpretation reduces the radicality of Heidegger's thinking, limiting it to our present way of seeing, or that it binds the interpretation to a way of thinking—in terms, namely, of the ontological difference— beyond which Heidegger later moved. In fact, however, precisely the reverse is true. By connecting our experience with seeing to the ontological difference, this interpretation questions, challenges, and interrupts this experience. It is a solicitation, effecting a violent breach in our habitual perceptual structures, forcing them to open up, making them tremble. Moreover, this connection makes it possible to consider historical transformations in perception that would correspond to the displacement of the ontological difference in the discourse of Heidegger's thinking.)

Now, I have said that, according to Heidegger, modernity is under the sway—I am tempted here to say, echoing Benjamin's critique of late modern capitalism, that it is under the spell—of the *Gestell*. In terms of our visual perception, this means that the perceptual formation of the ontological difference is—or tends to be, or is vulnerable to being—suppressed, so that the "play" and "give" in its opening differentiation into figure and ground gets restricted, narrowed, reified, tightened, and distorted, and the potential for violence inherent in the process of perceptual structuration, fixated in oppositional, confrontational relationships between a subject and an object, will be encouraged to show itself.[48]

In the epoch of the *Gestell*, the ground of the figure-ground structure is under constant frontal attack. Appropriated by the will to power, visual perception establishes its control over this structure by narrowing its line of sight to the figure on which it is focused, attempting, in effect, to reduce the ground to this figure—or even to occlude the ground altogether. The enframing of the *Gestell* "blocks [*verstellt*] the shining-forth" of the illumination that backgrounds all our visual structurations.[49] The will to power tries to impose this negation on the being of the ground, because the ground, being what it is, namely that which *cannot* be totalized and reified, objectified to satisfy the dictates of a metaphysics of presence, will always and forever elude its grasp. Absolute control is not possible: the ground cannot be turned into a figure—cannot be figured out. Thus, the attempt to seize control of the ground, to fixate it, can lead only to an experience of the ground as an abyss: the ground under such attack withdraws, its play eludes regulation, its dynamism (*energeia*) deconstructs all reifications, its openness defies domination and closure.

Corresponding to the violence in a vision driven by the will to power, the ground withholds its wealth—it becomes abyss, sheer *Abgrund*.

The ground will give itself *as* ground to our perception only insofar as its giving of itself is appropriately received by perception, and that means that its being, namely as grounding, must be respected; the ground must be allowed to presence *as* ground, that is, as different from (as deferred by, as being in deference to) the figures, the objects on which we focus. This calls for *Gelassenheit*, an attitude of letting-go and letting-be. How, then, can the capacity of visual perception for relating to its ground and matrix in the attitude and with the character of *Gelassenheit* be developed? This is a very difficult question. But it is perhaps the most crucial, most urgent question on which we need to work, if the wasteland of nihilism is not to continue to grow.

III

The present critique is not impugning the "nobility" of sight, not repudiating its potential. It is not even intended to deny the evolutionary position of superiority that vision has enjoyed among the five modalities of perception. It is, however, calling into question the long *hegemony* of vision in our world, calling attention to the fact that this hegemony, problematic enough by itself, has become particularly problematic inasmuch as the *character* of the vision which predominates in the ocularcentrism of late modernity is so decisively possessed, driven, by the will to power. Heidegger's critique is not, therefore, an attack on vision as such. On the contrary, it is intended to facilitate the recognition and development of a great potential inherent in vision.

I think it is appropriate to challenge the hegemony of vision—the ocularcentrism of our culture. And I think we need to examine very critically the *character* of vision that predominates today in our world. We urgently need a diagnosis of the psychosocial pathology of everyday seeing—and a critical examination of ourselves, and of our understanding of ourselves, as visionary beings. I think it can be argued, for example, that the vision which dominates our ocular culture is haunted by the specters of patriarchal rule: the rule of the masculine is both cause and effect of an ocularcentrism which privileges the autonomy-drive of vision and rewards its aggressiveness, its hunger for control. Similar arguments can be made concerning racism and capitalism. How do the specters of racism inhabit our way of seeing, and consequently continue to haunt us in the violence of our ocular paradigm? How has the hegemony of vision—vision with a very specific character—contributed to, and in turn been influenced by, the formation of capitalism—its processes, for example, of imaging? We need to *see* the connections these questions broach.

We also need a critical hermeneutical reading of the discourse of metaphysics, soliciting the ways vision and its language have figured, and continue to figure, in the formation and deformation of the discourse. It is hoped that this critical work, the need for which Heidegger understood, and which he himself began, will contribute to the release of the great potential in vision, making it possible for this potential, a crying need, to be engaged by the more progressive, emancipatory forces in our society and culture, and to be fulfilled, accordingly, within the still-unfinished project of the Enlightenment.

In "The End of Philosophy and the Task of Thinking," Heidegger says: "No outward appearance without light—Plato already knew this. But there is no light and brightness without the opening."[50] "Philosophy," he adds, "knows nothing of the opening [Lichtung]. Philosophy does speak about the light [Licht] of reason, but does not heed the opening of being." Connecting this criticism with an asseveration that could be interpreted—mistakenly, I believe—as an attack on the Enlightenment rather than as a more inclusive criticism of the narrowed vision of all modern philosophers, Heidegger then argues that the "lumen naturale" of philosophical thought in the seventeenth and eighteenth centuries "throws light only in openness [das Offene]. . . . [And yet this "natural light"] needs it in order to be able to illuminate what is present in the opening."[51] In relation to our vision, the forgetting of being (Seinsvergessenheit) is the occlusion of this open field of lighting, the givenness which we persist in taking for granted, in spite of its ultimate contingency.

Vision is a capacity; its nature constitutes a multiplicity of different developmental potentials—different possible directions for maturation. Since vision can be developed in different ways, how it develops is very much a question both for individual existence and for society. Which tendencies are encouraged and cultivated? Which tendencies are frowned upon, discouraged, and punished? To answer these questions, we need to examine the specific processes of socialization at work in different social and cultural formations; and we need to consider the relativity of these processes to different historical times.[52]

It is not at all necessary to conclude, from Heidegger's story of decline and fall, that the character of vision among the ancient Greeks was ethically superior to the modern, or closer to the truth of being. Reification and totalization were already at work in the everyday vision of the Greeks; likewise, there were, then as now, looks full of lust and envy, stares of malice and hate, glances of greed and avarice, eyes ruled only by the dreams of despotism. However, the increasing mechanization, technocratization, and capitalization of the modern world, historical achievements indebted, in part, to the power of vision—its ability to survey from afar, for example, and its foresight—increasingly affect, in turn, the very perception that made them possible, not only reinforcing the predispositions in vision that brought forth this world of science and capitalized technology, but even suppressing the other potentials and tendencies inherent in vision, destroying thereby the more balanced ordering of these potentials and tendencies that seems to have been possible in earlier epochs of perception.

Heidegger's *Seinsfrage,* his question(ing) of being, may be, and I would argue needs to be, thought in relation to our vision. For Heidegger, the *Seinsfrage* is a question addressed to us, and making a claim on us, as human beings. But, since human beings are embodied—endowed, for example, with a capacity for sight, the *Seinsfrage* needs to be thought *in terms of* our experience with seeing. The question(ing) of being makes a claim on our vision; it makes a claim on us as visionary beings: a claim or demand that calls for and calls forth a response. The claim that this question(ing) makes on us, in the dimension of our vision, touches and concerns the *character* of our seeing. That is to say, it concerns our capacity to develop our vision further: further in the direction of its openness. Thus, our vision—how we see, the character of our seeing—becomes our responsibility. Responsibility is the ability to be responsive, to respond appropriately. Since we are embodied beings, beings of vision, this responsibility involves our ability to respond appropriately even in the dimension of our embodiment—even in the field of our visionary being. We are responsible for our response-ability as beings gifted with vision.

Now, being, according to Heidegger, is the *Es gibt,* the "it gives" and "there is." A groundless "there is." There is no ultimate reason, no self-grounding ground, to account for why there is something—anything—rather than nothing at all. That there is—being—is therefore simply a given. More "metaphorically" considered, it is a gift. But gifts make claims. The gift, the sheer, contingent givenness of *being* makes a claim. And this claim presents us with questions that call upon us to question and examine ourselves. How are we responding to the claim? How should we respond? What kind of response would be appropriate? What kind of response would correspond to the gift?

In *Time and Being,* Heidegger says that it is necessary that we "show how this 'there is' can be experienced and seen [*wie sich dieses 'Es gibt' erfahren und erblicken lässt*]."[53] And he tells us that we must "try to look ahead [*vorzublicken*] to the It which—gives Being and time. Thus looking ahead [*vorblickend*], we become foresighted [*vorsichtig*] in still another sense. We try to bring the It and its giving into view [*in die Sicht*]. . . ."[54] Given that he explicitly states that this event of giving—the event by grace of which a field for our vision is first opened up, first cleared and lighted—must be understood (interpreted) in terms of how it is (or "can be") "experienced and seen," it would surely be a mistake to turn his words into tropes, binding them to a metaphorical function comfortably distinguished from the literal. The validity—or say the claim—in Heidegger's words must come, if it comes at all, precisely from its *practical bearing* on our experience, our lives as visionary beings, within the historical world of our seeing.

Here I want to ask a question that Heidegger himself never quite asked—a question that opens up a dimension of our experience that remains for the most part *unthought* in Heidegger's texts. For the vision of our eyes, what *is* being? How does being presence? The "gift" in question is, after all, a gift to the eyes: our eyes are *given* something to see. Moreover, they are *given* the lighting, the openness of a field of illumination, within which seeing first becomes a possibility. There is (*es gibt*) something for them to see—and there is (*es gibt*) the givenness of a circumambient illumination, such that, by grace of this lighting, we are enabled to see whatever is there. (In the modern discourse of philosophy, this "something" has often been regarded as a givenness reducible to "sense data," "impressions," or "atomic sensations." Heidegger's word *Geschick*, a sending or dispensation of being, radically contests this way of thinking about the given dimension of perceptual experience. It also contests the way in which, correlatively, this discourse has conceptualized the *reception* of this givenness. The "receptivity" of the senses is also very much at stake. In the *Beiträge*, Heidegger writes about *das Erdenken des Seyns*. How are we to think—responsively, receptively, and responsibly—from out of the *Seinsgeschick*, the dispensation of being?)

Derrida's "Sending: On Representation" is an insightful and thought-provoking commentary on the dispensation of being in an epoch of image and representation.[55] But he does not think this *renvoi* hermeneutically, through the phenomenology of the giving and givenness of the gift. So what I am proposing for our thought is that being *is* ("is," I mean, in the hermeneutical sense of *anwesen*) the lighting and clearing, *is* that which lights and illumines, that which for all beings present and absent, visible and invisible, opens up and inaugurates a visual field, a matrix open in its reach and range, its dimensionality, its possibilities, its prospects and promise. It is the primordial, groundless *Es gibt* that lays down and gathers into a whole a field of illumination within which, and by grace of which, an event of seeing, a moment of vision, can take place, and beings, coming to light, can become visible.[56] Itself groundless and indifferent, ontically indifferent, it is that gift of ambient illumination, of luminous clearing, which makes the ground of difference—that is to say, the opening spaciousness of the ontological difference, and in particular the differentiations that compose the figure-ground structuring of vision—possible.[57] This is the hermeneutical "truth" of being ("truth" understood in the sense of *alētheia*, not *orthotēs*): the visible truth of being, visible in its presencing unconcealment—and thus, too, its epochal withdrawal into hermeneutical concealment—for the eyes of a vision that is ontologically responsible, ontologically responsive, attempting to recollect the hermeneutical presencing of its background, the gift of the ontological difference.

As beings of vision, we are claimed by being: our being is questioned; the character, the *ethos* of our vision is called into question. Granted the gift of vision, we behold the world into which we are cast. Beholding what is, what is *given* to our eyes for their seeing, we are held in and held by their ontological beholdenness. Beholden to the being of beings, to that which grants all beings the conditions of visibility and invisibility, we receive through our eyes the *logos* and *nomos* of a hermeneutical assignment: to recognize and realize the ontological dimensionality of our vision, to see, through the structural differentiation of the figure-ground difference, the sheer openness of the ontological difference, that groundless event, that primal *Ereignis,* opening up, for our eyes, a luminous field. This gift of illumination solicits our capacity for enlightenment as beings gifted with a capacity for seeing.

In his commentary on Heraclitus, Heidegger says: "gods and men belong in the lighting not only as lighted and viewed, but also as invisible [*unscheinbaren*], bringing the lighting with them in their own way, preserving [*verwahren*] it and handing it down in its endurance [*in seinem Währen*]."[58] We are, as he also says in this text, "entrusted" (*zugetraut*) with this gift.[59] Will we then, we visionary beings, betray this entrustment? Or will we prove ourselves worthy of it? Will we preserve, in the way we see, a guardian awareness of the giving of this gift of light? And will we pass on this awareness, and the enlightenment it bestows, in the thinking of our philosophical discourse, and in the life of our culture? For Heidegger, these are the questions of being that test the enlightenment of our *ethos,* the character of our culture.

In *Being and Time,* Heidegger spoke of our *Schuldigkeit,* a word that has repeatedly been translated as "being-guilty." This word encodes the story of decline and fall. But perhaps it would be better to translate this word as "beholdenness," thereby setting out to tell a different story. For what I am trying to establish is that there is an implicit normativity in our perceptual experience. Thus, ethics and epistemology are equally primordial. What do we make of this? How are we to respond in an ontologically appropriate, ontologically responsible way? The dispensation, that gift of a field of light by grace of which we are enabled to see, is an entrustment. As visionary beings, we are entrusted with the realm of the visible and the invisible: we are, let us say, the "guardians" of this realm, entrusted with its truth. The responsibility we bear, by virtue of our beholdenness, is to respond to the dispensation in a way that is fitting, appropriate to the way in which it is, and has been, given: to develop our capacity to see this gift and make it visible, visible in its ecstatic dimensionality. (Here I am drawing our capacity for vision into the discursive field of the *Beiträge*: into the field of the *Ereignis* and the *Fügung*.)

Does Heidegger think, then, that the decline and fall can be reversed? Does he think that our vision can make an historical difference? Answering for him, I would say, perhaps. Perhaps, but only if our seeing were to become a *recollection* of being, gathering the unconcealment of being into our lives: a recollection not only in the sense of a retrieval in memory, reversing our "forgetfulness" of being, but also in the sense of a re-collecting of what has always already been collected, or gathered and laid down, for us—for our vision. What has already been given to us, namely, the ambient lighting, we habitually take for granted. This is the essence of our forgetfulness. Our vision would thus become ontologically responsive, ontologically responsible, ontologically appropriate, only insofar as (1) by the *virtue* of its character, the *way* in which it projects a figure-ground difference, gathering and laying down "for itself" a surrounding visual field, we not only (a) recollect the primordial event of being—the gift of a *prior* clearing, the unforeseeable opening-up of a field of illumination for the displays of the ontological difference, the sending of a radiant layout that gathers and collects our vision into its illumination—but also indeed (b) recollect this event *hermeneutically, as* that gift of a prior laying-down and gathering-collecting of light by *grace* of which alone we are enabled to see anything at all in the first place; and moreover, only insofar as (2) by *virtue* of our thoughtful gesture, the *way* in which our "own" vision gathers and lays down the vectors of its visual field, we *make* this gift, the dispensation of the ontological difference, *actually visible in the world,* visible, namely, *as* precisely that prior, more primordial laying-and-gathering of light by *grace* of which alone our sight is first rendered possible.

It is a question of actualizing the ontological relationship, the *homologein* between being and human beings, in and as our way of seeing.[60] To see in *this* way—gatheringly, re-collectingly—would be to see with a vision claimed and appropriated by the event of being. Is this possible for us—possible here, possible now, possible in our time? How can the gaze break through the metaphysical closure that casts our time in shadow, foreshadowing, perhaps, the end of modernity? How can our sight overcome its inveterate tendency to reduce the "ecstatic" dimensionality of its vision to the dimmer lighting characteristic of correctness? How can it become hermeneutical in response to the luminous solicitations of being?

Here it must be understood that there is *no* comportment, no responsiveness, which can actually be "ontologically appropriate," commensurate to the "there is," the giving of the gift of lighting. In relation to the (norm, the *metron* of the) immeasurable, an event the dimensions of which cannot be properly measured, there is no proper norm, and no mode of perception, that can possibly measure up. One can make the giving of this gift visible only hermeneutically, only with a proper mindfulness of a truth in unconcealment, *as* the invisible, the *impossibly* visible. The opening up of the field of vision, laying down the horizons of this field in a gathering of light and setting forth the ground of visibility in the ecstatic spacing of the ontological difference, is not "something" (some "thing") that can be made visible and seen the way we see the visible entities in our world. Thus it may be said that the experience of responding to the giving, the claim in the dispensation, is an experience of the sublime. For the attempt to recollect the giving of the lighting by virtue of an appropriately responsive vision is bound to be shattered: our capacity to see what it is given to us to see in our time is being stretched exceedingly, extended far beyond its limits.

I take it that "the moment of vision" refers, in *Being and Time*, to the achievement of a deep experiential understanding in relation to these questions. And I take it that his words refer to the actuality of our seeing—to what and how we see. But of course they also refer to what is possible and what is impossible. The *Seinsfrage* tests the *character* of our perceptiveness. Is this character determined by egoity? Or could it be determined, instead, by *Gelassenheit*? Is our vision to be limited to truth as correctness? Is it to be reduced to the gaze that (im)passively mirrors reality—the gaze represented by the correspondence theory of truth? Or could our vision be disclosive, interactive, participating in the hermeneutical event of disclosure, opened by a deeper understanding, opened to truth in the hermeneutic sense of *alētheia*, unconcealment? Our present historical situation—a world darkened by the shadow of nihilism—depends, perhaps, on our willingness to work on our capacity for seeing, with these questions in mind. In "Plato's Doctrine of Truth," Heidegger comments that "everything depends on the *orthotes*, the correctness of the look [*Blick*]."[61] If this gaze, a gaze that requires correctness, the plenitude of presence, inaugurates the history of the discourse of metaphysics, then Heidegger's work is a critique of the vision of truth that has dominated this discourse; but it is also an attempt to see with an "aletheic" gaze, a hermeneutical gaze that recollects the unconcealment of being—truth in *this* sense. The "truthful" gaze is thus a gaze that would hold itself open to the interplay of the visible and the invisible, the present and the absent—an interplay that is also made visible as the gift of the ontological difference, opening up a field of illumination for the enactment of human vision.

The will to power is very strong in vision. There is a very strong tendency in vision to grasp and fixate, to reify and totalize: a tendency to dominate, secure, and control, which eventually, because it was so extensively promoted, assumed a certain uncontested hegemony over our culture and its philosophical discourse, establishing, in keeping with the instrumental rationality of our culture and the technological character of our society, an ocularcentric metaphysics of presence.

The "will to power," crucial in the generation of this metaphysics of presence, seems to be much stronger in seeing than it is in listening—although it is at work, to be sure, in listening as well. If this is indeed the case, then first of all, the so-called postmodern problematization of modernity, insofar as it is justified, would seem to call, correspondingly, for the problematization of ocularcentrism, the hegemony of which, as our cultural paradigm for knowledge, truth, and reality, cannot be separated from the violence and nihilism circulating in our world. Second, this may be the time, the appropriate historical moment, to encourage and promote a shift in paradigms, a cultural drift that, to some extent, seems already to be taking place. I am referring, of course, to the drift from seeing to listening, and to the historical potential for a paradigm shift displacing vision and installing the very different influence of listening. Informed by an interactive and receptive normativity, listening generates a very different *episteme* and ontology—a very different metaphysics.[62] Today, moreover, it is becoming increasingly clear that we need the ethics and politics of a communicative rationality. Thus, I submit, the paradigm shift in question here could represent a truly progressive, emancipatory development of our historical potential.

It must, however, be emphasized that such a paradigm shift, were it to take place, would not in the slightest lift from us the task of changing the present character of our vision, and of bringing forth an ontological potential that so far we have not realized. In the *Beiträge*, Heidegger formulated some directives, *Weisungen*, which I would connect to our capacity for listening and seeing. In his later work, Heidegger formulated the task for thinking in terms of *das Geviert*, the fourfold. In the fourfold gathering-together of earth and sky, mortals and gods, he communicated his vision of a world in which *das Gestell* would no longer rule. (Heidegger never told us how he expected us to understand his references to "gods." I accordingly venture this: the "gods" are those extraordinary moments of local visionary unconcealment in which something of the greatest importance about the presencing of beings *as a whole* is given illumination.) Implicit in this allegorical vision, and still largely unthought, there are hints and traces of a different perceptual *Gestalt*, a different structuring enactment of our capacity for seeing. Perhaps what this suggests is that, even in the darkness of the modern epoch, Heidegger saw a potential for overcoming the *Gestell*, a way of seeing that imposes everywhere the destructiveness of nihilism, and that he may have glimpsed a certain potential for the emergence of a way of seeing whose character would contribute to the gathering of the fourfold—to the *flourishing* of earth and sky, gods and mortals.

Listening attentively to the roots of his words, Heidegger heard, in the German word for "perception" (*Wahrnehmung*), a sense radically different from that which prevails today, a normative sense that brings out the "pathology" in our inveterate perceptual habits: Perception involves keeping watch over and safeguarding (*wahren*) the truth (*das Wahre*), protecting and preserving (*bewahren, verwahren*) both that which is granted (*das Gewährte*) and that which endures (*währt*) in and as the granting.

Although Heidegger repeatedly insisted on the differences between Rilke and himself,[63] nothing, perhaps, comes closer to articulating for me the character of this new vision than Rilke's poem "The Turning" (*Die Wende*):

Animals trustfully stepped
into his open glance, grazing,
and captive lions
stared in as into inconceivable freedom;
birds flew straight through him,
big, as into children.[64]

Herein, however, is the projection of another chapter.

NOTES

1. Martin Heidegger, *An Introduction to Metaphysics* (New York: Doubleday, 1961), p. 49. Also see the German edition, *Einführung in die Metaphysik* (Tübingen: Max Niemeyer Verlag, 1953), p. 46.

2. Ibid., p. 55 (p. 51 in the German ed.).

3. Heidegger, *Beiträge zur Philosophie (Vom Ereignis)* (Frankfurt am Main: Klostermann, 1989), Gesamtausgabe, vol. 65, ed. Friedrich Wilhelm von Hermann.

4. See, for example, Heidegger, *Being and Time* (New York: Harper & Row, 1962), pp. 88, 98, 201; *Sein und Zeit* (Halle: Max Niemeyer Verlag, 1941), pp. 61, 69, 158, Heidegger correlates our present-at-hand ontology (*Vorhandensein*) with

seeing in the mode of staring. This correlation also figures in his discussion of the "theoretical attitude" as a way of looking at and seeing. See, in this regard, pp. 177, 412 (pp. 138, 361 in German), where the theoretical way of beholding is described as a "dimming down" of the world to what is purely present-at-hand. This "diminution" of light and visibility is likewise invoked in his critical analysis of truth as assertion and statement (*apophansis,* a Greek word that describes languaging as a process of coming to light and becoming visible: letting something be seen in its uncoveredness), where he says that, in "setting down the subject," assertion "dims entities down to focus" (p. 197; p. 155 in German). Also see pp. 214–217 (pp. 170–173), where he examines the character of seeing which takes place in "curiosity" (the "desire to see"), and p. 451 (p. 400), where he criticizes an "ocular" approach to historical research.

5. Ibid., pp. 186–188 (pp. 146–148 in German).

6. Ibid.

7. Ibid., p. 385 (p. 336 in German).

8. Heidegger, "Aletheia (Heraclitus, Fragment B16)," *Early Greek Thinking* (New York: Harper & Row, 1975), p. 122; *Vorträge und Aufsätze* (Pfullingen: Günther Neske, 1954), p. 281.

9. Heidegger, *Being and Time,* pp. 214–217; *Sein und Zeit,* pp. 170–173.

10. Heidegger, "What Are Poets For?" *Poetry, Language, Thought* (New York: Harper & Row, 1971); "Wozu Dichter?" *Holzwege* (Frankfurt am Main: Vittorio Klostermann, 1950), p. 292.

11. Heidegger, *An Introduction to Metaphysics,* p. 154 (p. 140 in German).

12. Ibid., pp. 154–155 (p. 141 in German).

13. Ibid., p. 155 (p. 141 in German).

14. Ibid., p. 151 (p. 138 in German).

15. Ibid., p. 158 (p. 144 in German).

16. Ibid., p. 50 (p. 46 in German).

17. Ibid.

18. Ibid., p. 159 (p. 145 in German).

19. Ibid., p. 158 (p. 144 in German).

20. Ibid., p. 159 (p. 145 in German).

21. Ibid.

22. Heidegger, "The Overcoming of Metaphysics," *The End of Philosophy* (New York: Harper & Row, 1973), p. 87. Also see "Überwindung der Metaphysik," *Vorträge und Aufsätze* (Pfullingen: Günther Neske, 1954), p. 74.

23. Heidegger, *An Introduction to Metaphysics,* p. 160 (p. 146 in German).

24. Ibid.

25. Ibid., p. 161 (p. 146 in German). Also see p. 156 (p. 142 in German):

> Truth that was originally unconcealment, a happening of the dominant essent itself, governed by gathering, now becomes an attribute of the logos. [At the same time, *logos* gets reduced to statement or proposition.] In becoming an attribute of statement, [however,] the truth not only shifts its abode; it changes its essence as well.

Truth as *alētheia,* unconcealment, becomes truth as correctness (*Richtigkeit*).

26. Ibid., p. 53 (p. 49 in German).

27. Ibid., p. 85 (pp. 76–77 in German).

28. Ibid.

29. Ibid., p. 86 (p. 77 in German).

30. Ibid., p. 87 (p. 78 in German).

31. Ibid., pp. 87, 89 (pp. 78, 79 in German).

32. Ibid., p. 111 (p. 101 in German). Also see p. 87 (p. 78).

33. See Thoreau's journal entry for June 21, 1852, in B. Torrey and F. Allen eds., *The Journal of Henrry David Thoreau*, vol. 2 (New York: Dover, 1906), p. 43.

34. Ibid., p. 88 (p. 79 in German).

35. Ibid., p. 52 (p. 48 in German).

36. Ibid.

37. Ibid.

38. Ibid.

39. Ibid. I have modified the English translation by Ralph Manheim.

40. Ibid., p. 93 (p. 84 in German).

41. Ibid.

42. Ibid., p. 114 (p. 104 in German). Also see p. 57 (p. 53).

43. Ibid., p. 99 (p. 89 in German).

44. Ibid., p. 99 (pp. 89–90 in German).

45. Ibid., p. 99 (p. 90 in German).

46. Heidegger, *Zur Seinsfrage* (Frankfurt am Main: Vittorio Klostermann, 1956), p. 21.

47. For a more detailed deployment of these concepts in accounting for the character of perception in modernity, the age or epoch of *das Gestell*, see Levin, *The Opening of Vision: Nihilism and the Postmodern Situation* (London and New York: Routledge, 1988).

48. See Robert Romanyshyn, "The Despotic Eye," in D. Krueger, ed., *The Changing Reality of Modern Man* (Capetown: Juta, 1984), and *Technology As Symptom and Dream* (London and New York: Routledge, 1990). Also see Martin Jay, "In the Empire of the Gaze: Foucault and the Denigration of Vision in Twentieth Century French Thought," in David Hoy, ed., *Foucault: A Critical Reader* (Oxford and New York: Basil Blackwell, 1986), pp. 175–204.

49. Heidegger, "The Question Concerning Technology," in *The Question Concerning Technology and Other Essays* (New York: Harper & Row, 1977), p. 28; *Die Technik und die Kehre* (Pfullingen: Günther Neske, 1962), p. 27.

50. Heidegger, "The End of Philosophy and the Task of Thinking," in *Basic Writings* (New York: Harper & Row, 1977), p. 386; *Zur Sache des Denkens* (Tübingen: Max Niemeyer Verlag, 1969), p. 73.

51. Ibid.

52. See, in this connection, Levin, "Justice in the Flesh," in G. Johnson and M. Smith, eds., *Ontology and Alterity in Merleau-Ponty* (Evanston: Northwestern University Press, 1990), pp. 35–44; and Levin, "Visions of Narcissism: Intersubjectivity and the Reversals of Reflection," in M. Dillon ed., *Merleau-Ponty Vivant* (Albany: State University of New York Press, 1990).

53. Heidegger, *On Time and Being* (New York: Harper & Row, 1972), p. 5;

Zur Sache des Denkens (Tübingen: Max Niemeyer, 1969), p. 5. Derrida has discussed the gift, the present, in this text in "Given Time: The Time of the King," *Critical Inquiry,* vol. 18, no. 2 (Winter 1992), pp. 161–187.

54. Ibid.

55. Jacques Derrida, "Sending: On Representation," *Social Research* 49 (1982): 294–326.

56. See Hans Blumenberg, "Light As a Metaphor for Truth," in this collection. Perhaps he is thinking of Heidegger when he writes that light "can be a dazzling superabundance, as well as an indefinite, omnipresent brightness containing all: the 'letting-appear' that does not itself appear, the inaccessible accessibility of things. . . . Light remains what it is while letting the infinite participate in it; it is consumption without loss."

57. What, then, is being for our ears, for our hearing? How does being, the being of beings, presence for our hearing? Hermeneutic phenomenology can show that it is in and as an auditory field, a field of sonorous energies, utterly open, that being presences for our hearing. Being is that (presencing) which first opens up a field of sound within which, and by grace of which, an event of hearing can take place, and the sounding-forth of beings can be audible. Here, the claim that being—the question(ing) of being—makes on our hearing is laid down, laid out, through the registering of our attunement, our *Gehörigkeit,* our belongingness and obedience, to the ontological attunement, the tone, set by the *Es gibt* of being. See Levin, *The Listening Self* (London: Routledge, 1989).

58. Heidegger, "Aletheia (Heraclitus, Fragment B16)," *Early Greek Thinking,* p. 121; *Vorträge und Aufsätze,* p. 279.

59. Ibid., p. 122 (p. 281 in German).

60. This "correlation," this relationship between (1) the gathering and laying-down (*legein*) of our seeing, a gesture by *virtue* of which, in projecting a visual field, a figure-ground difference, we recollect the gift of being to our eyes, and (2) the gathering and laying-down (*Legein*) of being, that *prior* clearing and lighting by *grace* of which our vision first becomes possible, is a phenomenological specification, an exemplification in the realm of vision, of the *homologein* that Heidegger discusses in his study on "Logos (Heraclitus, Fragment B50)," *Early Greek Thinking,* pp. 66–75. The ontological difference here is marked by my use of the words *virtue* (attributed to human beings) and *grace* (recollecting the gift, the *Geschick* of being).

61. Heidegger, "Plato's Doctrine of Truth," in H. Aiken and W. Barrett, eds., *Philosophy in the Twentieth Century* (New York: Harper and Row, 1962), vol. 3, p. 265. Also see pp. 261, 267. For the German, see *Platons Lehre von der Wahrheit* (Bern: Verlag A. Francke, 1947), p. 41.

62. See Heidegger's recognition, in *An Introduction to Metaphysics* (pp. 116–119, 141), of the historical need for an epistemology and ontology generated by a "receptive," participatory attitude. Also see pp. 109–111, 123 for his thoughts on listening and hearing. In *The Listening Self* (London and New York: Routledge, 1989), I have examined the question of the relationship between listening and metaphysics, and have attempted to lay out, in terms of a process

with four distinct stages of development, a praxis, a "practice of the self," in the course of which a historically different relationship to the being of beings may be achieved. The interpretation of this relationship is rendered in terms of the development of our capacity for listening, and involves a radical change in the structuring of figure and ground.

63. See Heidegger's objections to Rilke's articulation of "the Open" in *Parmenides* (Bloomington: Indiana University Press, 1992), pp. 151-161.

64. Rainer Maria Rilke, "The Turning," in *Letters of Rainer Maria Rilke 1910-1926* (New York: Norton, 1947), p. 116.

SEVEN

Time's Cinders

Herman Rapaport

In the summer term of 1930, Martin Heidegger delivered a course entitled *Vom Wesen der Menschlichen Freiheit* ("On the Essence of Human
Freedom") in which one already detects analyses which more than anticipate concerns which are broached in the *Beiträge zur Philosophie* of the
late 1930s and the seminars on the Pre-Socratics written during the
1940s. As in *Vom Wesen der Wahrheit* ("On the Essence of Truth"), delivered the following year, Heidegger was very interested in considering the
question of freedom in terms of Being as the unconcealment of Truth.
Both of the lecture courses invoke the phenomenon of lighting or illumination in discussing these issues. In the course on the essence of human
freedom, this illumination is spoken of in some rather suggestive para-
graphs in which Heidegger revises and goes beyond the *Daseinanalyse* of
time made in the closing sections of *Sein und Zeit* (*Being and Time*).
Whereas Heidegger closed his famous treatise by raising the question of
whether time could be considered the horizon of Being, the lecture
course on human freedom develops the thought that not only is time
such a horizon but that it is to be considered as a radiance throwing its
light on Being. However, if Being takes place under the firmament of
time, time also presents itself as a localization or particularization of a
Being whose breadth encompasses the wholeness of what is. Both Being
and time, therefore, may be considered horizons for one another. Hu-
mankind, Heidegger suggests, is what takes place in the openness between these two horizons, an openness which Heidegger wants to think
of in relation to freedom, and understands in terms of clarification, illumination, vision.

Although it is notable, and particularly in the context of the anthology for which this essay has been written, that Heidegger invokes a meta-phorics of light in order to discuss the clearing (*Lichtung*) or opening pertinent to the question of Being and time, my chief interest here is not in placing this metaphoric within a history of ideas—though there are some marked moments when, in fact, this occurs—or in settling the question of whether Heidegger is essentially ocularcentric or not. Rather, my main interest is to explain the moves and implications of one of Heidegger's more suggestive texts on time with respect to the figures of light and vision, and then, toward the end of the paper, to contrast Heidegger's conceptualizations with a notion of the cinder and the imagery of fire which informs Jacques Derrida's *Feu la cendre*, an essay which is in many respects a critique of Heidegger and, by implication, of his use of the figure of light. In *Feu la cendre* (1982), as in the later *De l'esprit* (1987), Derrida suggests that Heidegger's invocation of light, fire, and spirit conceals the figure of the cinder which Derrida associates with the crematoria of the Nazi death camps. Yet, it is this very disappropriative cinder which nevertheless is destined by the appropriative figure of light that illumines tracts like *Vom Wesen der Menschlichen Freiheit*, in which questions of human freedom and truth are raised. Even more significant for this essay is that, by considering the cinder, Derrida approaches the "hitherside" of a Heideggerian clearing which negotiates those two horizons, Being and time: what Emmanuel Levinas has termed the "otherwise than Being."

I

The course on the essence of human freedom begins with the familiar injunction that we must concern ourselves with the question of what beings are. And, not surprisingly, the question leads Heidegger to ask how Being is to be called and understood. Given these questions, Heidegger explains that human freedom will not be considered politically, but rather in the philosophical terms of one's freedom to pose ontological questions. This freedom is given only to human beings and, for that reason, affords *Dasein* a special status apart from other living beings, for we alone have been given the freedom not only to pose questions, but to ask them in such a way that we will eventually name and understand Being. Although this sounds uncontroversial enough, Heidegger asks his students to bear in mind that for him freedom does not refer to the pragmatics of simply initiating ontological questions; rather, he is referring to the interruption of a rift or opening whereby a sudden moment of clarification or illumination comes to pass in which Being is given as named or summoned. This opening is experienced as a sudden flash or lighting which clears the way for Being to appear, even if "Das Sein kommt dabei in die Sicht und in den Blick eines sich selbst noch ganz verborgenen Verstehens." ("In the process, Being comes into the sight and into the purview of an understanding still concealed to itself.")[1] In other words, if there is an opening or flash, there is still no automatic revelation with respect to achieving *Seinsverständnis,* since Being does not reveal itself to us of its own accord in a flash of light. Necessary is the naming or calling of Being.

> Wo philosophiert wird, kommt das Seinsverständnis zu Wort, Sein wird verstanden und irgendwie gegriffen und begriffen, gesehen im Lichte von . . . —wovon?

> [In philosophizing, the understanding of Being comes to speak, and Being is understood and somehow is grasped and comprehended, seen in the light of . . . —what?][2]

The understanding of Being is named through philosophizing and Being is thereby comprehended, seen in the light of. Heidegger breaks off momentarily in order to work through the imagery of light, and asks in what light the ancient Greek philosophers understood Being. That is, what is the nature of that lighting, clarification, or illumination through which the ancients could name Being? In asking this question Heidegger turns to the capacity of language to sight a predisclosive understanding of Being. The ancient Greek word *ousia,* for example, names Being from the side of things and as such initially acts as a predisclosive marker for Being. This, of course, is its strength: *ousia* is not a referent so much as a pointer or clue which anticipates and broaches naming, a term that shows us the way to what is concealed or forgotten whenever we consider Being: the permanence of what houses presencing. "Das Wort für Sein ist, und zwar schon in der alltäglichen Rede, ousia: Haus und Hof, Anwesen." ("The word for Being is—and already in everyday speech—ousia: house and domain, property.")[3] As a predisclosive word, *ousia* is akin to the opening or rift through which illumination or lighting comes to pass. That is, the predisclosive or anticipatory name makes it possible for an aspect of Being to appear which otherwise would remain concealed—in this case, the persistence of presencing which Heidegger speaks of as an *erhellende Licht* necessary for our understanding of Being.

Still, if language can name or disclose an aspect of Being, the *erhellende Licht* does not originate in language, but must be sought elsewhere.

> Wenn das Sein als beständige Anwesenheit verstanden wird: *Von woher empfängt solches Verstehen das erhellende Licht? In welchem Horizont bewegt sich das Seinsverständnis?*

[Yet if Being is understood as an abiding presence, *from where does such an understanding receive the light which illumines it? In what horizon is the understanding of Being moved?*][4]

If Being is to be understood as persistent presencing, from where does such an understanding get its brightening light? And in what horizon is the understanding of Being moved? At this juncture Heidegger offers the answers supplied by Plato and Aristotle, who thought of *ousia* largely in terms of presence and absence, *An-Wesenheit/Ab-wesenheit; Sein/Nichts; Bleiben/Nichtbleiben*. To comprehend *ousia* in that way, Heidegger says, was to mistakenly identify it too closely with *parousia,* a term which emphasized the thereness of what is.

Much of Heidegger's argument focuses on the conviction that Plato and Aristotle were much too hasty in considering ontology along pragmatic lines of distinguishing the difference between things which were ready to hand from things which were not. Heidegger contextualizes his objections to Plato in a brief examination of the *Euthydemus* at just that point when the Socratic conversation turns to the question of beauty and how it relates to the problem of difference. Of importance to Heidegger is how Socrates overlooks those aspects of *ousia* which point to its persistent presencing, its abidingness, and opts instead for a sharply defined opposition between what is there and what is not there. In Plato, Heidegger says, the standing or staying entirely depends upon a thing's *Entstehen* and *Vergehen*—its appearance as something that stands there before us or its disappearance as something which is no longer there. Hence Socrates has introduced the notion of *parousia* in place of *ousia* and thereby has forgotten or lost sight of that (as yet) inexplicable *erhellende Licht* which the persistence of presencing manifests. Heidegger's well-known objections—they turn up in many other texts, as well—are significant in that they motivate what will already in *Vom Wesen der Menschlichen Freiheit* be a dismantling of the difference between appearance (unconcealment) and disappearance (concealment).

Part of Heidegger's initial critique of Plato is that conceptions such as "reality," "completedness," "matter," "form," "energy," and "idea" have complex histories which are based on a conception of being that depends on the Socratic understanding of presence as what stands there: *Dastehen.* Moreover, in Aristotle the consequences of such an understanding become evident in terms of rigid perceptual dichotomies in which *das erhellende Licht* would be easily and mistakenly explained: for example, in terms of the visible and the invisible, the shown and the hidden, the unconcealed and the concealed. Aristotle, in particular, would be typical of one who had noticed but misunderstood *das erhellende Licht* with respect to what Heidegger calls the problem of the relation between

Being and truth. "Auch hier steht das Problem in der Helle des natür-
lichen alltäglichen Seinsverständnisses, ohne dass das Licht selbst
gelichtet wäre." ("But here too the problem [of the correspondence between Being and truth] stands in the clarity of the natural and everyday
understanding of Being, without the light itself being lit.")[5] Aristotle oc-
cludes our understanding of ontology when he maintains in book 9 of
the *Metaphysics* that "Being and non-being in the strictest sense are truth
and falsity," since "if the object is existent it exists in a particular way,
and if it does not exist in this way it does not exist at all; and truth means
thinking these objects, and falsity does not exist, nor error, but only ignorance,—and not an ignorance which is like blindness; for blindness is
akin to a total absence of the faculty of thinking."[6] According to Aristotle, error and falsity do not exist as such and are the total absence of
the faculty of thinking. Error and falsity therefore cannot tell us about
Being and non-Being. Similarly blindness: it cannot address ontology.
The question of Being and non-Being, therefore, depends upon an opening of vision, the capacity to see. This means that all thinking about
Being and non-Being has to be thought from the side of Being and the
visible. This ocularcentric approach is problematic, according to Heidegger, because it presumes that any understanding of Being depends
upon our perceiving some thing or entity which is always already standing before us and hence constituted prior to any reflection we might be
able to undertake with respect to the coming to appearance of beings or
things. To think of an opening of vision in terms of this Aristotelian *a
priori* would only be misleading; in fact, for Heidegger it would be exemplary of blindness insofar as this could be considered a modality of the
forgetting of being.

Also, there is a problem in Aristotelian metaphysics with respect to
time, since the givenness of "what is" in Aristotle's philosophy assumes
a unification of temporal moments that, once having appeared as self-
evidently given, discourages reflection or interrogation into temporality
as a manifold of moments that might not be inherently unified or bound
in the way that an Aristotelian conception of *Dastehen* would otherwise
suggest. The function of the critique of Aristotle is to allow Heidegger to
suggest that the presupposition that Being is inherently to be identified
with light may have been a mistake based on the sharp ontological classi-
fication which Aristotle made when he considered Being chiefly in opposition to non-Being and all the subordinate dichotomies which followed
from this.

Heidegger's third chapter of *Vom Wesen der Menschlichen Freiheit,* "Zur
Grundfrage der Philosophie," therefore broaches some of the more radical consequences of entertaining an inquiry into the temporality of being

with respect to the invocation of an opening or lighting that breaks entirely with a tradition of Aristotelian presuppositions.

Wenn Sein in der Helle von Beständigkeit und Anwesenheit steht, welches Licht ist die Quelle dieser Helle? Was kommt in dem zum Vorschein, was wir meinen mit 'Anwesenheit,' 'Beständigkeit'? Anwesenheit nennen wir auch Präsenz und Gegenwart. Diese unterschieden wir, wenn wir sie als solche fassen wollen, gegen Vergangenheit und Zukunft. Gegenwart, Anwesenheit, ist ein Charakter der *Zeit.* Und das 'beständig'? Beständigkeit meint das Fortwähren, das Immerwähren in jedem Jetzt. Das Jetzt ist gleichfalls eine Zeitbestimmung. Beständige Anwesenheit besagt sonach: die ganze Gegenwart, das Jetzige, das jetzig ist, beständig in jedem Jetzt. Beständige Anwesenheit bezeichnet dann das in jedem Jetzt (jederzeit) Jetzige. In der Helle, in der das als beständige Anwesenheit verstandene Sein steht, kommt das Licht zum Vorschein, das diese Helle spendet. Es ist die *Zeit* selbst. Das *Sein* wird, sowohl im vulgären Seinsverständnis als auch in der ausdrücklichen Seinsproblematik der Philosophie, *verstanden im Licht der Zeit.*

Wie kommt die Zeit dazu, als dieses Licht aufzuleuchten? Warum gerade die Zeit? Mehr noch, warum die Zeit gerade hinsichtlich des einen Charakters, der Gegenwart, des Jetzt? *Was ist überhaupt die Zeit selbst, daß sie als dieses Licht leuchtet* und *das Sein* zu erhellen vermag? *Wie kommen Sein und Zeit in diesen ursprünglichen Zusammenhang?* Welches ist dieser Zusammenhang? Was heißt Zeit? Was heißt Sein? Was heißt vor allem Sein *und* Zeit?

[If Being stands in the clarity of persistence and presence, what light is the source of this clarity? What, then, manifests itself in what we mean by "presence" and "persistence"? Presence is what we also call presencing and present. We distinguish the latter, the present, when we wish to take it as such, as opposed to the past and the future. The present and presence are characteristic of time. And "persistence"? Persistence signifies that something endures and always perdures in each now. But the now is itself also a temporal determination. Hence, persistent presence signifies: the whole present, the now which is now, persistent in each now. The persistent presence thus signifies what is any time in every now. In the clarity in which Being stands, understood as persistent presence, that light comes to the fore which dispenses this clarity. This is *time itself.* Both in the vulgar understanding of Being and in terms of the explicit ontological problematic of philosophy, *Being is understood in the light of time.*

But how does time come to shine as such a light? Why precisely time? What is more, why time precisely in view of the one attribute: the present, the now? *What is above all time itself, that it shines as this light and is able to illumine Being? How do Being and time come into such an originary relation?* What is this relation? What signifies time? What signifies Being? What signifies above all Being *and* time?][7]

These very important remarks directly follow from the last sentence of *Sein und Zeit*, in which Heidegger asks if time manifests itself as the horizon of *Being*. We may recall that earlier in the treatise Heidegger had considered temporality from the standpoint of a hermeneutics in which *Dasein* is capable of projecting itself beyond the now and in so doing comes to understand the temporal present in a "moment of vision" made possible by a complex convergence of different temporal horizons.[8] At one point Heidegger goes so far as to say that "Die ekstatische Zeitlichkeit lichtet das Da ursprünglich," suggesting that ecstatical temporality makes an originary clearing or lighting of the "there is" possible.[9] For that to occur, however, *Dasein* must be able to transcend its everyday experience of inhabiting a now that is unconcerned with those other horizons of temporality, which necessarily make up a fuller disclosure of our existence as such. In *Vom Wesen der Menschlichen Freiheit*, Heidegger has posed human freedom not in terms of *Dasein* and how it must come to grips with itself in moments of vision as a being which has existence, but rather in terms of how time comes to pass as a horizon of Being which needs to be considered in terms of lighting, clearing, illumination. In other words, whereas vision in *Sein und Zeit* is still being considered in terms of *Dasein*'s sense perception, in *Vom Wesen der Menschlichen Freiheit* lighting or brightening is considered much more as a trait of time or Being which, of course, *Dasein* does not literally "see" as such.

When Being stands in the brightness of persistence and presencing, what light makes up its source? This is the key question, which the passage will answer by supplying the word *time*. How do presencing and persisting come to light? Again, as time. For presence also suggests presentness as well as the present. We distinguish the present from the past and the future, and we therefore think of the present and presence as characteristics of time. Persistence refers to the continuation or ever-abidingness within every now, and this now is to be considered a determination of time. Following the *Daseinanalyse* of *Sein and Zeit*, Heidegger disarticulates or parcels out the notion of the now by suggesting that what persists as presence is a now-time which persists or continues in every now. It follows that for persistent presencing each now (each time or temporal horizon) nows. Heidegger then specifies that in the brightness, in which Being comes to stand as persistent presencing, a light afforded by the brightness appears, and again this is nothing less than time. Being, therefore, comes to be understood in the light of time, the very light which in *Sein und Zeit* was thought of as a horizon. Heidegger immediately follows these thoughts with some fundamental questions. How does time come to pass as that which illuminates? What is time that it can brighten

Being? What does it mean to speak of Being and time in such an originary relation? What is this relation? What does time signify? What does Being signify? Above all what is signified by Being *and* time?

Heidegger doesn't answer such questions directly but instead takes a detour in order to investigate what it means to imply that in *Sein und Zeit* not enough thought was given to the primordiality of the "and" which connects time to Being. Indeed, Heidegger is suspicious that this "and" presumes a causality or determinism that "forgets" a freedom or opening which releases time and Being from an essentialist relationship that had been presumed already in Plato's time. Moreover, the problem of time has traditionally been subordinated to the question of how humans experience temporality, and Heidegger clarifies that such an understanding of time is merely anthropological and will not get us far with respect to fathoming the *Wesen* or essence of time. Yet—and here comes the detour—Heidegger wants to explore how time corresponds or relates to us as beings who are human. This correspondence or *Zusammenhang* is itself to be considered in terms of the "and" which brings time into relationship with Being. In other words, to speak of the relation of time to Being, as Heidegger does in the long passage above, one must necessarily inquire into this correspondence as one within which not only the human subject, but its *Dasein*, comes into view as itself *Da* and *Sein,* time *and* Being. Of course, for this to be thought the subject has to be decentered; it cannot be thought of as a source or origin which thinks in terms of "my" time or "my" existence, since that brings about a reification which utterly forgets the much more primordial aspects of time and Being which Heidegger wants to discuss, namely, the containing breadth of Being—the *Aufs-Ganze-Gehen*—and the aggressive hold of temporal isolation, segmentation, or rootedness—the *An-die-Wurzel-Gehen*—which both make up the understanding-of-Being. Whereas Being opens out onto the whole or all of what is, time goes to the bottom or root of things. Both tendencies, Heidegger says, are in fact identical. "Die umgreifende Weite des Seins ist ein und das Selbe mit der angreifenden Vereinzelung der Zeit." ("The embracing amplitude of Being is one and the same with the penetrating particularity of time.")[10] *Da-Sein* as such is intimately positioned within this double directionality.

But even more to the main argument of Heidegger's course, *Da-Sein* (as *Dasein*) experiences an opening of vision (a *Blick*) wherein the question of the essence of freedom comes to pass in the opening or holding apart which is maintained by the "and" of time and Being as well as by the hyphen which separates *Da* and *Sein*. Heidegger argues, therefore, that freedom is not built into philosophy as a fundamental question, but that the key questions of metaphysics are grounded on the question of the essence of freedom which, as we have been told, is entirely situated in terms of the correspondence between Being and time, *Da* and *Sein*. In other words, freedom is not a characteristic that mankind has; rather, mankind is only possible given the openness or freedom without which mankind could not come forth out of the darkness. Freedom gives to *Dasein* the opportunity of understanding Being within the openness of beings, and hence *Dasein* can come to understand its relation to beings as wondrous, awesome, even monstrous.

> Der Mensch ist so ungeheuerlich, wie ein Gott nie sein kann, weil er ganz anders sein müßte. Dieses Ungeheuerliche, das wir da wirklich kennen und sind, kann solches nur sein als das Endlichste, aber in dieser Endlichkeit die existente Zusammenkunft des Widerstreitenden innerhalb des Seienden und deshalb die *Gelegenheit* und *Möglichkeit des Auseinanderbrechens und Aufbrechens* des Seienden *in seiner Viel – und Andersartigkeit*. Hier liegt zugleich das *Kernproblem* der *Möglichkeit der Wahrheit als Entborgenheit*.

> [Humankind is monstrous as a god can never be since he would have to be completely other. This monstrousness which we actually know and are can be such only as the most finite—but within this finitude it is the existent coming together: of the conflictual within beings and therefore the *occasion* and *possibility of a breaking apart or breaking open* of beings *in their diversity and alterity*. Here lies, at the same time, the *central problem of the possibility of truth as unconcealment.*][11]

The passage reflects a major departure from passages in *Sein und Zeit* in which Heidegger discusses *Dasein* as a consciousness of finitude and potentiality for being. In *Sein und Zeit* the understanding of Being, in particular, is described as an *Augenblick*, or moment of vision, in whose present *Dasein* has already exceeded itself ek-statically as that which has projected itself into temporalities before or beyond the present and has, thereby, glimpsed or grasped its own finitude.

> Das Phänomen des Augenblicks kann *grundsätzlich nicht* aus dem *Jetzt* aufgeklärt werden. Das Jetzt ist ein zeitliches Phänomen, das der Zeit als Innerzeitigkeit zugehört: das Jetzt, "in dem" etwas entsteht, vergeht oder vorhanden ist. "Im Augenblick" kann nichts vorkommen, sondern als eigentliche Gegen-wart läßt er *erst begegnen*, was als Zuhandenes oder Vorhandenes "in einer Zeit" sein kann.

> [The moment of vision is a phenomenon which *in principle* can *not* be clarified in terms of the "now." The "now" is a temporal phenomenon which belongs to time as within-time-ness: the "now" "in which" something arises, passes away, or is present-at-hand. "In the moment of vision" nothing can occur; but as an authentic present or waiting-towards, the moment of vision permits us *to encounter for the first time* what can be "in a time" as ready-to-hand or present-at-hand.][12]

Finitude expresses itself here as the arising and the passing away, what in the lecture course on human freedom Heidegger speaks of as the particularization or detachment of temporality. Whereas in *Sein und Zeit* the moment of vision follows from the disclosure of a now that is the "open" present in terms of which *Dasein* comes to an understanding of itself as finite (as *das Seiende*), in *Vom Wesen der Menschlichen Freiheit* the opening of vision bears on the difference between human beings and God. In short, it becomes a question of a de-monstration which that difference itself affords, and in which the human stands forth, grounded in a temporality that Heidegger speaks of as restrictive, retractive, particularizing, and isolating, if not also destructive.

The "now" in which we live is but a remnant or fragment of something much broader, to which the question of Being points. In this finitude of the now—which in the lecture course is ascribed to *Der Mensch*—there is the conjunction of contraries within *des Seienden* and hence the occasion and possibility of a breakdown or breakup of beings in their various (and often other) comportments. At this juncture, Heidegger says, we can see the possibility of truth as disclosure or *Entborgenheit* (unconcealment), a term Heidegger will develop at length in *Vom Wesen der Wahrheit*. Later, in the *Beiträge zur Philosophie,* he will address *Entborgenheit* as a characteristic of truth which discloses itself after its self-concealment. Such self-concealment, however, is broached by *Lichtung* and results in an openness or clearing that is to be deemed the emptiest of the empty. Yet, something has to be disclosed or unconcealed here as well, and Heidegger suggests that one cannot speak of such disclosure without recourse to a lexicon of lighting or illumination whose constituent terms concern the imagery of fire and sparks that in large part reintroduce an anthropomorphic and even ocularcentric notion of vision which had earlier been cleared away.

> Wie wenig aber auch die Leitvorstellung des Lichtes jenes Offene und seine Offenheit festhalten und ins Wissen heben konnte, zeigt sich darin, daß gerade die "Lichtung" und das "Gelichtete" nicht gefaßt wurde, sondern die Vorstellung sich entfaltete in der Richtung des Leuchtens und des Feuers und des Funkens, womit dann bald nur noch ein ursächliches Verhältnis der Erleuchtung maßgebend blieb, bis schleißlich alles in die Unbestimmtheit des "Bewußtseins" und der *perceptio* hinabglitt.

> [How little, though, the guiding conception could hold onto that opening and its openness and was able to raise it to knowledge, is indicated by the fact that precisely the "clearing" and the "cleared" was not grasped, but the presentation unfolded itself in the direction of the shining and the fire and the sparks, whereby only a causal connection of the illumination remained authoritative, until finally everything slipped down into the undeterminability of "consciousness" and *perceptio*.][13]

Important, of course, is that initially *Entborgenheit* took the place of the relatively crude "moment of vision" in *Sein und Zeit,* but by the later 1930s it would also function to conceal much of the argument concerning time and Being which was developed earlier in *Vom Wesen der Menschlichen Freiheit*—for example, the very advanced suggestion that Being is lighted or illuminated by a coming to pass of time whose moment can only be glimpsed in the afterburn of its having taken place, an afterburn which has cast a shadow on the difference of man and God: man's *monstrosity* with respect to Being, a monstrosity opened by that "freedom" which has been given in the contractions of time and the expansions of Being. In *Beiträge zur Philosophie* and the wartime seminars on the Pre-Socratics, the figure of the fire and its sparks will substitute a much more reductive and even far more subject-centered construction, which, as Jaques Derrida has argued, has a strong affinity with National Socialist rhetoric.

What Heidegger's *Beiträge* and later seminars do not acknowledge is that in revising the discourse of concealment and unconcealment, one is made to forget that a text like *Vom Wesen der Menschlichen Freiheit* was historically clairvoyant insofar as its understanding of freedom made conceivable a human monstrosity which Jacques Derrida would one day address in the name of the cinder, that figure which Heidegger's writings appear unable to think despite their invocation of fire.

II

In "Feu la cendre" Dasein is reinscribed into the image of the trace which follows the afterburn, the *il y a là cendre.*

> Il y a là cendre, une phrase dit ainsi ce qu'elle fait, ce qu'elle est. Elle s'incinère à la seconde, sous vos yeux. . . . La phrase dit ce qu'elle aura été, dès lors se donnant à elle-même, se donnant comme son propre nom, l'art consumé du secret: de l'exhibition savoir se garder.

> [Cinders there are, the sentence thus says what it does, what it is. It immediately incinerates itself, in front of your eyes. . . . The sentence says what it will have been, from the moment it gives itself up to itself, giving itself as its own proper name, the consumed (and consummate) art of the secret: of knowing how to keep itself from showing.][14]

The cinder is never entirely conceivable without fire. Hence "no cinder without fire." However, if this is "owed" to the fire, Derrida wants to think this debt as one that can be staged "sans l'ombre d'un sacrifice, à midi, sans dette, sans Phénix . . . au lieu d'aucun placement, le lieu seulement d'une incinération" ("without the shadow of a sacrifice, at noon, without debt, without the Phoenix . . . in the place of no emplacement, the place solely of an incineration").[15] Hence the sentence only avows an ongoing incineration, of which the sentence itself is an almost silent monument, indicating what is "there," the "there" (*là*) of the cinder.

In "Feu la cendre" Derrida wants to think the "otherwise" than Being, the *Seinsfrage* from the side of what follows the afterburn, the flash, or moment of illumination—what Derrida calls the *il y a là cendre*. Hence he asks if in fact the cinder takes place.

> Si un lieu même s'encercle de feu (tombe en cendre finalement, tombe en tant que nom), il n'est plus. Reste la cendre. Il y a là cendre, traduis, la cendre n'est pas, elle n'est pas ce qui est. Elle reste de ce qui n'est pas, pour ne rappeler au fond friable d'elle que non-être ou imprésence. L'être sans présence n'a pas été et ne sera pas plus là où il y a la cendre et parlerait cette autre mémoire. Là, où cendre veut dire la différence entre ce qui reste et ce qui est, y arrive-t-elle, là?

> [If a place is itself surrounded by fire (falls finally to ash, into a cinder tomb), it no longer is. Cinder remains, cinder there is, which we can translate: the cinder is not, is not what is. It remains *from* what is not, in order to recall at the delicate, charred bottom of itself only nonbeing or nonpresence. Being without presence has not been and will no longer be there where there is cinder and where this other memory would speak. There, where cinder means the difference between what remains and what is, will she ever reach it, there?][16]

Let us stop, for a moment, keeping in mind that Derrida will explicitly invoke the cinder in terms of the Holocaust. To put it bluntly, Derrida is asking over and over again how and whether the cinder of the crematorium "takes place." This is a troubling question—not least because of its openness—when we consider the power of those almost unspeakable place-names which have sheltered or preserved a sense of place for the cinder. Problematic for Derrida would be that in sheltering or in giving place to the cinder, the names which house the catastrophe provide not only a commemorative language in which the cinder is preserved (i.e., kept burning eternally), but a sacrificial place where "the truth" of Jewish experience, the German people, the Western tradition and so on can be said to take place. The assumption is, of course, that after the Holocaust we have the human (really political) freedom to think this truth, that history or time has given us the opening in which to think the cinder as something that is akin to everlasting spirit, that is, to the kind of Heideggerian lexicon within which it was concealed all along: in Derrida's words, "Esprit/âme/vie, Pneuma/phyché/zoè/bios, spiritus/anima/vita, Geist/Seele/Leben."[17] For Derrida, however, the cinder is the trait or trace of that lighting of spirit which resists such a historical incorporation.

In "Feu la cendre," therefore, Derrida is questioning how we can address the "truth" of the cinder. What speaks the cinder? And we could add, what speaks the guilt of Germany? What speaks the "truth" of what the German people have done? What speaks the "truth" of what the West, in terms of its historical development, has brought to pass as the Jewish experience of destruction? Is it possible to speak of a place where the cinder "is" or occurs as such? In sum, what clarity, clearing, or showing could bring this "truth" to light? Consider once more the cinder. It is not so much the other of Being than it is what has come to pass in the freedom or opening of a historical time, a coming to pass of that which has monstrosity, vastness, awesomeness. The *il y a là cendre* is the "there is" or monstration of horror, monstrosity, evil. The cinder is what remains of an evil that has come to appearance with respect to a human freedom opened in the difference of man and God.

Whereas the cinder is given or dispatched from the side of non-Being or nihilism, it too is something which has a persistent presence, which belongs to *das Seiendes,* and which has been lighted, though in the sense of being fired, incinerated, consumed in flame. Whereas for Heidegger *das Seiendes* manifests itself as present or now, for Derrida the cinder would be that example of *das Seiendes* which knows no present, but comes to pass in the temporal rift which elides placement in either the now or the afterward, as if the cinder could not take place as some thing which can be preserved, commemorated, or treasured up. Rather, the cinder is merely what *diese Helle spendet.* As such, the cinder comes about in the "and" of Being and time as the by-product or residual trace of human freedom; it partakes of a persistence and presence that does not meet all the conditions of what Heidegger calls *das Seiendes,* since the cinder is that which takes place without taking place as such.

The cinder, then, takes us from a consideration of Being *and* time to the destruction or dismantling of that *and,* since the cinder partakes of a different relation between Being and time than the beings of which Heidegger speaks in the lecture course on human freedom. The cinder, after all, is what no conjunction (or "and") can gather or pull together; it is what is opened—Derrida says the cinder is dissemination itself—as a monstrosity—a showing, demonstration, revelation, disclosure—that has no proper place, no proper time, no proper language, and no proper truth. If Derrida names the cinder, that name *cinder* is still a cinder of the cinder itself.[18] In short, the name *cinder* doesn't name anything but that which iteratively and paronomastically rescinds naming. In that sense, the naming of the cinder contrasts directly with what Heidegger has considered above, in terms of the naming of Being. "Mais l'urne de langage est si fragile. Elle s'effrite et tu souffles aussitôt dans une poussière de mots qui sont la cendre même." ("The urn of language is so fragile. It crumbles and immediately you blow into the dust of words which are the cinder itself.")[19] For this reason, Derrida will say:

> Dans cette phrase je vois: le tombeau d'un tombeau, le monument d'une tombe impossible—interdite, comme la mémoire d'un cénotaphe, la patience refusée du deuil, refusée aussi la lente décomposition abritée, située, logée, hospitalisée. . . . Une incinération célèbre peut-être le rien du tout, sa destruction sans retour mais folle de son désir et de sa ruse. . . . l'affirmation disséminale à corps perdu mais aussi tout le contraire, le non catégorique au labour du deuil, un non de feu.

> [In this sentence I see the tomb of a tomb, the monument of an impossible tomb—forbidden, like the memory of a cenotaph, denied the patience of mourning, denied also the slow decomposition that shelters, locates, lodges, hospitalizes. . . . An incineration celebrates perhaps the nothing of the all, its destruction without return but mad with its desire and with its cunning . . . the desperately disseminal affirmation but also just the opposite, the categorical "no" to the laborious work of mourning, a "no" of fire.][20]

The cinder, because it does not preserve or shelter, cannot be akin even to a predisclosive term like *ousia* (*Haus und Hof: Anwesend*), and therefore cannot be properly thought and hence mourned, for the cinder is the inappropriable, inhuman trace of that which has come to pass in the opening of vision, the flash of lightning, the rift of human freedom. It is an inappropriable materialization in the radiance of a temporal now in which presence and the present are withdrawn even as the persistence of that which is—of *das Seiendes*—remains. In this sense, the cinder might be thought of as the *retrait* of Being and time, of a holding back of *Haus und Hof* in the materialization of what persists as Being. This is the trait which Heidegger himself was not inclined to consider, the trait of a human freedom which comes to light as a monstration (but also de-monstration) that provides a clue to what Heidegger perceives in the lecture course as the difference between man and God.

Although the word *Holocaust* may well be invoked to house or contain this monstration in a temporality which we can safely seal off from ourselves, it could be thought of as a word which marks a lighting of time and a rescinding of Being that leaves the material trace of the cinder behind. Indeed, "Feu la cendre" even goes so far as to suggest that such a remainder means only that the fire itself is not extinguished, but remains withdrawn. If there is access to truth—*a-letheia*—it would have to be in terms of recollecting that the flames are never absent, that the fire, the light, the flash is what the *il y a là cendre* barely conceals. This is a thought which has also crossed Heidegger's mind in the lectures on

Heraclitus, when he speaks of lightning flashing in the sky, a lightning that is always held in reserve. In fact, at the close of "Logos," Heidegger tells us that he wants to stand in the "storm of Being" where the lightning bolts are manifest. However, at this much later juncture in Heidegger's thought, we can see where a decided reduction of the earlier discussion of Being *and* time has occurred for the sake of a lighting that will be identified with the logos or, more precisely, the *naming* of Being as the laying-to-rest that *gathers*. Moreover, in this bundling up of Being, Heidegger implicitly alludes to that standing in the storm of Being with which his rectoral address had ended, the lightning bolts retroactively resonating in such a way that they could, independently of any Heideggerian intention, commemorate a military organization instrumental in mass destruction. Here, of course, the opportunities for thinking the cinder have been largely foreclosed, both philosophically and politically. Yet, in *Vom Wesen der Menschlichen Freiheit* those opportunities are still available. The history of their eradication is something that merits further consideration within the context of Heidegger's seminars on Hölderlin, and also the seminars on Nietzsche and the Pre-Socratics. Indeed the study of such an eradication would bear on what Véronique Fóti has called, in the context of Heidegger's relation to Paul Celan, a path without issue. In glossing Celan's poem "Engführung," Fóti reminds us of this aspect of Heidegger. "In the face of the terrifying vision, one realizes that the path which leads to the moist eye is a path without issue."[21]

NOTES

1. Martin Heidegger, *Von Wesen der Menschlichen Freiheit (1930), Gesamtausgabe*, band 31 (Frankfurt am Main: Klostermann, 1982), p. 45. The translations from the German are my own; I am grateful to my colleague Sabine Gölz, for her many suggestions, which I have incorporated.

2. Ibid, p. 45.

3. Ibid, p. 55.

4. Ibid, p. 55.

5. Ibid, p. 93.

6. Aristotle, *Complete Works*, ed. Jonathan Barnes (Princeton: Princeton University Press, 1984), 9. 10. 1051b; 1052a1.

7. Heidegger, *Von Wesen*, pp. 114–115.

8. See, for example, *Sein und Zeit* (Tübingen: Max Niemeyer, 1984), p. 386; *Being and Time*, trans. J. Macquarrie and E. Robinson (New York: Harper & Row, 1962), p. 438.

9. *Sein und Zeit* (Frankfurt Am Main: Klostermann, 1984), p. 351; *Being and Time*, p. 402.

10. Heidegger, *Von Wesen,* p. 130.

11. Ibid., p. 135.

12. Heidegger, *Sein und Zeit,* p. 338; *Being and Time,* pp. 337–338.

13. Heidegger, *Beiträge zur Philosophie (Vom Ereignis)* in *Gesamtausgabe,* vol. 65 (Frankfurt am Main: Klostermann, 1989), p. 339.

14. French original and English translation in *Cinders,* trans. Ned Lukacher (Lincoln: University of Nebraska Press, 1992), p. 35.

15. The whole passage reads as follows in translation: "This is what is owed to the fire, and yet, if possible, without the shadow of a sacrifice, at noon, without debt, without the Phoenix, thus the unique phrase comes to set into place, in the place of no emplacement, the place solely of an incineration. The sentence avows only the ongoing incineration, of which it remains the almost silent monument: this can be 'there,' *là–*." Ibid., p. 37.

16. Ibid., p. 39.

17. Derrida, *De l'esprit* (Paris: Galilée, 1987), p. 119.

18. Derrida, *Cinders,* p. 49.

19. Ibid., p. 53.

20. Ibid., p. 55.

21. Véronique Fóti, *Heidegger and the Poets* (New Jersey: Humanities Press, 1992), pp. 91–92. Note that, in German, "path without issue" could be translated as *Holzweg.*

EIGHT

Derrida and the
Closure of Vision

John McCumber

Any attempt to clarify the status of vision in Derrida—vision itself, in the proper sense, true vision—runs straight into a curious problem. The topic is almost wholly absent from his writings prior to *La Vérité en peinture*.[1] Moreover, Derrida clearly has *reason* to avoid the topic of vision: he is a historian of philosophy, not a philosopher of the body. "Vision" can then enter into his thought, not as a topic in its own right, but only insofar as it affects the history of philosophy: the set of texts with which he deals. If philosophical texts were somehow paradigmatic objects of vision, we could obviously and directly learn about vision itself from Derrida's treatments of them. But they are not. Philosophical texts, while indisputably objects of vision, overlap only slightly with visual objects in general. As such objects they are quite special, while their strictly visual dimension does not yield significant insight into what they are. So there seems to be a gap between the nature of textuality and that of bodily experience: the two are not directly related. Derrida, by his emphasis on texts, seems to have closed himself off from our bodily experience of vision. To turn his discourse into a discourse on vision would be to inject a foreign problematic, to subject that discourse to a critical, perhaps even unfriendly, transformation.

But what if Derrida also has *reason* to be a historian of philosophy, rather than a philosopher of the body? What if there is an indirect relation between philosophical textuality and vision such that, while the latter may not tell us very much about the former, the former can tell us about the latter? What if there is a middle term, in virtue of which textuality turns out to illuminate corporeality in spite of their clear discrepancies? What if understanding philosophical texts which relate, somehow,

234

to vision somehow helps us to understand vision itself? In that case vision, though not explicitly part of Derrida's discourse, may yet be related to it. Our task would be, not to inject a wholly foreign problematic, but to ferret out the nature of that relation.

One of the things that Derrida refuses to close himself off from is the history of philosophy. He is by profession a historian of philosophy, and that is preeminently what he wishes both to understand and transform; the history of philosophy is to Derrida what sexuality was to Freud, or space-time to Einstein. His efforts, then, must be read together with and against the efforts of his predecessors—including in the present case particularly, but not exclusively, Hegel. Undertaking to write *only* on Derrida would thus commit the reverse of the previous error: instead of injecting him with an alien problematic, it would mean stripping him of his own.

I

The middle term which relates vision and textuality for Derrida is, I suggest, "metaphysics." For according to Derrida, those texts which constitute the history of philosophy do understand vision, in a way: in terms of a particular metaphor, to which it lends itself and of which philosophers have made recurrent use in constituting their inquiries as "metaphysical." This is the metaphor of the light of reason: "starting with its first words, metaphysics associates sight with knowledge."[2]

In various writings, Derrida traces this metaphor from the Platonic sun through clarity and distinctness in Descartes, to the "imperialism of theōria" in Husserl and finally to the light of disclosure in Heidegger.[3] It is no mere conceit:

> This metaphor of shadow and light (of self-showing and self-hiding) [is the] founding metaphor of occidental philosophy as metaphysics. . . . The entire history of our philosophy is a photology.[4]

It was thanks to taking vision as its (metaphorical) model for knowledge that philosophy became metaphysics. If vision itself is external to philosophy, then, a metaphorized version of vision is constitutive of it. Recognizing this metaphor can teach us about philosophy. But—once again—can it tell us anything about *vision*—nonmetaphorical vision, vision itself as we *properly* experience it—through the immediacy of our flesh?

As "la mythologie blanche" argues, we have reason to be suspicious of the very category of metaphor: Derrida does not in fact believe that there is any purely "proper" usage of a word, which can be opposed to its "metaphorical" senses. This means, in accordance with the Greek etymology in play here, that meta-phorical "carrying-over" operates in both directions. If what we call "metaphorical" uses of a word are carried over from their "literal" uses, then we must say that those "literal" uses are also carried over from the "metaphorical" ones. So vision itself, "properly" understood as a phenomenon of the body, is in truth merely an artifact of the metaphorical vision instituted by (and instituting) philosophy. Derrida's thought about vision, keyed to a view of it opened up metaphorically in the history of metaphysics, relates to "vision itself" because *vision itself is not biologically given*, but is mediated by—or disseminated through—the history of philosophy. That is why our critical transformation will not be an unfriendly one. Derrida has reason to be a historian of philosophy, rather than of the body, insofar as "vision" is a product, in fact a by-product, of a certain historical development in philosophy—one that also gave us "bodies" in the first place.

The philosophers' use of vision as a model for knowledge, then, gives us what we Westerners call "vision." Such vision has four main characteristics. First, it is centered on the notion of "presence," itself understood on two levels: temporally, as the independence of the present moment from past and future; and epistemologically, as the presence-to-self, or self-certainty, of consciousness. Both are available in the wink of an eye (the Heideggerean *Augenblick*) in which

> self-presence should produce itself in the undivided unity of a temporal present, in order to avoid entirely making itself known through the *procuration* of a sign.[5]

Second: The object of such vision—the particular kind of present at which it aims—is independent of its temporal context—and hence of all context. It is self-sufficient, then, against the flux of time. It is—form: "Form is presence itself. Formality is that which presents itself in the thing in general, *allows itself to be seen*, gives itself to thought."[6]

Third: If vision is knowledge, and vision delivers forms, then (as Aristotle argued in much detail)[7] the thing can be known only insofar as it is form. So understood, philosophy's founding assimilation of knowledge to vision is authorized by form: "The metaphysical domination of the concept of form cannot fail to give rise to a sort of submission to the gaze."[8] There is, of course, a price paid for this, and that is the suppression of the other of form: of matter. The visionary model for knowledge thus becomes complicitous with what Derrida calls, in *La Voix et le phénomène*, the "founding opposition of metaphysics," that of form and matter, and with the reduction of matter to unknowability.[9]

Fourth: sight, thus subjected to form, becomes sound. For to reduce a being to its form means to assimilate it to the knower, as Aristotle pointed out; and such assimilation can only be fully achieved when the object becomes, not merely assimilated to, but lodged within, the knower. Hence, for Aristotle, Derrida asks:

> But is sight enough? . . . For knowing how to learn, and learning how to know, sight, intelligence, and memory are not enough. We must also learn how to hear, and to listen. I might suggest somewhat playfully that we have to know how to shut our eyes in order to be better listeners.[10]

This reduction of sight to hearing is then the function of the "wink" of the eye, and is necessary—at the other end of metaphysics, in Husserl—to ideality itself:

> An ideal object is an object whose *monstration* can be repeated indefinitely, whose presence . . . is indefinitely reiterable precisely because, delivered from all worldly spatialization, it is a pure noema which I can express without (at least in appearance) having to pass by the world.[11]

The subjection of vision to form is thus only the first step toward a deeper subjection of vision to speech—in particular, to the "hearing oneself speak" which is for Derrida the *summum* of Husserlian self-presence and, as such, the ultimate stage of metaphysics.[12]

This subjection is also carried out, Derrida argues, by Hegel, in a way which reveals another of its sides. On Derrida's reading of Hegel, the visible thing, perceived across a distance, always presents itself with some opacity and contingency. The virtue of the word, belonging more intimately to the hearer (and the speaker), is—as with Husserl—to overcome such opacity so as to be fully present to thought. Sound is more transparent and illuminating than any vision, and hence can accomplish what vision tries to but cannot. Thus, the word does not transgress the norms of vision, but fulfills them: for Derrida's Hegel, "[hearing] is thus designated, in its excellence, according to optical language (*idea, theōria*)."[13] So sound, concludes Derrida, sublates vision for Hegel because it is actually more visionary than sight itself. In spite of Hegel's attempts to critique vision, knowledge for him, even philosophical knowledge, remains basically a form of *theōria*. His philosophy is as photological as any, if not more so.

What Hegel actually does with vision will be investigated later in this essay. For the moment, it is clear that the same metaphysical tradition which has delivered us vision as the vision of form—a vision "filled and satisfied by *présence*"[14]—has delivered sight over to sound, vision to the disponibility of the speaking voice. But this subjection of vision to voice is not one-sided, because in it vision is subjected to a sound which fulfills its own visionary imperative: that of form as assimilation of matter. So if vision is a transitional phenomenon within Western philosophy, that is because it cannot fulfill its own imperatives: it cannot fully close the gap between knower and known—or, as Derrida puts it with regard to Husserl, "vision was originarily the inadequation of interiority to exteriority."[15] Hence, we have here a bilevel hierarchy in which vision, the partial assimilation of known to knower, is completed by their full identification in voice.

I suggested earlier that the "metaphorical" vision of the philosophers could not, for Derrida, simply be contrasted with a "true" or "proper" vision. A somewhat different contrast, however, has now emerged: that between vision as it has been disseminated to us by the history of philosophy as metaphysics, and something that might turn out to be vision "uncontaminated" by that history. Such "uncontaminated" vision, whether or not and in whatever senses it might be biological or bodily, would simply be vision liberated from what might be called its metaphysical subjection to form and the voice. Derrida seeks such liberation: for he wants, not merely to trace out the origin of vision in the history of philosophy, but to critique that origin. For the "imperialism of *theōria*" carries with it a certain violence—the violence of the light, the suppression of matter. And, as Derrida writes:

> if light is the element of violence, then one must contest light with a certain other light, in order to avoid the worst violence.[16]

That critique will not be carried out from the standpoint of hearing, or indeed from any other sense. Indeed, the very distinction between vision and hearing has been called into question, because it is no more stable than the notoriously elusive line between interiority and exteriority, no more enduring than the wink of an eye. Nor will the critique of the appropriation of vision be carried out from the standpoint of the intellect—a standpoint which not only itself richly deserves Derridean criticism, but which has been defined by that very appropriation which is to be criticized. The critique of vision must then be carried out in the name of another sort of vision—sort of.

This is in general accord with Derrida's strategy of the double gesture. This strategy is a response to a problem of totality which Derrida's critique of metaphysics encounters. If metaphysics is the subjection of our language, cognition, society, and so forth to presence, then metaphysics should be criticized. But if metaphysics is also the subjection of *all* our language and concepts to presence, then there is no articulate way to fight it: we have no nonmetaphysical words in which to formulate an alternative, from the standpoint of which we could then criticize metaphysics. Derrida's response to this problem is that "metaphysics" is not a matter of which words and concepts we use, but of how we use them:

Each concept . . . belongs to a systematic sequence and itself constitutes a system of predicates. *There is no concept which is in itself metaphysical.* There is a work, which may or may not be metaphysical, on conceptual systems. Deconstruction does not consist in passing from one concept to another but in overturning and displacing a conceptual order.[17]

The answer is to use words in two ways at once: with their old, metaphysical meanings, and in ways that disrupt and transcend those meanings—without ever resolving themselves into new, precise (and hence metaphysical) meanings. Language thus has for Derrida two tasks, equiprimordially: to convey presence and to disrupt it. Applying this to "vision," we see that it must have two functions in Derrida's thought. One is to convey the metaphysical meaning whose genesis-by-metaphor I have retraced here, following Derrida. The other use is a disruptive and nonmetaphysical one. Such a use would convey the possibility of a vision which is not the vision of form.

But if form simply *is* that which presents itself to vision, "allows itself to be seen," how can there be vision which is not, somehow, of form? We seem to be trying to see nothing, which Plato's *Timaeus* defines as the problem of how to see the Receptacle: that "invisible and formless" something which contains all things and puts eternal essences into the play of Becoming.[18] The Platonic answer is that we become aware of the Receptacle, not directly, but by seeing things change, come to be, and pass away; and, according to the *Phaedo*, we see this, in turn, as the inability of sensible things to attain what they "reach out toward"—eternal perfection.[19] So for Derrida, disruptive vision would see its objects as reaching beyond themselves, but un-Platonically, with no promise of determinate fulfillment in this or any other world. Since we do not have the comfort of already knowing what those objects are reaching toward, our vision of them remains a vision of what we do not and cannot exactly see: a blindness, or better: a blind spot. Hence, nonmetaphysical (or, as I will call it, disruptive) vision is vision which is organized around its own blind spots.[20]

A blind spot is something we cannot see; and yet it is something which affects what we do see, the shape and scope of our visual field. Hence, it is something to which we should not willfully blind ourselves.[21] In the founding version of the founding metaphor—Plato's—it is the sun which cannot be seen, and which by virtue of that fact structures even the domain of Forms themselves, plenitude founded on something beyond Being:

> Presence disappearing into its own radiance, the hidden source of light, truth, and sense, the effacement of the face of the other: such would be the insistent *return* of what subjected the metaphor to philosophy.[22]

And this elusiveness is not the privileged characteristic of the source of Being and Truth; it is generalizable to all objects of sense:

> the *aisthêton* can always *not* present itself, can hide itself, absent itself. It does not give itself on command, and its presence cannot be mastered. The sun, from this point of view, is the sensible object *par excellence*.[23]

Thus generalized, the object of vision is no longer presence but something which is "visible" only in transition: *as* coming-from and going-to, without any determinate things that it comes from and goes to. Such an "object" is then not form but what Derrida calls the trace, which in fact is neither visual nor auditory because it is neither partially nor wholly assimilated: it is the "infinitely other" of Levinas.[24]

Disruptive vision is thus not blind to its own blind spots. Such blind spots can be found, to give two examples, in Hegel and Rousseau. In Hegel, it is the possibility of expenditure without reserve, of a loss that—contrary to what Derrida takes as the basic presupposition of Hegelianism—cannot be made up in any way. Because the possibility of such loss is incompatible with his own basic principle, Hegel cannot see it; but its very exclusion is what makes his own discourse possible.[25] For Rousseau, the concept of supplementarity is such an unseen: the strange logic of origins by which any origin—for example, natural man—is both, as *first* principle, an independent, self-contained plenitude—but, as *merely* first principle, in need of subsequent fulfillment by the rest of Rousseau's discourse. If natural man were not such a plenitude, there would be no point in Rousseau's attempt to return to him; but if he were not more than such a plenitude, there would be no point in Rousseau's discourse itself. Supplementarity is the "unseen which opens and limits visibility."[26]

Hence, the "vision" which organizes itself around its own blind spot is vision which is open to the trace itself: it is, in Derrida's words, "the system of an *écriture* and of a reading which we know . . . organize themselves around their own blind spots."[27]

Derrida's criticism of metaphysical vision is thus made, not from a standpoint supposed to be wholly beyond vision, or from that of a "purer" (intellectual) vision, but from the limits of such vision, the conditions under which it becomes impossible. It seems that his program is to accomplish for our reading eye what artists like Vasarely accomplish for our more broadly visual one: to show that the boundaries among its objects (forms or categories, words, or concepts) are unstable and questionable. Vasarely's vibrating colors and illusionistic patterns continually redraw their own boundaries, and in that way expose something of the nature of those colors. Such a critique of color—and all great artists engage in it—operates from the precise point where the distinctions among colors, and hence color itself as opposed to white light, become untenable.[28] Thus, if Vasarely shows the nature of color from the limits of vision, Derrida attempts to do the same, in a textual key: his critique of knowledge as intellectual vision is a summoning of such vision's limits.

Consider, for example, one of his most famous gestures: the replacement of the *e* in the French *différence* by *a*. This is not a simple orthographic change, for as Derrida notes the two words are pronounced exactly alike in French: the difference between *e* and *a* is in that perspective no difference. Derrida's gesture rather points to a place where *a* and *e* do not differ, where their distinction is questionable, where the line between them cannot be drawn but cannot simply be erased, either. The questioning of the distinction between *e* and *a* is thus conducted, not from the visual realm, but from the auditory: as inscriptions the two letters remain distinct, and it is from the aural point of view that we are invited to question that distinction. The "visual" is not for Derrida, as it is for Vasarely, a sphere so entirely cut off from all else that aural phenomena are of no significance for it. But the auditory realm is not some purer domain into which we can escape from the problems with vision; it is the subject merely of occasional episodic appeals, a useful contaminant.

The displacement of vision into the intellectual realm, which was supposed to make it still more visionary, thus includes for Derrida a contamination of it with certain phenomena of the sounding word: this is why so much of his work has to do with puns, which connect—yet insist on the distinctions among—words and concepts.[29] Hence, Derrida is able to use the auditory realm to critique the visual paradigm of knowledge, without positing it as some sort of pure domain where we could escape the problems of the visual: when we close our eyes, our blind spots remain. Indeed, they dance.

II

The question remains of the extent to which Derrida's disruptive vision really breaks, when all is said and done, with vision as philosophers have conceived it. It seems that it should, for vision traditionally conceived is metaphysical and Derrida wants to criticize metaphysics. But it also seems that it should not, because Derrida does not believe in definitive rupture, any more than in definitive closure.[30] Both sides of the question, in other words, are impelled by the double gesture, which means that no decisive answer can be given. We can begin to question Derrida's "break" with tradition by returning to philosophy's founding metaphor:

the gesture by which it takes knowledge to be like what it takes vision to be, and the resultant transition of vision into voice. In the modern age, Kant's *Critique of Pure Reason* presents, like Plato's *Symposium,* four aspects of vision that have traditionally found their way from the sensory up to the transcendental realm. First, we cannot see the momentary: vision requires relatively fixed objects (or, as the Greeks might say, no *horao* without *horizo*: I cannot see without determining). So for Plato, vision is ultimately only of the Forms, which are the only fully determinate and wholly stable things in his cosmos, and is carried out not by the physical but the metaphysical eye. The object of Kantian critique, the transcendental ego, persists, like the Forms, through change: it is a pure power of synthesis, and its modes of synthesizing—the categories of the understanding and the ideas of the will—are given independently of any material synthesized.[31] It thus remains fixable by the critical gaze, no matter what empirical contents it receives from sensation.

Second, the realm of vision lies homogeneously open to our gaze. We ordinarily see objects only perspectivally, of course. But what Aristotle called vision's proper objects,[32] the colors vision presents to the seer, are fully present at any stage: they lie entirely open to the knowing gaze, which therefore cannot be mistaken about them, and in this openness they are also homogeneously colors. And so the domain of Forms can be traversed by the metaphysical eye, once it has fixed on that domain at all. Similarly, the transcendental ego offers itself, fully outfitted with its categories and even with its categorical imperative, as a totality open all at once to the critical eye. No mode of synthesis is epistemically, or ontologically, prior to the others: all are homogeneous in being modes of synthesis.

Third, if the proper objects of the eye, as directly perceived sensory data, are wholly present to consciousness, they repose immediately on something which is radically other than they: what Heidegger eventually calls "earth," the massive materiality of the objects whose surfaces they color. The gap between physical being and what we see of that being is in fact so wide that Berkeley was able to argue that their relation could not be "causal" at all, from which he concluded that there are no physical objects.[33] For Plato, the Forms repose on a non-Something, a Good, which is "beyond Being and Substance," beyond any kind of determinate nature. As Heidegger notes in the case of Kant, the origin of the transcendental ego is also wholly hidden, the "hidden root" which Kant forbore to dig up.[34]

Fourth and finally, as an object of visionary knowledge, the Forms and the transcendental ego are given in an entirely private experience: Even though forms are "objectively" valid, what I know about them is mine alone, the object of no one else's knowledge, just as almost everyone can see colors but no one else can see the colors in *my* visual field. Hence, my reports on my visual field are "incorrigible": there is no way anyone else can say that I do not see the colors I think I see.

The displacement of vision into the intellectual realm means, for Kant as for Plato, that the object of knowledge is conceived in a certain way: as (1) stable, (2) homogenous, (3) immediately reposing on—or I will say grounded in—something far different from the object known itself, and (4) private.

The question then is: to what extent, if any, is Derrida's transgression of philosophy also a transgression of these four traditional characteristics of vision—of vision itself? This question can be sharpened. Situated within the displacement of vision, ocularcentric philosophy opened itself to certain criticisms—criticisms which turn out to be reprises of the four characteristics of the visionary paradigm I cited earlier. One is that its alleged vision of something permanent and enduring denies the radicality of time and history, dismissing them as effecting merely a set of changes that leave permanent essences untouched. A second is that philosophy's attempt to account for things in general leaves too many concrete differences out of play: just as all visual objects are equally and openly colors, so the philosophical intellect has a homogeneous field of objects, such as the Forms, or the categories, or Being. Third, philosophy seeks grounds which are, like the material objects that underlie our visual field, wholly other than what they ground, just as material objects are wholly unlike plays of color. This renders its attempt at accounting for things suspect, for what explanatory value does a ground have which is wholly other than its grounded? Fourth, ocularcentric philosophy grounds its certainties on the incorrigible reportage of the private intellectual eye, which is not open to correction by others, and is in that sense dangerously "monological."

All these charges are made openly by Hegel against Kant and his followers;[35] they hold as well against the visionary Plato (which is not to deny that there are other Platos, or indeed other Kants). Hence, it is perhaps Hegel who most clearly turns vision into voice. He does this in two steps. First, he identifies three of the above characteristics as proper, not to objects of knowledge, but to objects of vision.[36] For, as he points out, they do not hold for sounds. The sounding tone disappears as it arises, for example: it is the reverse of stability, which is proper to objects of vision. And it is vision which presents merely the surfaces of bodies, and the colors of those surfaces; sound arises as the vibration of part of a body, a part which (like the vocal chords) may not be immediately visible but is not wholly and in principle invisible, either. Beginning, not from the surface of bodies but from their interiors, it also arises in and as what is perceived: the vibrating body is not inaudible, as the seen object is invisible: it *is* what is heard; the origin of sound is not wholly other than sound. And (though Hegel does not stress this) sound does not appear as a single unity but is, from the birth of the hearer, sundered into at least two basically different components: the voice of the mother and all other sounds. Finally, sound is not always inescapably private. In particular, my own view of what I mean by my own words is not, for Hegel, incorrigible. If I can insist that what I have seen is what I have seen, even if others say they see it differently, what I mean by an utterance is by contrast what my hearers say I mean. If they disagree among themselves, then my meaning is not what I *or* any one of them think I mean, but the common core of their interpretations. If they agree among themselves and their interpretations have no common core, I have said nothing, a mere *Meinen* or *Bei-spiel.*

Hegel's second step (in my reconstruction here) is to claim that all four of these characteristics of sound as opposed to vision have philosophical significance.[37] Philosophy for him is to be radically temporal, the most fleeting possible organization of time. It should present, not the surface, but the inner nature of things. For only in this way can it be "expression."[38] Its task (the "toil of the Notion") is to play out fully the concrete differences of things, before allowing them to manifest their ultimate and "ideal" unity. And its objects have to be, not private perceptions, but public phenomena: words which, as soon as they are produced at all, no longer belong to the speaker in any privileged way.[39] These are the reasons why Hegel insisted that philosophy was primarily an oral/aural phenomenon, and that writing was a secondary mode of presentation: he was not mindlessly repeating the millenial prejudices of metaphysics. Indeed, it is possible that he was trying, long before Derrida, to expose and perhaps even to end them.

There is thus a full-blown philosophical critique of metaphysical vision prior to Derrida's deconstruction of it. Understanding Derrida's relation to the history of philosophy, including this critique, requires us to place him before the following trilemma: His thought remains keyed enough to vision to fall victim to those criticisms, in which case Derrida is a philosopher of consciousness, a pre-Hegelian like Kant and Plato. Or, his writing joins the Hegelian criticism of the philosophy of vision, in which case Derrida is not as "original" as he is often thought to be. Or, as we might judge from Derrida's remarks on Hegel, his own critique of vision goes beyond Hegel's, which is directed against intellectual vision but in the name of still purer intellectual vision.

We may take it that Derrida is outside philosophy (i.e. outside Hegel) enough that he does not repeat the sort of Hegelian criticisms I mentioned above: his critique of vision differs from Hegel's, and indeed encompasses Hegel's. But does his "program," limited to instating and re-stating the limits of intellectual vision through contamination with other realms, escape vision enough that Hegelian criticisms—ahistoricality, transcendentality, undifferentiatedness, and monology—cannot be made of it? If Hegel falls under Derrida's version of ocularcentrism, does Derrida fall under Hegel's?

Derrida's critique of what he calls "logocentrism," with its privileging of language as sound (*phonê*), and his accompanying valorization of *écriture* seem obviously to substitute something seen (writing) for something heard (logos). There are, to be sure, many qualifications to be made in such a statement: *écriture* is not, after all, something physically inscribed but a set of characteristics which applies to all textuality, and hence to all language that is textually structured, whether we see it or hear it. It is no more literally visual than was Plato's vision of the Forms: it is vision displaced, though in a different direction. This is why Rodolphe Gasché, in his magisterial study of the philosophical Derrida, can so plausibly locate him in what Gasché calls the philosophy of reflection.[40]

Consider, first, the set of *renvois* that constitute what Derrida calls *différance*. Nothing could be less stable. Yet at the end his book, Gasché refers to Derrida's various "infrastructures," including this one, as "quasi-transcendental."[41] To be sure, Gasché is not here attempting to reduce Derrida to a quasi-Kantian: two important features of *écriture* distinguish the two. One is that *écriture* gives, not merely the conditions of the possibility of traditional philosophical discourse (as would a Kantian type of "transcendental" structure) but the conditions of its impossibility as well: we might say that it gives, not merely its conditions, but its limits. And it does this in that the structures it circumscribes are not necessary concepts inherent in the mind as such, or indeed in anything else, but are the products of a "certain irreducible erratic contingency." The texts which they structure, then, they also destructure: possibility and impossibility are too deeply entwined for an account of the one to dispense with the other; and to meet the conditions of textual possibility is to fathom, in another way, the conditions of textual impossibility.

But insofar as it gives the conditions of the possibility-and-impossibility of textuality, indeed of philosophical discourse in general, must not *écriture* be itself unchanging—not an unchanging structure but, like Plato's sun, a sort of eternally occurrent, and in that way stable, de-structuring?[42] Is there not a kind of uniformity to the lability that Derrida introduces into the texts he writes on—whether of Plato, Rousseau, Kant, Hegel, Heidegger, or others—such that all the vibrations, the undertones and overtones, the resonances and dissonances he finds in them seem to take us, again and again, to the same nonplace: to what John Sallis has called "a wonder that one could never aspire to surpass"?[43] Then Derrida's *différance* would bear to Kant's categories the same sort of relation that Heidegger's "in-order-to" bears to Aristotle's concept of happiness—it holds the same place as the other, relatively well-defined concept, but holds it empty.[44] In this sense—that it always recurs in its own peculiar absence of structure—would not *différance* have its own, perhaps unique, sort of "stability"? Predicated on such a stable destabilizer, Derrida's program would ultimately be ahistorical in the sense that it would deny or overlook development: whatever is fed into it—whatever texts come under discussion—would exhibit the same basic "properties," or rather nonproperties. Plato, Aristotle, Kant, Hegel, and Heidegger would all present merely "empirical" variations on the same "transcendental" theme (of presence)—or, as he puts it, events of rupture in the more permanent chains of predicates that constitute the unity of metaphysics over time—rather than a historical development progressing, happily or not, from earlier to later.[45]

That deconstruction's accounts of what it aims to account for—the actual texts, as opposed to the infrastructures which operate within and on them—are undifferentiated (i.e. that "metaphysics" is for deconstruction a homogeneous realm of conceptual colorizations of presence) is an old criticism. What, it asks, is Derrida's warrant for his recurrent blanket characterizations of philosophy as the "metaphysics" of presence from Plato to Hegel? None is ever given.[46] Is this because to ask how metaphysics depends on presence would be as senseless as asking how colors depend on light?

As accounting for certain properties of philosophical texts, *différance* would be a certain sort of "ground" (or, as de-structuring, a nonground) for them. But such a "ground" is more than nonempirical, as were Plato's and Kant's transcendent/transcendental realms; it is wholly other than what reposes on it. To quote Gasché:

> The invisibility of the infrastructure . . . seems to be linked to a powerful motif in classical philosophy according to which what makes visibility possible must itself remain invisible. . . . Yet the motif of this invisible source of light, this unheard of source of speech, is only the negative image of what I have called the irreducible and originary doubling. . . . For structural reasons, that which, as the absolute ground, does not belong to the totality of what it makes possible cannot possibly offer itself to perception. . . . Consequently, to speak of this ground as the blinding origin of philosophy—that is, to subject it to the ethico-theoretical code of philosophy—is to continue to speak in the language of that which that origin makes possible.[47]

Thus, the infrastructures, as Gasché quotes Derrida,

> are "only general and formal predicative structures" that represent the "common root" of all predicates characterizing opposing terms.[48]

Gasché here at once subtracts visionary motifs from Derrida's account of the "unseen source" and reinstates them more deeply: visionary motifs do not apply to the unseen source because it is in fact the "negative image" of an unseen source. The specific problem to which Gasché attends here is the singularity of the term "the blinding origin of philosophy": the syntactical mark (the definite article) which suggests that the origin is somehow singular, undivided, a plenitude. The mutual otherness of structure and infrastructure which Gasché invokes is not a relation of "ground," any more than the unseen material being of an object, for Berkeley, "causes" the colors that present themselves to us. In each case, the ontological chasm between the two is too vast for "ground" (or "cause") to be used in marking the repose of a relation.

The fourth and final criticism concerns the modeling of ocularcentric philosophy on the privacy of the objects of vision. Consider what the *Phaedrus* calls the incapacity of texts to fight back—to correct partialities and idiosyncracies of interpretation. For Plato, such correction is the sovereign right of the speaker: I am allowed to explain what my words *really* mean if I speak them or am still present when they are read. For Hegel, as we saw, it is the right of the community: once my words have been spoken, they no longer belong to me, and their meaning is up to the community to decide. Derrida's readings have no such checks: even if his interpretations are successfully challenged, the challenge has no effect on them. Indeed, David Wood has written:

> Husserlians contest his reading of Husserl, de Man disputes his reading of Rousseau, Searle attacks his reading of Austin, and Derrida's treatment [sic] of Marx, Heidegger, and Freud have all had their critics. However, even if each of these responses were individually deserved, that would not necessarily constitute a cumulative case against deconstruction because they are each mounted on different grounds.[49]

It is not that the criticisms are justified, but that they miss the point. If one's own honest account of the ingredients of one's own visual field is incorrigible, so it seems are Derrida's: they recreate the texts they are about. That is perhaps as it should be, because as Wood finally remarks, the merits of Derrida's readings are pragmatic: the readings he produces have values other than their accuracy. But there does seem to be an ineluctable residuum of epistemological privacy, in the form of meaning-incorrigibility, in Derrida's program.

The texts which Derrida discusses are, of course, not private: they are public, indeed cultural, objects. But Derrida's ways of treating them are singular enough. To map the idiosyncracies of his readings of such thinkers as Aristotle, Husserl, Hegel, and Heidegger would be an immense task. True, in these interpretations, Derrida is not alone: his understanding of Aristotle, for example, follows Heidegger's; his account of Hegel is basically Kojèvian. But the "privacy" here need not be that of an individual, isolated ego. There are forms of communal privacy, such as sectarianism; and in its appeal to such privacy Derrida's thought seems, once again, to retain the ocularcentrism of the tradition. While visual forms are ingredients of the public world, our grasp of them is private: just so with Derrida's grasp of philosophical texts.

In sum: Derrida's critique of displaced vision, written from the limits of vision itself, does not evade the four criticisms of the visual paradigm in philosophy which I have noted above. We are tempted, indeed, to view those limits of vision as themselves temporal: as valorizing the vision that comes after vision, in the sense suggested by David M. Levin. When we stare at something long enough, Levin points out,

> instead of clear and distinct perception, [we find] blurring and confusion; . . . instead of stability and fixation at the far end of the gaze, we find a chaos of jerking, shifting forms, as the object of focus violently tears itself away.[50]

And then we blink. We are tempted to say that Derrida's unheard-of critique of vision has not so much escaped philosophy's traditional concern with vision of presence as given it a new twist: that he presents us with the millennial fatigue of the mind's eye: after centuries of trying to see absolute truth, it finds itself winking into *Götterdämmerung*, the dusk of difference.

NOTES

1. To which writings I, following Rodolphe Gasché, will unapologetically restrict myself: Gasché, *The Tain of the Mirror* (Cambridge, Mass.: Harvard University Press, 1986), p. 4.

2. Jacques Derrida, "The Principle of Reason: The University in the Eyes of Its Pupils," *Diacritics*, vol. 13, no. 3 (Fall 1983), p. 4.

3. Derrida, "La mythologie blanche," *Marges de la philosophie* (Paris: Minuit, 1972), p. 302 (Plato), 318–319 (Descartes); English translation, *Margins of Philosophy*, trans. Alan Bass (Chicago: University of Chicago Press, 1982), pp. 253–254, 266–267. See also Derrida, "Violence et métaphysique," *L'écriture et la différence*, p. 128 (Plato and Husserl), 131–132 (Heidegger); English translation, *Writing and Difference*, trans. Alan Bass (Chicago: Chicago University Press, 1978), pp. 85, 87–88. Page references to English translations will be given after a slash; the translations in this paper, however, are my own.

4. Derrida, "Forme et signification," in *l'Écriture et la différence*, p. 45/27.

5. Derrida, *La Voix et le phénomène* (Paris: Presses Universitaires de France, 1967), p. 67; English translation, *Speech and Phenomena*, trans. David B. Allison (Evanston: Northwestern University Press, 1973), p. 60.

6. Derrida, "Forme et vouloir-dire," in *Marges*, p. 188/158; emphasis added.

7. Aristotle, *Metaphysics* 7.2.

8. Derrida, "Forme et vouloir-dire," *Marges*, p. 188/158; cf. "La Mythologie blanche," p. 303/253 f.

9. Derrida, *La Voix et le phénomène*, p. 70/63.

10. Derrida, "The Principle of Reason," p. 4.

11. Derrida, *La Voix et le phénomène*,, p. 84/75.

12. Derrida, *La Voix et le phénomène*, pp. 78–97/70–87.

13. Derrida, "Le puits et la pyramide," in *Marges*, p. 108 n. 11/93 n. 21.

14. Derrida, *De la grammatologie* (Paris: Minuit, 1967), p. 164 n. 8; English translation, *Of Grammatology*, trans. Gayatri Chakravorty Spivak (Baltimore: Johns Hopkins University Press, 1976), p. 337 n. 8.

15. Derrida, "Violence et métaphysique," in *L'Écriture et la différence*, p. 177/120.

16. Ibid., p. 172/117.

17. Derrida, "Signature, événement, contexte," in *Marges* (Paris: Minuit, 1972), pp. 392–393/329; emphasis added.

18. Plato, *Timaeus* 49A–51D.

19. Plato, *Phaedo* 75A.

20. Derrida, "L'Exorbitant," *De la grammatologie*, p. 234/163.

21. Cf. the remarks on those who would blind themselves to the tissue, or textuality, of the literary text: ibid., p. 228/159.

22. Plato, *Republic* 507–509; Derrida, "La Mythologie blanche," in *Marges*, p. 320/268.

23. Derrida, "La Mythologie blanche," in *Marges*, p. 299/250.

24. Derrida, "L'Écriture avant la lettre," *De la grammatologie*, p. 95/65; "Violence et métaphysique," *L'Écriture et la différence*, p. 138/93.

25. Derrida, "De l'économie restreinte à l'économie générale," in *L'Écriture et la différence*, pp. 378, 380–382/257, 259–260.

26. Derrida, "L'Exorbitant," *De la grammatologie*, p. 234/163.

27. Ibid., p. 234/163.

28. As Gregory Ulmer has pointed out, many of Derrida's characteristic gestures are related to op art, which operates "the creation of visual effects through the manipulation of geometric forms, color dissonance, and kinetic elements, all exploiting the extreme limits of the psychology of optical effect or visual illusion." Gregory Ulmer, "Op Writing: Derrida's Solicitation of Theoria," in Mark Krupnick, ed., *Displacement: Derrida and After* (Bloomington: Indiana University Press, 1983), p. 39 and pp. 29–58 generally.

29. Ulmer makes punning central to Derrida's entire project (op. cit., p. 32). We need not go so far.

30. "I don't believe in decisive rupture. Breaks always reinscribe themselves in an older tissue which one must continue to undo, interminably; that is their

fate. This in no way denies the necessity and importance of certain breaks."
Derrida, *Positions* (Paris: Minuit, 1972), p. 35.

31. Immanuel Kant, *Kritik der reinen Vernunft* (Berlin Academy, "B" Edition, 1787), pp. 158–159.

32. Aristotle, *de Anima* 2.6.

33. David M. Armstrong, ed., *Berkeley's Philosophical Writings* (New York: Collier, 1965), pp. 41–128.

34. Martin Heidegger, *Kant und das Problem der Metaphysik* (Frankfurt am Main: Klostermann, 4th ed. extended 1973), pp. 155–165; English translation, *Kant and the Problem of Metaphysics*, trans. James S. Churchill (Bloomington: Indiana University Press, 1962), pp. 166–176.

35. They are to be found, for example, in the opening pages of the treatment of Kant in the *Lectures on the History of Philosophy*, at Hegel, *Werke*, ed. Eva Moldenhauer and Karl Markus Michel, 20 vols. (Frankfurt am Main: Suhrkamp, 1970–71), 20:330–332. All references to Hegel are to this edition. English translation, *Hegel's Lectures on the History of Philosophy*, trans. E. S. Haldane and Frances H. Simson, 3 vols. (New York: Humanities Press, 1974), 3:428–430.

36. *Werke*, 10:104–105. English translation, Hegel, *Philosophy of Spirit*, trans. William Wallace and A. V. Miller (Oxford: Clarendon Press, 1971), pp. 78–79.

37. See *Werke*, 10:246–249; English translation, *Hegel's Science of Logic*, trans. A. V. Miller (New York: Humanities Press, 1976), pp. 214–216.

38. See Charles Taylor, *Hegel* (Cambridge: Cambridge University Press, 1975), for an extended treatment of Hegelian philosophy as "expressive."

39. For this characteristic of the spoken word, see the account of Hegel in my *Poetic Interaction* (Chicago: University of Chicago Press, 1989), pp. 52–54.

40. Derrida, "Signature, événement, contexte," in *Marges*, pp. 378, 381/ 317–318, 320; *De la grammatologie*, p. 81/55. Rodolphe Gasché, *The Tain of the Mirror*, passim.

41. Gasché, *The Tain of the Mirror*, pp. 316–318.

42. Cf. Derrida, *De la grammatologie*, pp. 91–92/62–63; *Positions*, p. 39.

43. John Sallis, *Spacings* (Chicago: University of Chicago Press, 1987), p. 157; cf. Derrida, *La Voix et le phénomène*, p. 86.

44. Aristotle, *Nicomachean Ethics* 1.1; Heidegger *Sein und Zeit* (Tübingen: Niemeyer, 1967), pp. 63–89.

45. Derrida, "Le puits et la pyramide," in *Marges*, p. 82/72.

46. For instance at *De la grammatologie*, pp. 349–350/246: ". . . it is necessary to recuperate all the traits of . . . the metaphysics of presence, from Plato to Hegel, rhythmed by the articulation of presence into presence to self. The unity of this metaphysical tradition ought to be respected in its general permanence." David Wood, acknowledging the criticism, answers that presence is a "regulative" idea for Derrida: it determines his approach to the texts, which is to be judged pragmatically, on its fruits; but it is not something that needs actually to be attributed, "constitutively," to metaphysics. David Wood, *Philosophy at the Limit* (London: Unwin Hyman, 1990), p. 60. But this makes Derrida's project, like so many others, enabled by an exclusion—in this case of "constitutivity" from the idea of presence.

47. Gasché, *The Tain of the Mirror,* pp. 230–231.

48. Ibid., p. 156; the quotes are from Derrida, *La Voix et le phénomène,* p. 64/57.

49. David Wood, *Philosophy at the Limit,* p. 569. That Derrida systematically makes at least one large mistake, in all his readings of philosophers down through the tradition, is argued in my "Substance, Presence, Derrida," forthcoming. The mistake is a failure to distinguish "substance" from "presence."

50. David M. Levin, *The Opening of Vision* (London: Routledge, 1988), p. 69.

NINE

The Face and the Caress

Levinas's Ethical Alterations of Sensibility

Paul Davies

Sight is, to be sure, an openness and a consciousness, and all sensibility, open-ing as consciousness, is called vision; but even in its subordination to cognition sight maintains contact and proximity. The visible caresses the eye. One sees and hears like one touches.

LEVINAS[1]

The following remarks are mainly concerned with moving toward a read-ing of Levinas's 1967 essay "Language and Proximity," in particular a reading of the claim that "the visible caresses the eye" and that "one sees and hears like one touches." It is to be a matter, of course, of wondering what such a claim might mean, but—because Levinas is not simply setting out to provide a new philosophical account of sensibility, it is just as im-portant to understand why he makes the claim where and when he does—specifically, to understand why he makes it after the apparent de-lineation of "sensibility," "vision," and the "caress" in *Totality and Infinity*, a delineation which in that text seems necessary in order to secure the in-troduction of the thought of the "face of the Other."

I

At the very moment one is most inclined to resist it philosophically, there is surely something strangely compelling, indeed strangely convinc-ing, about Levinas's thought of the singular and irreducible alterity of *the* (singular) Other, a thought expressed most concisely in the description of the Other as face—expressed in those places, then, where it is impossi-ble to separate or to abstract the theme or the topic of alterity from the specific encounter with the other person, the other human being. For one has often had one's attention drawn to another's face, to its suffer-ing, its ecstasy, its difference. And who could doubt that to be looked at by an Other seems to be a special sort of experience or event? However fascinating one's own face can become if one stares at its reflection for any length of time, that fascination always has something to do with the realization that this surface, these features, this "look" are *mine*. However much I might think of myself as an Other during such reflective entrancement, there is always borne along with it the partly acknowledged qualification that I am *like* an Other to myself. It is *as though* I were other. The face of another, turned and turning toward me, can draw my attention in such a fashion that all and any context subsides or recedes from consciousness. In attending to it *as* face, as this face, it is not a matter of my recognizing the Other as a rational moral agent or subject, as being like me. The theoretical move by which, say, I infer his or her rights or recognize my duties is not presupposed in this encounter. I do not accept or acknowledge the Other's face because I am able to deduce that which—"behind the face"—unites us; a surface difference rendered intelligible by means of a deeper identity, the perpetual and noninterruptible possibility of a "we." The face can make me realize how all my attempts to think myself *with* this Other rest on something like the assumption that all "others" are really only *like* others, are not really and irreducibly other. The alterity of the face punctures this illusion. The face of another is never simply somewhere, it is always also behind or above the space within which I might think of myself and the Other as being together, as part of a collectivity, as commensurable. The face of the Other disrupts and is thus the alteration of the intersubjective and communicational spaces thematized by the philosophies of intersubjectivity and communication. For Levinas, insofar as all philosophy presupposes the conceptual reduction of the Other to such a space, to such a ground or essence, the "face" of the Other resists philosophy itself. It is not, properly speaking, a philosophical term at all, and is accordingly never properly spoken or said. The alterity which "faces" me faces a being (a subject) for whom being is exteriority. Being is exposure to an Other who is otherwise than being.

We could go on indefinitely, moving from what can seem to be the somehow obviously correct descriptions of the unique experience of another's face to the most difficult of formulations ("otherwise than being," "being is exteriority"). The question is whether such a move is entirely legitimate. Levinas's texts, from the first, warn us against thinking of the face as an object of experience, as something known or sensed. Indeed the difficulty and the deliberate awkwardness of a phrase such as "otherwise than being" derives from the way in which it requires us to relinquish such terms as "experience" or "event" when referring to the face. Yet what Levinas's texts do want to say about the face—that it implicates and obsesses me, that it is responded to from out of an originary passivity, that with regard to the active subject, the subject as agent, this response and this being implicated have always already occurred—seems to depend upon our initially reading it as drawing on a certain experience. It is as though even the most intricate and convoluted of Levinasian sentences looks to protect and to retrieve an intense obviousness: the face of the Other is different, different in a different way to any other difference. And if the obviousness of the difference of the face is always a partial paraphrase of every Levinasian statement, the question arises as to how it can be recognized. What "experience" serves and guarantees the always-in-part-correct translation: "otherwise than being" attempts to say the intense and irreducible difference of the other man or woman?

In many ways this is a familiar question. Pursued in a particular fashion it would bring us into the vicinity of Derrida's "Violence and Metaphysics" and to a particular presentation of the predicament of Levinas's argument. To take one example, consider the manner in which that argument impinges on the Husserlian reductions. How can one call a phenomenological "evidence" into question without in some way presuming a prior evidence? Must a reason not be given for breaking with the givenness of phenomena? In order to question the absolute authority accorded the language of appearing, in order to question the Husserlian coordinating of meaning with appearing so that it is only as an appearing to consciousness that an entity, a phenomenon, can be said to mean anything at all, must not the questionableness of appearing itself appear to consciousness? Such questions to Levinas—one way of taking the first step in the deconstructive reading—reinscribe the Levinasian terminology (the "face") within the language and the project of a descriptive phenomenology.

But the deconstructive reading must, of course, entail a second step, in this instance one that would mark the alteration—the Levinasian alteration—of "immediacy," "evidence," "givenness," "experience," and so on. If the first step attends to the inevitable appeal to a certain obviousness and suggests that the intelligibility of any account of the Other (the face of the Other) depends upon such an appeal, the second step shows how this obviousness and this appeal are themselves altered when thought with respect to Levinas's "Other." To appeal to a certain obviousness would not necessarily be to break with Levinas's ethics, nor need it be to return to some preethical and theoretical knowledge of the conditions of possibility of such an ethics, but rather it would involve thinking of the appeal as itself constituted by and for the ethical relation, as itself being made *for the Other*. It would involve recognizing that the "obvious" conceived as an intense and immediate commonality is always vulnerable to an interruption, and is thus never intense or immediate enough. To appeal to the obvious in order to account for one's capacity to consider such an interruption is to have begun to alter what the obvious and the appeal to it might possibly mean.

Something like a rule for reading Levinas seems to be unfolding here. One begins by reading that the face is not a phenomenon, that it is in no way the object of an experience. But one reads it, as it were, under the heading of an "as if": the experience of another's face, the phenomenon of another's face, is so extraordinary it is as if it were neither experience nor phenomenon. In other words, at first Levinas's denial of this language seems only, with regard to the face, to enforce a tacit repetition of it. As one continues to read, however, one finds that the implicit dependency upon an apparently rejected terminology cannot simply be defended by saying that the rejection was, after all, only apparent. The introduction of the face, the introduction of the phrase "the face of the Other" into a work of philosophy has the effect of altering the notion of "experience." Note that it is not a matter of expanding the notion of experience to accommodate the face, for if one were to approach the issue in this fashion one would have already admitted that the face is an object of experience. It makes no sense to speak of expanding "experience" here because as soon as one names that for which one is wishing to expand it one has already thought it (the named) as experienced, as experienceable. With the "face of the Other" Levinas seeks to mark an immediacy that is neither the immediacy of sensation, the passive reception of sense-data, nor the pretheoretical immediacy of being-in-the-world, nor indeed any immediacy ever thematized or thought by philosophy. If one can only ever say the sorts of immediacy it is not, one is perhaps only allowed to write it positively as an altered immediacy. In an attempt to protect and to comment on the radical paradoxicality Levinas is broaching here, Blanchot proposes thinking this immediacy in the past tense: an immediacy so intense and so immediate that it resists both the present and all presentation, an immediacy which after *Totality and Infinity* Levinas will explicitly negotiate by way of the "trace."

It is certainly the case that Levinas's vocabulary, constantly shifting and changing, grows deliberately and increasingly complex in the years between *Totality and Infinity* (1961) and *Otherwise Than Being, or Beyond Essence* (1974). It is a curious but genuinely philosophical development, one which seems to derive from Levinas's own reflections on the necessarily enigmatic presentation of his always enigmatic work, his "ethical" renewal of metaphysics. It is tempting to see this increased concern with textuality, this deliberate unpacking of the consequences of those moments where Levinas named language by way of the relation to the Other, as an acknowledging and a performing of the deconstructive double reading. Where once the talk might have been of a break away from ontology and phenomenology, it now slowly becomes a matter of a more reflective and indeed self-undermining "alteration" of ontology and phenomenology. Although such a view is neither unhelpful nor incorrect, it

can detract from what is most thought-provoking in these moments of
transition. In operating in a structural or quasi-structural manner (i.e., in
concentrating solely on the way in which any Levinasian "ethical" sentence must work) attention is drawn away from the specific topic which
informs, accompanies, and can perhaps be said to prompt the transition
from *Totality and Infinity* to *Otherwise Than Being*. That topic is sensibility.
It is in the context of a renewal of the issue of sensibility that Levinas
both reconsiders the role and the place of language in his work and introduces some of the most difficult and idiosyncratic changes in his own
language. At the very moment when Levinas, in deconstructive guise, is
being applauded for his increased sensitivity to language as the site of alterity, there is the danger of overlooking his claim that language is "contact," in other words, that language even in its now explicitly recognized
centrality cannot be separated from a certain tactility and so from a certain reconsideration of the tactile and of the sensible thought via the tactile. Here, at least from the purview of an initial reading of *Totality and
Infinity*, would be an unexpected congruence: the relation to the Other
(the "face to face" relation, the ethical relation), language, and the sensible brought together by means of a startling analysis of touch, of the caress. The crucial text is "Language and Proximity" which, along with
"Meaning and Sense" (1964), most clearly demonstrates and accounts
for what happens after *Totality and Infinity*.

                                    II

"The visible caresses the eye," "one sees and hears like one touches":
What is happening to vision when it can be legitimately likened to touch?
More generally, what sort of account of sense and sensibility could possibly justify or require this privileging of touch? Note, before knowing anything of the context, how it is not a simple overturning or reversal of a
traditional privileging of vision for, in spite of the specificity of the first
sentence ("The visible caresses the eye"), the ear as well as the eye is subsequently, indeed immediately, implicated ("One sees and hears like one
touches").

    I take it that what is thought of as the primacy of vision in philosophy
(a major part of what is going on, then, in a thought held to be "ocularcentric") involves both the interpretation of sensibility as primarily sight
and the interpretation of sight as that sense which transcends the sensible and so allows what is other than the sensible to be described in its
terms, that is, as a metaphorical seeing. All consciousness is thus vision.
Now the challenge to this primacy is in essence a challenge to the mastery that this interpretation of vision is said to accord to the subject, to

consciousness, to the one who—literally and metaphorically—sees. One form of this challenge is to displace this mastery by emphasizing a sense whose operation cannot be so easily separated from a certain passivity, namely hearing: the ear rather than the eye. The resultant metaphorics is familiar. It is a matter of a lingering attentiveness rather than a thematizing, all-encompassing gaze. This would be a strategic move, one judged more in keeping with a philosophy increasingly sensitive to the issue of language. The figure of thinking as hearing seems somehow, from the first, more compatible with what is to be thought as the linguisticality of the sensible.

Levinas's statements however seem to want to distance themselves from this simple opposition. Both seeing and hearing are to be re-thought—to be rethought an analogous to touching, to touching con-strued as caressing, where an analysis of the caress allows us to attend to what passes in sensibility (in seeing, hearing, touching, etc.) when sensibility is no longer simply identified with consciousness. Everything Levinas says about touch follows from this analysis. Yet to speak of touching in terms of caressing would seem to rule out the possibility of an involuntary touching. Is sensibility not thereby bound ever more tightly to the voluntaristic? If people are pressing against me in a crowd, it would seem reasonable to say that I cannot help touching them. But under what circumstances would it make sense to speak of my having to caress someone? Does not caressing consist of a conscious gesture? Is to caress not to touch meaningfully? Is it not always touching imbued with a sense, an intention? What could it mean to rethink seeing and hearing—also crucially and necessarily bound to the involuntary—as analogous to what seems to exclude the involuntary, and so presumably the passivity of the involuntary? But there is a slippage in our two sentences. "The vis-ible caresses the eye. One sees and hears like one touches." If the caress-ing of the eye by the visible describes seeing as touching, describes what happens when one sees like one touches, then presumably when one ac-tually and literally touches it is to be described as, say, the hand's being caressed. Note the fragmentation of the subject here. It is not synec-dochally present in "eye" and "hand." There is a thematic and syntactic break between the "one" of the second sentence and the "eye" of the first. If anything it is an absence of the subject that is metonymically marked by these terms. The visible caresses the eye. The audible caresses the ear. And, one assumes, the tangible caresses the hand. But we can describe the audible and the visible in this fashion only on the basis of the tangible being rethought by way of the caress. Therefore, strictly speaking, we would have to say, somewhat awkwardly, that the *caressable* caresses the hand. But what is the caressable? What could it be apart from a particular decision to impress upon or to intensify the tangible? Again, we seem to run up against not only a subject but a subject whose actions and intentions are necessary conditions—although obviously not sufficient conditions—for there being anything we might call caressable in the first place. Levinas's account of sensibility focuses on a reworking of a particular sense (touch) as the initially unequivocal act of a subject (the caress). His analysis of the caress will seek to show that caressing involves not only an absenting of that subject but also a disengaging of sensibility from consciousness. Caressing, literally and then metaphorically, will describe the continuing of consciousness in and from that disengagement. What passes in sensibility, the paradox one can begin to read in an analysis of the caress, induces a passivity wholly other to both that associated with the involuntary and that affirmed in the strategic opposing of passive, modest, and responsive hearing to active, arrogant seeing.

What passes, what comes to pass, in the caress (and so in sensibility considered by way of the caress) never gives itself as a theme or meaning and so drastically alters the relation that an always thematizing and meaning-giving consciousness has to sensibility. As one of the names for this altered relation, Levinas proposes "obsession." Consciousness, in caressing, is obsessed. Read in terms of this other passivity, the subject is defined solely as and by this obsession. To say that the visible caresses the eye is to say that what passes in the visible obsesses the subject, the subject who, thus obsessed, is never *there* to see or to know it, just as what passes is never *there* to be seen or known.

This renewal of the issue of sensibility in "Language and Proximity" is particularly surprising when one recalls the treatment of that issue in *Totality and Infinity,* where each sensory experience is grounded in the pretheoretical existence Levinas names and describes as "enjoyment." Everything seen, heard, or touched, prior to its being thematized as the object of a cognitive relation, falls within the purview of my "living from" the world, my being nourished and supported by the elements. Sensibility is the subject's relation to the elemental. There is then, from the first, a resistance within sensible life to thematization, to phenomenologization. "Sensation recovers a 'reality' when we see in it not the subjective counterpart of objective qualities, but an enjoyment 'anterior' to the crystallization of consciousness, I and non-I, into subject and object."[2]

Like Heidegger, and in a maneuver clearly reminiscent of *Being and Time,* Levinas argues that references to individual sensory experiences as well as to particular experiences of individual senses, rather than providing the basis for a philosophical understanding of the sensible, can themselves only be understood in terms of the lived existence which necessarily resists such individuation, such representation. Unlike Heidegger, however, Levinas insists that this existence is not essentially determined by its finitude and that finitude in and as sensibility is not anxious. Sensibility is finite "contentment," which is to say, emphasizing the positive connotation, "the finite as contentment."[3] Enjoyment is not life lived in the face of death. It is the absence of finality, the "not yet" of death, which gives to sensible life its sufficiency. Hence the deliberate prepositional alteration, living from (vivre de), not being-in or being-toward. Despite its own rigorous reduction of the theoretical mode, its suspension of the philosophical dispute which can only construe sensibility in terms of rationalism or empiricism, Being and Time would continue to organize the relations and structures it describes according to a residual intellectualism. Thus it is the very carefreeness of sensibility which one misses in the existential analytic of Dasein, of that being whose being is care, the carefreeness of an existence yet to be concerned about itself. "Sensibility, essentially naive, suffices to itself in a world insufficient for thought." It is to this secure world and to a life sustained by it, a life whose affectivities can never be "thought," that the face of the Other comes as absolute command and absolute disruption. And it is to the account of this world that Totality and Infinity appends an "account" of this coming. Recall that however novel Levinas's analyses of enjoyment and elemental life are, this altered sensibility leaves intact the metaphorical identification of thought, of theoretical consciousness, as vision. The ambiguity introduced by the face of the Other and introduced by this introduction derives from the claim that the face refers neither to enjoyment nor to vision.

III

At this point, it is worth becoming a little more schematic. The remainder of the paper proceeds in three stages: (1) It returns to the question of the introduction of the face, a question attentive to the immediacy of the face-to-face encounter in that introduction. If this immediacy is itself altered, is thus somehow other to the putative immediacies of everyday sensory experience, its coherence nonetheless seems to depend upon that experience. Here, then, we would repeat, but intentionally in its naivest form, the first step of the deconstructive reading. (2) The paper continues by proposing two possible answers to this question. One, the second step of the deconstructive reading, hints at the reflexivity of the introduction of the face, signaling its textual effects. The other, returning us to Totality and Infinity, suggests that the intelligibility and the legibility of that introduction might owe everything to the altered sensibility's (sensibility as enjoyment's) potential for a certain metaphoric transposition. Neither answer is wholly successful. Indeed, the latter seems to draw us back into the most familiar philosophical adaptation of sensibility. (3) The paper concludes by rereading the lines from "Language and Proximity." To argue that Levinas, after *Totality and Infinity*, completes the renewal of sensibility begun there, a completion which not only impinges on the manner in which we begin to read the introduction of the face but also explicitly obliges Levinas to address that reading and to provide a far subtler account of how philosophy is (able) to perform it.

(1) Introducing the Face

We return, then, to the questions with which we began, the questions we perhaps too quickly settled in our staging of the deconstructive reading both as a reading to be applied critically to Levinas's texts and, more importantly, as an index of Levinas's own itinerary.

During the course of his conversations with Levinas, Philippe Nemo mentions the "phenomenology of the face, that is [the] analysis of what happens when I look at the Other face to face."[4] Levinas, not surprisingly, challenges the use of "phenomenology." He wonders whether one can even "speak of a look turned toward the face." Such a look would notice the face, would register its features, its qualities. The potential for examination detracts from the puzzling immediacy of the encounter: "access to the face is straightaway ethical [*d'emblée éthique*]." Instead of being seen, the face commands. In its nakedness, its vulnerability, its lingering just this side of thematization, the face both invites and forbids any attempt to destroy it. The face commands. It speaks. Nemo responds to this move from vision to speech, from the face as an appearance to the face as prohibition, by remarking that "war stories tell us that it is difficult to kill someone who looks straight at you."[5] The dismissal of empirical evidence seems less easy here. Levinas repeats that the face is not seen, that vision is a search for adequation. And of course to describe the experience of being looked at by another is also to imagine having time to look, as it were, at the look of the other. To turn it into a phenomenon, an appearing to and for consciousness. So much is clear. But Levinas cannot rule out the power and force of those documentary references. This raises the question of how much the very notion of the face as it is introduced by Levinas relies upon the implicit assumption of such references and so is backed up by a certain body of evidence. It raises the question as to whether our reading of "The face speaks" depends upon a certain intuition of the face looking ("the face of the neighbor obsesses me. . . . 'He is looking at me'—everything in him looks at me; nothing is indifferent to me").[6]

When Levinas writes that access to the face is "straightaway ethical," there is a question as to what makes that "straightaway" (*d'emblée*) straightaway successful, straightaway intelligible. In asking about the peculiar force and attractiveness of this notion of the face, might it not be possible to identify a tension or ambiguity in the work Levinas requires of it? The face-to-face encounter is to be immediately intelligible, if only immediately intelligible as what is straightaway unintelligible, that is, "ethical" ("when I really stare, with a straightforwardness devoid of trickery or evasion, into [those] unguarded, absolutely unprotected eyes").[7] To introduce it must also be to introduce the most familiar of experiences, even at the very moment one withdraws it from the discourse of experience. It is also to suggest that philosophy necessarily violates the intensity of such an encounter, contextualizing it, thematizing the self or subject, the one who is faced, as a perpetually sense-bestowing agent and so construing the other as needing to be at all times endowed with a meaning. In letting be cited (if only by being unable to forbid its being cited, as is surely the case with Nemo's "war stories") the uniqueness or strangeness that is my being looked at by another, Levinas both wants to introduce something which might be said to be characterized by a certain self-evidence, and wants to call a certain self-evidence (the same self-evidence) into question. The reference to the "face" of the Other is not like G. E. Moore holding up his hand to illustrate something it would make no sense to doubt, something that is accepted regardless of the reaches of philosophical skepticism, because for Levinas the "face" is not an object of knowledge. Nonetheless it *would* on Levinas's own terms make no sense to doubt it. And this is the problem. This is why the simple Levinasian response, delimiting philosophy (phenomenology), reiterating the break with vision, does not serve as an answer. Something like the break with vision, the step from vision to "speech" ("the face speaks") is recalled and repeated, as though intuitively, as soon as one begins to talk oneself through a reading of Levinas. The "face" both is and is not the actual face of the actual Other who looks at me; displacing "vision" it nonetheless seems to owe its philosophical and rhetorical impact to it ("when I really stare, with a straightforwardness devoid of trickery or evasion, into [those] unguarded, absolutely unprotected eyes").

Consider a group of readers, unfamiliar with Levinas, coming to his work because they have heard that his concern is with "ethics," a concern they perhaps share. They find themselves taken with the elegance of his descriptions of the face-to-face encounter. They admit that here the other person is both vulnerable and inscrutable. They might even be willing to admit that, so encountered, the face has a disruptive effect on the social or political contexts within which the encounter takes place. But

they do not see why the face even in this most intense of settings does
not also and primarily signify a shared or common humanity.[8] They wonder how Levinas would respond to someone who disputed the account,
someone who claims to have no idea of what Levinas is talking about,
that the face of the Other has never evoked any of these responses in
him, that the poignancy of the encounter is clearly only accessible to
those of a certain sensitivity, a particular psychological propensity or inclination. What would Levinas reply? That such responsiveness is not a
matter of personal idiosyncracy or choice? That this interlocutor must be
lying? That we all know what it is to be "faced"? And even as we realize
that these would not be the appropriate answers, would we not want to
do more for the person who claims to know nothing of what Levinas
means by "the face of the Other" than to remind him that it is not a matter of knowledge anyway? If there is any argument that might be employed here, then surely Levinas has already conceded the point that a
shared rationality and so a symmetry is presupposed even at moments of
extreme asymmetry, something which at the very least allows us to assume, *as though* it were a given, that the phrase "The face speaks" still
sort of refers, even in what now has to be called nonreferring, to a certain experience.[9]

(2) The Dissociation of and from Sensibility

There would be at least two ways of responding to these matters. The
first response would entail a closer examination of the textual effects of
the introduction of the face. It would endeavor to show how the writing
of the face disrupts the context, the actual philosophical context, into
which it is written. It would thus rehearse the very disruption the text
seeks to comment upon. It is not because the face is something else that
I am unable to gesture toward the face of a person sitting with me in a
seminar and say, "Is this what you mean by the face of the Other?" That
"this" and that gesture already inscribe whatever they refer to into the
logic of exemplarity. They have already begun to philosophize. The face
of the Other has been replaced by a theme. What is wrong with remaining with this type of questioning is that it represents as a stage in
Levinas's argument or presentation a moment which itself only figures in
the argument or presentation under the guise of having "always already"
passed: the moment of Levinas's having recourse to my immediately understanding the altered immediacy of the ethical relation, an understanding which can only draw on my actual experiences of actual faces. The
step one seems to take, when reading Levinas, from "straightaway understanding" ethical immediacy as the disruption of what is elsewhere taken

as sensory immediacy to slowly beginning to rethink "ethics" and to re-constitute a relation to "ontology" is misleading. It is a fiction, a themati-zation of reading which never actually occurs like this. The moment of straightaway responding and straightaway understanding will always echo through every reading of Levinas's texts as an excessive moment, as both disruptive of the argumentation and that on the basis of which (and that for the sake of which) the argument is being made. To the reader who claims not to recognize the descriptions of the face, one would reply that he should follow the effect those descriptions are having in the text, not the extent to which they are successful in triggering particular mem-ories. That is, they should not be read as descriptions. The extraordinary intensity of Levinas's writing of and on the face should not be tracked down to an experience or assumed experience of looking or being looked at. It is the *writing* of the face, the fact that it is written, intro-duced here in this fashion, it is the experience of reading it which also mimics and repeats the interruption—the moment of obligation—which one represents to oneself as a visual experience. The face speaks, impli-cating me in the double bind of murder: the face, the only one it is both ethically possible and ethically impossible to murder. The writing of "The face speaks," the introduction of this phrase, implicates the reader in the double bind of legibility: to read it is to have already partially re-duced it to a theme, that is, to have read it for what it is not; not to read it is not to follow the impossibility of such a reduction. The face speaks: And when this is written as a phrase in Levinas's text, we might say that the phrase speaks, that is, signifies beyond and in spite of its reduction to a philosopheme.

A second response returns us to our topic, sensibility. It would recall that, in *Totality and Infinity*, the fullest introduction of the face comes after the account of enjoyment, and would ask whether this order was necessary. The third section of the book, "Exteriority and the Face," be-gins with a few pages entitled "Sensibility and the Face." Those pages open with the following two questions: "Is not the face given to vision? How does the epiphany as a face determine a relationship different from that which characterizes all our sensible experience?" A negative answer to the first question depends upon an answer's being found to the sec-ond. The retrieval of sensibility in terms of enjoyment is the first step to-ward such an answer. In other words it is not a persistent intuition which guarantees my accepting the introduction of the face. This would always already be a theoretical construction. What persists is better thought as the disruption of the already altered sensibility that is enjoyment: "we can speak of enjoyment or of sensation even in the domain of vision, when one has seen much, and the object revealed by the experience is steeped in the enjoyment of pure sensation."[10] The account of elemental life bears the introduction of the face at two step's remove from the common-sense intuitionist.

Each of these responses would, in its own way, rescue Levinasian asymmetry by providing an essentially ambiguous context (the text, elemental life), one to which all questions concerning the links between the face and vision or sensory experience can be delegated, and one which thus successfully dissociates the face from sensibility. But neither response is quite satisfactory. If the former does exhibit the sort of textual reflexivity to which Levinas himself becomes increasingly sensitive in and on the way to *Otherwise Than Being, or Beyond Essence,* it does so in almost complete indifference to the content of Levinas's analyses. (And, as we shall see, the increased sensitivity to the status of his work *as* text cannot be separated from the soon-to-be resumed analyses of sensibility.) It is the latter response, though, which raises the more serious worries.

Levinas's main aim in "Sensibility and the Face" is to show that although the notion of sensation has been "somewhat rehabilitated," it must always fall short of naming the relation to the face, the ethical relation. Sensation must always participate in the discourse of light which has defined it since Plato. Vision always discerns and receives beings in and from an illuminated space and against the backdrop of a horizon, a horizon which rules out the thought of beings as coming from elsewhere. They come as if from nowhere, as if from out of nothingness. The coming of the face as speech, as address, "cuts [*tranche*] across sensibility." To this extent, the relationship "which characterizes all our sensible experience" includes the relation with the elements. To the extent, however, that this latter ("somewhat rehabilitated") sensibility already subverts the characterization of consciousness as vision, it has already begun to suggest the possibility of another relationship. On the one hand, vision is a taking, a thematizing, of what appears. Vision, with touch, owes its philosophical privilege to the fact that it is not concerned with where this appearance comes from. It thus serves as the successful metaphor for a consciousness incapable of conceiving anywhere else a being could come from save the illuminated space across which the accumulating and illuminating gaze stretches: thinking as seeing and grasping sense. On the other hand, vision is one sense among others in the "experience . . . steeped in the enjoyment of pure sensation," where sensibility—just as in Heidegger's analyses of the ready-to-hand (*Zuhandenheit*)—can only be thought without thematic differentiation, a differentiation ruinous of it.

Phenomenology takes the active role consciousness plays in the accumulation of meaning to its limit. Vision—consciousness as vision—is inseparable from the attribution of meaning. The face disrupts the life of active, sense-bestowing consciousness by coming as a sense, a meaning, which signifies *by itself*. The face disrupts the life of enjoyment, the life of sensuous self-satisfaction, by coming as an unthematizable differentiation. The question here is whether in its difference from the thematizing vision metaphorized as consciousness, the "somewhat rehabilitated" sensibility does not serve to metaphorize the nonapprehension of the face. The point is elusive, but a moment's reflection will show that the distinction between the face (the unintelligibility of the face, its signifying *by itself*) and elemental life serves a similar function to the traditional distinction between consciousness (the intelligible) and the sensible. In each instance a certain transposition from the latter serves to say the former.

Although the face does not refer to enjoyment, is not a part of that elemental world from which I live, the description of that world, that sensibility—as essentially thematically undifferentiable, that is, nonphenomenologizable—gives rise to the thought of what resists philosophical thematization, the thought of an other. The Other, the face of the Other, grows legible by means of a partial analogy with this alterity held under the aegis of the elements. Contra Freud and Hegel, Levinas posits desire as excessive, that is, as not based on a lack. Living from the world, contented, my desire tends not toward something I would wish to add to my world but to what is other to the very logic of acquisition, of need and hoped-for satisfaction. Because the elements are so successfully suited to my needs, my desire is drawn elsewhere. Because my world is complete, it can be all the more unequivocally interrupted. Note however a slightly different emphasis. Because my world is, at base, the world of sensibility, a world marked by an alterity to perceptual thought, to consciousness, its disruption by the face of the Other—the introduction of this other alterity—can be stated. Is one then able to say that the face of the Other disengages me from the totality *as* sensibility disengages itself from thought in enjoyment? If this formula is too audacious, it is worth asking whether in the clear separation of the face from sensibility, there is not also the demarcating between two "spheres" necessary for metaphorization. Because consciousness does *not* see, it can be described as seeing metaphorically. Because the face is not "sensed" in the elemental life that is itself always already prior to and irreducible to consciousness, its "unintelligibility" can be described in terms borrowed from the description of that life. When, in *Totality and Infinity*, the face speaks, I am always already not yet the active subject fixed and thematized as philosophical consciousness. Even if to respond to the face is not something I can be said to do, even if it is not then an act which can be isolated and examined, it is something I can say to myself as a sort of "hearing." If I am right here, then Levinas's insistence on the distinction between the face

and sensibility in *Totality and Infinity* means that "The face speaks" is the
result of a choice of metaphor, a metaphor taken from and made possible by the renewal of sensibility in terms of elemental life. To be able to
comprehend the "unintelligibility" of the face from out of a certain alteration of sensibility, where the relation between the two is not one of con-
tiguity (the face "cuts [*tranche*] across sensibility"), is to introduce the sort
of transposition we know by and as the figure of metaphor. But if this is
the case then the step from the elemental to (let us say) the "unintelligible" is itself being thought on the basis of an analogy with the step from
the sensible (as traditionally understood) to the intelligible. It is still to
be dependent on the type of transposition, the type of distinction, determined by the discourse of light. Apropos of our earlier remarks on
choosing one sense over another as the metaphor for what is other than
the sensible, it would seem that nothing here quite protects Levinas from
being read as exercising just such a preference.

Al Lingis has suggested that there are two sensibilities operating in
Totality and Infinity: one, a sensibility toward the elemental (sensuous enjoyment); the other, a sensibility toward the face. He continues by noting
that in *Otherwise Than Being, or Beyond Essence* "Levinas set(s) out to show
that the space in which the sensuous material is laid out is already extended by the sense of alterity."[11] Lingis is correct to mark this change
but we would put it slightly differently. We would say, rather, that the account of sensibility in *Totality and Infinity* seems to encourage us to read
that responsiveness as a metaphorical sensibility. Consequently, when
Levinas, after *Totality and Infinity*, extends the account, it necessarily has
the effect of blurring the distinctions upon which metaphorical transposition relies. In other words, the return to sensibility is also in part a reflection upon the manner in which the face is to be introduced, the manner in which it is to be written.

(3) A Word on the Caress

"Language and Proximity" is an extraordinary essay. It seems both to
concede to the deconstructive reading we outlined earlier, learning from
it and rehearsing it, and to take its distance from a certain linguisticism
by concentrating on thinking language in and as sensibility. The essay begins with an extremely dense reading of Husserlian "passive synthesis."
This phrase serves as the title to the second section. Levinas, in effect,
performs a double reading of the way in which the thought of "passive
synthesis" addresses the issue of the origin of consciousness. On the one
hand, it will enable a certain phenomenological account to get off the
ground. It will allow phenomenology to mark the moment, the necessar-

ily inferred moment when an active subject (*the* active subject) distinct from time can be said to have come into being. In this respect, passive synthesis is introduced for the sake of what immediately follows it, namely a thematizable and separated consciousness. On the other hand, if prior to its proper phenomenological origin consciousness must think itself in, from, and as a preoriginary passivity, then the whole field of phenomenological research—the field consciousness serves as both limit and condition of possibility—might be said to bear the traces of this paradoxical precedence. Note that Levinas is effectively arguing that with "passive synthesis" phenomenology names and encounters the thought of its own interruptibility. It is a deconstructive reading *par excellence*.

"Language and Proximity" continues by thinking sensibility as itself the event of this interruption. "Sensibility" thus names not only a relation subservient to cognition but also a "proximity," a "contact" with a singular passing, a "contact" with *this* singular passing of what has always already made of the life of consciousness something more than a matter of knowledge. Something more which can perhaps only ever register as something less, as an absence. Never given as a theme or content, impervious to any noetico-noematic analysis content, how then do we write or say this passing immediacy of the sensible? If "proximity" is made to stand over and against "knowledge," it unfortunately bequeaths us no verb with which to describe the relation. Levinas answers: "sensibility must be interpreted as touch first of all."

In *Totality and Infinity*, Levinas made it clear: The face "is neither seen nor touched—for in visual or tactile sensation the identity of the I envelops the alterity of the object, which becomes precisely a content."[12] In "Language and Proximity," we will be invited to move through the following passages:

[a] Sight is, to be sure, an openness and a consciousness, and all sensibility, opening as a consciousness, is called vision; but even in its subordination to cognition sight maintains contact and proximity. The visible caresses the eye. One sees and hears like one touches.[13]

[b] In reality, the caress of the sensible awakens in a contact and tenderness, that is, proximity, awakens in the touched only starting with the human skin, a face, only with the approach of a neighbor.[14]

[c] Proximity, beyond intentionality, is the relationship with the neighbor in the moral sense of the term.[15]

[d] To approach the other is still to pursue what is already present, is still to seek what one has found, to not be able to have done with the neighbor. It is like caressing: the caress is the unity of approach and proximity.[16]

[e] Language, contact, is the obsession of an I "beset" [assiege] by the others.[17]

[f] The ethical language we resort to does not proceed from a special moral experience, independent of the description developed until then. It comes from the very meaning of approach, which contrasts with knowledge, of the face which contrasts with phenomena. Phenomenology can follow the reverting of thematization into ethics in the description of a face. Ethical language alone succeeds in being equal to the paradox into which phenomenology is abruptly thrown: starting with the neighbor, it reads this paradox in the midst of an absence which orders it as a face.[18]

Before commenting, all too briefly, on each of these passages, a few general remarks. There seems to be a confident distinction here between two vocabularies. On the one hand, intentionality, knowledge, the phenomenon, and phenomenology; on the other hand, proximity, approach, the face, and ethics or "ethical language." We have spoken of a tension between a traditional and a renewed or altered sensibility in *Totality and Infinity*. This tension which would hopefully result in the radical distinction Levinas wants to make between the face and sensibility seems to owe everything to the distinction with which it would need to break. How can these distinctions in "Language and Proximity" be said to have responded to this predicament? For, here again, sensibility—in the analysis of the caress—would seem to serve as the awkward mediator between the face and thought.

Totality and Infinity introduces the caress as the key term and feature of the "phenomenology of eros." In the erotic relation, the caress tends toward the beloved not in order to possess or to grasp him or her but in order to delight in the resistant alterity of the erotic Other. In eroticism, I encounter a differentiatable Other but not as a theme and not as simply part of elemental life. The specificity of the caress in eroticism already suggests a turning within elementality toward another sort of relationality. However, Levinas is firm. The other of eros is not the Other of ethics, the voluptuous nakedness caressed—not known—in eroticism is not the pristine vulnerable nakedness "heard"—not known—in the face.[19] Nevertheless, this specificity already gives to the experience of caressing the sense of the subject's undergoing a change. The erotic relation, Levinas says, is characterized by its essential anonymity. The becoming anonymous of the subject in eroticism is perhaps comparable to the becoming nothing but "for the other" in the ethical relation. Levinas writes that "the caress, like contact, is sensibility . . . but the caress transcends the sensible."[20] There would be two ways to read this transcendence. The first would see in it the very principle of metaphoric transposition, the move which gives the sensible to be used as metaphor. Insofar as Levinas continues to insist on the absolute distinction between the face and the lover, between ethics and erotics, it can be seen to reassert the dependency of the former on the figure of the metaphor. There is, however, another reading, one which stays with the caress itself. The caress caresses what ceaselessly evades it as sensibility, but where what ceaselessly evades it is nothing other than this ceaseless evasion. If we are entitled to use the word here, we might say that the caress attests truly to the alterity of the beloved in eroticism. That it is able to do this and to be described (as part of a phenomenology) as doing this suggests that it is always on the verge of blurring the distinctions Levinas is so keen on. A certain reading of the face depends upon its being kept apart from the self-transcending of sensibility in the erotic relation with the other. The phenomenology of eros, on this second reading, raises the suspicion that it cannot be so easily separated. If the first reading restates the relation, the separation, as metaphor, the second blurs that distinction and so requires another, less familiar, writing and reading of the face. This is what "Language and Proximity" seeks to provide.

It is not simply that after *Totality and Infinity* Levinas extends the caress to encompass ethics as well as erotics. Levinas implicitly confronts the question of what happens to sensibility if the caress can be described as transcending it. The answer is not, as it would seem to be in the very layout of *Totality and Infinity*, a more rigorous demarcation of the sensible, but rather a completed alteration of sensibility.

Note that, ironically, where Levinas appears to be explicitly metaphorical, *likening* the approach of the Other to caressing and *likening* language to contact, he is actually working to blur the distinctions which make metaphoricity possible. Whereas in *Totality and Infinity*, in transcending sensibility the caress was somehow distinguished from contact, as though it somehow ceased to be wholly identifiable with the sense of touch, here the analysis of the caress is bound to a rethinking of contact and touch themselves. The paradox which comes to thought in the description of the specific encounter with another that is eroticism, instead of being kept at bay as it was in *Totality and Infinity*, is now to be read. "Ethical language" (approach, proximity, responsibility, obsession, etc.), Levinas's vocabulary, is a language in the service of this reading, a reading which dissolves the figures which would keep that paradox at bay, the figures which would insist on introducing the face at the right time and in the right fashion.

From "sight" to "face": by way of conclusion, let us follow in a slightly more cautious tone the movement away from vision in the six passages we cited from "Language and Proximity." Notice how in [a] it is not a matter of opposing cognition to proximity. Notice, too, that it is not sim-

ply a matter of retrieving another sort of vision from that held to be subordinated to, and metaphorically identified with, cognition. "Even in its
subordination to cognition sight maintains contact and proximity." In
this maintaining, looking is akin to touching, which is understood as caressing rather than grasping. It is in the analysis of the caress, as [b]
makes clear, that one can begin to say something more about this contact and proximity, namely that it begins with the face, with the approach
of the neighbor. It is in [c] that we find the more recognizably Levinasian
wording. "Proximity, beyond intentionality, is the relationship with the
neighbor in the moral sense of the term." The question arises as to the
link, if any, between this "beyond" and the "even in its subordination" of
[a]. It would seem that the caress, that sensibility as touch, enjoins the
step away from sensibility. Vision would no longer be at issue. In [d],
however, at the very moment when Levinas's discourse seems freed from
the sensible, at the very moment when it moves into its account of the
paradoxical nature of "approach," a certain return or recoil occurs: "to
approach the other is like caressing: the caress is the unity of approach
and proximity." This is extraordinary. If the second part of this claim is
in some sense a justification for the first, it is in fact doing far more. It
not only intensifies the simile but turns the whole thing into something
other than a simile. The caress here resounds in and as the impossibility
of disentangling the ethical from the sensible. In the language of [a],
read from the standpoint of [d], the sensible—despite its subordination
to the intelligible, despite its being appropriated as metaphor—maintains
the ethical. For Levinas, too, this interweaving of the sensible and the
ethical must be attested to by language. Thus [e] inserts into the otherwise familiar statement "Language is the obsession of an I beset by the
others" the word "contact": language, that is, contact. Derrida and
Blanchot have at different times and in different ways expressed unease
with this word "contact" and with any move that would define language
as contact. In response to this unease, it is tempting either to overlook
the word in Levinas or to complicate it, to show how it has nothing whatsoever to do with the coinciding or the relationality one usually associates with contact. But it might in the end, as Blanchot, I think, comes to
realize, be more important to retain the unease, for in complicating the
way in which "language" and "alterity" are brought (written) together,
"contact" precludes any literal or metaphorical, any theoretical or
pretheoretical circumscribing of sensibility. Is this insistence on the ubiquity of the sensible not also one way in which we might distinguish the
"reading" mentioned in [f] from the deconstructive reading? The language Levinas introduces—and introduces with increased deliberation in
the essays of the 1960s—serves a reading of the paradoxes into which

phenomenology is thrown, a reading of those moments of a certain resistance, those moments where consciousness can only be said to be implicated, obsessed, obligated.

From "sight" to "face" by way of the "caress": There is no way in which we can any longer speak of a Levinasian break with vision (or ocularcentrism), no way in which we can distinguish between a good and a bad vision. In being likened to the caress, vision is not strictly speaking once again the unsuspecting victim of a certain metaphorization. It is being "read." Otherwise said: *In seeing, I am implicated. In being implicated, I am faced.*

NOTES

1. Levinas, *Collected Philosophical Papers* (Dordrecht: Martinus Nijhoff, 1987), p. 118.

2. Levinas, *Totality and Infinity* (Pittsburgh: Duquesne University Press, 1969), p. 188.

3. Ibid., p. 135.

4. Levinas, *Ethics and Infinity* (Pittsburgh: Duquesne University Press, 1985), p. 85.

5. Ibid., p. 86.

6. Levinas, *Otherwise Than Being, or Beyond Essence* (Dordrecht: M. Nijhoff, 1981), p. 93.

7. Levinas, *Difficult Freedom* (London: Athlone, 1990), p. 293.

8. In denying access even to talk of a common humanity, Levinas is not denying the humanity of the face, in fact the reverse. The face comes to me as the very limit of humanity, as humanity in and at the extreme, an extremity which denies me a reassuring humanism, that is, a humanism of the self. The extreme humanity of the Other faces me so as to undo the humanity I think of as my essence, my identity or truth. Faced by the Other, for me to be human is to be nothing but "for the Other"; the only humanism, a humanism of the other man. What interests us here is the memory of the step away from vision, the flicker of an intuition of the intensity of empirically "being faced," which surely inheres in every reading of "Faced by the Other" or "The face speaks."

9. Note that to introduce Levinas's assertion that "the whole body—a hand or a curve of the shoulder—can express as face" (*TI* 262) does not really help here. It is that "as face" and the suspicion that there would be no need to write "the face can express *as* face" which keeps in mind the actual face.

10. Levinas, *Totality and Infinity*, p. 188.

11. *Face to Face with Levinas*, ed. R. Cohen (Albany: SUNY Press, 1986), p. 227.

12. Levinas, *Totality and Infinity*, p. 194.

13. Levinas, *Collected Philosophical Papers*, p. 118.

14. Ibid.

15. Ibid., p. 119.

16. Ibid., p. 120.

17. Ibid., p. 123.

18. Ibid., p. 124.

19. And does not the fact that the quotation marks seem necessary around "heard" and not around "caressed" illustrate everything we are trying to say here?

20. *Totality and Infinity*, p. 257.

TEN

Foucault and the Eclipse of Vision

Thomas R. Flynn

Michel de Certeau was stating the obvious when he remarked that Foucault favors an ocular style in his writings. Among the tables and illustrations that abound in Foucault's works, de Certeau has identified in *Discipline and Punish*, for example, three variants of optical figures: representative tableaux like the horrifying account of the execution of a regicide in the eighteenth century, analytic lists of ideological "rules" and "principles" relating to a single phenomenon, and figurative images such as seventeenth-to-nineteenth-century engravings and photographs. But de Certeau drew a less obvious conclusion when he noted that Foucault uses vision to undermine vision: under his critical gaze, "the panoptical space of our contemporary scientific language . . . is colonized and vampirized."[1]

This opinion is shared by Martin Jay, who discovers a certain ambivalence regarding the ocular in Foucault's writings. At times, Foucault used the disruptive power of images, "especially against the claims of language to represent a perfectly self-contained and self-sufficient system." But Jay's thesis is that Foucault "remained very much in thrall to the antivisual discourse so pervasive in French thought in this century."[2]

What I wish to consider is the extent to which Foucault's ocular epistemology constitutes the *transformation* of an earlier visual approach and entails a *displacement* of the temporalizing logic of the subject by a spatializing rationality that could be called postmodern. After reflecting on what the "hegemony of vision" in the modern period broadly conceived might mean (I), I shall consider Foucault's use of "transformation" and "displacement" to understand the hegemony of vision in the modern era more narrowly understood, concentrating on his "archaeology of medical perception" in *The Birth of the Clinic* (II), and his later "genealogy of the penal system" in *Discipline and Punish* (III). I shall then turn to this transformation and displacement in Foucault's own thought, concluding with some observations about the viability of his middle way between formalism and dialectics (IV).

I

Aristotle considered sight the most noble of the senses because it approximates the intellect most closely by virtue of the relative immateriality of its knowing.[3] Because if its "dignity and certitude," Aquinas extends the term *sight* to the other senses and to intellectual cognition as well.[4] Unlike touch, sight does not have to relate to its object part-to-part, and unlike hearing, it is seemingly instantaneous in actualizing its proper object. Furthermore, sight leaves the visible undiminished by its action; it is the sense of "otherness." It seems to operate at a distance and through the most ethereal of mediums, light. In fact, an entire metaphysics of light permeated Occidental philosophy in the Middle Ages, sustained not only by Biblical texts but by light's own "imponderable materiality" which allotted it a bridge position in the hierarchy of being. The *lumen naturale* which Descartes appealed to for self-evident knowledge, had a venerable ancestry in medieval and classical thought. Whoever says "light" says "vision." So an ocular epistemology was scarcely a "modern" invention. Indeed, the culmination of created perfection in the Christian West was called the "Beatific *Vision*," which had its roots in the Biblical promise that the pure of heart "shall see God" (Mt. 5:8).

Of course, as his remarks on the Enlightenment indicate, Foucault sees the "modern" as more an attitude than an era. But when he indulges in periodization, he tends to locate the advent of modernity in the decades immediately before and after the French Revolution.[5] He notes a clear epistemological "break" with the "classical" age at this juncture. Still, given the common practice in the history of philosophy of calling "modern" the period that begins with "Descartes and His School" (Kuno Fischer), I shall begin by considering a cluster of characteristics that constitute the hegemony of vision which Foucault's "modern" attitude comprises, but which reach back to the seventeenth century or earlier.

Hegemonic vision denotes first the ideal of detached, disinterested awareness. This is what John Dewey characterized as the "spectator" theory of knowledge, and he saw its genesis in classical Greece. It implies that consciousness can hover over its object and simply illuminate its essence or form, without affecting the object in any other respect—what the Greeks called *theōria*—and that theory is superior to practice.

An epistemology of vision, secondly, places a premium on clarity and distinctness, on evidence as the self-transparency of the object, on the apodictic. Husserl epitomized this approach when he remarked that "immediate 'seeing,' not merely sensuous, experiential seeing, but seeing in the universal sense as an originally presentative consciousness of any kind whatsoever, is the ultimate legitimizing source of all rational assertions."[6] Insofar as this epistemology ascribes these features of "natural light" and "intuitive insight" to the translucency of consciousness, it tends toward foundationalism.

If philosophy in the West, as Whitehead suggests, is merely a series of footnotes to Plato, the footnoted text is ocular. The formalizing inclination which stems from the Platonic view that limitation is not imperfection, that the boundless is not perfect but chaotic, finds its epistemic correlate in the visual and in sight, the most discriminating of the senses. It is this Platonizing character of the traditional spectator view, which Dewey knew so well, that the "postmodern" wishes to combat.

The final feature of hegemonic vision that I wish to underline is its association with the Enlightenment itself. The very name betrays an ocular bias. Foucault was known for his ambivalent attitude toward this phenomenon. He respected the Enlightenment ideal of self-criticism and autonomy, the questioning of its own history and geography. But he rejected the "blackmail" of demanding in its name loyalty to the values of pure, universalizing Reason, acontextual knowledge, and historical progress: "Reason—the despotic enlightenment."[7]

It is the predominance of philosophies of consciousness since the seventeenth century that gives the hegemony of vision its peculiarly modern cast. The unblinking eye of Sartrean *pour-soi* is but the most recent in a long series of ontological and epistemic inventions that find their inspiration, if not their origin, in the Cartesian *cogito*. Setting aside Sartre's own complex and evolving position on the primacy of vision,[8] his looking/looked-at paradigm of interpersonal relations in *Being and Nothingness* articulates this link between consciousness and vision even as it shifts the relationship into a characteristically moral mode. In "objectifying" its referent, the Sartrean gaze alienates and dominates—a variation on a Hegelian theme that Foucault exploits in his power-knowledge dyad, as we shall see.

These, then, are the features of the optical epistemology that Foucault and many of his French contemporaries seek to combat. That his method of doing so is itself spatial and ocular raises more than the usual self-referential objection and must be addressed in its turn. But the shift from a detached, contemplative view to a dominating gaze is essential to Foucault's conception of modernity. Let us flesh this out with extended "archaeological" and "genealogical" examples.

II

Foucault, who "left it to the police" to check his identity papers, admitted to being a historian. But like every other potential label, this one must be applied to him with qualifications. In place of traditional history, he offers "archaeology," which describes the "archive" or set of effectively enunciated discourses that in fact establish the historical *a priori* (the rules of formation and transformation) for a given science, discipline, or practice. It is a method purged of all anthropologism, devoid of reference to the sovereign, totalizing subject.

Like his other archaeologies, Foucault's descriptive analysis of the medical gaze (*le regard*) centers on the difference and contrast between the classical period (roughly 1650–1800) and the modern (1800–1950), and deals with a level of discourse where "seeing and saying are still one."[9] Classical medicine was "nosological"; it was a medicine of species. True to Aristotle's dismissal of any science of the singular, this medicine treated the disease, not the patient. The doctor's perception of the symptoms led him to the essential characteristics that called for the generalized treatment. Like the natural historian, the classical doctor was interested in penetrating the vagaries of the individual instance to get at the necessary structures of the disease itself.

Toward the end of the eighteenth century the mind's eye of the physician, with its abstractive vision, gave way to the clinician's physical eye. Significantly, the latter brought to the object of investigation "nothing more than its own light" by means of which it "flickers around solid objects" (*BC* xiii, xiv). The enumeration of cases and probabilistic reasoning enter the scene. The case method allows the individual, *pace* Aristotle, to emerge as the object of scientific investigation.

But the shift was not simple. According to Foucault, the look gained its perspective from the political ideology of the Revolution:

> The ideological theme that guides all structural reforms from 1789 to Thermidor Year II is that of the sovereign liberty of truth; the majestic violence of light, which is itself supreme, brings to an end the bounded, dark kingdom of privileged knowledge and establishes the unimpeded empire of the gaze. [*BC* 39]

He describes this as "the great myth of the *free gaze* . . . a purified purifying gaze that, freed from darkness, dissipates darkness." He is quick to note that "the cosmological values implicit in the *Aufklärung* are still at work here" (*BC* 51–52). It is his thesis that the chief obstacle to the introduction of pathological anatomy into clinical medicine during this period was not religious intransigence or moral scruple but clinical thought itself: it was "interested in history, not geography" (*BC* 126).

What was called for was a "new, coherent, unitary model for the formation of medical objects, perceptions and concepts" (*BC* 51). The probing, cumulative, probabilistic gaze of the investigator would become the accepted practice, once the physician had learned how to see anew. The temporal exclusion of death from the discourse of pathology had to be overcome and a new spatiality of organs, sites, and causes introduced in order to bring pathological anatomy to the center of clinical medicine. As Foucault explains:

> The conflict [between anatomy and the clinic] was not between a young corpus of knowledge and old beliefs, but between two types of knowledge. Before pathological anatomy could be readmitted to the clinic, a mutual agreement had to be worked out: on the one hand, *new geographical lines,* and, on the other, a *new way of reading time.* In accordance with this litigious arrangement, the knowledge of the living, ambiguous disease could be aligned upon the white visibility of the dead. [*BC* 126, emphases mine]

In sum, "it is not a matter of the same game, somewhat improved, but of a quite different game" (137).

It is commonly supposed that the revolution in nineteenth-century medicine was brought about by the introduction of pathological anatomy, itself launched in 1801 by Bichat's influential counsel to "open up a few corpses." Foucault's concern is with the epistemic change that made this advice plausible. He sees it in the *spatialization* of the object of investigation. It was Broussais who completed this basic change, creating a "new organization of the medical gaze" by reversing Bichat's emphasis on the visibility-localization relationship: "It is because disease, in its nature, is local that it is, in a secondary way, visible. . . . Disease exists *in space* before it exists *for sight*" (*BC* 187, 188). This inversion of the commonly accepted relation between the conditioned and its conditions came to be a characteristically Foucauldian move in both his archaeologies and his genealogies.

Despite the error that the appearance of his general theory made "structurally necessary," Broussais's physiological medicine, the medicine of sick organs, brought "nosological" medicine to an end. Anticipating concepts and terminology from *The Order of Things,* Foucault concludes: "Broussais had fixed for his period the final element of *the way to see.* Since 1816, the doctor's gaze has been able to confront a sick organism. The historical and concrete *a priori* of the modern medical gaze was finally constituted" (*BC* 192).

"The anatomo-clinician's gaze has to *map a volume*" (*BC* 163). Its new semiology requires a sort of "sensorial triangulation" in that the ear and touch are added to sight. The invention of the stethoscope, for example, contributes to this "gaze" as does the active enlistment of the tactile surface. Still, Foucault insists, "the sensorial triangulation indispensable to anatomo-clinical perception remains under the dominant sign of the visible": first, because sound and touch merely make do in expectation of the "triumph of the gaze" which is the autopsy; second, because anatomy is concerned primarily with "spatial data that belong by right of origin to the gaze" (*BC* 165). Foucault speaks of the "absolute limit" set for anatomical analysis by the gaze (*BC* 167). The principle of visibility has its correlative in the differential reading of *cases* (*BC* 168), not as the mere instantiation of a rule or generality but as the constant possibility of an individual modulation. So "the figure of the visible invisible organizes anatomo-pathological perception" in the form of the knowledge of the individual (*BC* 170).

It may seem ironic that the victory of "geography" over "history" by which Foucault characterizes the revolution in modern medicine should likewise distinguish the "postmodern" method of this "new cartographer" himself.[10] His histories draw "new geographical lines" and present us with "a new way of reading time." How does one reconcile this apparent opposition between the "spatialized" thinking of anatomo-clinical perception and the totalizing, "temporalized" thought of the modern episteme as described in *The Order of Things*? Similarly, is there any significant difference between the clinical gaze correlative to this spatial field emerging in the nineteenth century and the vision whose hegemony Foucault is intent on combating?

The answer lies in the *diacritical*, comparatist nature of the clinical view, a stance adopted by Foucault in his "diagnostic" histories as well. He appeals to "the diacritical principle of medical observation: *the only pathological fact is a comparative fact*" (*BC* 134) in charting the difference between anatomical and clinical observation. The peculiarity of anatomo-clinical experience, he argues, lies in having applied the diacritical principle to a much more complex dimension: "that in which the recognizable forms of pathological history and the visible elements that it reveals on completion [viz., the cadaver] are articulated" (*BC* 135). Unlike the nosological intuition of his predecessors, Bichat's gaze operated on the surface, traversing the space of the disease that death had made coextensive with the organism and making a differential reading of the cases.

Describing his own method as "diagnostic," Foucault explains that it yields "a form of knowledge that defines and determines differences."[11] Thus his account of the specificity of the anatomo-clinical gaze, for example, gains its intelligibility precisely to the extent that it stands in contrast to the nosological view of the medicine of species. What he describes in the case of Bichat and Broussais is a *transformation* of the "absolutist" vision of classical medicine to the comparatist gaze of anatomy and physiology. Yet this is the kind of transformation his archaeologies exemplify, shifting from the *Wesensschau* of the phenomenologist and the intentional horizons of the hermeneut to the differential knowledge of the archaeologist.

In parallel fashion, there is a *displacement* of temporalizing accounts of the history of a disease in classical medicine effected by the *spatializing* gaze of the anatomo-clinician. The question from the medicine of species "What is wrong with you?" is supplanted by another from the medicine of sites, "Where does it hurt?" "The notion of *seat* has finally replaced that of *class*" (*BC* 140). This shift in the twin gears of seeing and saying is indicative, not only of an epistemic revolution in nineteenth-century medicine, but of the "postmodern" nature of Foucault's own thought. When he prefaces his study of clinical medicine with the injunction "We must place ourselves, and remain once and for all, at the level of the fundamental *spatialization* and *verbalization* of the pathological" (*BC* xi), he is characterizing his general approach to history as well.[12]

"The gaze that sees is the gaze that dominates" (*BC* 39). As if to counter the liberating pretensions of Enlightenment vision and to anticipate his subsequent genealogical claims regarding the correlation between knowledge and power, Foucault enunciates this thesis in his archaeology of medical perception. Gone is the transcendental subject whose perspectiveless view reveals the essences of things. Gone, too, is the detached, disinterested *conscience de survol* as Sartre and Merleau-Ponty called that awareness which seemed to hover above its objects. But he did not pursue the nondiscursive dimension of the "loquacious view" in this work as he would do in his genealogies.

III

A fear haunted the latter half of the eighteenth century: the fear of darkened spaces, of the pall of gloom which prevents the full visibility of things, men and truths. . . . The new political and moral order could not be established until these places were eradicated. . . . A form of power whose main instance is that of opinion will refuse to tolerate areas of darkness. If Bentham's project aroused interest, this was because it provided a formula applicable to many domains, the formula of "power through transparency," subjection by "illumination." In the Panopticon, there is used a form close to that of the castle—a keep surrounded by wells—to paradoxically create a space of exact legibility.[13]

Rather than containing the hegemony of vision in the modern period, the marriage of power and visibility that Bentham's panoptic principle achieved served to intensify it. Foucault's *Discipline and Punish: The Birth of the Prison,* subtitled in obvious parallel with his earlier work, offers a "genealogy" of the "carceral system" of which the prison formed the most obvious, but scarcely the most effective, instrument.

In a way that complements rather than counters his archaeological method, Foucault's genealogies draw our attention to the power relations operative at every phase of life in society. Bearing a prima facie resemblance to the "participant" theory of knowledge formulated by Dewey and others, his genealogical accounts differ from those of classical pragmatism to the extent that they emphasize the dimension of domination and control of other agents that practices of knowing entail. Like Darwinian pragmatism, genealogy sees struggle or warfare, not ideology or communication, as the proper model of social intelligibility. But like archaeology, it is rigorously nonteleological; it is especially hostile to the myth of social progress. So if Foucault continues to be a historian, it is now as "genealogist," laying bare the embarrassing secret of domination and control concealed by our most highminded purposes and stated intentions.

It is in this context that he undertakes his genealogy of the penal system. Typically, his analysis reverses the cause-effect relation usually attributed to penal reform, especially the utilitarian motivation of social betterment and reeducation through the ministration of newly generated social sciences. On the contrary, he sees the mass effort throughout the nineteenth century toward discipline and normalization—thoroughgoing instruments of observation and control—as expressing the self-custodial drive of a "carceral society" where "prisons resemble factories, schools, barracks, hospitals, which all resemble prisons."[14] The question he asks is how detention could change within the course of a few years from a rare punishment, reserved for the nobility, the insane, and the vagabond, to the accepted and preferred form of judicial sanction. What does this say about the epistemological status of crime, criminal, and court in modernity?

The terms *transformation* and *displacement,* missing from the archaeology of the clinic, are explicit in this genealogy. What Foucault is charting is a *displacement* in the point of punishment from body to body-*and*-soul in nineteenth-century practice as well as "a whole new system of truth," of knowledge, techniques, and "scientific" discourses concomitant to this displacement, which becomes entangled with the exercise of the *power* to punish.

His method aims to discover whether this focus on the soul, and with it the insertion of a body of "scientific" knowledge into the legal practice, is not the effect of a *transformation* of the way in which the body itself is invested by power relations (*DP* 24). An entire "political economy" of the body surfaces as the condition and context for the reformed systems of punishment that appear in the nineteenth century.

Foucault's book is noted for the "micro-physics of power" that in avowedly nominalist fashion ferrets out those instances where power is "expressed rather than possessed" (*DP* 26). His point is that "power" is not some abstract entity exercised by sovereign states in juridical, legislative, and executive manner. Rather, it names an indefinite complex of relations of domination and control, positive as well as negative, that connects every facet of society. The Rousseauean ideal of a fully transparent society that inspired the ideology of the Revolution of 1789 was but the incomplete articulation of this economy. It took the cool calculation of the utilitarian Bentham to link this with the power of surveillance. As Foucault remarks, "the tendency of Bentham's thought is archaic in the importance it gives to the gaze" (*P/K* 160).

The visibility of public executions in the seventeenth century was an exercise in sovereign power: the ruler displayed for all to see "the power relation that gave his force to the law" (*DP* 50). Foucault uncovers a whole "technology of representation" behind the art of punishing in the classical age: images linked by associations so disadvantageous as to rob the idea of crime of any attraction. This technology figured in the "economy of publicity" that was operative at the time.

The stated goal of punishment in the nineteenth century was the reform and reeducation of the criminal, his or her reconstitution as a productive member of society. Correspondingly, "the point of application of the penalty is not the representation, but the body, time, everyday gestures and activities; the soul, too, but insofar as it is the seat of habits. The body and the soul, as principles of behavior, form the element that is now proposed for punitive intervention" (*DP* 128). By a calculated control and apportionment of time (work schedules, periods of eating and rest, of schooling and prayer) and of space (the construction and allotment of spaces that permitted the greatest amount of potential surveillance), the bodies of the inmates of institutions (whether hospitals, factories, barracks, schools, or prisons) were rendered supple and docile, ready for the regimentation demanded by an industrial society. Not that there is a Marxist narrative afoot in Foucault's account; on the contrary, the rage for discipline *precedes* the demands of industrialization and to a large extent makes them possible. To be sure, Marx once said that a society only raises the kinds of problems it can solve. But in this case the answer is disciplinary, not economic; power, not productivity, is the great unthought of modernity.[15]

For modernity, vision has become supervision. The "hegemony" of vision in Foucault's modernity is the hegemony of power—a redundancy! Bentham's Panopticon, the architectural model for an institution in which the inmates are exposed to the possibility of constant surveillance so that they internalize this supervision as *self* control—this is the ideal, not only of the "carceral archipelago" (*DP* 297) that dotted the landscape of industrialized nations over the last two centuries, but also of the entire "carceral society" that has arisen on this model and the "disciplinary individual" who is both its creature and its apologist.[16]

The vehicles of this disciplinary economy are surveillance, normalization, and their synthesis, the examination. By "surveillance" Foucault means "hierarchical observation," like that facilitated in the layout of military camps, hospitals, workshops, asylums, and schools. By "normalizing judgment" he denotes the juridico-anthropological function of disciplinary power that joins the Law, the Word and Text, and Tradition by imposing new delimitations on each of these powers in modern society.

In one of the most brilliant passages from *Discipline and Punish*, Foucault discusses the normalizing gaze of the *examination*, which combines the techniques of an observing hierarchy with those of a normalizing judgment. From the daily rounds of the physician to reviews, tests and qualifying exams in barracks, schools and professional associations, here are united "the ceremony of power and the form of the experiment, the deployment of force and the establishment of truth" (*DP* 184). The various aspects of the power-knowledge dyad come to bear with the Benthamite principle of visibility: "The examination transformed the economy of visibility into the exercise of power" (*DP* 187). The hegemony of vision is not so much terminated as permeated by a more subtle exercise of power. Disciplinary power, unlike traditional sovereign power, is exercised through its invisibility while imposing compulsory visibility on its subjects—the grades are posted and/or the failed reveal themselves by their absence. Moreover, like the "clinical" sciences generally, the examination makes each individual a *case*. But in this new economy "describable individuality became a means of control and a method of domination," a fact that was only implicit in *Birth of the Clinic*. Each individual has a mass of documentation that fixes him or her for scrutiny. At this early stage such codes are crude anticipations of the thorough electronic "formalization" of the individual within the power systems that obtain today. The examination belongs to a modality of power for which individual difference is relevant (*DP* 192). In a disciplinary regime, power is exercised "by surveillance rather than ceremonies" (*DP* 193). It is such power and knowledge, Foucault has argued throughout his genealogies, that *constitute individuals* as correlatives.

Elsewhere Foucault has assumed the role of social critic by decrying the kind of individuality to which our society limits us.[17] Here he links that individualization to the hegemony of vision formalized in the examination. If the social contract has been regarded as the ideal foundation of law and political power in an individualistic age, he reminds us that "panopticism constituted the technique, universally widespread, of coercion." "The general juridical form that guaranteed a system of rights that were egalitarian in principle," he explains, "was supported by these tiny, everyday, physical mechanisms, by all those systems of micro-power that are essentially non-egalitarian and asymmetrical that we call the disciplines." Drawing a moral for which he became well known, Foucault adds: "The 'Enlightenment,' which discovered the liberties, also invented the disciplines" (*DP* 223).

IV

The ocular paradigm which Foucault believes has organized modernity, transforms and displaces concepts of the visual that marked the classical period and earlier. The language of the eye that dominated Western epistemology since the ancient Greeks, became the language of the "I" in the *cogito* and in the politics of possessive individualism. Foucault's archaeology of the medical gaze traced the transformation of that later vision and the displacement of its space in the modern episteme. His genealogy of the penal system revealed the transformation of the publicity of punishment into the subtle, normalizing gaze of the inspector and supervisor and the displacement of its object from the physical body to the body-soul as the stuff of which subjects are constituted.

In the course of these accounts, Foucault's own ocular proclivities have come to the fore. We are thus faced with the paradox mentioned earlier: that, in using the visual to undermine the visual, he disqualifies his own approach as well. How does he avoid the self-referential force of his own argument?

The answer, I have suggested, lies in the *diacritical* nature of his visual method, whether archaeological or genealogical. We noted that he adopts as his own the diacritical principle of medical observation that "the only pathological fact is a comparative fact" (*BC* 134). In his inaugural lecture at the Collège de France he credited George Dumézil for having taught him "to refer the system of functional correlations from one discourse to another by means of comparison." Dumézil likewise taught him "to describe the transformations of a discourse and its relations to the institution."[18] This nominalistic method freed vision from its Platonic perspective and held itself to the "surface" of events and practices, away from all the attributions of intention or influence that have muddied traditional intellectual history. By staying on the diagonal, following the comparatist lead of general geographers, as Paul Veyne suggests,[19] Foucault's diacritical vision *transforms* the intuitionist and foundationalist claims of ocular epistemologists without sacrificing the power of imagistic reasoning. In fact, it is precisely the *force* of the image that he exploits in his generous use of spatial metaphors.

But there is a concomitant *displacement* of the temporal by the spatial in Foucault's "histories." Just as geography (a medicine of sites) had to replace history (a medicine of the progression of a species) if pathological anatomy was to gain general acceptance in the clinic, so the spatialized "arguments" of Las Meninas, the Panopticon, and the various "triangles" and "quadrilaterals" that populate his writings are employed to replace the ordering temporality and totalizing subjectivity of the history of ideas. The very term *displacement* is a spatial word that connotes a power relationship as well. The resultant reasoning—which I am designating *postmodern*—proceeds more by association and juxtaposition than by causal attribution. And when necessities are appealed to, as they sometimes are, it is often retrospectively by pointing to "gaps" and "spaces" left by chance conjunctures or unexplained events. Even the strategical model employed in his genealogies implies power relations which are "both intentional and nonsubjective."[20]

What I have termed his "postmodern" spatialization of reason, with its diacritical vision and spatial paradigm, is Foucault's alternative to the leading methodologies of modernity, namely the formalism of the structuralists and the dialectics of the "humanists." It is to counter the axiomatization of the former and the totalizing character of the latter, I would argue, that he takes this spatializing turn. Not that he neglects time. *Pace* Paul Veyne, one could scarcely write history without it. But he dethrones Time and History from their ordering role in the human sciences in favor of the chance event, the contingent *a priori*, and the comparative fact. The Dionysian character of time is thus restored.[21]

But does spatialized reason really end the "hegemony of vision" that marks modernity in either the broad or the restricted sense? If "light" implies "vision" in historical discourse, does not "space" do so as well? Appeal to diacritical vision seems at first blush to avoid the features of ocularcentrism associated with modernism. But at what price? As I have argued elsewhere, the fundamental role of lived experience (*le vécu*) and its temporality in history is predicated on our basic ability to tell and follow stories.[22] This would seem to imply a "narrative vision" rather than a diacritical one and a "temporalized reason" rather than a spatialized one. Perhaps the challenge is to relate the narrative and the comparative, to pursue a plurality of plots simultaneously. Will this yield a new rationality, or just confusion?

Nor is it obvious that diacritical vision succeeds in transgressing the limits of ocularcentrism entirely. To be sure, it seems to avoid implicit appeal to totalizing consciousness and subjectivity. If strategies are possible without a strategist, so too are comparisons and contrasts. But the inevitability of the visibility-domination dyad looks suspiciously like the Sartrean looking/looked-at relationship, in that neither allows for positive reciprocity and mutuality. In Sartre's case, it was necessary to adopt an ontology and an epistemology of *praxis,* as he did in the *Critique of Dialectical Reason,* in order to warrant cooperation and what in his last interview he called "fraternity." Foucault never escapes the stage of reciprocal endangerment in his account of social interaction. For him, too, it appears that "hell is the other." But he allows no space for the generosity and communal effort that Sartre's Rousseauean ideal made possible. Without a utopian heaven, one cannot have a hell; for Foucault, the light-footed positivist, that's just the way it is. If this is not a victory for the visual, it is at least the triumph of the Other.

NOTES

1. Michel de Certeau, *Heterologies: Discourse on the Other,* trans. Brian Massumi (Minneapolis: University of Minnesota Press, 1986), pp. 192, 196.

2. Martin Jay, "In the Empire of the Gaze," in *Foucault: A Critical Reader,* ed. David Couzens Hoy (Oxford: Basil Blackwell, 1986) pp. 194–195.

3. See Hans Jonas, "The Nobility of Sight," in *The Phenomenon of Man: Toward a Philosophical Biology* (Chicago: University of Chicago Press, 1966), pp. 135–156.

4. Aquinas, *Sum. Theol.* 1. 67. 1, corp.

5. The phenomenon of the rupture between classicism and modernity "as a whole can be situated between easily assignable dates (the outer limits are the years 1775 and 1825)." Michel Foucault, *The Order of Things,* trans. anon. (New York: Random House Vintage Books, 1970), p. 221.

6. Edmund Husserl, *Ideas Pertaining to a Pure Phenomenology and to a Phenomenological Philosophy,* First Book, trans. F. Kersten (The Hague: Martinus Nijhoff, 1982), p. 36.

7. Foucault, introduction to Georges Canguilhem, *On the Normal and the Pathological,* trans. Carolyn R. Fawcett (Dordrecht: D. Reidel, 1978), p. xii.

8. For a defense of the thesis that Sartre's writings support two incompatible epistemologies, see my "Praxis and Vision: Elements of a Sartrean Epistemology" in *The Philosophical Forum* 8 (Fall 1976): 21–43.

9. Foucault, *The Birth of the Clinic: An Archaeology of Medical Perception,* trans. A. M. Sheridan Smith (New York: Random House Vintage Books, 1973), p. xi, hereafter cited as *BC.*

10. See Gilles Deleuze, "A New Cartographer," in *Foucault,* trans. Sean Hand (Minneapolis: University of Minnesota Press, 1988), pp. 23–44.

11. Foucault, "An Historian of Culture," in *Foucault Live,* trans. John Johnston et al. (New York: Semiotext(e) Foreign Agents Series, 1989), p. 73.

12. These last lines are taken from my essay "Foucault and the Spaces of History," *The Monist* 74, 2 (April, 1991), p. 170, where this thesis is developed at length.

13. Foucault, "The Eye of Power," in *Power/Knowledge: Selected Interviews and Other Writings 1972–1977*, trans. Colin Gordon et al. (New York: Pantheon Books, 1980), pp. 153–154, hereafter cited as *P/K*.

14. Foucault, *Discipline and Punish: The Birth of the Prison*, trans. Alan Sheridan (New York: Pantheon Books, 1977), p. 228, hereafter referred to as *DP*.

15. See David Couzens Hoy, "Foucault: Modern or Postmodern?" in Jonathan Arac, ed., *After Foucault: Humanistic Knowledge, Postmodern Challenges* (New Brunswick, N.J.: Rutgers University Press, 1988), p. 20.

16. The way had been carefully prepared in the eighteenth century. As Foucault observes: "A meticulous observation of detail, and at the same time a political awareness of these small things, for the control and use of men, emerge through the classical age bearing with them a whole set of techniques, a whole corpus of methods and knowledge, descriptions, plans and data. And from such trifles, no doubt, the man of modern humanism was born" (*DP* 141). On the "disciplinary individual" see *DP* 308.

17. See his interview, "On the Genealogy of Ethics," the afterword (1983) to Hubert L. Dreyfus and Paul Rabinow, *Michel Foucault: Beyond Structuralism and Hermeneutics*, 2d ed. (Chicago: University of Chicago Press, 1983), p. 216.

18. Foucault, "The Discourse on Language," published as an appendix to *The Archaeology of Knowledge*, trans. A. M. Sheridan Smith (New York: Harper Colophon, 1972), p. 235. Of course, his sympathy with Dumézil's methodology led to his being called a structuralist, a label he strenuously rejected.

19. Paul Veyne, *Writing History*, trans. Mina Moore-Rinvolucri (Middletown, Conn.: Wesleyan University Press, 1974), p. 284.

20. Foucault, *The History of Sexuality*, vol. 1, *An Introduction*, trans. Robert Hurley (New York: Random House Vintage Books, 1978), p. 94.

21. Even the existentialists had tamed the temporal into a principle of individuation by such ploys as "anticipatory resoluteness" (Heidegger) and "fundamental project" (Sartre).

22. See my "Michel Foucault and the Career of the Historical Event," in Bernard P. Dauenhauer, ed., *At the Nexus of Philosophy and History* (Athens: University of Georgia Press, 1987), pp. 195–198. I am following the general line of argument formulated by David Carr (*Time, Narrative, and History* [Bloomington: Indiana University Press, 1986]) and Paul Ricoeur (*Time and Narrative*, trans. Kathleen Blamey and David Pellauer, 3 vols. [Chicago: University of Chicago Press, 1984-1988]).

ELEVEN

Ocularcentrism and Social Criticism

Georgia Warnke

In a series of recent articles Martin Jay has focused on criticism of the ocularcentrism of Western culture.[1] By ocularcentrism, Jay means the epistemological privileging of vision that begins at least as early as Plato's notion that ethical universals must be accessible to "the mind's eye" and continues with the Renaissance, the invention of printing, and the development of the modern sciences. For Descartes, truth is associated with clear and distinct ideas discerned by a "steadfast mental gaze," while for Bacon objectivity is associated with observation, and objective knowledge is that knowledge obtained through sight. But such a privileging of sight has also inspired a deep distrust, a distrust that one can find in Bergson's work and that runs through the work of Wagner, Nietzsche, and Heidegger. More recently it has taken form in Foucault's analysis of modern surveillance techniques, in Guy Debord's condemnation of the society of the spectacle, and in Richard Rorty's critique of ocular metaphors in philosophy.[2] Many contemporary feminists, hermeneuticists, deconstructionists, and Marxists now attack any supposed association between vision and the critique of ideology. Marx could still rely on the power of the idea of clear vision in his comparison of ideology to a *camera obscura* that inverts the way "men and their circumstances" appear, just as the physical life-process inverts objects on the retina. For contemporary critics, however, ideology is no longer to be connected to distortions in vision but to distortions of language.

In Jay's view, such an analysis follows from a renewed respect for the truths of interpretation over the methods of scientific observation. Vision is conceived of as synchronic, antihistorical, and pointillist, "producing an external presence without any meaningful continuity between past and future."[3] Sight can only grasp external appearances and behavior, never inner meaning. It externalizes only the given moment and can never envision its context. In contrast, interpretation involves decoding meaning by listening to its expression, connecting meaning to what has been said or will be said and understanding the context of action or expression. For this reason, it seems to allow more space for sustained criticism. To connect ideology to obscured vision is to suppose that the social critic is somehow suited to seeing social reality for what it is. To connect ideology with language is to open up avenues for critical interpretation that focus on the kinds of discourses that have power in a culture or society and to claim that language includes hierarchical relations of domination. The overcoming of ideology is thus no longer associated with insight, clear vision, or even enlightenment. Social criticism does not reveal the truth of "men and their circumstances" for all to see. Instead, it cleans language and communication of their hidden relations to power.

But Jay himself is skeptical of this substitution. Agreeing with Hans Blumenberg, he suggests that to the extent that understanding and interpretation are linked to hearing rather than seeing, and to the extent, then, that they require us to connect up meanings expressed in the present to those expressed in the past and in tradition, they are also inherently conservative. In contrast, to privilege vision is to connect us more firmly to a present that we can see for ourselves and to sever the link to the authority of voices other than our own. Social emancipation, in Jay's view, is "our liberation from blind obedience to voices from the past."[4] For this reason, "We cannot entirely relinquish the cold eye of dispassionate analysis, losing the advantage given by gaining some perspective on a problem, in order to listen to each other." Rather, "as Ricouer has also often stressed, we need a moment of distantiation, a more synoptic overview, as one positive condition of all historical understanding."[5]

Jay finds support for this position in the social theory of Jürgen Habermas. On the one hand, Habermas follows other contemporary social critics in focusing on language and, in particular, on the way in which communication can be systematically distorted by relations of power and domination. Moreover, Habermas connects social emancipation to an ideal of unconstrained communication in which "the assumption of an undistorted speech situation in which the power of the better argument rather than prejudice, manipulation, or coercion creates a consensus of opinion about both cognitive and normative matters."[6] On the other hand, in spite of this emphasis on a communicative concept of reason, Jay contends that Habermas's social analysis still conceives of "a certain role for the objectivist epistemology that is so closely tied to the privileging of vision." Moreover, Jay suggests that, in recognizing this role,

Habermas marks his dissatisfaction with the truths of interpretation and, in particular, with the hermeneutic approach to social theory promoted by Hans-Georg Gadamer.

The question I want to ask in this essay, however, is: Just how tied to a privileging of vision over the truths of interpretation is Habermas's model of a critical social theory? I shall be arguing that Jay exaggerates the extent to which one might appeal to Habermas's work in an attempt to resuscitate the critical thrust of an objectivist epistemology, and that he accordingly plays down the overwhelmingly communicative aspects of Habermas's notion of ideology critique. But I shall also be arguing that there is another sense we might give to the idea of ocularcentrism, one that has to do less with an objectivist epistemology than with a kind of social and ethical perception. But if this extension to the idea of ocular-centrism makes sense, one question we might raise is whether Habermas's account of the critique of ideology grants enough importance to this sense of ocularcentrism or whether a recognition of its hold is not easier to find in Gadamer's hermeneutics. I shall start this essay by considering Habermas's criticism of Gadamer.

GADAMER VS. HABERMAS

Gadamer's *Truth and Method* is a critique of attempts to extend the "objectivist epistemology" of the natural sciences to the social sciences and humanities. In concert with neo-Wittgensteinian philosophy of the social sciences, Gadamer suggests that the observational methods of the natural sciences are suited only to formulating causal explanations for the occurrence of events. The social sciences, however, must also be concerned with a prior question, namely, with the question of the meaning events have or with the meaning of such text analogues as actions, practices, social norms, and principles. The meaning an event or occurrence has within the natural sciences is one that can be said to be determined by the natural scientific community alone. It is this community that determines how the phenomena under study are to be defined, what apparent causal connections should be investigated, and what the standards are for the confirmation and rejection of research hypotheses. But the meanings of the actions and practices studied by the social sciences are pre-constituted; they do not depend only on the definitions and purposes the scientific community brings to them. Rather, they possess prior meaning for the participants themselves, as part of a preexisting social context, language, and set of common understandings. Rocks and trees do not have a language they apply to themselves, but communities do; and the claim of both hermeneutics and neo-Wittgensteinian social science is that social science must take this language into account in order to describe the events it tries to explain causally. In other words, we must first determine what a particular action, practice, or norm is before we can explain why it happened or will happen under certain conditions; and this requires that we understand the context of actions, practices, and norms to which it belongs.

Habermas defends Gadamer and neo-Wittgensteinian social science on this point against efforts such as Theodore Abel's to discredit understanding or the "method of *Verstehen*" as, at best, a heuristic tool for setting up scientific hypotheses. In an essay first published in 1948, Abel characterizes an understanding of meaning as an act of imaginative identification with the subject under study. For example, we see our neighbor "rise from his desk by the window, walk to the woodshed, pick up an ax, and chop some wood." We subsequently observe him carrying the wood into the house, placing it in the fireplace, and lighting it. We internalize the motivation behind these various actions and thus hypothesize that our neighbor "began to feel chilly and, in order to get warm, lighted a fire." But we cannot verify the hypothesis by continuing to rely on our powers of identification or intuition. Instead, we have to employ "objective methods of observation."[7] And we have to be able to appeal to a general and well-confirmed causal law such as, "A person 'feeling cold' will . . . 'seek warmth.'"[8]

Still, as Habermas points out, Abel's example already skews his account of understanding. Because the person being observed is a member of the same culture to which his observer belongs, the example circumvents the very problem with which both hermeneutic and neo-Wittgensteinian accounts of understanding are concerned: namely, what does an event or a series of observed movements mean? Since Abel's subject is his neighbor, by empathizing with him, Abel can also take it for granted that the attempt to stay warm is a plausible motivation for making a fire and hence for gathering wood. He can also assume that wood has no sacred identification that would prohibit its instrumental use, that the person's behavior probably does not have either a religious or a sacrilegious meaning given its context, that the behavior does not involve playing a game or engaging in athletic activity for its own sake, and so on. In short, Abel already understands the range of meanings building a fire can have in the situation in question as well as the range of motivations that can be intelligibly connected to the activity, because he shares the norms, assumptions, and understandings of his subject. In cases such as Zande poison practices, in which chickens are killed and diagnosed in various, seemingly contradictory ways, or cases such as Tibetan legal practices in which root causes for an action can span lifetimes, anthropologists or social theorists cannot rely on such shared meanings, and understanding must be more systematically achieved.⁹ As Habermas puts it: "If Abel had chosen examples of actors from foreign cultures or distant epochs, it could scarcely have escaped him that he must first secure an understanding of non-trivial behavior maxims before he can apply them to meaningfully motivated action."¹⁰

Still, if an understanding of nontrivial behavior maxims must be secured before we can make statements about the causes of the behavior, neither hermeneutic nor neo-Wittgensteinian social science thinks that it can be secured by reexperiencing an event or practice as its participants experienced it. On the one hand, understanding behavior maxims requires an understanding of context, of the language of action within which the event has its meaning. On the other hand, interpreters cannot simply shed their own language, experiences, assumptions, and purposes to understand another culture or historical epoch the way its inhabitants understand it. Rather, they are socially and historically situated, and the concerns, assumptions, and life-involvements of that situation necessarily orient their understanding of any other situation. For example, the way in which Western anthropologists understand Tibetan legal practices will differ from the way the Tibetans themselves understand them because the aspects of those practices that seem odd or unintelligible to Westerners will differ from the aspects that concern the Tibetans themselves. The questions Westerners ask about these practices will center on the suffusion of legal maxims with religious purposes, the importance of such concepts as karma, the contrast between the figure of the Buddha and the Western attention to a "reasonable man" standard, the differing ideas of causation, and so on. These are questions Tibetans themselves neither could nor would ask. Still, they are questions without which it is hard to see how the practices could make any sense to contemporary Westerners at all.

Gadamer therefore takes it as a given that, although social scientific communities must attend to the language of action and practice of the community under study, they will also have their own research objectives and language, and that they will have to understand the actions, practices, and norms of the community under study in relation to these objectives and their linguistic framework. The context of that which is being studied must be brought into relation with the context within which the research objectives of the scientific or interpretive community are constituted. Interpreters cannot simply leave behind their own language and experience to understand the actions and practices of another time or culture as a native does, internally as it were. Neither can they simply impose their own language and experience on the alien time or culture, since its meanings are meanings that are preconstituted by a set of internal relations. Instead, interpreters must use the background of their own experience and practice, as a foil against which to clarify the meaning of the actions and practices of others. For Gadamer, then, understanding is a consensus on meaning reached through a kind of dialogue or virtual dialogue with a text or text analogue in which the meaning that is understood is a coordination of two distinct interpretive frameworks. Peter Winch makes a similar point in claiming that understanding involves a kind of merging of two language games: the one the social scientist has learned as part of the culture to which she belongs as a social scientist and the one she learns in learning how to participate in the culture she is studying.[11]

But Gadamer goes further. If meaning is a merging of interpretive contexts, then it can also involve a kind of education. Indeed, in conceiving of the understanding of meaning as a consensus achieved in dialogue, Gadamer's point is that the interpretive context of each partner to the interpretive dialogue necessarily changes. In coming to understand the meaning of an action or practice, I come to understand it in relation to actions and motivations for action with which I am more familiar; but I also understand these actions and motivations in relation to the action or practice I have come to understand. Hence, I can learn something about my own assumptions and concerns. If Tibetans understand causation differently than I do, I can also question my own conception. I can come to understand it as a cultural construct and question its legitimacy, necessity, or usefulness for scientific or legal purposes and the like. In other words, by coming to understand different actions and practices, I also acquire the capacity to understand my own in a different way. I understand the generality or particularity of my actions, practices, and norms; I learn to ask new questions about them and to conceive of different solutions to the conflicts they may produce. To this extent, by trying to understand other cultures and texts, we can also come to understand our own assumptions, prejudices, and concerns differently and, indeed, come to understand the way in which the meaning and context of different actions and practices set our own actions and practices in question.

But Gadamer goes even further. If understanding meaning involves educating ourselves, this is because understanding involves what he calls an anticipation of completeness or perfection [*der Vorgriff der Vollkommenheit*]. The point here is that the condition for the possibility of understanding a text or text analogue involves assuming its coherence, plausibility, and indeed significance for us. Otherwise, we have no standard for correcting our own misinterpretations of it. If we begin with the premise that a text or text analogue is part of a primitive or nonsecularized culture, for example, and that its alien character means that it cannot speak to our concerns, then we cannot test our assumptions either about the text or text analogue or about our own secularized culture. If we assume that the Tibetans do not understand causation because they look to root causes instead of proximate causes, then we can neither understand the way in which the idea of root causes in the law complements Tibetan religious beliefs nor the way in which our own views of causation in law might be modified. Indeed, Gadamer suggests that if what the text or text analogue seems to say to us appears patently incoherent or untrue, we must, at least initially, assume that the fault lies, not with the text, but with the assumptions we bring to it. Our inability to understand can be overcome only by listening more fully to the text or text analogue, changing the context within which we understand it, and trying harder to understand the meaning it has for us. As Charles Taylor charges: "in the sciences of man insofar as they are hermeneutical there can be a valid response to 'I don't understand' which takes the form, not only 'develop your intuitions,' but more radically 'change yourself.'"[12]

Still, Habermas's methodological reflections on the social sciences might be understood as arising from suspicions about just this charge. It seems to overlook the possibility that not all change may be rational, that what Gadamer sees as a "transformation into truth," insofar as we learn from what we are trying to understand, may be a transformation instead into falsity and ideological delusion. Suppose the transformation that is achieved by our efforts to learn from Tibetan legal practices changes our own conception of women? What do we have to learn from a conception of women that so emphasizes their caring and nurturing capacities that it precludes the possibility that they can serve as witnesses in court? Moreover, if we do try to learn from this conception, are we not prevented from understanding its possible connections to power and hierarchical domination in the society? If we are to conceive of meaning as a consensus brought about in dialogue, it appears that we must reckon with the possibility that this consensus may hide relations of coercion and that a deep understanding of meaning requires penetrating the surface meaning of what is said or done, to uncover hidden connections to power and domination.

This argument, at least, is the one Habermas brings against Gadamer. As I mentioned earlier, on Jay's view it requires restoring some of the critical distantiation from the phenomena we are studying, a distantiation that he associates with an objectivist epistemology and the privileging of vision. I want to explore this claim a bit further by examining the use Habermas makes of psychoanalytic theory as a model for a critical social science that can go beyond Gadamer's hermeneutics in distinguishing between a consensus on meaning and ideological force.

PSYCHOANALYTIC THEORY

Habermas claims that strictly hermeneutic attempts to understand meaning can be adequate only under certain conditions. If the meanings under study seem initially obscure and if hermeneutic understanding is nonetheless adequate to illuminate them, the initial obscurity is the result either of (1) their cultural, temporal, or social distance from us, or (2) of "openly pathological" elements that partially obfuscate them. In the first case, where we are trying to understand the meaning of a particular practice in a culturally or historically alien society, we can try to understand more of the experiential and social context in which the practice has its place, the other social practices in the society to which it is related and those to which it contrasts, the linguistic forms appropriate to it, and so on. In the course of these efforts it might also be apparent to us that certain activities related to the practice have a pathological character. In this second case, we can recognize that certain kinds of behavior are perversions of the meaning of the practice and should not be included in our account of its real meaning. Hence, we might, for example, exclude both voter apathy and stuffing the ballot box from our understanding of democracy, just as we might exclude Chinese incursions on Tibetan legal practices from our understanding of the practices themselves.

That which concerns Habermas, however, is the intrusion of "patterns of systematically distorted communication" into "pathologically unobtrusive speech." Here, pathological elements cannot be separated from nonpathological elements in the attempt to come to a consensus on meaning, because the pathological elements are part of the language of dialogue and consensus itself. Neither dialogue nor consensus is obviously disrupted by a failure to understand or a confused translation and hence there is no way, on the hermeneutic level itself, to recognize the distorted character of the dialogue or resulting consensus. As Habermas formulates this point:

> Hermeneutics has taught us that we are always a participant as long as we move within the natural language. . . . There is therefore no general criterion available to us which would allow us to determine when we are subject to the false consensus of a pseudo-normal understanding and consider something as a difficulty that can be resolved by hermeneutical means when, in fact, it requires systematic explanation.[13]

Gadamer admits that there may be texts and text analogues that can have no meaning for us and that we ought not to change in order to understand them. But he offers no criterion for deciding when this is the case; and Habermas's point is that hermeneutics can offer none. From within the parameters of a hermeneutic understanding, we can never know whether our failure to understand the text or text analogue in such cases is to be attributed to our failings as interpreters, failings that can be corrected by continued hermeneutic efforts alone, by our attempts to understand the truth of that which we are studying and to change ourselves so that we can understand it, or whether our failure is to be attributed to systematic distortions in that which we are trying to understand and hence in the hermeneutic "dialogue" itself. For this reason, Habermas thinks that a more theoretical approach to understanding is required from the start. In his view, we need a standard of undistorted communication to which we can appeal in order to recognize cases of systematically distorted communication. In addition, we need a theory that explains the possible sources for the distortions in communication and that, by explaining them, defuses their effect on the communication.

Freudian psychoanalysis offers Habermas a model of just this sort of theory. As understood by Alfred Lorenzer, Freudian theory explains distortions in communication as a confusion of two genetically consecutive stages in symbol formation: on the one hand, a prelinguistic level of symbol organization in which symbols are not yet integrated into any grammatical system, and on the other hand the properly linguistic level. At the prelinguistic level, symbols are still closely tied to specific scenes with such a highly charged affective meaning that the young child does not allow them to articulate themselves on the properly linguistic level. At the same time, meanings enter into this linguistic level surreptitiously and privatize the public meanings it contains, thereby causing systematic distortions in the language of communication. The important aspect of this sort of account is that it reverses the hermeneutic relation between understanding meaning and explaining events. The real meaning of a pathological action or expression is not the meaning it seems to have for the patient but the meaning it has as a confusion of linguistic levels. But this means that the action or expression is not understood in terms of its manifest content; it is rather understood from the start in causal terms, as a symptom or effect of a confusion of linguistic levels caused by the need to repress unwelcome drives.

> The what—the meaning-content of systematically distorted expressions—can only be "understood" when it is possible to answer, at the same time, the "why" question, i.e. to "explain" the emergence of the symptomatic scene by reference to the initial conditions of the distortion itself.[14]

Habermas cites two additional ways in which psychoanalytic explanation differs from hermeneutic understanding. Both ways center on the circumstance that the communication between analyst and patient proceeds under experimental conditions and hence does not fulfill the expectations of normal everyday communication. Through the intervention of the analyst the patient learns to articulate the unwelcome drives that had been repressed; in linguistic terms, he or she learns to retrieve the meaning-contents that have been systematically split off from the public language and become privatized. But in order for this retrieval to succeed, the analyst must take on the role of the conflict-charged primary object so that the communication that takes place between analyst and patient takes on the character of an original conflict scene for the patient. By relating this "transference" scene to the patient's symptomatic scenes outside of treatment and providing the connections between transference scene, original conflict scene, and symptomatic scene, the analyst can construct a scheme for translating the private language back into the public language and allow for the resymbolization of meaning.

But this circumstance means, first, that the analyst does not enter into the communication as an equal participant; his or her task is not to engage in the usual give and take of dialogue but rather to provide a backdrop for the patient's transference scenes and thereby construct a translation manual by which the patient can resymbolize lost meaning. Hence, the equality that exists in the hermeneutic relation between dialogue partners in which one can educate the other is undermined. The patient is not a full partner in the consensus on meaning, but a partially objectified event to be explained. Second, the analyst's purposes require that her attention be directed at only certain dimensions of the meaning of the patient's expressions, namely those that can be traced back to the conflictual object-relations of the patient's early development. Hence, the fullness of hermeneutic dialogue is restricted.

For a critical social theory, the model of Freudian psychoanalysis would seem to indicate the need for a similar explanatory framework. That is, what is needed is a critical theory of society that can explain manifest social meanings and shared social understandings as symptoms of underlying factors such as power and domination, which the meanings and social understandings cannot overtly express. Hence, a critical social theory will explain certain meanings as effects of pathology and specify the kinds of factors that can cause it. But neither characteristic seems to provide much support for Jay's suggestion that Habermas's account of the critique of ideology preserves a role for the privileging of vision. On Habermas's account, we need a theoretical starting point in order to penetrate systematically distorted communication; that starting point does incorporate elements of an explanatory science insofar as it involves the attempt to explain the causes and development of pathological symptoms with the help of a general theory. Still, this starting point does not mean that we move from speaking and hearing to observation; rather, we seem to move to a kind of theoretically informed listening in which the theorist approaches the expression of meaning within an explanatory context informed by a conception of communicative competence, on the one hand, and a schema of possible sources for systematic distortion on the other.

But, if Habermas's appeal to theory thus provides no basis for reinvoking the hegemony of the visual, might not his substitution of communicative conceptions for perceptual ones be a problem? The question here is whether a theory of communicative competence can do all the work Habermas assigns it or whether there is not a crucial role still to be played by some sort of moral and ethical perception. In order to clarify this concern, I need to elucidate briefly the standard of unconstrained communication that serves Habermas as the ideal against which distortions in communication can be measured. I shall then turn to the problems this standard might involve for the critique of ideology.

SOCIAL AND ETHICAL PERCEPTION

Habermas claims that what he terms "a critically enlightened hermeneutics" must both include "awareness of the conditions of the possibility of systematically distorted communication" and connect "the process of understanding to the principle of rational discourse according to which truth would be guaranteed only by that kind of consensus which was achieved under the idealized conditions of unconstrained communication free from domination and which could be maintained over time."[15] This notion of unconstrained communication serves as the standard for a communicative concept of rational justification. Theoretical and normative claims are rationally justified to the extent that they can gain assent in a discursive process in which "in principle, all those affected participate as free and equal members in a cooperative search for truth in which only the force of the better argument may hold sway."[16] Habermas specifies certain symmetry conditions that must hold for such discourses if they are to produce a rational consensus. Participants must have the same chances to contribute to the discourse, to make assertions, recommendations, and explanations, to challenge claims and proposed justifications, and to express feelings, wishes, and needs.[17] He also introduces a modified Kantian principle of universalization, "U," as a procedure

specifically of moral-practical discourse: "For a norm to be valid, the consequences and side-effects its general observance has for the satisfaction
of each's particular interests must be freely acceptable to all."[18]

Such a discursive account of rational justification allows us to distinguish between forced and unforced consensus on procedural grounds.
For any social meaning, we can ask whether it could have been assented
to under ideal conditions, or how

> the members of a social system, at a given stage in the development of pro-
> ductive forces, would have collectively and bindingly interpreted their
> needs (and which norms would they have accepted as justified) if they
> could and would have decided on the organization of social intercourse
> through discursive will-formation with adequate knowledge of the limiting
> conditions and functional imperatives of their society.[19]

The point here is that, where existing norms, practices, and institutions
could not have been agreed upon in a practical discourse sufficiently
fulfilling ideal conditions, then we have to acknowledge what Habermas calls the suppression of generalizable interests. The norms and institutions cannot be justified as the possible product of discursive will-
formation.

Still, one question that arises with regard to this analysis is why we
should suppose that the members of a social system, at a given stage in
the development of productive forces, should or would have collectively
and bindingly interpreted their needs in any one way, or that they should
or would have accepted one and the same set of norms as justified. If we
counterfactually suppose the elimination of all coercive features in the
process of discursive will-formation, does this entitle us to assume a collective interpretation of needs or a collective assent to the same set of
norms within a social system? At least within modern pluralistic societies,
is the problem not that different groups interpret their needs differently
and that they consider different norms justified? Why should they come
to agree through the force of the better argument? Will they not consider different arguments to be "better" because of the different assumptions, life-experiences, and values with which they begin?

It should be pointed out that, on Habermas's account, procedures of
discursive justification are not themselves supposed to generate norms.
They are meant simply to test norms that, for their part, have to be
brought to the test from the life-world of concrete practices and situations. Were we to test the assumptions of Tibetan legal practices in this
way, then we might find that they cannot be sustained once women are
allowed to raise their own challenges to the supposed dichotomy between caring for others and being able to tell the truth, when they are al-

lowed to articulate their needs and interests in a situation freed of fear, outright force or manipulation, and so on. Nevertheless, why suppose as even a regulative ideal that Tibetans could agree on a legitimate set of norms? And, in modern pluralistic societies, do we not possess such different values, interests, need-interpretations, and conceptions of the good life that we cannot together consider any set of norms to be justified? Will not any set violate the needs and interests of some group as it understands its needs and interests? And, do not our differences in these respects have less to do with questions of reason or ideology than with questions of orientation, sensibility, and indeed of differences in the way we "see" or understand things in general?

An example may help clarify the distinction with which I am concerned here between argument and a kind of ethical perception. Suppose a certain university has a rule according to which a student can obtain credit for the first semester of an introductory language course only if she takes the full year of the language. Now imagine a minority student who has been diligent and conscientious throughout her college career and has done very well. She has been awarded a scholarship to law school, which she cannot attend without aid, and the only condition of the scholarship is that she graduate on time as expected. But a month before she is to graduate the student discovers that she is one credit short of fulfilling her requirements because she took only one semester of an introductory French course in her freshman year and was never informed that she had not received credit for it. The college administrator in charge of academic affairs refuses to allow the student to graduate and supports this refusal with reasoned argumentation. The rule is a necessary one because the first semester of an introductory languages does not delve sufficiently far into the language to merit credit; the student is responsible for knowing all the academic rules of the college; and rules cannot be bent for women, minority students, and other groups.

The point of this example is that it is not clear that the college administrator's approach to the case can be simply dismissed as irrational. That is, it may be that the disgust I would feel at the college administrator's actions in this case does not support my convicting him of false consciousness, pathology, or reification. It may be that he simply takes certain rules and values more seriously than I do and, in general, sees the situation differently than I do. I might even agree with him that the rule about introductory courses is a good one in principle, that academic standards need to be maintained, that some part of fairness may dictate treating this student in the same way as we would treat a lazy student, and so on. If, still, I consider the administrator's action to be obscene, it may be simply because I view these considerations as less relevant and important than other considerations, such as the student's record over four years, fairness to the student, and so on. From my point of view, the college administrator has adopted an insensitive and unimaginative orientation to the situation and possesses a limited moral vision. But is he irrational or ideologically duped?

For Habermas, the issue this example raises is one that lies outside the domain of discursive justification because it involves, instead, a question of application. The assent of all concerned under ideal conditions is meant to determine the legitimacy of norms; it is not meant to contain prescriptions for their application to specific situations.[20] Hence, if the principle of individual responsibility for one's actions is legitimate it is because all concerned could assent to it as free and equal participants in a practical discourse; it is a separate question as to whether the principle can be applied to the case of a college student who does not know the rules that she should know about introductory language courses. Moreover, Habermas explicitly denies that even this separate question of application can be resolved by appealing to a moral agent's sensibilities or vision. Rather, he insists that "completely uncontemptible *topoi* are valid: for instance, the principles that all relevant aspects of a case must be considered . . . and that means should be proportionate to ends."[21]

But it is not clear that issues of justification can be so easily separated from those of application. In the first place, suppose we were to understand our different normative orientations toward the case of the college student as a problem limited to application, as a conflict in the ways we think an abstract and general principle—on the validity of which we do agree—is to be used to settle the question of her graduating. Still, what Habermas means by "completely uncontemptible *topoi*" remains unclear. While we may agree on a norm stipulating that all relevant aspects of a case must be considered in its adjudication, this norm would itself seem meaningless unless we could give more content to the notion of relevance. But here we may disagree. The college administrator thinks that considerations of fairness and equality are relevant, while we think the student's life and future are more relevant. The college administrator also thinks that the student's error is all that is at issue, while we assume that that error ought to be viewed within the context of the student's record as a whole. Hence, while we may agree that all relevant aspects of a case must be considered, we can still disagree on which aspects are relevant and how. Moreover, our understanding of relevance will depend not only on arguments but on our sense of things, the values we take seriously, the kinds of relationships we think are important, and in general our moral and social perspective. Similar disagreements would seem to arise in our efforts to decide on the means proportionate to a given end.

We can give arguments for why a certain means seems to us proportionate to the end but assent to such arguments seems already to presuppose a shared way of understanding and framing the issues at stake and a shared sense of what is and is not important.

In the second place, it is not clear that we can even understand the norms we are trying to justify independently of understanding their domains of application. Even if we are to accept the principle of equality as binding on our actions with regard to the student's mistake, we must first understand that principle. But, how can we understand it unless we know what sort of disputes it is supposed to adjudicate and how?[22] The issue is not simply how we are to apply the principle of equality; it is rather how we are to understand the principle itself or, in other words, what principal of equality *is* justified.

Habermas argues that in modern pluralistic societies, "as interests and value orientations become more differentiated," the norms to which we could all assent in a discursive process of will-formation "become ever more general and abstract."[23] He cites human rights as examples. But, if human rights can be morally grounded, we might still ask what these rights are. While we in the West, at least, might all agree on a right to free speech, others clearly do not and we can ourselves disagree on what counts as free speech and hence on what actions are supposed to be part of that freedom. As members of modern Western societies, we also understand the right to life differently, as the controversy over the morality of abortion makes clear. In this case, our normative differences seem to include differences on such questions as whether a right to life means that a fetus has a right to life, how such a right might be related to principles of individual liberty, whether principles of freedom mean that individuals are free to do what they want with their bodies as long as doing so does not affect others, and whether a fetus is to be seen as an other. Habermas may be correct in claiming that human rights are the basis for our legal system.[24] But the rights embedded there, as in the issue of the college student's graduating, are rights that we interpret, reinterpret, and debate in the course of our history and experience. Consequently, we must question the justificatory point of any rational consensus on norms that must abstract entirely from the issues of meaning and sensibility that arise in the course of trying to apply the norms.

Our normative differences seem to involve interpretive differences and these seem to involve differences in sensibility. We differ on the question of the morality of abortion, in part because we differ in the way we understand the rights and principles in question, and even on which rights and principles we think are in question. Moreover, our differences in these areas are connected to differences in our heritage and in our re-

ligious and ethical orientation. They are differences in value and vision
rather than differences in our capacity to follow the force of the better
argument, differences connected not to reason but to what we think is
important and to the context within which we frame the situation. Such
differences are not immutable. We can discard our heritage, come to understand the importance of different concerns, and realign our moral
perspective. But the point here is simply that the discursive procedures
to which Habermas appeals seem irrelevant to our differences in ethical
perspective. The appeal to reasons seems less significant than the character and vision of those making the appeal. Moreover, we seem to have to
share or come to share a common vision of things if we are to forge a
real agreement on moral norms. For where we do not share such a vision
it appears that we also cannot admit the force of the arguments to which
our interlocutors may appeal—arguments pointing to the purpose of the
rule about introductory languages, for example. Nor can our interlocutors admit the force of the considerations we may raise, those involving,
say, the work a student has done over the course of four years, or the
scholarship at stake.

But if our moral vision is not immutable and if discourse is, nonetheless, not the proper venue for its reassessment, how do we change our
perspectives? What is the proper model for normative justification or
normative change here? Habermas himself offers an interesting suggestion in distinguishing between practical discourse and aesthetic criticism.
Practical discourse pertains to the validity of normative statements about
"the hypothetical 'justice' of actions and of norms" while aesthetic criticism pertains to "evaluative statements" that involve a person's or
group's interpretations of its desires, feelings, and needs (*Bedürfnis-
natur*).[25] These interpretations are tied to one's identity and cultural heritage and bound up with specific values and conceptions of the good.
They therefore do not lend themselves to universal, rational consensus;
rather, our discussion with one another of these values and interpretations takes a form closer to that involved in discussions of art and literature. Suppose we are trying to persuade someone of the merit of a certain work of art. Here, the claims we make cannot be directly justified
with reasons or evidence. Instead, we refer to the emotions and desires
that the work evokes in us; we point to phenomena of color, movement,
dialogue, or form; we tell stories about the artist's life or the images represented or the history of art and we appeal to what we hope are our audience's assumptions and preferences. None of these considerations
have the direct force that reasons are supposed to have in practical discourse. If the stories we tell and the considerations we raise are to be
seen as a kind of argument, they are not the kind of argument our audi-

ence can reject only at the price of being irrational. Rather, they are meant to educate the perceptions and sensibilities of our audience and to encourage it to develop certain value-standards. A group's inability to develop the perceptions and sensibilities we have does not itself indicate that it is irrational or that we are. Hence, while according to Habermas the validity of a normative claim depends upon the possible ascent of a universal audience as free and equal participants in a practical discourse, with regard to discussions of art or value standards, he writes: "The circle of intersubjective recognition that forms around cultural values does not yet in any way imply a claim that they would meet with general assent within a culture, not to mention universal assent."[26]

In my view, this notion of aesthetic criticism might be extended to the question of moral consensus. If our ability to agree with one another with regard to fundamental norms of justice and morality depends, not only on the force of the better argument, but on a shared perception of things that allows us to see the force of the better argument, then the considerations we raise in the context of art might have a more general relevance. We can recognize the importance of education not only over art and value-standards but over moral norms and principles of justice; moreover, we can recognize that this education relies on the indirect rather than the direct force of reasons to transform the perspective we take on a principle or conflict. Jay notes that Gadamer uses an explicitly visual metaphor in connecting understanding (*Verständnis*) to an agreement on meaning reached through dialogue (*Einverständnis*). As we saw earlier, this agreement is meant to be a "transformation into truth" insofar as the understanding of each of the dialogue partners is changed and enriched as a consequence of the interchange between them. But it is also, Gadamer claims, a "fusion of horizons" in which one tries to bring one's own perspective on meaning into relation with another and, in so doing, comes to understand the way the other perspective relates to and expands one's initial view.

> The concept of horizon suggests itself [he writes] because it expresses the wide, superior vision that the person who is seeking to understand must have. To acquire a horizon means that one learns to look beyond what is close at hand—not in order to look away from it, but to see it better within a larger whole and in truer proportion.[27]

Jay himself seems to think that Gadamer's reliance on an ocular metaphor here indicates the hegemony of the visual or the extent to which even hermeneutics cannot escape the ocularcentrism associated with modern science. But in my view the notion of a fusion of horizons refers to a different form of ocularcentrism. Vision here does not create distance from what we are trying to understand; nor does it involve verifying external observations of behavior through comparative studies or statistical methods. Instead, it involves a kind of self-education of our sensibilities. The process by which one acquires a perspective is similar to the process of aesthetic criticism as Habermas conceives of it: namely, by including another horizon in one's view and expanding one's own vision through it. Thus, hermeneutics may successfully debunk one form of ocularcentrism, namely that involving the supposed objectivity of the methods of scientific observation, as Jay emphasizes. But, it does not dispense with a kind of extended form of ocularcentrism, namely that involved in the idea that agreements over norms can be undermined by deeper disagreements in moral, social, and political perspective and that the process of coming to share this kind of perspective has less to do with arguments than with the cultivation of perception and sensibility (*Bildung*) exemplified by an "aesthetic education."

Still, these claims seem to indicate that we may have come full circle in our reflections. The danger that Habermas originally saw in Gadamer's hermeneutics involved its inability to grasp possible distortions in hermeneutic understanding or consensus itself, insofar as hermeneutics remains on the level of meaning and ignores the conditions that may distort the process of reaching understanding. Jay claims that attention to these conditions requires some reliance on scientific methods of observation. Habermas, in contrast, seems to rely on a kind of listening informed by a theory of systematically distorted communication, on the one hand, and a standard of undistorted communication, on the other. But if we now contrast this communicative standard to a kind of moral and social perspective and if we emphasize the role of a form of moral education modeled on the aesthetic, then we seem to encounter just the problem Habermas tries to avoid, namely: how might we monitor what we may come to "see"? Might the horizon we inhabit at the end of our hermeneutic education not be more limiting than the one we inhabited at the start?

At times, Habermas seems to subject aesthetic criticism itself to the conditions of practical discourse. Thus he insists that value standards that fail to conform to wider community standards are irrational unless they have the "innovative" character of art;[28] elsewhere he writes that even an individual's own interpretation of his or her needs is "open to a revision process in which *all* participate";[29] and in *Legitimation Crisis,* he claims that the point of practical discourse is to transform subjective desires into generalizable ones.[30] In these passages, practical discourse is not simply a more universalistic mode of argumentation than is aesthetic criticism; it seems to trespass on the territory of aesthetic criticism by claiming itself as the means of transforming particular sensibilities, need-interpretations, and desires into universal ones. The point here seems to be that we can rely on the validity of our values, perceptions, and sensibility only if they pass the test of universalizability.

Habermas's argument for this position follows George Herbert Mead. Our individual sensibilities and perceptions are never purely individual, but are the result of our upbringing, heritage, and tradition. Hence, although we might see things in ways that differ from the way others do in the community to which we belong, the community already participates in the formation of our identity, and the parameters for our differences are themselves established by the language we speak and the cultural context in which we mature. By submitting our values and vision to the conditions of agreement in practical discourse, we are therefore only acknowledging the intersubjective dimensions those values and that vision already possess:

> Needs are interpreted in the light of cultural values and since these are always components of an intersubjectively shared tradition, the revision of need-interpreting values cannot be a matter over which the individual monologically disposes.[31]

Still, while we may not monologically dispose over our horizons and values, it is not clear that we can learn to renounce or expand them through practical discourse alone. We may not be solely responsible for our evaluative perspectives. But this does not mean that we can be simply *argued* out of them any more than we can be argued out of our heritage and experience themselves. With the notion of aesthetic criticism, Habermas seems to recognize that we also need a form of education that can enlarge the scope and depth of our vision, a form of education that can help us see our experience and heritage differently, just as we come to see the value or beauty of a work of art differently. The question returns: how might we check on the direction of this difference?

If, in contrast to Jay, we take Habermas as the advocate of a communicative reason and Gadamer as the advocate of the importance of social and moral perception, then the debate between the two seems to present us with a dilemma. On the one hand, Habermas's discourse ethics offers an ideal of consensus and political will-formation that tries to introduce reason into our social disputes by moving beyond a reliance on perspective and vision to develop a reliance on rational argumentation. The suspicion persists, however, that if we cannot come to see things in similar ways, our surface agreements on moral norms will be undermined by more fundamental disagreements having to do with the interpretation of the moral situation and the application of the moral norms. On the other hand, Gadamer's hermeneutics suggests a model of consensus and political will-formation that depends upon our coming to see things in similar ways and that appeals, therefore, to a fusion of horizons. The suspicion persists here, however, that horizons may be fused in ways that limit our vision and restrict future possibilities for expanding it. The dilemma, then, is that if we follow Habermas and abandon vision for the force of the better argument, our rational agreement on norms may be undermined by deeper divisions in evaluative perspective, while if we follow Gadamer and emphasize an education modeled on the aesthetic, we may come to an agreement that is simply obscene. Should we move, then, in the direction of combining the two by looking for standards of reasoned judgment within the process of fusing perceptions and sensibilities?

In my view, this third option might lead us to emphasize some sort of hermeneutic conversation. On the one hand, the goals of such conversation is that of a mutual education of our perceptions and sensibilities; we hope to gain increased capacities for moral insight, perception, and perspective from one another, just as we hope to gain aesthetic insight and perception from artists and art historians. On the other hand, we take from Habermas and from the critique of ideology in general an awareness that this mutual education can be systematically distorted by social and economic factors that operate behind its back. Consequently, we grant the importance of theoretically informed investigations into the sources of distortion and require of the aesthetic learning processes sought by hermeneutic conversation the same conditions of symmetry and equality that Habermas requires of practical discourse. These conditions may no longer lead to a collective and binding interpretation of needs; nor do they preclude differences in both our normative and our evaluative perspectives. But they do allow us to wonder how certain members of our society would *see* certain situations if constraints, for example on sexism, racism and the like, were no longer operative; and they allow us to pause, at least, before we take a college administrator's blind adherence to the rules as seriously as he does himself.

NOTES

1. Martin Jay, "Scopic Regimes of Modernity" in *Vision and Visuality, Discussions in Contemporary Culture 2*, ed. Hal Foster (Seattle: Bay Press, 1988); "The Rise of Hermeneutics and the Crisis of Ocularcentrism," in *Poetics Today*, vol. 9, no. 2 (1988); and "Ideology and Ocularcentrism: Is There Anything Behind the Mirror's Tain?" in Charles C. Lemert, ed., *Intellectuals and Politics: Social Theory in a Changing World* (Sage Publications, 1991).

2. See Jay, "Scopic Regimes of Modernity," p. 1.

3. Jay, "The Rise of Hermeneutics," p. 4.

4. Ibid., p. 7.

5. Jay, "Ideology and Ocularcentrism," p. 153.

6. Ibid., p. 151.

7. Theodore Abel, "The Operation called *Verstehen,*" in Fred Dallmayr and Thomas McCarthy, eds. *Understanding and Social Inquiry* (Notre Dame: Notre Dame University Press, 1977), p. 83.

8. Ibid., p. 84.

9. For an account of Zande witchcraft practices, see E. E. Evans-Prichard, *Witchcraft, Oracles and Magic Among the Azande* (Oxford: Oxford University Press, 1937). For an account of Tibetan legal practices see Rebecca French, "The Golden Yoke, A Legal Ethnography of Tibet Pre-1959" (Ph.D. diss., Yale University, 1990).

10. Jürgen Habermas, *Zur Logik der Sozialwissenschaften* (Frankfurt: Suhrkamp, 1970), p. 144.

11. See Peter Winch, "Understanding a Primitive Society," in *Understanding and Social Inquiry,* pp. 159–188.

12. Charles Taylor, "Interpretation and the Sciences of Man," in *Philosophical Papers 2, Philosophy and the Human Sciences* (Cambridge: Cambridge University Press, 1985), p. 54.

13. Habermas, "The Hermeneutic Claim to Universality" in *Contemporary Hermeneutics,* ed. Josef Bleicher (Routledge and Kegan Paul: London, 1980), p. 191.

14. Ibid., p. 194.

15. Ibid., p. 205.

16. Habermas, "Justice and Solidarity: On the Discussion Concerning Stage 6," in Thomas E. Wren, ed., *The Moral Domain: Essays on the Ongoing Discussion Between Philosophy and the Social Sciences* (Cambridge, Mass.: MIT Press, 1990), p. 235.

17. Habermas, "Diskursethik: Notizen zu einem Begrundungsprogramm," in *Moralbewusstsein und Kommunikatives Handeln* (Frankfurt: Suhrkamp, 1983), pp. 97–100.

18. Habermas, "Moralität und Sittlichkeit," in Wolfgang Kuhlmann, ed., *Moralität und Sittlichkeit* (Frankfurt: Suhrkamp, 1986), p. 18.

19. Habermas, *Legitimation Crisis,* trans. Thomas McCarthy (Boston: Beacon Press, 1973), p. 113.

20. See Habermas, "Justice and Solidarity," p. 50.

21. Habermas, "Moralität und Sittlichkeit," pp. 27–28.

22. See Hans-Georg Gadamer, *Truth and Method* (New York: Seabury Press, 1975), pp. 274–305.

23. Habermas, "Moralität und Sittlichkeit," p. 26.

24. Ibid., p. 26.

25. Habermas, *The Theory of Communicative Action,* trans. Thomas McCarthy (Boston: Beacon Press, 1984), p. 20.

26. Ibid.
27. Gadamer, *Truth and Method,* p. 272.
28. Habermas, *The Theory of Communicative Action,* p. 17.
29. Habermas, "Justice and Solidarity," p. 49.
30. Habermas, *Legitimation Crisis,* p. 109.
31. Habermas, "Diskursethik," p. 78.

TWELVE

Dream World of Mass Culture

Walter Benjamin's Theory of Modernity and the Dialectics of Seeing

Susan Buck-Morss

I

The Paris arcades, or *passages,* built in the early nineteenth century, were the earliest *ur*-shopping malls. They provided the central image for Walter Benjamin's major work, the *Passagen-Werk,* a study that remained unwritten and in fragments at the time of his suicide in 1940. These fragments—an enormous compendium of research notes and commentary— suggest a critical theory of modernity based on a materialist philosophy which, because it is concentrated in the experience of vision, can perhaps best be described as a "dialectics of seeing."

Benjamin saw in the Paris arcades "the original temple of commodity capitalism," all of the characteristics of commodity culture in embryonic form.[1] "Arcades—they beamed out onto the Paris of the Second Empire like fairy grottoes."[2] During the Second Empire of Napoleon III, this urban phantasmagoria burst out of the narrow confines of the original arcades, disseminating throughout Paris, where commodity display achieved ever grander, ever more pretentious forms. The passages "are the precursors of the department stores."[3] The phantasmagoria of display reached its apogee in the international expositions.

Wide-spanning glass windows originated in the arcades, as did window-shopping as the activity of the flaneur. But here display had not been a financial end in itself. The shops full of "novelties" and the pleasure establishments depended on a public clientele of the well-to-do. At world's fairs, in contrast, the commerce in commodities was not more significant than their phantasmagoric function as "folk-festivals" of capitalism whereby mass entertainment itself became big business. The international fairs were the origins of the "pleasure industry [*Vergnügungs-industrie*]," which

> refined and multiplied the varieties of reactive behavior of the masses. It thereby prepares the masses for adapting to advertisements. The connection between the advertising industry and world expositions is thus well-founded.[4]

At the fairs the crowd was conditioned to the principle of advertisements: "Look, but don't touch," and taught to derive pleasure from the spectacle alone.

There were 80,000 exhibitors at Paris's 1855 fair. In 1867, the fair's 15 million visitors included 400,000 French workers to whom free tickets had been distributed, while foreign workers were housed at French government expense. Proletarians were encouraged by the authorities to make the "pilgrimage" to these shrines of industry, to view on display the wonders that their own class had produced but could not afford to own, or to marvel at machines that would displace them. In the late nineteenth century, the world exposition took on an additional meaning. Not only did it provide a utopian fairyland that evoked the wonder of the masses. Each successive exposition was called upon to give visible "proof" of historical progress toward the realization of these utopian goals, by being more monumental, more spectacular than the last.

This physical transformation of urban space gave material form to the utopian dreams of the bourgeois Enlightenment the century before. The eighteenth century *philosophes* challenged the theological position that the heavenly and earthly cities were contradictory extremes, one full of sin and suffering, the other a place of redemption and eternal bliss. It called on human beings to use their own, God-given reason to create the "heavenly" city here and now. Material happiness was to be a basic goal for its construction. The industrial revolution seemed to make possible this practical realization of paradise. In the nineteenth century, capital cities throughout Europe, and ultimately throughout the world, were dramatically transformed into glittering showcases, displaying the promise of the new industry and technology for a heaven-on-earth—and no city glittered more brilliantly than Paris.

Urban brilliance and luxury were not new in history, but secular, public access to them was. The splendor of the modern city could be experienced by everyone who strolled its boulevards and parks, or visited its department stores, museums, art galleries, and national monuments. Paris, a "looking-glass city," dazzled the crowd but at the same time deceived it. The City of Light, it erased night's darkness—first with gas lanterns, then with electricity, then neon lights—in the space of a century. The City of Mirrors—in which the crowd itself became a spectacle—it reflected the image of people as consumers rather than producers, keeping the class relations of production virtually invisible on the looking-glass's other side.

Benjamin described the spectacle of Paris as a "phantasmagoria"—a magic-lantern show of optical illusions, rapidly changing size and blending into one another. Marx had used the term "phantasmagoria" to describe the deceptive appearance of commodities as "fetishes" in the market-place. The *Passagen-Werk* entries cite the relevant passages from *Capital* on the fetish-character of commodities, describing how exchange value obfuscates the source of the value of commodities in productive labor.[5] But for Benjamin, whose point of departure was a philosophy of historical experience rather than an economic analysis of capital, the key to the new urban phantasmagoria was not so much the commodity-in-the-market as the commodity-on-display, where exchange value no less than use value lost practical meaning, and purely representational value came to the fore. Moreover, when newness became a fetish, history itself became a manifestation of the commodity form.

Panoramas were a common attraction in the arcades, providing sweeping views that unrolled before the spectators, giving them the illusion of moving through the world at an accelerated rate. The experience corresponded to that of moving along a street of commodity display-windows. The *Arcades* project takes the reader on a "panoramic" tour of the *Urforms* of the phantasmagoria of progress which Benjamin unearthed in his (at the time very original) research. Following a principle of panoramic representation, the *Arcades* project provides a sense of that false, fetishized construction of history which Benjamin sought to interrupt with his use of critical, "dialectical" images.

II

With the concept of the "dialectical image," Benjamin consciously placed himself in close proximity not only to the Surrealists, but to the Baroque emblemists as well. The *Passagen-Werk*'s pictorial representations of ideas are undeniably modeled after those emblem books of the seventeenth century that had widespread appeal as perhaps the first genre of mass-publication. The gambler and the flaneur in the arcades project personify the empty time of modernity; the whore is an image of the commodity-form; decorative mirrors and bourgeois interiors are emblematic of bourgeois subjectivism; dust and wax-figures are signs of history's motionlessness; mechanical dolls are emblematic of workers' existence under industrialism; the store cashier is perceived "as living image, as allegory of the cash-box."[6] But, for Benjamin, the idea of "dialectical images" went beyond that of allegory. These images were to provide a critical understanding of modernity by juxtaposing, "stereoscopically," images of two time dimensions, his own world and its nineteenth-century origins, according to the cognitive principles of montage. Nineteenth-century objects were to be made visible as the originary, *Urphenomena* of the present. Thus, every assumption of progress or continuous development must be scrupulously rejected: "In order for a piece of the past to be touched by present actuality, there must exist no continuity between them."[7]

Benjamin noted: "'Construction' presupposes 'destruction.'"[8] Historical objects are first constituted in being "blasted" out of the historical continuum.[9] They have a "monadological structure," into which "all the forces and interests of history enter on a reduced scale."[10] Within these "small, singular moments the crystal of the total event is to be discovered."[11] "Truth . . . is bound to a temporal nucleus which is lodged in both the known and the knower."[12] In a tension-filled constellation with the present, this "temporal nucleus" becomes politically charged, polarized "dialectically," as "a force-field, in which the conflict between its fore- and after-history plays itself out."[13]

As fore-history, the objects are prototypes, *Urphenomena* that can be recognized as precursors of the present, no matter how distant or estranged they now appear. Benjamin implies that if the fore-history of an object reveals its possibility (including its utopian potential), its after-history is what, as an object of natural history, it has in fact become. Both are legible within the "monadological structure" of the historical object that has been "blasted free" of history's continuum. In the traces left by the object's after-history, the conditions of its decay and the manner of its cultural transmission, the utopian images of past objects can be read in the present as truth. It is the forceful confrontation of the fore- and after-life of the object that makes it "actual" in the political sense—as "presence of mind" (*Geistesgegenwart*)—and it is not progress but "actualization" in which *Ur*-history culminates.

"Thus, as a flashing image, recognizable now by the present [*im Jetzt der Erkennbarkeit*], the past is to be held fast."[14] Benjamin was counting on the shock of this recognition, in which history appears as a "constellation of danger."[15] Knowledge of the past is to place "the present in a critical condition" in order to jolt the dreaming collective into a political "awakening."[16] The presentation of the historical object within a charged force-field of past and present that produces political electricity in a "lightning-flash" of truth, is the "dialectical image."[17] Unlike Hegel's logic, it is "dialectics at a standstill":[18]

Where thought comes to a standstill in a constellation saturated with tensions, there appears the dialectical image. It is the caesura in the movement of thought. Its positioning, of course, is in no way arbitrary. In a word, it is to be sought at the point where the tension between the dialectical oppositions is the greatest. The dialectical image . . . is identical to the historical object; it justifies blasting the latter out of the continuum of history's course.[19]

Benjamin summarizes: "Re: the basic theory of historical materialism":

(1) The historical object is that for which the act of knowledge is carried out as its "rescue." (2) History decomposes into images, not into narratives. (3) Wherever a dialectical process is effected, we are dealing with a monad. (4) The materialist representation of history entails an immanent critique of the concept of progress. (5) Historical materialism supports its procedure on the foundation of experience, common sense, presence of mind, and the dialectic.[20]

All of this the "dialectical image" was to accomplish. "Common sense" (*gesunder Menschenverstand*) was not a simple, self-evident matter of reading meaning out of empirically given surfaces, specifically because the cognitive experience provided by the dialectical image was one of historical time as well as (or by means of) extension in space.

As an immediate, quasi-mystical apprehension, the dialectical image was intuitive. As a philosophical "construction," it was not. Benjamin's laborious and detailed study of past texts, his careful inventory of the fragmentary parts he gleaned from them, the planned use of these in deliberately constructed "constellations" were all sober, self-reflective procedures, which, he believed, were necessary in order to make visible a picture of truth that the fictions of conventional history-writing covered over. This debunking of fiction was in the spirit of the Enlightenment:

The entire ground must for once be reclaimed for reason, and cleared of the underbrush of delusion and myth. This is to be accomplished here for the nineteenth century.[21]

But it was Enlightenment in the era of fascism, pursued by the exiled thinker in a hostile intellectual world, against the tide of nihilism and irrationalism. Benjamin's description of critical reason differs markedly from that which had been articulated in the Enlightenment's sunnier days:

To reclaim those areas where formerly only delusion has grown. To forge ahead with the whetted axe of reason, and looking neither left nor right, so that one does not fall victim to the horrors beckoning from the depths of the primeval forest [*Urwald*].[22]

III

Benjamin's comments regarding the method of the *Passagen-Werk* were surely intended to provide the substance for the epistemological essay that he planned to write as "a separate chapter, either at the end or the beginning" of the work, which would be "put to the test in the material" that comprised the book as a whole.[23] These methodological deliberations are intensely vivid. For that reason they are not easily comprehended. How was this method to be "put to the test" on the historical material that Benjamin had compiled? How are we to understand the "dialectical image" as a form of philosophical representation? Was "dust" such an image?—What about fashion? the prostitute? expositions? commodities? the arcades themselves? Yes, surely. Not as these referents are empirically given, nor even as they are allegorically interpreted as emblematic of commodity society, but as they are dialectically constructed historical objects, politically charged monads, "blasted" out of history's continuum and made "actual" in the present. This construction of historical objects clearly involved the mediation of the author's imagination. The cognitive experience of history, no less than that of the empirical world, required the active intervention of the thinking subject. And yet Benjamin insisted, in accordance with the method of literary montage: "I have nothing to say, only to show."[24] Here, in what appear to be paradoxical extremes in Benjamin's method, is the source of a dilemma in interpretation. Are dialectical images in fact too subjective in their formulation? Or, are they not subjective enough?

The "dialectical image" has as many levels of logic as the Hegelian concept. It is a way of seeing, which crystallizes antithetical elements by providing the axes for their alignment. Benjamin's conception is essentially static (even as the truth which the dialectical image illuminates is historically fleeting), charting philosophical ideas visually within a non-reconciled and transitory field of opposition that can perhaps best be pictured in terms of coordinates of contradictory terms, the "synthesis" of which is not a movement toward resolution, but the point at which their axes intersect. In fact, it is as a simultaneity of crossing axes that the terms *continuity/discontinuity* appear in the very early *Passagen-Werk* notes, in connection with the dialectical "optics" of a modernity that is both ancient and new: they are to be understood as the "fundamental coordinates" of the modern world.[25]

Let us take a moment to develop the notion that coordinates structure Benjamin's thinking in the *Passagen-Werk*. His unfolding of concepts in their "extremes" can be visualized as antithetical polarities of axes which cross each other, revealing the dialectical moments of an "image" at the null-point. It can be argued that a pattern of coordinates functions as the invisible structure of the *Passagen-Werk*'s historical research, enabling the project's seemingly disparate, conceptual elements to cohere. The axes of these coordinates can be designated with the familiar Hegelian polarities: consciousness and reality. If the termini are to be antithetical extremes, we might name those on the axis of reality, *petrified nature/transitory nature,* while in the case of consciousness, the termini would be *dream/waking.* At the null-point where the coordinates intersect, we can place that "dialectical image" which by 1935 stood at the "midpoint" of the project: the *commodity.* Each field of the coordinates can then be said to describe one aspect of the physiognomic appearance of the commodity, showing its contradictory "faces": fetish and fossil; wish-image and ruin. In the positioning of the fields, those under the sign of transitoriness would need to be affirmed. The diagram represents this invisible inner structure of the *Passagen-Werk.*

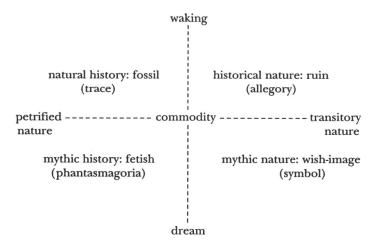

The *fossil* names the commodity in the discourse of *Ur*-history, as the visible remains of the "*Urphenomena.*" Even after his early, metaphoric *Ur*-landscape of consumer-dinosaurs and modern ice-ages recedes, Benjamin sustains the physiognomy of the fossil in the idea of the "trace" (*Spur*), the imprint of objects particularly visible in the plush of bourgeois interiors or the velvet lining of their casings (—here *Ur*-history turns into a detective story, with the historical "trace" a clue). The *fetish* is the key word of the commodity as mythic phantasmagoria, the arrested form of history. It corresponds to the reified form of new nature, condemned to the modern hell of the new as the always-the-same. But this fetishized phantasmagoria is also the form in which the human, socialist potential of industrial nature lies frozen, awaiting the collective political action that could awaken it. The *wish-image* is the transitory dream-form of that potential. In it, archaic meanings return in anticipation of the "dialectic" of awakening. The *ruin*, created intentionally in Baudelaire's allegorical poetry, is the form in which the wish-images of the past century appear, as rubble, in the present. But it refers also to the loosened building blocks (both semantic and material) out of which a new order can be constructed. Note that the figures of the collector, the rag-picker, and the detective wander through the fields of the fossil and ruin, while the fields of action of the prostitute, the gambler, and the flaneur are those of wish-images, and of the fetish as their phantasmagoric form. Haussmann builds the new phantasmagoria; Grandville represents it critically. Fourier's fantasies are wish-images, anticipations of the future expressed as dream-symbols; Baudelaire's images are ruins, failed material expressed as allegorical objects.

This whole elaborate structure of the *Passagen-Werk* was mediated by the temporal axis connecting the nineteenth century to Benjamin's "present," a dimension which, by transforming emblematic representation into a philosophy of history and historical image into political education, was to provide dialectical images with their explosive charge.

IV

Dialectical images were to reveal the truth of modernity, at once redemptively, as the expression of utopian longing, and critically, as the failure to fulfill that longing. This double interpretation involved a fusion of Marxism and theology. Yet the theological intent was to remain invisible, while the *visible* theoretical armature was a secular, socio-psychological theory of modernity as a dreamworld, in which dialectical images were to provide the impetus for a collective "awakening"—revolutionary class-consciousness. In his commentary in the *Passagen-Werk*, Benjamin went quite far in developing these ideas as he struggled to provide for himself a theoretical base which would support, nontheologically, the project's increasingly elaborate construction. His attempt was not entirely successful. The socio-psychological theory assembles elements of Surrealism and Proust, Marx and Freud with notions of historical generations and childhood cognition in a construct that is bound together more by literary than logical means. Yet the quality of historical experience which Benjamin was trying to capture in this theoretical montage *is* conveyed, and it is vital to his project. Moreover, the theory is unique in its approach to modern society, because it takes mass culture seriously not merely as the source of the phantasmagoria of false consciousness, but as the source of collective energy to overcome it.

Based on the writings of Max Weber, it has become a shibboleth in social theory that the essence of modernity is the demythification and disenchantment of the social world. In contrast, and in keeping with the Surrealist vision, Benjamin's central argument in the *Passagen-Werk* was that under conditions of capitalism, industrialization had brought about a *re*enchantment of the social world, and through it, a "reactivation of mythic powers."[26] Weber's thesis was based on the triumph of abstract, formal reason in the eighteenth and nineteenth centuries as the organizing principle of structures of production, markets, state bureaucracies, and also cultural forms like music and law. Benjamin would not have challenged these observations. But if social and cultural institutions had become rationalized, in its form this process nevertheless allowed content to be delivered up to very different forces. Underneath the surface of increasing systematic rationalization, on an unconscious "dream"-level, the new urban-industrial world had become fully reenchanted. Hence, Benjamin's *Arcades* project was to practice a dialectics of seeing that would enable people to wake up from that dream. In the modern city, as in the *Ur*-forests of another era, the "threatening and alluring face" of myth was everywhere alive.[27] It peered out of wall posters advertising "toothpaste for giants."[28] It whispered its presence in the most rationalized urban plans that, "with their uniform streets and endless rows of buildings, have realized the dreamed-of architecture of the ancients: the labyrinth."[29]

In the early nineteenth century, German Romantics, in protest against Enlightenment rationality, had called for a rebirth of mythology, and what Schelling termed a new, "universal symbolism," based on the "things of nature," which "both signify and are."[30] By the twentieth century, Benjamin was saying, the "new nature" of industrial culture had generated all the mythic power for a "universal symbolism" these Romantics might have desired. But Romanticism had falsely assumed that art would be the motor-force for a regeneration of mythology, rather than the creativity of industrialism, which was largely anonymous, and increasingly tied to technical skills. The Romantics wanted to root their "new mythology" in preindustrial, traditional culture. Benjamin rejected totally the social conservatism that by his own era volkish theories had assumed. The Surrealists also spoke of a "new mythology"—and got the matter straight. Rather than looking to folk culture for inspiration or, as with neoclassicism, tacking the symbols of ancient myths onto present forms, they viewed the constantly changing new nature of the industrial-urban landscape as itself marvelous and mythic.

A debunking irreverence toward traditional cultural values was fundamental to Surrealist humor. Whether the most-up-to-date banalities of
daily life are infused with the aura of the ancients, or whether the ancients are themselves brought up-to-date, the result is to bring myth, concrete nature, and history together in such a way that myth's claim to express transcendent, eternal truth is undermined—as in the logic that
leads from this claim to conservative or reactionary politics. Benjamin
comments: "Surrealism is the death of the last century through farce."[31]
But there is more to Surrealism's "new mythology" than the shock of
humor. If the modernist sentiment trivializes that which is conventionally
honored, the reverse is true as well: the trivial can become an object of
reverence. For Louis Aragon's peasant, the miraculous emanates from
the most mundane phenomena: a furrier shop, a high-hat, an electro-
scope with gold leaves, a hairdresser's display.[32]

If Aragon sees the modern world as mythic, he does not order this vision into a mythological system that would explain (and hence legitimate) the given. Rather, Aragon is recording a fact that the theory of instrumental rationality represses: Modern reality in this still-primitive
stage of industrialism *is* mythic, and to bring this to consciousness in no
way eliminates the possibility of a critique, for which, indeed, it is the
prerequisite.

V

Benjamin's enthusiastic response to Aragon did not prevent him from
recognizing, from the start, the dangers of Surrealism as a model for his
own work. Surrealists intentionally put themselves in a dream-state of
mind in order to record the images of what modern reality had become.
They reveled in this dream experience, which, for all their public display
of it, belonged to an individual, private world, wherein action had anar-
chistic political implications. Benjamin's insistence that the dream is, first
of all, historical, and second, always a collective phenomenon contrasted
significantly with their conception. This "dreaming collective" was, admittedly, "unconscious" in a double sense; on the one hand, because of
its distracted dreaming state, and on the other, because it was unconscious of itself, composed of atomized individuals, consumers who imagined their commodity-dreams to be uniquely personal (despite all objective evidence to the contrary), and who experienced their membership in
the collectivity only in an isolated, alienating sense, as an anonymous
component of the crowd.

Here was a fundamental contradiction in capitalist-industrial culture.
A mode of production that privileged private life and based its conception of the subject on the isolated individual had created brand-

new forms of social existence—urban spaces, architectural forms, mass-produced commodities, and infinitely reproduced "individual" experiences—that engendered identities and conformities in people's lives, but not social solidarity, no new level of collective *consciousness* concerning their commonality, and thus no way of waking up from the dream in which they were enveloped. Aragon unwittingly expressed this contradiction when he represented the new mythic experiences as individual even when they were sparked by common objects; his writing reflected the illusory experience of mass existence, rather than transcending it. Benjamin's goal was not to represent the dream, but to dispel it: dialectical images were to draw dream-images into an awakened state, and awakening was synonymous with historical knowledge:

> In the dialectical image, the past of a particular epoch . . . appears before the eyes of . . . [a particular, present epoch] in which humanity, rubbing its eyes, recognizes precisely this dream *as* a dream. It is in this moment that the historian takes upon himself the task of dream interpretation.[33]

Surrealists became "stuck in the realm of dreams."[34] Benjamin's intent, "in opposition to Aragon," was "not to let oneself be lulled sleepily within the 'dream' or 'mythology,'" but "to penetrate all this by the dialectic of awakening."[35] Such awakening began where the Surrealists and other avant-garde artists too often stopped short, because in rejecting cultural tradition they closed their eyes to history as well. Against the "mythology" of Aragon, the *Passagen-Werk* "is concerned with dissolving mythology into the space of history."[36]

It was crucial to Benjamin's conception that this "space of history" referred not only to the previous century, but to the ontogenetic, "natural" history of childhood—specifically, the childhood of his own generation, born at the century's close. In order to understand Benjamin's theory of the dreaming collective as source of revolutionary energy, we need to consider the significance of childhood for his theory of cognition. This is a detour that will return us to Surrealism with a clearer awareness of what Benjamin saw as the political potential of this intellectual movement.

VI

Children, according to Benjamin, are less intrigued by the preformed world that adults have created than by its waste products. They are drawn to the apparently valueless, intentionless things:

> In using these things they do not so much imitate the works of adults as bring together, in the artifacts produced in play, materials of widely differing kinds in a new intuitive relationship.[37]

Benjamin's cognitive approach to the discarded, overlooked phenomena of the nineteenth century was not different. No modern thinker, with the exception of Jean Piaget, took children as seriously as did Benjamin in developing a theory of cognition. Gershom Scholem attested to the significance of children for Benjamin and pointed out that he took seriously the cognitive process of remembering his own childhood.[38] Imagery from the child's world appears so persistently throughout Benjamin's opus that the omission of a serious discussion of its theoretical significance in practically all commentaries on Benjamin is remarkable—a symptom, perhaps, of precisely the repression of childhood and its cognitive modes which he considered a problem of the utmost political significance.

For both Piaget and Benjamin, children's cognition is a stage so completely overcome that to the adult it appears almost inexplicable. Piaget was content to see childhood thinking disappear. His own thinking reflected, on the axis of ontogenetic development, that assumption of history-as-progress which Benjamin considered the trademark of bourgeois false consciousness. Predictably, Benjamin's own interest was not in the sequential development of stages of an abstract, formal reason, but rather in what is *lost* along the way. What Benjamin found in the child's consciousness, badgered out of existence by bourgeois education and so crucial to redeem (albeit in new form), was precisely the unsevered connection between perception and action which distinguished revolutionary consciousness in adults. This connection is not causal in the behavioralist sense of a stimulus-response reaction. Instead it is an active, creative form of mimesis, involving the ability to make correspondences by means of spontaneous fantasy. Perception and active transformation are the two poles of children's cognition: "Every child's gesture is a creative impulse which corresponds exactly to the receptive one."[39]

Abstracting from all historical specificity, Piaget's experiments tested for the universal and predictable response, privileging precisely that abstract-formal rationality which Weber saw as the hallmark of modern reason. Benjamin was more interested in the creative spontaneity of response which bourgeois socialization destroyed. Piaget's theory treated cognition tied to action as only the most primitive cognitive form (—in the preverbal, sensory-motor period of child development), and ignored mimetic cognition once the child acquired language. In Piaget's tests, the child's fantastic play, the constitution of merely possible worlds, was likely to be registered as cognitive error. For Benjamin, in contrast, the primordial nature of motor reactions was a reason to pay attention to them. Evidence of the "mimetic faculty," they are the source of a language of gestures which Benjamin considered more basic to cognition than conceptual language.[40] Benjamin's idea of an "experiment" was to watch children's gestures in painting, dance, and particularly theatre, which allowed an "untamed release of children's fantasy."[41]

Children's cognition has revolutionary power because it is tactile, hence tied to action, and because, rather than accepting the given meaning of things, children get to know objects by laying hold of them and using them creatively, releasing from them new possibilities of meaning. Bourgeois socialization suppresses this activity: parroting back the "correct" answer, looking without touching, solving problems "in the head," sitting passively, learning to do without optical cues—these acquired behaviors go against the child's grain.[42] It might follow, moreover, that the triumph of such cognition in adults signals at the same time their defeat as revolutionary subjects. But, so long as there are children, this defeat can never be complete. Thus Benjamin avoided the pessimistic conclusion to which Adorno was led when he described the "extinction of the ego" as the horrifying result of history's "progress."[43] Benjamin's theory acknowledged that the relationship between consciousness and society on a historical level was interspersed with another dimension, the child's development, in which there is a relationship between consciousness and reality that has its own history. In children, the capacity for revolutionary transformation is present from the start. Hence, all children are "representatives of Paradise."[44]

Benjamin's appreciation of childhood cognition did not amount to a romanticization of childhood innocence. On the contrary, he believed that only people who are allowed to live out their childhood really grow up—and growing up is clearly the desired goal. Adults who observe children's behavior can learn to rediscover a mode of cognition that has deteriorated phylogenetically, and in the adult has sunk into the unconscious. A very brief piece, "On the Mimetic Faculty," written by Benjamin in 1933 and valued by him highly as a new, materialist formulation of his theory of language, speaks to this point precisely:

> Nature produces similarities. One has only to think of [the] mimickry [of, e.g., insects on leaves]. But the highest talent in producing similarities belongs to human beings. The gift of seeing similarities is merely a rudiment of the formerly powerful drive to make oneself similar, to act mimetically. Perhaps there is no higher human function that is not decisively determined, at least in part, by the mimetic capacity.
>
> This capacity, however, has a history, and indeed in a phylogenetic as well as an ontogenetic sense. For the latter, play is in many respects the schooling. Children's play is permeated everywhere by mimetic forms of behavior; and its realm is in no way limited to what one person can mimic about another. The child not only plays shopkeeper or teacher, but also windmill and railroad train.[45]

The development of mimetic cognitive skills has not been a constant in history. The oldest cognitive apparatuses of magical correspondences and analogies were clearly based on this skill. Indeed, as the practice whereby the expressive element in objects is brought to speech, human language is itself mimetic and magical in origin. Benjamin suggests that what appears to be the "decay of this capacity" in the "signworld (*Merkwelt*) of modern man" may be, rather, a new stage in its "transformation."[46] He holds open the possibility of a future development of mimetic expression the potentialities for which are far from exhausted. Nor are they limited to verbal language—as the new technologies of camera and film clearly demonstrate. These technologies provide human beings with unprecedented perceptual acuity, out of which, Benjamin believed, a less magical, more scientific form of the mimetic faculty was developing in his own era. He noted in the Artwork essay that the camera arrests the flow of perception and captures the most subtle physical gestures. "Through it we first experience an optical unconscious, as in psychoanalysis we first experience the instinctual unconscious."[47] Film educates our mimetic powers: "Within the enlargement, space is stretched out; within slow motion, movement expands," revealing "entirely new structural formations of matter":

> Thus it becomes clear that a different nature speaks to the camera than to the naked eye—different above all in this, that in place of space interwoven with the consciousness of human beings, one is presented with a space unconsciously interwoven.[48]

Now for the first time an analysis of this "unconsciously interwoven" space is possible. Like a surgeon, the cameraman "operatively penetrates into" the material, subjecting the actor's performance to a series of "optical tests."[49] Moreover, and of political importance, the world which opens up to the camera provides knowledge relevant to acting in it:

> Through close-ups of what it inventories, through accentuating the hidden details of props that for us are familiar objects, through exploration of banal milieus under the genial guide of the lens, film on the one hand increases our insight into the necessities that rule our lives, and on the other hand insures for us an immense and unexpected field of action.[50]

It is in this way that technological *re*production can give back to humanity that very capacity for experience which technological *production* threatens to take away. If industrialization has caused a crisis in perception due to the speeding-up of time and the fragmentation of space, film shows a healing potential by slowing down time and, through montage, constructing "synthetic realities" as new spatio-temporal orders, wherein "fragmented images" are brought together "according to a new law."[51] Both the assembly line and the urban crowd bombard the senses with disconnected images and shocklike stimuli. In a state of constant distraction the consciousness of the collective acts like a shock-absorber, registering sense impressions without really experiencing them: shocks are "intercepted, parried by consciousness," in order to prevent a traumatic effect.[52] Film provides the audience with a new capacity—to study modern existence from the position of an expert. The printed word shows itself more vulnerable in contrast:

> Printing, having found in the book a refuge in which to lead an autonomous existence, is pitilessly dragged out onto the street by advertisements . . . [which] force the printed word entirely into the dictatorial perpendicular. And before a child of our time finds his way clear to opening a book, his eyes have been exposed to such a blizzard of changing, colorful, conflicting letters that the chances of his penetrating the archaic stillness of the book are slight. Locust swarms of print, which already eclipse the sun of what is taken for intellect by city dwellers, will grow thicker with each succeeding year.[53]

Children instinctively mimic objects as a means of mastering their experiential world. Psychoanalytic theory tells us that the neurotic symptom similarly imitates a traumatic event in an (unsuccessful) attempt at psychic defense. Benjamin was suggesting that the new mimetic techniques could instruct the collective to employ this capacity effectively, not only as a defense against the trauma of industrialization, but as a means of reconstructing the capacity for experience that had been shattered by the process. The products of culture already showed signs of the development of this counterforce. Benjamin speculated:

> Perhaps the daily sight of a moving crowd once presented the eye with a spectacle to which it first had to adopt. . . . Then the assumption is not impossible that, having mastered this task, the eye welcomed opportunities to confirm its possession of its new ability. The method of impressionist painting, whereby the picture is assembled through a riot of flecks of color, would then be a reflection of experience with which the eye of a big-city dweller has become familiar.[54]

It is not surprising that Benjamin praised Charlie Chaplin's film performances on the same grounds. Chaplin rescued the capacity for experience by mimicking the fragmentation that threatened it.

> What is new in Chaplin's gestures: He breaks apart human motions of expression into a series of the smallest innervations. Every single one of his movements is put together from a series of hacked-up pieces of motion. Whether one focuses on his walk, on the way [he] handles his cane, or tips his hat—it is always the same jerky sequence of the smallest motions which raises the law of the filmic sequence of images to that of human motor actions.[55]

To recreate the new, technologically-mediated reality mimetically—to bring to human speech its expressive potential—is not to submit to its given forms, but to anticipate the human reappropriation of its power. Moreover (and this is the political point), such practice reestablishes the connection between imagination and physical innervation that in bourgeois culture has been snapped apart. Perception is no longer contemplative, but tied to action. Just this refusal to separate body and mind within cognitive experience characterizes Aragon's imagistic representation in *Le paysan de Paris*. Just this insistence that action is the sister of the dream is what Benjamin found irresistibly compelling in Surrealism's political stance. Political space can "no longer be gauged by contemplation." Rather, the intellectual must place him- [or her-] self, "even at the cost of his [or her] own creative development," in the "important points" of an "image-realm" in order to set this realm "into motion." Moreover:

> The collective is also corporeal. And the technological nature which will organize in its behalf, because it is totally real, politically and materially, can only be produced in that image-realm to which we have been acclimatized by profane illumination. Only within it, when body and image-realm so interpenetrate that all revolutionary tension becomes bodily, collective innervation, and all the bodily innervations of the collective become revolutionary discharge, has reality surpassed itself to the extent demanded by the *Communist Manifesto*. For the moment, only the Surrealists have understood the commands that now emanate from that realm.[56]

VII

The *Arcades* project was originally conceived as a "dialectical fairy-scene" (*dialektische Feerie*), so that the *Passagen-Werk* becomes a Marxian retelling of the story of Sleeping Beauty which was concerned with "waking up" from the collective dream of the commodity phantasmagoria. This, for Benjamin, was the "best example of a dialectical overturning."[57] We may note a key passage which locates the source of the dream-world that modern reality had become: "Capitalism was a natural phenomenon with which a new dream sleep fell over Europe, and with it, a reactivation of mythic powers."[58] The arcades, as "houses without exteriors," were themselves "just like dreams."[59] Indeed: "All collective architecture of the nineteenth century provides housing for the dreaming collective": "arcades, winter-gardens, panoramas, factories, wax-figure cabinets, casinos, railroad stations"—as well as museums, apartment interiors, department stores, and public spas.[60] Benjamin resurrects here an image of the body politic, out of fashion in political discourse since the Baroque era, in which the nineteenth-century dream-elements register the collective's vital signs:

The XIX century: a time-space [*Zeitraum*] (a time dream [*Zeit-traum*]) in which individual consciousness maintains itself ever more reflectively, whereas in contrast, the collective consciousness sinks into ever-deeper sleep. But just as the sleeping person (here like someone insane) sets out on the macrocosmic journey through his body, and just as the sounds and sensations of his own insides—which to the healthy, awake person blend together in a surge of health (blood pressure, intestinal movements, heartbeat and muscle sensations)—due to his unprecedently sharpened senses, generate hallucinations or dream-images which translate and explain [these sensations], so it is too with the dreaming collective, which in the arcade sinks into its own innards. This is what we have to pursue, in order to interpret the nineteenth century in fashion and advertisement, building and politics, as the consequence of [the collective's] dream-countenance.61

Benjamin observes: "The first stimulae for awakening deepen sleep."62 He is referring to the kitsch of the end of the century that thickened the dream-state. The proponents of *Jugendstil* rejected kitsch and tried to break out into "free air," but they understood this only as an ideational space, "the artificial brightness and isolation in which advertisements represented their objects": *Jugendstil* was thus only "the dream that one is awake."63 It was Surrealism, with its "radical concept of freedom,"64 that first sounded the rousing alarm; Benjamin's goal, within the "legacy of Surrealism," was to connect the shock of awakening with the discipline of remembering and thereby mobilize the historical objects.65

"With cunning [*mit List*], not without it, we absolve ourselves from the realm of dreams."66 The use of Hegel's term was intentional, but Benjamin's meaning was significantly different. According to Hegel, reason becomes conscious by working its way "with cunning" into history, using the passions and ambitions of unwitting historical subjects. But in Benjamin's dialectical fairy tale, cunning is the capacity, through "awakening," to *out*wit history, which has placed a spell on the dreaming collective, and has kept people *un*conscious.67 Hegel's "cunning of reason" literally deifies history, affirming the myth of progress. For Benjamin, cunning is the trick whereby the human subject gets the better of mythic powers. "Fairy tales," Benjamin wrote in his (1934) essay on Kafka, "are the way of handing down the tradition of victory over the [forces of myth]."68

The "trick" in Benjamin's fairy tale is to interpret out of mass culture's discards a politically empowering knowledge of the collective's own unconscious past. He believed he could do this because it is through such objects that the collective unconscious communicates across generations. New inventions conceived out of the fantasy of one generation, they are received within the childhood experience of another. Now (and this is one of the most intriguing aspects of Benjamin's theory) they enter a second dream-state: "The childhood experience of a generation has much in common with dream experience."[69] We are thus presented with a double dream theory, based on the childhood of an epoch, on the one hand, and that of a generation, on the other. If capitalism has been the source of the historical dream-state, this second one is of ontogenetic origins, and the two axes converge in a unique constellation for each generation. At this intersection between collective history and personal history, between society's dream and the dreams of childhood, the contents of the collective unconscious are transmitted: "Every epoch has this side turned toward dreams—the childlike side. For the preceding century it emerges very clearly in the arcades."[70]

Childhood is not merely the passive receptacle for the historical unconscious. Even the most practical, technical inventions are transformed in accord with its own temporal index, and this entails their reversion from historically specific images into archaic ones. From the child's position the whole span of history, from the most ancient to the most recent past, occurs in mythic time. No history recounts his or her lived experience. All of the past lies in an archaic realm of *Ur*-history. Within the phylogenetic axis, history manifests itself as progress, fashion, and newness. But it is just this that the cognitive experience of childhood reverses. The child's creative perception of objects in fact recollects the historical moment when the new technology was first conceived. "The child can in fact do something of which the adult is totally incapable: 'discover the new anew.'"[71] This discovery *re*invests objects with symbolic meaning and thus rescues for the collective memory their utopian signification.

Slumbering within objects, the utopian wish is awakened by a new generation, which "rescues" it by bringing the old "world of symbols" back to life. Here Benjamin's fairy tale may appear to come close to the theory, posited by Jung, of a collective unconscious containing innate, archetypal symbols. The difference is Benjamin's Marxist sensibility. When the child's fantasy is cathected onto the products of modern production, it reactivates the original promise of industrialism, slumbering in the lap of capitalism, to deliver a humane society out of material abundance. In terms of socialist, revolutionary politics, then, the rediscovery of these *Ur*-symbols in the most modern technological products has an absolutely contemporary relevance—and a politically explosive potential.

The biological task of awakening from childhood becomes a model for a collective, social awakening. But more: In the collective experience of a generation the two converge. The coming-to-consciousness of a generation is a politically empowering moment, historically unique, in which the new generation, in rebellion against the parental world, may awaken not only itself, but the slumbering utopian potential of the epoch. A material history that disenchants the new nature in order to free it from the spell of capitalism, and yet rescues all the power of enchantment for the purpose of social transformation: this was to have been the goal of Benjamin's fairy tale. At the moment of the collective's historical awakening, it was to provide a politically explosive answer to the socio-historical form of the child's question: Where did I come from? Where did modern existence, or more accurately, the images of the modern dream-world come from?

VIII

In his 1936 essay "The Storyteller," Benjamin described the fairy tale as a mode of cultural inheritance that, far from participating in the ideology of class domination, keeps alive the promise of liberation by showing that nature—animals and animated forces—prefers not to be "subservient to myth," but rather, "to be aligned with human beings" against myth.[72] In this sense, merely by rescuing for historical memory Fourier's visions of society, the historian becomes a teller of fairy tales. Fourier's utopian plans, in which nature and humanity are in fact allied, challenge the myth that industrialization had to develop as it has, that is, as a mode of dominating both human beings and the natural world, of which human beings are a part.

Of course, it is not to children that the fairy tale of the *Arcades* is to be told, but to those whose childhood is itself only a dream-memory. These memories are evidence that the "unfinished and commonplace, comforting and silly" world in which we have in fact lived is not without the momentary experience of utopia. At no time did Benjamin suggest that the child's mythic understanding was itself truth. But childhood catches historical objects in a web of meanings so that the grown generation has, subsequently, a psychic investment in them, lending them a higher degree of actuality now than in the past. Moreover—and this was no small part of Benjamin's "trick"—in the presence of the historical objects that populate a city, this generation not only recognizes its own youth, the most recent one, but also an earlier childhood speaks to it. It is thus as a "memory trace" that the discarded object possesses the potential for revolutionary motivation. Benjamin describes

> the two faces of the [*Arcades*] project: One, that which goes from the past into the present and which represents the arcades as precursors; and that which goes from the present into the past, in order to let the revolutionary completion of these "precursors" explode in the present. This [second] direction also understands the sorrowful, fascinated contemplation of the most recent past as its revolutionary explosion.[73]

IX

According to Benjamin, the cognitive axis of social history is necessary because it allows one to "recognize the sea in which we are journeying and the shore from which we pushed off."[74] Moreover, the allegorical, "sorrowful" contemplation of the past underscores the transiency of mythic images. But even within the symbolic, cognitive axis of childhood, Benjamin took great pains to demonstrate that its images were mediated at every point by history. In the *Passagen-Werk* he cited Ernst Bloch's insistence that the unconscious is an "'acquired condition'" in specific human beings.[75] Programmatically, those images of his own childhood which he recorded in the early 1930s were less of people than of those historically specific, urban spaces of turn-of-the-century Berlin which formed the settings for his experiences—parks, department stores, railroad stations, city streets, cafés, and school buildings. They concern as well the material products of industrialism—a wrought-iron door, the telephone, a chocolate-dispensing slot machine, Berlin's own arcades. The world of the modern city appears in these writings as a mythic and magical one in which the child Benjamin "discovers the new anew," and the adult Benjamin recognizes it as a rediscovery of the old.[76] The impulses of the unconscious are thus formed as a result of concrete, historical experiences, and are not (as with Jung's archetypes) biologically inherited.[77]

Benjamin observes that the dialectical "confrontation of the most recent past with the present is something historically new."[78] In fact, the intensification of mythic power in both dream-states is itself a function of history. When capitalism's new dream-sleep fell over Europe, *it* became the cause of a reactivation of mythic powers. Precisely the *city* landscape "confers on childhood memories a quality that makes them at once as evanescent and as alluringly tormenting as half-forgotten dreams."[79] Benjamin describes what has happened to memories in the modern era:

> The worlds of memory replace themselves more quickly, the mythic in them surfaces more quickly and crassly, [and] a totally different world of memory must be set up even faster against them. From the perspective of today's *Ur*-history, this is how the accelerated tempo of technology looks.[80]

By contrast, in the premodern era, collective formations of symbolic meaning were transferred consciously through the narration of tradition, guiding the new generation out of its childhood dream-state. Given modernity's rupture with tradition, this is no longer possible:

> Whereas . . . the traditional and religious upbringing of earlier generations interpreted these dreams for them, the present process of child-rearing

boils down simply to the distraction of children. Proust could appear as a phenomenon only in a generation that had lost all bodily, natural experience of remembering, and, poorer than before, was left to its own devices, and thus could only get a hold of the children's world in an isolated, scattered and pathological fashion.[81]

In a world of objects which changed its face drastically in the course of a generation, parents could no longer counsel their children, who were thus "left to their own devices." These devices can only remain "isolated," indeed "pathological," until they are organized collectively. Benjamin's fairy tale was conceived in response to this need.

The rupture with tradition was irrevocable. Far from lamenting the situation, Benjamin saw precisely here modernity's uniquely revolutionary potential. The traditional manner whereby the new generation was brought out of its childhood dream-world had the effect of perpetuating the social status quo. In contrast, the rupture with tradition freed symbolic powers from conservative restraints and made them available for the task of social transformation, that is, for a break with those social conditions of domination that, consistently, had been the source of tradition. Thus Benjamin insisted: "We must wake up from the world of our parents."[82]

X

Benjamin maintained the double dream theory outlined above at least until 1935, the year he completed his exposé of the *Arcades* project. At this point, the philological situation becomes murky. There are at least six copies of the 1935 exposé, with differences in wording significant enough to have caused the editor to include three of them in the published *Passagen-Werk*. All of these versions refer to the following: dreamworld, utopian wish-images, collective dream-consciousness, generations, and, most emphatically, the conception of dialectical thinking as a historical awakening sparked by the residues of mass culture. Noticeably absent is the image of the slumbering body-politic, as well as any reference to a "dialectical fairy-scene."

In a letter dated 18 August 1935, he explained that he had given up this earlier subtitle because it allowed only an "inexcusably literary" shaping of the material.[83] Did Benjamin give up his theory of the childhood dream-state as well? In the same letter he spoke of the absolute distinction between the *Arcades* project and forms (like *Berliner Kindheit um 1900*) which recounted childhood memories: "The *Ur*-history of the 19th century which is reflected in the gaze of the child playing on its threshold has a much different face than that which it engraves on the map of history."[84] He added that "making this knowledge clear to me" had been "an important function of [writing the exposé]."[85] If not only the too-literary form but also the theoretical content of the original conception had been abandoned, it would be difficult to justify his simultaneous claim, against Adorno's criticisms, that there had been "no word lost" from the original 1927–29 draft of the project. In fact Benjamin had not discarded the early notes and commentary dealing with the dream theory, and never did. Adorno's knowledge of these notes was limited to what Benjamin had read to him in Königstein in 1929. We do not know whether their discussions there included the childhood dream-state. We do know that the absence of it in the exposé was not what Adorno lamented when he accused Benjamin of betraying the early plan. It was the imagery of "negative theology"—the nineteenth-century commodity world as hell—that Adorno missed, not that of childhood and fairy tales.

Ironically, had Benjamin included an elaboration of the theory of the childhood inheritance of the collective dream, he might have warded off another of Adorno's criticisms, that with the "sacrifice of theology" Benjamin had "disenchanted" the idea of dialectical images by psychologizing them, to the point where the entire conception had become "de-dialecticized."[86] The double dream theory was complex and its expression was perhaps indeed "inexcusably literary," but without it, the revolutionary power of "dream images" had to be situated solely within the socio-historical axis, as if these existed ready-made in the actual nineteenth-century (un)conscious of the collective, rather than being created by the specific way the present generation inherited the "failed material" of the past. Adorno argued against the conception of a collective consciousness on Marxist grounds: "It should speak clearly and with sufficient warning that in the dreaming collective there is no room for class differences."[87]

There is no doubt that Benjamin took Adorno's criticisms of the 1935 exposé seriously. There is little doubt that he attempted to stick to his position despite them. The material relating to theoretical questions which he added to the *Passagen-Werk* after 1935 intensified a direction of research he had in fact already begun: to ground the basic premise of his dream-theory—that the nineteenth century was the origin of a collective dream from which an "awakened" present generation could derive revolutionary signification—in the theories of Marx and Freud. Interestingly (and dialectically), he found in Marx a justification for the conception of a collective dream, and in Freud an argument for the existence of class differences within it.

Of course Marx *had* spoken positively of a collective dream, and more than once. After 1935 Benjamin added to his manuscript the well-known quotation from Marx's early writings:

Our motto must . . . be: Reform of consciousness not by means of dogmas, but by analysing the mystical consciousness unclear to itself, whether it appears religiously or politically. It will then become clear that the world has long possessed in the form of a dream something of which it only has to become conscious in order to possess it in reality.[88]

And he chose as the inscription for his file on method (*Konvolut* N) Marx's statement: "'The reform of consciousness consists *only* therein, that one wakes the world . . . out of its dream of itself.'"[89] Benjamin claimed that Marx never intended a direct, causal relationship between substructure and superstructure: "Already the observation that the ideologies of the superstructure reflect [social] relations in a false and distorted form goes beyond this."[90] Freud's dream theory gave a ground for such distortion. Benjamin's direct references to Freudian theory remained limited and quite general. But on this point, even if direct indebtedness cannot be proven, there was a clear consensus. Freud argued that ideas in dreams are fulfillments of "wishes" which, due to ambivalent feelings, appear in censored, hence distorted form. The actual (latent) wish may be almost invisible at the manifest level, and is arrived at only after the dream's interpretation. Thus, a dream is a (disguised) fulfillment of a (suppressed or repressed) wish. If one takes the bourgeois class to be the generator of the collective dream, then the socialist tendencies of that industrialism which it itself created would seem to catch it, unavoidably, in a situation of ambivalent desire. The bourgeoisie desires to affirm that industrial production from which it is deriving profits; at the same time it wishes to deny the fact that industrialism creates the conditions which threaten the continuation of its own class rule.

Precisely this bourgeois class ambivalence is documented by a whole range of quotations which Benjamin included in the *Passagen-Werk* material at all stages of the project. Nineteenth-century utopian writings are the "depository of collective dreams," but they also come to the aid of the ruling class by fetishistically equating technological development with social progress (Saint-Simon). On the manifest level, the future *appears* as limitless progress and continuous change. But on the latent level (the level of the dreamer's true wish), it *expresses* the eternalization of bourgeois class domination.

An early (pre-June 1935) entry to the *Passagen-Werk* questions whether

. . . there could spring out of the repressed economic contents of consciousness of a collective, similarly to what Freud claims for [the] sexual [contents] of an individual consciousness . . . , a form of literature, a fantasy-imagining . . . [as] sublimation . . .[91]

A late formulation describes the ruling class's ambivalence which makes it block the realization of the very utopian dreams it has generated: "The bourgeoisie no longer dares to look in the eye the order of production which it has itself set into motion."[92] The culture of the nineteenth century unleashed an abundance of fantasies of the future, but it was at the same time "a vehement attempt to hold back the productive forces."[93] If on the manifest dream-level, changing fashion is a prefiguring of social transformation, on the latent level it is "a camouflage of very specific desires of the ruling class," a "figleaf" covering up the fact that, to cite Brecht, "'The rulers have a great aversion against violent changes.'"[94] Commodity fetishism (as well as urban "renewal") can be viewed as a textbook case of Freud's concept of displacement: Social relations of class exploitation are displaced onto relations between things, thus concealing the real situation with its dangerous potential for social revolution. It is politically significant that by the late nineteenth century, the bourgeois dream of democracy itself underwent this form of censorship: Freedom was equated with the ability to consume. Benjamin writes that *égalité* developed its own "phantasmagoria," and *la revolution* came to mean "clearance sale" in the nineteenth century.[95]

By the end of the century, the dream, clearly of bourgeois origins (and bourgeois in the latent wish that it expressed), had in fact become "collective," spreading to the working class as well. The mass marketing of dreams within a class system that prevented their realization in anything more than a distorted, dream-symbol form was quite obviously a growth industry. In his earliest notes, Benjamin interpreted "kitsch," the cluttered, aesthetic style of this mass marketing, as bourgeois class guilt, "the overproduction of commodities; the bad conscience of the producers."[96] The goal of course *was* material abundance, which is why the dream functioned legitimately on the manifest level of collective wish-image. But the commodity-form of the dream generated the expectation that the international, socialist goals of mass affluence could be delivered by national, capitalist means, and that expectation was a fatal blow to revolutionary working-class politics.

XI

The childhood of Benjamin's generation belonged to this end-of-the-century era of the first mass-marketing of dreams. Benjamin recalled that his introduction to civic life had been as a consumer. He remembered his "sense of impotence before the city," but also his "dreamy resistance" when out shopping with his mother. If, as has just been argued, Benjamin's theory of the collective dream did not disregard class distinctions, can the same be said of his theory of political awakening?

In his earliest notes, Benjamin indicated that the bourgeoisie who had generated the dream remained trapped within it:

Did not Marx teach us that the bourgeoisie can never come to a fully enlightened consciousness of itself? And if this is true, is one not justified in
connecting the idea of the dreaming collective (i.e., the bourgeois collective) onto his thesis?[97]

And immediately following:

Wouldn't it be possible, in addition, to show from the collected facts with
which this [Arcades] work is concerned how they appear in the process of
the proletariat's becoming self-conscious?[98]

Benjamin never implied that his experience of the city was anything but
class-bound. He admitted:

I never slept on the street in Berlin. . . . Only those for whom poverty or
vice turns the city into a landscape in which they stray from dark till sun-
rise know it in a way denied to me.[99]

And in the *Passagen-Werk*: "What do we know of the streetcorners, curb-
stones, heat, dirt, and edges of the stones under naked soles . . . ?"[100]

The class division was undeniable. Nevertheless, Benjamin felt that
there was a confluence in the *objective* position of intellectuals and artists
as cultural producers and the proletariat as industrial producers, due to
the specific constellation of economic and cultural history. The turn of
the century experienced a cultural "crisis," and close on its heels there
followed the economic one, a "shaking of commodity society" that set off
tremors in the collective dream.[101] Around this historical constellation
the experience of his generation congealed, and well into the 1930s
Benjamin found in it an extremely precarious cause for hope. Thus he
could write to Scholem in 1935: "I believe that [the *Passagen-Werk's*] conception, even if it is very personal in its origins, has as its object the decisive historical interests of our generation."[102]

For the proletariat, the discarded material of nineteenth-century culture symbolized a life that was still unattainable; for the bourgeois intellectual it represented the loss of what once was. Yet for both classes, the
revolution in style brought about by commodity culture was the dream-
form of social revolution—the only form possible within a bourgeois social context. The new generation experienced "the fashions of the most
recent past as the most thorough anti-aphrodisiac that can be imagined."[103] But precisely this was what made them "politically vital," so that
"the confrontation with the fashions of the past generation is an affair of
much greater meaning than has been supposed."[104] The discarded props
of the parental dream-world were material evidence that the phantasmagoria of progress had been a staged spectacle and not reality. At the
same time, as the stuff of childhood memories, these outmoded objects
retained semantic power as symbols. Benjamin commented that for

Kafka, "as only for 'our' generation . . . the horrifying furniture of the beginning of high capitalism was felt as the showplace of its brightest childhood experience."[105] The desire to recapture the lost world of childhood determines a generation's interest in the past. But it is the need of its members as adults that determines their desire to wake up.

XII

It is tempting to interpret Benjamin's *Passagen-Werk* within the context of present-day debates. But it would be misleading to argue either that the *Arcades* project, as a failed attempt, is a last grand effort in the modernist tradition, or that (precisely because of its failure as a complete, totalized form) it is a prototypically postmodern text. To be sure, Benjamin's philosophy departed from the idealism of the modern bourgeois tradition. But he would have just as surely rejected such quintessentially postmodernist philosophic slogans as "the death of the subject," "the emptiness of the sign," "the end of metaphysics," and "the linguistic turn," seeing these thematics as symptoms of a deficient social reality, not in themselves a new and higher stage of philosophical truth. His was a radical reconstruction of materialism that drew its inspiration from premodern theology, nineteenth-century socialist thought, and twentieth-century Surrealism, all three. He brought elements of these discourses together, not as a bricoleur who makes a pastiche out of conflicting traditions, but—almost Platonically—as someone convinced that "truth" lies in the elements themselves.

What was new about his philosophy was that it was a method of *seeing* the world in a certain way. The modernity about which he wrote is a world made visible to us through his eyes. For him, images are the realm not of the imaginary, but of the "real" (a term he would have understood simultaneously in a materialist and a metaphysical fashion). His "dialectics of seeing" is a powerful materialist method of transforming visual perception, one that he believed could compel a collective "awakening" from the soporific effects of mass culture, and inform and inspire revolutionary politics.

While rejecting the Enlightenment view of progress, Benjamin remained true to its utopian goals. In the service of these goals, he believed that philosophy was obliged to engage in a critique of culture. In executing this task, the *Passagen-Werk* provides evidence that for Benjamin it would make no sense to divide the era of capitalist culture into modernist formalism and postmodernist eclecticism, as both these tendencies were there from the start of industrial culture. These cultural forms refer not to chronological eras, but to contending positions in the century-long confrontation between art and technology. If modernism as an aesthetic "style" has expressed utopian and aesthetic form, postmodernism has acknowledged their nonidentity and kept fantasy alive. Each position thus represents a partial truth; each will recur "anew," so long as the contradictions of commodity society are not overcome.

NOTES

1. Walter Benjamin, *Gesammelte Schriften,* 7 vols., ed. Rolf Tiedemann and Hermann Schweppenhäuser, with the collaboration of Theodor W. Adorno and Gershom Scholem (Frankfurt am Main: Suhrkamp Verlag, 1972–), vol. 5, *Das Passagen-Werk,* ed. Rolf Tiedemann (1982), p. 86 (A2, 2, also L°, 28).

2. 5, p. 700 (Tla, 8).

3. 5, p. 45 (1935 exposé).

4. 5, p. 267 (G16, 7).

5. "It is only the particular social relation between people that here takes on the phantasmagoric form of a relation between things" (Marx, *Capital,* cited 5, p. 245 [G5, 1]).

6. 5, p. 1250 (exposé note no. 23).

7. 5, p. 587 (N7, 7).

8. 5, p. 587 (N7, 6).

9. "The destructive or critical moment in the materialist writing of history comes into play in that blasting apart of historical continuity with which, first and foremost, the historical object constitutes itself" (5, p. 594 [N10a, 1]).

10. 5, p. 594 (N10, 3).

11. 5, p. 575 (N2, 6).

12. 5, p. 578 (N3, 2).

13. 5, p. 587 (N7a, 1).

14. 5, pp. 591–592 (N9, 7; cf. Q°, 21 and Q°, 81).

15. 5, p. 587 (N7, 2: cf. O°, 5 and O°, 81).

16. See 5, p. 588 (N7a, 5) and p. 577 (N2a, 3).

17. 5, p. 570 (N1, 1; also N9, 7).

18. 5, p. 587 (N3, 1; cf. P°, 4).

19. 5, p. 595 (N10a, 3).

20. 5, pp. 595–596 (N11, 4).

21. 5, p. 571 (N1, 4).

22. 5, pp. 570–571 (N1, 4).

23. Letter, Benjamin to Adorno, 31 May 1935, 5, p. 1117.

24. 5, p. 574 (N1a, 8).

25. 5, p. 1011 (G°, 19). In this world, the old (the time of Hell), repeats itself in the new, but this repetition is one of "strict discontinuity": "the always-again-new is not the old that remains, nor the past that returns, but the one and the same crossed by countless intermittences" (ibid.).

26. 5, p. 494 (Kla, 8). Following Weber, one might argue that the charismatic leader becomes desirable as a way of breaking out of the iron cages of moder-

nity's rationalizations, whereas according to Benjamin, fascism is an *extension* of the reenchantment of the world and of mass man's illusory dream-state. For Adorno and Horkheimer, however, fascism is seen as an extension of modern rationality itself.

27. 5, p. 96 (K2a, 1).

28. *Einbahnstrasse*, 4, p. 132.

29. 5, p. 1007 (F°, 13).

30. Schelling, cited in Manfried Frank, *Der kommende Gott: Vorlesungen über die Neue Mythologie, I. Teil* (Frankfurt am Main: Edition Suhrkamp, 1982), pp. 198–199; ital. Schelling's.

31. 5, p. 584 (N5a, 2).

32. Louis Aragon, *Le paysan de Paris* [1962] (Paris: Gallimard, 1953), p. 142.

33. 5, p. 580 (N4, 1).

34. 5, p. 1014 (H°, 17; again N1, 9).

35. 5, p. 1214 (1935 exposé note no. 8).

36. 5, p. 1014 (H°, 17; again N1, 9).

37. *Einbahnstrasse*, 4, p. 93, trans. Edmund Jephcott and Kingsley Shorter in Walter Benjamin, *One Way Street and Other Writings* (London: NLB, 1979), p. 53.

38. Scholem, "Walter Benjamin," *On Jews and Judaism in Crisis: Selected Essays,* ed. Werner J. Dannhauser (New York: Schocken Books, 1976), p. 175. (The writings to which Scholem refers are "Berliner Chronik" and *Berliner Kindheit um 1900.*)

39. Walter Benjamin (with Asja Lacis), "Programm eines proletarischen Kindertheaters," 2, p. 766.

40. Cf. Benjamin, "Probleme der Sprachsoziologie" (1935), 3, p. 474.

41. "Programm eine proletarischen Kindertheaters," 2, p. 768.

42. Benjamin recalled his own schooling: "References to objects were no more to be found than references to history; nowhere did it offer the eye the slightest refuge, while the ear was helplessly abandoned to the clatter of idiotic harangues." ("Berliner Chronik," 6, p. 474, trans. Jephcott and Shorter, *One Way Street,* p. 303).

43. See Susan Buck-Morss, *The Origin of Negative Dialectics: Theodor W. Adorno, Walter Benjamin and the Frankfurt Institute* (New York: The Free Press, 1977), p. 171 and passim.

44. Notes to "Theses on History," 1, p. 1243.

45. "Über das mimetische Vermögen," 2, p. 210.

46. Ibid., p. 211.

47. Artwork essay, 1, p. 500.

48. Ibid.

49. Ibid., pp. 488, 496.

50. Ibid., p. 499.

51. Ibid., p. 495.

52. "Über einige Motive bei Baudelaire," 1, p. 614.

53. *Einbahnstrasse*, 4, p. 103, trans. Jephcott and Shorter, *One Way Street,* p. 62.

54. "Über einige Motive bei Baudelaire," 1, p. 628n.

55. Notes to the Artwork essay, 1, p. 1040.

56. "Der Sürrealismus," 2, pp. 309–310.

57. 5, p. 1002 [D°, 7]. I am indebted to Irving Wohlfarth for pointing out that Benjamin's choice of the word *Feerie* rather than fairy tale (*Märchen*) is meaningful. It suggests a "fairy-scene," a visual image, not a narration.

58. 5, p. 494 (Kla, 8). *Konvulut* K is entitled "Dream-City and Dream-House; Dreams of the Future, Anthropological Materialism, Jung."

59. 5, p. 513 (L1a, 1). Their overhead roof-lighting created the "underwater atmosphere of dreams" (O°, 46; cf. H°, 4).

60. See 5, p. 1012 (H°, 1), 5, p. 1002 (L1, 1), and see *Konvulut* L. Significantly, Benjamin does not mention the movie theater as the penultimate "dream-house." On the contrary, film in its technological reproduction of the collective dream-spaces provides the opposite effect: "Our taverns and our metropolitan streets, our offices and furnished rooms, our railroad stations and our factories appeared to have locked us up hopelessly. Then came the film and burst this prison-world asunder by the dynamite of the tenth of a second, so that now, in the midst of its far-flung ruins and debris, we calmly and adventurously go travelling." Artwork essay, 1, p. 500, trans. Harry Zohn in Walter Benjamin, *Illuminations*, ed. Hannah Arendt (New York: Schocken Books, 1969), p. 236.

61. 5, pp. 492–493 (K1, 4; cf. G°,14).

62. 5, p. 494 (Kla, 9; cf. O°, 69).

63. 5, p. 496 (K2, 6).

64. "Der Sürrealismus," 2, p. 307.

65. Letter, Benjamin to Scholem, 30 October 1928, 5, p. 1089.

66. 5, p. 234 (G1, 7; again 1935 exposé, note no. 8).

67. The goal of Benjamin's "new dialectical method of history writing" was "the art of experiencing the present as the waking world to which in truth that dream which we call the past [*Gewesenes*] relates" (5, p. 491 [K1, 3]). Cf. the earlier (more Surrealist) formulation: The "dialectical method of history" is "to suffer what has been with the intensity of a dream in order to experience the awakened world to which the dream connects" (F°, 6).

68. "Franz Kafka," 2, p. 415.

69. 5, p. 490 (K1; cf. F°, 7).

70. 5, p. 490 (K1, 1 cf. F°, 7).

71. 5, p. 493 (Kla, 3; cf. M°, 20).

72. "Der Erzähler" (1936), 2, p. 458.

73. 5, p. 1032 (O°, 56).

74. 5, p. 493 (Kla, 6).

75. Bloch (1935), cited 5, p. 497 (K2a, 5).

76. See 5, pp. 235–236 (Gla, 4). The child's inventive reception of mass-culture forms as a sign of nature reconciled with humanity indicates that childhood cognitive powers are not without an antidote to mass culture's manipulation.

77. In 1936 Benjamin proposed to Horkheimer an essay for the Institut on Klages and Jung: "It was to develop further the methodological considerations of the *Passagen-Werk*, confronting the concept of the dialectical image—the central epistemological category of the '*Passagen*'—with the archetypes of Jung and the

archaic images of Klages. Due to the intervention of Horkheimer this study was never executed" (ed. note, 5, p. 1145). Still, the *Passagen-Werk* material makes clear the line Benjamin's argument would have taken. Where Jung would see, for example, the recurrence of a utopian image as a "successful return" of unconscious contents, Benjamin, far closer to Freud (and Bloch), argued that its repetition was the sign of the continued social repression which prevented realizing utopian desires (K2a, 5). Or, where Jung would see the image of the beggar as an eternal symbol of a trans-historical truth about the collective psyche, for Benjamin the beggar was a historical figure, the persistence of which was a sign of the archaic state, not of the psyche, but of social reality, which remained at the mythic level of prehistory despite surface change: "As long as there is still one beggar, there still exists myth" (K6, 4).

78. 5, p. 1236 (version of the 1935 exposé).

79. "Berliner Chronik," 6, p. 489, trans. Jephcott and Shorter, *One Way Street*, p. 316.

80. 5, p. 576 (N2a, 2).

81. 5, p. 490 (K1, 1; again F°, 1).

82. 5, p. 1214 (1935 exposé note no. 8).

83. 5, p. 1138.

84. Letter, Benjamin to Karplus, 16 August 1935, 5, p. 1139.

85. 5, p. 1139.

86. Letter, Adorno to Benjamin, 2 August 1935, 5, p. 1129.

87. 5, p. 1129.

88. Marx, cited 5, p. 583 (N5a, 1).

89. Marx, cited 5, p. 570.

90. 5, p. 495 (K2, 5).

91. 5, p. 669 (R2, 2).

92. "Zentralpark," 1, p. 677 (cf. 5, p. 175 [D9, 3]).

93. 5, p. 1210 (1935 exposé note no. 5).

94. 5, p. 1215.

95. 5, p. 1000 (D°, 1).

96. 5, p. 1035 (P°, 6).

97. 5, p. 1033 (O°, 67).

98. 5, p. 1033 (O°, 67).

99. 6, p. 488, trans. Jephcott and Shorter, *One Way Street*, p. 316.

100. 5, p. 1018 (K°, 28).

101. 5, p. 59 (1935 exposé).

102. Letter, Benjamin to Scholem, 9 August 1935, 5, p. 1137.

103. 5, p. 130 (B9, 1; cf. B1a, 4).

104. 5, p. 113 (B1a, 4).

105. 5, p. 1018 (K°, 27).

THIRTEEN

The Despotic Eye and Its Shadow

Media Image in the Age of Literacy

Robert D. Romanyshyn

I. INTRODUCTION

Postmodernism . . . assumes the task of reinvestigating the crisis and trauma at the very heart of modernity; the postmodern [is] a testament to the fact that the end of modernity is . . . a symptom as it were of its own unconscious infancy which needs to be retrieved and reworked if we are not to be condemned to an obsessional fixation upon, and compulsive repetition of, the sense of its ending. In this respect, the task of a postmodern imagination might be to envision the end of modernity as a possibility of rebeginning.[1]

This quotation strongly suggests that the task of postmodernism is to attempt a therapeutics of culture. Such is the intention of this essay. It is an experiment in cultural therapeutics which begins not with the past but with how the past is present in the present as symptom. To say symptom in this manner, however, requires caution. At the outset we must eschew the primarily modern and mostly negative idea of the symptom, an idea which would invite us to evaluate the symptom in order to "cure" it, that is, dismiss it. In place of that idea we need to embrace the more difficult notion that the symptom is a vocation, a call to listen and give voice to what would otherwise remain silenced.

The experiment in this essay is to demonstrate media image consciousness, illustrated here via TV consciousness, as the symptomatic ending of modernity. Such an experiment, however, initially needs some justification, because the media image industry in general, and television in particular, seems so much to be an expression of modernity, and even the epitome of its values. I confess that I have no argument with this position. Television is the intensification of many of the values of modernity; indeed it is the incarnation of these values in the extreme. But that is precisely the sense of television as symptom. As exaggeration and caricature of the values of modernity, it brings those values to our attention, inviting us not to call them into question but to wonder about them, perhaps in some instances for the first time. As symptom, then, television asks for a hearing, not a judgment.

The hypothesis of this experiment is that television is the cultural unconscious of the book. It is the other side, the shadow side, of a book consciousness whose origins coincide with modernity. Through a double anamnesis of these origins, one through the *Meditations* of Descartes and the other through the fifteenth-century invention of linear perspective vision, we return to those generative sites of modernity in order to rework, to remember, these sites as also sites of initial forgettings. And in this work what we recover is the way in which the ocularcentrism of modernity, the hegemony of vision, the installation of the reign of the despotic eye, is also a verbocentrism, the consciousness of the book, and an egocentrism, the consciousness of a separated, detached atom of individuality.

Through this double anamnesis, the sense of modernity is presented in this essay as ego-ocular-verbocentrism. It is this gestalt out of which many of the unquestioned values of modernity arise. Television as the shadow of the book makes visible the pathology of verbo-ocular-ego consciousness by challenging its values of linear rationality, contextual coherence, narrative continuity, focused concentration, infinite progress, individual privacy, productive efficiency, detached comprehensiveness, and neutral objectivity. The challenge, of course, is not for the sake of negating these values. On the contrary, the challenge is for the sake of pointing up their symptomatic character, of remembering their genesis at those cultural-historical moments when things could have been otherwise. That these values have not been otherwise attests to the fact that these moments of genesis were also moments of forgetfulness, in which these values were transformed from perspectives into unquestioned cultural conventions, sedimented habits of mind. Moreover, the importance of this challenge should not be missed. It is important to take up this experiment, important to allow ourselves to be addressed by television as a symptom in place of simply castigating and dismissing it, because the recognition that things could have been otherwise reminds us of our responsibility for our creations. That television seems intent upon the destruction of the verbo-ocular-ego values of modernity invites from us not an unthinking, even self-righteous defense of those values, but an attentive response to our participation in the creation of those values. It is not safe simply to defend the book against television. On the contrary, we need to attend to how television, as the shadow of the book, as its symptomatic expression, calls us to become responsible by remembering what we have made.

In this essay, television as symbolic of the ending of modernity is presented as the symptomatic breakdown of modernity. Whether or not this breakdown is also a breakthrough to another kind of cultural consciousness, postmodern, remains for the reader to decide. In the closing words of this introduction, I will offer my own assessment of this experiment. For the moment, however, I want to summarize a few ways in which television consciousness, or media image consciousness in general, can be a breakthrough to a postmodern style.

The television experience can be a breakthrough to a postmodern style insofar as it breaks the gestalt of verbo-ocular-egocentrism, and in so doing redefines the ocularcentrism of modernity. If television is ocularcentric—and in many ways it is—it nevertheless revisions the eye. The eye of ego consciousness, the eye of the reader of the book, arises within a cultural-historical moment in which the ego as disembodied spectator is invited to keep his or her eye, singular, fixed, and distant, upon the world. The double anamnesis of this spectator eye makes these features quite clear. The television eye, the ocularcentrism of the television experience, is of a quite different sort. As the essay suggests, beginning with its opening image, the eye of television consciousness is *re-minded* of the body. Seduced by images, a seduction which to be sure is not without its problems, the eye of the television body is an emotional vision, a vision that is moved at a bodily level.

As emotional-rationality, the television body is not verbocentric. In place of a literate consciousness, the television body is an image consciousness. Drawing upon psychoanalysis, the television body is said to be more like the dream body than the waking body. Drawing also upon the preliterate body of poetic performance in Homeric Greece, the television body is said to be more akin to this body of orality, where knowing is emotional, participatory, and sensuous, rather than rational, detached, and logical, and where waking and dreaming are less clearly distinguished and are more confused. In these respects, the postmodernism of the television body is presented as a postliterate orality, a surreal reality in which the values of literacy are confused with a new, technologically produced orality.

Finally, television body consciousness can be postmodern insofar as it is the decentering of the ego. Just as the dream in psychoanalysis decentered the ego, television can move the ego out of its privacy and isolation into a kind of group—even tribal—consciousness, where the tension between fusion with the other and distance from the other is refigured. The figure of the borderline patient is offered as an illustration of this decentering of ego consciousness which the television experience brings. It is suggested that working with a borderline is more like watching television than it is like reading a book. The symptomatic value of television, then, might very well lie in its invitation toward another kind of consciousness now visible in our culture only as the pathology of the borderline.

Does this experiment in attending to the symptomatic character of television consciousness in particular, and media image consciousness in general, succeed? Does this effort to *re-member* out of forgetfulness the generative sites of modernity allow us to value the differences between modernity and postmodernity, especially with respect to its ocularcentric character, in place of evaluating them? The reader is the judge. Myself, I need to say that in praxis the experiment has not yet even begun. What I offer here is a possibility, a work to be done. To achieve it, however, would first require acknowledgment of this historical fact. Television and the media image industry have been and continue to be held captive by the forces of economic capitalism, in much the same way that psychoanalysis was taken captive. These forces have an inertial mass which makes them resistant to change. The dream in psychoanalysis, and of psychoanalysis, became profitable and so lost its symptomatic edge. So too have television and the media image industry. Revolutions in consciousness, shifts from a modern style to a postmodern one, have little if any chance of succeeding so long as there is money to be made in their exploitation. So far that seems to be the case, making television a mid-twentieth-century version of the therapy room, the place where the dream and the symptom are not only matters of profit but of amusement as well.

II. THE TELEVISION AND THE BOOK

Neil Postman's 1986 paperback edition of *Amusing Ourselves to Death* has a provocative and illuminating cover.[2] Framed within a square, which gives the potential reader of this book the impression that he or she is looking through a window, is what appears to be a nuclear family gathered together around a television set whose back faces us, the potential readers looking at this family looking at television. Besides this visual double play, one is also struck by the fact that each family member is headless! But there is no sense of shock or horror at their condition. They have not been decapitated. On the contrary, the scene is amusing, and inspires a question: Who are these people who, fully clothed and sitting upright, confront us watching them watching television? And here for the first time some sense of shock does enter. They are us, mindless zombies whose heads, whose capacities for critical discourse and discursive thinking, have atrophied into nothingness, perhaps for lack of use in the age of the entertaining image. Entranced and amused, they (we) sit passively and expectantly, waiting to be fed and to be filled with the glut of images dispensed by the tube. Information addicts, we might say, enslaved by the hypnotic power of the image!

Postman's book poses a serious question about the possibility of reasonable public discourse in what he calls the "Age of Show Business," and his analysis of how electronic media have refashioned matters of knowledge into matters of entertainment is difficult to fault. When he states, for example, that the nineteenth-century invention of the telegraph cut the connection between communication and transportation, between the message and the messenger, making it possible not only to transmit messages more quickly but also to transmit more messages, producing a flood of information which without local context has become increasingly irrelevant, trivial, and even incoherent, and which in its sheer volume has put us on overload and made us powerless in the face of it all, our daily experience with newspaper headlines, radio broadcasts, and television news from around the globe strongly supports him. When he describes how television in its "Now this" syndrome breaks the continuity of experience, fragmenting it into bits of information by presenting segments of news not only interrupted by commercials but also, like newspaper headlines, presented with no internal connection among them, offering as it were a collage of news events, our daily experience again confirms him. Or, when he argues that TV takes away any sense of reality by inviting us to attend to a news story about war followed by a commercial for fast food, presenting sequence without consequence, a pattern which is more like a dream or a fantasy than perceptual contact with the world, we are ready to agree. And finally, when he proposes that TV should, therefore, aspire to do nothing more than what it does best, which is to amuse, we are convinced by this proposal. After all, when coverage of the Persian Gulf War produces images of allied bombing missions spoken of in terms of video games, the line between matters of serious import and games, between fact and fiction, has been more than broken; it has been erased.

My intention is not to challenge Postman's diagnosis of our state of mind in the age of the media image. I applaud the diagnosis for its accuracy in portraying our current condition. I do wish, however, to differ with him about the prescription which follows his diagnosis, and about the anamnesis through which the diagnosis is made and from which the prescription follows.

That television should simply amuse, that it should abandon its pretense that it is or can be anything other than entertainment, is a prescription resulting from the way in which Postman uses the perspective of the book as a standard against which television is measured. The values of book literacy—linearity, coherence shaped by context, continuity, focused concentration, and privacy, to name only a few—are the presumed natural frame within which television consciousness, that is, consciousness shaped by the immediate image rather than the discursive word, is placed and judged in an essentially negative way. But is such a judgment a defensive reaction of typographical consciousness, of that kind of consciousness shaped these last four hundred years by the book, a consciousness for which loss of coherence, continuity, and context can only be experienced as a form of schizophrenia?

Postman, I believe, is guilty of this defensive reading in spite of the fact that he is aware of the historical and cultural character of the relationship between instruments of technology and styles of consciousness. Postman knows that cultural instruments are metaphors as well as mediums for experience, epistemologies incarnate, tools which not only inform us but formulate how we are in-formed. He knows this, yet the differences between book and television become for him matters of evaluation. I suppose, then, that unlike Plato he would not have banned the poets from the polis at that time when a shift occurred, from myth to logos, a shift engineered in large measure by the invention of the phonetic alphabet.[3] But defending the Homeric poets and mythic consciousness against the philosophers and rational consciousness then would have had, I suspect, as little impact as Postman's defense of typographic consciousness against media consciousness will have now.

In saying this, however, I do not mean to imply that we surrender ourselves to television consciousness as a matter of historical necessity or inevitability. That is not the point. The point is to appreciate whatever positive transformations in consciousness are being brought about by changes in our technological ways of knowing the world, and to appreciate that the instruments through which we encounter the world are made by us, even if for motives that are largely unknown. Television, like the book, incarnates a collective psychological condition. I want to propose, then, that before evaluating the differences, we value the difference in order to understand something of ourselves. I want to propose that the challenges which media culture pose today are symptoms. As such, "television" asks not for a diagnosis which would emphasize only what is wrong with it (and us), but for a hearing which would challenge the "book" to remember what *it* has (and we have) otherwise forgotten. The symptom, then, not as a sign of disease but as a vocation, as a call to remember.[4]

III. INTERLUDE

A reader, when starting a book, intends to make sense of it. Recently I attempted an experiment in what I called "complex reading," which invited graduate students in a class that was reading Freud's case histories to suspend this intention. Throughout the semester we tried to remain with the question of how the texts make sense of us even as we were trying to make sense of them. Five themes guided this experiment. For example, bracketing the effort to make sense of the text raised *anxiety* over the following issues: Where is one's reading going? Is the reading producing nonsense? How does the interplay of text, memory, fantasy, and feeling fit together? Is the text as repository of information being correctly interpreted? Is one doing a good job of reading, doing it efficiently, and finishing the task? In all these concerns, we learned how our trying to make sense of the text is "a means of mastery and control, the perspective of an ego consciousness in the stance of detached observer of the world." We also learned how the bracketing of this intention to make sense of the text, allowing the text to make sense of us as readers, challenged "the position of ego consciousness by undercutting its fantasies of power and progress, of virtue and purity, of efficiency and comprehensiveness," and revealed that these fantasies lie "behind the ideals of objective reading, of a finished text, of a correct interpretation."[5]

Television on a daily and hourly basis, already does to ego consciousness—to that consciousness which, as we shall see, historically has developed in relation to the book—what this experiment at complex reading did. It challenges the values and assumptions of ego consciousness, and in this respect it seems proper to say that *television is the shadow of the book*. As such, television (and the electronic media of the image in general, from television and film to neon advertising signs) makes visible the pathology of ego, literate, book consciousness, by bringing into question the values of linear rationality, contextual coherence, narrative continuity, infinite progress, individual privacy, productive efficiency, detached comprehensiveness, and neutral objectivity.

To attend to television as shadow is to approach it as a cultural symptom, and this approach is no more a celebration of the new in praise of progress than it is a defensive protection of the old. Rather it is a work of remembering, an anamnesis of the hidden in the given, an attending to how already in the givenness of the book the television is hidden, a witnessing to how book consciousness, the consciousness of the word, forgets and yet still remembers television consciousness, the consciousness of the image. J. F. Lyotard makes the point in this fashion:

> The modern is all too easily snapped up by the future, by all its values of pro-motion, pro-gram, pro-gress . . . dominated by a very strong emphasis on willful activism. Whereas the post-modern implies, in its very movement . . . a capacity to listen openly to what is hidden within the happenings of today. Post-modernism is deeply reflexive, in the sense of anamnesis or reminiscence, and that itself evinces what is best in modernity.[6]

Postman's question, therefore, of how rational public discourse is possible in the age of the media image is best served not by dismissing image media or confining them to amusement, but by recovering through the image media the cultural unconsciousness of the book. I would only add that it is important to be about this work of cultural anamnesis at this time. "In an age and at a time overtaken by linear and programmed thinking, by obsessions with the bottom line and the straight path, by a passion for straightening things out and straightening them up,"[7] we need to remember the complex character of psychological life and the way in which it twists, weaves, and blends together fact and fiction, sense and nonsense, continuity and discontinuity, order and chaos, reason and dream. It is important today because we have already missed one opportunity to do this work of re-membering. The dream of psychoanalysis, meant in both senses of its vision of the unconscious as the shadow of the ego and its appreciation of the dream as a royal road to this unconscious, has been appropriated and tamed insofar as psychoanalysis has become less a cultural critique and more an established profession in the service of this ego. We make sense today of the dream as much as we make sense of the text. Ignoring the shadow, however, it has returned with greater intensity and insistence. The TV, I am suggesting, is dream consciousness made public and visible. Can we afford the attempt to situate television consciousness within the confines of ego, literate, book consciousness as we have situated dream consciousness within the service of the ego? Can we dismiss TV consciousness's challenge to book consciousness by confining it to the task of amusement, as we have done with dream consciousness by confining it to the therapy room?

IV. FIRST RE-MEMBERING: THE *COGITO* PROJECT

Our anamnesis of book consciousness begins with that headless nuclear family in front of its television set. It begins with the claim that the members of this family are the descendants of Descartes. To appreciate this claim, we need to remember that moment in time when we, the children of his meditations, were being conceived. Specifically, we need to remember Descartes's *Meditations on First Philosophy* and especially that moment in the work when he sets his conditions for who and what the reader must be in order to read his book.

"I would not recommend it to any except to those who would want to meditate seriously along with me."[8] Those who are invited to read the text, those who are serious, are defined by what they are not. The instruction is a negative requirement, a requirement which asks the reader to purify himself or herself of something in order to read the text. Susan Bordo, in a provocative reading of Descartes's work, has also noted this theme of purification, and she places it within a psycho-historical framework which illuminates the *cogito* project in insightful fashion.[9] Along with her, we need to ask of what should the reader be purified so as not to contaminate the text? The answer is found in the figure from whom the serious reader is distinguished. It is found in the figure of the "vulgar." The serious reader is the one who is *not* vulgar, that is, the one who in an act of negation which purifies becomes "capable of freeing the mind from attachment to the senses."[10] The reader of Descartes's text turns out to be a disincarnate mind, a head minus the body, a bodyless reader.

It would seem at this point a false claim that the nuclear family looking at television are children of Descartes. They are headless bodies, while the reader of Descartes's text is a bodyless head. But the claim is not false, nor are the children faithless or rebellious. On the contrary, they are exactly what this kind of thinking had to produce—bastards, in the sense of unwanted and unintended offspring. "Monstrosities" might be better, except that it has too negative a connotation. Let us say they are Descartes's neurotic offspring, shadows which continuously remind practitioners of the *cogito* project of their vulgar heritage.

The *cogito* project establishes a way of thinking which takes leave of its senses. To take leave of one's senses is, however, a way of thinking shadowed by madness, and the headless bodies in front of their TV screen are one form of this madness: life as continuous, repetitive entertainment and amusement. Purifying itself of the body, the serious practitioner of the *cogito* project abandons the body which becomes, as I described elsewhere,[11] not only the corpse, the body as anatomical object, but also the consumer, the body as object of pleasure and profit. This corpse and the body addicted to pleasure are twins, the former the legitimated offspring of Cartesian vision and the latter the black sheep.

I am suggesting that the entertainment industry, incarnated in the electronic media of the image, is the shadow of that thinking which has taken leave of the senses. The technology of media culture as entertainment haunts a Cartesian consciousness which, in creating a thinking that is disincarnate, has also created a body fit only for amusement, a body of endless appetites addicted to its need for continuous stimulations and distractions. Postman, in his critique of the media image, says as much and adds the features of triviality and passivity to his description of media consciousness. Possessing an unlimited capacity for distraction from our boredom, we are also overwhelmed by the amount of information that is produced and made available. In the face of this information glut the capacity for distinguishing the true from the false is lost. Pieces of disconnected information without a surrounding context generate a mountain of trivial details, reducing us to passive consumers of advertised items and reported information, and rendering us powerless to frame any of it within a perspective. Reflecting on this state of affairs, Postman adds that the last refuge of the powerless individual in a culture of the image is pleasure. Pleased and entertained, we are narcotized against our condition of helplessness. Amused to death, we are distracted from our condition of indifference. Pleasure becomes the anodyne of the powerless. "Big Brother," Postman says, "turns out to be Howdy Doody."[12]

It is difficult to resist the rhetoric of Postman's critique, but we must recall here that his diagnosis rests upon a preference for the book which becomes the evaluating measure of television. Television, for Postman, is not the shadow of the book, a view which would lead to an equally critical questioning and diagnosis of book consciousness. On the contrary, he considers television the antithesis of the book, and its threatened elimination.

Distraction, triviality, and passivity are the judgments then of a book consciousness watching television. They are the diagnosed symptoms of the serious reader who has distanced herself or himself from the vulgar. The headless nuclear family watching television is the nightmare of the bodyless reader, the terrible image of what we become when we lose the book. We need to remember, however, the kinship between the two, the connection between that kind of thinking which, in splitting off the serious from the vulgar, the mind from flesh, reason from emotion, first created a mindless body and its needs for distraction, and then produced the means to do it. Indeed, we are called to this task of re-membrance in order not to take the easy path which would lead us to conclude that the fault and the danger are with the media of the image, and which would then make us forget that the danger and the fault are with that way of thinking which in taking leave of its senses has fashioned a body capable only of being stimulated and entertained. To do any less would leave that way of thinking safely in place. We need to remember that the fault is not with television itself. The fault is with that historically created situation within which Descartes's shadow children watching television were originally conceived.

V. SECOND RE-MEMBERING: ALBERTI'S WINDOW

If Descartes is the father of the body of amusement, the reluctant, unintentional author of the television body, of the body left behind by the flight of the *cogito* from the flesh, then Leon Battista Alberti, fifteenth-century artist, architect, and author is the father of that father, the grandfather of our nuclear family ensconced in front of its television. Our second re-membrance starts, therefore, with the claim that Alberti's codification of the laws of linear perspective vision inaugurates a psychology of distance between the eye of mind and the flesh of the world, upon which the *cogito* project of Descartes rests and of which it is an elaboration.

Linear perspective vision was a fifteenth-century artistic invention for representing three-dimensional depth on the two-dimensional canvas. It was a geometrization of vision which began as an invention and became a convention, a cultural habit of mind. We will not trace out here the full story of this shift from a technique or method to a world-view or metaphysics. Rather, we will concentrate on one aspect of Alberti's technique which prepared the ground for Descartes.[13]

Imagine that you are looking at the world through the lens of a camera. The scene which you see stretches out before you in such fashion that objects nearer to you are bigger while those farther away appear smaller. This is as it should be, for we have become used to the convention that size represents the distance from the perceiver. Indeed, this connection between size and distance seems a natural fact. Medieval, prelinear perspective paintings appear to us, therefore, as strange, as messengers of another world. And in fact they are of another world. Medieval men and women did not look at the world through a camera eye. We do habitually, even without the presence of the instrument. With Alberti the eye was beginning its education in a new way.

A camera is a little room, and the lens is a special kind of window which lets in the world as a matter of light. When Alberti described his procedures for making a perspective drawing, that is, a drawing in which things become smaller as they recede from the viewer, he invited his readers to imagine the canvas on which one would paint to be a window. In other words, Alberti began his perspective drawing by becoming a spectator on one side of a window looking at the world on the other side. A window, however, does not stand by itself. It is a frame within a wall attached to other walls. It is part of a room, and precisely that part which admits the world as a matter of light.

Linear perspective vision is an invitation to enter into a room and to become on this side of its window a spectator looking at a world transformed into a spectacle, that is, into a matter of light. It is an invitation to become a subject with his or her eye upon a world which now has become an object of vision. We have become quite accustomed to being in this little room, living in it as our outpost or outlook upon the world. We call it ego consciousness, and we locate it, uncritically, inside our heads which, like cameras themselves, have film inside them, have impressionable material called a brain.

Ego consciousness, consciousness as private, interior subjectivity, was initially invented and imagined by the artist as a way of envisioning the world as a matter of vision. The *cogito* of Descartes, the "I think therefore I am," begins as the eye of mind. And I say "eye of mind" because in looking at the world through a window, we are destined to lose touch with the world, except in those ways which matter for the eye alone. The eye, which of all the senses favors contact at a distance, already defines that contact in terms of its limits and its preferences. What is visible, observable, measurable, and quantifiable will increasingly become, therefore, the index of the real, while what is invisible and not observable, qualitative, and nonmeasurable (like the beauty and awe of the rainbow which Newton will later in another closed room quantify as the spectrum) will become at best subjective, secondary qualities projected onto the world now cleansed and purified of those qualities. In addition, this eye will exercise its preference for surfaces, transforming the invisible, imaginal depths of the world into a visible display of surface images, probing each and every surface and exposing beneath it only another surface ready and capable of being made into another piece of visibility. For the eye of mind behind the window, the world as a tension or play between visible surface and invisible depth will be eclipsed to become a project of progressively unveiling potential surfaces hidden beneath manifest surfaces. The instruments through which the eye of mind will enforce its project already demonstrate its vision. The telescope and the microscope, for example, will open surfaces only to reveal other surfaces, surfaces moreover from which the human body will become alien and distant. The world transformed into a matter of light will become the counterpart of a subject increasingly distant and withdrawn into its room of private subjectivity, a solitary, isolated atom of disincarnate individuality incapable of sensing and hence making sense of a world which has become measurably insensible. This subject with its eye upon the world is the start of the modern reign of the despotic eye, that eye of mind which in draining the world of its qualities purifies it of its substance, making it into a matter of light.

It is no accident of history that the subject spectator looking at the world through a window will also within his or her room begin to engage in another activity. At approximately the same time that Alberti's procedures are mapping the world as a geometric grid, laying it out in linear fashion, the book will be introduced and mass-produced. The linearity of the geometric world will find its counterpart in the linear literacy of the book, where line by line, sentence by sentence, the chronological structure of the book will mirror the sequential, ordered, linear structure of time in the sciences. In addition, the interiorization of individual subjectivity within the room of consciousness will find apt expression in the private act of reading and in silence, unlike the manuscript consciousness of the Middle Ages, where reading was done aloud.[14] The increasing standardization of grammar will also mirror the increasing homogenization of a world quantifiably defined. In these and in other respects too, linear vision will create an ego consciousness not only separate from the world and distant from the body, but also literate, private, and silent, an ego paradoxically standardized in its individuality.

The *cogito* project invites, as we saw, the serious reader to part company with the vulgar by taking leave of his or her senses. And this bodyless head, we also saw, leaves behind a body capable only of amusement. Alberti's window anticipates this project, creating a spectator for whom the world has become a matter for the eye alone. It is only a small step, I would suggest, from envisioning the world as a matter of light to the world becoming a *light matter,* which it is, in both senses, for our nuclear family looking at television.

VI. MEDIA AS SHADOW AND SYMPTOM

Television is a *light matter* and the parentage which we have traced of our nuclear family looking at television confirms it. It is a matter of light and a matter fit only to amuse. My claim, however, is that the first sense, which is descriptive, becomes in the second sense an evaluation, a judgment passed by the despotic eye. Against that judgment, I will attempt an experiment. I will suggest that television as a medium, along with film, is an evolution in human consciousness, a new style of consciousness, that is imprisoned in the heady eye of mind. The problem with television is that we treat it like a book, that we measure it by the book, by those patterns of consciousness appropriate to the isolated atom of individuality ensconced within the room of ego subjectivity. TV, however, is a challenge to ego consciousness, as much as it is a challenge to the political counterpart of ego consciousness, the individual nation-state. Indeed, I will go further and say that TV as a medium brings out such strong criticisms because it is the *breakdown* of literate, linear, ego consciousness, the consciousness of the book. The evolution is a revolution, akin in its implications to that earlier transformation in Platonic times from mythic to literate consciousness. Whether this breakdown can also be a *breakthrough* is what I will explore.

Near the very end of his *Meditations*, in the sixth and final one, Descartes returns to the issue of the difference between waking and dreaming, a difference which in the beginning of his work was central in securing the ego *cogito* from the shadows of doubt. Proclaiming his earlier efforts less than satisfactory, he says that now he has found a very notable and secure difference between them. Memory, he says, "can never bind and join our dreams together [one with another and all] with the course of our lives, as it habitually joins together what happens to us when we are awake."[15]

On the surface that is a key difference, and one that is phenomenologically astute, at least for that ego consciousness that has defined the project of modernity. Whether such a distinction, however, is as true for a nonliterate ego, or in preliterate cultures, is a debatable question, and certainly the Homeric epic poems, which historically precede literate consciousness, suggest otherwise. Eric Havelock and Julian Jaynes have both suggested that in oral culture the separation between dreaming and waking is less fixed. Indeed in his discussion of the psychology of the poetic performance, Havelock describes a state of waking consciousness characterized by a sense of possession. Poetic performance, like the dream, envelops, and the listener, like the dreamer who is fused with the dream, is fused with the singer. If this was "a life without self-examination," a critique which Plato made and which the literate ego of modernity resumes, it was, as Havelock acknowledges, nevertheless "a manipulation of the resources of the unconscious in harmony with the conscious [that is] unsurpassed."[16]

But we need not speculate on this matter of the preliterate mind, since the media image poses also for the postliterate mind a challenge to Descartes's difference between waking and dreaming. To appreciate this challenge we need to know what Descartes does with his idea about memory's function in waking and sleeping. Immediately after citing the failure of memory to weave our dreams together and to weave them into life, he says: "And so, in effect, if someone suddenly appeared to me when I was awake and (afterward) disappeared in the same way, as (do images that I see) in my sleep, so that I could not determine where he came from or where he went, it would not be without reason that I could consider it a ghost."[17]

But what after all is this experience—which if it happened to Descartes would convince him that he had seen a ghost and that he was therefore either mad or dreaming—but a description of the nuclear family in front of its television set switching channels with a remote control? What haunted Descartes, and necessitated for him a strict line between waking and sleeping, has become for us our daily fare. What the ego *cogito* of Descartes dreamed has become a reality which now threatens ego literate consciousness with the dream consciousness of television. TV consciousness, as Postman remarks, is discontinuous. But it is so for an ego that, educated in the model of the linear rationality of the book, separates itself from the episodic pattern of the dream. The television image, appearing and disappearing before me, is the ghost banished by Descartes. Television does on a daily basis exactly what Descartes feared, and in this respect it is a continuous witness to the fact that the *cogito* project contains in its origins its own undoing.

The nuclear family in front of its television set is neither sleeping nor insane. It is awake and it is dreaming. Television consciousness today haunts book consciousness because it eclipses those boundaries between waking and sleeping (reason and madness; fact and fiction) which ego literate consciousness so firmly established at the foundation of modernity. In doing so, it exposes the modern ego to a new sense of time, disrupting the familiar pattern of narrative and replacing it with the episodic pattern of the dream. Perhaps the term *replace* is not the best to describe the experience, because the medium of television does not so much eclipse the boundaries between waking and sleeping as confuse them. Television consciousness, as Donald Lowe remarks, is "a surreality," that is, an electronic media mentality superimposed on the older typographic mentality of the book.[18] The episodic pattern of time, more peculiar to the discontinuous medium of television, rests upon the still more familiar habits of narrative time, with its patterns of linear and even causal sequence. Watching television, then, exposes the ego to the bizarre experience of being awake in one's dreams. Or, watching television is akin to interpreting dreams, making sense of them, while dreaming. TV's coverage of the San Francisco earthquake in 1989 is a good example. The episodic and even random character of the events were plotted as a story line. We were watching chaos being ordered and order being dissolved again in chaos. Recent coverage of the Persian Gulf War is an even better example, since the illusion of being informed was continually broken. Coverage of that event did demonstrate that the accounts of the war were allusions to what remained frustratingly elusive. To be sure, some of this frustration can be attributed to the way in which the U.S. military restricted television coverage. But not all of it is explained in this fashion. Indeed, the frustration in this experience is built into the relation between the medium, with its multi-perspectival, collage type of consciousness, and the viewer, with his or her still relatively intact linear perspectival consciousness. The frustration belongs to the surreal quality of this relation which con-fuses or blends together episodic and story line time. And it is generated by the effort to dismiss this play of levels between a collage of images and the story line by forcing the former into the latter.

Before television, we had another instance of this frustrating effort. Freud's psychoanalysis also challenged the ego with the dream, discovering the multiple ways in which the ego's efforts to make sense of life and to bring order to it were illusions. Before dream consciousness had to become a cultural insistence, incarnating itself in the medium of television, it attempted to break through its separation from the ego by incarnating itself as a symptom in the body of the hysteric. In her symptoms she was suffering from reminiscences, Freud said with Breuer. She was suffering from memory, from time, becoming in a bodily way a collage of symptoms overdeter.nined in their meanings, threaded with events, wishes, dreams, and othe · symptoms, a constant interplay of allusions superimposed upon an ego consciousness unable to make sense of it all, a living, breathing surreal figure lost in the linear landscapes of the modern world. But Freud, the intrepid explorer of as-yet unmapped domains, did make the effort to make sense of it all. He interpreted the dream, transforming it as it were into a book, placing over it the narrative story line of a case history, and in so doing he got memory back on line, securing the hysteric's symptomatic sexuality in the past, erasing memory as presence of the past in the present.

In retrospect, Freud's effort was a mistake, generated by a literate ego consciousness too threateningly challenged by the dream. The hysteric's symptomatic sexuality was not a repressed past. It was, on the contrary, a fullness in the present. The hysteric suffered from memory, from time, and in that suffering she was an appeal addressed to the ego. She was the shadow of that ego reminding it that time and memory can become a disease when in an attempt to plot time as a line one lives outside of time, above it, detached from it. She was a shadow which, through her symptoms and dreams, was flooding the present with the full presence of past and future, presenting everything—event, memory, dream, wish, symptom—at once, recalling the ego out of its spectator detachment from life, re-minding its bookish distance with immediate sensual presence, re-membering that the past is not and never can be only a cause, and that the future is not and never can be a plot line of infinite progress subjected to one's will.

Diagnosing or treating the hysteric has in effect silenced the effort of the dream in psychoanalysis to breach the isolation of ego consciousness. Moreover, insofar as the media image has been co-opted by the capitalist mentality of consumption and profit, the television body, with its infinite appetite for distraction and amusement, has become first cousin to the hysteric body, with its symptomatic confusion of memory and event, fantasy and dream. In its resistance to dream consciousness, ego, literate, book consciousness has not, however, treated this symptom away. On the contrary, it has simply elevated it into a form of mass entertainment. Television has become the therapy room of the hysteric transformed into a public spectacle. Talk shows, as public confessionals for the secrets of the soul, have become a form of mass hysteria made palatable as amusement.

If, however, we have become insensitive to the mass hysteria disguised as entertainment which television consciousness induces, inculcating within us that same *belle indifference* so characteristic of the early hysteric, the media image persists as shadow of ego, literate, book consciousness at another level. In another symptomatic form, very much akin to the borderline, media image consciousness might very well be serving as a reminder of the unconscious legacy of literate consciousness.

The television experience is a radical separation of body and mind. On one hand, the headless *body* of the *cogito* seems fused with the emotional appeals of the media image, moved by these images without either judgment or reflection. On the other hand, the very absence of these capacities, so visible in the iconographic display of the *headless* body in front of its TV, betrays a distance between the person watching television and his or her emotionally infected body already fused with the television. Of the many complexities and difficulties which the borderline patient presents in psychotherapy, it is this tension of fusion and distance which often stands out. At one moment the therapist can be overwhelmed by the intense affects of his or her patient, engulfed either in a sea of abuse which often seems to threaten the therapist's own well-defended ego structures, or in a whirlpool of fascination at the patient's courage, spirit, insight, and secret knowledge. Commenting on the latter, Nathan Schwartz-Salant says in fact that the borderline often can envelop the therapist within an atmosphere which is experienced as "a link to the *numinosum,* the power of the gods and especially gods that the normal collective awareness has long since displaced."[19] However, at another moment, the next moment in fact, which shifts with the same rapidity as channels on a television, the therapist can feel herself to be in the presence of an absence so remarkable as to give the impression that the borderline individual is somehow less than human, a chillingly cold, aloof being from another world. At such moments the remark of the American psychiatrist Harry Stack Sullivan about schizophrenics, that we are all much more human than otherwise, seems off the mark. The therapist can, I believe, more easily recognize the absurd humanity of the schizophrenic than the borderline, for the schizophrenic, despite his or her bizarreness, escorts ego, literate consciousness only to the borders of order and chaos, whereas the borderline seems to be introducing another kind of order, an order that first erases the borderline and then confuses order and chaos in unexpected and unfamiliar ways. To be with a borderline is to be in a moment that is simultaneously "too full and too empty." It is to be in "a fairy tale world of abstract characters that then, quickly, turn back to flesh and blood reality."[20] No fairy tale that is merely being read evokes this experience. We are, on the contrary, describing here an experience more akin to the magic of television and movies, where the distance from the characters portrayed is eclipsed as these very same characters, like some ghosts haunting the world, emotionally impregnate one's body. The borderline individual radically challenges the comfortable distance and secure detachment of ego, literate consciousness. Being with a borderline is more like watching TV than it is like reading a book.

What the borderline challenges on the *idiographic* symptomatic level, the media image challenges on the *cultural* symptomatic level. On both levels we are being called to reimagine the separation and opposition of mind and body through this intense con-fusion of fusion and distance. On both levels we are being asked to attend to the shadow of ego, literate, spectator consciousness with its detached, despotic eye upon the world. The danger, of course, is that we will miss the opportunity, as happened with the hysteric. The borderline, then, will remain a negative diagnosis, and television an irritating distraction only to be dismissed by the more serious and sober-minded. The opportunity, however, is that on each level we might hear, as Schwartz-Salant does with the borderline, an appeal for union which this tension of fusion and distance dramatizes. We might hear an appeal for a sense of communion which the distance of ego, literate, book consciousness, ensconced behind its window, has shattered, and which the fusion of media image consciousness, seated as the headless nuclear family in front of its television set, dissolves.

VII. CONCLUSION:
TOWARD A POSTLITERATE ORALITY

The kind of consciousness which characterizes the media image, television consciousness for example, is a breakdown of the kind of consciousness which characterizes ego, literate consciousness, book consciousness for example. The remarks about the borderline propose, however, that breakdown can also be breakthrough. That the latter is resisted, however, is evidenced by the fate of psychoanalysis. Although Freud described the relation of transference between patient and therapist as a playground, the dream never quite made it into that arena of play. The dream in psychoanalysis remained for the ego a humiliation, a threat to its mastery and control, a matter of disguise, deception, illusion. That it was a way of playing with the ego, that it was a matter not of illusion but allusion to what remains elusive, was lost. The psychoanalyst as detective intended to uncover what the dream was hiding, making the ego of analysis a discoverer of buried secrets, forbidden wishes, arcane and illicit desires. As detective and discoverer, the ego of analysis made use of the dream in its search for origins and causes.

The dream, however, is an invitation which asks to be played with by a wakeful consciousness aware of its continuous and reciprocal relation of making the dream while being made by it. In doing so, the dream infects the seriousness of *cogito* consciousness with play, even as it undermines the idea of an origin outside that process which in searching for origins simultaneously creates the origins that are discovered. The dream, then, breaks through to a consciousness which in its playfulness is participatory, and which in its sense of participation accepts its oxymoronic character of created-discoveries, of serious-play, of constructed-origins. It breaks through to a consciousness which in its acceptance of paradox is radically metaphorical.[21]

Television consciousness certainly partakes of these features of the dream. It is no less participatory, especially at the level of the emotional body, working upon it in much the same fashion that the dream works upon the body. It is also oxymoronic insofar as it continuously presents us with those juxtapositions of experience—the news story followed by the commercial, for example—which to the serious eye of ego, literate consciousness seem only like an opposition. And it is finally radically metaphorical insofar as its images, like Magritte's pipe, are not what they appear to be and yet are. Or at least television consciousness might break through to these features which characterize much of postmodern consciousness, if its symptomatic character is attended as a vocation.

To call media image consciousness postmodern is not, however, sufficiently descriptive, for its postmodernism is a postliterate orality. The television body, like the dreaming body, is in many respects a re-presentation of the preliterate body of orality, of that body of speaking and listening which is always prior to the body of the text. The television body is this oracular body, the body which Havelock presents in his descriptions of poetic performance. It is a body which culturally and historically spirals out of the body of the book, out of the literate ego, a body which is not a repetition of preliterate orality but a re-membrance of that body, a re-play of it after the reign of the despotic eye. Like the body of poetic performance, the television body is emotional-rationality, drawn out of itself and into the world aesthetically, sensibly, as a matter of sense. It is also a body of group consciousness, a body already wedded via the sensuous and even erotic experience of the image to other bodies—a tribal body, then, immersed in a landscape that is more mythical than it is logical, and invited into action that is more ritual in texture than moral in outlook. That this kind of bodily presence to reality is open to exploitation and manipulation is obvious. Television has been manipulated, primarily by submitting to the industry of capitalism the potential of the medium to be a breakthrough to another kind of experience. But it need not do so. The use of television during the Vietnam War demonstrated its power to de-isolate the ego of literate consciousness and to create a coherent tribal identity, held together with a powerful myth of its place in history and prepared to act in such fashion that its emotional thought, contained within the space of dramatic ritual, was an important catalyst to stop that war.

As a psychotherapist with a perspective of psychopathology, and who attends to the symptomatic and shadow character of the symbols of culture, I believe we stand at a crossroads. The very same features of television consciousness described above were sufficient for Plato to ban the poet-singer from the polis. The danger was that in becoming enmeshed in the poet's song one would be diffused, distracted, unfocused, and without fixed moral direction. The danger was that one would become plural in place of the unified, self-contained, self-organized, and autonomous individual. For Plato there was a "direct connection . . . between rejection of the poets on the one hand and the affirmation of the psychology of the autonomous individual on the other."[22]

The history of the Western psyche shows the results of the exclusion of the poets from the polis. We have sketched it here in terms of Descartes's *cogito* project, Alberti's window, and the book. It is a history of a radical shift from ear to eye, and particularly to that eye of detached, spectator distance, a history of the despotic eye. Media image consciousness, especially the television, seems to be the shadow and the symptom of that eye, and in this respect a retuning of it. The images of television are no mere spectacles. They are spoken images, oracular insights, emotional visions. Perhaps with the television the poetic returns, or at least might do so. Notwithstanding Postman's criticism that today political discourse is not possible on television, television might be the means by which the poet is restored to the polis. Such a restoration would bring in its wake a re-membrance of the body's participation in vision, a re-minder which would restore a sense of limits to a vision which, detached from the body, developed a singular, fixed devotion to the infinite, pursued in a linear, active, willful fashion. Postman's criticisms of television as fostering distraction, passivity, and the trivial might then be reimagined. Distraction might be revalued as an appreciation for what lies off to the side, an attention to the oblique, an openness to allusion. Passivity might be restored as a balance to the hyperactivity of willful consciousness, an antidote to the ego as will to power, the development of an attitude of receptivity. And the trivial might be recovered as a sensitivity for the detail, a refound sense of the local so easily lost sight of in the big picture achieved with distance. Each and all might be rescued from the current negative condition assigned to them by an ego consciousness in its headlong pursuit of separating its vision of life from living.

NOTES

1. Richard Kearney, *The Wake of Imagination* (Minneapolis: University of Minnesota Press, 1988), p. 27.

2. Neil Postman, *Amusing Ourselves to Death* (New York: Penguin Books, 1986).

3. See Eric Havelock, *Preface to Plato* (Cambridge: Harvard University Press, 1963).

4. For a detailed discussion of this psychological approach to culture, see Robert Romanyshyn, *Technology As Symptom & Dream* (London, New York: Routledge, Chapman & Hall, 1989).

5. Romanyshyn, "Complex Knowing: Toward a Psychological Hermeneutics," *The Humanistic Psychologist* (Spring 1991), vol. 19, no. 1, pp. 10–29.

6. Quoted in Kearney, *The Wake of Imagination,* p. 27.

7. Romanyshyn, "Complex Knowing," p. 28.

8. René Descartes, *Meditations on First Philosophy,* trans. Laurence J. LaFleur (Indianapolis, New York: Bobbs-Merrill, 1969), p. 11.

9. Susan Bordo, *The Flight to Objectivity* (Albany: State University of New York Press, 1987).

10. Descartes, *Meditations,* p. 11.

11. See note 3.

12. Postman, *Amusing Ourselves to Death,* p. 111.

13. For a detailed account of Alberti's procedures, their meanings and cultural-historical implications, see Romanyshyn, *Technology As Symptom & Dream.*

14. See Marshall McLuhan, *The Guttenberg Galaxy* (New York: New American Library, 1969).

15. Descartes, *Meditations,* p. 85.

16. Havelock, *Preface to Plato,* p. 190. For a discussion of the views of Julian Jaynes, see Jaynes, *The Origin of Consciousness in the Breakdown of the Bicameral Mind* (Boston: Houghton Mifflin, 1976).

17. Descartes, *Meditations,* p. 85.

18. Donald M. Lowe, *History of Bourgeois Perception* (Chicago: University of Chicago Press, 1982), p. 9.

19. Nathan Schwartz-Salant, "The Dead Self in Borderline Personality Disorders," in David M. Levin, ed., *Pathologies of the Modern Self* (New York: New York University Press, 1987), p. 118.

20. Ibid.

21. For a discussion of the metaphorical character of psychological consciousness, see my earlier book, *Psychological Life: From Science to Metaphor* (Austin: University of Texas Press, 1982). In that work the hidden metaphoric character of modern scientific consciousness is indicated, suggesting that ego, literate consciousness already harbored within itself the seed of its own symptomatic undoing.

22. Havelock, *Preface to Plato,* p. 202.

FOURTEEN

Assisting at the Birth and Death of Philosophic Vision

Andrea Nye

> *If they managed to get their hands on the philosopher, all that remains to know is whether this impoverished effigy of a copula was not already dead and what in this hand-to-hand combat they stand to gain other than to tear themselves apart.*
>
> LUCE IRIGARAY COMMENTING ON THE DEATH OF PLATO'S SOCRATES
> (*Speculum* 457, 364)[1]

If it has been woman's work to assist at births, it is also for her to lay out the dead, arrange their limbs, mourn for a suitable length of time, and go on with the business of life. Both birth and death are painful processes; both require skill, tact, and soothing words. Both can shake men and women to their very souls. So it was with Plato when his teacher Socrates died. But he had little patience with the keening of women.[2] He made of that death a birth, of another life, after death, the life of philosophy. His obstetrics, much as it might have mimicked the midwifery of women, was meant to bring into the world a new kind of Being that could see with an eye dead to life and all its confusions but alive to the vision of an ideal landscape of Forms and Truths.

There are no assistants to this procedure as Plato describes it in the *Republic*'s allegory of the cave. The master-philosopher, alone, turns the neophyte philosopher around headfirst, forces him out and away from the flickering images cast on the wall of the cave—away from the posturing heroes, salacious gods, claptrap warriors, wily adventurers, seducers of nymphs that Greek men repeatedly copied in their actions and words. Alone, the teacher works the initiate into proper position at the back of the dark womb of the cave where there is hidden an exit, not down but up into the sunlight of Reason. And so in pain, dazzled by the sudden brightness, panting for breath, the philosopher is born to his new life.

It is this traumatic passage out of the deception and confusion of men's affairs and into the rigors of philosophy that Luce Irigaray attends in *Speculum*. Appropriate, because what does a man know about birth, about the skillful management necessary to insure a safe delivery, about what can go wrong, what may have already gone wrong even though it is not apparent at first—stillbirths, fatal deformities, missing hearts? And so at Plato's elbow appears Irigaray, the midwife, repeating, recording, commenting, and above all watching and listening, seemingly faithful to the text and to the intent. Seemingly, because there is something in her manner which might cause uneasiness for the Platonic obstetrician, a certain tone of tongue-in-cheek which, even as it appears to acknowledge the immense gravity of the occasion and the skill of the practitioner, introduces an irony punctuated here and there by a *sotto voce* murmur hard to catch. All of which suggests that this nurse-assistant is not so docile, so sincere in her wish to help, as one might have wished, that her very accuracy in following procedure exactly as the doctor orders goes too far, purposefully too far, so as to expose overtones, undertones, implications that would have been better left unmentioned.

In contrast to Irigaray's ambiguous assistance at a passage from one life to another, from one seeing to another, most commentary on the allegory of the cave has focused on the result of the Platonic passage: the mind, Reason, Western culture. The painful birth process recorded in the *Republic* is forgotten; in its place is the momentous "discovery" of a Truth which could not have been born like a mortal thing, but which must have been already there, inherent in the Aryan soul, or in the Greek language, which, as the only innately "scientific" language, is the most perfect expression of that soul.[3] Buried in grammar, so the argument goes, or in a certain grammar, waiting to be exhumed, was and is the object of true knowledge, the "universal."[4] Reason, which discovered this object, is no "foreign intruder who pressured his way into language,"[5] but was already there in the facility with which verbs and adjectives in Indo-European languages are nominalized into abstract substantives combinable in logical order.

The availability of a definite article in that family of languages allows reference to ordinary experience—"the horse" meaning "that horse"—to become reference to a transcendental object—"the Horse," and so brings to light a nobler object of contemplation. More important, the same article used generically allows a crucial transition from the particular, fallible judgments of practical life—"these are good men"—to the moral absolute—"the Good." Most profound of all, most valuable of all, it is claimed, is the Indo-European copula, the "this is a . . ." which points the way from unknowable particulars, visible to ordinarily fluid, flexible, relative sight, to the invisible universals which are the true reality. On this account, Plato's Forms were not so much born as they were mined, "brought to the surface,"[6] where they can be seen with the eye of mind, brought up to the light of reason in a labor which must always struggle against the "unscientific potentialities of early speech."[7]

There have been critics of the procedures Plato used to unearth the metaphysical "what is." Heidegger, for example, complained that Plato betrayed the memory of true "Being," partially intuited in Pre-Socratic philosophy and inherent in the Indo-European imagination. Being-as-Becoming, he claimed, was hidden in the root meaning of the Greek work for truth, ἀλήθεια, "unveiled" or "not hidden."[8] In its place, Plato projected a static simulacrum. The Heideggerian philosopher digs down into the Pre-Socratics φυσις or primal origin of the cosmos, to find the buried understanding of an emergence-of-Being whose understanding is no calm contemplation of stationary Form but a vision that might inspire instead a historic movement of becoming, such as fascism.[9] If the results are different, the process of discovery is the same: not the birth of a mortal Being, but a mining of what is eternally already there, latent in Indo-European grammar.

Irigaray revives the birth metaphor suppressed in these transcriptions of the Platonic ascent to Form onto the grammar of a family of languages. For her, Platonic midwifery is no discardable literary conceit, but marks the emergence of a new Being out of male hysteria and gynophobia. Irigaray, the psychoanalytic linguist, turns from the structure of language to the unconscious structure of the masculine mind. The coming into being of an unseeing vision of Truth as the epistemological paradigm for Western rationalism, as she observes it, is a symbolic birth, the acting out of a fantasy in which "foolish" men, having rejected the world of women and sexuality, and therefore trapped in a shadow theater of deceptive repeating images, are reborn under the guidance of the Platonic philosopher to a heaven of clear and distinct forms.

Already substituted for whatever unimaginable, unimageable form of expression is possible between child and mother, Irigaray's cave is the prison house of men's illusory representation, a nightmare world of echoes, reflections, fakes, fakes of fakes, copies of copies, traded back and forth by a congregation split between passive miming masses and the few "magicians" who work the mechanisms of projection. Because there is no reference to any material thing—all that is earthly and therefore womanly has already been erased in flight from the mother—reference is artificially produced, by maintaining a dividing line or wall between the signified devised by the magicians and the signifier viewed by the passive masses. This break, which maintains representation, is further articulated in the silences between remark and remark that allow a proposition to be reiterated. In the cave, language is the only material, requiring for support no more than the blank, anonymous back wall on which written or spoken sounds are inscribed.[10]

That men would feel an urgent need, even a compulsion, to escape such a bad dream is understandable:

> How can these prisoners, for whom only simulacres exist, only words bor-
> rowed from projected shadows, hallucinating with voices whose artifices of
> reproduction-production they do not understand, fascinated by spectacles
> whose mimetic techniques they have no means for evaluating, how can
> these fools, these children, deprived of all education, be freed from their
> chains, cured of their wandering? [*Speculum* 333, 268]

Plato's answer is, of course, the passage to a new life in philosophy,
which replaces any traumatic return to the mother's vagina-womb, invisible behind the blank, featureless screen of the cavern-womb on which
the "signfiers" that occupy men are projected. Irigaray's philosopher replaces the already rejected, unspeakable primal copulation of sexed bodies with the disembodied copula of logic. In the passage to rationality,
the cave's tricks of representation are not abandoned, but rectified in the
pseudo-cave of the vault of heaven. The minor trickery of the magicians
of representation is not exposed but replaced by a master trickery in
which the necessity for material reference, already reduced to a blank
medium of transmission, is eliminated. The eye of Reason requires no
medium, no surface, no backing, as the seer comes face to face with his
own image in an all-knowing, all powerful Father-God. Reflected and reflecting in the divine eye of the sun, he achieves a nonmaterial autonomy. The final, ineffable Platonic revelation is reserved for an elite few;
but those who remain at the lower level of names, definitions, and images also profit. Understanding that "what is" is, and "what is not" is not,
ordering their thinking according to the law of the excluded middle,
they are delivered from the proliferating, dizzying plurality of men's affairs in the city to the ordered homogeneity of Law. Now a new kind of
talk is possible. Not the disordered proliferation of "differance," but the
pederastic instruction of young men by those who are older and wiser.

Irigaray describes well, perhaps too well, the dazzling pyrotechnics of
the final Platonic revelation. The tricks of light, the flashes, blazes, repeating images, bursts of light as male eye meets male eye under the all-
seeing, all-annihilating eye of the Sun.[11] The dazzling éclat of the change
from diachronic discursivity to synchronic structure frees the speculative
constructions of metaphysics as well as the spectacular skills of technical
science, in which the copulating penis becomes the penetrating eye of a
voyeur. Vision, of all the senses, Irigaray agrees, is the proper organ for
this transformation. Vision alone allows the simultaneous presentation of
an array of objects in a coordinate field, placing them at a distance. This
distance is necessary for the mirroring that sustains theoretical projection. Vision alone promotes the illusion of autonomy that keeps the seeing subject and his material support unseen behind the scenes.[12] Vir-
tuosic, brilliant, Irigaray stimulates the photophallic effects of logic into a

final blaze of homoerotic ecstasy. Then silence, the anticlimax, the abortive retreat back down into the shadow box of men's affairs, the fatal confrontation with ordinary men from which the philosopher, if he is lucky, barely escapes with his life.[13]

Silence, death, the end of the story. Until the process begins again, in a reerection of theory and speculation, as Irigaray records, through Descartes, Hegel, Lacan, and presumably, forever, as long as there are men. There is another synchrony here, not of Reason and Form, but of eternal psychic drama, the spell of another dream of a dream, which prevents Irigaray from seeing what has actually happened to this philosophic subject born out of Plato's cave, from seeing how he has aged. Plato's universe of Reason, as Irigaray records it, is the vision of a young man shot through with eros. But I keep thinking of another man, a later version of this vision of a man, Ludwig Wittgenstein.

In Wittgenstein's *Tractatus,* the rectification Plato prescribed has rectified itself in the perfection and purification of a fully mathematicized photo-logicism. Gone is Plato's flickering Aryan fire, Sun-God, the glittering, blinding reflections of Form. Wittgenstein's metaphysical vision, finally removed from any reference to physical things, is detached from any spoken language, dependent on no metaphorical substratum for support. Only the purest of representational symmetry remains between logical form and the necessary form of the world.

1. The world is all that is the case.
1.1 The world is the totality of facts not things.
[*Tractatus* 1, 1.1][14]

In austerely numbered passages, the romantic passion of Plato's ascent is replaced by somber litany. The cave is gone, the χώρα, the material substratum still necessary in the cosmology of the *Timaeus* so that Form, "uncreated and indestructible, never receiving anything into itself from without, nor itself going out to any other," exists some*where*.[15] In the *Tractatus* there is no material with its own energy and principles, but only the purest of representation, only what Being must be if it is to be represented.

Withered away is the flesh of grammar, the Indo-European verbs and adjectives from which substantives of Forms might be derived:

> Language disguises thought. So much so, that from the outward form of the clothing, it is impossible to infer the form of the thought beneath it, because the outward form of the clothing is not designed to reveal the form of the body, but for different reasons. [*Tractatus* 4.002]

Ideal reality is no longer the shadow of any living or dead language, but colorless, undefinable geometrical space.[16] The new logical form is nei-

ther in "heaven" nor in "earth"; it is the configuration, the "concatenation"[17] of substanceless points, the abstract patterns of their possible ar-
rangement made visible in a notation from which all acoustic effects of
language have been erased. Objects are not substantial entities, but argument places in logical functions. Only skin and bones are left, the bones
of logical form, the parchment skin of logical notation; no clothing, and
not even any flesh or muscle intrudes between meaning and expression.
The great body of Western metaphysics, delivered by Plato, schooled by
the Scholastics, energized by the Enlightenment, drained of blood, lies
inert.

All that remains is the bare trick of representation, without the cave's
reflecting walls, without a heaven ruled by the Sun-God. Only the wall
erected between signifier and the signified is left, so that the effects of
mirroring can be achieved. If objects are not there to be represented, if
propositions are not resolvable into their constituents, "we could not
sketch any picture of the world (true or false)" (*Tractatus* 2.0212). The relation between signifier and signified cannot be physical resemblance.
Too fleshy and material, resemblance becomes a "rule of projection"
which maps reality onto a notation, a reality that is only the projection of
what is necessary for that notation's representation.

In Wittgenstein's *Tractatus,* the crude trickery of Plato's magicians is
replaced not with the fireworks of revelation but with logical semantics.
From that vantage, there will be no more dangerous and frustrating returns to the affairs of the city, no more climaxes of sublimated desire, no
more ecstatic communion eye-to-eye with God. Only a showing and articulation of logical form. What can be said can be said clearly. "What we
cannot speak about we must pass over in silence" (*Tractatus* 7). If there is
debris left behind here, it is no longer matter, the afterbirth of the *chora,*
but life itself, as what matters and has meaning. The self, value, God,
death, will, all are outside the limits of logical language, of what can be
said (*Tractatus* 6.373–7). Even thinking is gone, replaced by the static
limits of what can be thought (*Tractatus* 4.1121, 4.114). There is no
agency, only the automatism of a mechanism into which are fed bits of
information that correspond to the objects of discourse of a theory.

The eye that projects reality, that has its view outside the world, seeing
the world as a "limited whole, sub specie aeterni" (*Tractatus* 6.45), is the
eye of a dead man. The metaphysician's philosophic vision is finally
blind. This was the danger Hans Jonas warned about even as he praised
the "nobility" of metaphysical vision as the preferred vehicle of Western
rationalism. Although there might be "biological" advantage in the visual
ability to survey a field of objects from a removed, invulnerable position,
at the same time vision which is detached from the body and the other

senses can be the least realistic sense. Separated from the object seen, the seer can only confirm what he sees. Touch, on the other hand, is "true contact" with reality, a contact which is both contact with another and contact with self. In the very effortlessness of detached vision, reality fades away, "denuded of its raw power," its causality made invisible.[18]

If, in Plato's heaven, the dream of a seeing mortal body remained, in Wittgenstein's logic it has disappeared. There is no perspective. Not only the movement of a body around, toward, away from an object—which reduces vision to a string of discursive images—is gone, but also the movement of the eyes themselves, *two* eyes which focus like pincers on an object of interest and, in the strain of that grasp, are affected just as the fingers which grip a stick are affected. The unseeable form of the real in *Tractatus* is monocular, the "eye and the visual field." Its center is one "I" which projects its objects but cannot focus, which cannot see itself seeing, and so cannot see what is outside its own fixed gaze (*Tractatus* 5.633).

The metaphysician cannot see himself. The trick of representation requires that the wall between what is represented and the symbols which represent not be breached. There can be no looking behind the wall to what the magicians are doing:

> So we cannot say in logic, "the world has this in it and this, but not that."
>
> For that would appear to presuppose that we were excluding certain possibilities, and this cannot be the case since it would require that logic could go beyond the limits of the world; for only in that way could it view those limits from the other side as well. [*Tractatus* 5.5571]

Nor did Plato invite his chosen students to look behind the wall, where the magicians did their tricks, to expose the mechanisms of deception; his interest was not to expose representation but to transport it to a higher sphere where the Father-Sun-God provides a self-validating representation of a Form of forms that can be authoritatively divided and represented. The eye of the *Tractatus* has no such counterpart. A fixed point "without extension," it has no place and no existence even in heaven. "The subject does not belong to the world: rather it is a limit of the world" (*Tractatus* 5.632).

Utterly removed from the world, the "world" of the logical subject is what is the case, and what is the case is always what was the case under "specie aeterne," a static projection of the possibility of life, a life which is over, a life in which the self is only a "report":

> If I wrote a book called *The World As I Found It*, I should have to include a report on my body, and should have to say which parts were subordinate

to my will, and which were not, etc., this being a method of isolating the subject, or rather showing that in an important sense there is no subject; for it alone could *not* be mentioned in that book. [*Tractatus* 5.631]

A life frozen into its final form, incapable of thought. "There is no such thing as the subject that thinks or entertains ideas" (*Tractatus* 5.631).[19] If Plato's philosopher shares the excitement of birth, this is the silence of the grave.

But we know that it was not the end. Philosophy went on. Wittgenstein went on, rising from the dead end of the *Tractatus* to write his later philosophy, a philosophy that gave birth to new movements of ordinary-language philosophy and speech-act theory. There is such a thing as the walking dead, men dead for all purposes of life, but who give a semblance of vitality. After all, what is a dead man who is still alive to do, someone who has lost his self, his will, his god, and all meaning or value? He might have to learn "forms of life," playing "language games" so that he appears like everyone else; he might have to follow the rules of proper usage so that he is not so much a freak. In all of this, there is no question of a living subject speaking to others for their response to what he says. Whatever thoughts, beliefs, intentions, and expectations the living man might have remain nonentities, null and void, inexpressible in any language.[20]

But even after the pretense of language games, more, much more happens, in one sense of "happens." Speech-act theory glosses the inert semantic core of the *Tractatus* with rules that govern "how to do things with words."[21] Cognitive psychologists give the mind new mechanical existence as the functional states of neural or computer hardware. Scientific realists wire the existence of objects onto the accepted procedures of science. In structural linguistics, logical semantics proclaims itself a science by discovering the ultimate simples of plus-and-minus phonetic features that structure speech. Deconstructionalists mount a rearguard action, staging a defiant return to the decentered, disordered representations of Plato's cave. Back in the cave, Foucaultians explain how paradigms of discourse are embedded in disciplinary procedures that keep the bodies of prisoners chained in their seats. And finally Lacan, whose oppressive shadow so haunts Irigaray, in a masterly move fuses the logical semantics of the linguists with Plato's Father-God. Claiming that the ultimate meaning of the foundational tautology *"what is" is* is the self-identity of the paternal phallus, he grounds semantic structure of plus-and-minus features in a primordial alternation of male phallic presence and female lack. Placed, one by one, at the keyhole of Wittgenstein's solipsistic world-view, Lacan's subjects, dead to the world, take up positions "constructed in the language." In all these cases, the architecture of the final vision of the *Tractatus* remains. Reference, removed from meanings generated in speech between diverse others, is to nothing. There is no other way it can be in a life after death.

Irigaray, the feminine analyst, herself suffers from the paralysis induced by this draining away of life. Almost unnoticeable, at the bottom of the last page, in the smallest of prints, she describes her feminine function:

> The/a woman performing in relation to the elaboration of theory a function both from outside mutely sustaining all systematicity, and from the maternal ground (still) silent from which is nourished all foundation, does not have to conduct herself in the proper manner as it is coded in theory. Confronting, in this way, yet another time, the imagination of the "subject"—in its masculine connotations—and that which would be, will be perhaps, the "feminine" imagination. . . . If this causes, in the resistance found there, the "discomfort of a distortion" if possible unreducible, then perhaps? something of the "difference between the sexes has taken place also in language." [*Speculum* 458, 365]

Irigaray, as midwife, participates in the Platonic drama. Trapped in the closed orbit of synchronic psychoanalysis, the resisting philosophical subject and the feminine analyst struggling to "reinscribe" the feminine are antagonistic partners in an interminable psychoanalysis.[22] Always the stasis of masculine reason asserts itself, always the feminine intrudes and derails; the only sign of life is a passing "discomfort."

On this view, no feminist metaphysics, no feminist philosophy is possible. The woman must play her proper part in the recurring symbolic order, suffering and disrupting the philosophizing of men, over and over, again and again.

> Since, yet again, "reasonable" words—which anyway she can arrange only by mimicking—cannot translate that which pulses, clamors, and is suspended, floating, in the cryptic trajectories of hysterical latent suffering. Then . . . to put all sense inside out, front to back, high to low. To *shake it radically*, to report there, reimport there, the crises which her "body" suffers in its impotence to say what it is that agitates it. [*Speculum* 176, 142]

A woman may mimic "reason," exposing its feints and avoidances, or she may suffer inarticulately. She, along with the philosophers, has been born into a kind of living death, barely alive, without the ability to speak her pain, without the ability to tell a story the way it happened and make a judgment, without a politics that does not mime the artifice of representation but knocks it away.

Is there any alternative? Irigaray herself makes a tentative suggestion, one that, unfortunately, she does not pursue: we must interpret the interests in the game. To whom accrue the profits from the credit invested in such a metaphoricity, in such cordonages and definitions of the pieces of a game, in the attribution of these different criteria to the pieces of chess, in this hierarchy of values as stakes, rules, balance in the affair? [*Speculum* 335, 270]

Beyond the imaginary man of Plato's cave, trapped in infantile rejection of the mother, were other men, real men with interests and stakes that were not imaginary but real. Irigaray hints at what might have revealed those interests and made the dream-man a reality. If the prisoners in the cave, before the philosopher intervenes, "had talked to each other, at least at this point in Socrates' story, they would have interpreted, and unmasked, the mimetic functioning that organizes this cave" (*Speculum* 319, 257). The real, not symbolic, alternative to the duality of foolish disordered talk and its counterpart, ordered philosophic metaphysics, is not the suffering of the feminine body, victim in life of the dream projects of men, but interpersonal speaking in which all can be heard, freed from the representational paradigm. Irigaray herself points out some of the ways in which such a conversing might interrupt the synchrony of both illogical and logical discourse:

> What passes, comes to pass, in conversation, is not reducible to the neutral blank, silence, interval, which allow the discrimination or framing of remarks and their repetition and sustains the fiction of terms specific to each one and each thing capable of being reproduced as such. [In conversation] the complexity of effects of retroaction, and also, inevitably in the drama, the interventions of factors of multi-determination and overdetermination, burst open the present of production-reproduction. Not only in the gap, the pretended break and articulation between a present and a past—an imitator and an imitated, a signifier and a signified—but also in the present's retaking up, repeating, specularizing the past, this past defined as a present having already taken place, conversing, by deploying, unfolding, would open into an abyss this present or this past in the suspension of insoluble, undecidable correlations between a "has been" and a "would have been," as well as between a "would have been" and a "has been." [*Speculum* 319, 257]

What you have said is what I would have said, perhaps, if I had been there, and what I would have said, having heard you, is something different again. What has been would have been different if we had spoken. Moving relations between speakers, different perspectives on events, the layering of time, allow thought to move forward and judgments to be made. These effects of communication resist both the proliferation of manipulated illogical discourses and the rectification and monocularity of logical form.

What would they have said to each other, those prisoners, those living Greek men to whom Plato addressed his teachings? What would they have talked about if they had spoken to each other, if they had not been captivated by images, if they had been able to bypass the "function of representation to sanction, organize, regulate, arbitrate relations, between men?" (*Speculum* 329, 265). Would they have analyzed the imaginary complexes of their masculine unconscious with Irigaray? Would they have noted the Lacanian phallacity of Plato's Forms and bowed before the *jouissance* of women? These motifs are from our time, objects of interest in our twentieth century, not in theirs. Their history is also our history, but it is those Greek men, different from us, who would have had to speak together about their situation. How did they live, or fail to live, and who were these magicians who entranced them?

In the *Republic* Plato makes it clear who, in his judgment, were the magicians. Greek men were entranced by heroic myths repeated over and over in the hypnotic rhythms of the poets:

> the trailings of Hector's body round the grave of Patroclus and the slaughter of living captives upon his pyre, all these we will affirm to be lies, nor will we suffer our youth to believe that Achilles . . . was of so perturbed a spirit as to be affected with two contradictory maladies, the greed that becomes no free man and at the same time overweening arrogance toward gods and men. . . . Neither, then, must we believe this, or suffer it to be said, that Theseus, the son of Poseidon, and Pirithous, the son of Zeus, attempted such dreadful rapes, or that any other child of a god or hero would have brought himself to accomplish the terrible and impious deeds that they now falsely relate of them. [*Republic* 391B–D]

Thoughtlessly, in disastrous and wasteful foreign adventures, in political posturing and maneuvering, Greek men mimicked the fictional heroes of the *Odyssey* and *Iliad*. Over and over, the shades of Agamemnon, Menelaus, and Achilles repeated the follies of the Trojan war. Driven by covetousness, greed, lust, and a shallow reflex of honor that demanded retribution even for the misfortunes they brought on themselves, men jeopardized the autonomy of Athens and the proper government of the state. In the city there was civil strife, abroad ill-advised expeditions of conquest. And so Plato's authoritarian remedy: it is not that Greek men should give up representation or mimicking and find a forum for realistic and democratic discussion of civic matters, but rather other "nobler" images should be substituted to captivate their already captivated vision. As Plato explains it in the *Statesman*: "The soul full of vigor and courage will be made gentle by its grasp of this truth, and there is nothing as well calculated as this to make it a willing member of a community based on justice" [*Statesman* 309E].

To "analyze" this substitution as a projection of the Phallus above and beyond diverse expressions of masculinity in men's affairs effaces the specific methods by which Plato proposed to deliver his philosopher-king. As explained in the *Republic,* the exit from the confusions of the cave was to be achieved by way of a particular pedagogy. Men would be introduced to a nobler vision than that of the imperfect warriors of myth, as presented by Homer. "What studies have the power to effect this? What would be the study that would draw the soul away from the world of becoming to the world of being?" Plato asks (*Republic* 521D). Rigorous physical training might be sufficient for the exploits of Homeric heroes, but it administers only to the body, not the mind. The transition to political order can best be brought about, Plato concludes, by military *science,* by a mathematics of "number and calculation." This is the knowledge that the generals of myth lack:

> Palamedes in the play is always making Agamemnon appear a most ridiculous general. Have you not noticed that he affirms that by the invention of number he marshaled the troops in the army at Troy in ranks and companies and enumerated the ships and everything else as if before that they hadn't been counted, and Agamemnon apparently did not know how many feet he had if he couldn't count? And yet what sort of general do you think he would be in that case? [*Republic* 522D]

Planning battle formations, deploying troops, counting enemy forces, these require mathematics, require a geometer's eye that can project mathematical relations. To the general, men are not just men; it is the exact calculation of their massing that is important. In this way the military man already has his eyes turned away from particular living bodies and toward abstractions. Unlike Agamemnon, the posturing hero, who didn't know how many feet he had, the man of reason is practiced in the "nobility" of vision. He draws back a distance from battle so as to survey the whole field; he takes up a position invulnerable to attack by enemy forces. He objectifies the forces he commands in clearly defined units so as to plot exactly their deployment. He counts ships, forces, weapons.

> The qualities of number appear to lead to the apprehension of truth. . . . Then, as it seems, these would be among the studies we are seeking. For a soldier must learn them in order to marshal his troops, and a philosopher because he must rise out of the region of generation and lay hold of essences or he can never become a true reckoner. . . . Our guardian is soldier and philosopher in one. [*Republic* 525B]

If Plato was the first to recommend this transition to a reasoned science of war and the promotion of the skills necessary for its elaboration, he was not the last. Throughout the history of scientific Western reason, there continued to be a close correlation between the needs of the battle-field and advances in science. It is the general's eye that is "noble, ready to be converted, turned," in his later years, to the government of the state. His eye has already been weaned from the "world of becoming" (*Republic* 518C). He is ready to put his whole soul to the reordering of society. In contrast to the vulgar arithmetic of "merchants or hucksters," which provides no basis for a conversion to metaphysics (*Republic* 525C), the general's mathematics is abstract in the requisite way. His skill of reckoning "never acquiesces if anyone proffers to it in the discussion numbers attached to visible and tangible bodies" (*Republic* 525D). To him, "one" battalion, "one" company are "units which can only be conceived by thought. . . . Each unit is equal to every other without the slightest difference and admitting no division into parts" (*Republic* 526A). This is why, skilled in his military art, the general is ready to move on, from the "bringing of troops into column and line" to the proper ordering of society (*Republic* 526D). Plato's soldier-philosopher has an interest in the rectification of representations; he profits from the investment he has made in years of training in the arts of war. This may be why the most profound successes of the Western culture which takes Plato as its founder are in military conquest. The metaphysician's eye is a refinement of the general's eye: abstract, all-encompassing, unemotional, pitiless.

It is not just that the Platonic philosopher has turned away from women's sexual pleasure, or the Mother—although he may have done that too—but he has turned away from all of life, from births, deaths, marriage, love, friendship, community relations, work, and labor. What he does *not* see is not the "bodies" of women—which he may see well enough—but the graceful forms of life of an older Mediterranean matri-focal culture, under seige in Homer's epics and now either destroyed or co-opted by the dominant Hellenic culture. If, in Plato's story, the posturing hero Agamemnon is transformed into an efficient military dictator, what is omitted is not Clytemnestra's "copulation" with Aegisthus, but something much more important: her judgment on and execution of her husband, Agamemnon, the general responsible for the carnage of the Trojan war as well as for the death of their daughter.

The antidote for this failure to live in the world of speaking, living human beings is not the imposition of another kind of death. Would it have helped the understanding of Greek men if, as some have suggested, they had taken another one of their senses as fetish, such as hearing, and so instituted a nonocular metaphysics?[23] Any attempt to found meaning in a single sense traps the subject inside himself and closes off the possibility of speaking with others. For the objects of interest about which people can speak are never accessible only to one sense but to several, never accessible to one person only but to many. The object of any one sense or any one vision must be finally ineffable, uncapturable in words, images, or theory. When the focus shifts, as it must, away from the object of knowledge to the formal structure of language, that structure, ungrounded in living speech, becomes the shell of solipsism, one man's projection of what only he can understand, regardless of how many others he may induce to mimic him.[24]

But what if, as Irigaray suggested, at some point in the story, before the imposition of "martial law," Greek men had spoken of what was happening to them? What if, turning away from heroic tales to each other, they looked, not at imagined ideal Forms, but rather at themselves, to see not the imagined shades of heroes, but visible and tangible bodies, the bodies of men? Men who see with "arrogant eyes."[25] Men who in their anxious, defensive surveying of the visual field of battle had lost the ability to look each other (or anyone) "in the eye."[26] Might they have seen themselves, as Clytemnestra, or any Greek woman, might have seen them?

What if, to go even further, mimicking neither Agamemnon and Achilles, who quarrel over the body of a woman as booty of war, nor the model husband, master of wife and slaves, of Aristotle's *Politics*, Greek men had turned to *speak* to the women, who had been there all along? In such a speaking, the "I" would not have been a single "eye," from which the cone of vision reaches into eternity, blind to everything in its periphery, but rather two eyes, which act like a pincers to grasp what is of common interest. The "I" would not have been the monocular subject who never catches a glimpse of himself as he retreats successively behind his representations, but an "I" in relation to you's and she's, themselves in relation, you to us, he to it, it to me. If such a subject does not constitute his language, he is not constituted in it either; he speaks it, alive to the circuit of assertion and response. His meanings are not his epitaph written on stone, but are constantly reworked and remade in the revolving cycle of communication and thought without which the "human body is a corpse" and the "human mind is dead."[27]

Would have beens. But if such a speech is hardly possible now for the ancient Athenians to whom Plato directed his teaching, it may still be possible for those of us who are alive in the numbing shadow of Wittgenstein, who share with him the nihilism of modern mass warfare and the alienation of those who are taught to despise the sexed bodies of living men and women, who share with him the living death of contemporary analytic philosophy. If the Platonic philosopher's dying vision was briefly illuminated by a transcendent sun, the post-Wittgensteinian philosopher's eyes are fixed and staring. Might his remains be decently laid to rest, might his wake be celebrated among the living?

Ο ἀποθαηένος δὲ ηιλεῖ, γιατὶ δεύ ἔχει στοηα
γιατι τόνε σκεπάζουνε ηὲ πέτρες και ηὲ χῶηα.

The dead man does not speak, because he has no mouth,
and because they are covering him with rocks and with earth.

Greek Funeral Lament[28]

NOTES

1. Page references to Irigaray in the text are to the *Speculum d L'autre Femme* (Paris: Minuit, 1974) (my translations), followed by page references to the English version, *Speculum of the Other Woman,* trans. G. C. Gill (Ithaca, N.Y.: Cornell University Press, 1985).

2. See the *Republic,* book 3, 387E (all references to Plato's dialogues are to *The Collected Dialogues of Plato,* ed. E. Hamilton and H. Cairns [Princeton, N.J.: Princeton University Press, 1973]): "Then we should be right in doing away with the lamentations of men of note and in attributing them to women—and not to the most worthy of them either—and to inferior men, in order that those whom we say we are breeding for the guardianship of the land may disdain to act like these."

3. Bruno Snell, *The Discovery of the Mind* (New York: Harper, 1960). "Greek is the only language which allows us to trace the true relation between speech and the rise of science; for in no other tongue did the concepts of science grow straight from the body of the language. In Greece and only in Greece, did theoretic thought emerge without outside influence, and nowhere else was there an autochthonous formation of scientific terms."

4. Although Snell (chap. 10, "The Origin of Scientific Thought") acknowledges that the generic use of the article is not found in Hesiod or Homer or the Pre-Socratics and only very tenuously in Greek drama, he insists that Plato did not disfigure usage but discovered something already there potentially in the language.

5. Snell, *Discovery,* p. 235.

6. Ibid.

7. Ibid., p. 244.

8. "Meaning" must be understood here in its Heideggerian sense. Heidegger argued that the Greek word ἀλήθεια was a compound of the privative ἀ and ληθ. Pressed by classicists who cited overwhelming evidence that the word was never used in Homer or any other early source in a privative sense, but always meant "correct" or "reliable," Heidegger retreated to another sense of *meaning,* in which meanings, although they are not, and have never been, part of any known *use* of a word, are latent in a language. Not only Plato missed the true meaning of ἀλήθεια; so did all Greek speakers. See Heidegger's "Platons Lehre von der Wahrheit," in *Wegmarken* (Frankfurt am Main: Victtorio Klosterman, 1967), Paul

Friedlander's critique in *Plato: An Introduction* (New York: Harper & Row, 1958), and then Heidegger's qualified retraction in *Zur Sache des Denkens* (Tübingen: Max Niemeyer Verlag, 1969).

9. On Hitler's plebiscite of November 12, 1933, Heidegger commented: "The German people have been called to the polls by the Führer. But this is not a demand that the Führer addresses to the people; on the contrary it gives to the people the most immediate possibility of making the highest of free decisions: the people all together will decide if it wishes its proper *Dasein* or if it does not wish it. Tomorrow, the people choose nothing less than its future" (my translation from *Le Debat* 48, [January–February 1988], pp. 184–185). If his remarks are not mandated by the existential philosophy of *Being and Time*, they reflect its spirit: the West has lost the "rootedness in Being" which, Heidegger argues, can be found in Pre-Socratics like Parmenides. Man can be rescued from the nihilism of critical reason when a "historic" people is reunited with Being or "destiny." The German people are in a special position to accomplish this because of what Heidegger took as the roots of the German language in Greek and the German folk's historic destiny. Later, disillusionment with some aspects of fascism, reminiscent of Plato's failure in Syracuse (see Letter 7), caused Heidegger to retreat to the safer, more metaphysical revelation of Being in German Romantic poetry, holding in reserve for an unknown future a revived earthly realization of Becoming. See Hannah Arendt's account of his various positions, as caused by a "professional deformation" shared by other philosophers, in "Martin Heidegger at Eighty," *New York Review of Books* 17, no. 5 (October 1971).

10. Irigaray and others have called attention to the function of the χώρα in the cosmology of the *Timaeus*. For Irigaray it is symbolic of the repressed feminine body. The cave is a model of male "hysteria"—womb-craziness, womb-aversion, denial of the mother's body. For Julia Kristeva (*Desire in Language* [New Haven: Yale University Press, 1980], pp. 6–7), the *chora* is the semiotic maternal. In a close hermeneutical reading of the text, Gadamer (*Dialogue and Dialectic: Eight Hermeneutic Studies in Plato*, trans. P. C. Smith [New Haven: Yale University Press, 1980], p. 178) argues that the *chora* represents a break between two not completely compatible accounts of the origin of the cosmos: one mythic in which the demiurge fashions forms, one mathematical, reached not by the intuition of any god's intentions but by rational deduction. In this mathematical account, the *chora* is credited with an active principle of foment and change which preorders natural elements in the same way that "grain is shaken and winnowed by fans and other instruments" (*Timaeus* 52E). In this formal ordering, Plato's god must "persuade" matter and create within certain natural limits. I might add to these readings the actual Greek use of χώρα as the living communal and social space of the village or region, which is the matrix of shared meanings.

11. See Irigaray's ". . . And If, Taking the Eye of a Man Recently Dead" in *Speculum* for an exploration of the strange hypnotic quality of this romance.

12. The defense cited most often of the superior phenomenology of vision is Hans Jonas's "The Nobility of Sight" (*Philosophy and Phenomenological Research*, vol. 14, no. 4 (1954), pp. 507–519), reprinted in Stuart Spicker, ed., *The Philosophy of the Body: Rejections of Cartesian Dualism* (New York: Quandrangle/New

York Times, 1970), pp. 312–333. Jonas argues that only sight guarantees "independence from the transitory event of sense affectation" (p. 508). The "passive" sense of hearing registers a transitory event, itself only the effect of an object; touch produces objects and is active, but involves an intercourse with the object which leaves the agent vulnerable to being affected himself. In contrast, vision opens an autonomous gaze to infinity and so gives rise to the philosopher's eternal truth and nonmaterial form.

13. The paradigm example is Plato's attempt to influence the politics at Syracuse, which led to an ignominious retreat. See his account in Letter 7.

14. References to the *Tractatus* in the text are to *Tractatus Logico-Philosophicus*, trans. D. F. Pears and B. F. McGuinn (London: Routledge & Kegan Paul, 1961).

15. "What is neither in heaven nor in earth has no existence" (Plato, *Timaeus* 52).

16. There has been much debate as to the identity of the simple objects whose configuration is mirrored in Wittgenstein's elementary propositions. That Russell and other positivists were mistaken in taking them as sense data is now generally acknowledged. Similarly the physicalist argument that they are atoms or atomic particles fails; Wittgenstein's objects have meaning only in the context of a proposition (3.3), which can say only how things are and not what they are (3.221). In my judgment the most plausible interpretation is that of Leonard Goddard and Brenda Judge in *The Metaphysics of Wittgenstein's "Tractatus"* (Australasian Association of Philosophy Monograph Series, no. 1, June 1982), who argue that many of the paradoxical qualities of Wittgenstein's objects disappear if they are taken as geometrical points.

17. Compare Irigaray's description of the prisoners in the cave as being enchained by "the effects of a certain language, of certain norms of language, that one calls sometimes, or for example, *concatenation* (*Speculum* 321, 259) with the *Tractatus* 2.03: "In a state of affairs objects fit into one another like the links of a chain."

18. See Jonas, "The Nobility of Sight," pp. 516–517.

19. Another way to make the point is to consider the technical problems in translating intensive language into logical notation, problems which seem to indicate that a thinking subject has a certain irreducible subjectivity. "It is clear, however, that 'A believes that p,' 'A has the thought p,' and 'A says p' are of the form '"p" says p'" (5.541). In this translation, thinking is erased and only representation is left. The sign "p" represents the fact 'p'.

20. As Peter Carruthers argues, defending the semantics of the *Tractatus* (*The Metaphysics of the Tractatus* [Cambridge: Cambridge University Press, 1990]), there is no essential conflict between early and late Wittgenstein. In *Philosophical Investigations*, the strictures against ostensive definition are still there, as well as the insistence that ideas are not expressible in language. The only change is Wittgenstein's recognition of a multiplicity of uses. Underlying these uses, however, if there is to be truth there will be still the propositional core ordered by a semantics such as that in the *Tractatus*, as is clear in post-Wittgensteinian semantics.

21. See for the classic expositions John Searle, *Speech Acts* (London: Cam-

bridge University Press, 1970); John Austin, *How to Do Things with Words* (Cambridge: Harvard University Press, 1962).

22. Irigaray's treatment of Freud could be compared. In *Speculum,* she presents the Freudian text as a reenactment of Plato's dream scene of avoidance rather than as the statement of a man in a given historical situation. See, for a contrasting historical analysis, Marie Balmary, *Psychoanalyzing Psychoanalysis,* trans. Ned Lukacher (Baltimore: Johns Hopkins Press, 1982). In pursuance of professional success and driven by his own familial conflicts, Freud denies the facts of sexual abuse which his women patients recount to him, deciding that their problem is an imaginary complex.

23. See Evelyn Fox Keller's conclusion to "The Mind's Eye," Sandra Harding and Merrill Hintikka, eds., *Discovering Reality* (Dordrecht: D. Reidel, 1983), p. 221, and Hannah Arendt's argument in *Thinking* (New York: Harcourt, Brace, Jovanovich, 1978), p. 111. Both more or less reject the suggestion. Keller argues that the problem is not a patriarchal imposition of the vision motif so much as a distortion in our understanding of vision, while Arendt argues that "the difficulties created by metaphors drawn from the sense of hearing would be as great as the difficulties created by the metaphor of vision." As Arendt has pointed out, although in Heidegger the vision metaphor has "shrunk" to a moment of illumination succeeded by the "ringing of silence," the thinker is reduced to "an immobile mental state of sheer receptivity" (pp. 122–123).

24. This is the point at which the arguments of the *Investigations* extinguish even this spark of life. There can be no private language. A solipsistic projection has no meaning even to the eye projecting; thus, we are left with only the constituent rules of speech acts.

25. Marilyn Frye's phrase. See her contrast of "the arrogant eye" with "the loving eye" in *The Politics of Reality* (Trumansburg, N.Y.: Crossing Press, 1983), pp. 66–83.

26. See Keller's discussion of the vision paradigm in "The Mind's Eye." Keller argues that in the original Platonic metaphor of vision, surveying is combined with communion. This element, still present in some forms of scientific research, is missing in Jonas's philosophical account of the distancing and invulnerability of vision.

27. Arendt. *Thinking,* p. 123.

28. From Loring Danforth, *The Death Rituals of Rural Greece* (Princeton: Princeton University Press, 1982), opposite plate 16.

FIFTEEN

His Master's Eye

Mieke Bal

INTRODUCTION

Is vision as a mode of representation, knowledge, and sexual relationality especially pervasive in modernity? And is it bound up with patriarchy? Both these questions, and the answers given to them, are predicated upon the assumption that it is possible to define vision in some unified if not essentialist way. This paper does not endorse that assumption. Instead, it presents the argument that differentiating modes if not kinds of vision—multiplying perspectives, proliferating points of view—may be a more useful strategy for examining the ideological, epistemological, and representational implications of dominating modes of vision, including their illusory monopoly.

The argument for a differentiating conception of vision is made through an in-depth analysis of two culturally powerful and integrative "cases": the painting *Danae* by Rembrandt and its seventeenth- and twentieth-century reception, and the painting *Olympia* by Manet, the scandal surrounding its reception, and the analysis of that scandal in present-day art history.

I. A VISION THAT IS NOT (ONE)

Is there an inherent connection between vision and patriarchal power? This is often assumed to be the case, for example in the wake of Laura Mulvey's 1975 article, although not without qualifications.[1] The assumption underlying the suspicion is that vision is an essentially unified mode of perception and interpretation. But as has become clear in so many other areas of thought, unification (e.g. of "man," "woman," "language," or "life") tends to promote in and of itself a usurpation of power, if only through rendering invisible other aspects, elements, or positions within the unified category. Instead, therefore, I would like to address the question of vision's relation to power with the explicit aim of differentiating various modes of vision. I consider attention to such differentiations itself a more effective contribution to the rupturing of monopolies than their acceptance, albeit in their critical denunciation.

There is a second reason not to begin by assuming vision to be a single mode. As current debates about the authenticity of Rembrandt's paintings suggest, philosophical analysis of and speculation about vision seem a world apart from the practice of regulating vision in society, in this case in the world of High Art. If philosophy analyzes the relations between vision and power, knowledge, and subjection, in art history these relations are just lived out. And because of the elitism and the prestige that surround High Art, its effect as ideological model, and its pragmatic promotion of submission, High Art is an uncommonly relevant social issue. I will therefore attempt to keep together the philosophical-theoretical issues of vision in modernity with the practice of connoisseurship and art history's problematic attempts to move beyond this practice, in turn considered as a representative practice of dealing with gender and sexuality. I will discuss two famous "cases": the one surrounding Rembrandt's *Danae*, painted in the early days of the modern era and recognized as a masterpiece, and the one surrounding Manet's *Olympia*, painted roughly two centuries later, where the issues addressed in the *Danae* are exacerbated to the point of self-cancellation.

II. PORTRAIT OF THE EXPERT AS AN OLD MAN

One of the main characters in the discussions on vision is still the art-historian connoisseur, scholar, or layman. In order to get the issues clear, let me open with a quote from an expert's book on art in Western civilization, Sir Kenneth Clark's *Feminine Beauty*.

> The closest Rembrandt came to a statement of his ideal was the *Danae* in the Hermitage, where he certainly wished to make the figure as beautiful as he could. But his love of truth got the better of him. She is sensuous and desirable, but beautiful is not the word that comes to one's mind.[2]

Needless to say, the very title of Clark's book is programmatic of the tradition, in the modern era in Western culture, of subjecting important issues like representation, value, and sexuality to a confining and naive unification. The critic's assumption of self-evident expertise, and his unacknowledged projections onto the artist through a gaze that shifts from the area of art to that of sexuality, from beauty in one domain to beauty in another,[3] and from attraction—ultimately a communicative position—to truth, are typical of that tradition. In it, the positions are clearly distributed: patriarchal power is held by a figure whose paternal position remains unquestioned, and thereby unseen. This textual fragment, then, serves as an emblem of the expert posing as an old man.

The painting in question is Rembrandt's *Danae* (fig. 15.1, p. 385), still examined by the Rembrandt Research Project in the early 1980s and reported on in volume 3 of *Corpus*[4] but apparently destroyed since then. The quote from Clark makes a good case for the point I have made elsewhere about projection as a function of realism.[5] Words like *wished* and *love of truth* are evidence of this projection. Clark's response to the painting/woman, whatever it is, is attributed by projection to the artist: *He* wanted to make a statement on beauty, but *he* was too honest to disregard truth. That the "truth" in question is a misogynistic one—a hardly concealed disgust—is barely a coincidence; in fact, as I hope to demonstrate, realism and misogyny collude in the history of art history. The artist is always seen as a clone of the critic: here, a woman-lover, a connoisseur of female beauty, an honest person, and all for clinging to the "truth" of women's deficient beauty without reflecting on the standards by which her beauty is measured; sensitive to the visual appeal and aware of the difference between artistic beauty and sexual attraction. An astonishingly modern Rembrandt and a surprisingly self-centered and simple man emerge from this picture. This, then, is realism: the unreflected appeal to "common sense" judgments, to an unquestionable *doxa* according to which painting and model are identical, whereas beauty and truth are opposed when it comes to women. A "common sense" whose communality is limited by gender and class divisions.

This reflection can be analyzed in terms of a poststructuralist philosophical distrust of vision, but it cannot be wished away. I take it at face value and as representative of the kind of vision Foucault's antiocularism argues against.[6] Martin Jay frames Foucault's distrust of trust in vision by placing it within the contemporary, philosophical, "French" discourse questioning sight; and John Rajchman reminds us of the danger that connecting a distrust of sight with a distrust of rationality can lead to a charge against French thought akin to the charge of antirationalism often mounted against things critical. In conjunction with these two views but shifting the issue slightly, I wish to place that framing discourse in opposition to the powerful platitudes, the *doxa* it argues against.

III. SETTING VISION AGAINST VISION

Vision can be powerful or be a tool of power only if it is considered a form of communication. At least two views of communication have become generally accepted, and both are equally problematic. When we think of communication, we think first of all of language. The standard view of communication is Roman Jakobson's model. According to this model, a message, say the text, an utterance, an image, is sent by a sender, a speaker, to a receiver, reader, listener, or viewer. In order to be understandable, this message must refer to the reality which sender and receiver share, at least in part. This reality is called the context. Furthermore, the message must be transmitted through a material channel, the medium, to which the receiver has access, and be set in a code to which the receiver must possess the key.

However, this model can account only for ideal, totally successful communication, wherein the message arrives unharmed at its destination and is decoded according to the intention of the sender. The receiver is totally passive, a container rather than a subject, and the sender is omnipotent. We all know, of course, that reality is not so ideal—nor so oedipal—and that messages hardly ever arrive complete and undamaged. Nor is the sender ever completely aware of all aspects of his or her message. The receiver is not passive. The sender takes into account what she or he assumes the receiver wishes or is able to hear, read, or see. The receiver approaches the message from within her or his own context and preoccupations. Yet most of art history and much of literary interpretation still aims at "restoring" this ideal communication by retrieving the "original" intention and context. This is why the critic's practice of projection, "finding" the artist's intention in the work (see the Clark passage) is still a predominant and accepted mode of thinking.

This model obscures both the sender's manipulation of the receiver *and* the receiver's manipulation of the sender. Manipulation is an instance not only of historical agency, but also of the historical embeddedness of that agency. Genuine *historical* inquiry should be concerned with the *interaction* between work and audience, and not so much with authorial intention, which is always really a projection. These matters do not pass unnoticed, but by virtue of the dominance of the Jakobsonian model, the interactions of real communication are seen as merely deviant disturbances, as "noise." The sender-orientation of the model is not really challenged.

Yet the Jakobsonian model is not the only available one any more. Recent interest in visuality, in particular in film theory, has provided an alternative model. Feminist inquiries into the power relations that obtain in the domain of visual culture emphasize these relations in communication. Thus an alternative model is taking shape, in which visual communication is represented as a counterpart of the linguistic idealistic model. This alternative model is *voyeurism*. While the linguistic model tends to obscure the operations of power in communication, this visual model tends to reduce looking to power only, to an absolute subject-object relation, wherein the viewer/receiver has total power and the object of the look does not even participate in the communication. This model is in fact based on noncommunication.

Between these two models, the difference is irreducible, and both pose serious drawbacks to any complex, historical, and politically aware analysis of art. A serious examination of the possible exchange between these two models is imperative for the development of a nonidealized and noncensoring view of painting, and for the recognition of other modes of vision. Such a mediation may be offered by recent work in visual analysis, notably by Norman Bryson. Bryson argues for a more differentiated vision, a vision perhaps already explored by Rembrandt.[7]

Rembrandt's nudes have provoked many comments, from his era to the present. One reaction has been criticism of his "realism," a realism which resulted in the representation of the ugly aspects of bodies, like stretch marks and the imprints of garters—to mention the well-known objections by Andries Pels in a poem of the mid-seventeenth century.

> When he a naked woman, as it sometimes happened,
> Would paint, chose no Greek Venus as a model,
>
> But sooner a washerwoman, or a peat-treader from a barn,
> calling his error imitation of Nature,
> Everything else invention. Sagging breasts,
> Wrenched hands, even the pinch of the sausages [the mark of the pinches]
> Of the stays of the stomach, or the garter on the leg[8]

And lest one should think, moved by an unacceptable evolutionism, that this type of realism in the service of misogyny is outdated, we can still read a modern version of the Pels tradition in Clark. Although the connoisseur of women that emerges from the texts is different—Pels's hostility seems more overt—the link between realism, class bias, and misogyny is evident in both.

These two gentlemanly responses confirm the existence of the bond between vision and patriarchy. But denouncing that as a statement on vision in general serves the interest of precisely the power game that is denounced. In Norman Bryson's terms, these reactions verbalize the gaze, the look that denies its historicity and embodiment and objectifies the contemplated object. The solidarity between this gaze and Foucault's panoptic, medical, and evidence-producing gazes is obvious. This gaze is bound up with power-knowledge—realism in art is congenial to positivism in science—and is still so pervasive that the first move in undermining it is to show that it is not the only possible or reasonable kind of gaze—and that it has a vested interest in pretending that it is.

Bryson distinguishes the gaze from the glance, the involved look where viewers, aware of and bodily participating in the process of looking, engage in interactions of various kinds, put themselves at risk, and do not need, therefore, to deny the work of representation, including its most material aspects, like brush, pen, or pencilwork. The virtue in this mode of looking is that the awareness of one's own engagement in the act of looking entails the recognition that what one sees is a representation, not an objective reality. And, of course, this mode of looking does not fit the Jacobsonian model of communication too smoothly.

IV. REVISITING THE *DANAE*

As soon as we address Rembrandt's nudes from the position of the glance we are hit by the insistence with which the many drawings and sketches of the so-called ugly female body relate to the representation of looking itself. Elsewhere, I have conducted a detailed analysis of some of these works in order to point out the effect of the glance as a mode of looking.[9] To suggest the effectivity of such an analysis we need to assess the status of the viewer as *reader*.

In keeping with my view of narrative[10] and in order to break away from an unexamined positivist conception of sight, I will use the term *focalizer*, which refers to an agent *in* the work who represents various modes of attention, including the visual, and who thereby offers positions of viewing to the real viewer. As such, this agent is a possible mediator between the two poles of the linguistic communication model, and between the two opposed models of language and voyeurism. Reading a work by analyzing the focalization that marks its representation is therefore a double mediation. First of all, such a reading mediates between sender and receiver by pausing at the sites of available viewing positions and giving the real viewer the freedom to choose and hence to act. But second, such a reading mediates between discourse and image, because the narrativization of the viewing process that it entails introduces the mobility, the instability, and the sequential temporality of the process of reading. As we will see, reading the focalizer involves undermining the asymmetrical gaze, and blocking the temptations of voyeurism.

The naked woman in the *Danae* in the Hermitage in St. Petersburg looks away from the viewer. More importantly, the look of the figure is narratively embedded in a structure of focalization that changes the voyeurism generated by the display of her body. In fact, at first sight, the painting comes close to voyeurism; it thematizes it. The woman is represented as naked in her most private space, on her bed. But her naked-

Figure 15.1. *Danae.* Rembrandt van Rijn, 1636.

ness does not make her passive. Her beauty, desired by both the lover Zeus[11] and the viewer, is not an object to be taken in. She disposes of it herself.

Let us look at some details. The shower of gold in which Zeus is supposed to approach the woman takes the form of a sheen. But this sheen, the border of light, so crucially Rembrandtian, dissolves into futility. For in spite of deceptive appearances, it is not Zeus's gold that illuminates the woman; her light is disseminated throughout all the corners of the space. Zeus's sheen coincides with the limit of the space in which the woman is enclosed—the sheen delimits her private space and thus emphasizes the form of the opening in which the woman's feet disappear— her opening. Thus the pretextual story and *its* internal focalizer are undermined.

The hand the woman raises directs us. In combination with the look of the servant behind the curtain, an internal focalizer, the hand sends away the voyeuristic gaze. The implied onlooker is forced to follow the narrative structure of focalization and look, with the servant, with the woman, somewhere else. Had the internal focalizer not been represented, then the gesture would have been deprived of its narrative status and become empty, a pretext for a better look at her body.[12] The powerful arm which makes us aware of this woman's self-disposal certainly does not preclude the viewing of her body, but it does encourage awareness of that act of viewing: from the gaze to the glance.

The two delegated focalizers, the *putto* and the servant, form an insistent triangle with the female body as its base, paralleling and reversing the triangle of the exit-vagina-curtain. The *putto*, pre-text of the "symbol" of a forbidden sexuality that is iconed by his tied hands, also offers a possibility of viewing—but it is, of course, an immature, childish one. He is not looking at the woman's body (although he wrings his hands in despair over this lack), but at the bonds on his hands, which thus prohibit both touching *and* looking. Exasperated by the interdiction, the *putto* is visually self-enclosed.

This is not a coincidence. According to Freud, looking is a "natural" extension of touching, while according to the opponents of pornography, touching is an inevitable extension of looking.[13] This tension, which produces the present state of an important feminist debate, cannot be resolved, because both positions rest on incompatible premises. This tension is simply there as a cultural contradiction, textualizing the *Danae* in the 1990s: modernizing it.

The servant, whose intent look cannot but direct the viewer's look, is engaged in looking *elsewhere*. This figure looks toward the limit between outside and inside, the frame of the situation of voyeurism as well as of the pre-textual episode. The revisions to the painting done in 1643 emphasize this figure more. In their inevitable compulsion to interpret by projecting authorial intention, the writers of the Rembrandt Research Project estimate that

> the reason for the drastic changes Rembrandt made to the picture may well have been his desire to have the light fall in from between the back curtains, drawn further apart, and to involve the old woman in the new lighting.[14]

They do express in this interpretation their own sense of meaningfulness; in other words, they *read* the work, placing the figure in closer connection to the other elements, "words" if you like, on the painted surface: "today she provides . . . a clear link between Danae and the light falling through the open curtain."[15]

Pursuing this reading, but attempting not to project a verbal story

with too much certainty, I feel that the face of this "officially" female figure seems strangely masculine; moreover, a strong similarity, if not with
the artist's face, at least with the beret which he so often dons in his self-
portraits, is hard to overlook. Reread in the 1990s, in an age of feminist
concerns regarding gender identity and the body, the figure represents
the conflation of genders and of sender—the artist—and receiver—the
viewer. This seems significant for a figure who is in charge of representing looking between the gaze and the glance, and of linking light, the
embodiment of the lover as well as the precondition of looking and, in
Rembrandt, of representation, and of sight. She or he looks not at the
body but at the place to which the powerful arm of the woman sends his
or her eyes: outside of the bedroom.

These two stories—the textual, verbal pre-text and the story of the visual present—collude *and* collide in the work's textuality. They are in tension, but not in contradiction. They produce a new story, the text of the
Danae: Zeus, invisible as he is, thus becomes the pre-text the woman uses
to get rid of the indiscreet viewer. The woman who at first sight seemed
to be on display as spectacle takes over and dominates both viewer and
lover. Her sex, prefigured by the slippers and magnified by the opening
of the curtain at the other end of the diagonal of viewing, is central in
the framed text. Her sex is turned toward the viewer, but it can be seen
by neither viewer nor lover, because the viewer is sent away, while the
lover comes from the other side/sight. The viewer, again, receives the
"freedom" to choose a mode of looking flung into his or her face. Each
mode comes with a price.

The position of the viewer has thus flipped to the other side as well.
Far from representing the construction of a female object for the
voyeuristic gaze, then, what the *Danae* stands for is the construction of a
masculine viewer whose visual potency is extremely problematic. While
the ideal communication of a transparent message—female beauty—is disturbed by the woman's counteraction, which specifies the status and possession of that beauty, the opposite model, voyeurism and the subordination of the passive female object it entails, has similarly been disturbed.
The painting, if about anything, is about manipulating and blocking,
demonstrating and disturbing, both visual communication and the distri-
bution of power between the genders. And it is that meaning that has
been consistently emphasized in the 1643 reworking.

V. THE INTERESTS OF REALISM

As these remarks suggest, the issue of the submission of the female body
to a penetrating gaze as an inevitable function of realism is fore-

grounded in this work rather than just displayed as "natural." Clark's dis-
content with the work can be speculatively explained as an irritation at
being provoked into self-reflection, at being denied easy access to visual-
and-sexual pleasure. Paradoxically, not-being-able-to-see comes with the
enforcement of communication. For an all-too-brief moment, the power
positions are reversed, and the gentleman must submit to she who
should submit to him. We are far removed from Giorgione's *Sleeping
Venus*, who already began to awake in Titian's *Urbino Venus*, and who is
here fully alert and active while still lying naked on her bed, as if to fore-
ground her allegiance with, and revenge for, her more passive and submissive predecessors.

Let me speculate, for the sake of the demonstration, that this painting
is *modern* in this specific sense. It is modern, not because it serves the interests of the alleged hegemony of vision and its entanglement in relations of power but, on the contrary, because it already challenges that
hegemony, not by escaping vision but by changing and differentiating its
modes. After the *Danae*, I am suggesting, vision is no more what it used
to be: the combination of illusionism and power-knowledge it was on its
way to becoming after the great inventions of the Renaissance, including
the discovery of linear perspective, that mastertrope of realism.

What is designated by the word *realism* is no more unified than what is
designated by "looking." Without systematically surveying the question, I
can think of at least six different conceptions of realism:

1. Realism serves the interests of dominant moral and political structures: as the debate on Corneille's *Le cid* (almost contemporary with the
making of the *Danae*) suggests, what is real translates into what is acceptable; *vraisemblance* is decency. The debate on *Le cid* quickly became a
scandal. The issue, of course, was a woman's autonomous sexual preference: Chimene's decision to marry the man who killed her father.[16]

2. Realism serves the illusion of iconicity, based on a grave misread-
ing of that concept in the work of Charles S. Peirce. Although many of
the key theoretical terms in Peirce's elaborate typologies of signs have
not been commonly taken up by art critics, the most famous of these,
icon, index, symbol, have been over-extended because of their support for
realism. Therefore I quote Peirce's own definitions, because iconicity
cannot be understood outside of the typology of which it is one term,
and because this typology is frequently misunderstood:

> An *icon* is a sign which would possess the character which renders it signifi-
> cant, even though its object had no existence; such as a lead-pencil streak
> as representing a geometric line. An *index* is a sign which would, at once,
> lose the character which makes it a sign if its object were removed, but
> would not lose that character if there were no interpretant. Such, for exam-

ple, is a piece of mould with a bullet-hole in it as a sign of a shot; for without the shot there would have been no hole; but there is a hole there, whether anybody has the sense to attribute it to a shot or not. A *symbol* is a sign which would lose the character which renders it a sign if there were no interpretant. Such is any utterance of speech which signifies what it does only by virtue of its being understood to have that signification.[17]

First of all, any identification of icon and the entire domain of the visual is wrong.[18] As Peirce clearly states, the iconic is a quality of the sign in relation to its object; it is best seen as a sign capable of evoking nonexistent objects because it proposes to imagine an object similar to the sign itself. Iconicity is in the first place a mode of reading, based on a hypothetical similarity between sign and object. Thus, we think we know the face of a self-portraitist, say Rembrandt, even though other painters have presented a face of Rembrandt quite different from his self-portrait, just because we adopt the iconic way of reading when we look at Rembrandt self-portraits.[19]

But the example of portraits might wrongly suggest that the icon is predicated upon the degree of "realism" of the image. An abstract element like a triangular composition can become an iconic sign whenever we take it as a ground to interpret the image in relation to it, dividing the represented space into three interrelated areas. (Leo Steinberg, for example, makes this division in his paper on *Las Meninas*.)[20] Instead of visuality in general, or realism for that matter, the decision to suppose that the image refers to something on the basis of likeness is the iconic act, and a sense of specularity is its result. For our discussion, the iconic illusion tempts Pels and Clark—and the critics of *Olympia*—to think that they are seeing a likeness (but a likeness they deem flawed) to a desirable woman, instead of appreciating the fact that they are reading a "text" made up of signs, some of which can lure one into that illusion, even while others rupture it.

3. Realism promotes the use of art, politically biased as it is, to serve as documentary. Here, realism links up with ethnography, collecting artifacts as a form of colonialism, and an epistemological position that disavows knowledge's involvement in the practice of high art. Thus, as Linda Nochlin tells us, the curator of a recent show on French Orientalism opposed "aesthetic quality to historical interest." That gesture exploits opposition as a mode of argumentation which obscures all questions concerning whose reality is being documented.[21] It also obscures the fact that this use of art colludes with art's passing itself off as science. The visual culture in which Orientalism art functioned—and, as such oppositional statements demonstrate, still functions—capitalizes on the visual positivism current in science to hold onto the metaphors of the mind's eye and the nobility of vision.

4. Realism serves the interest of mystification in what it conceals and obscures. Thus it reveals not only what is "there" but also what is not there. The ambition to represent the "essence of the Orient" is at the same time an assertive way of not representing change, of not representing the history of the Orient nor of Orientalism, of not representing the Orientalist gaze.

5. Realism is even more aggressively political than that, specifically in its preference for details: it serves what Barthes termed an *effect of the real*, a mode of interpretation that willingly neglects the content of a representation in order to instill the notion that "this is reality." In Barthes's analysis, the denotation—what is actually represented—disappears to form a connotation—"this is reality," which displaces the denotation and hence becomes one itself.[22] Linda Nochlin's analysis of a painting by Gerome rightly emphasizes how the realist detail of broken tiles makes the painting look like a photograph. But Barthes's analysis makes this effect a little too innocent. For this reality-effect is *thereby* an effective means of reinserting the denotation—or rather, a further connotation—which states that since Orientals neglect their tiles, they "really" are lazy. And physical decay, with the help of the iconic illusion, further promotes the notion of moral decay—which, in turn, justifies colonialism. The effect of the real, both in practice and in its theoretical status, functions like a Freudian denial, an attempt to stop meaning which cannot be stopped.

6. The complicity between realism and colonialism makes the conjunction of the two in the sixteenth and seventeenth, and again in the nineteenth, centuries, a suspicious coincidence. One side of realism is its collusion with the aesthetic of the *pittoresque*, the representation of details connoting otherness in terms of derogatory and then idealized categories such as poverty. The interest in the *pittoresque* in turn colludes with the rise of ethnography as a discipline that is predicated upon the destruction of the cultures it studies. It may be illuminating to stop and think about the representation of a female body in the tradition of "the nude" as a potentially *pittoresque* mode. Just like the shabby huts that look so pretty on pictures, suggesting the contentment and even the superiority of the objectified poor, the objectified but submissive, passive woman on display is pretty precisely *because* she is passive. Danae resists that *pittoresque*. And so does Olympia. Thus these pictures denounce the oppressive fantasy character of realism.

From these remarks, one can safely conclude that realism is hardly a suitable category for use in analysis. Whether it be viewed in opposition to fantasy, to distortion, or to fiction, it always ends up on top subsuming, under its protecting wings, the very category it is opposed to. Realism has been a powerful urge in the modern era, both in the broader conception—since the Renaissance—and in the more limited one—from the mid-nineteenth century on. But if the above diagnosis of realism's politics is in the least convincing, then, lest we endorse a conspiracy theory of power, we must expect the conjunction between realism and modernity to show breaks, interruptions, if not moments of incommensurability. And indeed, modernity strikes back when this imperialistic subsuming flaunts itself too shamelessly. Manet's scandalous refiguring of the *Danae*'s protest presents such a case, where vision is pitted against itself so as to show its dividedness.

VI. MANET, HIS PAINTING AND HIS CRITICS

There is one way of avoiding evolutionism in an account of modernity, and that is to reverse the perspective and suggest that it is a feature of modernity to foresee what later critics, condescending from an evolutionist understanding, think they discover in an older work, and respond to it beforehand.[23] That is what I have been suggesting in my reading of the *Danae*: it is as if the woman in the picture is aware of Clark's attempt to subject her to his master's gaze, and responds to it by dismissing him. This complicating representation of a visual regime to come is as much part of the visual discourse of the time as is the one this representation polemically responds to.

John Rajchman's survey of Foucault's more constructive accounts of vision provides a clear understanding of the reasons why, for all Foucault's distrust of vision, his work must also be seen as a powerful tool for working critically with vision in ways that allow more complicated and differentiated conceptions of it. His notion that visuality and visibility are quite like discursive formations is indispensable for any historical account of visual art that is simultaneously a historical account of vision. As Rajchman lucidly puts it:

> Foucault's hypothesis was that there exists a sort of "positive unconscious" of vision which determines not what is seen, but what *can* be seen. His idea is that not all ways of visualizing or rendering visible are possible at once. A period only lets some things be seen and not others. It "illuminates" some things and so casts others in the shade. There is much more regularity, much more *constraint*, in what we can see than we suppose. To see is always to think, since what is seeable is part of what "structures thought in advance." And conversely to think is always to see.[24]

I would like to take this view—and the term is chosen intentionally—to look at Manet's *Olympia* in conjunction with recent thought about that work. I will argue that the painting addresses two issues at once. First, it pursues the difficulty of vision as a communicative act, involving the

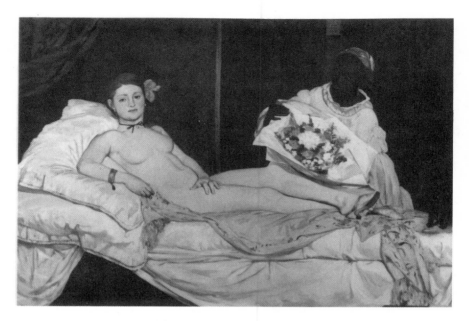

Figure 15.2. *Olympia*. Edouard Manet, 1863.

agency of *both* parties and thus preventing the objectification and the sexual subjection of the represented woman. More radically than the *Danae* it suggests that the regime in which it functions does not allow a communicative functioning of vision. It simultaneously displays and refuses that difficulty, and remains in the negativity that results. At the same time it addresses that difficulty more explicitly than the *Danae,* and on more levels at once: on the level of representation and on the level of its own medium.

Rather than narrative focalization and dramatical gesture, then, line, surface, and color are the means by which this painting flaunts its self-subversion. These medium-bound aspects however, work so powerfully because they become semiotic: line signifies dividing line; surface, superficiality, and color, color. And while Manet's contemporary critics could only get enraged by it, late twentieth-century art historians, more sophisticated in their disciplinary methodology, fail to see what it is exactly that those critics could not see.

The *Olympia* has become a "case" in cultural criticism and theory because another art historian with the name of Clark, T. J. Clark, has written a long analysis of this work which has become as famous as it is controversial. One of the critics who took issue with it is literary scholar Charles Bernheimer, who blames Clark for having too narrowly focused on class, thus repressing the gender issue the painting obviously puts on the carpet. It is immediately clear from this admittedly biased account that, of the tripartite concerns of contemporary feminism, namely race, class, and gender, the first is not addressed at all whereas the second and third elements have been separated.

Bernheimer's assessment of Clark's limitations makes just as good a case as Clark's own piece for Foucault's notion that a period's visual discourse allows only certain things to be seen. Both critics demonstrate a clear and surprising blindness. Clark is unable to see (enough of) gender, although he blatantly focuses on it, thematically by reading the image through the history of prostitution and methodically by using a psychoanalytically informed mode of reading in responding to Manet's critics. Clark does, of course, see gender in *Olympia,* but not in his own category of class analysis, prostitution. Bernheimer, on the other hand, is unable to see to what extent Clark does address gender, because he is himself caught up in an unacknowledged gender position which blinds him to Clark's mix. Both critics' blindness is at its most blatant when they are unable to see the issue of race, in other words, color. They both call the painting modern but fail to see why it is so.

Let me first characterize the discourses in which the critical arguments are couched. Clark's chapter can be easily divided: twenty pages in which the problem (the scandal) is posed (78–98); two pages of methodological considerations, mainly suggesting a symptomatic reading of the critical texts which, so far, he has not carried out (98–100); then about twelve pages on the history of prostitution in general (100–111), six on prostitution in art (111–116) and two in *Olympia* (116–117), fourteen on the nude in art (118–132) and then, finally, six pages only—by far the most engaging of the chapter—offer an analysis of the painting (133–139). The final seven pages are devoted to another critic, praised for being the only real critic of the painting (144).

The larger part of Clark's discourse exemplifies a certain positivist-inductivist mode of argumentation that consists of collecting a massive amount of evidence. This has problems in itself, raising questions of epistemology and of gender politics. His sixty-seven-page chapter begins with a statement of the scandal, consisting a good twenty pages of quotations of insults of the most offensive misogynistic kind. Clark, of course, is critical of those statements, but he quotes them nevertheless in full; much more, one feels, than is necessary to make his point. This exuberance falls under a problematic I have discussed elsewhere: that of the politics of citation. The argument against this strategy leads up to three claims, increasingly strong: (1) the critical text almost disappears under the weight of the quotes; (2) it is contaminated by a kind of reveling in other people's objectionable discourse; (3) criticism becomes a pretext that enables the critic simultaneously to endorse the objectionable position and to disavow it. The rhetoric conveys the objectionable material and does nothing to prevent readings that revel in it. This strong claim entails a kind of negative catharsis: it is not the case that by "working through" the objectionable desire one cleanses oneself of it; on the contrary, the gesture of cleansing—of critiquing—in fact smears the dirt around.[25] Although I prefer to give a good critic like Clark the benefit of the doubt and offer him a place under the weakest claim, it is not hard to realize how one easily moves from the first to the second, and then to the third.

Prostitution, Clark argues, is an issue of class. And he draws a distinction between the ordinary prostitute and the *courtisane*. The distinction coincides with that in art between ordinary nakedness and the elevated genre of the nude, and many of the critics he quotes suggest such a collusion between the two class systems. Both, of course, have a lot to do with gender. And while it seems obvious that one cannot discuss prostitution without addressing gender, there are moments when one feels, like Bernheimer, that the one does disappear behind the other. But my problem with the chapter is not that; rather than for a class bias and for a subsequent gender blindness, I would indict Clark for another, more deceptive and hence more powerful bias, a professional one raving in the vanguard of art history: a contextualist bias.

The problems that arise in the contextualist study of texts and images have been pointed out very sharply by Jonathan Culler in the preface to a collection of his essays:

> context is not fundamentally different from what it contextualizes; context is not given but produced; what belongs to a context is determined by interpretive strategies; contexts are as much in need of elucidation as events; and the meaning of a context is determined by events.[26]

And this view has been applied to problems in art history by Bryson.

The consequence of this bias becomes immediately clear: the context of prostitution is built around Clark's interpretation of *Olympia* as a protective belt is built around a research paradigm. The building blocks are the twenty pages of quotations; the relevance of the topic is stated twice, quite casually and with a symptomatic certainty that indexically refers to the concomitant lack of self-reflection; and it is *never* argued: "It was also a picture of a prostitute, we can be fairly certain of that" and "Olympia was a prostitute."[27] The only implicit evidence comes from the quotes, which are thereby turned from object of analysis into evidence for it. Moreover, the phrases just cited leave the semiotic location of prostitution ambiguous: is the painted woman presented as a prostitute, is the model one? Although the former is often implied, the latter is not denied, and the use of the past tense in the quotation about *Olympia* can even be seen as a parapraxis: willy-nilly, Clark is speaking of a real historical woman, even though her status as a prostitute has existed only in fantasy.[28]

So far, the two problems with Clark's piece are both bound up with epistemological positions. His positivism entails the problem of exuberant quoting and its sexist effect, while his contextualism misleads him into assuming *Olympia*/Olympia's prostitution to be a fact. And since everything else he writes is derived from that notion, his argument flounders, even if, thanks to his skill as a reader, many brilliant observations on the painting, condensed in pages 133–139, retain great value. Whereas Clark's discourse is burdened with the problems of positivism and contextualism, Bernheimer's psychoanalytic interpretation is tainted with an oedipal "anxiety of influence."

Although coming from a different, less positivistic, and more analytic tradition than Clark, Bernheimer writes a discourse that is contaminated by Clark's in two ways, First, he also and quite uselessly quotes the critics' badmouthing. The most poignant case occurs when, like a naughty boy, he copies Clark's equally naughty series of dirty words for prostitutes without mentioning his source.[29] This contamination makes him endorse without hesitation Clark's compromising citation politics, his assumption of the woman's low status, and other elements such as (most problematically) the black woman's status as a servant, on which I shall say more shortly. The second contamination consists in his oedipal engagement with Clark's text. While leaning heavily against it, he also distorts it quite grossly, thus setting Clark up as the antagonist he needs in order to define his own position; yet staying within the paradigm of the opposition he first simplifies—class versus gender—he is unable to stand outside Clark's paradigm.

This frequently used critical strategy is oedipal in structure, for if oedipalism consists in wishing to kill the father in order to take his place, the domination of the father-position remains in place. By misrepresenting Clark's argument, Bernheimer makes us misread Clark.[30] His extensive borrowing is justified by an opposition to the predecessor, combated on his own—reduced—terms. The most blatant, almost comical symptom of this oedipalism occurs when he argues with Clark about the possibility that Olympia is, after all, as elevated as a *courtisane*, for how else would she be wealthy enough to have a black servant?[31]

VII. MANET TALKS BACK, AND SO DOES "OLYMPIA"

In order to avoid the kind of oedipal discourse I just pointed out in Bernheimer, it is necessary to address the critical discourses head on, but instead of opposing these on their own terms, we need to take them as part of the problem to be explained, as part of the "case." Neither of these critics seems willing to reconsider the commonplace assumption that Olympia is venal—*courtisane* or prostitute, she remains for sale—and that the black woman is a servant—also for sale. Both see the relation between the two, if any, as symbolizing sexuality, and both assume the viewer to be male.[32] Reading the painting through the critics (i.e. taking the work to answer them), requires an attitude toward the critics that is both serious and critical: an attitude that questions their assumptions but must also account for their reasons. As becomes more than clear from Manet's quoted contemporaries, the primary problem with the painting is its lack of realism. Thus a first entrance into the work is to find an alternative for realism, rather than staying with the negativity of that lack. That alternative, of course, is self-reflexivity.

A second, related problem is the sense of ambiguity, incoherence, and fracture the painting conveys. This is measured against an unspoken expectation of denotative clarity and wholeness, and Bernheimer's suggestion that the concept of the uncanny is a helpful code to read the painting makes a lot of sense in this respect. The question one can derive from these two issues is, how can this painting be described in a language that mitigates both the centralizing of the single white woman in the picture and the anatomical vocabulary in which "she" is described?

First, then, let us consider realism and its alternative. The nude, Clark notes, is disintegrating as a genre in the 1860s. The problem is caused by the tension between the two kinds of beauty involved in it and the predicament it thereby inflicts on realism:

> If it is chaste, and it sometimes is, it is rigid and inanimate with its own decorum; and if it engages with sexuality, it does so in ways which verge on violence or burlesque.[33]

He goes on to quote a description of another painting which makes clear where the stakes are. I am reluctant to repeat such statements, but this case deserves some analysis for its exemplary demonstration of realism's complicity with the patriarchal dread of otherness:

> The pose is bizarre, I grant you; the head horrible, certainly; and let us agree that the body is hardly seductive, if you insist. But what admirable drawing.[34]

Writing in 1869, the author of this statement goes on to praise the shifting tones of the flesh, the modeling, the fineness of the belly, the hollow of the breasts. "How palpably the nude's flesh sinks into those fine red cushions!" And after shifting back to the woman he had first written off, he ends up formulating the program of a realism that essentializes the other: "It really is the woman of the Orient, in all her softness and bestiality."[35]

This realist project is damaged by individualizing realism, and individualization is the problem of *Olympia*, according to both Clark and Bernheimer. As Bernheimer rightly states—but forgetting that Clark was trying to say the same thing:[36] "But individualization does not entail readability."[37] In other words, realism is not a project of approaching reality but of promoting ways of reading as the only possible ones; and the last clause in Hache's criticism makes clear what that reading does to reality.

The problem of realism becomes entirely focused on the uncanny when anxiety is caused by the woman's look, a look which, according to Clark, "is not evidently feminine"; but "surely Olympia's sexual identity is not in doubt; it is how it belongs to her that is the problem."[38] And Bernheimer, in one of his by-now familiar (pun intended) moves, sets out to contradict and ends up appropriating this doubt when he writes:

> But I think that in an important sense Olympia's sexual identity *is* in doubt. Her depiction, as I read it, deliberately activates in the male viewer doubts whether her sexuality can indeed *belong* to her.[39]

True, the question whether her sexuality belongs to her is a relevant one; for this naked woman is on display as a sexual being, as a nude who foregrounds problems in aesthetics, yet also naked. Thus it is not the male viewer who wonders to whom her sexuality belongs—an ambiguous phrase anyway. That is, unfortunately for that viewer, beyond doubt. Given that it belongs to her in the mode of synecdoche—it is part of her—the very fact of her display points to a painful awareness of visual appropriation. And that awareness makes it hard to sustain.

This leads us from the question of realism to that of ambiguity. One prime example is the woman's look. The look is daunting—it has made critics angry, doubtlessly for not being sufficiently submissive, encouraging, condoning, or complicit with the visual intrusion. It is unreadable because it is both offensively impolite and at the same time self-enclosed. For from afar she seems to look at the viewer in challenge and refusal; but in close-up the look is directed nowhere if not at some inner vision, an anticipation of some pleasure no viewer of the painting will participate in. The doubt cast by critics on her sexuality is displaced from the doubt that they, the viewers, can own it. If, as I think we should, we take this look as a sign, not a thing—something which means something to someone in some respect or capacity[40]—the look in this painting foregrounds the impossibility of reconciling these two meanings. That is what makes the look hard to sustain—and the sexuality difficult to acknowledge. It separates two worlds, and the space between the two is predicated upon gender. What belongs to her—and that property is hardly in doubt—is an undeniably female body, including its sexual potential. It does not belong to the viewer, who can look from a distance and be scorned, or try to get closer, and be dismissed. It is not the sexual identity of the woman in Clark's and Bernheimer's terms that is in doubt—is she a woman or a man—but rather her sexual identity in the sense of what kind of sexuality she might be interested in.

Facing the tradition of viewing naked women on display and discussing them in the terms amply evidenced by Clark, leaves a woman—and an ambitious painter trying to probe the modalities of vision—several options for protest. The *Danae* demonstrated one of those: a theatrical acting out of the refusal to be looked at, complete with stage props supporting her agency. In the age of *Olympia*, when mythology has caught up with reality and the social traffic in women has taken such a complicated shape, a female figure destined to reenact Danae's agency under new conditions will have to be more complicated. This nineteenth-century Danae cannot dismiss the gaze, for the only figurations she disposes of are those the tradition has handed on. And the nude, in trouble though it may be just at this time, has won over Danae's attempt at emptying it out.

Danae's well-modeled flesh missed its target: its defiance was not appreciated by Kenneth Clark because his visual access to it was obfuscated. Hence, Manet avoided such flesh. Instead, this work offers sharp lines, which divide the body into anatomically analyzed parts, emphasizing the fact that lines really do divide. The surfaces don't match the lines, are not properly delineated by them. And lines fail where they are needed—to divide stomach from belly from thigh—and are in excess elsewhere—at shoulder and nipple, all too sharp; and also on the belly, suggesting the presence of some body hair. Finally, the surfaces are flat, defying the depth that realism demands. This work uses the means of the medium—line, surface, color—to frustrate the male viewer, eager to see the beauty of female flesh. This is what arouses the anger.

When separated from questions of race, a high degree of class and gender awareness does not guarantee that the critics will be able to address *critically* the issues of class and gender. What neither critic is able to see is the literalization of that other element of the medium, color. Clark offers a wonderful analysis of one of the key ambiguities in the painting: Olympia's hair. That hair, he argues, is hard to see. Chestnut brown, it hardly stands out against the brown background, the unpainted wooden back of a screen. The hair melts with the wood—almost. What the ambiguity does to the viewer is clearly and convincingly described by

Clark. When the viewer does not see the hair, he will find the head too hard—too "lined"—and when his visual efforts to engage with the nuances of the representation finally make the hair visible, the reward is softness: femininity without the threat of harshness and androgyny.

Clark does not address the question whether seeing the hair entails a change of class; an upward mobility from prostitute to *courtisane*, to phrase it in his terms. But the harshness that was the major inscription of class on the body yields to a more generalized sense of pleasing femininity, more pleasing to male eyes. This detail hints at a program: to reward a mode of looking that engages with the work's work, and that thereby allows the figure to become different from what she seems.

How could Clark not pursue this exciting efficacy of color and see what happens to the other woman in the picture? That other woman, reduced to the status of stage prop,[41] now becomes more important, more central, and more meaningful, just like the servant in the *Danae*, who became an artist after the light had enhanced her or his position. What light was for the *Danae*, color is for *Olympia*. For the black woman's face is exactly as (in)visible, hidden and shown in the same way. The chestnut-brown rhymes with the brown-dark green. Color, it turns out, divides the painting's background into two areas, both dark, both hard to see, and both making the crucial elements in the representation hard to see. Seeing color: could that be the clue to this painting's modernity?

Once made visible, the black woman's face becomes truly engaging. For, suggesting an alternative to the frustrated voyeur, she really looks at the white woman. If one takes up the clue offered by this internal focalizer, the look suggested is friendly, perhaps erotic, but not in a colonizing way. And in her are inscribed the signs of ambiguity that allow for an altogether different reading. She brings in flowers left by a client, our critics write. But her body suggests a sitting position. She may not be serving, but visiting. The flowers, echoing those on the bedspread and the single but emphatically exotic flower in Olympia's hair, may be hers; hers to give. The hand of her black friend, clearly drawn and thus distinct from Olympia's awkwardly represented hands, covers/displays what has been read as a metaphor for female genitalia. She has her hand on the top corner of that huge vagina—the place where female pleasure is engendered. The friendly look enables an erotic, lesbian reading, but does not enforce it. In addition, if the black woman is seen as *visiting* the white woman, then the latter's look at the viewer, either defiant or dreamy, can also be read as punctual instead of durative: a response to an intrusive interruption in her engagement with her visiting friend. Thus this look, too, embodies an alternative mode of looking: hesitant, mobile, historically positioned, inscribed in time.

VIII. MODES OF VISION

I do not need to impose, on a painting that has suffered so many impositions, a lesbian reading, to make my point about differentiating modes of vision, although I would like to emphasize how its possibility occurred. The point is, engaging with color makes something visible: a racial otherness not to be dismissed automatically, as in the realm of household colonialism, but rather to be appreciated as engaging. The mode of vision I am trying to describe is also an epistemology: a different way of getting to know. The epistemology that is being tested here is based on relationality, or more precisely, on the model of friendship.[42] Friendship requires getting to know other people in a dialogic mode. In the visual domain, this means a seeing radically different from the voyeuristic, asymmetrical mode that has for too long been hegemonic. The dialogical mode of looking in a nuanced way emblematizes, among other things, the "closer look" at (issues of) color that feminism today recommends. And it calls for a suspension of what we *think* we see, for a recognition of historical positionality, and for an appreciation of relations of reciprocity.

We have here a painting about two women. Each of them is inscribed in a tradition that exploits and scorns them. Whatever sophisticated theoretical framework is brought to bear on the painting by today's connoisseurs, these two women remain locked up in their position of exploitation. The problem with the two readings I have discussed is that each in its own way relies upon an unexamined context: historical knowledge for Clark, psychoanalysis for Bernheimer. Both entertain an insufficiently critical relation to previous texts taken as contexts, forgetting to heed Culler's warning that context is not given but produced. In their studies, "context" becomes the projection of an obsession that has so little to do with what is visually there that their acts of looking become at times acts of unlooking. The fact that both critics have relevant and sharp observations to offer about the painting doesn't help, for these observations are imprisoned in contexts that function as mechanisms of defense. Both critics use context as a means to look away from the works of art in order to confine image to what they already know: the familiar territory of patriarchal appropriation. This is not good art-historical seeing. I contend that history can be done better justice. *Olympia* responds to Giorgione's *Venus* through Rembrandt's *Danae,* each work adding a dimension to the problematic of looking at/from gender. That, I wish to emphasize, is historical looking.

But there are many other ways of looking around; only we don't see them, because there are certain gazes that take all the authority. What do we want to say about the glance that the black woman casts at the white woman in the *Olympia*? Is that a glance of desire, of engagement, of friendship; or is it one of curiosity, of jealousy, of contempt? Manet didn't specify it, and in the principle of ambiguity he offered a pluraliza- tion of vision that, I like to think, characterizes modernity, in spite of at- tempts to unify it, for better or for worse. Manet was aware of the sign systems that made his culture shaky, and like Rembrandt, he demon- strated an interest in modes of looking. What happens between the two women when they are made visible by a viewer, male or female, who is willing to engage with color, can be safely left to them. Prostitution and household service remain visible as allusions to what it is that these women must exist against.

For we cannot reinvent vision; it was already there before us. But as these two cases demonstrate, vision can be pluralized so as to deprive the colonizing, patriarchal gaze of its authority. And one way to do that is to keep connected the three burning issues of race, class, and gender in feminism.

NOTES

1. See Laura Mulvey, "Visual Pleasure and Narrative Cinema," *Screen* 16 (1975): 6–18; see Evelyn Fox Keller and Christine R. Grontkowski, "The Mind's Eye," in *Discovering Reality*, ed. Sandra Harding and Merrill B. Hintikka (London: D. Reidel, 1983), pp. 207–224.

2. See Kenneth Clark, *Feminine Beauty* (New York: Rizzoli, 1980), p. 23.

3. See Gill Saunders's study of the nude, among many others: *The Nude: A New Perspective* (Philadelphia: Harper & Row, 1989). In a brilliant study of the work of Francis Bacon as cultural critique, Van Alphen discusses what happens when men decide not to take that sexual-aesthetic division of labor for granted: Ernst Van Alphen, *Francis Bacon and the Loss of Self* (London: Reaktion Books, 1992).

4. J. Bruyn, B. Haak, S. H. Levie et al., *A Corpus of Rembrandt Paintings*. Stichting Rembrandt Research Project (The Hague: Martinus Nijhoff, 1982– 1989).

5. See my recent study, *Reading "Rembrandt": Beyond the Word-Image Opposition* (New York: Cambridge University Press, 1991).

6. See Martin Jay, "In the Empire of the Gaze: Foucault and the Denigration of Vision in Twentieth-Century French Thought," David Couzens Hoy, ed., *Foucault: A Critical Reader* (Oxford: Basil, 1986).

7. See Norman Bryson, *Vision and Painting. The Logic of the Gaze* (London: Macmillan, 1983) and "The Gaze in the Expanded Field," in Hal Foster, ed., 87–114. For a good collection on this movement in art history, see Bryson, *Calligram: Essays in the New Art History from France* (Cambridge: Cambridge University Press, 1988).

8. Quoted in Svetlana Alpers, *Rembrandt's Enterprise: The Studio and Market* (Chicago: University of Chicago Press, 1988).

9. See *Reading "Rembrandt."*

10. See my *Narratology: Introduction to the Theory of Narrative*, trans. Christine van Boheemen (Toronto: University of Toronto Press, 1992) and *On Story-Telling: Essays in Narratology*, ed. David Jobling (Sonoma: Polebridge Press, 1991).

11. Like so many stories from antiquity which thematize vision as a function of sexuality, this one has a long story of exploitation in the history of art. For an overview of the story and the iconographic tradition, see Erwin Panofsky, "Der gefesselte Eros (zur Genealogie von Rembrandts Danae)," *Oud Holland* 50: 193–217. Panofsky takes the stability of the theme a bit too much for granted; see Madelyn Millner Kahr, "Danae: Virtuous, Voluptuous, Venal Woman," *Art Bulletin* 60: 43–55, for the changing meaning of the theme from chastity to venal sex.

12. I have discussed such a case of an "empty" raising of the arm in *Reading "Rembrandt,"* pp. 146–147.

13. Sigmund Freud, 1905, *Three Essays on the Theory of Sexuality*. SE VII, 125–243.

14. Bruyn, *Corpus*, p. 217.

15. Bruyn, *Corpus*, p. 219.

16. The play's heroine, Chimene, decides to marry the hero, Rodrigue, who has killed her father to revenge his own father's humiliation. The scandal is that she would do this rather than hire some suitor to take revenge. The scandal was phrased in terms of *vraisemblance*. Chimene's choice in sexual matters was simply unthinkable. The issue was, of course, honor, that ideologeme of patriarchy that helps oedipalism stay in place.

17. Charles Sanders Peirce, "Logic as Semiotic," in Robert E. Innis, ed., *Semiotics: An Introductory Anthology*. (Bloomington: Indiana University Press, 1984), pp. 9–10.

18. This is the grave error of Louis Marin's influential "Toward a Theory of Reading in the Visual Arts: Poussin's *The Arcadian Shepherds*," most recently reprinted in Bryson, ed., *Calligram*. See also his "The Iconic Text and the Theory of Enunciation: Luca Signorelli at Loreto (Circa 1479–1484)," *New Literary History* 14 (1983): 253–296. For Marin, the "iconic text" is the visual text. Thus the sign-status of the icon is obscured, while the importance of the other two signs in visual art, the index and the symbol, are underestimated. And an onto-logical distinction inevitably returns between verbal texts as symbolic and visual texts as merely "natural."

19. This example is mentioned by Svetlana Alpers in *Rembrandt's Enterprise*. For a study of Rembrandt's self-portraits, see H. Perry Chapman, *Rembrandt's Self-Portraits* (Princeton: Princeton University Press, 1990). I have proposed a semiotic perspective on his self-portraits, related to psychoanalysis, in *Reading "Rembrandt."*

20. "Velasquez's *Las Meninas*," *October* 19:45–54. Steinberg published this paper, written long before, after reading (and, one presumes, being amused by) the somewhat hot-headed publications on this painting by critics of Foucault's opening chapter in *The Order of Things*, trans. Alan Sheridon (New York: Vintage Books), pp. 3–16. Both John Searle ("*Las Meninas* and the Paradoxes of Pictorial Representation," *Critical Inquiry* 6 (1980): 477–488) and, more strongly, Joel

Snyder and Ted Cohen ("Reflections on Las Meninas: Paradox Lost," *Critical Inquiry* 7 (1980): 429–447) demonstrate how upsetting it is if the "truth in painting" is under menace. See my analysis of this debate in *Reading "Rembrandt."*

21. See Linda Nochlin's sharp analysis of orientalism and its reception, in *The Politics of Vision: Essays on Nineteenth-Century Art and Society* (New York: Harper & Row, 1988); the case of Rosenthal's oppositional statement is discussed on p. 34.

22. See Roland Barthes, "L'effet de réel," *Communications* (1968), pp. 84–89 (English: "The Reality Effect") in Barthes, *The Rusttle of Language*, trans. Richard Howard (New York: Hill and Wang).

23. This is the idea underlying Michael Holly's recent work on the historiography of art. See her "Cultural History As a Work of Art: Jacob Burckhart and Henry Adams," *Style* (1988), pp. 209–218; "Past Looking," *Critical Inquiry* 16, no. 2 (1990): 371–396; "Vision and Revision in the History of Art," in *Theory Between the Disciplines*, ed. Martin Kreiswirth and Marc Cheetham (Ann Arbor: University of Michigan Press, 1990).

24. John Rajchman, "Foucault's Art of Seeing," *October* (Spring 1988), pp. 89–117.

25. See my analysis of a few samples of postcolonial critique featuring this problem, in "The Politics of Citation," *Diacritics* (Spring 1991).

26. Jonathan Culler, *Framing the Sign: Criticism and Its Institutions* (Norman: University of Oklahoma Press, 1988).

27. T. J. Clark, *The Painting of Modern Life: Paris in the Art of Manet and His Followers* (London: Thames & Hudson, 1985), pp. 85, 100.

28. Clark never reflects on this ambiguity even when he names the model as Victorine Meurend, and he refrains from specifying her relationship to Manet: a colleague, a fellow artist.

29. Charles Bernheimer, "Manet's *Olympia*: The Figuration of Scandal," *Poetics Today* 10, no. 2 (1989): 225–278, 261.

30. Bernheimer, "Manet's *Olympia,*" pp. 260–261; Clark, *Painting of Modern Life*, p. 109.

31. Bernheimer argues this on page 262, and again on 272, and sees in the black woman's presence as an indicator of Olympia's class mobility "damaging consequences" for Clark's argument. The black woman's class is thus more firmly fixed.

32. Bernheimer ends with the question what would happen if the viewer were female, and I give him credit for the suggestion. But his answer—femininity as masquerade—hardly allows for a serious consideration of the two women's interaction.

33. Clark, p. 128.

34. Eduard Hache, quoted in Clark, p. 128.

35. Hache in Clark, p. 129.

36. Clark, p. 133.

37. Bernheimer, "Manet's *Olympia,*" p. 259.

38. Clark, p. 132.

39. Bernheimer, "Manet's *Olympia,*" p. 259; first emphasis Bernheimer's, second mine.

40. Peirce's definition of the sign; see Peirce in Innis, *Semiotics*.

41. Clark, p. 146.

42. For friendship as a model for epistemology, see Lorraine Code, *What Can She Know? Feminist Epistemology and the Construction of Knowledge* (Ithaca and London: Cornell University Press, 1991).

INDEX

Designer: U.C. Press Staff
Compositor: Prestige Typography
Text: 10/12 Baskerville
Display: Baskerville
Printer: Maple-Vail Book Manufacturing Group
Binder: Maple-Vail Book Manufacturing Group